Decision Support Systems in Smart Computing

D1867862

Scrivener Publishing
100 Cummings Center, Suite 541J
Beverly, MA 01915-6106

Studies in Computational Intelligence and Smart Technologies

Series Editor(s): Harish Garg: harishg58iitr@gmail.com

This book series aims to bring together all the valuable contributions that focus on the recent developments in the field of computational intelligence as well as smart technologies and allied areas. The aim of this series is to consider cutting-edge technologies and explain their significance in terms of models, algorithms, theoretical concept related to computational engineering. It covers research related to the different databases and their applications to computational theory, machine learning, decision-support systems, artificial intelligence, knowledge-based systems, pattern recognition, fuzzy theory, meta-heuristic search, optimization, cognitive engineering, swarm intelligence, and other algorithms. Overall, the aim is to provide a unique platform for the technical solution related to the problems in the field of computational engineering.

Publishers at Scrivener
Martin Scrivener (martin@scrivenerpublishing.com)
Phillip Carmical (pcarmical@scrivenerpublishing.com)

Decision Support Systems in Smart Computing

Embracing Uncertainty and Challenges

Edited by

Harish Garg
Thapar Institute of Engineering and Technology, Patiala, Punjab, India

Scrivener Publishing

WILEY

This edition first published 2026 by John Wiley & Sons, Inc., 111 River Street, Hoboken, NJ 07030, USA and Scrivener Publishing LLC, 100 Cummings Center, Suite 541J, Beverly, MA 01915, USA
© 2026 Scrivener Publishing LLC
For more information about Scrivener publications please visit www.scrivenerpublishing.com.

All rights reserved. No part of this publication may be reproduced, stored in a retrieval system, or transmitted, in any form or by any means, electronic, mechanical, photocopying, recording, or otherwise, except as permitted by law. Advice on how to obtain permission to reuse material from this title is available at http://www.wiley.com/go/permissions.

Wiley Global Headquarters
111 River Street, Hoboken, NJ 07030, USA

For details of our global editorial offices, customer services, and more information about Wiley products visit us at www.wiley.com.

The manufacturer's authorized representative according to the EU General Product Safety Regulation is Wiley-VCH GmbH, Boschstr. 12, 69469 Weinheim, Germany, e-mail: Product_Safety@wiley.com.

Limit of Liability/Disclaimer of Warranty
While the publisher and authors have used their best efforts in preparing this work, they make no representations or warranties with respect to the accuracy or completeness of the contents of this work and specifically disclaim all warranties, including without limitation any implied warranties of merchantability or fitness for a particular purpose. No warranty may be created or extended by sales representatives, written sales materials, or promotional statements for this work. The fact that an organization, website, or product is referred to in this work as a citation and/or potential source of further information does not mean that the publisher and authors endorse the information or services the organization, website, or product may provide or recommendations it may make. This work is sold with the understanding that the publisher is not engaged in rendering professional services. The advice and strategies contained herein may not be suitable for your situation. You should consult with a specialist where appropriate. Neither the publisher nor authors shall be liable for any loss of profit or any other commercial damages, including but not limited to special, incidental, consequential, or other damages. Further, readers should be aware that websites listed in this work may have changed or disappeared between when this work was written and when it is read.

Library of Congress Cataloging-in-Publication Data

ISBN 978-1-394-39941-3

Cover image: Generated with AI using Adobe Firefly
Cover design by Russell Richardson

Set in size of 11pt and Minion Pro by Manila Typesetting Company, Makati, Philippines

Printed in the USA

10 9 8 7 6 5 4 3 2 1

Contents

Preface

In an age marked by rapid technological advancements, volatile global trends, and increasingly complex decision environments, the role of Decision Support Systems (DSS) has never been more critical. From managing the intricacies of sustainable development to optimizing urban infrastructure and healthcare, DSS frameworks—especially those grounded in fuzzy logic and soft computing paradigms—offer indispensable tools for navigating uncertainty and complexity.

This volume brings together a collection of pioneering research contributions that explore both the theoretical foundations and real-world applications of intelligent decision-making methodologies. At the core of these contributions lies a common theme: the imperative to model, manage, and make informed decisions under conditions that are inherently imprecise, ambiguous, or conflicting conditions that traditional models often struggle to address.

The book is organized into seven parts, each addressing a crucial domain in which decision support plays a transformative role:

- Part I lays the foundation with cutting-edge methodologies in fuzzy decision-making, highlighting advancements in fuzzy linear programming, type-2 intuitionistic sets, and fuzzy AHP-TOPSIS integrations.
- Part II focuses on supply chain and logistics, where researchers tackle sustainability, risk, and supplier selection through fuzzy machine learning, MCDM, and group decision analysis.
- Part III delves into sustainable development and environmental decision-making, presenting hybrid methods for transportation, innovation adoption, and urban pollution assessment.
- Part IV turns attention to smart cities and urban systems, offering novel fuzzy models for parking, infrastructure,

and graph networks that underpin future-ready urban management.
- Part V presents DSS innovations in healthcare and medical applications, addressing digital healthcare, complex pregnancy evaluation, and knowledge-based decision systems.
- Part VI explores applications in education and public services, emphasizing the role of DSS in managing national educational resources.
- Part VII concludes with advanced fuzzy and soft computing techniques, featuring cutting-edge models using Fermatean, Dombi, and pentagonal fuzzy numbers for emergency and replacement decision-making.

Each chapter is authored by leading experts and research scholars from around the world, providing both academic rigor and practical relevance. The diversity of application areas covered, ranging from urban planning and logistics to healthcare and environmental sustainability, demonstrates the growing reach and versatility of intelligent decision systems.

We hope this book serves not only as a comprehensive reference for researchers, students, and professionals but also as a catalyst for future explorations in this dynamic and multidisciplinary field. As we embrace the uncertainties and challenges of modern-day decision-making, may these contributions inspire further innovation at the intersection of smart computing, data-driven insights, and human judgment.

We extend our heartfelt gratitude to all contributing authors whose efforts have made this volume possible. We are also grateful to the referees for their valuable and highly appreciated works contributed to select the high quality of chapters published in this book. Last but not the least, we would like to also thank Martin Scrivener and the team at Scrivener Publishing for their support through the process of editing this book.

Harish Garg
Patiala, India
July 2026

Part I

FOUNDATIONS AND METHODOLOGIES IN FUZZY DECISION-MAKING

1

A Methodology for *A Posteriori* Decision Making in Fuzzy Linear Programming

Boris Pérez-Cañedo[1,2*], Eduardo René Concepción-Morales[3] and José Luis Verdegay[4†]

[1]*Models of Decision and Optimization (MODO) Research Group, University of Granada, Granada, Spain*
[2]*Department of Mathematics, University of Cienfuegos, Cienfuegos, Cuba*
[3]*Department of Informatics, University of Cienfuegos, Cienfuegos, Cuba*
[4]*Department of Computer Science and Artificial Intelligence, University of Granada, Granada, Spain*

Abstract

A posteriori decision-making for multi-objective optimization problems relies on evaluating a set of alternative solutions against defined criteria. However, a limitation arises when some objective functions are unquantifiable due to subjective considerations or because they remain unknown to the decision-maker during initial problem formulation. This paper addresses this gap in the context of linear programming by introducing a methodology that consists of the integration of fuzzy techniques with Modeling to Generate Alternatives (MGA) to effectively incorporate subjective and unmodeled objectives. Specifically, the proposed methodology:

(1) employs fuzzy numbers to represent subjectivity within quantifiable objectives and constraints; (2) utilizes fuzzy logic to capture unmodeled objectives *via* fuzzy propositions; and (3) applies the MGA technique to generate a diverse set of near-optimal solutions expected to perform well when evaluated against the unmodeled objectives. An illustrative example demonstrates that the proposed methodology successfully generates alternatives that satisfy both modeled and unmodeled objectives, overcoming the limitations of conventional methods.

**Corresponding author*: bpcanedo@gmail.com
†*Corresponding author*: verdegay@decsai.ugr.es

Harish Garg (ed.) Decision Support Systems in Smart Computing: Embracing Uncertainty and Challenges, (3–26) © 2026 Scrivener Publishing LLC

Keywords: *A posteriori* decision-making, fuzzy linear programming, fuzzy logic, fuzzy proposition, modeling to generate alternatives

1.1 Introduction

Optimization is a ubiquitous practice in virtually all fields of science and engineering. Numerous techniques have been developed for it, from purely mathematical approaches to others inspired by nature or social phenomena [8, 19]. To solve an optimization problem, the first step is to create a model that serves as an abstraction of the real-world scenario, capturing key aspects while omitting less relevant features. This model consists of three fundamental components: the decision variables, a set of constraints that limit the possible values of these variables, and objective functions that evaluate the quality of the possible solutions. The goal is to identify an optimal solution (that maximizes or minimizes the objective functions) within the set of all feasible solutions. However, in practice, the less relevant features of the real-world scenario are not the only ones that we omit. Often, we are forced to omit relevant features, either because we cannot express them in a desirable form that makes the resulting mathematical model solvable with the available methods or because they are simply unknown at the time the problem needs to be solved. For example, we may only be able to describe the constraints and objectives of our problem in natural language in a vague manner. Furthermore, even if we know and can express without vagueness all the equations that describe our problem in terms of their forms (e.g., linear or quadratic), there may still be vagueness in the coefficients of these equations.

A multi-objective optimization (MOO) problem is inherently tied to a multi-criteria *a posteriori* decision-making problem. The latter involves a set of alternatives, represented by the efficient points of the MOO problem identified by the search algorithm, and their corresponding consequences, resulting from the execution of each alternative. These consequences, typically estimated through the evaluation of the objective functions, form the basis for the final decision. Lastly, a set of criteria is used to evaluate and compare the alternatives, where each criterion offers a different perspective for the selection of the most suitable alternative [9, 24, 32]. Several methods exist to perform this task, e.g., Simple Multi-Attribute Rating Technique (SMART), Preference Ranking Organization METHod for Enrichment Evaluation (PROMETHEE), and ELimination and Choice Expressing the REality (ELECTRE) [18, 34]. But what can we do when we find ourselves in the situation described above, i.e., we do not know all the objective functions or they are described in natural language only vaguely?

Brill *et al.* [6, 7] proposed a technique named *Modeling to Generate Alternatives* (MGA) to cope with unknown or ill-defined objective functions called "unmodeled objectives" in their framework. The MGA technique systematically generates a limited set of alternative solutions that perform well within the modeled (known) objective space and are maximally different in the decision space. These alternatives achieve comparable performance on the modeled objectives but differ significantly in their impact on unmodeled objectives. This enables decision-makers to explore the decision space for high-quality solutions while considering the unmodeled objectives *a posteriori* [40].

With regard to handling vagueness in decision-making, Fuzzy Set theory [38], proposed by Lotfi A. Zadeh in 1965, has shown remarkable success in real-world applications [25]. In particular, the field of fuzzy optimization has accumulated a considerable body of research to which new approaches and techniques are continually being added [14]. Fuzzy linear programming (FLP) is an established mathematical framework for addressing vagueness in optimization, which has its roots in the 1974 works of Tanaka *et al.* [33] and Zimmermann [41]. Although an exhaustive classification of FLP models and methods is beyond the scope of this paper, we note and share the authors' findings in [14] that methods are being proposed to solve FLP problems with multiple objective functions [3, 29], fuzzy set generalizations as model parameters and decision variables [1, 2], and fuzzy number ordering approaches such as ranking functions [1, 5] and lexicographic ranking [23, 27, 29], which shows that the field is currently active. The interested reader is referred to recent literature reviews provided in [12, 16], where several FLP methods are discussed along with some numerical examples. Zadeh's work on fuzzy sets [38] gave birth to fuzzy logic. In the author's words: "fuzzy logic is a precise logic of imprecision and approximate reasoning" [39]. It seeks to formalize the human capability to converse, reason, and make rational decisions in an environment of imprecision, uncertainty, incomplete information, conflicting information, partial truth, and partial possibility [39].

In this paper, we make the following contributions:

- A methodology that combines MGA, FLP, and Fuzzy Logic to address optimization problems where all components are described in natural language only vaguely.

- Our approach specifically enables *a posteriori* decision-making for scenarios where the optimization model is fundamentally vague or ill-defined, extending beyond imprecise coefficients to encompass unknown, poorly specified, or linguistically described objectives and constraints at the modeling stage.
- The methodology facilitates the systematic generation of high-quality, maximally different alternative solutions that perform well on modeled objectives (*via* FLP) while exploring significant variations in the decision space (*via* MGA), empowering decision-makers to evaluate options considering unmodeled objectives and vague criteria *a posteriori*.

The rest of the paper is organized as follows. All the abbreviations used throughout the paper are presented in Section 1.2. Section 1.3 presents the preliminary concepts. The proposed methodology is developed in Section 1.4. Section 1.5 illustrates the working of the methodology with a simple two-period fish harvesting problem in fuzzy environment. Conclusions and future research lines are discussed in Section 1.6.

1.2 List of Abbreviations

MOO	Multi-Objective Optimization
SMART	Simple Multi-Attribute Rating Technique
PROMETHEE	Preference Ranking Organization METHod for Enrichment Evaluation
ELECTRE	ELimination and Choice Expressing the REality
MGA	Modeling to Generate Alternatives
FLP	Fuzzy Linear Programming
TFN	Triangular Fuzzy Number

1.3 Preliminaries

In this section, we present the basic definitions used in the rest of the paper. Most of them have been taken from [10, 38] and the textbooks [11, 20]. The notation used follows that introduced in [28].

Definition 1.1: A fuzzy set $\tilde{A}$ in a space of points X, with elements denoted generically by x, is characterized by a membership function $\mu_{\tilde{A}} : X \rightarrow [0,1]$, with the value of $\mu_{\tilde{A}}(x)$ at x representing the grade of membership of x in $\tilde{A}$.

Definition 1.2: A fuzzy set $\tilde{A}$. is convex if and only if $\mu_{\tilde{A}}(\lambda x_1 + (1-\lambda)x_2) \geq \min\left(\mu_{\tilde{A}}(x_1), \mu_{\tilde{A}}(x_2)\right)$ for all $x_1, x_2 \in X$ and $\lambda \in [0, 1]$.

Definition 1.3: A fuzzy set $\tilde{A}$ is normal if $\sup\limits_{x\in X}\left(\mu_{\tilde{A}}(x)\right) = 1$, where sup denotes supremum.

Definition 1.4: The core of a fuzzy set $\tilde{A}$ is the crisp set $C(\tilde{A}) = \left\{x \in X \mid \mu_{\tilde{A}}(x) = 1\right\}$.

Definition 1.5: A fuzzy number is a convex normalized fuzzy set of the real line with a singleton core, whose membership function is at least piecewise continuous.

Definition 1.6: A fuzzy number $\tilde{a} = (\underline{a}, a, \overline{a})$ is said to be a triangular fuzzy number (TFN) if its membership function is given by:

$$\mu_{\tilde{a}}(x) = \begin{cases} \dfrac{x - \underline{a}}{a - \underline{a}} & \text{if } \underline{a} \leq x \leq a, \\ \dfrac{\overline{a} - x}{\overline{a} - a} & \text{if } a \leq x \leq \overline{a}, \\ 0 & \text{otherwise.} \end{cases}$$

Definition 1.7: A TFN $\tilde{a} = (\underline{a}, a, \overline{a})$ is said to be non-negative (denoted by $\tilde{a} \geq 0$) if $\underline{a} \geq 0$.

Definition 1.8: Let $\tilde{a} = (\underline{a}, a, \overline{a})$ and $\tilde{b} = (\underline{b}, b, \overline{b})$ be any TFNs, then $\tilde{a} = \tilde{b}$ if and only if $\underline{a} = \underline{b}$, $a = b$ and $\overline{a} = \overline{b}$.

Definition 1.9: For any two TFNs $\tilde{a} = (\underline{a}, a, \overline{a})$ and $\tilde{b} = (\underline{b}, b, \overline{b})$, fuzzy addition $\oplus$, subtraction $\ominus$, multiplication $\otimes$, and multiplication by a scalar $\times$ are given respectively as: $\tilde{a} \oplus \tilde{b} = \left(\underline{a} + \underline{b}, a + b, \overline{a} + \overline{b}\right)$; $\tilde{a} \ominus \tilde{b} = \left(\underline{a} - \overline{b}, a - b, \overline{a} - \underline{b}\right)$; $\tilde{a} \otimes \tilde{b} = \left(\underline{a}\underline{b}, ab, \overline{a}\overline{b}\right)$ if $\tilde{b} \geq 0$ and $\underline{a} \geq 0$; $\tilde{a} \otimes \tilde{b} = \left(\underline{a}\overline{b}, ab, \overline{a}\overline{b}\right)$ if $\tilde{b} \geq 0$, $\underline{a} < 0$, and $\overline{a} \geq 0$; $\tilde{a} \otimes \tilde{b} = \left(\underline{a}\overline{b}, ab, \overline{a}\underline{b}\right)$ if $\tilde{b} \geq 0$ and $\overline{a} < 0$; and $\lambda \times \tilde{a} = (\lambda\underline{a}, \lambda a, \lambda\overline{a})$ if $\lambda \geq 0$, $(\lambda\overline{a}, \lambda a, \lambda\underline{a})$ otherwise.

Definition 1.10*([28])*: For an arbitrary TFN $\tilde{a} = (\underline{a}, a, \overline{a})$, let $f_k(\tilde{a}) = w_{k1}\underline{a} + w_{k2}a + w_{k3}\overline{a}$ for k = 1, 2, 3 be three linear functions of the parameters of $\tilde{a}$ with each w_{kr} chosen such that matrix $[w_{kr}]$ is non-singular. Furthermore, let $\leq_{\text{lex}}$ denote the lexicographic order relation on $\mathfrak{R}^3$. Given two TFNs $\tilde{a}$ and $\tilde{b}$, then:

1. $\tilde{a} \prec \tilde{b}$ if and only if $\left(f_k(\tilde{a})\right)_{k=1}^{3} <_{\text{lex}} \left(f_k(\tilde{b})\right)_{k=1}^{3}$;
2. $\tilde{a} \preccurlyeq \tilde{b}$ if and only if $\left(f_k(\tilde{a})\right)_{k=1}^{3} <_{\text{lex}} \left(f_k(\tilde{b})\right)_{k=1}^{3}$ or $\left(f_k(\tilde{a})\right)_{k=1}^{3} = \left(f_k(\tilde{b})\right)_{k=1}^{3}$.

The lexicographic order relation $\preccurlyeq$ satisfies the total order properties [18]; i.e., $\preccurlyeq$ is reflexive, transitive, anti-symmetric, and complete. There are several lexicographic order relations in the literature, see e.g. [13, 35, 36]. It has been shown that they have several advantages, including simplicity, consistency with human intuition, and power of discrimination [13, 30].

Definition 1.11: Given two TFNs $\tilde{a}$ and $\tilde{b}$, then:

1. $\max\{\tilde{a},\tilde{b}\} = \begin{cases} \tilde{a} & \text{if } \tilde{b} \preccurlyeq \tilde{a}, \\ \tilde{b} & \text{otherwise;} \end{cases}$

2. $\min\{\tilde{a},\tilde{b}\} = \begin{cases} \tilde{a} & \text{if } \tilde{a} \preccurlyeq \tilde{b}, \\ \tilde{b} & \text{otherwise.} \end{cases}$

Definition 1.12*([22])*: For two TFNs $\tilde{a}$ and $\tilde{b}$, the absolute distance between $\tilde{a}$ and $\tilde{b}$ is defined as follows:

$$\text{ABS}(\tilde{a},\tilde{b}) = |a-b| + |\overline{a}-\overline{b}| + |\underline{a}-\underline{b}|.$$

1.4 Methodology for *A Posteriori* Decision-Making

In real-world optimization, not all relevant objective functions can be precisely defined or mathematically formulated at the time of solving a problem. An *a posteriori* decision-making approach addresses this challenge by generating alternative solutions to the problem, allowing decision-makers to evaluate trade-offs and incorporate additional knowledge after optimization. In this section, the problem of *a posteriori* decision-making in FLP is formally raised and a methodology for its solution is proposed.

1.4.1 Outline of the Proposed Methodology

Consider the multi-objective fuzzy optimization problem (1.1).

$$\min \left(\bigoplus_{j=1}^{n} \tilde{c}_j \otimes \tilde{x}_j, U_1(\tilde{x}), U_2(\tilde{x}), \ldots, U_{p\geq 1}(\tilde{x}) \right)$$
$$\text{s.t. } \tilde{x} \in \tilde{X} = \left\{ \tilde{x} : \bigoplus_{j=1}^{n} \tilde{a}_{ij} \otimes \tilde{x}_j \{\preccurlyeq, =, \succcurlyeq\} \tilde{b}_i,\ i=1,2,\ldots,m;\ \tilde{x}_j \geq 0,\ j=1,2,\ldots,n \right\}. \tag{1.1}$$

We call the first objective function "modeled objective" and assume that the other objective functions U_1 to U_p are not available when the problem needs to be solved or are more easily expressed in natural language, and therefore we call them "unmodeled objectives".

One way of tackling problem (1.1), under the given assumptions, is to look for multiple solutions to the single-objective FLP problem

$$\min \bigoplus_{j=1}^{n} \tilde{c}_j \otimes \tilde{x}_j$$
$$\text{s.t. } \tilde{x} \in \tilde{X}. \tag{1.2}$$

Let us denote them by $\tilde{x}^{(1)}, \tilde{x}^{(2)}$ up to $\tilde{x}^{(n_a+1)}$ for some integer $n_a \geq 1$ and assume that $\tilde{x}^{(1)}$ is optimal. Starting from $\tilde{x}^{(2)}$, the solutions need not solve optimally problem (1.2). There may not be multiple optimal solutions at all. What is important is that these solutions are all close to each other in the objective space and as far apart as possible in the decision variables space to represent valid alternatives for a decision-maker. From a practical perspective, by being close in the objective space we mean that they are considered "equally" good with respect to the modeled objective. With these solutions calculated beforehand, the decision-maker can take precautionary measures about what is needed to implement any of the solutions and make informed decisions *a posteriori* when the objective functions U_1 to U_p become available. At this point, the decision-maker will need to solve a multi-criteria decision-making problem, in which the objective functions U_1 to U_p act as the set of criteria to measure the quality of the solutions across p dimensions. We notice that some of the objective functions are or could become available only as subjective descriptions in natural language of the characteristics that a solution to the problem must have. Consequently, to solve problem (1.1), we need:

- A method to solve FLP problem (1.2) optimally.
- A procedure to generate alternative solutions to FLP problem (1.2) in the sense described above.
- A method to handle subjective descriptions in the unmodeled objective functions U_1 to U_p.
- A multi-criteria decision-making method.

Below we make a selection of the necessary methods. Figure 1.1 summarizes the steps of the proposed methodology.

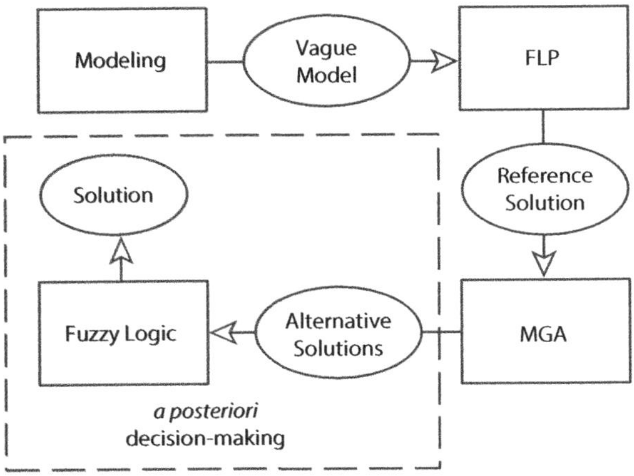

Figure 1.1 Steps of the proposed methodology.

1.4.2 Method for FLP

Let us focus on FLP problem (1.2) and introduce $\tilde{z} = \bigoplus_{j=1}^{n} \tilde{c}_j \otimes \tilde{x}_j$ and $\tilde{a}_i = \bigoplus_{j=1}^{n} \tilde{a}_{ij} \otimes \tilde{x}_j$ for clarity. In addition, let $I_{=}$, $I_{\preccurlyeq}$, and $I_{\succcurlyeq}$ denote the index sets of the equality, less-than-or-equal-to, and greater-than-or-equal-to constraints of FLP problem (1.2), respectively. Using Definitions 1.8 and 1.10, in [27], the authors proposed the following transformation.

$$\begin{aligned} &\operatorname{lex\,min}\left(f_k(\tilde{z})\right)_{k=1}^{3} \\ &\quad \text{s.t.}\left(f_k(\tilde{a}_i)\right)_{k=1}^{3}\{\leq_{\text{lex}},\geq_{\text{lex}}\}\left(f_k(\tilde{b}_i)\right)_{k=1}^{3} \text{ for } i \in I_{\preccurlyeq} \cup I_{\succcurlyeq}, \\ &\quad \underline{a}_i(\tilde{x}) = \underline{b}_i,\ a_i(\tilde{x}) = b_i, \text{ and } \overline{a}_i(\tilde{x}) = \overline{b}_i \text{ for } i \in I_{=}. \end{aligned} \tag{1.3}$$

To handle the lexicographic constraints, problem (1.3) is further transformed into problem (1.4), where ϵ and L are positive constants sufficiently small and large, respectively.

$$
\begin{aligned}
&\operatorname{lex\,min}\left(f_k(\tilde{z})\right)_{k=1}^{3} \\
&\quad \text{s.t.} -L\sum_{r=1}^{k-1} y_{ir} + \epsilon y_{ik} \le f_k(\tilde{b}_i) - f_k(\tilde{a}_i) \le L y_{ik} \\
&\quad \text{for } k = 1,2,3 \text{ and } i \in I_{\preccurlyeq}, \\
&\quad -L\sum_{r=1}^{k-1} y_{ir} + \epsilon y_{ik} \le f_k(\tilde{a}_i) - f_k(\tilde{b}_i) \le L y_{ik} \\
&\quad \text{for } k = 1,2,3 \text{ and } i \in I_{\succcurlyeq}, \\
&\quad \underline{a}_i(\tilde{x}) = \underline{b}_i,\ a_i(\tilde{x}) = b_i, \text{ and } \overline{a}_i(\tilde{x}) = \overline{b}_i \text{ for } i \in I_{=}, \\
&\quad y_{ik} \in \{0,1\} \text{ for } k = 1,2,3 \text{ and } i \in I_{\preccurlyeq} \cup I_{\succcurlyeq}.
\end{aligned}
\tag{1.4}
$$

The lexicographic method guarantees optimal solutions with unique fuzzy objective function values, which is not guaranteed by the methods that use linear ranking functions. This has theoretical and practical implications as shown in [27, 29]. We further clarify the implications in our case in Section 1.4.4.

1.4.3 Alternative Solutions Generation

Applying the MGA approach to problem (1.1) consists of solving, as many times as the number of desired alternatives (namely, from $k = 1$ to n_a), the problem:

$$
\begin{aligned}
&\max \sum_{q=1}^{k}\sum_{j=1}^{n} \operatorname{ABS}\left(\tilde{x}_j^{(q)}, \tilde{x}_j^{(k+1)}\right) \\
&\text{s.t.} \bigoplus_{j=1}^{n} \tilde{c}_j \otimes \tilde{x}_j^{(k+1)} \preccurlyeq \bigoplus_{j=1}^{n} \tilde{c}_j \otimes \tilde{x}_j^{(1)} \oplus \tilde{d}, \\
&\tilde{x}^{(k+1)} \in \tilde{X},
\end{aligned}
\tag{1.5}
$$

where $\tilde{x}^{(1)}$ is an optimal (or reference) solution to problem (1.2), $\tilde{x}^{(2)}$ to $\tilde{x}^{(k)}$ are (alternative) already available solutions to problem (1.2) obtained by iteratively solving problem (1.5), $\tilde{x}^{(k+1)}$ is a new (alternative) solution—the actual decision variable of problem (1.5)—, and $\tilde{d}$ is an allowed deviation from the optimal (or reference) objective function value of problem (1.2). It is clear from the formulation of problem (1.5) that each new alternative obtained from its solution will be as far apart from the rest of the alternatives as possible in the decision space while guaranteeing comparable performance on the modeled objective.

1.4.4 Handling the Unmodeled Objectives *Via* Fuzzy Propositions

A fuzzy proposition is a statement p whose truth or falsity is expressed to varying degrees [21]. When falsity and truth are represented by the values 0 and 1, respectively, the degree of truth of p, denoted as truth(p), is quantified by a number within the interval [0, 1]. Canonical fuzzy propositions can be categorized into the following types [21]:

Unconditional and Unqualified Propositions

$$p : V \text{ is } \tilde{F},$$

where V is a variable that takes values in a universe of discourse X, and $\tilde{F}$ is a fuzzy set in X that represents a fuzzy predicate. Fuzzy predicates include linguistic terms such as *Low*, *Medium*, and *High*. The truth value of p is equal to the degree of membership of x in $\tilde{F}$, denoted $\text{truth}(p) = \mu_{\tilde{F}}(x)$.

Unconditional and Truth-Qualified Propositions

$$p : \left(V \text{ is } \tilde{F}\right) \text{ is } \tilde{S},$$

where $\tilde{S}$ is a fuzzy set, with membership function $\mu_{\tilde{S}}$, that represents a fuzzy truth qualifier [21]. Truth qualifiers include linguistic terms such as *Very True*, *Fairly True*, *Very False*, and *Fairly False*. The degree of truth of a truth-qualified proposition p is given by $\text{truth}(p) = \mu_{\tilde{S}}\left(\mu_{\tilde{F}}(x)\right)$.

Conditional and Unqualified Propositions

$$p : \text{if } V \text{ is } \tilde{F}, \text{ then } W \text{ is } \tilde{G},$$

where V and W are variables that take values in sets X and Y, respectively, and $\tilde{F}$ and $\tilde{G}$ are fuzzy sets on X and Y, respectively. The degree of truth of p is given by $\text{truth}(p) = I(\mu_{\tilde{F}}(x), \mu_{\tilde{G}}(y))$ and I is a fuzzy implication (see [4]).

Conditional and Truth-Qualified Propositions

$$p:\left(\text{if } V \text{ is } \tilde{F}, \text{ then } W \text{ is } \tilde{G}\right) \text{ is } \tilde{S}.$$

The degree of truth of this proposition is given by truth $(p) = \mu_{\tilde{S}}\left(I(\mu_{\tilde{F}}(x), \mu_{\tilde{G}}(y))\right)$.

Furthermore, fuzzy propositions may be compound, i.e., obtained by a combination of canonical propositions using the logical connectives **and**, **or**, **implies**, **and** not (see Zadeh's logical connectives in Table 1.1 and reference [21]).

We notice that since we are solving FLP problems, the solutions will be fuzzy subsets of the universes of discourse. So, we need to clarify what it means, for example, $\mu_{\tilde{F}}(\tilde{x})$ for a generic fuzzy subset $\tilde{x}$ of X.

To define $\mu_{\tilde{F}}(\tilde{x})$ for a generic fuzzy subset (fuzzy number) $\tilde{x}$ of X, we follow an approach similar to the one in [37] for vocabulary matching. Hence,

$$\mu_{\tilde{F}}(\tilde{x}) = \max_{x \in X} \min\left(\mu_{\tilde{x}}(x), \mu_{\tilde{F}}(x)\right).$$

Thus, we could calculate, e.g. in a fish harvesting problem, the degree of truth of the proposition "The biomass is *High*" in the case we have described the actual biomass as *around* 900 metric tons (see Figure 1.2).

In Section 1.4.2, we touched upon the fact that the lexicographic method for FLP guarantees solutions with unique optimal objective function values and the popular ranking function-based methods do not. Research has shown that the latter methods could yield suboptimal (or intuitively suboptimal) solutions [27] and dominated ones in the multi-objective case [29]. This happens because ranking functions can map different fuzzy numbers into the same real number. The lexicographic methods, on the other hand, use multiple comparison indexes in an attempt to discriminate between different fuzzy numbers. When the conditions of Definition 1.10 hold, uniqueness is guaranteed. Now, since we will evaluate the degree of truth with which a solution to an FLP problem satisfies a proposition (or a set of them) and

Table 1.1 Zadeh's logical connectives.

and	**or**	**not**	**implies**
min(*x*, *y*)	*max*(*x*, *y*)	1 − *x*	*max*(1 − *x*, *min*(*x*, *y*))

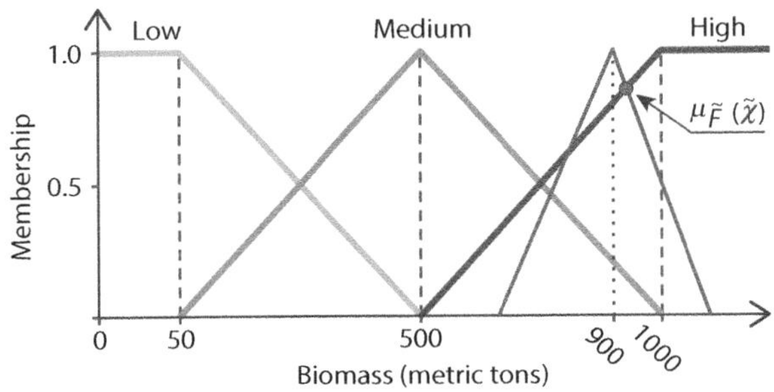

Figure 1.2 Degree of truth of the proposition "The biomass is *High*" when the biomass is *around* 900 metric tons.

decide on it, we should be interested in the optimality and uniqueness of the objective function value; otherwise, the degree of truth will not be unique, which could lead to different (suboptimal) decisions.

1.4.5 Decision-Making

Let us describe the unmodeled objectives U_1 to U_p using the fuzzy propositions p_1 to p_p, respectively. To make a decision *a posteriori*, a set of feasible solutions to problem (1.1) $\tilde{S} = \{\tilde{x}^{(1)}, \tilde{x}^{(2)}, \ldots, \tilde{x}^{(n_a)}\}$ is obtained using the MGA approach. Then, a decision matrix $D = [d_{ij}]_{n_a \times p}$ is constructed by determining the degree of truth d_{ij} to which the solution $\tilde{x}^{(i)}$ satisfies the proposition p_j. Using the **and** connective, or a suitable aggregation operator (see [26] and [17]), an *a posteriori* solution $\tilde{x}^*$ is then drawn from the set $\{\tilde{x}^{(q)} \in \tilde{S}$: **and**$(d_{i1}, d_{i2}, \ldots, d_{i,p}) \leq$ **and** $(d_{q1}, d_{q2}, \ldots, d_{q,p})$ for all $i = 1, 2, \ldots, n_a\}$—i.e., a solution $\tilde{x}^* \in \tilde{S}$ is chosen such that it maximizes the overall degree of truth of the propositions. The overall degree of truth gives the aggregate compatibility of a solution to the problem with the propositions that define the unmodeled objectives. A more compatible solution is preferable. At this point, we would like to stress that other methods from the multi-criteria decision-making field could be used as well to make the final decision. Here, however, we choose the **and** connective as the aggregation operator, since we are dealing with degrees of truth.

1.5 Illustrative Example

Let us consider, just for the sake of illustration, the following fuzzy version of a simple two-period fish harvesting problem.

$$\begin{aligned}\max\ & (\tilde{x}_1 \oplus \tilde{x}_2, U_1, U_2, U_3)\\ \text{s.t. } & \tilde{I}_1 \oplus \tilde{r}_1 \otimes \tilde{I}_1 = \tilde{x}_1 \oplus \tilde{I}_2,\\ & \tilde{I}_2 \oplus \tilde{r}_2 \otimes \tilde{I}_2 = \tilde{x}_2 \oplus \tilde{I}_3,\\ & \tilde{I}_1 = (950, 1000, 1050),\end{aligned}$$

where $\tilde{I}_j, \tilde{r}_j$, and $\tilde{x}_j$ denote the initial biomass (metric tons), fish reproduction rate, and capture in period j, respectively. We assume that the biomass at the beginning of the first period is the TFN (950, 1000, 1050), $\tilde{r}_1 = (0.15, 0.20, 0.25)$, and $\tilde{r}_2 = (0.10, 0.15, 0.20)$. The modeled objective is to maximize capture, and the unmodeled objectives are to comply with three regulations that aim to ensure that the stock remains economically viable, namely

- if $\tilde{I}_1$ is *High* **and** $\tilde{r}_1$ is *Low*, then $\tilde{x}_1$ is *Low* **or** $\tilde{x}_1$ is *Medium*,
- if $\tilde{I}_2$ is *High* **and** $\tilde{r}_2$ is *Low*, then $\tilde{x}_2$ is *Low* **or** $\tilde{x}_2$ is *Medium*, and
- $\tilde{I}_3$ is *Medium* **or** $\tilde{I}_3$ is *High*.

We remark that, in the general case, these regulations may not be known in advance to the decision-maker for multiple reasons; they could, e.g., change with the decision-making context [26].

1.5.1 Determination of a Reference Solution

The first step of the proposed methodology is to find an optimal solution to the problem.

$$\begin{aligned}\max\ & \tilde{x}_1 \oplus \tilde{x}_2\\ \text{s.t. } & \tilde{I}_1 \oplus \tilde{r}_1 \otimes \tilde{I}_1 = \tilde{x}_1 \oplus \tilde{I}_2,\\ & \tilde{I}_2 \oplus \tilde{r}_2 \otimes \tilde{I}_2 = \tilde{x}_2 \oplus \tilde{I}_3,\\ & \tilde{I}_1 = (950, 1000, 1050).\end{aligned}$$

We use the lexicographic method from Section 1.4.2 and get $\tilde{x}_1 = (0,0,0)$, $\tilde{x}_2 = (1201.75, 1380.0, 1575.0)$, $\tilde{I}_2 = (1092.5, 1200.0, 1312.5)$, and $\tilde{I}_3 = (0, 0, 0)$. We see that this solution leaves the stock at zero; hence, it is not economically viable to capture everything in the second period.

1.5.2 Alternative Solutions Generation

In the second step of the proposed methodology, we find alternative solutions to the fish harvesting problem by solving the following problem iteratively.

$$\max \sum_{q=1}^{k} \Big(\mathrm{ABS}\left(\tilde{x}_1^{(q)}, \tilde{x}_1^{(k+1)}\right) + \mathrm{ABS}\left(\tilde{x}_2^{(q)}, \tilde{x}_2^{(k+1)}\right) + \mathrm{ABS}\left(\tilde{I}_2^{(q)}, \tilde{I}_2^{(k+1)}\right)$$
$$+\mathrm{ABS}\left(\tilde{I}_3^{(q)}, \tilde{I}_2^{(k+1)}\right)\Big)$$
$$\text{s.t. } \tilde{I}_1 \oplus \tilde{r}_1 \otimes \tilde{I}_1 = \tilde{x}_1^{(k+1)} \oplus \tilde{I}_2^{(k+1)},$$
$$\tilde{I}_2^{(k+1)} \oplus \tilde{r}_2 \otimes \tilde{I}_2^{(k+1)} = \tilde{x}_2^{(k+1)} \oplus \tilde{I}_3^{(k+1)},$$
$$\tilde{x}_1^{(k+1)} \oplus \tilde{x}_2^{(k+1)} \oplus \tilde{d} \succcurlyeq (1201.75, 1380.0, 1575.0),$$
$$\tilde{I}_1 = (950, 1000, 1050).$$

Notice that, besides adding the superscript $(k+1)$ to the variables to denote the iteration, we now have an objective function that seeks to maximize the distance between the new solution to the problem and those obtained in past iterations. Plus, we added a new constraint to allow deviations from the optimal objective function value of the fish harvesting problem. Table 1.2 shows several alternative solutions obtained for varying values of the deviation parameter $\tilde{d}$.[1]

1.5.3 Handling the Unmodeled Objectives

Let us suppose that to describe the amount of biomass the decision-maker uses the linguistic terms *Low*, *Medium*, and *High* with membership functions

$$\mu_{low}(x) = \min\left(1, \max(0, (500 - x)/500)\right),$$
$$\mu_{medium}(x) = \max\left(0, \min(x/500, (1000 - x)/500)\right),$$
$$\mu_{high}(x) = \max\left(0, \min(1, (x - 500)/500)\right),$$

[1]Actually, we generated ten solutions per deviation value and kept the ones with degree of truth ≥ 0.30.

Table 1.2 Alternative solutions.

Deviation	Alternatives				
	$\tilde{x}_1$	$\tilde{x}_2$	$\tilde{I}_2$	$\tilde{I}_3$	Modeled objective
(180.26, 207, 236.25)	(957.51, 1065.01, 1065.01)	(0.0, 0.0, 0.0)	(134.98, 134.98, 247.48)	(148.48, 155.23, 296.98)	(957.51, 1065.01, 1065.01)
(240.35, 276, 315)	(0.00, 0.00, 0.00)	(627.61, 805.86, 805.86)	(1092.49, 1199.99, 1312.49)	(574.13, 574.13, 769.13)	(627.61, 805.86, 805.86)
	(680.67, 788.17, 788.17)	(0.00, 0.00, 0.00)	(411.82, 411.82, 524.32)	(453.00, 473.59, 629.18)	(680.67, 788.17, 788.17)
	(0.00, 0.00, 0.00)	(578.86, 757.11, 952.11)	(1092.49, 1199.99, 1312.49)	(622.88, 622.88, 622.88)	(578.86, 757.11, 952.11)
(300.43, 345, 393.75)	(957.51, 1065.01, 1065.01)	(0.0, 0.0, 0.0)	(134.98, 134.98, 247.48)	(148.48, 155.23, 296.98)	(957.51, 1065.01, 1065.01)
(360.52, 414, 472.5)	(0.0, 0.0, 0.0)	(489.19, 667.44, 667.44)	(1092.5, 1200.0, 1312.5)	(712.55, 712.55, 907.55)	(489.19, 667.44, 667.44)
	(542.25, 649.75, 649.75)	(0.0, 0.0, 0.0)	(550.24, 550.24, 662.74)	(605.26, 632.77, 795.28)	(542.25, 649.75, 649.75)
	(0.0, 0.0, 0.0)	(440.44, 618.69, 813.69)	(1092.5, 1200.0, 1312.5)	(761.30, 761.30, 761.30)	(440.44, 618.69, 813.69)
(420.61, 483, 551.25)	(0.0, 0.0, 0.0)	(766.03, 944.28, 944.28)	(1092.5, 1200.0, 1312.5)	(435.71, 435.71, 630.71)	(766.03, 944.28, 944.28)
	(0.0, 0.0, 0.0)	(717.28, 895.53, 1090.53)	(1092.5, 1200.0, 1312.5)	(484.46, 484.46, 484.46)	(717.28, 895.53, 1090.53)

(Continued)

Table 1.2 Alternative solutions. (*Continued*)

Deviation	Alternatives $\tilde{x}_1$	$\tilde{x}_2$	$\tilde{I}_2$	$\tilde{I}_3$	Modeled objective
	(819.09, 926.59, 926.59)	(0.00, 0.00, 0.00)	(273.40, 273.40, 385.90)	(300.74, 314.41, 463.08)	(819.09, 926.59, 926.59)
(480.7, 552, 630)	(0.0, 0.0, 0.0)	(212.35, 390.60, 390.60)	(1092.5, 1200.0, 1312.5)	(989.39, 989.39, 1184.39)	(212.35, 390.60, 390.60)
	(265.42, 372.92, 372.92)	(0.0, 0.0, 0.0)	(827.07, 827.07, 939.57)	(909.78, 951.13, 1127.49)	(265.42, 372.92, 372.92)
	(0.0, 0.0, 0.0)	(163.60, 341.85, 536.85)	(1092.5, 1200.0, 1312.5)	(1038.14, 1038.14, 1038.14)	(163.60, 341.85, 536.85)
(540.78, 621, 708.75)	(0.0, 0.0, 0.0)	(589.47, 767.72, 767.72)	(1092.5, 1200.0, 1312.5)	(612.27, 612.27, 807.27)	(589.47, 767.72, 767.72)
	(642.53, 750.03, 750.03)	(0.0, 0.0, 0.0)	(449.96, 449.96, 562.46)	(494.95, 517.45, 674.95)	(642.53, 750.03, 750.03)
	(0.0, 0.0, 0.0)	(540.72, 718.97, 913.97)	(1092.5, 1200.0, 1312.5)	(661.02, 661.02, 661.02)	(540.72, 718.97, 913.97)
	(0.0, 0.0, 0.0)	(723.16, 723.16, 723.16)	(1092.5, 1200.0, 1312.49)	(478.58, 656.83, 851.83)	(723.16, 723.16, 723.16)
(600.87, 690, 787.5)	(0.0, 0.0, 0.0)	(723.16, 723.16, 723.16)	(1092.5, 1200.0, 1312.49)	(478.58, 656.83, 851.83)	(723.16, 723.16, 723.16)
	(1002.94, 1002.94, 1115.44)	(0.0, 0.0, 0.0)	(89.55, 197.05, 197.05)	(98.51, 226.61, 236.46)	(1002.94, 1002.94, 1115.44)

(*Continued*)

Table 1.2 Alternative solutions. (*Continued*)

Deviation	**Alternatives** $\tilde{x}_1$	$\tilde{x}_2$	$\tilde{I}_2$	$\tilde{I}_3$	**Modeled objective**
	(0.0, 0.0, 0.0)	(0.0, 41.42, 41.42)	(1092.5, 1200.0, 1312.5)	(1201.75, 1338.57, 1533.57)	(0.0, 41.42, 41.42)
	(922.31, 1029.81, 1142.31)	(0.0, 0.0, 0.0)	(170.18, 170.18, 170.18)	(187.19, 195.70, 204.21)	(922.31, 1029.81, 1142.31)
	(1031.06, 1031.06, 1031.06)	(0.0, 0.0, 0.0)	(61.43, 168.93, 281.43)	(67.57, 194.27, 337.71)	(1031.06, 1031.06, 1031.06)
	(0.0, 0.0, 0.0)	(0.0, 0.0, 124.27)	(1092.5, 1200.0, 1312.5)	(1201.75, 1380.0, 1450.72)	(0.0, 0.0, 124.27)
	(1002.94, 1002.94, 1115.44)	(0.0, 0.0, 0.0)	(89.55, 197.05, 197.05)	(98.51, 226.61, 236.46)	(1002.94, 1002.94, 1115.44)
	(0.0, 0.0, 0.0)	(31.06, 31.06, 31.06)	(1092.5, 1200.0, 1312.5)	(1170.68, 1348.93, 1543.93)	(31.06, 31.06, 31.06)

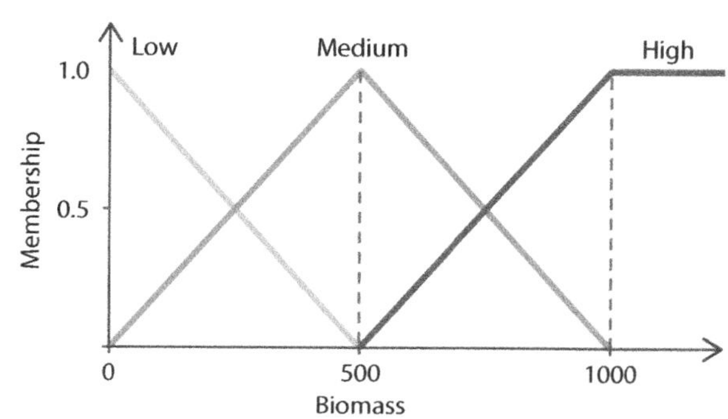

Figure 1.3 Linguistic terms set used to describe the biomass in the fish harvesting problem.

Table 1.3 Individual and overall degrees of truth of every alternative solution.

	Alternatives		Propositions			
No.	**Deviation**	**Modeled objective**	**First**	**Second**	**Third**	**Overall**
1	(180.26, 207, 236.25)	(957.51, 1065.01, 1065.01)	0.36	1	0.46	0.36
2	(240.35, 276, 315)	(627.61, 805.86, 805.86)	0.63	0.54	0.85	0.54
3		(680.67, 788.17, 788.17)	0.52	0.96	0.95	0.52
4		(578.86, 757.11, 952.11)	0.63	0.62	0.75	0.62
5	(300.43, 345, 393.75)	(957.51, 1065.01, 1065.01)	0.36	1	0.46	0.36
6	(360.52, 414, 472.5)	(489.19, 667.44, 667.44)	0.63	0.72	0.58	0.58
7		(542.25, 649.75, 649.75)	0.63	0.73	0.74	0.63
8		(440.44, 618.69, 813.69)	0.63	0.72	0.52	0.52
9	(420.61, 483, 551.25)	(766.03, 944.28, 944.28)	0.63	0.34	0.9	0.34
10		(717.28, 895.53, 1090.53)	0.63	0.41	0.96	0.41
11		(819.09, 926.59, 926.59)	0.36	1	0.71	0.36
12	(480.7, 552, 630)	(212.35, 390.60, 390.60)	0.63	0.72	0.98	0.63
13		(265.42, 372.92, 372.92)	0.63	0.71	0.92	0.63
14		(163.60, 341.85, 536.85)	0.63	0.72	1	0.63
15	(540.78, 621, 708.75)	(589.47, 767.72, 767.72)	0.63	0.6	0.77	0.6
16		(642.53, 750.03, 750.03)	0.58	0.89	0.96	0.58
17		(540.72, 718.97, 913.97)	0.63	0.67	0.67	0.63
18		(723.16, 723.16, 723.16)	0.63	0.55	0.76	0.55
19	(600.87, 690, 787.5)	(723.16, 723.16, 723.16)	0.63	0.55	0.76	0.55
20		(1002.94, 1002.94, 1115.44)	0.36	1	0.46	0.36
21		(0.0, 41.42, 41.42)	0.63	0.72	0.99	0.63
22		(922.31, 1029.81, 1142.31)	0.36	1	0.4	0.36
23		(1031.06, 1031.06, 1031.06)	0.36	1	0.52	0.36
24		(0.0, 0.0, 124.27)	0.63	0.72	0.99	0.63
25		(1002.94, 1002.94, 1115.44)	0.36	1	0.46	0.36
26		(31.06, 31.06, 31.06)	0.63	0.72	0.99	0.63

respectively (see Figure 1.3). The number of terms and their definitions is both subjective and application-dependent. Similarly, to describe *Low* in the case of the reproduction rates $\tilde{r}_1$ and $\tilde{r}_2$, the decision-maker could use the membership function $\mu_{low}(x) = \max\left(0, (0.5 - x)/0.5\right)$. We can now use these membership functions along with Zadeh's logical connectives to handle the regulations (unmodeled objectives), which have been expressed as fuzzy propositions.

1.5.4 Decision-Making

Table 1.3 shows the degrees of truth to which each solution in Table 1.2 satisfies the unmodeled objectives. The "Overall" column gives the aggregate degree of truth obtained with the **and** connective. The decision-maker can now analyze these results for each deviation level and decide according to the maximum degree of truth criterion. In case of ties, since we are maximizing capture, the decision could be made based on the "Modeled objective" column. Notice that, in this case, the nature of the unmodeled objectives-the fact that they are regulations-establishes an explicit priority structure in which they have certain precedence over the modeled objective. Based on this observation, if we allow a deviation from the optimal objective function value of up to (240.35, 276, 315) (around 20% of the optimal value), then we should opt for solution No. 4 with an overall degree of truth equal to 0.62. According to Table 1.2, this solution requires not capturing during the first period and capturing *around* 757.11 metric tons during the second. Similarly, we could analyze other deviation levels and make a decision accordingly.

1.6 Conclusions and Future Work

This paper presented a methodology for *a posteriori* decision-making in FLP, addressing the challenges posed by unmodeled objectives and vagueness in problem formulation. By integrating fuzzy numbers into the mathematical model, fuzzy logic for handling qualitative and unmodeled objectives, and the MGA technique to provide decision-makers with sets of diverse solutions, the proposed methodology enables a more comprehensive evaluation of optimization problems in uncertain environments. A two-period fish harvesting problem demonstrated the applicability of the methodology. The results underscore the importance of considering unmodeled objectives in decision-making, as they can significantly impact the final choice of solution.

Future research directions include extending the methodology to the multiobjective case, nonlinear programming problems, and other fuzzy sets generalizations and uncertainty modeling approaches, such as Pythagorean fuzzy sets [2], Z-numbers [1], and rough sets [15]. Furthermore, empirical studies across various application domains, including transportation and tourism [26, 31], could provide deeper insights into the practical benefits and limitations of the proposed methodology. Finally, given that the fuzzy optimization problems are transformed into equivalent mixed-integer linear programming problems, improving the computational efficiency of the methodology remains an important challenge crucial for real-world applications. We envision the use of metaheuristic methods to handle these problems efficiently.

Acknowledgments

This research was funded by MICIU/AEI /10.13039/501100011033, including FEDER Funds, UE grant number PID2023-146575NB-I00.

AI disclosure statement: The author confirms that no artificial intelligence (AI)-generated content or AI-assisted writing tools were used in the preparation of this chapter (including summaries and the abstract). All text, analysis, and conclusions are the result of the author's original work.

References

1. Akram, M. and Ullah, I., Solution of z-number-based multiobjective linear programming models with different membership functions. *Inf. Sci.*, 659, 1–22, 2024, doi: 10.1016/j.ins.2024.120100.
2. Akram, M., Ullah, I., Alharbi, M.G., Methods for solving lr-type pythagorean fuzzy linear programming problems with mixed constraints. *Math. Probl. Eng.*, 2021, 1, 1–29, 2021, doi: 10.1155/2021/4306058.
3. Arana-Jiménez, M., Fuzzy pareto solutions in fully fuzzy multiobjective linear programming, in: *Optimization of Complex Systems: Theory, Models, Algorithms and Applications*, H.A.L. Thi, H.M. Le, T.P. Dinh (Eds.), pp. 509–517, Springer International Publishing, Cham, 2020, ISBN 978-3-030-21803-4.
4. Baczyński, M. and Jayaram, B., *Fuzzy Implications, volume 231 of Studies in Fuzziness and Soft Computing*, Springer-Verlag, Berlin, Heidelberg, 2008, ISBN 978-3-540-69080-1. doi: 10.1007/978-3-540-69082-5.

5. Behera, D. and Thomas, R., Epistemic uncertainty based linear programming problem and its solution. *Int. J. Mach. Learn. Cybern.*, 15, 6, 2337–2346, 2024, doi: 10.1007/s13042-023-02033-y.
6. Downey Brill, E., Chang, S.-Y., Hopkins, L.D., Modeling to generate alternatives: The hsj approach and an illustration using a problem in land use planning. *Manage. Sci.*, 28, 3, 221–235, 1982, doi: 10.1287/mnsc.28.3.221.
7. Downey Brill, E., Flach, J.M., Hopkins, L.D., Ranjithan, S., MGA: a decision support system for complex, incompletely defined problems. *IEEE Trans. Syst. Man Cybern.*, 20, 4, 745–757, 1990, doi: 10.1109/21.105076.
8. Cuevas, E., Luque, A., Castañeda, B.M., Rivera, B., *Metaheuristic Algorithms: New Methods, Evaluation, and Performance Analysis*, 1 edition, Studies in Computational Intelligence. Springer Nature Switzerland, Cham, Switzerland, 2024, ISBN 9783031630538. doi: 10.1007/978-3-031-63053-8.
9. David, D. and Alamoodi, A., A bibliometric analysis of research on multiple criteria decision making with emphasis on energy sector between (2019-2023). *Appl. Data Sci. Anal.*, 2023, 143–149, 2023, doi: 10.58496/ADSA/2023/013. URL https://journals. mesopotamian.press/index.php/ADSA/article/view/190.
10. Dubois, D. and Prade, H., Operations on fuzzy numbers. *Int. J. Syst. Sci.*, 9, 6, 613–626, 1978, doi: 10.1080/00207727808941724.
11. Dubois, D. and Prade, H., *Fuzzy Sets and Systems: Theory and Applications*, Academic Press, New York, 1980.
12. Ebrahimnejad, A. and Verdegay, J.L., *Fuzzy Sets-Based Methods and Techniques for Modern Analytics*, 1 edition, *volume 364 of Studies in Fuzziness and Soft Computing*, Springer International Publishing, Cham, 2018, doi: 10.1007/978-3-319-73903-8.
13. Farhadinia, B., Ranking fuzzy numbers based on lexicographical ordering. *Int. J. Appl. Math. Comput. Sci.*, 5, 4, 248–251, 2009.
14. Figueroa–García, J.C., Hernández, G., Franco, C., A review on history, trends and perspectives of fuzzy linear programming. *Oper. Res. Perspect.*, 9, 1–14, 2022, doi: 10.1016/j.orp.2022.100247.
15. Garg, H., Alodhaibi, S.S., Khalifa, H.A.E.-W., Study on multi-objective nonlinear programming problem with rough parameters. *J. Intell. Fuzzy Syst.*, 42, 4, 3591–3604, 2022, doi: 10.3233/JIFS-211747.
16. Ghanbari, R., Ghorbani-Moghadam, K., Mahdavi-Amiri, N., De Baets, B., Fuzzy linear programming problems: models and solutions. *Soft Comput.*, 24, 13, 10043–10073, 2020, doi: 10.1007/s00500-019-04519-w.
17. Grabisch, M., Marichal, J.-L., Mesiar, R., Pap, E., *Aggregation functions*, Encyclopedia of Mathematics and its Applications. Cambridge University Press, Cambridge, UK, 2009, ISBN 978-0-521-51926-7. URL https://www.cambridge.org/9780521519267.
18. Greco, S., Ehrgott, M., Figueira, J.R., *Multiple Criteria Decision Analysis, volume 233 of International Series in Operations Research & Management*

Science, Springer New York, New York, NY, 2016, ISBN 978-1-4939-3093-7. doi: 10.1007/978-1-4939-3094-4.

19. Hamid, F. (Ed.), *Optimization Essentials: Theory, Tools, and Applications*, 1 edition, International Series in Operations Research & Management Science. Springer Nature Singapore, Singapore, 2024, ISBN 9789819954919. doi:10.1007/978-981-99-5491-9.
20. Hanss, M., *Applied Fuzzy Arithmetic*, Springer-Verlag, Berlin/Heidelberg, 2005, doi: 10.1007/b138914.
21. Klir, G.J. and Yuan, B., *Fuzzy Sets and Fuzzy Logic: Theory and Applications*, Prentice Hall PTR, New Jersey, NJ, 1995, ISBN 0-13-101171-5.
22. Li, J., Zeng, W., Xie, J., Yin, Q., A new fuzzy regression model based on least absolute deviation. *Eng. Appl. Artif. Intell.*, 52, 54–64, 2016, doi: 10.1016/j.engappai.2016.02.009.
23. Malik, M., Gupta, S.K., Arana-Jiménez, M., Developing solution algorithm for lr-type fully interval-valued intuitionistic fuzzy linear programming problems using lexicographic-ranking method. *Comput. Appl. Math.*, 42, 6, 1–55, 2023, doi: 10.1007/ s40314-023-02408-5.
24. Parreiras, R.O., Maciel, J.H.R.D., Vasconcelos, J.A., The a posteriori decision in multiobjective optimization problems with smarts, promethee ii, and a fuzzy algorithm. *IEEE Trans. Magn.*, 42, 4, 1139–1142, 2006, doi: 10.1109/TMAG.2006.871986.
25. Pedrycz, W., *An Introduction to Computing with Fuzzy Sets: Analysis, Design, and Applications*, Springer International Publishing, Cham, 2021, ISBN 9783030528003. doi: 10.1007/978-3-030-52800-3.
26. Pérez-Cañedo, B., Porras, C., Pelta, D.A., Verdegay, J.L., Modeling contexts as fuzzy propositions in optimization problems. *IEEE Trans. Fuzzy Syst.*, 31, 5, 1474–1483, 2023, doi: 10.1109/TFUZZ.2022.3203786.
27. Pérez-Cañedo, B. and Concepción-Morales, E.R., A method to find the unique optimal fuzzy value of fully fuzzy linear programming problems with inequality constraints having unrestricted L-R fuzzy parameters and decision variables. *Expert Syst. Appl.*, 123, 256–269, 2019, doi: 10.1016/j.eswa.2019.01.041.
28. Pérez-Cañedo, B., Verdegay, J.L., Rosete, A., Concepción-Morales, E.R., Fully Fuzzy Multi-objective Berth Allocation Problem, in: *Hybrid Artificial Intelligent Systems. HAIS 2020, volume 12344 of Lecture Notes In Computer Science*, E.A. de la Cal, J.R.V. Flecha, H. Quintián, E. Corchado (Eds.), pp. 261–272, Springer, Cham, 2020, ISBN 978-3-030-61705-9. doi: 10.1007/978-3-030-61705-9 22.
29. Pérez-Cañedo, B., Verdegay, J.L., Concepción-Morales, E.R., An *E*-constraint method for multiobjective linear programming in intuitionistic fuzzy environment. *Int. J. Intell. Syst.*, 2023, 1, 1–14, 2023, doi: 10.1155/2023/9677396.
30. Salas-Molina, F., Reig-Mullor, J., Pla-Santamaria, D., Garcia-Bernabeu, A., On the conditions for total orderings in lexico-graphic methods to rank

fuzzy numbers. *Int. J. Fuzzy Syst.*, 26, 5, 1417–1427, 2024, doi: 10.1007/s40815-023-01676-x.

31. Sirbiladze, G., Garg, H., Ghvaberidze, B., Matsaberidze, B., Khutsishvili, I., Midodashvili, B., Uncertainty modeling in multi-objective vehicle routing problem under extreme environment. *Artif. Intell. Rev.*, 55, 8, 6673–6707, 2022, doi: 10.1007/ s10462-022-10169-6.
32. Talib, H.M., Albahri, A.S., Edoh, T.O.C., Fuzzy decision-making framework for sensitively prioritizing autism patients with moderate emergency level. *Appl. Data Sci. Anal.*, 2023, 16–41, 2023, doi: 10.58496/ADSA/2023/002.
33. Tanaka, H., Okuda, T., Asai, K., On Fuzzy-Mathematical Programming. *J. Cybern.*, 3, 4, 37–46, 1974, doi: 10.1080/01969727308545912.
34. Tian, H., Zhang, S., Garg, H., Liu, X., An extended seca-gdm method considering flexible linguistic scale optimization and its application in occupational health and safety risk assessment. *Alexandria Eng. J.*, 88, 317–330, 2024, doi: 10.1016/j.aej.2024.01.026.
35. Wang, M.-L., Wang, H.-F., Chih-Lung, L., Ranking fuzzy number based on lexicographic screening procedure. *Int. J. Inf. Technol. Decis. Making*, 4, 4, 663–678, 2005, doi: 10.1142/S0219622005001696.
36. Wang, W. and Wang, Z., Total orderings defined on the set of all fuzzy numbers. *Fuzzy Sets Syst.*, 243, 131–141, 2014, doi: 10.1016/j.fss.2013.09.005.
37. Watada, J. and Pedrycz, W., A fuzzy regression approach to acquisition of linguistic rules, in: *Handbook of Granular Computing*, chapter 32, W. Pedrycz, A. Skowron, V. Kreinovich (Eds.), pp. 719–732, John Wiley & Sons, Ltd, New Jersey, NJ, 2008, ISBN 9780470724163. doi: 10.1002/9780470724163.ch32.
38. Zadeh, L.A., Fuzzy sets. *Inf. Control*, 8, 3, 338–353, 1965, doi: 10.1016/S0019-9958(65)90241-X.
39. Zadeh, L.A., Is there a need for fuzzy logic? *Inf. Sci.*, 178, 13, 2751–2779, 2008, doi: 10.1016/j.ins.2008.02.012.
40. Zechman, E.M. and Ranji Ranjithan, S., An evolutionary algorithm to generate alternatives (eaga) for engineering optimization problems. *Eng. Optim.*, 36, 5, 539–553, 2004, doi: 10.1080/03052150410001704863.
41. Zimmermann, H.-J., Optimization in fuzzy environment, in: *XXI Int. TIMS and 46th In ORSA Conference*, San Juan, Puerto Rico, 1974.

2

Interval-Valued Proportional Spherical Fuzzy AHP and TOPSIS Methodology: A Case Study for Smart City Park Planning

Selcuk Cebi[1,2], Irem Ucal Sari[3], Başar Öztayşi[4], Sezi Çevik Onar[4] and Cengiz Kahraman[4*]

[1]*Yildiz Technical University, Industrial Engineering Department, Istanbul, Türkiye*
[2]*Industrial Data Analytics and Decision Support Systems Center, Azerbaijan State University of Economics, Baku, Azerbaijan*
[3]*Baskent University, Industrial Engineering Department, Ankara, Türkiye*
[4]*Istanbul Technical University, Industrial Engineering Department, Istanbul, Türkiye*

Abstract
Rapid urbanization has led to increased pressure on city infrastructure, particularly in managing transportation and parking. Efficient parking management plays a critical role in reducing traffic, promoting environmental sustainability, and improving the overall urban experience. As cities aim to adopt smarter and more sustainable practices, choosing the right parking technologies becomes a complex problem involving multiple criteria and uncertainty. This uses the combination of Analytic Hierarchy Process (AHP) and the Technique for Order Preference by Similarity to Ideal Solution (TOPSIS) for choosing the right parking technologies. The uncertainties and imprecision in the decision-making process are represented with Interval-Valued Proportional Spherical Fuzzy Sets (IVPSFS). This model allows experts to express their evaluations more accurately even when there is ambiguity and little data. This integration enables us to better handle uncertainty, hesitation, and incomplete information, especially in urban planning scenarios where decision makers' judgments are often linguistic and have imprecision. A case study is presented to compare three common parking technology alternatives, namely image processing systems, sensor-based methods, and radar/LiDAR solutions, based on criteria including cost, durability, maintenance, data

**Corresponding author*: kahramanc@itu.edu.tr

Harish Garg (ed.) Decision Support Systems in Smart Computing: Embracing Uncertainty and Challenges, (27–68) © 2026 Scrivener Publishing LLC

accuracy, and security. The findings offer practical insights for urban planners and decision-makers involved in the development of smart parking systems. The proposed methodology offers a flexible and realistic decision-support tool for urban planners and policymakers aiming to develop sustainable and efficient smart city infrastructures.

Keywords: Smart city, smart parking, proportional spherical fuzzy sets, MCDM

List of Abbreviations

AI	Artificial Intelligence
AHP	Analytic Hierarchy Process
CPS	Cyber-Physical Systems
DL	Deep Learning
IoT	Internet of Things
PSFN	Proportional Spherical Fuzzy Number
IVPSFS	Interval-Valued Proportional Spherical Fuzzy Sets
IVSFS	Interval-Valued Spherical Fuzzy Sets
IVSF	Interval-Valued Spherical Fuzzy
MCDM	Multi-Criteria Decision Making
MADM	Multi-Attribute Decision Making
ML	Machine Learning
SBS	Sensor-Based Systems
TOPSIS	Technique for Order Preference by Similarity to Ideal Solution

2.1 Introduction

Cities around the world are expanding rapidly, bringing with them new challenges in urban living. As populations grow and vehicle ownership increases, traffic congestion and inefficient parking have become pressing issues for many municipalities. One critical aspect of urban mobility that requires urgent attention is parking management. In many cities, the lack of available and efficiently used parking spaces contributes to traffic problems, air pollution, and driver frustration. These issues highlight the need for smarter and more sustainable parking solutions.

To overcome these challenges, urban planners and local governments are turning to technology-driven solutions within the broader vision of smart cities. Smart parking systems are designed to improve the management of parking spaces by using digital technologies such as sensors, data analytics, and networked communication tools. The smart parking systems focus on reducing the time spent looking for parking, ease congestion, lower fuel consumption, and enhancing the overall urban experience. They also provide city authorities with real-time data to manage parking demand more effectively.

However, building an effective smart parking system goes beyond simply adopting new technology. It requires careful planning and coordination across multiple domains, including environmental considerations, infrastructure compatibility, user convenience, cost-efficiency, and long-term sustainability. Moreover, the implementation of such systems involves diverse stakeholders (urban planners, engineers, municipal officials, and local residents) each with different perspectives and priorities. Balancing these interests often involves uncertainty and incomplete information, which makes decision-making particularly difficult.

Traditional decision-making approaches struggle to manage the complexity and uncertainty inherent in urban planning and smart city projects. Multi-Criteria Decision Making (MCDM) methods usually propose a constructed approach to prioritizing and ranking options, yet, they often fall short when dealing with qualitative and linguistic expert judgments. To overcome this limitation, fuzzy logic techniques have become increasingly popular. Fuzzy set theory, which originated with Zadeh [46], has developed significantly over the years to address the multidimensional nature of decision problems. Early fuzzy sets focused on representing uncertainty through one-dimensional membership functions. However, as decision problems became more complex, extensions like intuitionistic fuzzy sets [5], Pythagorean fuzzy sets [43], and spherical fuzzy sets [20] were introduced. Spherical fuzzy sets, in particular, stand out because they can represent membership, non-membership, and hesitation all within a single three-dimensional space. One of the latest advancements in this area is interval-valued proportional spherical fuzzy sets (IVPSFS) [19], which combine the large domain of classical spherical fuzzy sets with a proportional allocation mechanism that allows experts to make their evaluations more accurately, reflecting their true thinking patterns.

Among the diverse analytical tools available for supporting complex decisions in urban environments, AHP and TOPSIS have gained significant prominence in the context of smart city planning. AHP is widely recognized for its structured and hierarchical decomposition of complex problems, enabling decision-makers to evaluate the relative importance of criteria using pairwise comparisons. It facilitates a clear prioritization of decision factors, even when they are qualitative in nature. On the other hand,

TOPSIS offers a robust mechanism for ranking alternatives based on their distance from ideal and negative-ideal solutions, allowing for an intuitive and performance-oriented evaluation of competing options. When combined, AHP and TOPSIS provide a powerful synergy: AHP derives precise weights for the decision criteria, while TOPSIS uses those weights to identify the most preferable alternative. In the context of smart city applications—such as smart parking systems—these methods are especially valuable due to their ability to handle multidimensional evaluation, incorporate expert judgment, and deal with uncertainty. Their integration within an IVPSFS framework further enhances their applicability, enabling more nuanced and accurate decision-making in environments where data is imprecise or incomplete.

This chapter presents a decision-making approach that combines the AHP and the TOPSIS under the IVPSFS environment. The method is applied to a real-world case study involving the evaluation of smart parking technologies. Three alternatives, namely image processing systems, sensor-based solutions, and radar/LiDAR technologies, are assessed based on five key criteria: data accuracy, durability, cost, maintenance requirements, and data security. The results aim to support city authorities in selecting the most suitable technology for smart parking implementation, ensuring more efficient and sustainable urban development.

The main objectives of this study are as follows:

- To develop an integrated MCDM model by combining AHP and TOPSIS within the framework of IVPSFS, allowing for better managing uncertainty and impreciseness in the expert judgments.
- To design a practical decision-support methodology that enables experts and urban planners to evaluate smart parking technologies based on multiple, often conflicting, criteria.
- To apply the proposed methodology to a real-world case study involving the selection of optimal parking space identification technologies in a smart city context.
- To provide actionable insights and a replicable evaluation framework for municipalities and decision-makers aiming to implement efficient and sustainable smart parking systems.

The rest of the chapter is organized as follows: Section 2.2 provides literature review on smart computing methods. Section 2.3 examines the smart city concept and analyzes existing studies. Section 2.4 first presents the preliminaries related to proportional spherical fuzzy sets, then details the formulation and implementation steps of the proposed IVPSF-AHP and IVPSF-TOPSIS methods. Section 2.5 applies these methods to a comparative case study on Free Park Space Identification. Finally, Section 2.6 concludes the chapter with a summary of findings and implications.

2.2 Smart Computing, Methods, Technologies Literature Review

Smart computing refers to a new-generation technological paradigm that integrates hardware, software, and networking components to enable information systems to perceive real-world contexts in real time. By leveraging advanced analytics and contextual awareness, smart computing supports users in making more informed and intelligent decisions, ultimately contributing to the optimization of dynamic and ongoing processes [24]. The platform on which smart computing is executed should be capable of receiving an input problem, analyzing the situation, and making a decision that generates a valuable solution. While the decision-making process is the primary focus in such applications, software and hardware components are also critical to create the input for an acceptable decision [28]. The literature involves various application areas for smart computing. Smart cities, smart healthcare, smart transportation, industry 4.0, smart agriculture, and smart education are among the application domains of smart computing.

The literature identifies a wide range of technologies employed in smart computing applications. These applications typically integrate sensor-based systems, the Internet of Things (IoT), edge computing, cyber-physical systems (CPS), machine learning, cognitive computing, big data analytics, cloud computing, blockchain and artificial intelligence (AI). Sensor-based systems (SBS) are computational systems that rely on sensors to collect data from their environment in real time. SBS processes sensory input—such as temperature, motion, pressure, location, or biometric signals—to monitor, analyze, and often react to changes in their surroundings. They form the foundational layer for many smart applications by enabling context-awareness, automation, and intelligent decision-making [23, 38]. SBS are essential for enabling smart computing environments to sense and adapt to real-world conditions dynamically. They serve as the sensory foundation that fuels intelligent responses in automated systems. Another important technology is the Internet of Things (IoT) [13]. In the context of smart computing, IoT serves as the foundational input mechanism, feeding continuous streams of environmental, biometric, or operational data which will later be analyzed and used for smart computing applications. IoT enables seamless connectivity between the physical and digital worlds in smart computing ecosystems. It provides the high-frequency, real-time data essential for intelligent analysis and decision-making.

Cyber-Physical Systems (CPS) are among the most commonly adopted technologies in smart computing. CPS are integrated systems where computation, networking, and physical processes are combined [36]. CPS involve embedded sensors and output devices that monitor and control physical elements, with real-time interaction between the software and physical environment. CPS bridge the gap between computational intelligence and physical action, allowing smart systems to perceive and act within their environment. They are the operational backbone of many smart applications in fields like healthcare, manufacturing, and mobility.

Cloud computing is a way of providing easy, on-demand access to shared resources like networks, servers, storage, applications, and services, which can be quickly set up or released with little effort or help from the provider [11]. Cloud computing empowers smart computing systems with virtually unlimited processing and storage capacity. It facilitates the centralized handling of massive data volumes generated by IoT and sensor networks.

Another important technology in smart computing is edge computing, which suggests a decentralized computing paradigm in which data analysis and processing are done at or near the physical location where the data is generated [1]. Generally, edge devices or local edge servers are used instead of centralized cloud infrastructure. Edge computing improves system performance by minimizing latency, reducing bandwidth usage, enhancing privacy and security. Edge computing is crucial for smart systems requiring real-time responsiveness, such as autonomous vehicles or health monitors. It allows smart computing applications to act instantly and locally, even in limited connectivity scenarios.

Blockchain is a decentralized and distributed ledger technology that records transactions or data in a series of cryptographically linked blocks. Each block contains a timestamp, transaction data, and a hash of the previous block, ensuring data integrity, transparency, and immutability without the need for a central authority [25]. In smart computing environments involving multiple stakeholders, blockchain ensures secure, verifiable, and tamper-proof data transactions. It is particularly important for trust, authentication, and auditability in decentralized systems.

Big Data Analytics is the process of analyzing massive, complex, and varied datasets with advanced analytical methods to reveal hidden patterns, correlations, trends, and other insights that can support decision-making and action [17]. Big Data Analytics enables smart computing systems to extract meaningful patterns and insights from large-scale, high-velocity, and heterogeneous data, supporting intelligent, real-time, and context-aware decision-making. It transforms raw, chaotic data into actionable knowledge that drives smart behavior in computing systems. Without big data analytics, smart systems cannot adapt effectively to evolving conditions or user needs.

Cognitive computing refers to computational systems that mimic human cognitive abilities such as reasoning, perception, learning, and decision-making [31]. Cognitive computing is generally used to understand unstructured data, interact naturally with users, learn from interactions, and provide context-aware insights and recommendations. This technology allows smart computing systems to interpret ambiguous or incomplete information and still deliver intelligent responses. It enhances the human-like reasoning capacity of automated systems in dynamic environments.

Machine learning is a computational approach that enables systems to automatically identify patterns in data and make decisions or predictions without the need for explicit programming for each specific task [29]. Machine learning enables smart computing systems by finding patterns in data, and making intelligent decisions autonomously. It equips smart computing with the ability to evolve and improve based on experience. As a result, systems become more accurate, personalized, and efficient over time.

Artificial Intelligence (AI) is a branch of computer science dedicated to creating systems that can carry out tasks normally requiring human intelligence, such as reasoning, learning from experience, understanding natural language, recognizing patterns, and making independent decisions [45]. AI represents the cognitive engine of smart computing, enabling autonomous decision-making across complex and uncertain domains. It integrates all other technologies by providing high-level intelligence and adaptability.

Studies on smart computing represent the multidisciplinary nature of the field. In a recent study, Si *et al.* [34] focus on theft detection problem in smart grids and propose a smart computing framework involving deep learning and cloud computing. The framework is capable of handling massive data generated in the smart grids and automatically detecting theft activities. In another recent study, Butt *et al.* [9] propose a fog-enabled smart surveillance approach to enhance responsiveness and efficiency for intelligent transportation systems. The proposed approach utilizes IoT,

RFID-based monitoring, and fog computing and it provides efficiency by reducing response time, optimizing resource usage. The analysis based on one simulation shows that the proposed approach outperforms traditional cloud-only deployments. Healthcare is an important domain for smart computing, for example Xu *et al.* [42] present a smart computing infrastructure based on CPS in the field of healthcare. The system integrates deep learning, big data analytics, and artificial intelligence technologies to process health data. Data collected from IoT sensors, are processed by both cloud and edge computing to enable real-time health monitoring. In another recent study, Batra *et al.* [7] focus on the integration of AI within the architecture of CPS for smart cities. The authors provide insights about the synergistic use of technologies such as IoT, AI, big data analytics, and edge computing within CPS, emphasizing their roles in urban environments for real-time data sensing, predictive analytics, and decision support. In another study on smart transportation, Ali *et al.* [2] propose an integrated approach for enhancing smart transportation systems using big data analytics and cloud computing. The authors focus on collecting real-time traffic data and environmental data through IoT-enabled sensors and processing it in cloud infrastructures for smart transportation decisions. Smart healthcare also focuses on wearable technologies. In a recent study, Taha *et al.* [35] provide a comprehensive overview of nanophotonic smart contact lenses which shows a high potential on enriching smart healthcare with wearable technology.

A literature review on Scopus database shows 2794 papers on Smart Computing. The literature review is later limited to specific technologies. Results reveal that the most commonly mentioned technologies in smart computing domain are cloud computing, internet of things, edge computing, and machine learning. While cloud computing takes place in 47% of the smart computing papers, Internet of Things takes place in 33%, edge computing in 29% and machine learning is referenced in 14% of smart computing papers. The number of papers using specific technologies in smart computing is listed in Figure 2.1.

In order to illustrate trends in smart computing technologies, annual publication counts are compiled and examined. Figure 2.2 highlights how academic interest in these technologies has evolved over the past decade.

Among the others, Cloud Computing and Artificial intelligence have been frequently referenced in the field for the last decade. On the other hand, blockchain and edge computing have gained attraction especially after 2017. It can be concluded that they moved from a lesser-known topic to a key research focus. IOT, sensor-based systems and cyber-physical systems have been in the focus of studies for the last decade but it can be

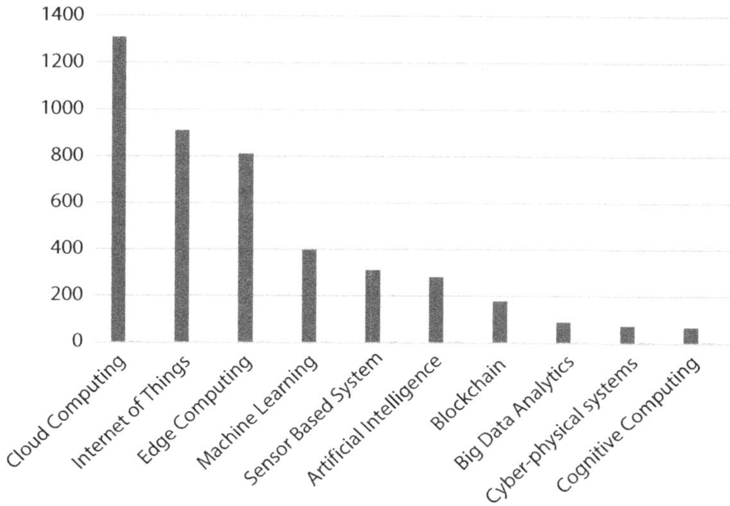

Figure 2.1 Number of papers published using specific technologies.

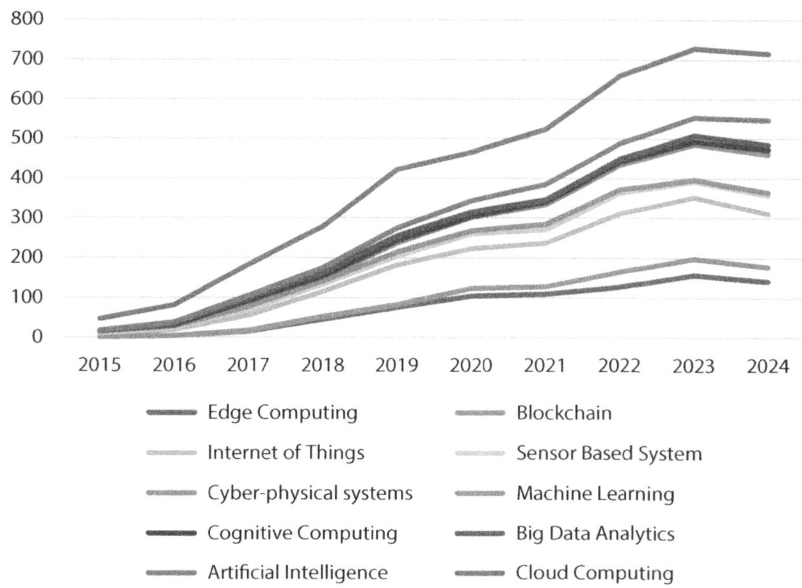

Figure 2.2 Trends on specific technology usage on smart computing papers in the last 10 years.

observed that the topics have become more popular especially after 2021. Big data analytics, machine learning and cognitive computing technologies also gain important attention as a part of data interpretation and decision-making tools.

Beyond the foundational technologies enabling data collection and processing, MCDM or Multi-Attribute Decision-Making (MADM) methods are critical for optimizing outcomes in smart computing applications. These techniques evaluate trade-offs between conflicting objectives (e.g., cost, efficiency, privacy) in complex systems. Mohammed *et al.* [27] review MCDM/MADM technologies in the field of software engineering. David and Alamoodi [15] present a bibliometric analysis of research from the past five years focusing on MCDM in relation to its use and applications in the energy sector. A statistical study of influential publications, journals, countries/territories, and authors is carried out first. Then, an analysis is performed based on four distinct time periods to determine the evolving patterns of authors' cooperation structure and study themes. Aljanabi [3] offers an in-depth examination of decision-making research in civil engineering. Wang *et al.* [40] present a new CODAS method that applies the Heronian Minkowski distance operator within T-spherical fuzzy sets, strengthening group decision-making through this framework. Gao *et al.* [18] propose a hybrid BWM-Entropy-COPRAS model based on spherical fuzzy sets to support the selection of digital supply chain partners. This approach provides a balanced integration of expert judgment and objective data. Kaur and Garg [22] developed an algorithm for autonomous vehicle parking that utilizes adjustable probabilistic neutrosophic hesitant fuzzy sets. These studies show that fuzzy MCDM methods are efficient tools for handling complex problems under uncertainty.

2.3 Smart Cities Literature Review

Smart city concept is an urban development that combines communication and information technologies for improving cities' livability, efficiency, and sustainability [16]. Smart cities concept gained popularity at the end of 2000s. Both the advancements in technologies and the need for optimizing the scarce resources made smart city concept very popular. There is a rapid urbanization in the world, which creates challenges in many areas such as transportation and waste management. Smart cities are considered as a successful way to deal with those challenges [41]. Therefore, the studies on smart cities have increased rapidly over the years. In order to see the major concepts in Smart City literature, we conducted a literature review by using Scopus database accessed on May 5, 2025. We look at the articles, books and book chapters that use "smart city" in the title. The query we have used is (TITLE("smart city") AND (LIMIT-TO (DOCTYPE,"ar") OR LIMIT-TO (DOCTYPE,"ch") OR LIMIT-TO (DOCTYPE,"re") OR LIMIT-TO (DOCTYPE,"ed") OR LIMIT-TO (DOCTYPE,"bk")) AND (LIMIT-TO (LANGUAGE,"English"))). A total of 10938 papers are analyzed for thematic analysis using VOSViewer software.

Figure 2.3 shows the increasing interest on "smart city" interest over the years based on Scopus database analysis.

In order to see the main themes and clusters, we have to look at the co-occurrence of the keywords in the literature by using VOSViewer. VOSViewer enables visualizing bibliometric networks [39]. We look at the co-occurrence of the keyword by using fractional counting, the threshold is selected as 30. The illustration of the results is given in Figure 2.4.

When we look at Figure 2.4, we see that technology such as IoT and Big data is an important aspect of a smart city. Similarly, smart cities are often associated with sustainability and sustainable development. Energy efficiency, policy and renewable usage are also other concepts that are commonly associated with smart cities. Being transparent and ensuring security is also important for smart cities. by using Technologies such as blockchains and cryptography these aspects can be met. Not only IoT but maintaining connectivity by using sensor networks and optimizing them using various smart techniques such as deep learning and intelligent systems are crucial for an efficient smart city.

The solutions of the technology firms and their collaborations with the major technology companies popularize and increase the usage of sensors,

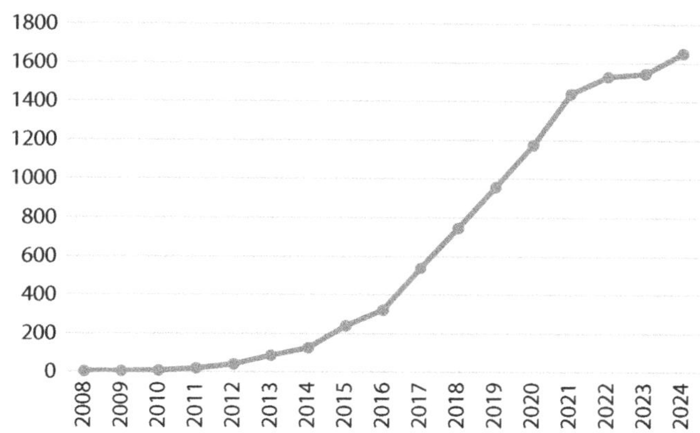

Figure 2.3 Number of papers published over the years on smart cities.

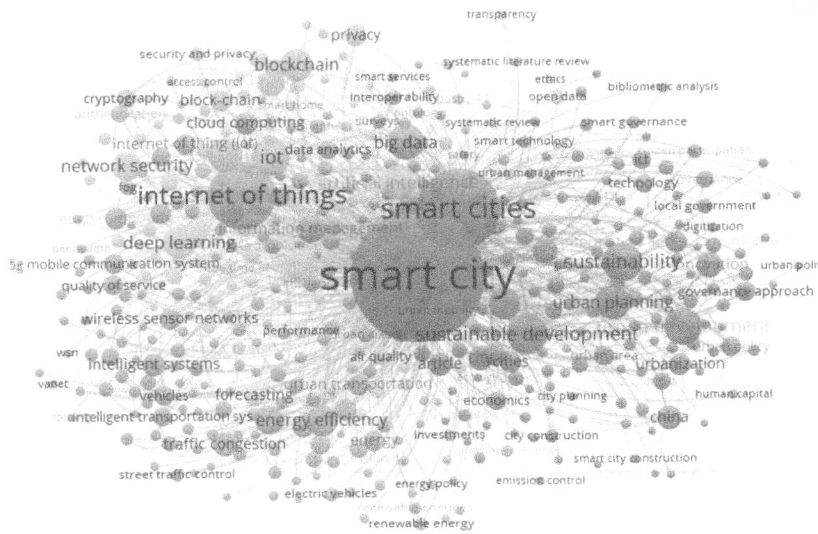

Figure 2.4 Smart city co-occurrence of keywords (based on VOSViewer).

networks, and analytics for solving problems of the cities and making them smarter [41]. The concepts such as "digital city" and "intelligent city" are also used to define either connectivity or the usage of analytical techniques. The major focus of these studies and smart cities is to overcome challenges resulting from increasing population and existence of many complex infrastructures in the cities [8, 14].

In literature various academic fields use the term smart city and try to overcome various problems of the cities. Although smart city term has been used for over a decade, there is no single definition which is accepted by all the academic fields [41]. The early studies emphasize the role of information technologies and infrastructure such as sensor networks [8]. Whereas the recent studies see smart cities as a way to increase quality of life, and ensure transparency, democracy, and safety [14]. Using technology such as sensors, IoT, and networks to achieve a more sustainable and improved quality of life has become the main focus of smart city concepts. Today smart city is defined as an integrated system of physical, social, and digital elements that work together to fulfill urban needs [37].

Recent studies on smart cities highlight the necessity for holistic, and inclusive methods that combine advanced technologies with resilience and human involvement. Lytras [26] defines the future of smart cities around three key pillars: technology (such as AI, metaverse, cloud computing), human and social connectivity (inclusiveness, co-designed policies), and focusing on sustainability and innovation. The quality of life of the people living in cities is seriously affected by problems such as air pollution, and climate change. Smart energy solutions such as smart grids or optimizing renewable energy sources become important [33]. Not only physical problems but also social problems such as security can be solved by smart surveillance systems. Similarly, the problems of disadvantaged groups within a city can be solved and inclusivity can be achieved with smart city structures [4]. Emerging technologies and their usage are always at the heart of the smart city concept. The solutions such as improving traffic lighting systems with IoT sensors in traffic lights are considered as the main application areas in smart cities. Technology such as 5G wireless networks has created further opportunities to improve urban life [8]. Not only connectivity but also cloud computing and big data analytics are used to process information and create intelligence for the city [14]. Especially, recent developments in data computing and storage, AI technologies and Metaverse also create many new opportunities for smart cities. Many smart city operations centers now integrate AI-driven dashboards for monitoring city KPIs [33]. Yet, these technologies also create security and privacy problems which should be handled by competent human resources. Thus, we should invest not only in infrastructure, but also in skills needed to use them effectively [10]. For instance, many UK cities have focused on developing open data portals and innovative ecosystems to leverage technological solutions [8]. Governance of smart cities involves setting standards for privacy, security, and ethics and an effective urban governance is crucial for a smart city [12]. Especially, the problems related with cybersecurity can drastically affect the population of the cities.

MCDM techniques are increasingly used to support smart city planning and operations. Ates and Önder [6] claim that resilience in cities can be reached through by considering climatic and geographical attributes of the cities. They propose an AHP-based framework for evaluation of smart city projects, they claim that the criteria should integrate geographical and cultural characteristics along with local architectural knowledge and sustainable urban planning into smart city frameworks to guarantee the resilience. Kamvysi *et al.* [21] developed a QFD-AHP-ANP integrated framework to support smart technology selection with city-specific needs, demonstrated through an application in Thessaloniki. Zhao *et al.* [47] built a hybrid EW-G1 and TOPSIS-Utility Theory model for risk-sharing in public-private partnership (PPP) smart city projects. They focus on fairness and complexity in stakeholder responsibilities. Yenkar and Sawarkar [44] combine MCC and two-level MCDM (AHP, TOPSIS) to prioritize urgent urban complaints shared *via* Twitter. This approach enables timely municipal responses.

2.4 Preliminaries: Interval Valued Spherical Fuzzy Sets

The definition of IVSFS, arithmetic operations, aggregation and defuzzification operations are given in the following.

Definition 1. An IVSFS $\tilde{A}_S$ of the universe of discourse X is defined as;

$$\tilde{A}_S = \left\{ \langle x, \left(\begin{array}{c} \left[\mu^L_{\tilde{A}_S}(x), \mu^U_{\tilde{A}_S}(x)\right], \left[v^L_{\tilde{A}_S}(x), v^U_{\tilde{A}_S}(x)\right], \\ \left[\pi^L_{\tilde{A}_S}(x), \pi^U_{\tilde{A}_S}(x)\right] \end{array} \right) \middle| x \in X \right\} \tag{2.1}$$

where, $0 \le \mu^L_{\tilde{A}_S}(x) \le \mu^U_{\tilde{A}_S}(x) \le 1$, $0 \le v^L_{\tilde{A}_S}(x) \le v^U_{\tilde{A}_S}(x) \le 1$ and $0 \le \left(\mu^U_{\tilde{A}_S}(x)\right)^2 + \left(v^U_{\tilde{A}_S}(x)\right)^2 + \left(\pi^U_{\tilde{A}_S}(x)\right)^2 \le 1$.

For each $x \in X$, $\mu^U_{\tilde{A}_S}(x)$, $v^U_{\tilde{A}_S}(x)$ and $\pi^U_{\tilde{A}_S}(x)$ are the upper degrees of "membership", "non-membership" and "hesitancy" respectively of x to $\tilde{A}_S$. For each $x \in X$, if $\mu^L_{\tilde{A}_S}(x) = \mu^U_{\tilde{A}_S}(x)$, $v^L_{\tilde{A}_S}(x) = v^U_{\tilde{A}_S}(x)$ and $\pi^L_{\tilde{A}_S}(x) = \pi^U_{\tilde{A}_S}(x)$ then, IVSFS $\tilde{A}_S$ becomes a SVSFS.

For an IVSFS $\tilde{A}_S$,

$$\tilde{A}_s = \langle \left[\mu^L_{\tilde{A}_S}(x), \mu^U_{\tilde{A}_S}(x)\right], \left[v^L_{\tilde{A}_S}(x), v^U_{\tilde{A}_S}(x)\right], \left[\pi^L_{\tilde{A}_S}(x), \pi^U_{\tilde{A}_S}(x)\right] \rangle \tag{2.2}$$

is called an IVSF number. For simplicity, Eq. (2.2) is given as

$$\tilde{a} = \langle [a, b], [c, d], [e, f] \rangle \tag{2.3}$$

where $[a,b] \subset [0,1]$, $[c,d] \subset [0,1]$, $[e,f] \subset [0,1]$ and $b^2 + d^2 + f^2 \le 1$.

Some basic operations are defined over IVSFS as follows:
Addition;

$$\tilde{a}_1 \oplus \tilde{a}_2 \Big[((a_1)^2+(a_2)^2-(a_1)^2(a_2)^2)^{\frac{1}{2}},((b_1)^2+(b_2)^2-(b_1)^2(b_2)^2)^{1/2}\Big],$$
$$[c_1c_2,d_1d_2],\Big[\big((1-(a_2)^2(e_1)^2+(1-(a_1)^2(e_2)^2-(e_1)^2(e_2)^2)\big)^{1/2},$$
$$((1-(b_2)^2)(f_1)^2+(1-(b_1)^2)(f_2)^2-(f_1)^2(f_2)^2))^{1/2}\Big] \tag{2.4}$$

Multiplication;

$$\tilde{a}_1 \otimes \tilde{a}_2 = [a_1a_2,b_1b_2],\Big[((c_1)^2+(c_2)^2-(c_1)^2(c_2)^2)^{1/2},((d_1)^2+(d_2)^2-(d_1)^2(d_2)^2)^{1/2}\Big],$$
$$\Big[\big((1-(c_2)^2)(e_1)^2+(1-(c_1)^2)(e_2)^2-(e_1)^2(e_2)^2)\big)^{1/2},$$
$$\big((1-(d_2)^2)(f_1)^2+(1-(d_1)^2)(f_2)^2-(f_1)^2(f_2)^2)\big)^{1/2}\Big] \tag{2.5}$$

Multiplication by a scalar; $\lambda > 0$

$$\lambda.\tilde{a} = \Big\{\Big[\big(1-(1-a^2)^\lambda\big)^{\frac{1}{2}},\big(1-(1-b^2)^\lambda\big)^{\frac{1}{2}}\Big],\big[c^\lambda,d^\lambda\big],\Big[\big((1-a^2)^\lambda-(1-a^2-e^2)^\lambda\big)^{1/2},$$
$$\big((1-b^2)^\lambda-(1-b^2-f^2)^\lambda\big)^{1/2}\Big]\Big\} \tag{2.6}$$

λth **Power of** $\tilde{a};\lambda > 0$

$$\tilde{a}^\lambda = \Big\{\big[a^\lambda,b^\lambda\big],\Big[\big(1-(1-c^2)^\lambda\big)^{1/2},\big(1-(1-d^2)^\lambda\big)^{1/2}\Big],\Big[\big((1-c^2)^\lambda -$$
$$(1-c^2-e^2)^\lambda\big)^{1/2},\big((1-d^2)^\lambda-(1-d^2-f^2)^\lambda\big)^{1/2}\Big]\Big\} \tag{2.7}$$

Definition 2. Let $\tilde{a}_j = \langle[a_j,b_j],[c_j,d_j],[e_j,f_j]\rangle$ be pairs of Interval-valued Spherical Weighted Arithmetic Mean (IVSWAM) with respect to, $w_j=(w_1,w_2,\ldots\ldots,w_n)$; $w_j \in [0,1]$; $\sum_{j=1}^n w_j = 1$, IVSWAM is defined as;

$$\text{IVSWAM}_w(\tilde{a}_1,\ldots\ldots,\tilde{a}_n) = w_1\tilde{a}_1 \oplus w_2\tilde{a}_2 \oplus \ldots\ldots \oplus w_n\tilde{a}_n$$
$$= \left\{\left[\left(1-\prod_{j=1}^{n}\left(1-a_j^2\right)^{wj}\right)^{1/2}, \left(1-\prod_{j=1}^{n}\left(1-b_j^2\right)^{wj}\right)^{1/2}\right], \left[\prod_{j=1}^{n} c_j^{wj}, \prod_{j=1}^{n} d_j^{wj}\right],\right.$$
$$\left.\left[\left(\prod_{j=1}^{n}\left(1-a_j^2\right)^{wj} - \prod_{j=1}^{n}\left(1-a_j^2-e_j^2\right)^{wj}\right)^{1/2}, \left(\prod_{j=1}^{n}\left(1-b_j^2\right)^{wj} - \prod_{j=1}^{n}\left(1-b_j^2-f_j^2\right)^{wj}\right)^{1/2}\right]\right\} \tag{2.8}$$

Definition 3. Let $\tilde{a}_j = \langle [a_j, b_j], [c_j, d_j], [e_j, f_j] \rangle$ be a collection of Interval-Valued Spherical Weighted Geometric Mean (IVSWGM) with respect to, $w_j = (w_1, w_2, \ldots\ldots, w_n)$; $w_j \in [0,1]$; $\sum_{j=1}^{n} w_j = 1$, IVSWGM is defined as;

$$\text{IVSWGM}_w(\tilde{a}_1,\ldots\ldots,\tilde{a}_n) = \tilde{a}_1^{w_1} \otimes \tilde{a}_2^{w_2} \otimes \ldots\ldots \otimes \tilde{a}_n^{w_n}$$
$$= \left\{\left[\prod_{j=1}^{n} a_j^{wj}, \prod_{j=1}^{n} b_j^{wj}\right], \left[\left(1-\prod_{j=1}^{n}\left(1-c_j^2\right)^{wj}\right)^{1/2}, \left(1-\prod_{j=1}^{n}\left(1-d_j^2\right)^{wj}\right)^{1/2}\right],\right.$$
$$\left.\left[\left(\prod_{j=1}^{n}\left(1-c_j^2\right)^{wj} - \prod_{j=1}^{n}\left(1-c_j^2-e_j^2\right)^{wj}\right)^{1/2}, \left(\prod_{j=1}^{n}\left(1-d_j^2\right)^{wj} - \prod_{j=1}^{n}\left(1-d_j^2-f_j^2\right)^{wj}\right)^{1/2}\right]\right\} \tag{2.9}$$

Definition 4. The score function of IVSFS number a is defined as

$$Score(\tilde{a}) = S(\tilde{a}) = \frac{a^2 + b^2 - c^2 - d^2 - (e/2)^2 - (f/2)^2}{2} \tag{2.10}$$

where $Score(\tilde{a}) = S(\tilde{a}) \in [-1, +1]$.

Definition 5. The accuracy function of IVSFS number a is defined as;

$$Accuracy(\tilde{a}) = H(\tilde{a}) = \frac{a^2 + b^2 + c^2 + d^2 + e^2 + f^2}{2} \tag{2.11}$$

where $H(\tilde{a}) \in [0,1]$.
Note that: $\tilde{a}_1 < \tilde{a}_2$ if and only if $S(\tilde{a}_1) < S(\tilde{a}_2)$ or $S(\tilde{a}_1) = S(\tilde{a}_2)$ and $H(\tilde{a}_1) < H(\tilde{a}_2)$.

2.5 IVPSF AHP and TOPSIS Methodology

In this section first, the preliminaries are given for single-valued and interval-valued proportional spherical fuzzy sets. Then the interval valued proportional spherical fuzzy AHP and interval valued proportional spherical fuzzy TOPSIS methodologies are proposed.

2.5.1 Single-Valued Proportional Spherical Fuzzy Sets

Consider the spherical fuzzy set $\tilde{S} = \{\langle x; \mu_{\tilde{S}}(x), h_{\tilde{S}}(x), v_{\tilde{S}}(x)\rangle | x \in X\}$. Assume that the expert judges the proportions between $\mu_{\tilde{S}}(x), v_{\tilde{S}}(x)$ and $h_{\tilde{S}}(x)$ as in Equations 2.12–2.14:

$$\mu(x) = k_1 r_{\tilde{S}}(x) \tag{2.12}$$

and

$$h(x) = k_2 r_{\tilde{S}}(x) \tag{2.13}$$

and

$$v(x) = k_3 r_{\tilde{S}}(x) \tag{2.14}$$

satisfying

$$\left(r_{\tilde{S}}(x)\right)^2 + \left(k_1 r_{\tilde{S}}(x)\right)^2 + \left(k_2 r_{\tilde{S}}(x)\right)^2 + \left(k_3 r_{\tilde{S}}(x)\right)^2 = 1 \tag{2.15}$$

The refusal degree can be given by Equation 2.16:

$$r_{\tilde{S}}(x) = \sqrt{\frac{1}{1 + (k_1)^2 + (k_2)^2 + (k_3)^2}} \tag{2.16}$$

Then, each element in the set $\tilde{S}$ can be represented by

$$\tilde{S}=\left\{\langle x;k_1\sqrt{\frac{1}{1+(k_1)^2+(k_2)^2+(k_3)^2}},k_2\sqrt{\frac{1}{1+(k_1)^2+(k_2)^2+(k_3)^2}},k_3\sqrt{\frac{1}{1+(k_1)^2+(k_2)^2+(k_3)^2}}\rangle \,|x\in X\right\} \tag{2.17}$$

Let $\tilde{A}$ and $\tilde{B}$ be two spherical fuzzy sets. Addition and multiplication operations are defined as in Equations 2.18 and 2.19, respectively.

$$\tilde{A}+\tilde{B}=\left(\begin{array}{c} x;\,k_{A1}\sqrt{\frac{1}{1+(k_{A1})^2+(k_{A2})^2+(k_{A3})^2}}+k_{B1}\sqrt{\frac{1}{1+(k_{B1})^2+(k_{B2})^2+(k_{B3})^2}}- \\ k_{A1}\sqrt{\frac{1}{1+(k_{A1})^2+(k_{A2})^2+(k_{A3})^2}}\times k_{B1}\sqrt{\frac{1}{1+(k_{B1})^2+(k_{B2})^2+(k_{B3})^2}}, \\ k_{A2}\sqrt{\frac{1}{1+(k_{A1})^2+(k_{A2})^2+(k_{A3})^2}}\times k_{B2}\sqrt{\frac{1}{1+(k_{B1})^2+(k_{B2})^2+(k_{B3})^2}}, \\ k_{A3}\sqrt{\frac{1}{1+(k_{A1})^2+(k_{A2})^2+(k_{A3})^2}}\times k_{B3}\sqrt{\frac{1}{1+(k_{B1})^2+(k_{B2})^2+(k_{B3})^2}} \end{array}\middle| x\in X\right) \tag{2.18}$$

$$\tilde{A}\times\tilde{B}=\left(\begin{array}{c} x;\,k_{A1}\sqrt{\frac{1}{1+(k_{A1})^2+(k_{A2})^2+(k_{A3})^2}}\times k_{B1}\sqrt{\frac{1}{1+(k_{B1})^2+(k_{B2})^2+(k_{B3})^2}}, \\ \Big(\frac{{k_{A2}}^2}{1+(k_{A1})^2+(k_{A2})^2+(k_{A3})^2}+\frac{{k_{B2}}^2}{1+(k_{B1})^2+(k_{B2})^2+(k_{B3})^2}- \\ \frac{{k_{A2}}^2}{1+(k_{A1})^2+(k_{A2})^2+(k_{A3})^2}\times\frac{{k_{B2}}^2}{1+(k_{B1})^2+(k_{B2})^2+(k_{B3})^2}\Big)^{1/2}, \\ \Big(\frac{{k_{A3}}^2}{1+(k_{A1})^2+(k_{A2})^2+(k_{A3})^2}+\frac{{k_{B3}}^2}{1+(k_{B1})^2+(k_{B2})^2+(k_{B3})^2}- \\ \frac{{k_{A3}}^2}{1+(k_{A1})^2+(k_{A2})^2+(k_{A3})^2}\times\frac{{k_{B3}}^2}{1+(k_{B1})^2+(k_{B2})^2+(k_{B3})^2}\Big)^{1/2} \end{array}\middle| x\in X\right) \tag{2.19}$$

The multiplication by a constant and power operation is given by Equations 2.20 and 2.21, respectively.

$$\lambda\tilde{A}=\left\langle\left(1-\left(1-k_{A1}\sqrt{\frac{1}{1+(k_{A1})^2+(k_{A2})^2+(k_{A3})^2}}\right)^{\lambda}\right)^{1/2},\left(k_{A2}\sqrt{\frac{1}{1+(k_{A1})^2+(k_{A2})^2+(k_{A3})^2}}\right)^{\lambda},\left(k_{A3}\sqrt{\frac{1}{1+(k_{A1})^2+(k_{A2})^2+(k_{A3})^2}}\right)^{\lambda}\right\rangle \tag{2.20}$$

$$\tilde{A}^{\lambda}=<\left(k_{A1}\sqrt{\frac{1}{1+(k_{A1})^2+(k_{A2})^2+(k_{A3})^2}}\right)^{\lambda},\left(1-\left(1-k_{A2}\sqrt{\frac{1}{1+(k_{A1})^2+(k_{A2})^2+(k_{A3})^2}}\right)^{\lambda}\right)^{1/2},$$
$$\left(1-\left(1-k_{A3}\sqrt{\frac{1}{1+(k_{A1})^2+(k_{A2})^2+(k_{A3})^2}}\right)^{\lambda}\right)^{1/2}> \tag{2.21}$$

Definition 6. Let α_j $(j=1,2,\ldots,n)$ be a collection of PSFNs. The proportional spherical fuzzy weighted averaging (PSFWA) operator is a mapping $PS^n \to PS$ such that

$$PSFWA_w(\alpha_1,\alpha_2,\ldots,\alpha_n)=\oplus_{j=1}^{n}\left(w_j\alpha_j\right) \tag{2.22}$$

where $w=(w_1,w_2,\ldots,w_n)^T$ is the weight vector of $\alpha_j(j=1,2,\ldots,n)$ and $w_j>0,\sum_{j=1}^{n}w_j=1$. Then

$$PSFWA_w(\alpha_1,\alpha_2,\ldots,\alpha_n)=\left(\begin{array}{c}(1-\Pi_{j=1}^{n}\left(1-k_{1j}\sqrt{\frac{1}{1+(k_{1j})^2+(k_{2j})^2+(k_{3j})^2}}\right)^{w_j})^{1/2},\Pi_{j=1}^{n}\left(k_{2j}\sqrt{\frac{1}{1+(k_{1j})^2+(k_{2j})^2+(k_{3j})^2}}\right)^{w_j},\\ \Pi_{j=1}^{n}\left(k_{3j}\sqrt{\frac{1}{1+(k_{1j})^2+(k_{2j})^2+(k_{3j})^2}}\right)^{w_j}\end{array}\right) \tag{2.23}$$

Definition 7. Let $\alpha_j\ (j=1,2,\ldots,n)$ be a collection of PSFNs. The proportional spherical fuzzy weighted geometric (PSFWG) operator is a mapping $PS^n \rightarrow PS$ such that

$$PPiFWG_w(\alpha_1,\alpha_2,\ldots,\alpha_n)=\otimes_{j=1}^{n}\left(\alpha_j\right)^{w_j} \tag{2.24}$$

where $w=(w_1,w_2,\ldots,w_n)^T$ is the weight vector of $\alpha_j\ (j=1,2,\ldots,n)$ and $w_j>0,\sum_{j=1}^{n}w_j=1$. Then

$$PSFWG_w(\alpha_1,\alpha_2,\ldots,\alpha_n)=\left(\Pi_{j=1}^{n}\left(k_{1j}\sqrt{\frac{1}{1+(k_{1j})^2+(k_{2j})^2+(k_{3j})^2}}\right)^{w_j},(1-\Pi_{j=1}^{n}\left(1-k_{2j}\sqrt{\frac{1}{1+(k_{1j})^2+(k_{2j})^2+(k_{3j})^2}}\right)^{w_j})^{\frac{1}{2}},\right.$$
$$\left.(1-\Pi_{j=1}^{n}\left(1-k_{3j}\sqrt{\frac{1}{1+(k_{1j})^2+(k_{2j})^2+(k_{3j})^2}}\right)^{w_j})^{1/2}\right) \tag{2.25}$$

Definition 8. Let a full PSFN be $\tilde{A}=(k_{A1},k_{A2},k_{A3})$. The score $(S_{\tilde{A}})$ and accuracy functions $(Ac_{\tilde{A}})$ are defined as in Equation 2.26 and Equation 2.27, respectively.

$$S_{\tilde{A}}=\left(k_{A1}\sqrt{\frac{1}{1+(k_{A1})^2+(k_{A2})^2+(k_{A3})^2}}-\frac{k_{A2}}{2}\sqrt{\frac{1}{1+(k_{A1})^2+(k_{A2})^2+(k_{A3})^2}}\right)^2-\left(k_{A3}\sqrt{\frac{1}{1+(k_{A1})^2+(k_{A2})^2+(k_{A3})^2}}-\right.$$
$$\left.-\frac{k_{A2}}{2}\sqrt{\frac{1}{1+(k_{A1})^2+(k_{A2})^2+(k_{A3})^2}}\right)^2" \tag{2.26}$$

$$Ac_{\tilde{A}}=\frac{{k_{A1}}^2}{1+(k_{A1})^2+(k_{A2})^2+(k_{A3})^2}+\frac{{k_{A2}}^2}{1+(k_{A1})^2+(k_{A2})^2+(k_{A3})^2}$$
$$+\frac{{k_{A3}}^2}{1+(k_{A1})^2+(k_{A2})^2+(k_{A3})^2} \tag{2.27}$$

Definition 9: Let $x\in X$ be a universe set and $\tilde{A}$ and $\tilde{B}$ be two spherical fuzzy numbers. Then normalized Euclidean distance $d_E(\tilde{A},\tilde{B})$ is given by Equation 2.28.

$$dE(\tilde{A},\tilde{B}) = \sqrt{\frac{1}{n}\sum_{i=1}^{n}\left[\begin{array}{l}\left(\frac{k_{A1i}^{2}}{1+(k_{A1i})^2+(k_{A2i})^2+(k_{A3i})^2}-\frac{k_{B1i}^{2}}{1+(k_{B1i})^2+(k_{B2i})^2+(k_{B3i})^2}\right)^2+\\ \left(\frac{k_{A2i}^{2}}{1+(k_{A1i})^2+(k_{A2i})^2+(k_{A3i})^2}-\frac{k_{B2i}^{2}}{1+(k_{B1i})^2+(k_{B2i})^2+(k_{B3i})^2}\right)^2+\\ \left(\frac{k_{A3i}^{2}}{1+(k_{A1i})^2+(k_{A2i})^2+(k_{A3i})^2}-\frac{k_{B3i}^{2}}{1+(k_{B1i})^2+(k_{B2i})^2+(k_{B3i})^2}\right)^2\end{array}\right]} \tag{2.28}$$

2.5.2 Interval Valued Proportional Spherical Fuzzy Sets (IVPSFS)

Let the interval valued proportional spherical set $\tilde{A}$ be defined as in Equation 2.29. Equations 2.30–2.36 transform an IVPSFS to an IVSFS:

$$\tilde{A}_p = \left(\left[k_{\mu L}, k_{\mu U}\right], [k_{hL}, k_{hU}], [k_{vL}, k_{vU}]\right) \tag{2.29}$$

$$\tilde{A}_I = ([\mu_L, \mu_U], [h_L, h_U], [v_L, v_U]) \tag{2.30}$$

where

$$\mu_L = \frac{k_{\mu L}}{\sqrt{1+(k_{\mu L})^2+(k_{\mu U})^2+(k_{\pi L})^2+(k_{\pi L})^2+(k_{vU})^2+(k_{vL})^2}} \tag{2.31}$$

$$\mu_U = \frac{k_{\mu U}}{\sqrt{1+(k_{\mu L})^2+(k_{\mu U})^2+(k_{\pi L})^2+(k_{\pi L})^2+(k_{vU})^2+(k_{vL})^2}} \tag{2.32}$$

$$h_L = \frac{k_{hL}}{\sqrt{1+(k_{\mu L})^2+(k_{\mu U})^2+(k_{\pi L})^2+(k_{\pi L})^2+(k_{vU})^2+(k_{vL})^2}} \tag{2.33}$$

$$h_U = \frac{h_{hU}}{\sqrt{1+(k_{\mu L})^2+(k_{\mu U})^2+(k_{\pi L})^2+(k_{\pi L})^2+(k_{vU})^2+(k_{vL})^2}} \tag{2.34}$$

$$v_L = \frac{k_{vL}}{\sqrt{1+\left(k_{\mu L}\right)^2+\left(k_{\mu U}\right)^2+(k_{\pi L})^2+(k_{\pi L})^2+(k_{vU})^2+(k_{vL})^2}} \tag{2.35}$$

$$v_U = \frac{k_{vU}}{\sqrt{1+\left(k_{\mu L}\right)^2+\left(k_{\mu U}\right)^2+(k_{\pi L})^2+(k_{\pi L})^2+(k_{vU})^2+(k_{vL})^2}} \tag{2.36}$$

Definition 10: Let $\tilde{\alpha}_1 = \langle[a_1,b_1],[c_1,d_1],[e_1,f_1]\rangle$ and $\tilde{\alpha}_2 = \langle[a_2,b_2],[c_2,d_2],[e_2,f_2]\rangle$ be t IVSF numbers, the distance between $\tilde{\alpha}_1$ and $\tilde{\alpha}_2$ is given in Equation 2.37 [30]:

$$d(\tilde{\alpha}_1,\tilde{\alpha}_2) = \frac{1}{4}\left(\left|a_1^2-a_2^2\right|+\left|b_1^2-b_2^2\right|+\left|c_1^2-c_2^2\right|+\left|d_1^2-d_2^2\right|+\left|e_1^2-e_2^2\right|+\left|f_1^2-f_2^2\right|\right) \tag{2.37}$$

2.5.3 IVPSF AHP

The steps of the proposed IVPSF AHP method are presented below:

Step 1. Construct the hierarchy of the problem including n criteria (j=1, 2,…, n) and m alternatives (i=1, 2,.., m). Each main criterion may have s sub-criteria (t=1,2,…, s).
Step 2. Construct the IVPSF pairwise comparison matrices $\tilde{P}$ based on the hierarchy

For the main criteria:

$$\tilde{P}_{kn} = \begin{bmatrix} & c1 & cj & cn \\ c1 & \left(\left[k_{11\mu L}, k_{11\mu U}\right], [k_{11hL}, k_{11hU}], [k_{11vL}, k_{11vU}]\right) & \cdots & \left(\left[k_{1n\mu L}, k_{1n\mu U}\right], [k_{1nhL}, k_{1nhU}], [k_{1nvL}, k_{1nvU}]\right) \\ cj & \vdots & \ddots & \vdots \\ cn & \left(\left[k_{n1\mu L}, k_{n1\mu U}\right], [k_{n1hL}, k_{n1hU}], [k_{n1vL}, k_{n1vU}]\right) & \cdots & \left(\left[k_{nn\mu L}, k_{nn\mu U}\right], [k_{nnhL}, k_{nnhU}], [k_{nnvL}, k_{nnvU}]\right) \end{bmatrix}$$

For the sub-criteria:

$$\tilde{P}_{ks} = \begin{bmatrix} & c1 & ct & cs \\ c1 & \left(\left[k_{11\mu L}, k_{11\mu U}\right], [k_{11hL}, k_{11hU}], [k_{11vL}, k_{11vU}]\right) & \cdots & \left(\left[k_{1s\mu L}, k_{1s\mu U}\right], [k_{1shL}, k_{1shU}], [k_{1svL}, k_{1svU}]\right) \\ ct & \vdots & \ddots & \vdots \\ cs & \left(\left[k_{s1\mu L}, k_{s1\mu U}\right], [k_{s1hL}, k_{s1hU}], [k_{s1vL}, k_{s1vU}]\right) & \cdots & \left(\left[k_{ss\mu L}, k_{ss\mu U}\right], [k_{sshL}, k_{sshU}], [k_{ssvL}, k_{ssvU}]\right) \end{bmatrix}$$

For the alternatives:

$$\tilde{P}_{km} = \begin{bmatrix} & c1 & ci & cm \\ c1 & \left(\left[k_{11\mu L}, k_{11\mu U}\right], [k_{11hL}, k_{11hU}], [k_{11vL}, k_{11vU}]\right) & \cdots & \left(\left[k_{1m\mu L}, k_{1m\mu U}\right], [k_{1mhL}, k_{1mhU}], [k_{1mvL}, k_{1mvU}]\right) \\ ci & \vdots & \ddots & \vdots \\ cm & \left(\left[k_{m1\mu L}, k_{m1\mu U}\right], [k_{m1hL}, k_{m1hU}], [k_{m1vL}, k_{m1vU}]\right) & \cdots & \left(\left[k_{mm\mu L}, k_{mm\mu U}\right], [k_{mmhL}, k_{mmhU}], [k_{mmvL}, k_{mmvU}]\right) \end{bmatrix}$$

Step 3. Convert the IVPSF matrices to the IVSF pairwise comparison matrices $\tilde{P}$.

For the main criteria:

$$\tilde{P}_{n} = \begin{bmatrix} & c1 & cj & cn \\ c1 & ([\mu_{11L}, \mu_{11U}], [h_{11L}, h_{11U}], [v_{11L}, v_{11U}]) & \cdots & ([\mu_{1nL}, \mu_{1nU}], [h_{1nL}, h_{1nU}], [v_{1nL}, v_{1nU}]) \\ cj & \vdots & \ddots & \vdots \\ cn & ([\mu_{n1L}, \mu_{n1U}], [h_{n1L}, h_{n1U}], [v_{n1L}, v_{n1U}]) & \cdots & ([\mu_{nnL}, \mu_{nnU}], [h_{nnL}, h_{nnU}], [v_{nnL}, v_{nnU}]) \end{bmatrix}$$

For the sub-criteria:

$$\tilde{P}_s = \begin{bmatrix} & c1 & ct & cs \\ c1 & ([\mu_{11L},\mu_{11U}],[h_{11L},h_{11U}],[v_{11L},v_{11U}]) & \cdots & ([\mu_{1sL},\mu_{1sU}],[h_{1sL},h_{1sU}],[v_{1sL},v_{1sU}]) \\ ct & \vdots & \ddots & \vdots \\ cs & ([\mu_{s1L},\mu_{s1U}],[h_{s1L},h_{s1U}],[v_{s1L},v_{s1U}]) & \cdots & ([\mu_{ssL},\mu_{ssU}],[h_{ssL},h_{ssU}],[v_{ssL},v_{ssU}]) \end{bmatrix}$$

For the alternatives:

$$\tilde{P}_m = \begin{bmatrix} & c1 & ci & cm \\ c1 & ([\mu_{11L},\mu_{11U}],[h_{11L},h_{11U}],[v_{11L},v_{11U}]) & \cdots & ([\mu_{1mL},\mu_{1mU}],[h_{1mL},h_{1mU}],[v_{1mL},v_{1mU}]) \\ ci & \vdots & \ddots & \vdots \\ cm & ([\mu_{m1L},\mu_{m1U}],[h_{m1L},h_{m1U}],[v_{m1L},v_{m1U}]) & \cdots & ([\mu_{mmL},\mu_{mmU}],[h_{mmL},h_{mmU}],[v_{mmL},v_{mmU}]) \end{bmatrix}$$

Step 4. Defuzzify the pairwise comparison matrices in Step 3 based on Equation 2.27 and obtain the regression function between AHP scale and the defuzzified values.

Equation 2.38 is used for the defuzzification of IVPSF numbers. Assume an IVPSF number $\tilde{A}_p = \left(\left[k_{\mu L}, k_{\mu U}\right],[k_{hL},k_{hU}],[k_{vL},k_{vU}]\right)$. Then, the defuzzification of $\tilde{A}_p$ is realized based on Equations 2.30–2.36.

$$\text{Deff}\left(\tilde{A}_p\right) = \frac{(\mu_L)^2 + (\mu_U)^2 + \left(\frac{h_U}{2}\right)^2 + \left(\frac{h_L}{2}\right)^2 - (v_L)^2 - (v_U)^2}{2} \tag{2.38}$$

A regression analysis between the defuzzified values and AHP scale in Table 2.1 produces quadratic and cubic functions given by Figures 2.5 and 2.6, respectively.

We prefer the cubic function given by Equation 2.39 since it better fits the data between the defuzzified values and AHP scale.

$$AHPV = 0.9291 + 5.950 Deff\left(\tilde{A}_p\right) + 14.67 Deff\left(\tilde{A}_p\right)^2 + 11.96 Deff\left(\tilde{A}_p\right)^3 \tag{2.39}$$

Using Equation 2.39, any IVPSF number can be converted to its corresponding value in AHP scale. For instance, an intermediate value between H and VH may be ([5.5, 6.5], [2.5, 3.5], [3, 3.5]). Its corresponding IVSF number becomes ([0.517, 0.611], [0.235, 0.329], [0.282, 0.329]).

Table 2.1 IVSF linguistic scale.

Linguistic term	Abbr.	IVPSF number	Defuzzified value, $Deff\left(\tilde{A}_p\right)$	AHP scale, *AHPV*
Absolutely Low Importance	AL	([0, 1],[0, 1],[8, 9])	-0.4856	1/9
Too Low Importance	TL	([1, 2],[1, 2],[7, 8])	-0.4304	1/7
Very Low Importance	VL	([2, 3],[2, 3],[6, 7])	-0.3069	1/5
Low Importance	L	([3, 4],[3, 4],[5, 6])	-0.1328	1/3
Medium Importance	M	([4, 5],[4, 5],[4, 5])	0.0413	1
High Importance	H	([5, 6],[3, 4],[3, 4])	0.1886	3
Very high Importance	VH	([6, 7],[2, 3],[2, 3])	0.3359	5
Too High Importance	TH	([7, 8],[1, 2],[1, 2])	0.4405	7
Absolutely High Importance	AH	([8, 9],[0, 1],[0, 1])	0.4873	9

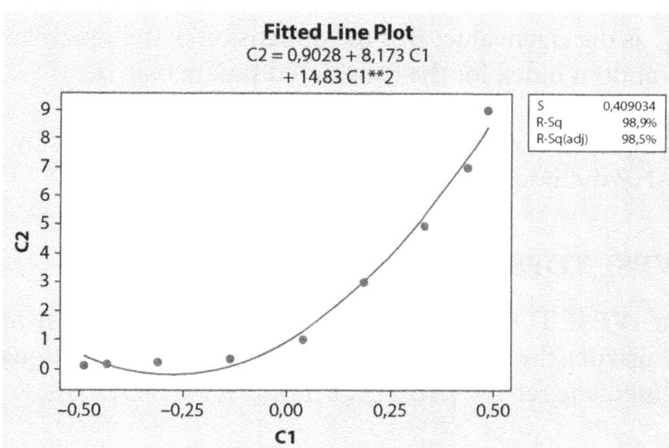

Figure 2.5 Quadratic regression function.

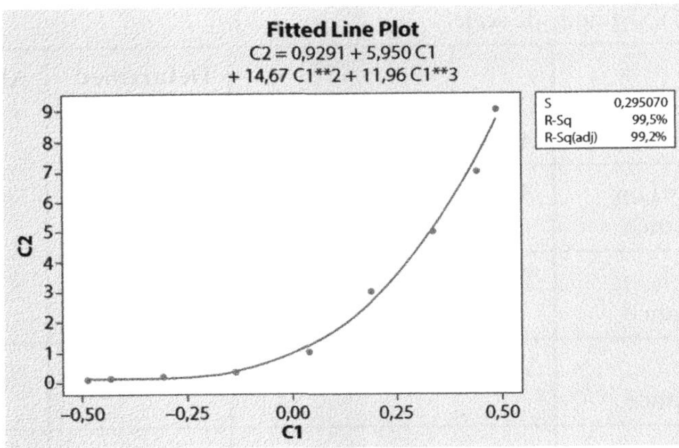

Figure 2.6 Cubic regression function.

The defuzzified value of this IVSF number is 0.2467. The corresponding AHP scale value of the IVPSF number is 3.469.

Step 5. Apply the consistency check of the judgments assigned by the expert.

Consistency of a crisp decision matrix is measured by Equation 2.40 [32] and the matrix is corrected if the consistency ratio (CI) is larger than 0.10.

$$CR = \left(\frac{\lambda_{max} - n}{n-1}\right)/RI \tag{2.40}$$

where λ_{max} is the eigenvalue; n is the dimension of the square matrix; and RI is the random index for the considered square matrix.

Step 6. Compute the weights of the criteria and alternatives by following the crisp AHP method.

2.5.4 IVPSF TOPSIS

Steps of the IVPSF TOPSIS method are presented in the following.

Step 1. Construct the IVPSF decision matrix as given by Equation 2.41 using the linguistic set $L = \{AL, TL, VL, L, M, H, VH, TH, AH\}$.

$\tilde{D}_L =$ (2.41)

	C_1	C_2	$\cdots$	C_n
A_1	l_{11}	l_{12}	$\cdots$	l_{1n}
A_2	l_{21}	l_{22}	$\cdots$	l_{2n}
$\vdots$	$\cdots$	$\cdots$	l_{ij}	$\cdots$
A_m	l_{m1}	l_{m2}	$\cdots$	l_{mn}

Step 2. Replace the linguistic terms with their corresponding IVPSF numbers given in Table 2.1 and obtain the IVPSF decision matrix $\tilde{D}_P$ (Equation 2.42).

$\tilde{D}_P =$ (2.42)

	C_1	C_2	$\cdots$	C_n
A_1	p_{11}	p_{12}	$\cdots$	p_{1n}
A_2	p_{21}	p_{22}	$\cdots$	p_{2n}
$\vdots$	$\cdots$	$\cdots$	p_{ij}	$\cdots$
A_m	p_{m1}	p_{m2}	$\cdots$	p_{mn}

Step 3. Convert IVPSF numbers to IVSF numbers by using Equations 2.30–2.36 to obtain the interval-valued spherical fuzzy $\tilde{D}_S$ (Equation 2.43).

$\tilde{D}_S =$ (2.43)

	C_1	C_2	$\cdots$	C_n
A_1	s_{11}	s_{12}	$\cdots$	s_{1n}
A_2	s_{21}	s_{22}	$\cdots$	s_{2n}
$\vdots$	$\cdots$	$\cdots$	s_{ij}	$\cdots$
A_m	s_{m1}	s_{m2}	$\cdots$	s_{mn}

Step 4. Obtain the weighted decision matrix $\tilde{D}_w$ in Equation 2.44 based on Equation 2.45.

$\tilde{D}_w =$ (2.44)

	C_1	C_2	$\cdots$	C_n
A_1	$\tilde{s}w_{11}$	$\tilde{s}w_{12}$	$\cdots$	$\tilde{s}w_{1n}$
A_2	$\tilde{s}w_{21}$	$\tilde{s}w_{22}$	$\cdots$	$\tilde{s}w_{2n}$
$\vdots$	$\cdots$	$\cdots$	$\tilde{s}w_{ij}$	$\vdots$
A_m	$\tilde{s}w_{m1}$	$\tilde{s}w_{m2}$	$\cdots$	$\tilde{s}w_{mn}$

$$\tilde{s}_{wij} = \tilde{s}_{ij} \times w_j, j = 1,2,\ldots,n; i = 1,2,\ldots,m$$

$$= \left\{ \left[\left(1-\left(1-\mu^2_{\tilde{s}w,L}\right)^w\right)^{1/2}, \left(1-\left(1-\mu^2_{\tilde{s}w,U}\right)^w\right)^{1/2} \right], \left[\left(1-\left(1-v^2_{\tilde{s}w,L}\right)^w\right)^{1/2}, \right. \right.$$

$$\left. \left(1-\left(1-\mu^2_{\tilde{s}w,U}\right)^w\right)^{1/2} \right], \left[\left(\left(1-\mu^2_{\tilde{s}w,L}\right)^w - \left(1-\mu^2_{\tilde{s}w,L} - \pi^2_{\tilde{s}w,L}\right)^w \right)^{1/2}, \right.$$

$$\left. \left. \left(\left(1-\mu^2_{\tilde{s}w,U}\right)^w - \left(1-\mu^2_{\tilde{s}w,U} - \pi^2_{\tilde{s}w,U}\right)^w \right)^{1/2} \right] \right\} \tag{2.45}$$

Step 5. Defuzzify IVSF numbers by using Equation 2.38 to obtain the crisp decision matrix D (Equation 2.46).

$D =$ (2.46)

	C_1	C_2	$\cdots$	C_n
A_1	d_{11}	d_{12}	$\cdots$	d_{1n}
A_2	d_{21}	d_{22}	$\cdots$	d_{2n}
$\vdots$	$\cdots$	$\cdots$	d_{ij}	$\vdots$
A_m	d_{m1}	d_{m2}	$\cdots$	d_{mn}

Step 6. Find the positive ideal solution (PIS) and negative ideal solution (NIS) as in Equations 2.47 and 2.48.

For PIS,

$$A^* = \{d_1^*, \ldots, d_n^*\} \tag{2.47}$$

where

$$d_j^* = \{ max\,(d_{ij})\, if\ j \in J\, ;\ min\left(d_{ij}\right) if\ j \in J'\}$$

For NIS,

$$A^- = \{ d_1^-, \ldots, d_n^- \} \tag{2.48}$$

where

$$d_j^- = \{ min\,(d_{ij})\, if\ j \in J\, ;\ max\left(d_{ij}\right) if\ j \in J'\}$$

where J represents the benefit criteria and J′ represents the cost criteria.

Step 7. Determine the corresponding fuzzy values of crisp ideal solutions.

Compute the distances of each alternative to PIS and NIS as in Equations 2.49 and 2.50.

$$S_i^* = \sum D(d^*, \tilde{s}_{w_{ij}}),\ i = 1, \ldots, m \tag{2.49}$$

where

$$\boldsymbol{D}\left(\boldsymbol{d}^*, \tilde{\boldsymbol{s}}_{\boldsymbol{w}_{ij}}\right) = \frac{\mathbf{1}}{\mathbf{4n}} \sum_{j=1}^{n} \left| \mu_{\tilde{s}_w,L}^2 - \left(\mu_{jL}^*\right)^2 \right| + \left| \mu_{\tilde{s}_w,U}^2 - \left(\mu_{jU}^*\right)^2 \right|$$
$$+ \left| \boldsymbol{v}_{\tilde{s}_w,L}^2 - \left(\boldsymbol{v}_{jL}^*\right)^2 \right| + \left| \boldsymbol{v}_{\tilde{s}_w,U}^2 - \left(\boldsymbol{v}_{jU}^*\right)^2 \right| + \left| \pi_{\tilde{s}_w,K}^2 - \left(\pi_{jL}^*\right)^2 \right| + \left| \pi_{\tilde{s}_w,U}^2 - \left(\pi_{jU}^*\right)^2 \right|, \forall \boldsymbol{j}$$

For the IVSF-NIS:

$$S_i' = \sum D(d^-, \tilde{s}_{w_{ij}}),\ i = 1, \ldots, m \tag{2.50}$$

where

$$D\left(d^{-},\tilde{s}_{w_{ij}}\right)=\frac{1}{4n}\sum_{j=1}^{n}\left|\mu_{\tilde{s}_w,L}^{2}-\left(\mu_{jL}^{*}\right)^{2}\right|+\left|\mu_{\tilde{s}_w,U}^{2}-\left(\mu_{jU}^{*}\right)^{2}\right|+\left|v_{\tilde{s}_w,L}^{2}-\left(v_{jL}^{*}\right)^{2}\right|$$
$$+\left|v_{\tilde{s}_w,U}^{2}-\left(v_{jU}^{*}\right)^{2}\right|+\left|\pi_{\tilde{s}_w,L}^{2}-\left(\pi_{jL}^{*}\right)^{2}\right|+\left|\pi_{\tilde{s}_w,U}^{2}-\left(\pi_{jU}^{*}\right)^{2}\right|,\forall j$$

Step 8. Compute the similarity to ideal solution for each alternative as in Equation 2.51 and rank the alternatives from the largest to the smallest. The largest value indicates the best alternative.

$$C_i^{*}=\frac{S_i'}{S_i^{*}+S_i'} \tag{2.51}$$

2.6 A Comparative Analysis of Free Park Space Identification Methods

With the increasing number of vehicles and urbanization, the accurate identification of free parking spaces is critical to reduce traffic congestion and improve the quality of urban life. In this context, the evaluation of free parking space identification methods should be done by considering various criteria. One of the primary criteria is the data accuracy (Ac-C1) which refers to determining the rate at which the system can accurately detect empty parking spaces and is one of the key determinants of user satisfaction. Durability (Dr-C2) describes the performance of the system against different environmental conditions (rain, snow, extreme temperatures, etc.). The installation and operation cost (IOC-C3), which refers to the initial investment and sustainability costs of the system. Maintenance requirement (MR-C4) includes the frequency of technical support and maintenance needed for the regular operation of the system. Finally, data security (DS-C5) is important in terms of protecting the collected parking data from unauthorized access and ensuring confidentiality. The free parking space identification method evaluations based on these criteria will increase the efficiency of urban transportation, improve user experience and contribute to smart city applications.

Basically 3 main systems are used as free parking space identification methods. These are;

1. Image Processing (Computer Vision) Methods (IP-A1): By taking live image stream through cameras placed in the parking lot, empty or occupied parking spaces are detected with deep learning algorithms (for example CNN - Convolutional Neural Networks).
2. Sensor-Based Methods (SB-A2): A magnetic sensor, ultrasonic sensor or pressure sensor is placed in each parking space. When the vehicle comes and goes, the sensors detect empty/occupied information.
3. Radar and LiDAR-Based Methods (LR-A3): Radar or LiDAR sensors are used to detect object density and location in the parking lot. It is especially used in the entrance-exit tracking of parking lots or in open areas.

2.6.1 Determining Importance Degree of Free Parking Space Evaluation Criteria Using IVPSF AHP

Step 1. There are basically 5 criteria and 3 alternative technologies in the decision problem, the details of which are stated above. The hierarchical structure of these criteria is shown in Figure 2.7.

Step 2. First, the pairwise comparison matrix of the criteria given in Table 2.2 was constructed using IVPSF. The evaluations were made by a panel of five experts working in the smart transportation departments of various

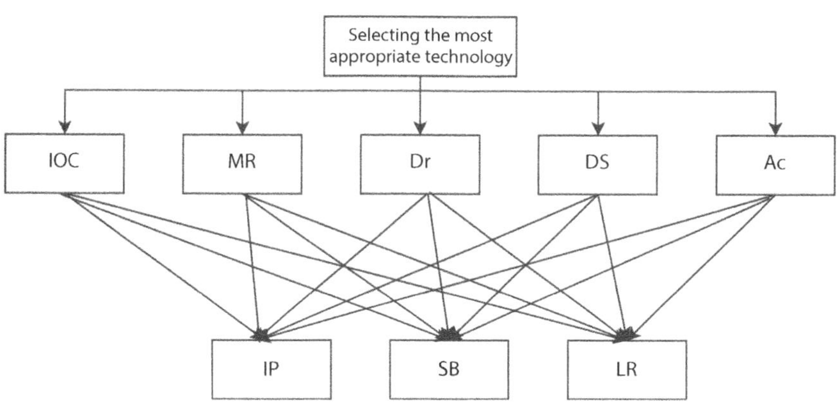

Figure 2.7 The hierarchical structure of decision problem.

Table 2.2 Pairwise comparisons.

	C1	C2	C3	C4	C5
C1	([4,5],[4,5],[4,5])	([5,6],[3,4],[3,4])	([3,4],[3,4],[5,6])	([5,6],[3,4],[3,4])	([6,7],[2,3],[2,3])
C2	([3,4],[3,4],[5,6])	([4,5],[4,5],[4,5])	([2,3],[2,3],[6,7])	([3,4],[3,4],[5,6])	([5,6],[3,4],[3,4])
C3	([3,4],[3,4],[5,6])	([5,6],[3,4],[3,4])	([4,5],[4,5],[4,5])	([5,6],[3,4],[3,4])	([6,7],[2,3],[2,3])
C4	([2,3],[2,3],[6,7])	([3,4],[3,4],[5,6])	([3,4],[3,4],[5,6])	([4,5],[4,5],[4,5])	([5,6],[3,4],[3,4])
C5	([2,3],[2,3],[6,7])	([3,4],[3,4],[5,6])	([2,3],[2,3],[6,7])	([3,4],[3,4],[5,6])	([4,5],[4,5],[4,5])

municipalities. The expert team consisted of a civil engineer specialized in transportation systems, two electronics and communication engineers with expertise in signal processing, a computer engineer specialized in image processing, and an electrical engineer responsible for maintenance and infrastructure systems.

Table 2.3 IVSF for pairwise comparisons.

	C1	C2	C3	C4	C5
C1	([0.359,0.449], [0.359, 0.449], [0.359, 0.449])	([0.472,0.567], [0.283, 0.378], [0.283, 0.378])	([0.283,0.378], [0.283, 0.378], [0.472, 0.567])	([0.472,0.567], [0.283, 0.378], [0.283, 0.378])	([0.567,0.661], [0.189, 0.283], [0.189, 0.283])
C2	([0.283,0.378], [0.283, 0.378], [0.472, 0.567])	([0.359,0.449], [0.359, 0.449], [0.359, 0.449])	([0.189,0.283], [0.189, 0.283], [0.567, 0.661])	([0.283,0.378], [0.283, 0.378], [0.472, 0.567])	([0.472,0.567], [0.283, 0.378], [0.283, 0.378])
C3	([0.283,0.378], [0.283, 0.378], [0.472, 0.567])	([0.472,0.567], [0.283, 0.378], [0.283, 0.378])	([0.359,0.449], [0.359, 0.449], [0.359, 0.449])	([0.472,0.567], [0.283, 0.378], [0.283, 0.378])	([0.567,0.661], [0.189, 0.283], [0.189, 0.283])
C4	([0.189,0.283], [0.189, 0.283], [0.567, 0.661])	([0.283,0.378], [0.283, 0.378], [0.472, 0.567])	([0.283,0.378], [0.283, 0.378], [0.472, 0.567])	([0.359,0.449], [0.359, 0.449], [0.359, 0.449])	([0.472,0.567], [0.283, 0.378], [0.283, 0.378])
C5	([0.189,0.283], [0.189, 0.283], [0.567, 0.661])	([0.283,0.378], [0.283, 0.378], [0.472, 0.567])	([0.189,0.283], [0.189, 0.283], [0.567, 0.661])	([0.283,0.378], [0.283, 0.378], [0.472, 0.567])	([0.359,0.449], [0.359, 0.449], [0.359, 0.449])

Step 3. Each IVPSF number is converted into IVSF form as given in Table 2.3.
Step 4. The IVSF matrices are converted to crisp values as given in Table 2.4 by using Equation 2.38. Then, these crisp values are converted to the Saaty's AHP scale using the regression function given by Equation 2.39 as given in Table 2.5.
Step 5. The consistency of the comparisons made by the experts is checked using Equation 2.40. Based on the calculation, the consistency index (CI) is found to be 0.017. Since the random index (RI) is 1.12, the consistency ratio (CI/RI) is 0.02. This indicates that the comparison matrix is consistent.
Step 6. The criteria weights are derived from the refined comparison matrices according to the classical AHP method, as follows: Data Accuracy (Ac-C1) – 0.42, Durability (Dr-C2) – 0.16, Installation and Operation Cost (IOC-C3) – 0.26, Maintenance Requirement (MR-C4) – 0.10, and Data Security (DS-C5) – 0.06. The obtained weights indicate that the most important factor in evaluating criteria is Data Accuracy (Ac-C1), while maintenance requirement (MR-C4) and data security (DS-C5) have lower weights.

Table 2.4 Defuzzified value.

	C1	C2	C3	C4	C5
C1	0.041	0.189	-0.13	0.189	0.336
C2	-0.133	0.041	-0.31	-0.133	0.189
C3	-0.133	0.189	0.041	0.189	0.336
C4	-0.307	-0.133	-0.13	0.041	0.189
C5	-0.307	-0.133	-0.31	-0.133	0.041

Table 2.5 Saaty's AHP scale.

	C1	C2	C3	C4	C5
C1	1.00	3.00	2.00	4.00	5.00
C2	0.33	1.00	0.50	2.00	3.00
C3	0.50	2.00	1.00	3.00	4.00
C4	0.25	0.50	0.33	1.00	2.00
C5	0.20	0.33	0.25	0.50	1.00

2.6.2 Analysis of Free Park Space Identification Methods Using IVPSF TOPSIS

Step 1. Having completed the criteria weightings, the expert team defined in the previous section made their evaluations by consensus for the three alternative technologies defined above. The evaluation made by the team is given in Table 2.6.

Step 2. Each linguistic term in Table 2.6 is converted into its corresponding IVPSF numerical value using Table 2.1. Table 2.7 presents the IVPSF values.

Step 3. The IVPSF values are transformed into IVSF values using Equations 30–36, as given in Table 2.8.

Step 4. The weighted decision matrix given in Table 2.9 is obtained by using Equation 2.45.

Step 5. The IVSF values are defuzzified using Equation 2.38 to generate the crisp decision matrix (Table 2.10).

Table 2.6 Expert preferences.

	Ac-C1	Dr-C2	IOC-C3	MR-C4	DS-C5
IP-A1	VH	M	M	H	H
SB-A2	M	H	VH	M	L
LR-A3	AH	VH	L	M	H

Table 2.7 IVPSF-based decision matrix.

	A1	A2	A3
C1	([6,7],[2,3],[2,3])	([4,5],[4,5],[4,5])	([8,9],[0,1],[0,1])
C2	([4,5],[4,5],[4,5])	([5,6],[3,4],[3,4])	([6,7],[2,3],[2,3])
C3	([4,5],[4,5],[4,5])	([6,7],[2,3],[2,3])	([3,4],[3,4],[5,6])
C4	([5,6],[3,4],[3,4])	([4,5],[4,5],[4,5])	([4,5],[4,5],[4,5])
C5	([5,6],[3,4],[3,4])	([3,4],[3,4],[5,6])	([5,6],[3,4],[3,4])

Table 2.8 IVSF-based decision matrix.

	A1	A2	A3
C1	([0.567, 0.661], [0.189, 0.283],[0.189,0.283])	([0.359, 0.449],[0.359, 0.449],[0.359,0.449])	([0.658, 0.74], [0,0.082], [0,0.082])
C2	([0.359, 0.449], [0.359, 0.449],[0.359,0.449])	([0.472, 0.567], [0.283, 0.378],[0.283,0.378])	([0.567, 0.661], [0.189, 0.283],[0.189, 0.283])
C3	([0.359, 0.449], [0.359, 0.449],[0.359,0.449])	([0.567, 0.661], [0.189, 0.283],[0.189,0.283])	([0.283, 0.378], [0.283, 0.378],[0.472, 0.567])
C4	([0.472, 0.567], [0.283, 0.378],[0.283,0.378])	([0.359, 0.449], [0.359, 0.449],[0.359,0.449])	([0.359, 0.449], [0.359, 0.449], [0.359, 0.449])
C5	([0.472, 0.567],[0.283, 0.378],[0.283,0.378])	([0.283, 0.378], [0.283, 0.378],[0.472,0.567])	([0.472,0.567], [0.283, 0.378],[0.283, 0.378])

Table 2.9 Weighted decision matrix.

	A1	A2	A3
C1	([0.388, 0.463], [0.138, 0.222], [0.123, 0.186])	([0.237,0.3],[0.248, 0.324], [0.237, 0.3])	([0.46, 0.532], [0,0.067], [0,0.053])
C2	([0.148, 0.188], [0.157, 0.21], [0.148, 0.188])	([0.199,0.245], [0.129, 0.187], [0.115, 0.156])	([0.245,0.297], [0.09, 0.149], [0.076, 0.115])
C3	([0.188, 0.238], [0.198, 0.262], [0.188, 0.238])	([0.31,0.373], [0.112, 0.184], [0.097, 0.147])	([0.147, 0.198], [0.152, 0.211], [0.252, 0.31])
C4	([0.158, 0.195], [0.103, 0.15], [0.091, 0.124])	([0.117,0.149], [0.125, 0.167], [0.117, 0.149])	([0.117, 0.149], [0.125, 0.167], [0.117, 0.149])
C5	([0.123, 0.152], [0.08, 0.117], [0.071, 0.096])	([0.071, 0.096], [0.074, 0.104], [0.123, 0.152])	([0.123, 0.152], [0.08, 0.117], [0.071, 0.096])

Table 2.10 Weighted crisp decision matrix.

	C1	C2	C3	C4	C5
A1	0.1662	0.0086	0.0135	0.0238	0.0144
A2	0.0208	0.0375	0.1078	0.0055	-0.0099
A3	0.2466	0.0683	-0.0409	0.0055	0.0144

Table 2.11 Distances of each alternative to PIS and NIS.

	Criteria weights are not equal			**Criteria weights are equal**		
	S*	S-	C	S*	S-	C
A1	0.0299	0.0365	0.5501	0.1077	0.1179	0.5225
A2	0.0558	0.0065	0.1037	0.1720	0.0429	0.1995
A3	0.0000	0.0623	1.0000	0.0000	0.2149	1.0000

Step 5. The Positive Ideal Solution (PIS) and Negative Ideal Solution (NIS) using Equations 2.47 and 2.48 are identified as $A^* = \{0.42466, 0.0683, -0.0409, 0.0055, 0.0144\}$ and $A^- = \{0.0208, 0.0086, 0.1078, 0.0238, -0.0099\}$, respectively.

Step 6. The distances of each alternative to both the PIS and NIS are calculated by using Equations 2.49 and 2.50.

Step 7. The similarity to the ideal solution for each alternative is determined using Equation 2.49, as shown in Table 2.11. The Radar and LiDAR-based method is the most appropriate and closest to the ideal solution across all criteria. Therefore, it stands out as the most effective and recommended technology. This result holds for the case where all criteria are equally weighted. When the criteria weights calculated in Section 2.6.1 are included in the evaluation, it is clearly seen that The Radar and LiDAR-based method still remains the best choice.

2.7 Conclusion

In conclusion, as cities continue to grow and evolve, the challenges of urbanization require innovative solutions that blend technology, data, and strategic planning. The concept of smart cities offers a powerful framework for addressing the many complexities of urban life, from improving efficiency in transportation and energy management to enhancing public safety and promoting sustainability. However, the transformation into a smart city is not solely about the adoption of new technologies; it requires thoughtful integration of social, environmental, and economic goals to ensure holistic urban development.

One key area where smart city technologies can make a significant impact is in parking management. The design and implementation of smart parking systems are essential for improving traffic flow, reducing congestion, and optimizing urban space usage. These systems can integrate advanced technologies such as sensors, image processing, and IoT-based monitoring to enhance efficiency and provide real-time information to drivers. However, creating effective parking solutions requires careful consideration of various factors, including location, accessibility, cost, security, and the impact on the environment.

As urban planners, engineers, and policymakers tackle these challenges, traditional decision-making tools often fall short in handling the complexity and uncertainty of such multifaceted issues. The uncertainty and complexity inherent in smart city applications, like parking system design, call for advanced decision-support methods that can accommodate diverse stakeholder opinions and account for qualitative, uncertain data. Fuzzy logic-based decision-making techniques, such as spherical fuzzy sets and interval-valued proportional spherical fuzzy sets (IVPSFS), provide a promising solution. These techniques allow for a more flexible and realistic representation of expert judgments, helping decision-makers account for uncertainty in their evaluations.

By integrating these advanced decision-making methods, municipalities can better address the needs of various stakeholders and make more informed, balanced decisions about the implementation of smart parking systems. The findings from this chapter, including the case study on smart parking technologies, provide valuable insights for municipal teams and urban planners. These methods can guide the development of smarter, more efficient, and sustainable parking solutions that help optimize urban spaces and improve the quality of urban life.

In future studies, the evaluation process could be extended by including more parking technologies and decision criteria that reflect the needs of different cities. It would be useful to consider user feedback, long-term maintenance results, and environmental factors in further research. Comparing smart parking projects in different cities over time can also offer valuable insights for improving planning and decision-making.

AI disclosure statement: The author confirms that no artificial intelligence (AI)-generated content or AI-assisted writing tools were used in the preparation of this chapter (including summaries and the abstract). All text, analysis, and conclusions are the result of the author's original work.

References

1. Akram, A., Azeem, Q., Ali, S., Muntaha, S.T., Haider, H., Iqbal, J., Younis, W., A Review on Hybrid Cloud-Fog-Edge Architectures for Efficient and Scalable Smart Home IoT Systems. *Spec. Eng. Sci.*, 3, 4, 812–817, 2025.
2. Ali, M.H., Jaber, M.M., Abd, S.K., Alkhayyat, A., Albaghdadi, M.F., Big data analysis and cloud computing for smart transportation system integration. *Multimedia Tools Appl.*, 1–18, 2022, https://doi.org/10.1007/s11042-022-13700-7.
3. Aljanabi, M., Navigating the Landscape: A Comprehensive Bibliometric Analysis of Decision-Making Research in Civil Engineering. *Mesopotamian J. Civ. Eng.*, 2023, 35–43, 2023.
4. Allam, Z., Sharifi, A., Bibri, S.E., Jones, D.S., Krogstie, J., The Metaverse as a Virtual Form of Smart Cities: Opportunities and Challenges for Environmental, Economic, and Social Sustainability in Urban Futures. *Smart Cities*, 5, 771–801, 2022, https://doi.org/10.3390/smartcities5030040.
5. Atanassov, K., Intuitionistic fuzzy sets. *Fuzzy Set Syst.*, 20, 1, 87–96, 1986.
6. Ates, M. and Önder, D.E., A local smart city approach in the context of smart environment and urban resilience. *Int. J. Disaster Resil. Built Environ.*, 14, 3, 266–284, 2023, https://doi.org/10.1108/IJDRBE-07-2021-0064.
7. Batra, I., Malik, U., Sharma, S., Sharma, C., Sanwar, A.S.M., Explainable Artificial Intelligence into Cyber-Physical System Architecture of Smart Cities: Technologies, Challenges, and Opportunities. *J. Electr. Syst.*, 20, 2, 2342–2362, 2024.
8. Brown, W., King, M., Goh, Y.M., UK smart cities present and future: An analysis of British smart cities through current and emerging technologies and practices. *Emerald Open Res.*, 2, 4, 25, 2020, DOI: 10.35241/emeraldopenres.13415.2.
9. Butt, A.U.R., Saba, T., Khan, I., Mahmood, T., Khan, A.R., Singh, S.K., Ullah, I., Proactive and data-centric Internet of Things-based fog computing architecture for effective policing in smart cities. *Comput. Electr. Eng.*, *123*, 110030, 2025.
10. Choma, J. and Zaina, L., Investigating quality aspects for UX evaluation of IoT applications in smart city environments. *Sci. Comput. Program.*, 245, Article 103319, 2025, DOI: 10.1016/j.scico.2023.103319.
11. Cloud, H., The nist definition of cloud computing. National institute of science and technology, special publication, 800(2011), 145, 2011.

12. Correia, D., Lourenço Marques, J., Teixeira, L., A framework to guide and support the design of a smart city based on the PDCA cycle approach. *J. Syst. Inf. Technol.*, 27, 1, 65–93, 2025, https://doi.org/10.1108/JSIT-02-2022-0055.
13. Costa, G.P., Sakata, G.Y.A., Oliveira, L.F.P.D., Chaves, M.E., Duarte, L.F., Matulovic, M., Morais, F.J., FarmSync: Ecosystem for Environmental Monitoring of Barns in Agribusiness. *AgriEngineering*, 7, 4, 124, 2025.
14. Dadwal, Sumesh, IoT (Internet of Thing), Cloud Computing and the Elementary Building Blocks Of Smart Sustainable Cities, in: *Technology and Talent Strategies for Sustainable Smart Cities: Digital Futures*. Sumesh Dadwal, Hamid Jahankhani, Bowen Gordon, Imad Nawaz (eds.), vol. 1, 1, pp. 1–34, Emerald Publishing Limited, Leeds (UK), 2023.
15. David, D. and Alamoodi, A., A bibliometric analysis of research on multiple criteria decision making with emphasis on Energy Sector between (2019-2023). *Appl. Data Sci. Anal.*, 2023, 143–149, 2023.
16. Dirks, S., Gurdgiev, C., Keeling, M., Smarter Cities for Smarter Growth: How Cities Can Optimize Their Systems for the Talent-Based Economy (May 1, 2010), IBM Institute for Business Value, May 2010, Available at SSRN: https://ssrn.com/abstract=2001907.
17. El-Sayed, A., Abougabal, M., Lazem, S., Practical big data techniques for end-to-end machine learning deployment: a comprehensive review. *Discover Data*, 3, 1, 11, 2025.
18. Gao, K., Liu, T.T., Rong, Y., Simic, V., Garg, H., Senapati, T., A novel BWMEntropyCOPRAS group decision framework with spherical fuzzy information for digital supply chain partner selection. *Complex Intell. Syst.*, 10, 6983–7008, 2024, https://doi.org/10.1007/s40747-024-01500-5.
19. Kahraman, C., Proportional Fuzzy Set Extensions and Imprecise Proportions. *Informatica*, 35, 2, 311–339, 2024.
20. Kahraman, C. and Kutlu Gündogdu, F., *From 1D to 3D membership: spherical fuzzy sets, BOS / SOR 2018, Polish Operational and Systems Research Society*, Palais Staszic, Warsaw, Poland, September 24th – 26th 2018.
21. Kamvysi, K., Tsironis, L.K., Gotzamani, K., An integrated QFD framework for smart city strategy development. *TQM J.*, 37, 5, 1203–1226, 2025, https://doi.org/10.1108/TQM-07-2023-0223.
22. Kaur, G. and Garg, H., A novel algorithm for autonomous parking vehicles using adjustable probabilistic neutrosophic hesitant fuzzy set features. *Expert Syst. Appl.*, 226, 120101, 2023, https://doi.org/10.1016/j.eswa.2023.120101.
23. Khan, M. and Hossni, Y., A comparative analysis of LSTM models aided with attention and squeeze and excitation blocks for activity recognition. *Sci. Rep.*, 15, 1, 3858, 2025.
24. Kurmude, K.D.V., Kakarwal, S.N., Deshmukh, R.R., Smart Computing: An Integrated Approach of Computing, CSI Communications, pp. 10–11, 2019.
25. Liang, W., Liu, Y., Yang, C., Xie, S., Li, K., Susilo, W., On identity, transaction, and smart contract privacy on permissioned and permissionless blockchain: A comprehensive survey. *ACM Comput. Surv.*, 56, 12, 1–35, 2024.

26. Lytras, M.D., Future Smart Cities Research: Identifying the Next Generation Challenges, in: *Smart Cities and Digital Transformation*, pp. 1–11, Emerald Publishing Limited, Howard House, Wagon Lane, Bingley BD16 1WA, UK, 2023, hiips://doi.org/10.1108/978-1-80455-994-920231001.
27. Mohammed, S.Y., Oleiwi, A.K., Kh. Asman, T., Saleh, H.M., Mahmood, A.M., Avci, I., A Survey of MCDM-Based Software Engineering Method. *Babylonian J. Math.*, 2023, 13–18, 2024.
28. Mukherjee, A. and Dey, N., *Smart computing with open source platforms*, Boca Raton, FL, USA, CRC Press, 2019.
29. Murphy, K.P., *Machine learning: a probabilistic perspective*, MIT Press, Cambridge, Massachusetts, USA, 2012.
30. Peng, X. and Yang, Y., Fundamental properties of interval-valued Pythagorean fuzzy aggregation operators. *Int. J. Intell. Syst.*, 31, 5, 444–487, 2016.
31. Popov, D., Terentev, E., Serenko, D., Sochenkov, I., Buyanov, I., Transferring Natural Language Datasets Between Languages Using Large Language Models for Modern Decision Support and Sci-Tech Analytical Systems. *Big Data Cognit. Comput.*, 9, 5, 116, 2025.
32. Saaty, T.L., A scaling method for priorities in hierarchical structures. *J. Math. Psychol.*, 15, 3, 234–281, 1977, https://doi.org/10.1016/0022-2496(77)90033-5.
33. Sharifi, A., Amirzadeh, M., Khavarian-Garmsir, A.R., The Metaverse as a future form of smart cities: A systematic literature review of co-benefits and trade-offs for sustainable development goals. *Cities*, 161, Article 105879, 2025, DOI: 10.1016/j.cities.2023.105879.
34. Si, Z., Liu, Z., Mu, C., Wang, M., Gong, T., Xia, X., Xiao, Y., A new deep learning based electricity theft detection framework for smart grids in cloud computing. *Comput. Stand. Interfaces, 94*, 104007, 2025.
35. Taha, B.A., Abdulateef, S.A., Addie, A.J., Muneam, S.A., Muneam, N.A., Haider, A.J., Arsad, N., Paradigm of Nanophotonics Integrated Smart Contact Lenses: A New Frontier in Wearable Healthcare. *Mater. Res. Bull.*, 113511, 2025.
36. Taimun, M.T.Y., Sharan, S.M.I., Azad, M.A., Joarder, M.M.I., Smart Maintenance and Reliability Engineering in Manufacturing. *Saudi J. Eng. Technol.*, 10, 4, 189–199, 2025.
37. Ulyaa, A., Susanto, T.D., Dharmawan, Y.S., Pribadi, A., Subriadi, S., Major dimensions of smart city: A systematic literature review. *Procedia Comput. Sci.*, 234, 996–1003, 2024, DOI: 10.1016/j.procs.2023.07.122.
38. Vajpayee, D., Gupta, N., Joshi, V., Digital Transformation in Mechatronics: ICT Applications in Automation and Robotics, in: *2024 IEEE 4th International Conference on ICT in Business Industry & Government (ICTBIG)*, IEEE, pp. 1–8, 2024.
39. Van Eck, N.J. and Waltman, L., Visualizing bibliometric networks, in: *Measuring scholarly impact: Methods and practice*, Y. Ding, R. Rousseau, D. Wolfram (Eds.), pp. 285–320, Springer, Cham, Switzerland, 2014.

40. Wang, H., Feng, L., Deveci, M., Ullah, K., Garg, H., A novel CODAS approach based on Heronian Minkowski distance operator for Tspherical fuzzy multiple attribute group decisionmaking. *Expert Syst. Appl.*, 226, 122928, 2024, https://doi.org/10.1016/j.eswa.2023.122928.
41. Warnecke, D., Wittstock, R., Teuteberg, F., Benchmarking of European smart cities – a maturity model and web-based self-assessment tool. *Sustain. Account. Manag. Policy J.*, 10, 4, 654–684, 2019. DOI: 10.1108/SAMPJ-03-2018-0057.
42. Xu, W., Xu, H., Zhang, J., Cyber Physical System Based Smart Healthcare System with Deep Learning Architectures with Data Analytics, in: *Wireless Personal Communications*, pp. 1–20, Springer Science and Business Media LLC, Berlin/Heidelberg, Germany, 2024.
43. Yager, R.R., Pythagorean fuzzy subsets. *IFSA world congress and NAFIPS annual meeting (IFSA/NAFIPS), 2013 Joint*, IEEE, pp. 57–61, 2013.
44. Yenkar, P.P. and Sawarkar, S.D., A novel ensemble approach based on MCC and MCDM methods for prioritizing tweets mentioning urban issues in smart city. *Kybernetes*, 52, 9, 3613–3646, 2023, https://doi.org/10.1108/K-08-2021-0785.
45. Yim, I.H.Y. and Su, J., Artificial intelligence literacy education in primary schools: a review. *Int. J. Technol. Des. Educ.*, 1–30, 2025. 10.1007/s10798-025-09979-w.
46. Zadeh, L.A., Fuzzy sets. *Inf. Control*, 8, 3, 338–353, 1965.
47. Zhao, H., Cheng, X., Gao, J., Yu, G., A study on risk sharing of smart city PPP projects based on EW-G1 and TOPSIS-UT: a case study in China. *Kybernetes*, 54, 3, 1470–1494, 2025, https://doi.org/10.1108/K-05-2023-0824.

3

A Novel Measure and Modified Root Assessment Method for Type-2 Intuitionistic Fuzzy Sets in Multi-Standard Evaluation Making for Solid Waste Management

Barathi Gnanavelu and Jagadeeswari Murugan*

Department of Mathematics, School of Advanced Sciences, Vellore Institute of Technology, Vellore, India

Abstract

Solid waste management has considerable challenges, mostly involving complicated and undetermined factors. Effective decision-making in solid waste management requires a precise interpretation of the differences between criteria. This research proposes a new method for solid waste management decision-making that explains the type-2 intuitionistic fuzzy set to secure the internal ambiguities. The modification of the new formula is made to measure the natural intricacy of solid waste management assessments. This method adequately finds the uncertainty associated with both association and non-association rates at the secondary membership values, while maintaining computational ability. The modified RAM method is capable of producing meaningful rankings for the alternatives of solid waste management.

***Keywords*:** Type-2 intuitionistic fuzzy sets, modified RAM method, multi-criteria decision-making, sustainable solid waste management

**Corresponding author*: jagadeeswari.m@vit.ac.in

Harish Garg (ed.) Decision Support Systems in Smart Computing: Embracing Uncertainty and Challenges, (69–92) © 2026 Scrivener Publishing LLC

3.1 Introduction

Solid waste management (SWM) poses a critical challenge to policymakers and environmentalists due to its complexity of factors like environmental, economic, and social concerns. The 2020-21 annual progress report by the national environmental regulatory authority of India indicated that the total quantity of waste generated was 160,038.9 tons per day (TPD) [4]. By 2030, the overall production of solid waste is predicted to exceed 165 million tons (MT). Waste collection, shipment, treatment, and disposal demand careful planning and preparation across all stages to guarantee sustainable development, cost-effectiveness, administrative consent, and public acceptance. Considering these challenges, administrators must carefully judge conflicting data to restrict environmental damage and health risks.

To deal with the complex challenges of solid waste management, the widely used methodology is multi-criteria decision-making (MCDM). It is a branch of decision theory and a popular field of mathematical optimization, which selects the best option from a set of possible options based on multiple criteria [36]. In decision theory, multi-standard evaluation-making is a prominent field involving a finite number of alternatives that contradict each other and may have distinct metric values. When the difficulty level of evaluation-making increases, it becomes impractical for a specific choice to fulfill the contradicting criteria. Weightage is given to the MCDM method to deal with day-to-day problems when tradeoffs between solutions are considered. The multi-standard evaluation-making approach has attained remarkable attention across various fields, and it is progressing at a rapid pace. A few of the popular MCDM techniques include Best-Worst Method (BWM), Measurement of Alternatives and Ranking according to Compromise Solution (MARCOS), Combined Compromise Solution (CoCoSo), and Evaluation based on Distance from Average Solution (EDAS).

Powerful evaluation-making in solid waste management requires exact clarification of the difference among standards. Evaluation of solid waste management includes uncertainty and hesitation, which are common in real-world scenarios. Experts may pick up intuitive judgment. To overcome the limitations of these multi-standard evaluation-making methods, this analysis uses the root assessment method (RAM) which was introduced by Alireza Sotoudeh-Anvari in September 2023. RAM introduced a new compensation degree to evaluate the beneficial with the non-beneficial alternatives, which was not defined in the earlier MCDM methods. The other MCDM methods like technique for order of preference by similarity to ideal solution (TOPSIS) [5], and ViseKriterijumska Optimizacija I Kompromisno Resenje (VIKOR), have the rank reversal approach, which is prevented in the RAM method. A Decision Maker (DM) without any theoretical background can also interpret the RAM results.

Originally, fuzzy membership values, as suggested by Zadeh [45], have been popularly used to find the administrators' choices. Nevertheless, conventional fuzzy sets declined to elucidate the degree of hesitation in human awareness. To refine this limitation, intuitionistic fuzzy set which was introduced by Atanassov [2], integrates belongingness, non-belongingness, as well as hesitation degrees. This method facilitates the evaluation makers to explicitly recognize their preferences more specifically through the level of conflict.

In decision-making, uncertainty can be expressed in different forms like incomplete, partial, vague, not fully reliable, deficient, imprecise, fragmentary data [45]. In situations where uncertainty exists, it's more accurate to use fuzzy sets than traditional sets because they allow for degrees of membership. The uncertainty is represented by values within the interval [0,1] for type-1 fuzzy sets, but hesitation does not emerge. Intuitionistic fuzzy sets (IFS), which were introduced to improve upon type-1 fuzzy sets, include membership, non-membership degrees, and hesitation factor. Type-2 fuzzy sets provide a more flexible approach by allowing the membership function to be a fuzzy set, which makes them more effective for handling deep uncertainty. Non-belongingness plays an equivalent role in our regular activities during the progress of evaluation-making. To address this problem, Singh and Garg [30] extended type-2 fuzzy set (T2FS) to type-2 intuitionistic fuzzy set (T2IFS) by adding the hesitation degree into the concept of T2FS. Among the most effective methods, T2IFS is a very powerful method for modeling complicated decision-making issues. Since SWM decisions involve uncertainty in expert opinions, T2IFS can provide a more realistic and flexible framework for evaluation.

In a type-2 intuitionistic fuzzy set environment, by Singh and Garg [15], formulations of similarity measures are defined with properties, and an algorithm for solving the group decision-making method is explained to rank the alternatives. Research has been done to assess the solid waste management techniques using intuitionistic fuzzy set with Multi-objective optimization based on ratio analysis plus full multiplicative form (MULTIMOORA) approach based on aggregation operators by Harish Garg and Dimple Rani [14]. A case study based on interval type-2 fuzzy with analytical hierarchy process (AHP) approach is used to find the supplier selection in fuzzy environment [9].

This study aims to provide a more accurate and uncertainty-based decision-making framework for decision makers in SWM. As a result, MCDM methods have become essential for solving real-world problems where compromise solutions must be considered. Since the 1970s, the MCDM approach has gained significant attention across various domains, and its development continues at a rapid pace. To date, over 300 MCDM techniques have been proposed, with methods such as analytical hierarchy process (AHP), TOPSIS, Best-Worst Method (BWM), Step-wise Weight Assessment Ratio Analysis (SWARA), Full Consistency Method (FUCOM), Combined Compromise Solution (CoCoSo), Level Based Weight Assessment (LBWA), Multi-Attributive Border Approximation Area Comparison (MABAC), Measurement of Alternatives and Ranking according to the Compromise Solution (MARCOS), Proximity Indexed Value (PIV), COmplex PRoportional ASsessment with Grey relations (COPRAS-G), and Evaluation Based on Distance from Average Solution (EDAS) [48] being introduced by researchers recently. Among these methods, RAM is a new method for making decisions with many factors (MCDM). It figures out how good each choice is by combining its scores on different criteria, and then ranks the choices based on these overall scores. It does this using a straightforward formula: it increases the score for good things and decreases it for bad things. Essentially, RAM blends different ways of combining criteria, allowing for some trade-offs while still providing a clear and meaningful ranking [33].

3.1.1 Research Gap and Motivation Behind the Study

Despite extensive work on MCDM, several research gaps remain:

- Most of the existing methods inadequately represent hesitation and ambiguity in decision makers' evaluations.
- Under fuzzy logic, most of the common score functions often fail to differentiate between close alternatives.
- There is a lack of advanced methods in MCDM that integrate type-2 intuitionistic fuzzy set (T2IFS) with robust ranking methods such as RAM.

Motivation:

- To manage uncertainty, a type-2 fuzzy set can be used as a tool.

- Type-2 fuzzy sets have the secondary membership degree, which can capture more uncertainty in real-life fields such as engineering, social sciences, arts, humanities, computer sciences, medical sciences, physical sciences, business, and management.
- Due to the difficulties in computation and its three-dimensional nature, type-2 fuzzy sets are not widely used in many fields like type-1 fuzzy sets. This motivated us to apply type-2 fuzzy sets to the solid waste management system.
- In the decision-making field, there are only 134 articles till 2022 [10]. This research combines applications of type-2 fuzzy sets with novel RAM method.

3.1.2 Objectives of the Study

- The main objective is to modify the latest MCDM method, RAM, using the generalized modified score function(GMSF).
- To apply the modified RAM method with Type-2 intuitionistic fuzzy sets for finding rankings.
- Establishing the modified RAM results by considering an example using solid waste management.

3.2 Preliminary Considerations

3.2.1 Fuzzy Logic Concepts

This section covers some primary concepts related to fuzzy sets of type-1, fuzzy intuitionistic sets, fuzzy sets of type-2(T2FS), as well as intuitionistic fuzzy sets of type-2(IFST2), the score functions are defined across the domain of discourse.

Definition 2.1.1. (Fuzzy set) [45] A fuzzy set F defined over the domain of discourse V is represented with its belongingness function $M_F(\breve{c})$ as below

$$F=\{f(\breve{c},M_F(\breve{c}))|\forall\breve{c}\in V\},M_F(\breve{c})\in[0,1] \tag{3.1}$$

Definition 2.1.2. (Intuitionistic fuzzy set) [2] In the domain of discourse V, the fuzzy intuitionistic set (IFS) F is defined as

$$F = \{\breve{c}, M_F(\breve{c})), N_F(\breve{c}))|\breve{c} \in V\}, \tag{3.2}$$

where the belongingness and non-belongingness function maps to values ranging from 0 and 1 with the condition that the sum of them is ≤ 1 for all values in the domain of discourse.

Definition 2.1.3. (Type-2 fuzzy set) [22] In the domain of discourse V, type-2 fuzzy set (T2FS) with its belongingness function is expressed as

$$F = \{((\breve{c}, V), M_F(\breve{c}, V))|\forall\breve{c} \in V\}, \tag{3.3}$$

where the domain of discourse belongs to the primary membership and $M_F(\breve{c}, V)$, takes the values from 0 to 1 called as the secondary belongingness function.

In T2FS, the non-membership degree is not playing any role in representing the element. In real-life decision-making, the level of nonmembership has an identically significant part. Adding non-membership to the fuzzy set of type-2, [30] the approach of intuitionistic fuzzy set of type-2 can be derived.

Definition 2.1.4. (Type-2 intuitionistic fuzzy set) [30] In the domain of discourse V, a collection of paired memberships of F is stated as

$$F = \{(\breve{c}, M_F(\breve{c}), f_{\breve{c}}(M_F)), N_F(\breve{c}), t_{\breve{c}}(N_F)|\breve{c} \in V, M_F \in j_{\breve{c}}^1, N_F \in j_{\breve{c}}^2\} \tag{3.4}$$

where M_F, N_F represent the primary association function and primary non-association functions of the set F, $f_{\breve{c}}(M_F)$ and $t_{\breve{c}}(N_F)$ are the secondary association and non-association functions lie within the range 0 and 1 with the condition that average of association and non-association of both degrees is less than or equal to 1.

3.2.2 Fuzzy Score Functions

The generalized score function to compare the interval-valued intuitionistic fuzzy sets (IVIFS) [47], with the evaluation and precision functions corresponding to a few metric methods discussed by different authors, is given as below.

Definition 2.2.1. (Score function) [42] Let $F = \langle[p, q], [r, s]\rangle$ be an intuitionistic interval-valued fuzzy set, then the evaluation function is defined as

$$G(F) = \frac{p+q-r-s}{2}, S(F) \in [-1, 1] \tag{3.5}$$

Definition 2.2.2. (Accuracy function) [42] Let $F = \langle[p, q], [r, s]\rangle$ be an IVIFS, then the accuracy function is devised as

$$H(F) = \frac{p+q+r+s}{2}, H(F) \in [0, 1] \tag{3.6}$$

Definition 2.2.3. (Novel accuracy function) [44] Let $F = \langle[p, q], [r, s]\rangle$ be an IIVFS, the novel precision function is formulated as

$$\mathrm{M}(F) = \frac{p-(1-p-r)+q-(1-q-s)}{2}, \mathrm{M}(F) \in [-1, 1] \tag{3.7}$$

Definition 2.2.4. (Modified Accuracy function) [25] Let $F = \langle[p, q], [r, s]\rangle$ be an IVIFS, then the accuracy function is given as

$$\mathrm{L}(F) = \frac{p+q-s(1-q)-r(1-p)}{2}, \mathrm{L}(F) \in [-1, 1] \tag{3.8}$$

Definition 2.2.5. (Improved score function) [3] For the IVIFS $F = \langle[p, q], [r, s]\rangle$, the improved evaluation function is described as

$$\mathrm{I}(F) = \frac{\mathrm{p}+\mathrm{p}(1-\mathrm{p}-\mathrm{r})+\mathrm{q}+\mathrm{q}(1-\mathrm{q}-\mathrm{s})}{2}, \mathrm{I}(F) \in [0, 1] \tag{3.9}$$

Definition 2.2.6. (Generalized Enhanced Score Operation) [13] An intuitionistic interval-valued fuzzy measure over $F = \langle[p, q], [r, s]\rangle$ with uncertainty level gives the generalized enhanced evaluation operation as

$$\mathrm{GES}(F)=\frac{p+q}{2}+k_1p(1-p-r)+k_2q(1-q-s),\mathrm{GES}(F)\in[0,1] \tag{3.10}$$

The GES functions attitudinal characters are represented by $k_1 + k_2 = 1$, $k_1, k_2 \geq 0$, which gives the mean value adjusted by weights, a weighted average of the hesitation level among the association and non-association functions. While $k_1 = k_2 = \frac{1}{2}$, the generalized enhanced score operation becomes improved score operation. Accordingly, the enhanced score operation can be treated as a specific instance of the score operation.

3.3 Objective of Generalized Modified Score Function

Zadeh presented the theory of fuzzy sets of type-2 as an extended version of the fuzzy sets of type- 1 (ordinary fuzzy set). The association values of the collection whose membership grades themselves are fuzzy sets of type-1, which are described by the main and auxiliary association functions and the footprint of indeterminacy, are known as T2FSs [6]. The overview of type-2 fuzzy sets was presented by Mendel [22]. Fuzzy sets of type-2 stand as a vigorous tool, yet their difficult computations make them impossible to apply in practice. As a result, interval type-2 fuzzy sets (IT2FS), a simpler version with membership values in the range 0 and 1, are widely used. Traditional fuzzy sets, the extent to which an element is not a part of the set is simply the opposite of its membership degree. However, this doesn't always reflect real-world situations where uncertainty exists. To address this, Atanassov introduced intuitionistic fuzzy sets (IFS). These sets explicitly define both a membership degree and a non-membership degree, providing a more nuanced way to model real-world problems where both belongingness and non-belongingness are considered equally important. In this paper, the notion of fuzzy set of type-2 and intuitionistic sets is combined by taking the association values for type-2 trapezoidal intuitionistic fuzzy numbers to proceed with the multi-subjective evaluation-making method.

The existing ranking and precision functions suggested by different researchers are inadequate for ranking alternatives, as they fail to differentiate between pairs of interval-valued intuitionistic fuzzy numbers (IVIFNs) [1, 43, 46] effectively. This reservation features the need for more expedition to develop a more precise evaluation function for identifying an ideal option between advantageous alternatives. To sort out this problem, Harish Garg [13] introduced a new generalized improved score (GIS) function, which considers the level of hesitation among the association and non-association operations of interval-valued intuitionistic fuzzy sets.

Definition 3.3.1 (Generalized modified score function) The generalized modified score (GMS) function is defined as follows: Consider the type-2 intuitionistic fuzzy number in trapezoidal form $F = \langle [p, q, r, s], [t, u, v, w] \rangle$ then the generalized modified score function is derived to find the crisp value based on unknown degree as

$$\mathrm{GMS}(F) = \frac{p+q+r+s}{4} + k_1 \cdot \frac{p+q}{2} \cdot 1 - \frac{p+q}{2} - \frac{t+u}{2} + k_2 \cdot \frac{r+s}{2} \cdot 1 - \frac{r+s}{2} - \frac{v+w}{2}$$

Where:

- $k_1 + k_2 = 1$, and $k_1, k_2 \in [0, 1]$ are ideological parameters, which allow decision makers to prioritize early or late trapezoidal sections.
- The average membership degrees are represented by the first term.
- The weighted hesitation between membership and non-membership across the trapezoidal numbers is represented by the second and third terms.
- The final score $\mathrm{GMS}(F) \in [0, 1]$, making it suitable for normalized scoring and comparison.

Properties of the Proposed GMS Function

The Generalized Modified Score (GMS) function satisfies the following properties:

1. **Boundedness:** This property ensures compatibility with normalized MCDM algorithms and maintains interpretability in the range [0, 1].i.e., $0 \leq \mathrm{GMS}(F) \leq 1$

Proof: The first term $\frac{p+q+r+s}{4} \in [0,1]$, as all components lie in [0, 1].

For the second and third terms, note that: $0 \le \frac{p+q}{2}, \frac{r+s}{2} \le 1$ and $0 \le \frac{t+u}{2}, \frac{v+w}{2} \le 1$.

The inner expressions: $1 - \frac{p+q}{2} - \frac{t+u}{2}$ and $1 - \frac{r+s}{2} - \frac{v+w}{2}$ are also bounded within [0, 1] because membership plus non-membership of an intuitionistic fuzzy set is at most 1. Therefore, the product terms: $\left(\frac{p+q}{2} \cdot \left(1 - \frac{p+q}{2} - \frac{t+u}{2}\right)\right)$ and $\left(\frac{r+s}{2} \cdot \left(1 - \frac{r+s}{2} - \frac{v+w}{2}\right)\right)$ are both non-negative and bounded. Since $k_1, k_2 \in [0, 1]$, their weighted contributions to GMS are bounded. Thus, the sum of all three components remains in the interval [0, 1]. Therefore, we conclude that GMS (F) is bounded.

2. Monotonicity:

This property ensures the ranking of the function. Let $F_1 = \langle [p_1, q_1, r_1, s_1], [t_1, u_1, v_1, w_1] \rangle$ and $F_2 = \langle [p_2, q_2, r_2, s_2], [t_2, u_2, v_2, w_2] \rangle$ be two type-2 trapezoidal intuitionistic fuzzy numbers. If $p_1 \ge p_2, q_1 \ge q_2, r_1 \ge r_2, s_1 \ge s_2$ and $t_1 \le t_2, u_1 \le u_2, v_1 \le v_2, w_1 \le w_2$, then, GMS ($F_1$) ≥ GMS ($F_2$).

Proof:

We analyze the changes in increasing membership parameters and decreasing non-membership parameters on each component of GMS.

Average Membership Term: $\frac{p_1 + q_1 + r_1 + s_1}{4} \ge \frac{p_2 + q_2 + r_2 + s_2}{4}$ because $p_1 \ge p_2, q_1 \ge q_2, r_1 \ge r_2, s_1 \ge s_2$ and First Hesitation Term: $\frac{p+q}{2} \cdot \left(1 - \frac{p+q}{2} - \frac{t+u}{2}\right)$

As $p + q$ increases and $t + u$ decreases, this expression either increases or remains unchanged due to the convex shape of the product. The Second Hesitation Term: $\frac{r+s}{2} \cdot \left(1 - \frac{r+s}{2} - \frac{v+w}{2}\right)$ behaves similarly. Larger $r + s$ and smaller $v + w$ lead to a larger or equal score. Finally, each term in the GMS function either increases or remains unchanged when membership values increase and non-membership values decrease.

Hence, we conclude that, if $F_1 \ge F_2$ in membership and $F_1 \le F_2$ in non-membership, then GMS(F_1) ≥ GMS(F_2).

3. Discrimination:

The proposed GMS function has a strong discriminative quality in contrast to the classical score functions. It effectively differentiates between alternatives even when their membership intervals are similar, but their hesitation or non-membership components differ.

4. Flexibility through k_1, k_2:
The inclusion of attitudinal parameters k_1 and k_2 with $k_1 + k_2 = 1$ enables the function to adapt to different decision-making preferences:

- $k_1 > k_2$: Prioritizes early membership information.
- $k_1 = k_2$: Treats both sides equally.
- $k_1 < k_2$: Gives more importance to the tail segment.

5. Idempotency for Crisp Values:
If the T2TIFN F degenerates into a crisp value such that $p = q = r = s = \mu$, and $t = u = v = w = \nu$, with $\mu + \nu \leq 1$, then the GMS reduces to: $\text{GMS}(F) = \mu + \mu(1 - \mu - \nu)(k_1 + k_2) = \mu + \mu(1 - \mu - \nu)$, since $k_1 + k_2 = 1$.

Hence, GMS remains consistent with the classical membership value under non-fuzzy input, showing $\text{GMS}(F) \rightarrow \mu$ when $\nu = 1 - \mu$. This demonstrates that the function naturally integrates classical decision models when uncertainty vanishes.

3.4 A Multi-Criteria Decision-Making Problem Using Modified RAM Procedure

3.4.1 Modified RAM Procedure

The RAM method is a unique MCDM technique that measures the utility value of all options by combining scores from different selection criteria. The final ranking is based on these utilitarian values, having an aggregation coefficient whose value is directly proportional to advantageous criteria, considering both the compensatory and partial compensatory attributes. Compared to traditional methods, RAM uses a unique compensation procedure. In that compensation between the beneficial criteria is accepted, whereas poor results within the beneficial characteristics cannot be balanced completely by outstanding performance in non-beneficial criteria. This method confirms that alternatives having high scores in beneficial criteria are chosen over those that score well with cost-related criteria but not in beneficial features.

Consider a multi-standard evaluation-making problem with a finite number of y options P_u $(u = 1, 2, \ldots, y)$ and a finite number of z standards

Q_v ($v = 1, 2, \ldots, z$). The standards can be split into two parts, such as favorable standards, that include gain and productivity, whose top scores are required, whereas non-favorable standards, such as cost and uncertainty, whose minimum values are optimal, have been considered. Consider s_{uv} as the value of uth option in v^{th} evaluation criterion, a result matrix for y options and z subjects can be constructed as below

$$D = \begin{bmatrix} s_{11} & s_{12} & \cdots & s_{1z} \\ s_{21} & s_{22} & \cdots & s_{2z} \\ \vdots & \vdots & \ddots & \vdots \\ s_{y1} & s_{y2} & \cdots & s_{yz} \end{bmatrix}$$

In this matrix, Q_{uv} represents the output measure P_u with the standard value of Q_v. Directly modify the proceedings from RAM that are applied to hierarchize the considered options. Modified RAM follows these steps.

Step 1: The evaluation matrix is normalized through the linear sum standardization form

$$Q_{uv} = \frac{s_{uv}}{\sum_{u=1}^{y} s_{uv}}, (v=1,2,\ldots, z) \tag{3.11}$$

Step 2: The standardized evaluation matrix is computed by employing Definition 3.3.1.

Step 3: Calculate the average of standardized evaluations for appropriate and non-appropriate standards of uth option by applying the equations below

$$+u(S) = \sum_{v=1}^{z} y_{+uv} \tag{3.12}$$

$$-u(S) = \sum_{v=1}^{z} y_{-uv} \tag{3.13}$$

In the above equations, $+u(S)$ is the sum which represents the standardized values of appropriate options and $-u(S)$ is the average of standardized values of the non-appropriate criteria.

Step 4: Calculate the total score for each alternative by applying the aggregating function provided below

$$RI_u = \sqrt[(-u(S))+2]{(+u(S))+2}, (u = 1,2,\ldots,y) \tag{3.14}$$

Step 5: The value of RI_u is used to rank the alternatives. A larger RI_u involves more advanced priority of alternatives. Conversely, a better option indicates the higher value of RI_u. By applying the generalized modified score function for normalization, the members of the evaluation matrix take the limit range from 0 to 1.

3.4.2 Multi-Standard Evaluation Making Problem Using Generalized Modified Score Function for Solid Waste Management

Management of solid waste in municipalities (MSWM) is a big threat for developing cities and nations, which requires effective planning and execution. Countries with different social, economic, and environmental circumstances do not rely on the best possible solution to handle the waste. Selecting the suitable disposal method is difficult and has multiple characteristics, when the information is not clear or uncertain. This type of evaluation-making, where multiple criteria must be considered, is known as a multi-standard evaluation-making issue. This method provides a more refined ranking system by introducing a generalized modified score function (GMSF).

The management of solid waste remains a critical issue in environmental studies due to its complexity. Solid waste is an unavoidable byproduct generated from residential, industrial, and institutional sources. With the rising global population and increasing industrial activities, effective solid waste management (SWM) has become an urgent concern. This study employs the root assessment method (RAM) combined with type-2 intuitionistic fuzzy sets (T2IFS) to systematically evaluate sustainable SWM alternatives. By incorporating uncertainty-based decision making, the proposed approach offers a structured framework for evaluating SWM strategies based on multiple criteria, leading to a more informed and precise selection process.

Step 1: Determine the weights of the evaluation criteria and form a set of supervisors and identify the review parameters. Assign verbal terms for the

Table 3.1 Verbal terms and corresponding fuzzy assessment ranges.

Verbal terms	Fuzzy assessment range
Negligible (N)	[0.0 – 0.2]
Marginal (M)	[0.2 – 0.4]
Average (A)	[0.4 – 0.6]
Considerable (C)	[0.6 – 0.8]
Severe (S)	[0.8 – 1.0]

Table 3.2 Verbal scale representation of T2IFS membership values.

Criteria / Options	Environmental impact (+)	Cost efficiency (-)	Social acceptability (+)	Energy recovery (+)	Operational cost (-)
Land-filling	(M,A)	(C,M)	(A,M)	(A,M)	(S,N)
Incineration	(C,M)	(A,M)	(C,M)	(C,M)	(A,M)
Recycling	(S,N)	(M,A)	(S,N)	(C,M)	(M,A)
Composting	(C,N)	(A,M)	(C,N)	(S,N)	(A,M)
Waste-to-Energy	(C,N)	(S,N)	(S,N)	(C,N)	(C,M)

weighting of criteria. The corresponding fuzzy score ranges for the verbal terms are defined and organized in Table 3.1.

Step 2: Construct the primary evaluation matrix using type-2 intuitionistic fuzzy sets (T2IFS), by selecting appropriate verbal terms for each alternative concerning each criterion as in Table 3.2.

Step 3: Form the fuzzy evaluation matrix by representing membership (M_L, M_U) and non-membership (N_L, N_U) values as in Table 3.3. Type -2 intuitionistic fuzzy values are considered in the form of trapezoidal belongingness and non-belongingness values. The belongingness and non-belongingness values are assigned in the range [0, 1] and the non-membership values include the degree of hesitancy also. In a practical environment, it is not possible to represent a T2IFS directly.

Table 3.3 T2IFS initial decision matrix for solid waste management.

Criteria / Options	Environmental impact (+)	Cost efficiency (-)
Land-filling	(0.2,0.225,0.325,0.4), (0.4,0.45,0.55,0.6)	(0.6,0.625,0.65,0.7), (0.2,0.225.275,0.3)
Incineration	(0.6,0.625,0.65,0.7), (0.2,0.225,0.275,0.3)	(0.5,0.525,0.575,0.6), (0.3,0.325,0.350,0.4)
Recycling	(0.8,0.825,0.875,0.9), (0.0,0.025,0.05,0.1)	(0.3,0.325,0.350,0.4), (0.5,0.525,0.575,0.6)
Composting	(0.7,0.725,0.775,0.8), (0.1,0.125,0.15,0.2)	(0.4,0.425,0.450,0.5), (0.3,0.325,0.350,0.4)
Waste-to-energy	(0.6,0.625,0.675,0.7), (0.1,0.125,0.175,0.2)	(0.8,0.825,0.875,0.9), (0,0.025,0.05,0.1)

Criteria / Options	Societal acceptance (+)	Energy recovery (+)
Land-filling	(0.4,0.425,0.450,0.5), (0.3,0.325,0.350,0.4)	(0.4,0.425,0.450,0.5), (0.3,0.325,0.350,0.4)
Incineration	(0.6,0.625,0.650,0.7),(0. 2,0.225,0.275,0.3)	(0.6,0.625,0.650,0.7), (0.2,0.225,0.275,0.3)
Recycling	(0.8,0.825,0.875,0.9), (0.0,0.025,0.05,0.1)	(0.6,0.625,0.650,0.7), (0.2,0.225,0.275,0.3)
Composting	(0.7,0.725,0.775,0.8), (0.1,0.125,0.150,0.2)	(0.8,0.825,0.875,0.9), (0,0.025,0.05,0.1)
Waste-to-energy	(0.9,0.925,0.935,0.95), (0.0,0.025,0.035,0.05)	(0.7,0.725,0.775,0.8), (0.0,0.125,0.150,0.2)

Criteria / Options	Operational cost (-)
Land-filling	(0.6,0.625,0.65,0.7), (0.1,0.125,0.150,0.2)
Incineration	(0.4,0.425,0.450,0.5), (0.3,0.325,0.350,0.4)
Recycling	(0.3,0.325,0.350,0.4), (0.4,0.425,0.450,0.5)
Composting	(0.5,0.525,0.575,0.6), (0.2,0.225,0.275,0.3)
Waste-to-energy	(0.6,0.625,0.675,0.7), (0.2,0.225,0.275,0.3)

Here the trapezoidal valued membership and non-membership values are considered in the initial decision matrix.

Step 4: Apply the generalized modified score function to transform type-2 intuitionistic fuzzy values into crisp values as in Table 3.4. Construct a crisp decision matrix by calculating the score for each alternative and criterion by Definition 3.3.1.
Step 5: Normalize the decision matrix by using the linear summation formula from RAM (given in Section 3.4.1) as in Table 3.5. To find each element of the crisp decision matrix, use the normalization formula and ensure that beneficial criteria are maximized and non-beneficial criteria are minimized.
Step 6: Compute the sum of beneficial and non-beneficial criteria by calculating the total sum of standardized values for optimized factors ($+u(S)$) and non-optimized factors ($-u(S)$). Then compute the assigned score of $\{+u(S) + 2\}$ and $\{-u(S) + 2\}$ for further processing.
Step 7: Apply the modified root assessment method formula to compute the final RAM score for each alternative using the radical expression which is given in Equation 3.14. The alternatives based on the computed RAM scores can be arranged in ascending order to find the ranks.
Step 8: Once the arrangement of the modified RAM scores in ascending order has been done, the top-ranked alternative in the RAM score is considered as the most suitable for solid waste management. In this example, recycling attained the highest score of 1.5505 and took first place, composting with a score of 1.5149 in the second place, incineration with a score of 1.4897 in the third place, waste-to-energy arrived at the fourth place

Table 3.4 Crisp decision matrix for solid waste management alternatives.

Criteria / Options	Env. impact (+)	Cost eff. (-)	Soc. accept. (+)	Energy recovery (+)	Oper. cost (-)
Landfilling	0.3373	0.712	0.536	0.536	0.774
Incineration	0.710	0.606	0.710	0.710	0.536
Recycling	0.937	0.378	0.938	0.710	0.415
Composting	0.827	0.536	0.827	0.938	0.657
Waste-to-Energy	0.777	0.938	0.969	0.845	0.710
TOTAL	**3.589**	**3.170**	**3.980**	**3.739**	**3.093**

Table 3.5 Normalized decision matrix for solid waste management alternatives.

Options \ Criteria	Env. impact (+)	Cost eff. (-)	Soc. accept. (+)	Energy recovery (+)	Oper. cost (-)
Landfilling	0.094	0.225	0.135	0.143	0.250
Incineration	0.198	0.191	0.178	0.190	0.173
Recycling	0.261	0.119	0.236	0.190	0.134
Composting	0.230	0.169	0.208	0.251	0.213
Waste-to-Energy	0.217	0.296	0.243	0.226	0.230

Table 3.6 Final root assessment scores for solid waste management alternatives.

Options	$\{+u(S)\}$	$\{-u(S)\}$	$\{+u(S)\}+2$	$\{-u(S)\}+2$	**RAM**
Landfilling	0.372	0.475	2.372	2.475	**1.4176**
Incineration	0.566	0.364	2.566	2.364	**1.4897**
Recycling	0.687	0.253	2.687	2.253	**1.5505**
Composting	0.689	0.382	2.689	2.382	**1.5149**
Waste-to-Energy	0.686	0.525	2.686	2.525	**1.4788**

with a score of 1.4788, followed by landfill with a score of 1.4176 in the fifth position as in Table 3.6.

3.4.3 Comparison with Existing Methods

In this study, four different MCDM methods — WASPAS, SAW, TOPSIS, and WPM — were applied in conjunction with the proposed modified RAM method to compare the score functions and rank the solid waste management (SWM) attributes. The ranking methods were analyzed based on a decision matrix derived from Type-2 Intuitionistic Fuzzy Sets (T2IFS).

The comparison based on the performance score as given in Table 3.7 gives the ranking as in Table 3.8, which shows that the modified RAM method aligns with the rankings of SAW, TOPSIS, and WPM. Incineration was ranked first only by WASPAS, indicating its sensitivity to multiplicative scoring components. Landfilling was unanimously ranked last by all

Table 3.7 Comparison of MCDM methods based on performance scores.

Options	WASPAS	SAW	TOPSIS	WPM	Proposed RAM
Land Filling	1.3089	0.875	0.6523	0.8754	1.4176
Incineration	1.4682	0.920	0.7654	0.9153	1.4897
Recycling	1.3931	0.985	0.8921	0.9871	1.5505
Composting	1.4014	0.950	0.8576	0.9536	1.5149
Waste to Energy	1.3230	0.910	0.7345	0.9032	1.4788

Table 3.8 Ranking comparison of MCDM methods for SWM alternatives.

Options	WASPAS	SAW	TOPSIS	WPM	Proposed RAM
Land Filling	5	5	5	5	5
Incineration	1	3	3	3	3
Recycling	3	1	1	1	1
Composting	2	2	2	2	2
Waste to Energy	4	4	4	4	4

methods, confirming its lower sustainability. RAM, TOPSIS, and WPM exhibited strong consistency in their rankings. WASPAS, although powerful, showed some deviation in rank placement due to its hybrid structure.

Proposed RAM method demonstrated the highest suitability for fuzzy and uncertainty in environments like solid waste management. Due to its root-based scoring, modified RAM offers strong interpretability and is easiest to explain to non-expert stakeholders. Among all the methods tested, the proposed RAM method provided a balanced, stable, and interpretable ranking that aligns well with sustainable waste management principles and fuzzy logic modeling. It consistently recognized top-performing alternatives, handled hesitation in expert judgment effectively, and maintained ranking clarity.

3.4.4 Merits of the Proposed Work

- Uses T2IFS to deal with uncertainty in expert opinions.
- Provides a balanced evaluation by integrating beneficial and non-beneficial criteria.
- Uses an intuitive and mathematically easier ranking procedure for clarity and interpretability.
- Combines the expressive power of T2IFS with the modified RAM method for efficient decision-making.
- Introduces a generalized modified score function that balances both positive and negative assessment scores.
- Under fluctuating expert opinions, this method ensures robustness and consistency in decision outcomes.
- This method can be applied to any domain having linguistic or interval-valued inputs, not limited to solid waste management.

3.5 Conclusion

Effective solid waste management is a demanding challenge that needs a dynamic idea along with an organized and supervised assessment process. In this study, a modified form of the Root Assessment Method is applied using Type-2 Intuitionistic Fuzzy Sets to determine sustainable solid waste management (SWM) alternatives under uncertainty. The suggested technique combines fuzzy logic with decision-making techniques to handle estimated and ambiguous information, ensuring a more extensive evaluation. By normalizing decision criteria, calculating the sum of scores, and ranking alternatives, this modified assessment method provides a balanced approach to inspect the most suitable waste management action. The findings establish that this method strengthens the decision-making process by considering both beneficial and non-beneficial criteria.

Major Contributions:

- Development of a new Generalized Modified Score function for T2IFNs.
- Integration of T2IFS and modified RAM method for simple and effective ranking method.
- Comparative validation against established methods like TOPSIS, SAW, WASPAS, WPM.

3.6 Findings and Future Work

In unpredictable situations, the proposed approach is applied to improve the rank consistency.

The calculations are simple, but at the same time, they can maintain hesitancy and uncertainty. This novel modified RAM method can be used in decision-making environments for large-scale group decision-making, and this modified RAM with AI models is applied to optimize real-time waste management techniques. In future research, further refine this method by incorporating additional sustainability elements and day-to-day case studies to ratify its appropriateness.

3.7 Acknowledgment

The authors express their heartfelt thanks to the experts who contributed in this research with their insightful opinions and evaluations. They also express their sincere appreciation to the peer reviewers for their valuable comments, which helped to improve the paper. Additionally, the authors sincerely thank VIT for providing the Faculty Seed Grant (RGEMS) 2023-24 (Sanction no.SG20230026), along with the necessary resources and guidance for this research.

AI disclosure statement: The author acknowledges the use of AI-based tools for minor language editing or grammatical correction. However, all intellectual contributions, analyses, and conclusions presented in this chapter are entirely the author's own.

References

1. Abdullah, L., *et al.*, An interval-valued intuitionistic fuzzy DEMATEL method combined with Choquet integral for sustainable solid waste management. *Eng. Appl. Artif. Intell.*, 82, 207–215, 2019.
2. Atanassov, K., Intuitionistic fuzzy sets. *Int. J. Bioautomation*, 20, 1–5, 2016.
3. Bai, Z., An interval-valued intuitionistic fuzzy TOPSIS method based on an improved score function. *Sci. World J.*, 2013, 1, 879089, 2013.
4. Central Pollution Control Board, Annual Report (2020-21). Tech. rep. Accessed: March 2025, Government of India, 2021, url: https://cpcb.nic.in/.

5. Boran, F.E., *et al.*, A multi-criteria intuitionistic fuzzy group decision making for supplier selection with TOPSIS method. *Expert Syst. Appl.*, 36, 8, 11363–11368, 2009.
6. Chen, T.-Y., A comparative analysis of score functions for multiple criteria decision making in intuitionistic fuzzy settings. *Inf. Sci.*, 181, 17, 3652–3676, 2011.
7. Chen, Z., *et al.*, Entropy measures of type-2 intuitionistic fuzzy sets and type-2 triangular intuitionistic trapezodial fuzzy sets. *J. Syst. Eng. Electron.*, 26, 4, 774–793, 2015.
8. Cherif, S., *et al.*, New fuzzy similarity measures: From intuitionistic to type-2 fuzzy sets, in: *2017 IEEE International Conference on Fuzzy Systems (FUZZ-IEEE)*, IEEE, pp. 1–6, 2017.
9. Choudhury, S., *et al.*, Interval type 2 fuzzy based AHP approach: A case study. *Int. J. Fuzzy Syst. Appl. (IJFSA)*, 11, 1, 1–16, 2022.
10. De, A.K., Chakraborty, D., Biswas, A., Literature review on type-2 fuzzy set theory. *Soft Comput.*, 26, 18, 9049–9068, 2022.
11. Ekmekçioğlu, M., Kaya, T., Kahraman, C., Fuzzy multicriteria disposal method and site selection for municipal solid waste. *Waste Manage. (Oxford)*, 30, 8-9, 1729–1736, 2010.
12. Feng, F., *et al.*, Minkowski weighted score functions of intuitionistic fuzzy values. *Mathematics, 8*, 7, 1143, 2020.
13. Garg, H., A new generalized improved score function of interval-valued intuitionistic fuzzy sets and applications in expert systems. *Appl. Soft Comput.*, 38, 988–999, 2016.
14. Garg, H. and Rani, D., An efficient intuitionistic fuzzy MULTIMOORA approach based on novel aggregation operators for the assessment of solid waste management techniques. *Appl. Intell.*, 1–34, 2022.
15. Garg, H. and Singh, S., Algorithm for solving group decision-making problems based on the similarity measures under type 2 intuitionistic fuzzy sets environment. *Soft Comput.*, 24, 10, 7361–7381, 2020.
16. Jana, D.K., Novel arithmetic operations on type-2 intuitionistic fuzzy and its applications to transportation problem. *Pac. Sci. Rev. A: Nat. Sci. Eng*, 18, 3, 178–189, 2016.
17. Kaneesamkandi, Z., *et al.*, Methodology for assessment of alternative waste treatment strategies using entropy weights. *Sustainability*, 12, 16, 6689, 2020.
18. Kharat, M.G., *et al.*, Fuzzy multi-criteria decision analysis for environmentally con- scious solid waste treatment and disposal technology selection. *Technol. Soc.*, 57, 20–29, 2019.
19. Li, Z., *et al.*, Crisp and fuzzy optimization models for sustainable municipal solid waste management. *J. Cleaner Prod.*, 370, 133536–56, 2022.
20. Liu, Y. and Jiang, W., A new distance measure of interval-valued intuitionistic fuzzy sets and its application in decision making. *Soft Comput.*, 24, 6987–7003, 2020.

21. Magdalena, L., *et al.*, Different Types of Entropy Measures for Type-2 Fuzzy Sets. *Axioms*, 13, 8, 556–60, 2024.
22. Mendel, J.M. and John, R.I.B., Type-2 fuzzy sets made simple. *IEEE Trans. Fuzzy Syst.*, 10, 2, 117–127, 2002.
23. Mishra, A.R., *et al.*, Entropy and discrimination measures based q-rung orthopair fuzzy MULTIMOORA framework for selecting solid waste disposal method. *Environ. Sci. Pollut. Res.*, 30, 5, 12988–13011, 2023.
24. Mittal, K., *et al.*, A comprehensive review on type 2 fuzzy logic applications: Past, present and future. *Eng. Appl. Artif. Intell.*, 95, 103916, 2020.
25. Lakshmana Gomathi Nayagam, V., Muralikrishnan, S., Sivaraman, G., Multi-criteria decision-making method based on interval-valued intuitionistic fuzzy sets. *Expert Syst. Appl.*, 38, 3, 1464–1467, 2011.
26. Rajesh, K. and Srinivasan, R., Interval-valued Intuitionistic Fuzzy Sets of Second Type. *Adv. Fuzzy Math.*, 12, 4, 845–853, 2017.
27. Roy, J., Adhikary, K., Kar, S., Credibilistic TOPSIS model for evaluation and selection of municipal solid waste disposal methods, in: *Advances in Waste Management: Select Proceedings of Recycle 2016*, pp. 243–261, Springer, 2019.
28. Setiawansyah, S., Integration of Root Assessment Method and Entropy Weighting in Determining Business Location Selection. *J. Artif. Intell. Technol. Inf.*, 2, 4, 209–221, 2024.
29. Shanta, M.H., Choudhury, I.A., Salman, S., Municipal solid waste management: Identification and analysis of technology selection criteria using Fuzzy Delphi and Fuzzy DEMATEL technique. *Heliyon*, 10, 1, 2024.
30. Singh, S. and Garg, H., Distance measures between type-2 intuitionistic fuzzy sets and their application to multicriteria decision-making process. *Appl. Intell.*, 46, 788–799, 2017.
31. Singh, S. and Garg, H., Symmetric triangular interval type-2 intuitionistic fuzzy sets with their applications in multi criteria decision making. *Symmetry*, 10, 9, 401–410, 2018.
32. Sola, H.B., *et al.*, Interval type-2 fuzzy sets are generalization of interval-valued fuzzy sets: Toward a wider view on their relationship. *IEEE Trans. Fuzzy Syst.*, 23, 5, 1876–1882, 2014.
33. Sotoudeh-Anvari, A., Root Assessment Method (RAM): A novel multi-criteria decision making method and its applications in sustainability challenges. *J. Cleaner Prod.*, 423, 138695–105, 2023.
34. Surajit, D.S., *et al.*, Intuitionistic type-2 fuzzy set and its properties. *MDPI*, 11, 808–812, 2019.
35. Thilagasree, C.S., *et al.*, Analysis of municipal solid waste as a source of energy production using fuzzy decision system. *Appl. Soft Comput.*, 163, 111917–935, 2024.
36. Triantaphyllou, E. and Triantaphyllou, E., *Multi-criteria decision making methods*, Springer, Berlin, Germany, 2000.
37. Trung, D.D., *et al.*, Using the root assessment method to choose the optimal solution for mushroom cultivation. *Yugosl. J. Oper. Res.*, 7–14, 2024.

38. Wang, J., *et al.*, Multi-criteria decision-making method based on type-2 fuzzy sets. *Filomat*, 31, 2, 431–450, 2017.
39. Wibowo, S., Deng, H., Zhang, X., Evaluating the performance of e-waste recycling programs using fuzzy multiattribute group decision making model, in: *2014 9th IEEE Conference on Industrial Electronics and Applications*, IEEE, pp. 1989–1994, 2014.
40. Wibowo, S., Deng, H., Zhang, X., Fuzzy multicriteria decision support for solid waste disposal method and site selection, in: *2014 9th IEEE Conference on Industrial Electronics and Applications*, IEEE, pp. 1774–1779, 2014.
41. Wibowo, S. and Grandhi, S., A multicriteria group decision making approach for selecting e-waste recycling company, in: *2015 IEEE 10th Conference on Industrial Electronics and Applications (ICIEA)*, IEEE, pp. 849–854, 2015.
42. Xu, Z., Methods for aggregating interval-valued intuitionistic fuzzy information and their application to decision making. *Control Decis.*, 22, 2, 215–219, 2007, S1402758.
43. Yang, Y., *et al.*, Commentary on a new generalized improved score function of interval-valued intuitionistic fuzzy sets and applications in expert systems. *Appl. Soft Comput.*, 49, 611–615, 2016.
44. Ye, J., Multicriteria fuzzy decision-making method based on a novel accuracy function under interval-valued intuitionistic fuzzy environment. *Expert Syst. Appl.*, 36, 3, 6899–6902, 2009.
45. Zadeh, L.A., Fuzzy sets. *Inf. Control*, 8, 3, 338–353, 1965.
46. Zhang, F., *et al.*, Commentary on "A new generalized improved score function of interval-valued intuitionistic fuzzy sets and applications in expert systems"[Appl. Soft Comput., 2016 (38) 988–999]. *Appl. Soft Comput.*, 52, 48–52, 2017.
47. Zhang, F., *et al.*, Generalized score functions on interval-valued intuitionistic fuzzy sets with preference parameters for different types of decision makers and their application. *Appl. Intell.*, 48, 4084–4095, 2018.
48. Zhang, W., Zhang, X., Chen, D., Causal neural fuzzy inference modeling of missing data in implicit recommendation system. *Knowledge-Based Syst.*, 222, 106678–86, 2021.
49. Zhang, Z., *et al.*, A type of score function on intuitionistic fuzzy sets with double parameters and its application to pattern recognition and medical diagnosis. *Procedia Eng.*, 29, 4336–4342, 2012.

4

Fuzzy Logic Systems for Decision-Making Applications

Jitender Kaushal

Department of Electrical Engineering, Chandigarh University, Mohali, India

Abstract

Fuzzy logic systems have grown as an effective tool for decision-making in contexts marked by uncertainty and imprecision. In contrast to classical logic, which is based on binary values, fuzzy logic utilizes degrees of truth, facilitating a more human-like reasoning approach. This chapter examines the core principles of fuzzy logic, encompassing fuzzy sets, membership functions, and fuzzy inference systems, with an emphasis on their application in multi-criteria decision-making (MCDM). The aim is to establish a systematic framework for fuzzy decision-making, illustrating its applicability in practical scenarios like medical treatment choices. The methodology combines fuzzy discrete event systems (FDES) with fuzzy technique for order of preference by similarity to ideal solution (Fuzzy TOPSIS) to simulate decision-making in difficult situations. A case study on clinical decision-making is presented, evaluating various treatment options – surgery, radiation, and medication based on factors like success rate, side effects, and recovery time. The findings demonstrate that medication is the most effective treatment option, followed by surgery, with radiation being the least favorable. Subsequent studies will concentrate on combining fuzzy logic with artificial intelligence and machine learning to improve adaptive decision-making. The integration of IoT-driven real-time analytics is anticipated to enhance decision-support systems in dynamic sectors like healthcare, industrial automation, and autonomous systems.

***Keywords*:** Fuzzy logic, decision-making systems, fuzzy inference systems, multi-criteria decision-making (MCDM), membership functions, fuzzy discrete event systems (FDES), Fuzzy TOPSIS

Email: jitender.e14621@cumail.in; ORCID: https://orcid.org/0000-0002-8383-7791

Harish Garg (ed.) Decision Support Systems in Smart Computing: Embracing Uncertainty and Challenges, (93–120) © 2026 Scrivener Publishing LLC

4.1 Introduction

Decision-making is a crucial component of human cognition and artificial intelligence, impacting many fields, from industrial automation to medical diagnostics. Conventional decision-making frameworks, typically reliant on binary logic and deterministic models, inadequately address uncertainty and imprecision. Conversely, fuzzy logic systems have arisen as a potent alternative, facilitating more adaptable and human-like decision-making processes.

Fuzzy logic has achieved extensive utilization in decision-making applications owing to its capacity to manage uncertainty and imprecision. In the past five years, researchers have investigated innovative applications and approaches to enhance the efficiency and precision of fuzzy logic-based systems. A primary focus has been to deepen the mathematical foundations of fuzzy logic to improve decision-making processes in diverse fields [1]. It is presented that a revised architecture for uncertain rule-based fuzzy systems, offering a more resilient basis for managing linguistic uncertainty and ambiguous input [3]. It is further developed that the theoretical dimensions of fuzzy sets and logic, enhancing their relevance in AI-driven decision-making frameworks [2]. These advancements have established a more systematic foundation for multi-criteria decision-making (MCDM), facilitating improved practical application of fuzzy systems in healthcare, supply chain management, and industrial automation.

Despite these gains, a considerable disparity persists in the integration of fuzzy logic with contemporary AI methodologies to improve decision automation and predictive modeling. The authors have examined soft consensus models within a fuzzy context to enhance decision-making processes, observing a deficiency in adaptable frameworks capable of dynamically responding to real-time decision situations [5]. It is investigated that fuzzy MCDM techniques for supplier selection, highlighting that the majority of models continue to depend on static decision parameters, which may be wasteful in dynamic business contexts [6]. These findings underscore the necessity for adaptive fuzzy logic models capable of learning and evolving through real-time feedback, an issue that remains predominantly unsolved.

Researchers have proposed various innovative approaches and computer models to address this gap. The authors have presented a heterogeneous fuzzy technique for order of preference by similarity to ideal solution (Fuzzy TOPSIS) methodology, enhancing MCDM by incorporating several fuzzy sets to address distinct decision criteria [7]. It is further developed that fuzzy multi-criteria decision-making techniques by integrating linguistic variables and hybrid fuzzy systems to enhance precision and relevance in practical applications [11]. The authors have introduced an intuitionistic fuzzy aggregation model that enhances uncertainty management through the integration of membership and non-membership degrees, rendering it very useful for risk assessment applications [12]. These methodological breakthroughs illustrate the ongoing evolution of fuzzy logic, effectively resolving existing deficiencies in decision-making processes.

The results of these novel techniques have been evaluated across multiple industries, showing measurable enhancements in decision-making precision and dependability. The authors have performed a bibliometric analysis of fuzzy decision-making in complex systems, demonstrating that fuzzy logic frameworks have enhanced risk assessment, quality control, and strategic planning in sectors including manufacturing and logistics [9]. The authors have assessed interval type-2 fuzzy sets for multi-criteria decision-making, indicating their efficacy in enhancing choice results amid uncertainty [10]. These findings underscore the adaptability of fuzzy logic in managing intricate decision-making processes, especially in areas characterized by imprecise, incomplete, or dynamic data.

The integration of fuzzy logic with AI-driven systems is one of its most potential applications. It is investigated that the interplay between fuzzy logic and artificial intelligence, illustrating how fuzzy models might augment machine learning algorithms to manage uncertainty in decision-making processes [8]. It is formulated that an enhanced VIKOR approach for multi-criteria decision-making within interval-valued intuitionistic fuzzy contexts, rendering it a significant instrument for medical decision-making and financial risk evaluations [13]. It is employed that a fuzzy evaluation model in supply chain management, demonstrating the optimization of risk management in global trade networks. These applications represent a significant transition towards hybrid fuzzy-AI systems, which are expected to be crucial in the future of autonomous decision-making [14].

In the future, fuzzy logic is anticipated to advance through the incorporation of big data analytics, the Internet of Things, and deep learning models. The authors have examined the application of fuzzy set theory in social sciences, highlighting the necessity for multidisciplinary study to fully realize its potential in policy-making and human behavior studies [15]. The continuous development of real-time adaptive fuzzy models, in computational intelligence applications, will reinforce the significance of fuzzy logic in decision-making across various domains [4]. These advancements are expected to influence the future of automated and intelligent decision-support systems, allowing them to manage ambiguity, adapt to changing data, and improve predictive ability in complex situations.

Recent advancements in fuzzy logic systems have concentrated on improving real-time adaptability and handling high-dimensional input in dynamic settings. A novel Adaptive Dynamic Attribute and Rule (ADAR) management system is developed, which dynamically optimizes fuzzy rule bases and input attributes, particularly beneficial for decision-making with extensive datasets [16]. Likewise, it is established that learning-inspired fuzzy controllers designed for oscillatory systems provide enhanced robustness and responsiveness in automation tasks [17]. Fuzzy attention mechanisms are integrated into Transformer-based time series models, enhancing uncertainty management in forecasting and classification tasks through a model designated as FANTF [18].

Research has highlighted the integration of fuzzy logic with other soft computing methodologies. A full assessment of type-3 fuzzy logic systems is done, highlighting their superior ability to model uncertainty in intricate control applications [19]. A 2024 study in Neural Computing and Applications introduced a type-2 fuzzy-based adaptive module that dynamically modifies parameters in metaheuristic optimization algorithms, thereby improving convergence reliability in multi-objective choice scenarios [20]. Complex intuitionistic fuzzy rough sets are employed to assess AI architectures for autonomous vehicles, demonstrating the promise of fuzzy MCDM in safety-critical systems [21].

Fuzzy logic is increasingly being adopted in application-centric research within specific fields. A Mamdani-type fuzzy logic controller has been applied for airplane landing gear systems, enhancing dependability in mission-critical automation [22]. An expert advising system created at the Centre for Advanced Manufacturing Technologies in 2025 utilized fuzzy AHP to optimize material selection in additive manufacturing, effectively managing qualitative decision criteria [23]. BMC Medical Informatics introduced a fuzzy MCDM-based framework for customizing care plans for the elderly, providing real-time adaptation to individual patient data [24].

Ultimately, sophisticated uncertainty management has been accomplished by the integration of fuzzy logic with neutrosophic sets. A neutrosophic fuzzy decision-making model for site selection is presented, which more successfully addresses indeterminacy in environmental and infrastructural data compared to typical fuzzy systems [25]. These new directives together demonstrate a paradigm shift towards advanced, hybrid, and adaptive fuzzy systems that better correspond with the complexities of contemporary intelligent decision-making contexts.

Fuzzy logic systems fundamentally consist of essential elements, including fuzzy sets, membership functions, and fuzzy inference systems. These components jointly facilitate the modeling of ambiguous and imprecise information, enhancing decision-making in dynamic and uncertain contexts. Membership functions delineate the extent to which input is associated with a specific fuzzy set, whereas fuzzy inference systems employ a collection of rules to analyze inputs and provide corresponding outputs. By incorporating these components, fuzzy logic systems may proficiently manage intricate decision-making tasks that conventional binary logic cannot adequately solve. A prominent application of fuzzy logic is in MCDM, which involves the simultaneous consideration of many competing criteria. MCDM is essential in multiple domains, including business analytics, engineering design, and resource allocation. Fuzzy logic augments MCDM by integrating subjective preferences and expert insights into the decision-making process, thus enhancing the dependability and adaptability of solutions. In addition to MCDM, fuzzy logic systems have proven effective in other practical applications. Industrial process control utilizes fuzzy controllers to enhance performance under unpredictable situations, whilst autonomous systems depend on fuzzy logic for navigation and obstacle evasion. Fuzzy logic facilitates the evaluation of uncertain scenarios in risk assessment, improving predictive modeling and strategic planning. The healthcare sector benefits from fuzzy-based diagnostic tools that aid medical practitioners in conducting more precise and individualized patient evaluations.

A significant research gap remains in the dynamic adaptability and integration of fuzzy logic with contemporary computational intelligence methodologies, including deep learning, neural-symbolic systems, and reinforcement learning. This chapter tackles existing research deficiencies by investigating and proposing innovative adaptive and hybrid fuzzy logic models that incorporate AI techniques to facilitate real-time, context-aware decision-making. These contributions provide a foundation for the advancement of fuzzy systems capable of effectively managing uncertainty, variability, and high-dimensional inputs–challenges characteristic of contemporary intelligent systems.

This chapter primarily contributes by offering a thorough overview of recent research, pinpointing existing limits in traditional fuzzy systems, and suggesting avenues for developing adaptive, hybrid, and scalable decision-support architectures. This chapter contextualizes fuzzy logic within the contemporary AI landscape, providing researchers and practitioners with insights and methodologies to create intelligent systems that are both theoretically sound and pragmatically robust in uncertain real-world environments.

Moreover, computational complexity may emerge while managing extensive fuzzy systems. Nevertheless, developments in computational tools, such as MATLAB's Fuzzy Logic Toolbox and open-source software, have considerably streamlined the development and implementation of fuzzy systems. As artificial intelligence advances, fuzzy logic remains an essential element in improving decision-making frameworks. Emerging trends indicate a heightened integration of fuzzy logic with machine learning and deep learning methodologies, resulting in more intelligent and adaptive systems. This chapter examines recent accomplishments and prospective research trajectories, highlighting the escalating significance of fuzzy logic in tackling the issues presented by a more unpredictable environment.

4.1.1 Objectives

This study establishes a comprehensive fuzzy logic framework to aid treatment selection for patients with intricate health conditions within the realm of clinical decision-making under uncertainty. It employs a Fuzzy Discrete Event System (FDES) to represent patient health states and assess the effects of treatments on clinical outcomes and quality of life. A patient preference-based methodology is introduced to reconcile clinical recovery with long-term well-being, facilitating personalized treatment options aligned with individual priorities. Furthermore, the Fuzzy TOPSIS method is utilized to rank various medical treatments by analyzing success rates, side effects, and recovery durations, thereby ensuring systematic, data-driven, and patient-centered decision support.

- To create a fuzzy discrete event system (FDES) model for the dynamic evaluation of clinical status and quality of life in patients, facilitating personalized treatment decisions *via* state-transition matrices, health indicators, and defuzzification methods.
- To develop a patient-centered treatment selection framework that incorporates clinical outcomes and long-term quality of life through a fuzzy multi-criteria methodology.
- To use Fuzzy TOPSIS to compare and rank medical treatments under unclear and contradictory clinical criteria to improve treatment planning through data-driven and uncertainty-aware medical decision-making.

The subsequent sections of this chapter methodically explain the incorporation of fuzzy logic into clinical decision-making. Section 4.2 outlines the fundamental concepts of fuzzy logic, highlighting the significance of membership functions, which are crucial for representing ambiguity in real-world data. Section 4.3 explores fuzzy sets, providing the mathematical foundation required for addressing imprecision in healthcare evaluations. Section 4.4 introduces the concept of FDES, an effective modeling framework for simulating transitions in patient health updates over time. Section 4.5 illustrates the application of FDES through a comprehensive clinical scenario, encompassing the depiction of patient status, assessment of treatment alternatives, and their impact on quality of life, resulting in a case study. Section 4.6 examines the fuzzy TOPSIS method to facilitate multi-criteria medical treatment decisions, integrating fuzzy decision matrices and analyzing findings that underscore the model's effectiveness. Finally, Section 4.7 concludes by summarizing the insights gained and outlines prospective future directions for the enhancement of fuzzy logic applications in customized healthcare.

4.2 Principles of Fuzzy Logic

Fuzzy logic is predicated on the core principle of fuzzy sets, which enhances classical set theory by permitting partial membership. A fuzzy set $\boldsymbol{A}$ within a universal set $\boldsymbol{X}$ is characterized by a membership function $\mu_A(\boldsymbol{x})$, as delineated in Equation (4.1), which assigns each element $\boldsymbol{x}$ in $\boldsymbol{X}$ a value ranging from **0** to **1**:

$$\mu_A(x): X \rightarrow [0,1] \tag{4.1}$$

In contrast to classical sets, where an element either belongs or does not belong to a set (i.e. $\mu_A(\boldsymbol{x})$ is either **0** or **1**), fuzzy sets facilitate incremental transitions, rendering them more appropriate for managing inaccuracy.

4.2.1 Membership Functions

Membership functions outline the extent to which an input correlates with a fuzzy set. The predominant categories of membership functions have been defined as follows.

4.2.1.1 Triangular Membership Function

According to Equation (4.2), ***a*** represents the lower limit at which membership initiates at **0**. ***b*** represents the point at which membership attains a value of **1**. ***c*** represents the upper limit at which membership reverts to zero.

$$\mu_A(x) = \begin{cases} 0, x \le a \\ \dfrac{x-a}{b-a}, a < x \le b \\ \dfrac{c-x}{c-b}, b < x \le c \\ 0, x > c \end{cases} \tag{4.2}$$

In Figure 4.1(a), the x-axis denotes the input variable "input1", which ranges from 0 to 1. The y-axis denotes the degree of membership, varying

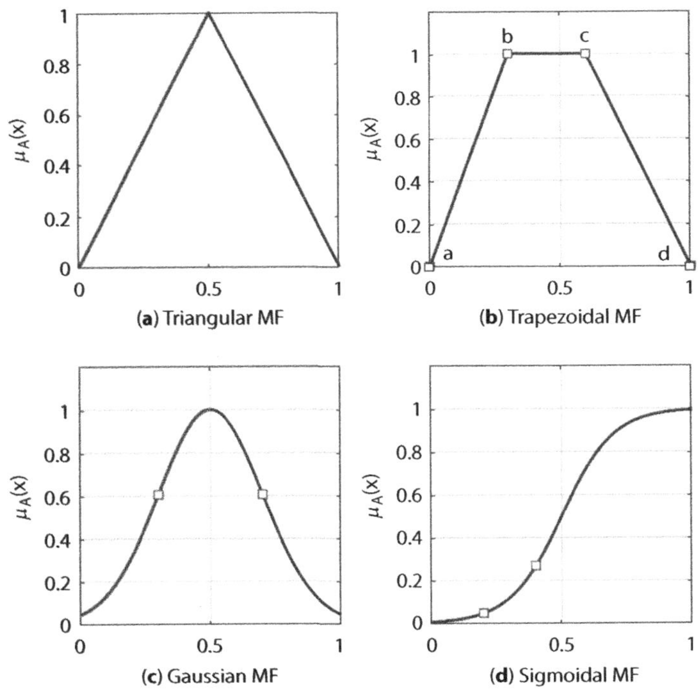

Figure 4.1 Representation of (a) triangular, (b) trapezoidal, (c) Gaussian, and (d) sigmoidal membership functions (MFs).

from 0 to 1. The maximum value (membership = 1) is attained when x = 0.5, indicating that this value is entirely encompassed within the fuzzy set. The membership degree progressively diminishes on both ends, becoming 0 at x = 0 and x = 1. Triangular membership functions are extensively utilized in fuzzy control systems and decision-making applications because of their simplicity and computational efficiency. They are especially beneficial in fuzzy inference systems (FIS) for defining linguistic variables such as low, medium, and high, where seamless transitions between categories are required.

A fuzzy set with a triangle membership function is one in which the degree of membership grows linearly up to a maximum and then falls symmetrically. It is an essential component of fuzzy logic systems that deal with imprecision and uncertainty in decision-making.

4.2.1.2 *Trapezoidal Membership Function*

In Figure 4.1(b), the function forms a trapezoidal shape as shown in Equation (4.3), with a flat top at the membership degree of 1 and sides that increase and decrease linearly. Left endpoint (a), flat top start (b), flat top end (c), and right endpoint (d) are the four critical points that characterize it.

$$\mu_A(x) = \begin{cases} 0, x \le a \\ \dfrac{x-a}{b-a}, a < x \le b \\ 1, b < x \le c \\ \dfrac{d-x}{d-c}, c < x \le d \\ 0, x > d \end{cases} \tag{4.3}$$

where ***a*** is the lower bound where membership starts at 0. ***b*** is the start of full membership (flat top begins). ***c*** is the end of full membership (flat top ends). ***d*** is the upper bound where membership returns to 0.

Fuzzy control systems and decision-making applications utilize trapezoidal membership functions when a range of values should be fully represented instead of only one peak, as is the case with the triangular function. Linguistic variables like low, medium, and high can be defined with their help, as certain values progressively fall into the fuzzy set, and others are entirely symbolic. Notable examples of common uses include multi-criteria decision-making (MCDM), expert systems, and fuzzy logic controllers.

The trapezoidal membership function is a crucial tool in fuzzy logic applications, facilitating smoother transitions, and enhanced flexibility compared to triangular membership functions. The flat top guarantees comprehensive consideration of a spectrum of values in decision-making, rendering it optimal for practical fuzzy inference systems.

4.2.1.3 Gaussian Membership Function

The symmetrical Gaussian (bell-shaped) curve is shown in Figure 4.1(c), and centered at the function's maximum, describing its behavior. This curve is perfect for fuzzy logic applications that require smooth transitions because it climbs and drops gradually without any abrupt shifts. A Gaussian membership function $\mu_A(x)$ is typically defined by Equation (4.4).

$$\mu_A(x) = e^{-\frac{(x-c)^2}{2\sigma^2}} \tag{4.4}$$

where $\boldsymbol{c}$ is the mean and $\boldsymbol{\sigma}$ is the standard deviation.

In FIS, Gaussian membership functions are widely utilized, especially in AI, control systems, and pattern recognition. With their seamless transition between fuzzy sets, they effectively manage uncertainty and imprecision. It is helpful in neural-fuzzy systems, which combine neural networks with machine-learning models using fuzzy logic. The Gaussian membership function is favored when a smooth and intuitive representation of fuzzy sets is necessary. Its continuous nature renders it exceptionally successful in intricate decision-making applications, such as medical diagnostics, image processing, and adaptive control systems.

4.2.1.4 Sigmoidal Membership Function

The function exhibits a sigmoidal curve, marked by a slow rise from 0 to 1. Figure 4.1(d) represents a sigmoidal membership function, which is widely used in fuzzy logic systems for defining smooth transitions between fuzzy sets. It is monotonic, indicating that it consistently increases without any decline. The function commences at a minimal membership value and progressively ascends, attaining full membership value (1) at the upper limit. A sigmoidal membership function $\mu_A(x)$ is represented by Equation (4.5).

$$\mu_A(x) = \frac{1}{1 + e^{-\alpha(x-c)}} \tag{4.5}$$

where α is the slope of the function and c represents the center of the transition.

Sigmoidal membership functions are effective for representing smooth transitions and are frequently utilized in neural networks and fuzzy inference systems. They can signify both ascending and descending trends contingent upon the sign of α.

Sigmoidal membership functions are commonly used in fuzzy inference systems (FIS) for cases where a gradual change from non-membership to full membership is needed. They are widely used in classification problems, neural networks, and control systems, where progressive decision boundaries are required. This function is especially useful for defining fuzzy concepts like "high temperature," "strong signal," or "large size", where the transition from low to high should be smooth rather than abrupt.

Sigmoidal membership functions are frequently employed in FIS when a gradual transition from non-membership to complete membership is required. They are extensively utilized in classification problems, neural networks, and control systems when incremental decision boundaries are necessary. This function is particularly advantageous for defining ambiguous notions such as "high temperature", "strong signal", or "large size", where the shift from low to high should be gradual rather than sudden.

The sigmoidal membership function facilitates a seamless and progressive transition across fuzzy sets, rendering it suitable for applications necessitating soft decision boundaries. It is widely utilized in adaptive fuzzy systems, medical diagnostics, and machine learning frameworks.

4.3 Fuzzy Sets

Fuzzy set theory is a fundamental concept in fuzzy logic systems. In contrast to classical (crisp) sets, where an element is either a member or not a member of a set, fuzzy sets permit partial membership. This property renders fuzzy sets exceptionally adept at managing uncertainty, imprecision, and ambiguity, which are prevalent in real-world decision-making contexts.

A fuzzy set ***A*** in a universe of discourse ***X*** is defined by Equation (4.6).

$$A = \{(x, \mu_A(x)) | x \in X, \mu_A(x) \in [0,1]\} \tag{4.6}$$

where x is an element of the set X. $\mu_A(x)$ denotes the membership function that allocates a degree of membership. $\mu_A(x) = 0$ signifies the no membership. $\mu_A(x) = 1$ signifies full membership. $0 < \mu_A(x) < 1$ denotes partial membership.

Suppose if A is the fuzzy set "Tall Persons", then:

- A person with a height of 5.5 feet might have $\mu_A(5.5) = 0.4$ (partially tall).
- A person with a height of 6.5 feet might have $\mu_A(6.5) = 0.9$ (almost fully tall).

This adaptability renders fuzzy sets appropriate for representing ambiguous and uncertain real-world ideas.

Fuzzy sets are extensively utilized in practical decision-making applications, encompassing:

- Industrial Control Systems: Automation of processes in chemical facilities, robotics, and intelligent systems.
- Medical Diagnosis: Managing ambiguous symptoms and illness advancement.
- Risk Assessment: Decision-making in finance, project management, and disaster forecasting.
- AI and Machine Learning: Enhancing human-like decision-making capabilities in AI systems.
- Autonomous Systems: Navigation and decision-making in autonomous vehicles.

Fuzzy set theory enhances classical set theory by permitting progressive membership instead of rigid binary classification. Fuzzy sets are vital for managing uncertainty and imprecision, which is critical for intelligent decision-making across diverse fields.

This section serves a fundamental purpose in the proposed chapter by providing the theoretical foundations essential for comprehending fuzzy logic-based decision models. It introduces the fundamental concept of partial membership, differentiating fuzzy sets from traditional binary sets, and clarifies how this adaptability facilitates the representation and use of ambiguous or imprecise information, an inherent characteristic in medical and real-world contexts. This section theoretically defines fuzzy sets and contextualizes their importance through relatable instances, such as assessing the notion of "tallness." Moreover, it underscores the extensive applicability of fuzzy sets in diverse fields, such as medical diagnosis and artificial intelligence, hence validating their significance in healthcare decision-making models addressed in subsequent sections. This part prepares readers for advanced modeling techniques like FDES and Fuzzy TOPSIS by elucidating how fuzziness may be quantified and applied to enhance decision-making quality in complicated, uncertain situations.

4.4 Decision-Making Using Fuzzy Discrete Event Systems

FIS is a rule-based framework that translates inputs into outputs utilizing the principles of fuzzy logic. In contrast to conventional Boolean logic systems, FIS integrates degrees of truth in its decision-making processes. Fuzzy logic offers a proficient method for managing uncertainty in decision-making processes. In contrast to classical logic, which functions with binary true/false values, fuzzy logic accommodates varying degrees of truth, facilitating more human-like reasoning. In the context of discrete event systems (DES), fuzzy logic improves decision-making by integrating uncertainty, imprecision, and subjective criteria into system design and analysis.

4.4.1 Fuzzy Discrete Event Systems (FDES)

Discrete event systems (DES) are dynamic systems in which state transitions transpire at distinct time intervals in reaction to certain stimuli. Conventional DES models depend on clear transitions, constraining their capacity to manage imprecise or ambiguous inputs. The incorporation of fuzzy logic into discrete event systems (DES) produces fuzzy discrete event systems (FDES), wherein state transitions and event occurrences are regulated by fuzzy rules. FDES models are especially advantageous in contexts necessitating real-time decision-making, including manufacturing systems, communication networks, and autonomous control systems.

4.4.2 Mathematical Foundation of FDES

A fuzzy discrete event system is represented using mathematical Equation (4.7), which shows the relationship between various variables.

$$F = (X, \Sigma, \delta, \mu, x_0) \tag{4.7}$$

where X signifies a finite set of states, Σ indicates a finite number of events, δ represents the state transition function, μ is the fuzzy membership function that defines the degree of truth for each state, and x_0 identifies the initial state.

In contrast to traditional DES, where transitions are either deterministic or probabilistic, FDES features transitions that occur with a certain likelihood, governed by fuzzy rules.

4.4.3 Fuzzy State Transition Model

The state transition in an FDES follows a fuzzy inference mechanism, which is defined by Equation (4.8).

$$\mu_{x'} = \max(\min(\mu_x, \mu_\sigma)), \quad \forall\, x \in X, \sigma \in \Sigma \tag{4.8}$$

where μ_σ denotes the fuzzy membership value associated with an event that initiates the transition. This method ensures that state alterations are represented using fuzzy truth values instead of binary conditions.

FDES is extensively utilized throughout diverse domains necessitating adaptable decision-making systems, including:

- Industrial Process Control – Regulating production operations among ambiguous sensor data.
- Autonomous Systems – Facilitating adaptive behavior in robots and autonomous vehicles.
- Healthcare Diagnostics – Facilitating medical decision-making amidst unclear symptoms.
- Risk Assessment – Analyzing financial or environmental hazards through ambiguous criteria.

Fuzzy discrete event systems offer a robust framework for decision-making in uncertain conditions. Through the integration of fuzzy sets, inference techniques, and state transition models, FDES facilitates efficient decision-making across multiple domains. Future research may concentrate on augmenting computational efficiency and incorporating machine learning methodologies to refine fuzzy-based decision models.

4.5 FDES Model for Clinical Status and Quality of Life – An Example

This example presents a Fuzzy Discrete Event System (FDES) model to evaluate the clinical condition of individuals diagnosed with aggressive, early-stage cancer. The FDES framework facilitates a systematic and quantitative assessment of illness progression and treatment effectiveness through the use of fuzzy states and state-transition matrices.

4.5.1 Clinical Status Representation

The patient's clinical status is represented by four fuzzy states, each defined by a peak membership value.

Healthy (μ_h) with a maximum value of 4
Good (μ_g) with a maximum value of 3
Fair (μ_f) with a maximum value of 2
Poor (μ_p) with a maximum value of 1

The fuzzy state vector Q, which denotes patient status, is defined as follows: $Q = [\mu_h, \mu_g, \mu_f, \mu_p]$ signify the membership values for each respective state. A reduced value of μ_h, μ_g *and* μ_f alongside an elevated μ_p indicates a more severe situation. The fuzzy state vector is defuzzified using the centroid approach to yield a precise health index, which ranges [1 to 4], with lower values signifying poorer health conditions.

Initial Clinical State
Prior to treatment, the initial state vector $q_{0,c}$ is determined as, $q_{0,c} = [0, 0.2, 0.7, 0.1]$. Defuzzification produces an initial health index of 2.1, classifying the patient as in a Fair condition.

4.5.2 Treatment Options and State Transition

The patient considers two treatment options:

i. Surgical excision of malignant tissues.
ii. Radiation therapy to target and eradicate cancer cells.

Each alternative is represented as a fuzzy state-transition matrix constructed from past patient data. The transition matrices α_c (for surgery) and β_c (for radiation) delineate the probability of individuals transitioning between states following treatment. The expected post-treatment states for both choices are calculated using max-product composition.

Post-operative health index: 2.6737
Post-radiation health index: 2.2667

Surgery yields a superior health score compared to radiation, indicating its greater efficacy for clinical recovery.

4.5.3 Quality of Life Evaluation

In addition to clinical efficacy, treatment options must also take into account the patient's long-term quality of life (QoL), which is characterized by three ambiguous states:

- High (μ_h) with a peak at 3
- Medium (μ_m) with a peak at 2
- Low (μ_l) with a peak at 1

The initial quality-of-life state $q_{0,l}$ is defined as: $q_{0,l} = [0.1, 0.5, 0.4]$. Defuzzification provides an initial QoL index of 1.7 (Medium state).

Impact of Treatment on Quality of Life
Separate state-transition matrices α_l (surgery) and β_l (radiation) model the long-term quality-of-life changes. The post-treatment QoL indices are:

- Post-surgery QoL index: 1.5211
- Post-radiation QoL index: 1.6559

Radiation has a superior quality of life score compared to surgery, suggesting reduced long-term adverse side effects.

Treatment Decision Framework
Surgery provides superior clinical control; however, it may adversely affect the quality of life more than radiation therapy. A treatment preference function is introduced to equilibrate these factors using Equations (4.9) and (4.10):

$$F_\alpha(\theta) = \theta x_{\alpha,c} + (1-\theta) y_{\alpha,l} \tag{4.9}$$

$$F_\beta(\theta) = \theta x_{\beta,c} + (1-\theta) y_{\beta,l} \tag{4.10}$$

where $\theta\ (0 \le \theta \le 1)$ is a patient preference factor which can be understood as:

Higher θ: Emphasizes clinical enhancement (prefers surgical intervention).
Lower θ: Emphasizes quality of life (prefers radiation).

It is shown in Figure 4.2 that the analysis of these functions indicates that for $\theta > 0.25$, surgery is the preferable intervention, whereas for $\theta < 0.25$, radiation is more advantageous.

The FDES-based methodology offers a systematic decision-making framework for choosing the most effective cancer treatment by incorporating clinical efficacy and quality of life factors. The approach facilitates quantitative assessment of patient conditions and treatment effects, hence enhancing informed and individualized decision-making.

4.5.4 Case Study

It illustrates how mathematical frameworks can be employed to inform clinical decision-making by incorporating patient-specific variables. The graph clearly indicates that treatment options should be flexible and tailored according to patient priorities and risk evaluations. This crossing point offers a quantitative foundation for assessing when a therapy modification is necessary, underscoring that patient-centered decision-making can be enhanced through systematic, data-informed approaches.

Figure 4.2 shows the relationship between two treatment preferences, radiation preference, and surgery preference, and a patient weighting factor, denoted as θ. The x-axis shows the patient weighting factor, which is likely to influence the choice between the two treatment options. The y-axis shows the preference score for each treatment option, though the exact unit of measurement is not specified. This could be a utility score, the outcome of a risk-benefit analysis, or some other decision-making metric. Figure 4.2 shows that when $\theta > 0.25$, surgery is the better intervention, but radiation is better when $\theta < 0.25$, according to the study of these functions.

The two treatment preference lines demonstrate distinct growth trajectories. The blue line (Surgery Preference) commences at a lower score when $\theta = 0$ and ascends linearly with increasing θ, indicating that as the patient's

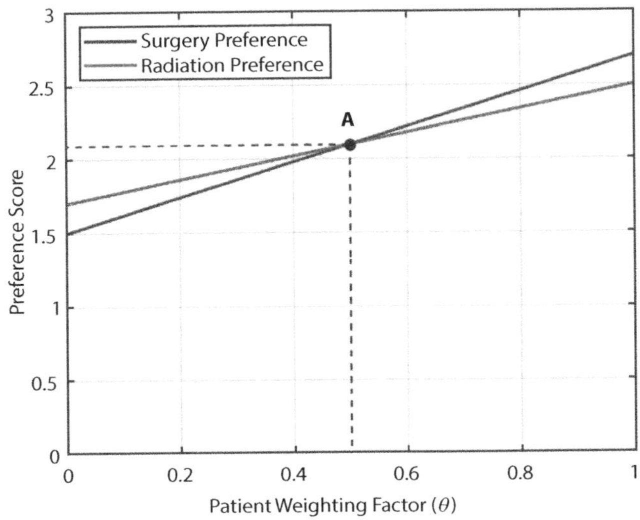

Figure 4.2 Treatment selection criteria based on the choices for surgery and radiation preferences.

weighting factor rises, so does the inclination towards surgery. Conversely, the red line (Radiation Preference) initiates at a higher score than surgery at $\theta = 0$ but progresses at a more gradual pace relative to the surgery preference line. This trend signifies that radiation is initially favored but does not experience as pronounced an increase in preference as surgery over time. The two lines intersect at a specific value of θ (approximately between 0.3 and 0.4), denoting the point at which the preference for surgery eclipses that of radiation.

The intersection point (A) indicates the value of θ at which the preference ratings for surgery and radiation are equivalent. Below this threshold, radiation is the more advantageous choice, as its preference score surpasses that of surgery. Conversely, beyond this threshold, surgical intervention emerges as the more favored treatment, indicating a change in the decision-making of patients or clinicians. The dotted lines running from point (A) to the axes delineate the precise values at which this transition transpires, offering a clear visual depiction of the decision boundary. The preference scores escalate with θ, although surgery demonstrates a more pronounced ascent, signifying that as the weighting factor amplifies, surgery is increasingly favored over radiation. Consequently, this form of analysis can aid in medical decision-making, enabling practitioners to customize therapy recommendations based on patient-specific weighting variables.

4.6 Fuzzy Decision-Making for Medical Treatment Selection Using Fuzzy TOPSIS

In medical decision-making, choosing the most suitable treatment for patients necessitates the assessment of various conflicting criteria, including success rate, side effects, and recovery duration. Conventional decision-making models may inadequately address the intrinsic uncertainty and ambiguity present in patient preferences and medical data. This study employs the fuzzy technique for order of preference by similarity to ideal solution (Fuzzy TOPSIS) to systematically rank medical treatments according to multiple criteria. The objective is to aid clinicians in making informed, data-driven decisions while accounting for the imprecise nature of medical parameters.

The methodology employs the Fuzzy TOPSIS approach, utilizing fuzzy numbers to denote ambiguous decision parameters. The procedure comprises the subsequent essential stages:

i. Data Collection and Decision Matrix Development: A decision matrix is created to assess treatments based on several criteria utilizing fuzzy numbers.
ii. Fuzzy Normalization: The decision matrix undergoes normalization to facilitate comparability across varying scales.
iii. Weighted Normalization: Criteria weights are utilized to signify the relative significance of each medical criterion.
iv. Fuzzy Positive Ideal Solution (FPIS) and Fuzzy Negative Ideal Solution (FNIS): The optimal (ideal) and suboptimal (anti-ideal) treatment alternatives are identified.
v. Distance Calculation: The Euclidean distance between each treatment option and both the ideal and anti-ideal solutions is calculated.
vi. Closeness Coefficient Calculation: The ultimate ranking is established by assessing the proximity of each treatment to the optimal answer.

4.6.1 Fuzzy Decision Matrix

Table 4.1 shows a decision matrix that serves as a systematic framework for assessing various medical treatments through the application of fuzzy numbers. The three therapy modalities – Surgery, Radiation, and Medication—are evaluated according to three essential medical criteria: Success Rate, Adverse Effects, and Recovery Duration. Each criterion is articulated as a fuzzy number (L, M, U), denoting the minimum (L), most probable (M), and maximum (U) anticipated values. This method enables us to address the intrinsic ambiguity and variability in medical decision-making, guaranteeing that the assessment is not purely deterministic but rather a flexible and realistic depiction of clinical situations.

The imprecise criteria weights, denoted as (L, M, U), indicate the relative significance of each component in the decision-making process. Table 4.2 presents the weights assigned to three criteria: success rate, side effects, and recovery time. In this scenario, success rate and recovery time are prioritized over side effects, indicating that a treatment characterized by a high success rate and expedited recovery is typically favored, despite the presence of significant side effects. This rating scheme corresponds with actual physician preferences, prioritizing effectiveness and patient recovery over negligible unwanted effects. By including these weights into the decision matrix, we standardize the influence of each criterion and guarantee an equitable evaluation of various treatment alternatives.

The structured fuzzy TOPSIS methodology identifies the optimal treatment option by computing the proximity coefficient to both the ideal solution and the anti-ideal solution. According to the findings, medication is identified as the most effective treatment, followed by surgery, whereas radiation is ranked the least effective. This result indicates that Medication achieves an optimal equilibrium among elevated success rates, minimum adverse effects, and expedited recovery, rendering it the most favored option in this particular context. The findings illustrate the efficacy of fuzzy logic in medical decision-making by accommodating uncertainty, expert

Table 4.1 Data representation of fuzzy decision matrix for three criteria.

Criteria	Surgery (L, M, U)	Radiation (L, M, U)	Medication (L, M, U)
Success Rate	(0.6, 0.8, 1.0)	(0.5, 0.7, 0.9)	(0.7, 0.9, 1.0)
Side Effects	(0.3, 0.5, 0.7)	(0.4, 0.6, 0.8)	(0.2, 0.4, 0.6)
Recovery Time	(0.4, 0.6, 0.8)	(0.3, 0.5, 0.7)	(0.5, 0.7, 0.9)

Table 4.2 Criteria weights for the execution of fuzzy logic model.

Criteria	Weight (L, M, U)
Success Rate	(0.3, 0.5, 0.7)
Side Effects	(0.2, 0.4, 0.6)
Recovery Time	(0.3, 0.5, 0.7)

opinion, and diverse patient requirements in a systematic and computationally efficient way.

4.6.2 Results and Discussion

After executing the MATLAB implementation, the subsequent results are obtained.

Closeness Coefficients (A Higher Value Indicates Superior Performance)
Operative Procedure: 0.67
Radiation level: 0.58
Medication dosage: 0.72

The ranking, as presented in Table 4.3, demonstrates that medication is the optimal treatment option according to the specified criteria, followed by surgery, whereas radiation occupies the lowest position. This is mainly attributable to the elevated success rate and diminished side effects linked to the medication, as indicated by the ambiguous criteria weights.

A bar chart is shown in Figure 4.3, which is generated in MATLAB software to illustrate the proximity coefficients of each treatment option. The tallest bar signifies the superior option, affirming that Medication is the

Table 4.3 Final treatment ranking (best to worst).

Treatment option(s)	Ranking order
Medication (T3)	0.62
Surgical Procedure (T1)	0.38
Radiation (T2)	0.34

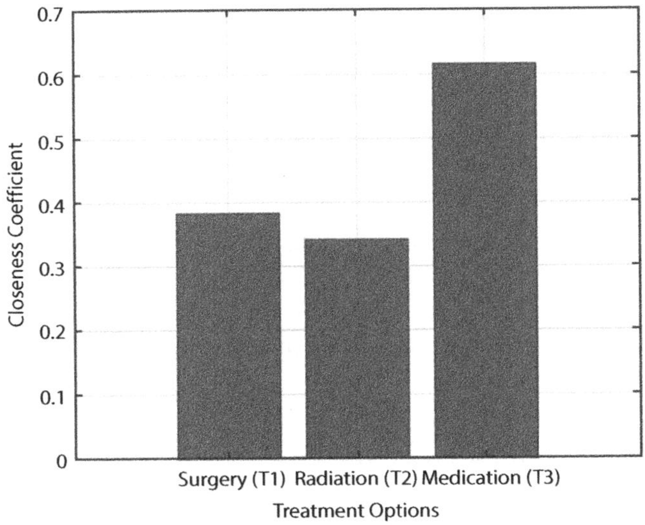

Figure 4.3 Fuzzy TOPSIS decision for medical treatments.

optimal choice. The findings confirm that the Fuzzy TOPSIS method accurately addresses decision uncertainty and delivers an impartial ranking of treatments. The method can be further refined by incorporating more medical parameters and expert opinions for enhanced decision support.

The use of Fuzzy TOPSIS in medical therapy selection was proven in this study. A strong and organized method for dealing with uncertainty in clinical decisions is offered by the suggested model, which incorporates fuzzy logic into multi-criteria decision-making. According to the findings, medication is the therapy of choice, followed by surgery, and radiation comes in last. Improving the decision-making accuracy can be achieved by expanding the existing MATLAB framework to include more criteria and real-world clinical information. This method provides a helpful decision-support tool for doctors when they have to choose the best course of therapy depending on a number of competing priorities.

4.6.3 Comparative Analysis of Fuzzy TOPSIS with Analytical Hierarchy Process (AHP) for Medical Treatment Selection

In medical decision-making, choosing the appropriate treatment frequently entails various conflicting criteria, along with intrinsic uncertainty and ambiguity in clinical data. Conventional multi-criteria decision-making (MCDM) methods, such as the Analytic Hierarchy Process (AHP), offer a systematic approach for selecting alternatives; nevertheless, they frequently struggle to accommodate imperfect information and subjective expert assessments. This section provides an analytical comparison of the classic AHP method and the Fuzzy TOPSIS approach introduced in this work. The aim is to emphasize the benefits of integrating fuzzy logic in addressing ambiguity, improving decision robustness, and generating more realistic treatment rankings. This study anticipates that Fuzzy TOPSIS will exhibit enhanced performance in representing real-world medical situations by providing increased flexibility, precision, and dependability in the decision-making process.

Table 4.4 compares Fuzzy TOPSIS and AHP in critical aspects, demonstrating that Fuzzy TOPSIS is more appropriate for managing uncertainty,

Table 4.4 Comparative analysis: Fuzzy TOPSIS vs. AHP for medical treatment selection.

Aspect	Fuzzy TOPSIS	AHP (analytic hierarchy process)
Uncertainty Handling	Employs fuzzy numbers (L, M, U) to signify ambiguity in data and preferences.	Processes precise data; ill-equipped for ambiguous or inaccurate assessments.
Criteria Comparison	No requirement for a comprehensive pairwise comparison.	More criteria require pairwise comparisons, increasing complexity.
Ease of Implementation	Simple in MATLAB or spreadsheets.	Time-consuming and complicated, with many options or criteria.
Ranking Robustness	Fuzziness makes rankings more realistic and steady.	Depending on the consistency ratio, inconsistent inputs can influence rankings.
Scalability	Adapts to more options and criteria.	Scaling is difficult owing to the exponential comparison increase.
Suitability for Medical Decision-Making	Perfect for expert perspectives, patient preferences, and clinical ambiguity.	Poor adaptability to subjective and confusing healthcare circumstances.

scalability, and medical decision-making. In Table 4.5, the ranking results of treatment options are presented. Medication is consistently preferred over Surgery and Radiation in both methodologies. This alignment bolsters the validity and robustness of Fuzzy TOPSIS, particularly in uncertain clinical environments.

Figure 4.4 presents a comparison examination of three medical treatment modalities- Medication (T3), Surgery (T1), and Radiation (T2)- utilizing two major multi-criteria decision-making methodologies: Fuzzy TOPSIS and Analytic Hierarchy Process (AHP). The bar chart illustrates that Medication regularly achieves the highest ranking in both methodologies,

Table 4.5 Comparative assessment of treatment options using Fuzzy TOPSIS and AHP methodologies.

Treatment option	Fuzzy TOPSIS (closeness coefficient)	AHP (normalized priority score)
Medication (T3)	0.62	0.46
Surgery (T1)	0.38	0.35
Radiation (T2)	0.34	0.19

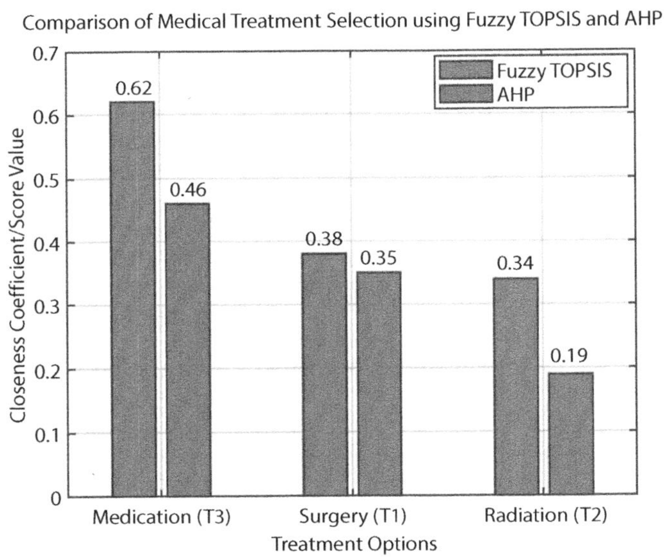

Figure 4.4 Comparative ranking of treatments using Fuzzy TOPSIS and AHP.

with a closeness coefficient of 0.62 in Fuzzy TOPSIS and a normalized score of 0.46 in AHP, signifying its optimal balance of efficacy, minimum adverse effects, and expedited recovery. Surgery receives middling ratings, however, Radiation is placed lowest in both models, underscoring its comparative deficiencies across the specified parameters. This visual comparison confirms the efficacy of Fuzzy TOPSIS in managing uncertainty and producing outcomes consistent with expert-driven AHP evaluations.

Fuzzy TOPSIS addresses the intrinsic uncertainty and expert variability in medical parameters, which AHP could not accommodate. In both methodologies, Medication is prioritized; however, Fuzzy TOPSIS offers a more refined interpretation by proximity to the optimal solution. The measured ambiguity in decision weights and treatment efficacy guarantees that Fuzzy TOPSIS more precisely reflects actual clinical decision-making behavior. This chapter presents the Fuzzy TOPSIS technique, which addresses expert ambiguity and patient variability, resulting in a more adaptable, dependable, and clinically relevant ranking of treatments. This renders it exceptionally appropriate for contemporary, patient-focused medical settings where uncertainty can make precision less accurate.

4.6.4 Merits of the Proposed Work

- Incorporates fuzzy logic to effectively manage the inherent uncertainty and imprecision in clinical decision-making.
- Utilizes Fuzzy TOPSIS, which enables a data-driven and adaptable multi-criteria assessment of medical treatments.
- Improves scalability by eliminating the necessity for exhaustive pairwise comparisons, thereby demonstrating superior performance over traditional AHP.
- Offers treatment rankings that are clinically possible and are substantiated by closeness coefficients that are consistent with patient-centric factors and expert intuition.
- Provides a computationally efficient model that is readily implementable in MATLAB, rendering it suitable for real-world healthcare applications.
- Facilitates customization in accordance with evolving clinical data, patient preferences, and expert opinion, thereby guaranteeing adaptability to complicated medical scenarios.

4.7 Conclusions

Fuzzy logic systems have demonstrated considerable efficacy in decision-making applications, particularly in contexts marked by uncertainty and imprecision. These models may emulate human-like reasoning and handle imprecise or ambiguous data by utilizing fuzzy sets, membership functions, and fuzzy inference methods. This chapter has examined the fundamental principles of fuzzy logic, emphasizing its importance in multi-criteria decision-making (MCDM) applications. By integrating fuzzy logic into discrete event systems (DES) and the Fuzzy TOPSIS framework, we have illustrated how these methodologies improve decision-making in intricate situations, such as the selection of medical treatments.

The comparative evaluation of Fuzzy TOPSIS and AHP emphasizes the superiority of fuzzy-based decision-making in the management of uncertainty and ambiguity in the selection of medical treatments. By integrating imprecise inputs, expert judgments, and patient-specific factors, Fuzzy TOPSIS generated more realistic and stable evaluations. This was effectively illustrated in the case study, where medication was identified as the most appropriate option. This method outperforms traditional methods such as AHP, which frequently encounter data vagueness and necessitate extensive pairwise comparisons. Nevertheless, the current model's dependence on static weight assignments and pre-assigned ambiguous numbers is a significant limitation. If not validated properly, these factors may bias the decision outcome. Furthermore, the model does not yet incorporate real-time clinical feedback or dynamically alter patient conditions.

Future Scope

Future research should concentrate on the integration of fuzzy logic with advanced artificial intelligence techniques, such as deep learning and machine learning, in order to improve the adaptability and robustness of fuzzy decision-making systems in medical and other fields. This would enable the automatic designation of weights, the generation of rules, and the continuous acquisition of knowledge from patient data. The decision process could be rendered more personalized and responsive by incorporating real-time data streams from IoT-enabled medical devices. Further, the clinical relevance of the model will be enhanced by its extension to longitudinal patient surveillance and decision-making across multiple treatment phases. Ultimately, the system will require empirical validation through clinical trials and expert feedback to be refined and to facilitate its broader adoption in intelligent healthcare decision support.

AI disclosure statement: The author confirms that no artificial intelligence (AI)-generated content or AI-assisted writing tools were used in the preparation of this chapter (including summaries and the abstract). All text, analysis, and conclusions are the result of the author's original work.

References

1. Jana, S., Mallik, B.B., Sarkar, A., Jana, C. (Eds.), *Applications of Fuzzy Logic in Decision Making and Management Science*, Springer, 2025.
2. Zadeh, L.A., *Fuzzy Sets and Fuzzy Logic: Theory and Applications*, World Scientific, 2020.
3. Mendel, J.M., *Uncertain Rule-Based Fuzzy Systems: Introduction and New Directions*, 2nd ed., Springer, 2021.
4. Kacprzyk, J. and Pedrycz, W. (Eds.), *Springer Handbook of Computational Intelligence*, Springer, 2022.
5. Herrera-Viedma, E., Cabrerizo, F.J., Kacprzyk, J., Pedrycz, W., A review of soft consensus models in a fuzzy environment. *Inf. Fusion*, 64, 44–52, 2020.
6. Liu, P. and Liu, X., Fuzzy multi-criteria decision making with applications to supplier selection. *Appl. Soft Comput.*, 101, 107045, 2021.
7. Zhang, Z. and Zhou, S., A novel fuzzy TOPSIS approach for multi-criteria decision making with heterogeneous information. *Expert Syst. Appl.*, 186, 115735, 2022.
8. Torra, V., Narukawa, Y., Lopez, D., *Fuzzy Logic in Artificial Intelligence*, Springer, 2023.
9. Wang, X. and Li, D., Fuzzy decision making in complex systems: A bibliometric analysis. *Int. J. Fuzzy Syst.*, 22, 1376–1392, 2020.
10. Chen, S.M. and Lee, L.W., Fuzzy multiple criteria decision making based on interval type-2 fuzzy sets. *Inf. Sci.*, 546, 356–372, 2021.
11. Kahraman, C. and Öztayşi, B. (Eds.), *Fuzzy Multi-Criteria Decision Making: Theory and Applications with Recent Developments*, 2nd ed., Springer, 2022.
12. Xu, Z. and Chen, J., *Intuitionistic Fuzzy Information Aggregation: Theory and Applications*, Springer, 2023.
13. Garg, H. and Rani, P., An extended VIKOR method for multi-criteria decision-making under interval-valued intuitionistic fuzzy environment. *Comput. Ind. Eng.*, 152, 107023, 2021.
14. Liu, F. and Liu, J., Fuzzy comprehensive evaluation method for risk assessment in supply chain management. *J. Intell. Fuzzy Syst.*, 42, 3, 2297–2308, 2022.

15. Peng, X. and Yang, Y., *Fuzzy Set Theory: Applications in the Social Sciences*, Routledge, 2024.
16. Liu, K.E., Ma, J., Lai, E.M.K., *A Dynamic Fuzzy Rule and Attribute Management Framework for Fuzzy Inference Systems in High-Dimensional Data*, pp. 1–27, 2025.
17. Melhaoui, M., Rhiat, M., Oukili, M., *et al.*, Hybrid fuzzy logic approach for enhanced MPPT control in PV systems. *Sci. Rep.*, 15, 19235, 2025.
18. Tong, J., Xie, L., Yang, W., Zhang, K., Zhao, J., Enhancing time series forecasting: A hierarchical transformer with probabilistic decomposition representation. *Inf. Sci.*, 647, 2023.
19. Castillo, O., Valdez, F., Melin, P., Ding, W., A survey on type-3 fuzzy logic systems and their control applications. *IEEE/CAA J. Autom. Sin.*, 11, 8, 1744–1756, Aug. 2024.
20. Mortazavi, A., A novel type-2 decision mechanism for dynamic parameter adaptation: theory and application in mathematical and structural problems. *Neural Comput. Appl.*, 36, 19729–19757, 2024.
21. Mahmood, T., Idrees, A., Hayat, K., Ashiq, M., Rehman, U.U., Selection of AI Architecture for Autonomous Vehicles Using Complex Intuitionistic Fuzzy Rough Decision Making. *World Electr. Veh. J.*, *15*, 9, 402, 2024.
22. Dagal, I., Mbasso, W.F., Ambe, H., *et al.*, Adaptive Fuzzy Logic Control Framework for Aircraft Landing Gear Automation: Optimized Design, Real-Time Response, and Enhanced Safety. *Int. J. Aeronaut. Space Sci.*, 2025.
23. Skrzek, K., Mazgajczyk, E., Dybała, B., Application of Fuzzy Logic-Based Expert Advisory Systems in Optimizing the Decision-Making Process for Material Selection in Additive Manufacturing. *Materials (Basel Switzerland)*, *18*, 2, 324, 2025.
24. Aljohani, A., AI-Driven decision-making for personalized elderly care: a fuzzy MCDM-based framework for enhancing treatment recommendations. *BMC Med. Inf. Decis. Making*, 25, 119, 2025.
25. Biswas, A., Gazi, K.H., Bhaduri, P., Mondal, S.P., Neutrosophic fuzzy decision-making framework for site selection. *J. Decis. Anal. Intell. Comput.*, *4*, 1, 187–215, 2024.

Part II

SUPPLY CHAIN, LOGISTICS, AND INDUSTRY APPLICATIONS

5

Risk Prioritization and Mitigation in Cold Supply Chain Distribution: A Best–Worst Method Approach

Irem Helvacioglu[1,2] and Muhammet Gul[3*]

[1]Department of Transportation and Logistics, Istanbul University, Institute of Social Sciences, Istanbul, Türkiye
[2]Bandırma Onyedi Eylül University, Ömer Seyfettin Faculty of Applied Sciences, Department of International Trade and Logistics, Bandirma, Balikesir, Türkiye
[3]Department of Transportation and Logistics, Istanbul University, Faculty of Transportation and Logistics, Istanbul, Türkiye

Abstract

In addition to the inherent complexity of supply chains, cold supply chains (CSC) introduce the critical requirement of maintaining specific temperature conditions throughout the entire process. Meeting this requirement within such a complex structure carries numerous risks. This chapter investigates the way a corporation operating a CSC distributes its products and highlights the risks involved in this approach. In this context, 12 risks arising in the distribution process of the CSC and 24 risk mitigation strategies have been identified under four main criteria groups through literature review and expert opinions. The identified risks and risk mitigation strategies have been prioritized by weighting them using the Best–Worst Method (BWM). Based on the results, "Planning risks" and "Planning strategies" emerged as the most prioritized in the main criteria group, while the priority rankings of the sub-criteria varied. The results of this study are expected to assist companies in the CSC sector identify risks related to their distribution methods and making strategic decisions based on the prioritization of these risks. Furthermore, this study is expected to contribute to the existing body of knowledge and literature by focusing specifically on the distribution channel.

Keywords: Cold supply chain, distribution logistics, risk prioritization, best–worst method

**Corresponding author*: muhammetgul@istanbul.edu.tr

Harish Garg (ed.) Decision Support Systems in Smart Computing: Embracing Uncertainty and Challenges, (123–150) © 2026 Scrivener Publishing LLC

5.1 Introduction

Technological developments and globalization have greatly complicated and dynamically modified supply chain management [16, 49]. Companies have to guarantee sustainability, resilience, and efficiency of their supply chains while still negotiating a market getting more and more competitive. Among these, CSCs provide specific challenges due to their exact temperature and handling requirements. Temperature-sensitive products such as food, pharmaceuticals, and some chemicals depend on these chains to be transferred to the ultimate user without spoiling or quality degradation. Any disruption in this chain could lead to major financial losses, legislation non-compliance, and perhaps hazards to public health.

The CSC is inherently more sensitive than conventional supply chains and depends on exact environmental conditions and specialized logistics [1]. Product integrity may be compromised by temperature excursions, equipment failures, delayed transportation, storage errors, and supply chain delays. Consequently, the business's financial and reputational integrity was also compromised [8]. Additionally, external factors such as climate variability, regulatory changes, and energy price fluctuations further complicate risk management efforts [56, 58]. The interdependence of various hazards makes their evaluation and prioritizing challenging but essential work. Without a purposeful approach to assessing and reducing these risks companies could find it challenging to ensure operational continuity, regulatory compliance and general supply chain resilience. Businesses want to minimize risks in order to make their operations more efficient. At this point, determining the priorities of emerging risks and focusing on the risk factors that most affect operations within the scope of risk management is a critical process. Effective risk management in CSC distribution requires a dual approach: (1) Risk Prioritization – Identifying and ranking the most critical risks to allocate resources effectively. (2) Risk Mitigation Action Ranking – Evaluating and prioritizing the most effective strategies to minimize or eliminate these risks.

This study extensively investigates and ranks both distribution risks and risk mitigation strategies in the CSC using the BWM, Multi-Criteria Decision-Making (MCDM) method, therefore reaching these aims. Traditional risk assessment methods often assume equal weighting of risk factors or rely on subjective expert judgments that can lead to inconsistencies [43]. In contrast, BWM offers a more structured approach by requiring decision-makers to compare risks and mitigation actions against the most and least critical factors. This method reduces inconsistency in expert evaluations, requires fewer pairwise comparisons than conventional MCDM techniques, and provides more reliable weighting results [43]. By applying BWM, this study aims to: (1) Identify the most significant risks in CSC distribution. (2) By prioritizing these risks, ensure that decision-makers focus on the most pressing threats. (3) Evaluate risk mitigation strategies. (4) Rank these strategies guiding businesses toward the most effective strategies to enhance supply chain resilience.

The results of this study are expected to contribute both theoretically and practically by providing a structured decision-making framework for risk management in CSC distribution. This research will offer valuable insights for industry practitioners, supply chain managers, and policy-makers, helping them develop targeted strategies to enhance operational efficiency, minimize losses, and strengthen the overall robustness of CSC networks.

5.2 Basic Preliminaries and Definitions

This section introduces the basic concepts related to the theme of this chapter and their meanings as used in this study.

Risk management: *The entirety of management approaches planned in a manner most suitable for the structure of a business in order to control risks that may arise in the supply chain of that business.*
Risk assessment: *Refers to the process of identifying and analyzing risks that may arise in the supply chain.*
Risk prioritization: *A process of determining the priorities of risks arising in the supply chain using various methods. This provides outputs that indicate which risks to focus on more in risk management.*
Risk mitigation: *Evaluating and prioritizing the most effective strategies to minimize or eliminate supply chain risks.*
Cold supply chain: *A variety of supply chains consisting of perishable products such as food and pharmaceuticals that require specific temperatures to be maintained.*
Distribution risks: *Risks that occur in the distribution process of the supply chain.*

Technical risks and strategies: *Refers to risks arising from technical causes in the supply chain and strategies to mitigate these risks.*
Operational risks and strategies: *Refers to risks arising from operational activities in the supply chain and strategies to mitigate these risks.*
Planning risks and strategies: *Refers to the risks arising in the planning process for activities and operations carried out in the supply chain and the strategies for mitigating these risks.*
External risks: *Refers to risks that do not originate from the supply chain itself but arise due to external factors.*
Management strategies: *Refers to strategies arising from management approaches to risks arising in the supply chain.*
Sanitation: *In the food industry, sanitation refers to "the creation and maintenance of hygienic and healthy conditions" [30].*
Near miss incidents: *Refers to a dangerous situation, event, or unsafe action that could have caused an accident if the sequence of actions had not been interrupted [22].*
Pre-cooling: *Refers to the removal of heat from freshly harvested products before transport or storage in order to reduce spoilage [9, 21].*
Thermal boxes: *Especially used in cold chain logistics, these are insulated transport boxes designed to keep products at a constant temperature for a certain period of time.*
Participative management approach: *It refers to a management style in which managers make decisions together with employees, trust their initiative, and decisions are made through group discussions and experience sharing [28].*

5.2.1 List of Abbreviations

AHP	Analytic Hierarchy Process
BWM	Best–Worst Method
COPRAS	Complex Proportional Assessment
CSC	Cold Supply Chain
DANP	DEMATEL-based Analytic Network Process
DEMATEL	Decision-Making Trial and Evaluation Laboratory
FMEA	Failure Modes and Effect Analysis
GPS	Global Positioning System
IMS	Information Management Systems
MCDM	Multi-Criteria Decision-Making

PROMETHEE	Preference Ranking Organization Method for Enrichment Evaluation
SWARA	Step-Wise Weight Assessment Ratio Analysis
TOPSIS	Fuzzy Technique for Order Preference by Similarity to Ideal Solution
VIKOR	VlseKriterijumska Optimizacija I Kompromisno Resenje

5.3 Literature Review

Risks can arise at all stages of the supply chain due to various factors, and the scope of these risks and their consequences can vary. Effective management of these risks is essential for an efficient supply chain. Based on their comprehensive literature review, Ho *et al.* [19] defined supply chain risk management as "an inter-organizational collaborative endeavor utilizing quantitative and qualitative risk management methodologies to identify, evaluate, mitigate, and monitor unexpected macro and micro-level events or conditions that might adversely impact any part of a supply chain". In line with this definition, all elements that could negatively affect the supply chain are included in the scope of risk management. Even risks that may seem small compared to others in the supply chain can have significant consequences. Additionally, any risk that occurs in the supply chain affects numerous factors, such as operating costs, production, product quality, delivery times, and brand reputation [55]. On the other hand, the cold chain is a type of supply chain that involves temperature control during the supply chain process for perishable products [47]. Accordingly, risk management in the cold supply chain brings with it different risks and, consequently, different impacts at all stages in order to maintain product temperature. All these effects emerge as the primary factors. They make supply chain risk management indispensable for businesses. As a crucial element influencing the efficiency and effectiveness of a business's supply chain, risk management is increasingly becoming a primary research topic in academic literature and within the industry [17].

This literature review includes the studies conducted on the subject in two stages. First, studies using MCDM were analyzed, followed by those studies using BWM. The CSC is a temperature-controlled system that ensures the continuous storage and distribution of food products by maintaining the required temperature throughout the process until they reach the point of consumption [3]. Studies of this complex construction have shown several risks [25]. As a relatively new discipline, MCDM approaches have also been frequently used in studies both individually and in hybrid forms and have shown development [37]. Khan *et al.* [25] used the Analytic Hierarchy Process (AHP) to identify risks in the supply chain and as a result, they determined the most important risk dimensions among the 17 risks identified. Sarpkaya and Temur [46] used Decision-Making Trial and Evaluation Laboratory (DEMATEL) to measure the effect of strategic decision alternatives on each other in the CSC and VlseKriterijumska Optimizacija I Kompromisno Resenje (VIKOR) method to rank and select these alternatives. Shen and Liao [48] used AHP method to evaluate the main risks of food CSCs in their study. Mukherjee *et al.* [33] used Fuzzy TOPSIS to identify and prioritize operational supply chain risk factors in their studies. Altubaishe and Desai [2] proposed an approach that includes AHP, Preference Ranking Organization Method for Enrichment Evaluation (PROMETHEE), and FMEA methods within the scope of risk assessment in supplier selection. Sudarmin and Ardi [50] used DEMATEL-based Analytic Network Process (DANP) to assess the risks in vaccine supply chains that require temperature control. Among the studies in the literature, some researchers grouped risks as "Financial risks, Delivery risks, Technological capability risks, Environmental risks, Quality risks and Social risks" [4]. In this study, while evaluating the risks in the CSC, the focus was on the distribution process and hierarchical groupings were determined in this context. In some studies, while CSC risks have been evaluated using MCDM methods, the criteria have been determined under sustainability conditions. This situation is consistent with the growing interest in the transformation and improvement of traditional supply chain models through digital technology, the circular economy, manufacturing, and sustainable development [15]. Kumar, Tyagi, and Sacheva [26] applied a hybrid approach incorporating the Step-Wise Weight Assessment Ratio Analysis (SWARA) and Complex Proportional Assessment (COPRAS) methods to identify and assess the critical challenges of the CSC in terms of sustainability. Similarly, Liao *et al.* [27] utilized the AHP and Fuzzy Technique for Order Preference by Similarity to Ideal Solution (TOPSIS) methods to identify systematic best practices in fresh food supply chains, which they characterized as having negative attributes concerning sustainability.

In addition, there are also studies in which BWM has been used on the relevant topic. Kumar *et al.* [59] employed fuzzy BWM in their study to identify risks that emerged during the COVID-19 period within perishable food supply chains. Paillin *et al.* [38] utilized BWM to assess risk factors in the agricultural supply chain. Similarly, Masudin *et al.* [31] applied fuzzy BWM to identify and evaluate risks in the halal meat supply chain. According to the studies investigated, there are only a few studies that apply the BWM method, a new tool that can optimize multi-criteria decisions in supply chain risk management. In the future, BWM can be widely applied in sustainable supply chain management. It is also noted that the literature lacks contributions that integrate barriers and challenges with strategies and analyses using an integrated MCDM methodology [39].

This study aims to identify effective risks as well as strategies to mitigate these risks in order to increase the resilience and sustainability of CSCs, which can be exposed to many negative impacts, particularly from in-process elements and external factors. Studies in the literature risk evaluation and risk mitigation strategies generally address the entire supply chain. In addition to these studies in the literature, this study focuses on the distribution process to determine risks in the CSCs and evaluate risk mitigation strategies that can be applied in CSCs with BWM, which is an effective MCDM method. The identification of risks and risk mitigation strategies in this study is supported by a comprehensive literature review and expert opinions. While the identified risks relate to the temperature control of perishable products - one of the CSCs main objectives – the study also provides a detailed framework covering all potential risks arising from operational processes, technical elements, external factors and planning processes. The risk mitigation strategies presented in this study adopt a similar framework for operational, technical, planning, and supply chain management processes, taking a proactive approach. In addition, the risk mitigation strategies are associated with the identified risks and are also subjected to evaluation. In the study, a hierarchy of CSC distribution risks has been established and, in this context, the study is expected to contribute to future studies and decision processes in CSC management. In this respect, the study contributes to future research and decision-making processes in CSC risk management by creating a hierarchical model for CSC deployment risks as a guiding framework.

5.4 Methodology

In the study, risks and risk mitigation strategies were determined by the relevant literature and expert opinions. The calculation and prioritization of the weights of the identified risks and risk mitigation strategies were carried out with BWM. Detailed information on the method and the specific implementation steps followed are illustrated in Figure 5.1.

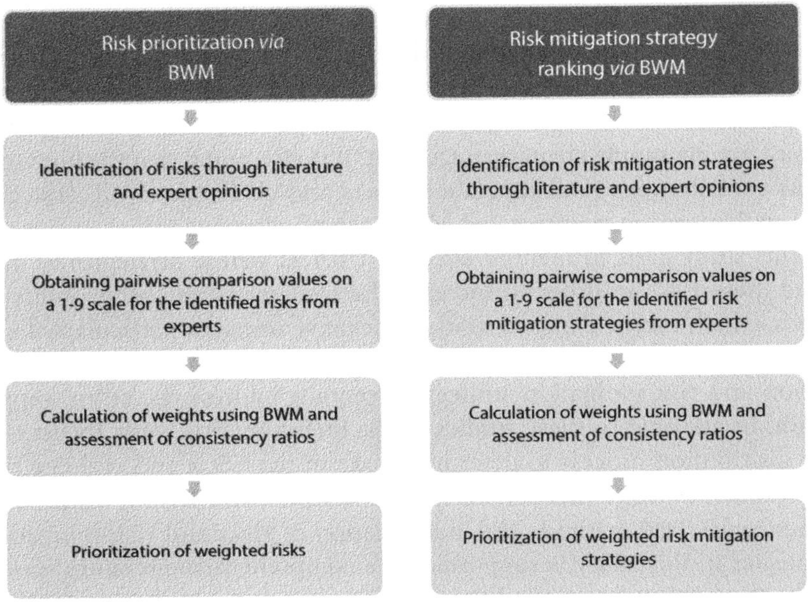

Figure 5.1 Implementation steps of the methodology.

5.4.1 Basic Preliminaries

This section provides basic information about the approach used in the study, along with detailed information on the method and application steps.

5.4.1.1 Multi-Criteria Decision-Making

MCDM is a modern decision science tool that supports decision makers who are faced with multiple decision criteria and multiple decision alternatives [54]. In recent years, many decision-making methods supporting decisions under multi-criteria conditions have emerged [57]. In this study, BWM was employed as a current approach among multi-criteria decision-making methods.

5.4.1.2 Best–Worst Method

In the MCDM methods, alternatives consisting of a set of criteria are evaluated in order to select the best alternative. According to BWM, firstly the best (most important) and worst (least important) criteria are determined by a decision maker. Subsequently, the criteria are subjected to pairwise comparisons on a 1-9 scale. These comparisons are converted into weights through the maximin problem. The method also includes a proposed consistency ratio to test the reliability of the weights. In this study, BWM was preferred due to its ability to achieve more consistent results with fewer comparisons [42]. The linear BWM steps are given below [38]:

1. **Identification of relevant risk factors:** At this stage, risk factors are identified in terms of Technical risks (A), Operational risks (B), Planning risks (C), External risks (D); risk mitigation strategies are identified in terms of Operational strategies (A), Management strategies (B), Planning strategies (C), Technical strategies (D) and verified by experts.
2. **Selection of the best and worst risk factors:** The expert selects the "best" and "worst" risk factors from the identified risk factors. In the case of a tie, it can be decided at random whether the risk factor is the best or the worst. The decision maker is fully responsible for this.
3. **Determination of the preference of the best risk factor over all other risk factors:** In this step, a pairwise comparison is made between the "best" risk factor and the "other" factors (j = 1,2,...,n). This is then constructed as a row vector as in Equation 5.1.

$$A_B = (a_{B1}, a_{B2}, \ldots, a_{Bn}) \tag{5.1}$$

   Here, $a_{(Bj)}$ represents the best preference of risk factor B over risk factor j.
4. **Determination of the preference of all risk factors in relation to the worst risk factor:** In this step, a pairwise comparative assessment is made between the "worst" risk factor and the "other" factors (j = 1,2,...,n). This is then constructed as a column vector as in Equation 5.2.

$$A_w = \begin{pmatrix} a_{1W} \\ a_{2W} \\ \cdots \\ a_{nW} \end{pmatrix} \tag{5.2}$$

Here, a_{jw} represents the preference level of the worst risk factor W over the risk factor j.

5. **Development of the optimization model and determination of the optimal weights for each risk factor:** In this stage, an optimization model will be created to calculate the weight of each risk factor, as represented by Equation 5.3. The formulation for determining the optimal weight is modeled as follows:

$$\min \max_j \left\{ \left| \frac{w_B}{w_j} - a_{Bj} \right|, \left| \frac{wB}{wj} - a_{Bj} \right| \right\} \tag{5.3}$$

Subject to

$$\sum_J w_j = 1$$

$$W_j \geq 0, \quad \text{for } \forall \text{ j}$$

It is then transformed into a linear model as follows;

$$\min \varepsilon^L$$

Subject to

$$\left| W_B - a_{Bj} w_j \right| \leq \varepsilon^L, \; for \; \forall \; j$$

$$\sum_J w_j = 1$$

$$W_j \geq 0, \quad \text{for } \forall \text{ j}$$

6. **Consistency check:** The resolution of this issue is contingent upon the optimal weights ($w_1^*, w_2^*, \ldots, w_n^*$) and ε^{L*}. The value $\varepsilon^{L*} \in [0,1]$ serves as an indicator of the consistency of pairwise comparisons. In this context, values that approximate zero on the real number line signify a high level of consistency.

5.5 Results

This chapter presents the results in two parts. Firstly, within the scope of the study, distribution risks in the CSC were identified with the relevant literature and expert opinions and were then prioritized according to their importance levels by calculating their weights using BWM. Secondly, the CSC's risk mitigation strategies were determined in a similar way and analyzed with BWM. The identified risks and risk mitigation strategies were categorized hierarchically under four criteria. To contribute to existing literature and to assist industry practitioners, the results also include a table that associates the identified risks with their corresponding risk mitigation strategies. The relevant table also incorporates risk mitigation strategies based on both literature and expert opinions.

As part of the process of gathering expert opinions and evaluations for this study, experts were selected based on their professional experience and expertise in CSCs, as well as their ability to anticipate risks in distribution processes, given their professional roles. This selection process aimed to ensure that the insights provided were grounded in practical knowledge and industry-specific expertise. Table 5.1 presents detailed information on the identified experts.

The first expert was identified through professional networks which served as a key starting point for the study. Subsequently, additional participants were brought in through a snowball sampling approach, allowing for the inclusion of highly relevant and experienced professionals who could contribute valuable insights to the research. This approach helped to ensure a diverse yet specialized panel of experts, thereby strengthening the reliability of the results.

To ensure the reliability and consistency of the study, a three-stage online survey was applied to three experts identified within the scope of the relevant criteria. In the first stage, in addition to the literature in the

Table 5.1 Information about the experts.

	Experience (years)	Professional position in the business	The supply chain structure of the organization
Expert 1	26	Sales operations manager	CSC
Expert 2	17	Logistics fleet team leader	CSC
Expert 3	15	Logistics planning manager	CSC

field, expert opinions were consulted to identify distribution risks and risk mitigation strategies in the CSC. The second stage involved making comparisons of the best-to-others and worst-to-others for the identified risks, while the third stage involved making the same comparisons for risk mitigation strategies.

The identified risks were categorized under four main risk criteria: Technical risks (A), Operational risks (B), Planning risks (C) and External risks (D). Subsequently, these identified risk criteria were evaluated by decision-makers using the BWM method. Table 5.2 presents the risks associated with the main criteria identified within this scope.

The representation of the identified risks under the main criteria in a hierarchical structure is as shown in Figure 5.2. According to this, distribution risks in the CSC are determined as a total of 12 sub-risk criteria under four main risk criteria.

The values of the prioritization of the identified risk criteria by BWM are shown in Table 5.3.

At the same time, for each assessment by three experts, the consistency ratio was calculated simultaneously. The consistency ratios of the five

Table 5.2 Distribution risks in the CSC.

Related risk description	Source (Literature/ expert opinion)
Malfunction (A.1)	Expert Opinion
Using inappropriate transport equipment (A.2)	[41]
Failure to maintain the required temperature level (A.3)	[23]
Failure to ensure vehicle occupancy (B.1)	Expert Opinion
Delayed delivery of raw material supply vehicle (B.2)	Expert Opinion
Failure to complete delivery on time (B.3)	[24]
Lack of sanitation (B.4)	[13]
Failures in production planning (C.1)	Expert Opinion
Failure to have vehicles ready for timely use (C.2)	[42]
Lack of training (C.3)	[13]
Traffic/Traffic Accident (D.1)	Expert Opinion
Loss/Damage (D.2)	[10]

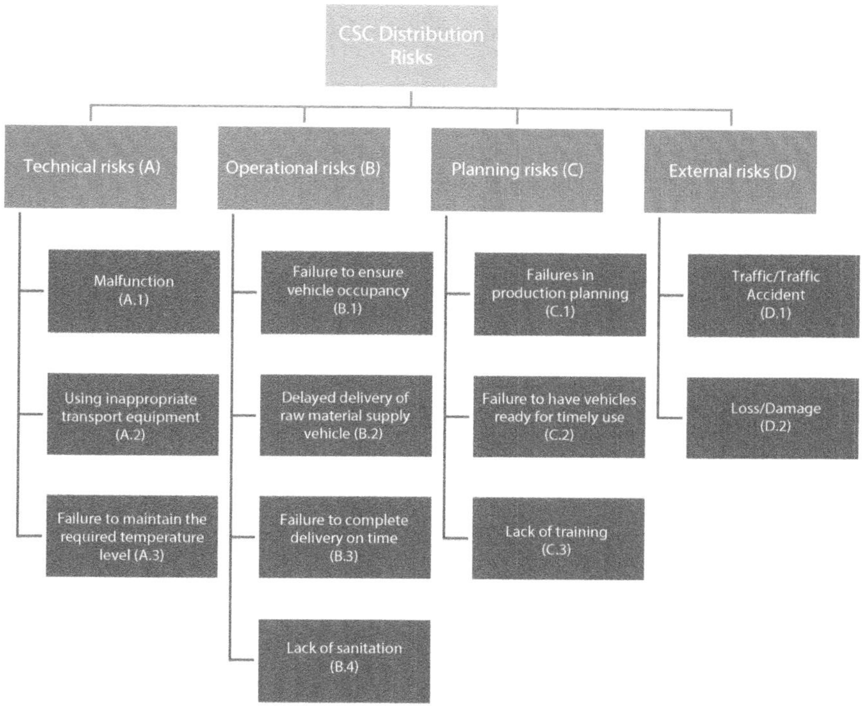

Figure 5.2 CSC distribution risks in a hierarchy.

comparisons made by Expert 1 are 0.069, 0.097, 0.208, 0.097 and 0.000, respectively. The consistency ratios of the five comparisons performed by Expert 2 are 0.119, 0.119, 0.214, 0.097 and 0.000, respectively. The consistency ratios of the five comparisons made by Expert 3 are 0.142, 0.047, 0.142, 0.097 and 0.000, respectively.

The prioritization of the main and sub-risk criteria, the averages of which were calculated by taking the evaluations of the decision makers, according to these values is as shown in Table 5.4.

Accordingly, the risk mitigation strategies determined by referring to expert opinion and literature in the field and the previously determined risk criteria were associated with the risk criteria as shown in Table 5.5. The risk mitigation strategies against distribution risks in the CSC, which were analyzed and expert opinion was taken, were determined within the proactive scope. Accordingly, the associated strategies are strategies to reduce the probability of realization of the related risks.

Table 5.3 Risk criteria and weight values.

Identified risk	Weight value
A	0.081
B	0.302
C	0.529
D	0.088
A.1	0.688
A.2	0.130
A.3	0.181
B.1	0.582
B.2	0.111
B.3	0.190
B.4	0.117
C.1	0.726
C.2	0.202
C.3	0.071
D.1	0.866
D.2	0.134

Table 5.4 Risk prioritization.

Main risk criteria	C>B>D>A
Sub-criteria related to the main risk criterion (A)	A.1> A.3> A.2
Sub-criteria related to the main risk criterion (B)	B.1> B.3> B.4> B.2
Sub-criteria related to the main risk criterion (C)	C.1> C.2> C.3
Sub-criteria related to the main risk criterion (D)	D.1> D.2

Table 5.5 Association of CSC distribution risks and risk mitigation strategies.

Distribution risks	Risk mitigation strategies
Malfunction (A.1)	▪ Redundancy and flexibility [12, 44, 52] ▪ Establishing appropriate "checklists" for the machines, tools and processes used to carry out the relevant activities in order to prevent "near-miss" incidents handled within the scope of risk management (Expert Opinion)
Risk of unsuitable transport equipment (A.2)	▪ Establishing appropriate "checklists" for the machines, tools and processes used to carry out the relevant activities in order to prevent "near-miss" incidents handled within the scope of risk management (Expert Opinion) ▪ Audit procedures (Expert Opinion)
Failure to maintain the required temperature level (A.3)	▪ Refrigerated transport systems and temperature control [35] ▪ Fast distribution and insulated vehicles [35] ▪ Establishing appropriate "checklists" for the machines, tools and processes used to carry out the relevant activities in order to prevent "near-miss" incidents handled within the scope of risk management (Expert Opinion) ▪ Pre-cooling integrated with continuous monitoring and control mechanisms in transport and storage processes (Expert Opinion) ▪ Use of vehicle tracking system to ensure temperature monitoring in vehicles used in transport (Expert Opinion) ▪ Transport of products in thermal boxes, especially in e-commerce orders (Expert Opinion)
Failure to ensure vehicle occupancy (B.1)	▪ Consolidating demand [5] ▪ Developing operational and tactical policies to address the downward slope in demand and Bullwhip effects [6]

(*Continued*)

Table 5.5 Association of CSC distribution risks and risk mitigation strategies. (*Continued*)

Distribution risks	Risk mitigation strategies
Inability of the raw material supplier to deliver on time (B.2) (outsourcing)	▪ Information sharing, trust relationships, co-operation and transparency [11, 29, 34, 45] ▪ Multiple supplier strategy/Substitute suppliers [11, 32, 53] ▪ Continuous risk monitoring and assessment [36]
Failure to realize delivery on time (B.3)	▪ Real-time replanning of routes with IoT [7] ▪ Organizing customer groups during transport [7] ▪ Continuous risk monitoring and assessment [36] ▪ Redundancy and flexibility [12, 44, 52] ▪ Efficient transport [40] ▪ Establishing appropriate "checklists" for the machines, tools and processes used to carry out the relevant activities in order to prevent "near-miss" incidents handled within the scope of risk management (Expert Opinion)
Lack of sanitation (B.4)	▪ Routine maintenance of manufacturing equipment and sanitary transport [31] ▪ Hygiene maintenance, use of clean containers for storage [40]
Production planning errors (C.1)	▪ Establishing appropriate "checklists" for the machines, tools and processes used to carry out the relevant activities in order to prevent "near-miss" incidents handled within the scope of risk management (Expert Opinion) ▪ Multiple supplier strategy/Substitute suppliers [11, 32] ▪ Benchmarking supply chain practices [51] ▪ Redundancy and flexibility [12, 44, 52] ▪ Flexible capacity and improved planning [14] ▪ Maintenance of information management systems (IMS) [40] ▪ Inventory management [40]

(*Continued*)

Table 5.5 Association of CSC distribution risks and risk mitigation strategies. (*Continued*)

Distribution risks	Risk mitigation strategies
Vehicles are not ready for use on time (C.2)	▪ Continuous risk monitoring and assessment [36] ▪ Establishing appropriate "checklists" for the machines, tools and processes used to perform the relevant activities in order to prevent "near-miss" incidents addressed within the scope of risk management (Expert Opinion) ▪ Redundancy and flexibility [12, 44, 52] ▪ Fleet management [40]
Lack of training (C.3)	▪ Education and communication [18, 20] ▪ Participative management approach [14]
Traffic/Traffic Accident (D.1)	▪ GPS usage (Expert Opinion) ▪ Route optimization (Expert Opinion) ▪ Insurance (Expert Opinion)
Loss/Damage (D.2)	▪ Redundancy and flexibility [12, 44, 52]

In order to prioritize the identified risk mitigation strategies, a different hierarchical grouping was performed. Accordingly, the main risk mitigation strategies were determined under four main criteria: Operational strategies (A), Management strategies (B), Planning strategies (C) and Technical strategies (D). Under these four main risk mitigation strategies, 24 risk mitigation strategies determined by literature and expert opinion were grouped. These strategies are shown in Figure 5.3 under the main risk mitigation strategies.

The importance values of the risk mitigation strategies identified for the distribution process of the CSC were determined based on survey data collected from decision-makers. The obtained data were analyzed using the BWM to determine the weights of the main and sub-risk mitigation strategies. Average weight values were calculated, and based on these average values, the risk mitigation strategies were ranked according to their level of importance. These average values of risk mitigation strategies are as shown in Table 5.6.

At the same time, the consistency ratio was calculated for each of the three experts' assessments. The consistency ratios for the five comparisons performed by Expert 1 are 0.166, 0.285, 0.303, 0.285 and 0.208, respectively. The consistency ratios of the five comparisons performed by Expert 2 were

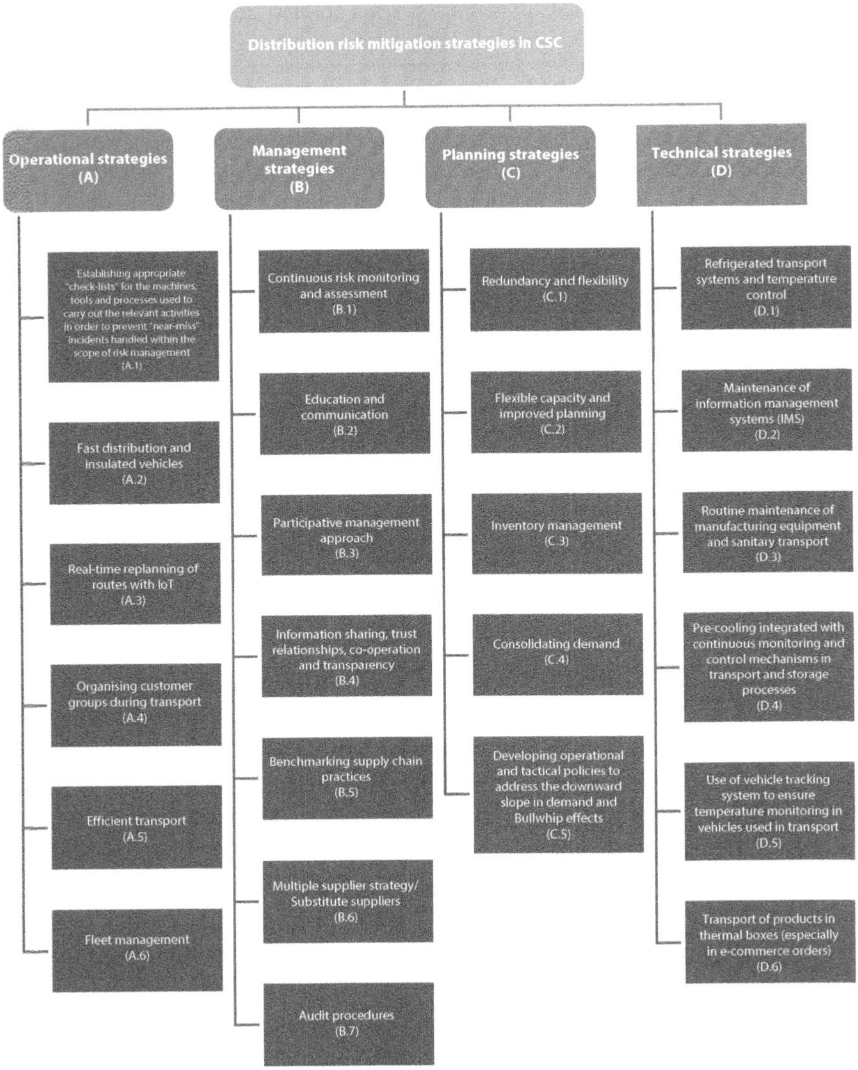

Figure 5.3 Distribution risk mitigation strategies in CSC.

0.071, 0.291, 0.222, 0.214 and 0.214, respectively. The consistency ratios of the five comparisons performed by Expert 3 are 0.036, 0.208, 0.303, 0.222 and 0.222, respectively.

According to these values, the prioritization of the main and sub risk criteria, whose averages are calculated by taking the decision makers evaluations, is shown in Table 5.7.

Table 5.6 Weight values of risk mitigation strategies.

Identified risk mitigation strategy	Weight value
A	0.276
B	0,060
C	0.560
D	0.106
A.1	0,290
A.2	0.126
A.3	0.086
A.4	0.039
A.5	0.074
A.6	0.384
B.1	0.305
B.2	0.036
B.3	0.070
B.4	0.082
B.5	0.137
B.6	0.269
B.7	0.099
C.1	0.134
C.2	0.189
C.3	0.515
C.4	0.110
C.5	0.051
D.1	0.096
D.2	0.224
D.3	0.423
D.4	0.141
D.5	0.077
D.6	0.039

Table 5.7 Prioritization of risk mitigation strategies.

Main risk mitigation strategies	**C>A>D>B**
Sub-strategies linked to the main risk mitigation strategies (A)	A.6>A.1>A.2>A.3>A.5>A.4
Sub-strategies linked to the main risk mitigation strategies (B)	B.1>B.6>B.5>B.7>B.4>B.3>B.2
Sub-strategies linked to the main risk mitigation strategies (C)	C.3>C.2>C.2>C.1>C.4>C.5
Sub-strategies linked to the main risk mitigation strategies (D)	D.3>D.2>D.4>D.1>D.5>D.6

5.6 Discussion

According to the results of the risk prioritization, "Planning risks" stand out compared to other risk groups in terms of the potential risks that may arise in the distribution process of the CSC, while their level of importance is similar to that of "Operational risks". The ranking of sub-criteria determined based on the main risk criteria also varies across different groups.

The main risk mitigation strategies were ranked as follows as a result of the prioritization of risk mitigation strategies: "Planning strategies", "Operational strategies", "Technical strategies", and "Management strategies". Similarly, in risk prioritization, 'Planning' held the highest priority closely followed by operational risks. However, in risk mitigation strategies, the importance gap widened further. The fact that "planning strategies" are more important than other risk mitigation strategies shows that the most effective measure that can be taken against the risks that may occur in the distribution processes of the CSC is the activities to be carried out within the scope of planning. Planning risk mitigation strategies compared to other main risk mitigation strategy groups stand out for having reserves and an adaptation level against changes in process elements such as transport vehicles, loading equipment, packaging, products to be distributed, flexibility in vehicle and product capacities, correct planning to optimize demand with minimum cost, obtaining time and cost advantages through consolidation rather than single demands for products to be distributed, and implementing policies to prevent risks in the distribution process from affecting further links in the supply chain. When the strategies in this group are prioritized, inventory management is seen to be of significant importance. This is followed by flexible capacity and more accurate planning, redundancy and flexibility, consolidating demand, and developing operational and tactical policies to address the downward slope in demand and bullwhip effects.

Following planning risks, the second highest priority main risk mitigation strategy category is operational strategies. Taking expert opinions into account, it has been determined that "near miss" incidents, which are generally examined in occupational health and safety within quality management, can be evaluated in supply chain distribution processes and for the vehicles and equipment used in these processes. Accordingly, as a risk mitigation strategy, it is suggested to create checklists for the relevant processes, tools and equipment that may cause disruption in the processes. For example, periodic control of the items that can be itemized such as damage, malfunction and technical settings for insulated vehicles used in the distribution phase through checklists will prevent near-miss incidents damaging risk occurrences. In addition, operational risk mitigation strategies include fast distribution to save time and prevent product deterioration, real-time route planning using insulated transport vehicles and Internet of Things (IoT) technology, organizing customer groups for distribution to multiple demand points, and ensuring efficient transportation and effective fleet management. The following strategies are prioritized: "fleet management"; "establishing appropriate checklists for the machines, vehicles and processes used to carry out the relevant activities, in order to prevent 'near-miss' incidents handled within the scope of risk management"; "fast distribution and insulated vehicles"; "real-time replanning of routes with IoT"; "efficient transportation"; and "organizing customer groups during transportation".

Technical strategies, which are the third priority criteria as the main risk mitigation strategy, are critical for maintaining product temperatures throughout the entire supply chain as well as the distribution phase of CSCs. These risk mitigation strategies include refrigerated transport systems and temperature control provided during the process, periodic maintenance of information management systems used in related processes in order not to cause wrong results, regular maintenance of production equipment in order not to disrupt distribution processes in case of malfunction and damage, and ensuring hygiene in transport, Planning at which stage and how often pre-cooling will be carried out in order to ensure that the product to be transported reaches the distribution process in a healthy way, ensuring instant temperature control with vehicle tracking systems that provide many information such as fuel, mileage, temperature of the vehicle used in transportation, and the use of thermal boxes against the risk of deterioration of products, especially in the distribution of small amounts of e-commerce orders. The prioritization of the related risk mitigation strategies is "Routine maintenance of manufacturing equipment and sanitary transport", "Maintenance of information management systems (IMS)", "Pre-cooling integrated with continuous monitoring and control mechanisms in transport and storage processes", "Refrigerated transport systems and temperature control", "Use of vehicle tracking systems to ensure temperature monitoring in vehicles used in transport" and "Transport of products in thermal boxes (especially in e-commerce orders)".

Several key measures are included under the main risk mitigation strategies of management: continuous risk analysis and assessment related to distribution processes; training programs aimed at developing a skilled workforce; and effective communication. Furthermore, senior management should adopt a participative approach to strategic decision-making, incorporating input and suggestions from all stakeholders. It is also emphasized that ensuring continuous information sharing, trust relationships, collaboration, and transparency among all employees, suppliers and stakeholders involved in the process is essential. Furthermore, the management risk mitigation strategy incorporates benchmarking supply chain practices to maximize distribution process efficiency, maintaining multiple suppliers to mitigate the impact of unforeseen demand fluctuations and supplier-related issues, and establishing audit procedures to ensure process compliance. The following strategies are prioritized: "Continuous risk analysis and assessment", "Multiple supplier strategy/substitute suppliers", "Benchmarking supply chain practices", "Audit procedures", "Information sharing, trust relations, cooperation and transparency", "Participative management approach" and "Training and communication".

All the strategies evaluated in this study are those that should be implemented to mitigate risks in CSCs. The structure of the company will affect the choice of these techniques. Expert opinions feel that the relevance values assigned to the highly prioritized strategies were high since failure to apply these strategies could result in more severe repercussions and more risks, hence their mitigating more difficult.

In this context, the risks assessed within the distribution process of the CSC and the priorities of risk mitigation strategies are of great importance in optimizing the activities carried out by companies in their distribution process. The results obtained indicate the risks and risk mitigation strategies that companies should focus on in their decision-making processes. In addition to the relevant results, strategies targeting different risks for businesses with different structures are comprehensively related as shown in Table 5.5. Furthermore, it is anticipated that the findings of this study will contribute to future studies on the CSC, distribution process, and risk management in the relevant literature.

5.7 Conclusion

CSCs are a set of activities in which time sensitivity and temperature control are absolutely important at all phases. Especially in the distribution stage, the movement, handling, and packing of items must be done in the most suitable way, considering the product characteristics and without excluding the temperature element. Of considerable relevance also are the technical inspection and maintenance of the equipment and vehicles utilized, the design of procedures, the qualifications of people engaged in these processes, the efficient planning and management of operations, etc.

In this context, this chapter addresses the risks that could arise during the CSC distribution phase, together with their respective risk mitigation strategies. Based on past research and expert opinions, the risks and mitigation strategies for the CSC distribution phase have been proactively identified. To calculate the weightings of these risks and mitigation strategies and to establish their prioritization, the BWM (a contemporary multi-criteria decision-making approach) has been utilized.

The results in this chapter are divided into two sections: risks and risk mitigation strategies. The identified risks and risk mitigation strategies are grouped under four main criteria, with 12 risks and 24 risk mitigation strategies categorized under these criteria. The identified risks and risk mitigation strategies were analyzed using the BWM. When calculating criteria weights using the BWM, the consistency ratios obtained through the method were taken into account. Accordingly, the consistency ratios of the risks and risk mitigation strategies, for which the weights had been determined ranged between 0 and 1. Following the verification of these ratios, prioritization of the risks and risk mitigation strategies was conducted based on their average values. In addition to these analyses, the study also includes a matching table that associates the identified risks with their corresponding risk mitigation strategies.

Recognizing risks within their own operations is crucial for businesses with CSCs, as these risks directly impact time, cost, demand fulfillment, and customer satisfaction. Failure to identify these risks can have an adverse effect on business processes. The risk mitigation strategies prioritized in this study may vary depending on the structure of businesses. Adopting and implementing risk mitigation strategies that are tailored to their operational frameworks will help businesses prevent losses caused by emerging risks. This will enhance their competitive advantage and contribute to their sustainability.

This chapter identifies risks and risk mitigation strategies in the CSC's distribution phase which are expected to inform relevant literature and the strategic decision-making procedures of business practitioners. Future studies in this area could adopt a broader approach by including several phases of the CSC, providing a more comprehensive and cohesive perspective. Including a greater spectrum of decision-makers would improve the dependability and completeness of the results by extending the study. Furthermore, diversified methodologies could offer more thorough understanding of risk priority in this field. Beyond the conventional BWM applied in this study, future research could investigate alternative or improved variants of the approach to improve the assessment process. In the context of risk assessment and mitigation strategies, Layered BWM could be employed to account for future scenarios, enabling a structured evaluation of risks under different conditions. For global supply chains, where efficiency in decision-making is critical, Parsimonious BWM could provide a practical alternative by reducing the cognitive burden extensive pairwise comparisons. Advancing research in these areas will contribute to enhancing the effectiveness, efficiency, and flexibility of risk management strategies in the CSC, ultimately strengthening its resilience and sustainability.

AI disclosure statement: The author acknowledges the use of AI-based tools for minor language editing or grammatical correction. However, all intellectual contributions, analyses, and conclusions presented in this chapter are entirely the author's own.

References

1. Ali, I., Nagalingam, S., Gurd, B., A resilience model for cold chain logistics of perishable products. *Int. J. Logist. Manage.*, 29, 3, 922–941, 2018, https://doi.org/10.1108/IJLM-06-2017-0147.

2. Altubaishe, B. and Desai, S., Multicriteria decision making in supply chain management using FMEA and hybrid AHP-PROMETHEE algorithms. *Sensors, 23*, 8, 4041, 1–21, 2023, https://doi.org/10.3390/s23084041.
3. Arora, M., Kumar, R., Garg, C.P., Sharma, N., Sarfraz, M., Study of issues in cold chain using fuzzy environment. *Qual. Quant.*, 58, 5395–5419, 2024, https://doi.org/10.1007/s11135-024-01901-1.
4. Arslan, O., Karakurt, N., Cem, E., Cebi, S., Risk analysis in the food cold chain using Decomposed fuzzy set-based FMEA approach. *Sustainability*, 15, 17, 13169, 1–20, 2023, https://doi.org/10.3390/su151713169.
5. Ballou, R.H. and Burnetas, A., Planning multiple location inventories. *J. Bus. Logist.*, 24, 2, 65–89, 2003, https://doi.org/10.1002/j.2158-1592.2003.tb00046.x.
6. Bamakan, S.M.H., Malekinejad, P., Ziaeian, M., Motavali, A., Bullwhip effect reduction map for COVID-19 vaccine supply chain. *Sustainable Oper. Comput.*, 2, 139–148, 2021, https://doi.org/10.1016/j.susoc.2021.07.001.
7. Bogataj, D., Hudoklin, D., Bogataj, M., Dimovski, V., Colnar, S., Risk mitigation in a meat supply chain with options of redirection. *Sustainability*, 12, 20, 1–23, 8690, 2020, https://doi.org/10.3390/su12208690.
8. Bou Bouazzi, I., Zaidi, M., Shati, R.A., Bedywi, L., Alahmari, S., Al Qahtani, R., Asiri, S., Medication cold chain improvement by using IoT-based smart tracking: a case study in KSA. *Eng. Res. Express*, 7, 1, 1–27, 015266, 2025, https://doi.org/10.1088/2631-8695/adb5d8.
9. Brosnan, T. and Sun, D.W., Precooling techniques and applications for horticultural products—a review. *Int. J. Refrig., 24*, 2, 154–170, 2001, https://doi.org/10.1016/S0140-7007(00)00017-7.
10. Cavinato, J.L., Supply chain logistics risks: From the back room to the board room. *Int. J. Phys. Distrib. Logist. Manage.*, 34, 5, 383–387, 2004, https://doi.org/10.1108/09600030410545427.
11. Chopra, S. and Sodhi, M.S., Managing risk to avoid supply-chain breakdown. *MIT Sloan Manage. Rev.*, 2004.
12. Christopher, M. and Peck, H., Building the resilient supply chain. *Int. J. Logist. Manage.*, 15, 2, 1–14, 2004, https://doi.org/10.1108/09574090410700275.
13. Dagsuyu, C., Derse, O., Oturakci, M., Integrated risk prioritization and action selection for cold chain. *Environ. Sci. Pollut. Res.*, 28, 13, 15646–15658, 2021, https://doi.org/10.1007/s11356-021-12733-z.
14. Diabat, A., Govindan, K., Panicker, V.V., Supply chain risk management and its mitigation in a food industry. *Int. J. Prod. Res.*, 50, 11, 3039–3050, 2012, https://doi.org/10.1080/00207543.2011.588619.
15. Gao, K., Liu, T., Rong, Y., Simic, V., Garg, H., Senapati, T., A novel BWM-entropy-COPRAS group decision framework with spherical fuzzy information for digital supply chain partner selection. *Complex Intell. Syst., 10*, 5, 6983–7008, 2024, https://doi.org/10.1007/s40747-024-01500-5.

16. Gunasekaran, A., Subramanian, N., Rahman, S., Supply chain resilience: role of complexities and strategies. *Int. J. Prod. Res.*, 53, 22, 6809–6819, 2015, https://doi.org/10.1080/00207543.2015.1093667.
17. Gurtu, A. and Johny, J., Supply chain risk management: Literature review. *Risks*, 9, 1, 16, 2023, https://doi.org/10.3390/risks9010016.
18. Hecht, A.A., Biehl, E., Barnett, D.J., Neff, R.A., Urban food supply chain resilience for crises threatening food security: a qualitative study. *J. Acad. Nutr. Diet.*, 119, 2, 211–224, 2019, https://doi.org/10.1016/j.jand.2018.09.001.
19. Ho, W., Zheng, T., Yildiz, H., Talluri, S., Supply chain risk management: a literature review. *Int. J. Prod. Res.*, 53, 16, 5031–5069, 2015, https://doi.org/10.1080/00207543.2015.1030467.
20. Ivanov, D., Viable supply chain model: integrating agility, resilience and sustainability perspectives—lessons from and thinking beyond the COVID-19 pandemic. *Ann. Oper. Res.*, 319, 1, 1411–1431, 2022, https://doi.org/10.1007/s10479-021-04181-2.
21. Janick, J., *Horticultural science*, 4th Ed., p. 550±1, Freeman WH, New York, 1986.
22. Jones, S., Kirchsteiger, C., Bjerke, W., The importance of near miss reporting to further improve safety performance. *J. Loss Prev. Process Ind.*, *12*, 1, 59–67, 1999, https://doi.org/10.1016/S0950-4230(98)00038-2.
23. Khan, A.U., Ali, Y., Pamucar, D., Vasa, L., Risk management for cold supply chain: Case of a developing country. *Acta Polytech. Hung.*, 19, 8, 161–185, 2022.
24. Khan, S., Haleem, A., Khan, M.I., Risk management in Halal supply chain: an integrated fuzzy Delphi and DEMATEL approach. *J. Modell. Manage.*, *16*, 1, 172–214, 2021, https://doi.org/10.1108/JM2-09-2019-0228.
25. Khan, W., Khan, S., Dhamija, A., Haseeb, M., Ansari, S.A., Risk assessment in livestock supply chain using the MCDM method: a case of emerging economy. *Environ. Sci. Pollut. Res.*, 30, 8, 20688–20703, 2023, https://doi.org/10.1007/s11356-022-23640-2.
26. Kumar, N., Tyagi, M., Sachdeva, A., A sustainable framework development and assessment for enhancing the environmental performance of cold supply chain. *Manage. Environ. Qual. Int. J.*, 34, 4, 1077–1110, 2023, https://doi.org/10.1108/MEQ-03-2022-0046.
27. Liao, J., Tang, J., Vinelli, A., Xie, R., A hybrid sustainability performance measurement approach for fresh food cold supply chains. *J. Cleaner Prod.*, 398, 1–22, 136466, 2023, https://doi.org/10.1016/j.jclepro.2023.136466.
28. Likert, R., *New patterns of management*, McGraw-Hill, New York, 1961.
29. Majumdar, A., Sinha, S.K., Govindan, K., Prioritising risk mitigation strategies for environmentally sustainable clothing supply chains: Insights from selected organisational theories. *Sustainable Prod. Consumption*, *28*, 543–555, 2021, https://doi.org/10.1016/j.spc.2021.06.021.
30. Marriott, N.G., Gravani, R.B., Schilling, M.W., *Principles of food sanitation*, vol. 22, Springer, USA, 2006.

31. Masudin, I., Zuliana, P.E., Utama, D.M., Restuputri, D.P., Assessment and risk mitigation on halal meat supply chain using fuzzy best-worst method (BWM) and risk mitigation number (RMN). *J. Islam. Mark.*, 15, 3, 842–865, 2024, https://doi.org/10.1016/j.spc.2021.06.021.
32. McFarlan, W., Li and Fung (A): Internet issues. Harvard Business School case 9, 301-009, 2002.
33. Mukherjee, S., De, A., Roy, S., Supply chain risk prioritization: a multi-criteria based intuitionistic fuzzy topsis approach. *Int. J. Qual. Reliab. Manage.*, 41, 6, 1693–1725, 2024, https://doi.org/10.1108/IJQRM-07-2023-0214.
34. Muzvondiwa, E., Strategies for Preventing and Mitigating the Effects of Agro-Food Supply Chain Disruptions, Walden Dissertations and Doctoral Studies, 4392, 2017.
35. Nasir, T., Quaddus, M., Shamsuddoha, M., Dairy supply chain risk management in Bangladesh: field studies of factors and variables. *J. Teknik Industri J. Keilmuan Aplikasi Teknik Industri*, 16, 2, 127–138, 2014, https://doi.org/10.9744/jti.16.2.127-138.
36. Norrman, A. and Jansson, U., Ericsson's proactive supply chain risk management approach after a serious sub-supplier accident. *Int. J. Phys. Distrib. Logist. Manage.*, 34, 5, 434–456, 2004, https://doi.org/10.1108/09600030410545463.
37. Oleiwi, A.K., Saleh, H.M., Mahmood, A.M., Avci, I., A survey of MCDM-based software engineering method. *Babylonian J. Math.*, 13–18, 2024, https://doi.org/10.58496/MJCS/2022/000.
38. Paillin, D.B., Machfud, M., Hardjomidjojo, H., Romli, M., Tupan, J.M., Supply chain risk assessment using best worst method: a case study of agroindustry skipjack tuna in Ambon-Indonesia. *Acta Logist. (AL)*, 11, 3, 361–371, 2024, https://doi.org/10.22306/al.v11i3.521.
39. Paul, A., Shukla, N., Paul, S.K., Trianni, A., Sustainable supply chain management and multi-criteria decision-making methods: A systematic review. *Sustainability*, 13, 13, 7104, 2021.
40. Prakash, S., Soni, G., Rathore, A.P.S., Singh, S., Risk analysis and mitigation for perishable food supply chain: a case of dairy industry. *Benchmarking Int. J.*, *24*, 1, 2–23, 2017, https://doi.org/10.1108/BIJ-07-2015-0070.
41. QingYing, Z. and Zhimin, H., HACCP and the risk assessment of cold-chain. *IJ Wireless Microwave Technol.*, *1*, 1, 67–71, 2011, https://doi.org/10.5815/ijwmt.2011.01.10.
42. Rathore, R., Thakkar, J.J., Jha, J.K., A quantitative risk assessment methodology and evaluation of food supply chain. *Int. J. Logist. Manage.*, 28, 4, 1272–1293, 2017, https://doi.org/10.1108/IJLM-08-2016-0198.
43. Rezaei, J., Best-worst multi-criteria decision-making method. *Omega*, 53, 49–57, 2015, https://doi.org/10.1016/j.omega.2014.11.009.
44. Rice, J.B. and Caniato, F., Building a secure and resilient supply network. *Supply Chain Manage. Rev.*, 7, 5, 22–30, 2003.
45. Sahay, B.S., Supply chain collaboration: the key to value creation. *Work Study*, 52, 2, 76–83, 2003, https://doi.org/10.1108/00438020310462872.

46. Sarpkaya, D. and Temur, G.T., Prioritizing strategic decisions in cold supply chain by DEMATEL and VIKOR. *Proceedings Book*, pp. 135–146, 2021.
47. Shabani, A., Torabipour, S.M.R., Saen, R.F., A new super-efficiency dual-role FDH procedure: an application in dairy cold chain for vehicle selection. *Int. J. Ship. Transport Logist.*, 71, 4, 426–456, 2015, https://doi.org/10.1504/IJSTL.2015.069678.
48. Shen, Y. and Liao, K., An application of analytic hierarchy process and entropy weight method in food cold chain risk evaluation model. *Front. Psychol.*, 13, 1–13, 825696, 2022, https://doi.org/10.3389/fpsyg.2022.825696.
49. Silvestre, B.S., Sustainable supply chain management in emerging economies: Environmental turbulence, institutional voids and sustainability trajectories. *Int. J. Prod. Econ.*, 167, 156–169, 2015, https://doi.org/10.1016/j.ijpe.2015.05.025.
50. Sudarmin, A.C. and Ardi, R., DEMATEL-based analytic network process (ANP) approach to assess the vaccine supply chain risk in Indonesia. *IEEE international conference on industrial engineering and engineering management (IEEM)*, pp. 726–730, 2020.
51. Székely, F. and Knirsch, M., Responsible leadership and corporate social responsibility: Metrics for sustainable performance. *Eur. Manage. J.*, 23, 6, 628–647, 2005, https://doi.org/10.1016/j.emj.2005.10.009.
52. Taleb, N.N., Goldstein, D.G., Spitznagel, M.W., The six mistakes executives make in risk management. *Harv. Bus. Rev.*, 87, 10, 78–81, 2009.
53. Tang, C.S., Perspectives in supply chain risk management. *Int. J. Prod. Econ.*, 103, 2, 451–488, 2006, https://doi.org/10.1016/j.ijpe.2005.12.006.
54. Toloie-Eshlaghy, A. and Homayonfar, M., MCDM methodologies and applications: a literature review from 1999 to 2009. *Res. J. Int. Stud.*, *21*, 21, 86–137, 2011.
55. Waters, D., *Supply chain risk management: vulnerability and resilience in logistics*, Kogan Page Publishers, London, 2011.
56. Xu, W., Zhang, Z., Gong, D., Guan, X., Neural network model for the risk prediction in cold chain logistics. *Int. J. Multimedia Ubiquitous Eng.*, 9, 8, 111–124, 2014, http://dx.doi.org/10.14257/ijmue.9.8.2014.
57. Zavadskas, E.K. and Turskis, Z., Multiple criteria decision making (MCDM) methods in economics: an overview. *Technol. Econ. Dev. Econ.*, *17*, 2, 397–427, 2011, https://doi.org/10.3846/20294913.2011.593291.
58. Zhang, H., Qiu, B., Zhang, K., A new risk assessment model for agricultural products cold chain logistics. *Ind. Manage. Data Syst.*, 117, 9, 1800–1816, 2017, https://doi.org/10.1108/IMDS-03-2016-0098.
59. Kumar, A., Mangla, S.K., Kumar, P., Song, M., Mitigate risks in perishable food supply chains: Learning from COVID-19. *Technol. Forecast. Soc. Change*, 166, 120643, 2021.

6

Fuzzy Machine Learning Integrated MCDM in Sustainable Supplier Selection of Healthcare Industries

Nivetha Martin[1]* and Akbar Rezaei[2]

[1]*Department of Mathematics, Arul Anandar College (Autonomous), Madurai, Tamil Nadu, India*
[2]*Department of Mathematics, Payame Noour University, Tehran, Iran*

Abstract

The choice of eco-friendly supplier is one of the intricate challenges of the healthcare industry as the selection process involves several criteria of selection. As the traditional selection methods fall short of addressing the uncertain decision-making circumstances, this research work contributes an unified method of choosing supplier using both machine learning (ML) and multi-criteria decision methods with fuzzy representations. This study considers criteria of different domains with special focus on sustainability features. Fuzzy decision trees are applied to determine the core criteria and the MCDM approach of Fuzzy AROMAN (Alternative Ranking Order Method Accounting for Two-Step Normalization) is used in ranking the course of actions. The experimental results showcase the capability of the developed integrated framework in obtaining consistent and reliable solutions to the supplier selection. Comparative analysis demonstrates that this integrated approach outperforms deterministic methods in handling imprecision and vagueness. This work certainly contributes to enhanced decision-making systems of deriving ideal solutions to the problem of supplier selection.

Keywords: Fuzzy sets, machine learning, MCDM, supplier selection, healthcare industry

**Corresponding author*: nivetha.martin710@gmail.com

Harish Garg (ed.) Decision Support Systems in Smart Computing: Embracing Uncertainty and Challenges, (151–180) © 2026 Scrivener Publishing LLC

6.1 Introduction

The operative of the health care engineering solely depends on the right selection of suppliers contributing to sustainable supply chain management. Decision-making on sustainable healthcare suppliers is crucial and critical as it encompasses several considerations of criteria [36]. Sustainability-based selection requires multiple criteria encircling economic, environmental, quality, risk, and logistic aspects. As the concerns of sustainability and complexities are growing in healthcare operations, it is essential to develop a more adaptive and intelligent approach to supplier selection. The traditional decision-making procedure often lacks the competency in handling uncertainty and complexity in criterion selection. Also, the selection will be based on limited data sets. The challenging hurdles of decision-making drive the need of developing a fuzzy integrated or hybrid approach to handle ambiguity in prioritizing criteria and ranking the suppliers.

Supplier selection generally functions in two segments in which the initial stage considers selection of criteria and the second phase ranks the suppliers based on the core criteria. Decision-making with precision and robustness is the core element of a fuzzy hybrid decision approach. Evolving hybrid methods with the integration of fuzzy machine learning and MCDM enhances the caliber of the model. Decision-making methods embracing fuzzy logic facilitate the decision makers in evaluating subjective and imprecise data. Fuzzy-based machine learning approaches are flexible in drawing patterns using past data of supplier performances. Furthermore, the integration of MCDM methods helps in prioritizing the suppliers. Despite existing diverse machine learning algorithms and MCDM methods, this research work proposes a hybrid approach integrating Fuzzy Decision Trees with Fuzzy AROMAN.

Fuzzy Decision Trees are more competent in determining the feature or the criterion weights and Fuzzy AROMAN is used in ranking the alternatives using two-way normalization approach [15]. This integrated approach is more advantageous as it is potent in dealing with subjective evaluation and incomplete data sets. The drawbacks of conventional Decision-making approach in criterion selection are well handled by this hybrid approach. This two-phase hybrid approach provides opportunities to consider factors related to sustainable healthcare supplier selection. The combined decision-making method ascertains enhanced accuracy, elasticity, and accountability in supplier selection thereby facilitating the healthcare institutions in reaching both operational efficacy and sustainability.

The other aspects of this study are organized into various segments. The related work is deliberated in Section 6.2. The basic preliminaries of MCDM are discussed in Section 6.3. The procedure of the combined approach is discussed in Section 6.4. The implementation of the proposed method is well substantiated with healthcare supplier selection in Section 6.5. The findings are discoursed in Section 6.6. Industrial implications are briefed in Section 6.7 and the final segment summarizes the work.

6.2 Review of Earlier Works

This section presents the review of literature of the applications of different MCDM methods applied in healthcare supplier selection. The applications of decision trees in healthcare systems and supplier selection are also discussed. The unexplored aspects and ground-breaking of this research work are also presented.

6.2.1 MCDM in Health Care Supplier Selection

The choice of suppliers in the healthcare industry involves the interventions of diverse MCDM methods. Yazdani *et al.* [66] proposed an integrated Decision-making model with fuzzy logic. Goh *et al.* discussed the operational framework of supplier choice with fuzzy-based MCDM environment [23]. Stević *et al.* ranked the suppliers based on compromise solutions [60]. Sumrit briefed on fuzzy vendor-managed inventory in healthcare [61]. Garcia *et al.* conceptualized a multitude criteria approach of selecting suppliers in the healthcare sector [21]. Kumcu and Ozyoruk applied Analytical Hierarchy Process with Goal Programming in supplier selection [38].

Chen *et al.* employed fuzzy group decision making of TOPSIS method in selecting suppliers. Boz *et al.* applied an innovative approach in choosing suppliers considering logistics 4.0 [9]. Goncu and Cetin applied DEMATEL ANP in supplier selection in healthcare enterprises [24]. Kumari *et al.* used blockchain in supplier selection [37]. Salimian *et al.* employed VIKOR and MARCOS-based interval-valued intuitionistic fuzzy models in selection of suppliers of healthcare devices [56]. Rod and Naenna discoursed on supplier selection with special reference to Thailand healthcare sector [54]. Pamucar *et al.* applied novel fuzzy rough sets-based decision-making on supplier selection during pandemic [49]. Chakraborty *et al.* compared the potency of fuzzy method [11]. Mohamed at al applied genetic algorithm and blockchain technology [43, 44]. Nayeri *et al.* developed a data-grounded model in selecting the suppliers [45]. Debnath *et al.*

applied a combination of decision-making methods [17]. Abbaspour and Rezaee applied game game-based fuzzy cognitive map approach in healthcare decisions [1]. Bhosale and Umpa applied Analytic Hierarchy Process and TOPSIS under a fuzzy stochastic system in supplier selection [5]. Otay *et al.* applied Interval-Valued Pythagorean Fuzzy AHP and CODAS in selecting the suppliers [48].

Chakraborty *et al.* developed an combined G-MACONT method under both crisp and intuitionistic environments [12]. Dai *et al.* applied SMAA-MABAC approach to handle uncertainties in supplier selection [16]. Saha *et al.* developed Generalized Dombi-based probabilistic method [55]. Pethaperumal *et al.* employed multi-fuzzy soft set [51]. Bhosale and Umap made a supplier selection using TOPSIS under an intuitionistic fuzzy environment [7]. Alrasheedi *et al.* used Fermatean oriented approach for sustainable supplier evaluation [3]. Liu *et al.* modeled a novel multi-attribute group decision-making technique in choosing suppliers [41]. Wang *et al.* framed a model to make green supplier selection [64]. Bhosale and Umap developed a fuzzy-based Analytical Hierarchy Process in selection [6, 8]. Shahab *et al.* formulated a gamified approach with Pythagorean operators [57]. Khalil *et al.* applied an analytical hierarchy process in dental healthcare supplier selection [35]. Rishabh and Das applied AHP and TOPSIS in a hybridized metaheuristic environment in supplier selection [53]. Jana *et al.* applied fuzzy MABAC for supplier selection [30]. Liang *et al.* applied PROMTHEE method in supplier selection [40]. Talib *et al.* employed a fuzzy-based decision-making framework for handling health issues of autism patients [62]. Tian *et al.* framed an extended decision-making method based on SECA-GDM to make optimal decisions in occupational health [63].

6.2.2 Decision Trees in Health Care Systems and Supplier Selection

Karatas *et al.* discussed big data analysis for addressing the challenges and perspectives for the healthcare industry [33]. Decision trees are applied in diverse aspects of healthcare systems. Levashenko *et al.* employed fuzzy decision trees in healthcare consistency [39]. Khan *et al.* employed fuzzy decision trees in envisaging the subsistence rate of breast cancer [36]. Kelarev *et al.* made an experimental study using decision trees and ensembles in observing diabetic patients [34]. Drousiotis *et al.* employed an intrinsically interpretable decision tree for healthcare applications [18]. Panwar *et al.* used AI-driven decision trees in securing patient data [50].

Soni *et al.* applied decision trees for making asthma predictions [59]. Zachariah *et al.* applied decision trees in combination with neural networks in making predictions of healthcare-associated urinary tract infections [67]. Hendriks *et al.* employed a data-driven model in making evaluations of cancer [27]. Giri *et al.* used JSON-based decision trees in remote healthcare [22]. In addition, decision trees are also applied in supplier selection. Wu integrated decision trees with Data Envelopment Analysis (DEA) and neural networks in supplier selection [65]. Sim and Wong applied a fuzzy decision tree in optimal supplier selection [58]. Ishak and Wijaya used a decision tree in spare part supplier selection [29]. Mahmoudifard *et al.* leveraged the decision tree as a tool to evaluate supplier performance [42].

FAROMAN Applications in Decision-Making

Boskovic *et al.* introduced AROMAN and it is employed in ranking the alternatives. Researchers have applied FAROMAN in decision-making. Cubranic *et al.* applied in professional driver selection [15]. Nikolic *et al.* used interval-valued fuzzy AROMAN decision-making to enhance the sustainability of the postal networks [46]. Alrasheedi *et al.* used interval valued AROMAN in selecting sustainable wastewater treatment technology [2]. Dundar assessed impacts of entrepreneurship training using fuzzy BWM and AROMAN [19]. Kara *et al.* employed a spherical fuzzy-based DIBR II-AROMAN model for evaluating sustainability performance [32]. Gurol *et al.* used intuitionistic fuzzy AROMAN in selecting pallet pooling service providers [25]. Hu *et al.* applied intuitionistic fuzzy SWARA-AROMAN for sports event management [28]. Riaz *et al.* applied an AI-Driven LOPCOW-AROMAN Framework with intuitionistic representations in healthcare [52]. Olteanu *et al.* employed Fuzzy-MEREC-AROMAN in prioritizing European investment sectors [47]. Anjum *et al.* applied Pythagorean fuzzy CRITIC-AROMAN in making optimal decisions on transportation systems [4]. Table 6.1 contains the expanded forms of the acronyms of MCDM methods mentioned above.

6.2.3 Existing Gaps and Novel Contributions

From the aforementioned literature the following research gaps are identified

- AROMAN both in crisp and fuzzy is not applied in healthcare systems
- Neither Fuzzy Decision Trees nor Fuzzy AROMAN is applied in healthcare supplier selection

Table 6.1 Abbreviations of MCDM methods.

Acronyms	Full form
AHP	Analytic Hierarchy Process
ANP	Analytic Network Process
TOPSIS	Technique for Order of Preference by Similarity to Ideal Solution
VIKOR	VlseKriterijumska Optimizacija I Kompromisno Resenje (Serbian)
PROMETHEE	Preference Ranking Organization Method for Enrichment Evaluation
DEMATEL	Decision Making Trial and Evaluation Laboratory
CODAS	COmbinative Distance-based ASsessment
MABAC	Multi-Attributive Border Approximation area Comparison
BWM	Best-Worst Method
SWARA	Step-wise Weight Assessment Ratio Analysis
CRITIC	Criteria Importance Through Intercriteria Correlation
SMAA	Stochastic Multi-criteria Acceptability Analysis
MARCOS	Measurement Alternatives and Ranking according to Compromise Solution
SPC-MARCOS	Single-Point Centered MARCOS
SECA-GDM	Simplified Evaluation by Criteria Aggregation - Group Decision Making
G-MACONT	Generalized Multi-Attribute COmparative Normalization Technique
DIBR II	Double Intuitionistic Based Ranking (Second Version)
AROMAN	Atanassov's Ranking Order-based Method for Alternative Negotiation
FAROMAN	Fuzzy AROMAN
LOPCOW	Logarithmic Percentage-Change Driven Objective Weighting
MEREC	Method based on the Removal Effects of Criteria

- Fuzzy Decision Trees are not integrated with FAROMAN to evolve an integrated approach.

The above gaps are bridged in this research work and the significant contributions made are as follows

- A hybrid two-phase decision-making approach is developed with the application of Fuzzy Decision trees in the first phase to choose the critical criteria and Fuzzy AROMAN in the second phase to rank the suppliers.
- Integration of ML and MCDM in healthcare systems.

6.3 Preliminaries

The basic concepts of MCDM and fuzzy logic are related to this work.

6.3.1 Multi-Criteria Decision Making (MCDM)

This primarily refers to a set of diverse methodologies to prioritize the alternatives based on conflicting and interdependent criteria.

6.3.2 Key Components of MCDM

The key components of MCDM are characterized as Alternatives, Criteria, Weights, and Decision Matrix.

- Alternatives refer to the options available to choose.
- Criteria are the factors or the attributes that facilitate in evaluating the alternatives.
- Weights are the numerical values that signify the importance of criteria.
- Decision matrix is the initially constructed matrix consisting of mapping between the alternatives to the criterion satisfaction.

6.3.3 General Steps in MCDM

There are several MCDM methods, however the below steps are more common in all methods.

- Problem definition
- Identification of criteria and alternatives.
- Weight assignment
- Normalization
- Aggregation and ranking

6.3.4 Fuzzy Set

Let X be a universe of discourse. A fuzzy set $\tilde{A}$ in X is defined by a membership function:

$\mu_{\tilde{A}} : X \rightarrow [0,1]$, where $\mu_{\tilde{A}}$ denotes the membership value of x ∈ X.

6.3.5 Fuzzy Logic

Fuzzy logic is basically an extension of Boolean logic is termed as many-valued logic with rules of inference.

6.3.6 Linguistic Variable

A variable assuming linguistic values describing qualitative and subjective feedback.

For example, Very Good, Medium, Fair, Low, Very Poor.

6.4 Methodology

This section discusses the procedure of the proposed hybrid decision-making method involving two phases with fuzzy representations to rank the healthcare suppliers. This hybrid method involves both machine learning and multi-criteria decision-making steps. The first phase comprises Fuzzy Decision Trees approach in minimizing the criterion count. The second phase involves Fuzzy AROMAN to rank the alternatives.

6.4.1 Phase I: Fuzzy Decision Trees in Criterion Reduction [58]

Step 1: Data Processing

Let us consider a feature dataset X of the form $X = \{x_1, x_2, ..x_n\}$ and label set $Y = \{y_1, y_2,..y_m\}$. Each of the features is represented using fuzzy linguistic variable and each of the feature xi is mapped into High (H), Medium (M) and Low (L). The triangular fuzzy numbers are used to quantify the linguistic representations. The criteria or the features required for ranking the suppliers are decided based on the domains of Economic, Environmental, Quality, Compliance and Logistics.

Step 2: Calculation of Fuzzy Entropy
Fuzzy entropy for each of the node N in the decision tree is measured to find the impurity of the node using (1)

$$H(N) = -\sum_{i=1}^{m} \mu_{A_i}(x) \log(\mu_{A_i}(x)) \tag{6.1}$$

Where $\mu_{A_i}(x)$ is the membership value of each of the class Ai and m is the count of the classes in the data set.

Step 3: Computation of Information Gain
For each of the features or the criteria, the information gain, IG (N,F) is computed

$$IG(N,F) = H(N) - \sum_{v \in V} \frac{|N_v|}{|N|} H(N_v) \tag{6.2}$$

Where, V is the possible values of the Feature F, N_v is the count of samples in node N with value v and $|N|$ represents the count of samples in node N

Step 4: Determination of Fuzzy Gain Ratio
The fuzzy gain ratio FGR (N,F) is computed to determine the bias toward the attributes with many values.

$$GR(N,F) = \frac{IG(N,F)}{IV(F)} \tag{6.3}$$

IV (F) is the essential value of the feature is defined as $IV(F) = -\sum_{v \in V} \frac{|N_v|}{|N|} \log \frac{|N_v|}{|N|}$

Step 5 Ranking the Features based on FGR
The fuzzy gain ratio which is characterized as the score values calculated for each of the features and based on these score values, each of the features is ranked. The features or the criteria with highest values are determined to be more significant.

6.4.2 Phase II: Fuzzy AROMAN in Ranking the Supplier [15]

Step 1: Framing of decision-making matrix G
A matrix G = [g_{ij}] with m alternatives and n criteria is formulated initially.

$$G = [g_{ij}]_{mxn} = \begin{bmatrix} g_{11} & \cdots & g_{1n} \\ \vdots & \ddots & \vdots \\ g_{m1} & \cdots & g_{mn} \end{bmatrix}$$

In this matrix G, each entry is an linguistic variable and it is quantified using triangular fuzzy numbers of the form (l,m,n). The matrix is quantified using triangular fuzzy numbers and then defuzzied using centroid method of the form $\frac{(l+m+n)}{3}$.

Step 2: Normalization of the matrix R
Linear normalization technique is used to determine the normalized matrix R with max-min operations.

$$\text{Benefit criteria} \quad r_{ij} = \frac{g_{ij} - min\ g_{ij}}{max\ g_{ij} - min\ g_{ij}}$$

$$\text{Cost criteria} \quad r_{ij} = \frac{max\ g_{ij} - g_{ij}}{max\ g_{ij} - min\ g_{ij}}$$

Step 3: Normalize the matrix again using vector normalization methods

$$\text{Benefit criteria} \quad n_{ij} = \frac{g_{ij}}{\sqrt{\sum_{i=1}^{m} g_{ij}^2}}$$

$$\text{Cost criteria} \quad n_{ij} = 1 - \frac{g_{ij}}{\sqrt{\sum_{i=1}^{m} g_{ij}^2}}$$

Step 4: Aggregation of normalization value
The normalization values are aggregated using

$$t_{ij}^{norm} = \frac{\beta t_{ij} + (1-\beta)t_{ij}^{*}}{2} i = 1,2,\dots m; j = 1,2,\dots n$$

β denotes the weight which varies between 0 and 1.

Step 5: Computation of weighted normalized matrix
The normalized matrix is converted to weighted normalized form considering equal weights

$$\hat{t}_{ij} = W_{ij}.t_{ij}^{norm} i = 1,2,\dots m; \quad j = 1,2,\dots n$$

$$L_i = \sum_j \hat{t}_{ij}^{(min)} \; i = 1,2,\dots m; \quad j \in cost\ criteria$$

$$A_i = \sum_j \hat{t}_{ij}^{(max)} \; i = 1,2,\dots m; \quad j \in benefit\ criteria$$

Step 6: Ranking of the alternatives
The resultant values of criteria function (R_i) are computed.

$$R_i = L_i^{\lambda} + A_i^{(1-\lambda)} i = 1,2,\dots\dots m$$

The optimal ranking of the alternatives is performed in decreasing order of the values of Ri.

The above-described two-phase fuzzy-based decision-making approach is applied in ranking the healthcare suppliers.

6.5 Hybrid Decision-Making Approach in Supplier Selection

6.5.1 Problem Description

Let us examine the decision-making problem of healthcare supplier selection for purchasingedical equipment and other required healthcare materials. The criteria of selecting the suppliers are categorized into five domains namely Economic, Environmental, Quality, Compliance and Logistics. The sub-criterion under each of the criterion dimensions is presented in Table 6.2. The selection of suppliers based on all the criteria mentioned in table is a hurdling task and hence it is essential to reduce the count of criteria. To make so, a hybrid decision-making method with two phases is required to rank the alternatives. The first phase must reduce the criteria and facilitate in identifying the core criteria of supplier selection and the latter phase ranks the alternatives. The hybrid method involves fuzzy-based Decision Trees in the first phase to obtain the critical criteria based on fuzzy data sets. In the second phase, fuzzy integrated FAROMAN is applied to rank the suppliers.

Table 6.2 Description of criteria.

Criterion domain	Sub-criterion		Description
Economic	EC1	Financial Stability	Ability of the suppliers to meet financial commitments.
	EC2	Cost Efficiency	Effective pricing
	EC3	Lead Time	Rate of order accomplishment
	EC4	Cost of Ownership	Meeting long-term expenses
	EC5	Contract Flexibility	Adaptability in pricing modalities
Environmental	EN1	Carbon Footprint	Mitigation of emissions
	EN2	Resource Utilization	Effective utilization of resources
	EN3	Energy Efficacy	Minimization of energy utility
	EN4	Sustainable Sourcing	Relying on eco-friendly energy sources
	EN5	Renewable Energy Adoption	Green energy utilization

(Continued)

Table 6.2 Description of criteria. (*Continued*)

Criterion domain	**Sub-criterion**		**Description**
Quality	Q1	Material Consistency	Quality of the raw materials
	Q2	Performance Stability	Competency of the products
	Q3	Service Reliability	Service mechanisms of the supplier
	Q4	Innovation Capability	Innovative attributes of the product
	Q5	Traceability	Ability to track the products
Compliance	C1	Environmental standards	Meeting the environmental regulations
	C2	Risk Management Strategy	Devising of suitable strategies in risk handling
	C3	Ethical Sourcing	Adherence to ethical aspects
	C4	Supplier Transparency	Openness in business transactions
	C5	Data Security	Data protection
Logistics	L1	Delivery Pattern	Optimal delivery time
	L2	Inventory Management Capability	Effective handling of resources to avoid shortages
	L3	Supply Chain Resilience	Potency to handle disruptions
	L4 L5	Geographical Proximity	Consideration of supplier's location
		Sustainable Transportation	Eco-friendly practices

6.5.2 Phase I Fuzzy Decision Trees in Criterion Reduction

In this phase the possible criteria that shall be considered for health care supplier selection are chosen and presented in Table 6.2. Among the listed 25 criteria, significant criteria are chosen for the next phase of ranking.

The above criteria are determined based on the experts in healthcare sector. The particulars of the experts are furnished in Table 6.3.

With the help of these experts, the required data is collected as linguistic variables of the forms (High – H, Medium – M and Low – L) and a sample of it is presented in Table 6.4.

Triangular fuzzy membership functions are used to handle the linguistic variables and the graphical representations are presented in Figure 6.1.

Employing Fuzzy Decision Trees, the score values of the criteria are determined and it is depicted graphically in Figure 6.2.

The score values of the criteria are presented in Table 6.5.

The criteria with highest score values under each of the domains are identified as the core criteria to be considered in healthcare supplier selection. The decision makers have a variety of choices in criterion selection, they shall either select one to three criteria of highest values under each domain or either eliminate the criteria with very least score values. For the second phase, the two criteria under each domain with maximum score values are chosen for ranking the alternatives.

6.5.3 Phase II: Fuzzy AROMAN in Ranking the Supplier

The criteria considered for ranking are EC2, EC3, EN3, EN4, Q3, Q4, C3, C4, L1, L2.

The criterion weights are presented in Table 6.6.

The initial decision-making matrix with linguistic variables showcasing the criterion satisfaction of the healthcare suppliers as alternatives is presented in Table 6.7.

Table 6.3 Expert's profile.

Expert	Years of experience	Expertise
Expert - I	15	Research and Development, Healthcare Principles, Risk Management
Expert - II	14	Supply chain, Inventory Management
Expert - III	12	Quality Management, Eco-practices
Expert - IV	10	Product Design, Budgeting

Table 6.4 Sample data.

S. no.	EC1	EC2	EC3	EC4	EC5	EN1	EN2	EN3	EN4	EN5	Q1	Q2	Q3	Q4	Q5
1	H	M	H	H	H	M	H	H	H	H	M	H	H	H	H
2	M	M	L	M	L	M	M	L	M	L	M	L	M	L	M
3	H	M	H	H	H	H	H	M	H	H	H	M	H	H	M
4	M	M	M	M	M	M	M	M	M	M	M	M	M	M	M
5	L	L	L	L	L	L	L	L	L	L	L	L	L	L	L
6	H	H	H	M	H	H	M	H	M	H	H	H	M	H	M
7	M	H	M	H	M	M	H	M	H	M	M	H	M	H	M
8	L	M	L	M	L	M	M	L	M	L	M	M	L	M	L
9	H	H	H	H	H	H	H	H	H	H	H	H	H	H	H
10	M	M	M	M	M	M	M	M	M	M	M	M	M	M	M

(Continued)

Table 6.4 Sample data. *(Continued)*

S. no.	C1	C2	C3	C4	C5	L1	L2	L3	L4	L5	Output
1	H	M	H	H	H	H	H	M	H	M	Preferred
2	L	M	M	L	M	M	M	M	M	L	Accepted
3	H	H	M	H	H	H	H	H	H	H	Preferred
4	M	M	M	M	M	M	M	M	M	M	Accepted
5	L	L	L	L	L	L	L	L	L	L	Rejected
6	M	M	H	H	H	M	H	H	H	M	Preferred
7	M	H	M	M	M	M	H	M	M	H	Accepted
8	M	L	M	M	L	M	M	M	L	M	Rejected
9	H	H	H	H	H	H	H	H	H	H	Preferred
10	M	M	M	M	M	M	M	M	M	M	Accepted

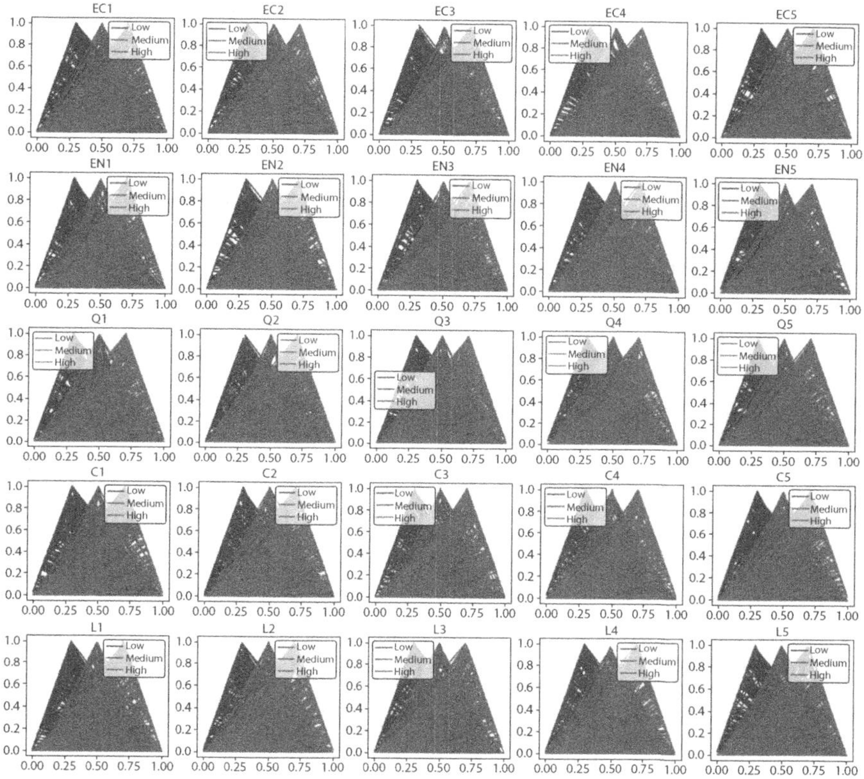

Figure 6.1 Triangular fuzzy representations of linguistic variables.

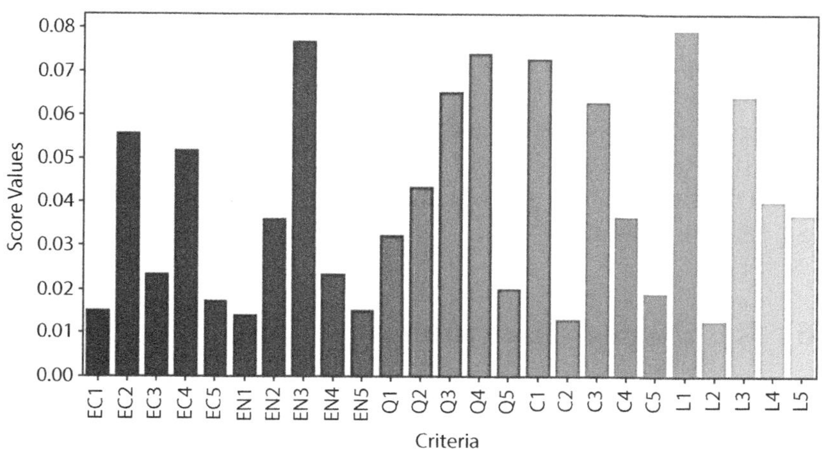

Figure 6.2 Fuzzy decision tree-based score values of the criteria.

Table 6.5 Score values of the criteria.

Criteria	**EC1**	**EC2**	**EC3**	**EC4**	**EC5**
Score Values	0.055	0.05	0.023	0.017	0.013
Criteria	**EN1**	**EN2**	**EN3**	**EN4**	**EN5**
Score Values	0.014	0.035	0.069	0.065	0.015
Criteria	**Q1**	**Q2**	**Q3**	**Q4**	**Q5**
Score Values	0.032	0.043	0.072	0.073	0.02
Criteria	**C1**	**C2**	**C3**	**C4**	**C5**
Score Values	0.013	0.019	0.036	0.063	0.019
Criteria	**L1**	**L2**	**L3**	**L4**	**L5**
Score Values	0.076	0.064	0.015	0.04	0.037

Table 6.6 Core criterion weights.

Criteria	**EC2**	**EC3**	**EN3**	**EN4**	**Q3**	**Q4**	**C3**	**C4**	**L1**	**L2**
Weights	0.07	0.05	0.12	0.10	0.09	0.13	0.06	0.15	0.14	0.11

The linguistic variables are represented using triangular fuzzy numbers and the above matrix is modified based on the graphical representation in Figure 6.3 as follows. The linguistic variables are modified and presented in Table 6.8.

The combined weighted normalized matrix is presented in Table 6.9 using steps 2–5.

The score values of the alternatives and the rankings are presented in Table 6.10 using step 6.

From the findings, it is inferred that, the supplier S3 ranks first followed by S4, S6, S10, S8 and so.

6.6 Results and Discussions

The two-phase integrated fuzzy-based decision-making approach is applied to minimize the criterion count. As mentioned earlier, the number of criteria considered for ranking shall be modified based on the choice of the

Table 6.7 Initial linguistic decision matrix.

	EC2	EC3	EN3	EN4	Q3	Q4	C3	C4	L1	L2
Suppliers	**CC**	**CC**	**BC**	**BC**	**BC**	**BC**	**BC**	**BC**	**BC**	**BC**
S1	VH	H	M	L	VL	M	H	L	VH	H
S2	M	L	VL	M	H	L	M	VL	M	L
S3	VH	VH	H	M	VH	H	VH	VH	VH	VH
S4	M	M	H	M	VH	M	H	M	H	M
S5	VL	VL	VL	L	VL	M	VL	M	M	M
S6	VH	VH	M	H	M	H	VH	M	VH	M
S7	M	M	H	M	M	M	M	M	M	H
S8	VL	M	L	M	VL	M	L	M	M	H
S9	VH	VH	VH	H	M	M	H	VH	M	H
S10	M	M	L	L	VL	H	M	H	H	M

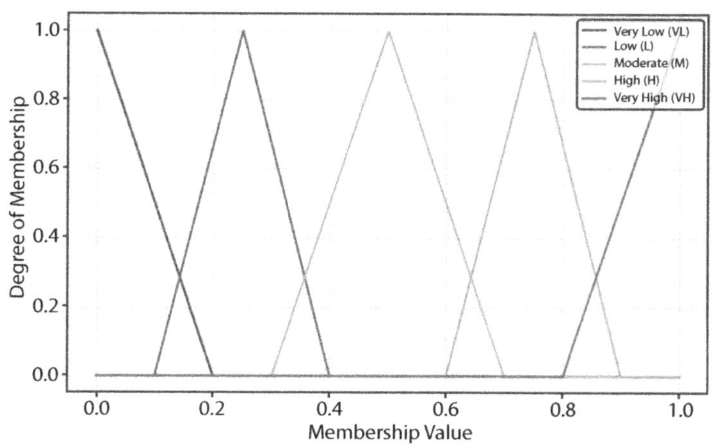

Figure 6.3 Fuzzy triangular representation of 5-point linguistic variable.

Table 6.8 Modified decision matrix.

Suppliers	EC2	EC3	EN3	EN4	Q3	Q4	C3	C4	L1	L2
S1	0.9	0.75	0.5	0.3	0.1	0.5	0.75	0.3	0.9	0.75
S2	0.5	0.3	0.1	0.5	0.75	0.3	0.5	0.1	0.5	0.3
S3	0.9	0.9	0.75	0.5	0.9	0.75	0.9	0.9	0.9	0.9
S4	0.5	0.5	0.75	0.5	0.9	0.5	0.75	0.5	0.75	0.5
S5	0.1	0.1	0.1	0.3	0.1	0.5	0.1	0.5	0.5	0.5
S6	0.9	0.9	0.5	0.75	0.5	0.75	0.9	0.5	0.9	0.5
S7	0.5	0.5	0.75	0.5	0.5	0.5	0.5	0.5	0.5	0.75
S8	0.1	0.5	0.3	0.5	0.1	0.5	0.3	0.5	0.5	0.75
S9	0.9	0.9	0.9	0.75	0.5	0.5	0.75	0.9	0.5	0.75
S10	0.5	0.5	0.3	0.3	0.1	0.75	0.5	0.75	0.75	0.5

Table 6.9 Weighted normalized matrix.

Suppliers	EC2	EC3	EN3	EN4	Q3	Q4	C3	C4	L1	L2
S1	0.014	0.016	0.149	0.047	0.045	0.114	0.07	0.109	0.184	0.122
S2	0.039	0.039	0.09	0.087	0.103	0.062	0.056	0.075	0.062	0.053
S3	0.014	0.01	0.161	0.087	0.114	0.175	0.078	0.193	0.184	0.143
S4	0.039	0.028	0.101	0.087	0.114	0.114	0.07	0.14	0.14	0.085
S5	0.07	0.05	0.06	0.047	0.045	0.114	0.03	0.14	0.062	0.085
S6	0.014	0.01	0.172	0.133	0.083	0.175	0.078	0.14	0.184	0.085
S7	0.039	0.028	0.101	0.087	0.083	0.114	0.056	0.14	0.062	0.122
S8	0.07	0.028	0.117	0.087	0.045	0.114	0.044	0.14	0.062	0.122
S9	0.014	0.01	0.153	0.133	0.083	0.114	0.07	0.193	0.062	0.122
S10	0.039	0.028	0.117	0.047	0.045	0.175	0.056	0.174	0.14	0.085

decision maker. Suppose if conventional or the crisp representations-based decision trees are used with numerical quantities, then the score values of the criteria obtained are pictorially represented in Figure 6.4.

From the above figure it is very difficult to determine the core criteria essential for ranking the alternatives as most of the criterion score values

Table 6.10 Positioning the alternatives.

Course of actions	Summation of the cost criteria	Summation of the benefit criteria	Score values	Position
S1	0.030062	0.840715	1.090289	9
S2	0.077852	0.587144	1.045272	10
S3	0.023746	1.134571	1.219259	1
S4	0.067329	0.850497	1.181702	2
S5	0.120293	0.582249	1.109885	8
S6	0.023746	1.049754	1.178671	3
S7	0.067329	0.765836	1.134599	6
S8	0.098259	0.730309	1.168044	5
S9	0.023746	0.930286	1.118609	7
S10	0.067329	0.838961	1.175426	4

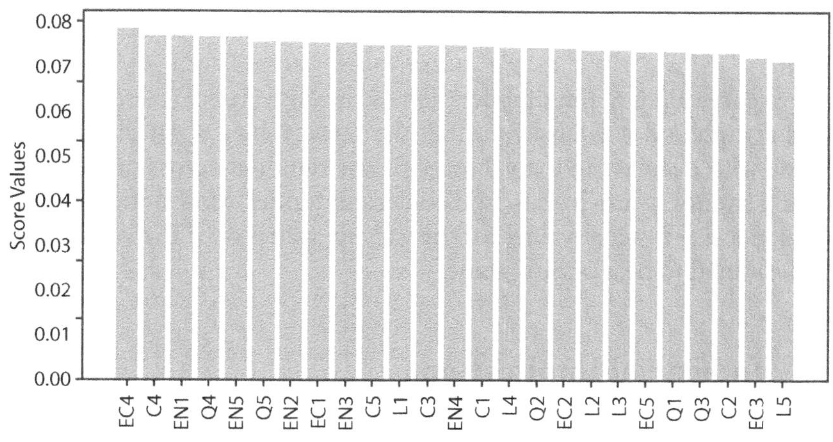

Figure 6.4 Feature score value using crisp decision trees.

are alike. This makes the choosing of core criteria complex. Hence fuzzy-based decision trees are applied to accommodate uncertainty and imprecision in expert's feedback. This makes decision-making more compatible and flexible in identifying the core criteria of ranking the alternatives.

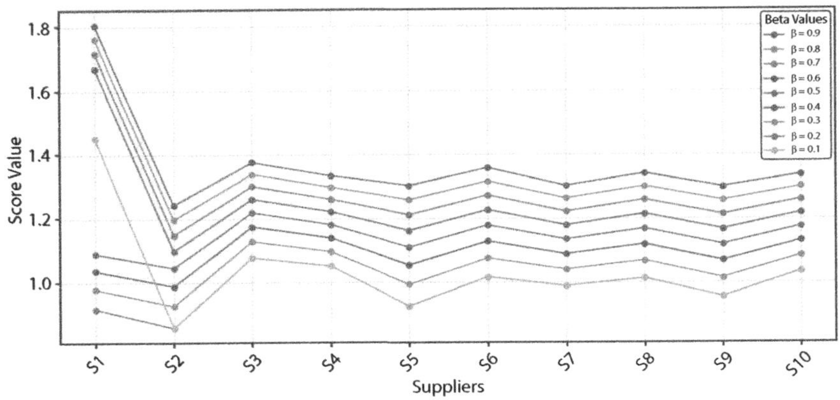

Figure 6.5 Supplier scores vs. β values.

The blend of fuzzy logic with the decision trees makes the framework more adaptive and dynamic.

On other hand Fuzzy AROMAN method facilitates in ranking the alternatives. The consistency of the ranking is ascertained by performing a sensitivity analysis for varying values of β and it is presented in Figure 6.5. The varying β represents the risk attitude of the decision makers. This analysis is a step to ensure the credibility and transparency of the decision support system.

The score values of the suppliers across various values of β are visualized in this graph and it is observed that the score values of all the suppliers decline with decrease in the values of β. The rankings across different values of β signify a more robust and consistent model. Most of the suppliers exhibit consistent score values for the varying values of β. The value $\beta = 0.5$ is determined to be a critical point.

6.7 Industrial Implications

The proposed two-phase fuzzy-based decision-making approach has several industrial implications as this method minimizes the complexity in ranking the suppliers. This integrated method is competent in dealing with the intricate decision environment involving uncertainty and conflicting criteria. This method effectively tackles the challenges in criterion reduction and ranking the alternatives of suppliers. The fusion of ML with MCDM methods offers a more comprehensive solution to the problems of subjectivity of expert's judgments. In the context of healthcare industries, the decision on optimal ranking of the supplier alternatives may not be quantifiable well always with the crisp values. Hence, it is essential to use fuzzy representations to enhance optimality and consistency in ranking results.

With special reference to healthcare context, the quality of supply materials is very significant. The proposed integrated model is highly effective in addressing intricacies caused by conflicting, interdependent criteria. As criterion selection is more critical, the techniques of machine learning minimize the risks in choosing the set of important criteria. The optimal criterion reduction conserves time and energy efficacy which in turn improves functionality of the supplier selection. Furthermore, the methodology of the proposed integrated model is more compatible and adaptable as it scales to the requirements of the industries. Also, this method improves operational efficiency, minimizes costs and promotes the sustainability of the supply chain. On the whole, this integrated framework supports data-driven decision making with more reliable and transparent results facilitating the decision makers in devising optimal policies in supplier selection.

Conclusion

This study discusses a fuzzy-based integrated method of supplier selection associating machine learning and MCDM. The application of this integrated method is applied to healthcare supplier selection. The efficacy of fuzzy-based integrated approach is compared with crisp representations and it is inferred that the fuzzy representations are more compatible and feasible than conventional approach. This proposed decision-making method shall be modified by employing other ML algorithms and MCDM methods. This two-phase integrated approach unveils the development of a new genre decision-making approach of supplier selection. The industrial implications of this research work are more resonating as the proposed model has more competency in handling conflicting criteria and intricate decision-making circumstances.

This research work shall be further explored with the integration of enhanced explainable artificial intelligence approaches to improve transparency and consistency in supplier selections. Furthermore, this research work shall also be extended to handle the real-time data of dynamic supplier environments considering criterion weights and supplier performance over a period of time. The higher order uncertainties shall be dealt with the extension of fuzzy representations to intuitionistic and neutrosophic expressions.

AI disclosure statement: The author confirms that no artificial intelligence (AI)-generated content or AI-assisted writing tools were used in the preparation of this chapter (including summaries and the abstract). All text, analysis, and conclusions are the result of the author's original work.

Bibliography

1. Abbaspour Onari, M. and Jahangoshai Rezaee, M., Implementing bargaining game-based fuzzy cognitive map and mixed-motive games for group decisions in the healthcare supplier selection. *Artif. Intell. Rev.*, *56*, 10, 11739–11772, 2023.
2. Alrasheedi, A.F., Mishra, A.R., Pamucar, D., Devi, S., Cavallaro, F., Interval-valued intuitionistic fuzzy AROMAN method and its application in sustainable wastewater treatment technology selection. *J. Intell. Fuzzy Syst.*, *46*, 3, 7199–7222, 2024.
3. Alrasheedi, A.F., Rani, P., Mishra, A.R., Alshamrani, A.M., Cavallaro, F., Fermatean fuzzy distance and Sugeno–Weber operators-based SPC-MARCOS approach for sustainable supplier evaluation in the healthcare supply chain. *Sci. Rep.*, *14*, 1, 27373, 2024.
4. Anjum, M., Simic, V., Min, H., Kraiem, N., Transformative Pathways to Metaverse Integration in Intelligent Transportation Systems Using Pythagorean Fuzzy CRITIC-AROMAN Method. *IEEE Access*, *12*, 119383–119404, 2024.
5. Bhosale, T. and Umap, H., Evaluation and Selection of Supplier in A Healthcare Supply Chain using Analytic Hierarchy Process under Fuzzy Stochastic Environment. *Aligarh J. Stat.*, *43*, 117–138, 2023.
6. Bhosale, T. and Umap, H., Evaluation and selection of supplier in a healthcare supply chain using TOPSIS under fuzzy environment. *AIP Conf. Proc.*, 2812, 1, 2023, August, AIP Publishing.
7. Bhosale, T. and Umap, H., Evaluating and Selecting a Supplier in a Healthcare Supply Chain Using the Technique for Order Performance by Similarity to Ideal Solution Under Intuitionistic Fuzzy Environment. *Int. J. Fuzzy Log. Intell. Syst.*, *24*, 1, 19–29, 2024.
8. Bhosale, T.S. and Umap, H.P., Evaluation and Selection of Supplier in a Healthcare Supply Chain Using Analytic Hierarchy Process Under Fuzzy Environment. *Int. J. Agric. Stat. Sci.*, *20*, 2, 363–372, 2024.
9. Boz, E., Çizmecioğlu, S., Çalık, A., A novel MDCM approach for sustainable supplier selection in healthcare system in the era of logistics 4.0. *Sustainability*, *14*, 21, 13839, 2022.

10. Cañizares Galarza, F., Neto Mullo, B., Ramos Argilagos, M., Information Fusion from Multimodal Clinical Sensors for Effective Supplier Decision-Making in Healthcare. *Fusion Pract. Appl.*, *14*, 1, 149–157, 2024.
11. Chakraborty, S., Raut, R.D., Rofin, T.M., Chatterjee, S., Chakraborty, S., A comparative analysis of Multi-Attributive Border Approximation Area Comparison (MABAC) model for healthcare supplier selection in fuzzy environments. *Decis. Anal. J.*, *8*, 100290, 2023.
12. Chakraborty, S., Raut, R.D., Rofin, T.M., Chakraborty, S., An integrated G-MACONT approach for healthcare supplier selection. *Grey Syst. Theory Appl.*, *14*, 2, 318–336, 2024.
13. Chakraborty, S., Raut, R.D., Rofin, T.M., Chakraborty, S., On solving a healthcare supplier selection problem using MCDM methods in intuitionistic fuzzy environment. *Opsearch*, *61*, 2, 680–708, 2024.
14. Chen, T., Wang, Y.C., Wu, H.C., Analyzing the impact of vaccine availability on alternative supplier selection amid the covid-19 pandemic: a cFGM-FTOPSIS-FWI approach. *Healthcare (Basel)*, *9*, 1, 71–80, 20212021.
15. Čubranić-Dobrodolac, M., Jovčić, S., Bošković, S., Babić, D., A decision-making model for professional drivers selection: A hybridized fuzzy–AROMAN–Fuller approach. *Mathematics*, *11*, 13, 2831, 2023.
16. Dai, X., Li, H., Zhou, L., Wu, Q., The SMAA-MABAC approach for healthcare supplier selection in belief distribution environment with uncertainties. *Eng. Appl. Artif. Intell.*, *129*, 107654, 2024.
17. Debnath, B., Bari, A.M., Haq, M.M., de Jesus Pacheco, D.A., Khan, M.A., An integrated stepwise weight assessment ratio analysis and weighted aggregated sum product assessment framework for sustainable supplier selection in the healthcare supply chains. *Supply Chain Anal.*, *1*, 100001, 2023.
18. Drousiotis, E., Joyce, D., Varsi, A., Spirakis, P., Maskell, S., Intrinsically Interpretable Decision Trees for Healthcare Applications, 2024, https://doi.org/10.21203/rs.3.rs-4608203/v1.
19. Dündar, S., Evaluation of hands-on entrepreneurship trainings on the basis of provinces, NUTS-I and NUTS-II regions by fuzzy BWM and AROMAN methods. *Pamukkale Üniv. Sos. Bilim. Enst. Derg.*, 61, 371–391, 2024.
20. Fallah, H., Sadigh, A.N., Jolai, F., Risk Analysis for Determining Number of Suppliers and amount of Purchase from each Supplier in Discount Environment with Decision Tree Method. *Asia Pac. Ind. Eng. Manage. Soc.*, 2009.
21. García-Alcaráz, J.L., Maldonado-Macías, A.A., Alor-Hernández, G., García-Alcaraz, P., Jiménez-Macías, E., Supplier Selection in the Healthcare Sector: A Multi-Criteria Proposal, in: *Handbook of Research on Interdisciplinary Approaches to Decision Making for Sustainable Supply Chains*, pp. 652–674, IGI Global Scientific Publishing, 2020.
22. Giri, S., Kumar, S., Roy, M., Dynamic service deployment using JSON based decision trees in remote healthcare, in: *2016 10th International Conference on Intelligent Systems and Control (ISCO)*, pp. 1–6, IEEE, 2016, January.

23. Goh, M., Shuya, Z., de Souza, R., Operational framework for healthcare supplier selection under a fuzzy multi-criteria environment, in: *Symposium on Logistics (ISL 2018) Big Data Enabled Supply Chain Innovations*, 2018.
24. Göncü, K.K. and Çetin, O., A decision model for supplier selection criteria in healthcare enterprises with dematel ANP method. *Sustainability*, *14*, 21, 13912, 2022.
25. Gürol, P., Yurdabak, S., Gül, A.Y., Çakmak, E., Pallet pooling service provider selection with an intuitionistic fuzzy-based AROMAN model. *J. Cleaner Prod.*, 498, 20, 145189, 2025.
26. Harikrishnan, R., Shivdas, A., Ananthu, S., Redefining supplier selection in healthcare sector: a novel framework for supplier classification. *J. Health Organ. Manage.*, 2025, https://doi.org/10.1108/JHOM-05-2024-0189.
27. Hendriks, M.P., Data-driven Decision Support for Multidisciplinary Clinical Decision-making & Reporting in Breast Cancer, University of Twente, 2024.
28. Hu, L., Yu, Q., Jana, C., Simic, V., Bin-Mohsin, B., An Intuitionistic Fuzzy SWARA-AROMAN Decision-Making Framework for Sports Event Management. *IEEE Access*, *12*, 57711–57726, 2024.
29. Ishak, A. and Wijaya, T., Spare part supplier selection model using decision tree classification techniques: J48 Algorithm. *IOP Conf. Ser.: Mater. Sci. Eng.*, 801, 1, 012118, 2020, May, IOP Publishing.
30. Jana, C., Garg, H., Pal, M., Sarkar, B., Wei, G., MABAC framework for logarithmic bipolar fuzzy multiple attribute group decision-making for supplier selection. *Complex Intell. Syst.*, *10*, 1, 273–288, 2024.
31. Kabak, M., Aktas, A., Park, C.S.Y., A Hybrid Supplier Evaluation Model for Personal Protective Equipment Procurement to Healthcare Employees, in: *International Conference on Management Science and Engineering Management*, pp. 596–606, Springer International Publishing, Cham, 2022, July
32. Kara, K., Yalçın, G.C., Simic, V., Yıldırım, A.T., Pamucar, D., Siarry, P., A spherical fuzzy-based DIBR II-AROMAN model for sustainability performance benchmarking of wind energy power plants. *Expert Syst. Appl.*, *253*, 124300, 2024.
33. Karatas, M., Eriskin, L., Deveci, M., Pamucar, D., Garg, H., Big Data for Healthcare Industry 4.0: Applications, challenges and future perspectives. *Expert Syst. Appl.*, *200*, 116912, 2022.
34. Kelarev, A.V., Stranieri, A., Yearwood, J.L., Jelinek, H.F., Empirical study of decision trees and ensemble classifiers for monitoring of diabetes patients in pervasive healthcare, in: *2012 15th International Conference on Network-Based Information Systems*, pp. 441–446, IEEE, 2012, September.
35. Khalil, B., Arayes, M.A., Shehadeh, R., Analytic Hierarchical Process-Based Supplier Selection in Dental Healthcare, 2024, https://hdl.handle.net/20.500.11888/18614.
36. Khan, M.U., Choi, J.P., Shin, H., Kim, M., Predicting breast cancer survivability using fuzzy decision trees for personalized healthcare, in: *2008 30th*

annual international conference of the IEEE engineering in medicine and biology society, pp. 5148–5151, IEEE, 2008, August.

37. Kumari, T., Singh, M., Baranwal, G., Tripathi, A.K., Supplier selection in healthcare using blockchain, in: *2022 IEEE 1st Global Emerging Technology Blockchain Forum: Blockchain & Beyond (iGETblockchain)*, pp. 1–6, IEEE, 2022, November.
38. Kumcu, S. and Özyörük, B., Supplier selection with ahp and 0-1 goal programming: an application in healthcare industry. *Mersin Univ. J. Marit. Fac.*, *2*, 2, 50–61, 2020.
39. Levashenko, V., Zaitseva, E., Kvassay, M., Deserno, T.M., Reliability estimation of healthcare systems using fuzzy decision trees, in: *2016 Federated Conference on Computer Science and Information Systems (FedCSIS)*, pp. 331–340, IEEE, 2016, September.
40. Liang, D., Fu, Y., Garg, H., A novel robustness PROMETHEE method by learning interactive criteria and historical information for blockchain technology-enhanced supplier selection. *Expert Syst. Appl.*, 235, 121107, 2024.
41. Liu, P., Khan, Q., Jamil, A., Haq, I.U., Hussain, F., Ullah, Z., A novel MAGDM technique based on q-rung orthopair fuzzy Aczel-Alsina power Heronian mean for sustainable supplier selection in organ transplantation networks for healthcare devices. *Int. J. Fuzzy Syst.*, *26*, 1, 121–153, 2024.
42. Mahmoudifard, S.M., Shabanpour, R., Golshani, N., Mohammadian, K., Mohammadian, A., Supplier Evaluation Problem, a Decision Tree and an Ordered Probit Analysis on a Freight Establishment Survey, 2017, No. 17-01210.
43. Mohamed, M.F., Eltoukhy, M.M., Al Ruqeishi, K., Salah, A., An adapted multi-objective genetic algorithm for healthcare supplier selection decision. *Mathematics*, *11*, 6, 1537, 2023.
44. Mohamed, M., Elsayed, A., Voskoglou, M., Collaboration of vague theory and mathematical techniques for optimizing healthcare by recommending optimal blockchain supplier. *Sustainable Mach. Intell. J.*, *6*, 5–1, 2024.
45. Nayeri, S., Khoei, M.A., Rouhani-Tazangi, M.R., GhanavatiNejad, M., Rahmani, M., Tirkolaee, E.B., A data-driven model for sustainable and resilient supplier selection and order allocation problem in a responsive supply chain: A case study of healthcare system. *Eng. Appl. Artif. Intell.*, *124*, 106511, 2023.
46. Nikolić, I., Milutinović, J., Božanić, D., Dobrodolac, M., Using an interval type-2 fuzzy AROMAN decision-making method to improve the sustainability of the postal network in rural areas. *Mathematics*, *11*, 14, 3105, 2023.
47. Olteanu, A.L., Ionaşcu, A.E., Cosma, S., Barbu, C.A., Popa, A., Cioroiu, C.G., Goswami, S.S., Prioritizing the European Investment Sectors Based on Different Economic, Social, and Governance Factors Using a Fuzzy-MEREC-AROMAN Decision-Making Model. *Sustainability*, *16*, 17, 7790, 2024.
48. Otay, I., Bulut, B., Barutbaş, K., Arat, A.E., Tekin, E., Gürz, Z.S., A Novel Decision-Making Framework Based on Interval-Valued Pythagorean Fuzzy

AHP and CODAS: An Application to Healthcare Supplier Selection, in: *International Conference on Intelligent and Fuzzy Systems*, pp. 124–132, Springer Nature Switzerland, Cham, 2023, August.

49. Pamucar, D., Torkayesh, A.E., Biswas, S., Supplier selection in healthcare supply chain management during the COVID-19 pandemic: a novel fuzzy rough decision-making approach. *Ann. Oper. Res.*, *328*, 1, 977–1019, 2023.
50. Panwar, N., Kumar, N., Kumar, M.S., Rafeeq, M., Rajeswari, P., Meenakshi, S., AI-Driven Healthcare Infrastructure for Smart Cities Using Privacy Preserved Decision Trees to Secure the Patient Data, in: *2024 15th International Conference on Computing Communication and Networking Technologies (ICCCNT)*, pp. 1–6, IEEE, 2024, June.
51. Pethaperumal, M., Jayakumar, V., Edalatpanah, S.A., Mohideen, A.B.K., Annamalai, S., An enhanced MADM with L q* q-Rung orthopair multi-fuzzy soft set in healthcare supplier selection. *J. Intell. Fuzzy Syst. (Preprint)*, 1–12, 2024.
52. Riaz, M., Qamar, F., Tariq, S., Alsager, K., AI-Driven LOPCOW-AROMAN Framework and Topological Data Analysis Using Circular Intuitionistic Fuzzy Information: Healthcare Supply Chain Innovation. *Mathematics*, *12*, 22, 3593, 2024.
53. Rishabh, R. and Das, K.N., Selection of a Suitable Healthcare Supplier Using AHP and TOPSIS Methods Hybridized in Metaheuristic Environment. *SN Comput. Sci.*, *6*, 2, 1–17, 2025.
54. Rod-Iw, R. and Naenna, T., Medical supplies lot-sizing with supplier selection in Thailand healthcare supply chain sector. *Int. J. Serv. Oper. Manage.*, *42*, 1, 129–150, 2022.
55. Saha, A., Debnath, B.K., Chatterjee, P., Panaiyappan, A.K., Das, S., Anusha, G., Generalized Dombi-based probabilistic hesitant fuzzy consensus reaching model for supplier selection under healthcare supply chain framework. *Eng. Appl. Artif. Intell.*, *133*, 107966, 2024.
56. Salimian, S., Mousavi, S.M., Antucheviciene, J., An interval-valued intuitionistic fuzzy model based on extended VIKOR and MARCOS for sustainable supplier selection in organ transplantation networks for healthcare devices. *Sustainability*, *14*, 7, 3795, 2022.
57. Shahab, S., Anjum, M., Dutta, A.K., Ahmad, S., Gamified approach towards optimizing supplier selection through Pythagorean Fuzzy soft-max aggregation operators for healthcare applications. *AIMS Math.*, *9*, 3, 6738–6771, 2024.
58. Sim, H.K. and Wong, Z.X., Fuzzy Decision Tree Approach for Optimal Supplier Base. *Appl. Mech. Mater.*, *315*, 283–287, 2013.
59. Soni, T., Gupta, D., Dutta, M., Machine Learning in Healthcare: Decision Trees for Asthma Risk Prediction, in: *2024 4th International Conference on Sustainable Expert Systems (ICSES)*, pp. 1211–1214, IEEE, 2024, October.
60. Stević, Z., Pamučar, D., Puška, A., Chatterjee, P., Sustainable supplier selection in healthcare industries using a new MCDM method: Measurement of

alternatives and ranking according to COmpromise solution (MARCOS). *Comput. Ind. Eng.*, *140*, 106231, 2020.

61. Sumrit, D., Supplier selection for vendor-managed inventory in healthcare using fuzzy multi-criteria decision-making approach. *Decis. Sci. Lett.*, *9*, 2, 233–256, 2020.
62. Talib, H.M., Albahri, A.S., Thierry, O.C., Fuzzy decision-making framework for sensitively prioritizing autism patients with moderate emergency level. *Appl. Data Sci. Anal.*, *2023*, 16–41, 2023.
63. Tian, H., Zhang, S., Garg, H., Liu, X., An extended SECA-GDM method considering flexible linguistic scale optimization and its application in occupational health and safety risk assessment. *Alexandria Eng. J.*, *88*, 317–330, 2024.
64. Wang, L., Zong, C., Shao, L., Liu, Z., An improved multi-attribute group decision-making method for selecting the green supplier of community elderly healthcare service. *Front. Energy Res.*, *12*, 1323742, 2024.
65. Wu, D., Supplier selection: A hybrid model using DEA, decision tree and neural network. *Expert Syst. Appl.*, *36*, 5, 9105–9112, 2009.
66. Yazdani, M., Torkayesh, A.E., Chatterjee, P., An integrated decision-making model for supplier evaluation in public healthcare system: the case study of a Spanish hospital. *J. Enterp. Inf. Manage.*, *33*, 5, 965–989, 2020.
67. Zachariah, P., Buenaventura, E.M.S., Liu, J., Cohen, B., Yao, D., Larson, E., 2107. Decision Trees vs. Neural Networks for Supervised Machine Learning-Based Prediction of Healthcare-Associated Urinary Tract Infections, in: *Open Forum Infectious Diseases*, vol. 5, No. Suppl 1, p. S618, 2018, November.

7

Green Supplier Selection Using a Preference Method: Complete Pre-Order and Geometrical Representation Analyses

Lazim Abdullah[1]*, Hazwani Hashim[2], Noor Azzah Awang[3], Norsyahidah Zulkifli[4] and Nor Liyana Amalini Mohd Kamal[5]

[1]*Faculty of Computer Science and Mathematics, Universiti Malaysia Terengganu, Kuala Nerus, Terengganu, Malaysia*
[2]*Faculty of Computer and Mathematical Sciences, Universiti Teknologi MARA (UiTM), Machang, Kelantan, Malaysia*
[3]*Faculty of Computer and Mathematical Sciences, UniversitiTeknologi MARA (UiTM), Shah Alam, Selangor, Malaysia*
[4]*Department of Mathematical Science, Faculty of Science, Universiti Teknologi Malaysia, Skudai, Johor, Malaysia*
[5]*Faculty of Computer and Mathematical Sciences, UniversitiTeknologi MARA (UiTM), Negeri Sembilan Branch, Rembau, Negeri Sembilan, Malaysia*

Abstract
In the past ten years, increasing concern for environmental sustainability has drawn significant interest from both academics and industry professionals toward green supply chain management. Traditionally, most organizations have evaluated supplier performance based on economic criteria such as cost, quality, and delivery. However, concerns have been raised regarding the integration of environmental protection as a key criterion in supplier selection. This paper develops an evaluation framework for green supplier selection using the Preference Ranking Organization Method for Enrichment Evaluation (PROMETHEE) technique. PROMETHEE is employed to determine the weights of green supplier selection criteria, which are characterized by specific preference functions. A semi-structured interview with five decision-makers was conducted to gather expert judgments on the importance of ten green supplier criteria. In this study, an eight-stage PROMETHEE framework, incorporating two symmetrical preference

**Corresponding author*: lazim_m@umt.edu.my

Harish Garg (ed.) Decision Support Systems in Smart Computing: Embracing Uncertainty and Challenges, (181–218) © 2026 Scrivener Publishing LLC

functions, is employed to assess supplier performance across the selected criteria. The analysis determines the most suitable green supplier, with the option having the greatest net flow placed at the top position among the four alternatives. A key novelty of the work is the combined use of several visualization techniques such as the GAIA plane, the network of distances, and the walking weights approach to confirm and strengthen the overall ranking results. These visual and analytical representations consistently affirm the robustness of the selection outcome. The findings highlight the effectiveness of the proposed approach in supporting practical and environmentally conscious supplier selection decisions. However, the results are subject to limitations related to the types of preference functions used and the ambiguity surrounding the conceptualization of green criteria. Future research could explore alternative preference functions and examine their applicability across multiple variables within the broader concept of green in organizational contexts.

Keywords: Supplier selection, decision making, preference function, green criteria, criteria weights

7.1 Introduction

It is generally accepted that economic gains from business activities have increased global prosperity and improved living conditions. However, business activities have also led to the direct and indirect destruction of the environment and the perpetuation of social inequality [1]. Some organizations continue to assert that environmental degradation is not caused by their business operations. Nevertheless, the business landscape today is vastly different from that of the past. Resource constraints, technological proliferation, emerging markets, and disruptive business models are new developments that compel us to reconsider the relationship between business and environmental issues. Many companies have begun to focus on producing green commodities to meet consumers' needs and expectations, aiming to achieve and maintain profitability in the global market [2]. Although increased investment in green products and processes may initially reduce business performance, in the long run, green practices enhance corporate reputation, ultimately enabling a balanced achievement of social, environmental, and economic performance.

There are numerous strategies to strengthen the balance between social, environmental, and economic objectives. Green supply chain management (GSCM) is one such emerging strategy, wherein environmental awareness is embedded within business models. The development of environmental thinking and strategic alignment through GSCM has become a critical task for modern enterprises [3]. Companies offering environmentally friendly goods and services gain additional recognition and competitive advantage. The growing significance of GSCM lies in its ability to foster cooperation among environmentally responsible suppliers for long-term commercial success [4]. Supplier selection is a vital operational activity in building a green supply chain. Organizations expect green suppliers to meet sustainability goals by reducing environmental harm while still supporting economic outcomes. As a result, supplier selection in a green context requires embedding environmental factors into supply chain relationships [5]. This consideration is essential because suppliers play a major role in shaping the overall environmental performance of a company's supply chain [6]. Hence, evaluating suppliers should account for both ecological and financial aspects at the same time [7]. According to Luthra *et al.* [8], six major dimensions of GSCM can be distinguished. These include practices such as green purchasing, sourcing of environmentally friendly raw materials, and eco-oriented product design and development. Additionally, emphasis is also placed on green-oriented manufacturing, environmentally responsible transportation, and sustainable process planning. Collectively, these criteria highlight the complexity of selecting suitable green suppliers. Consequently, the decision process is more accurately viewed as a multi-criteria problem, involving several sustainability dimensions, different supplier options, and the participation of multiple decision-makers [9].

A broad spectrum of multi-criteria decision-making (MCDM) techniques has been adopted in the literature to support green supplier assessment. Recent studies highlight applications of hybrid MABAC [10], fuzzy AHP [11], fuzzy TODIM [12], CODAS [13], Fermatean Fuzzy Schweizer–Sklar operators [14], and the combined TOPSIS-GRA method [15]. These examples underscore the essential role of MCDM approaches in supplier selection research. Among these methods, PROMETHEE has gained attention for its use of preference functions, partial pre-order, and complete pre-order rankings. The method, formally known as the Preference Ranking Organization Method for Enrichment Evaluation, is recognized for being both conceptually straightforward and computationally efficient. Originally introduced by Brans [16] and later enhanced in collaboration with Vincke [17], PROMETHEE has been successfully applied across diverse decision-making contexts such as the regeneration of granular activated carbon [18], assessment of energy efficiency initiatives [19], and analysis of tourism competitiveness [20]. In recent years, numerous PROMETHEE extensions and hybrid models have emerged, underscoring the growing popularity of this approach. According to Balali *et al.* [21], PROMETHEE offers three main advantages: it does not require trade-offs between criteria, it retains a large amount of decision-making information, and it is user-friendly. Its outranking relationships are determined through positive and negative flows derived from pairwise comparisons using preference and indifference thresholds. For typical applications, six types of nonlinear preference functions defined on a range from 0 to 1 constitute exclusive features of PROMETHEE.

A unique aspect of the PROMETHEE method, unlike many other approaches within Multi-Criteria Decision Analysis (MCDA) under the broader MCDM family, is its capacity to convert differences in preferences between alternatives into numerical values using preference functions. The flexibility of employing both linear and non-linear preference functions to capture the nature of these deviations, combined with the growing importance of environmental considerations in supplier evaluation, forms a strong foundation for this research. In this study, the PROMETHEE method is applied using Type IV (Level Preference Function) and Type V (Linear Preference Function with Indifference Area), with the preference functions dynamically selected based on the specific characteristics of each evaluation criterion. These functions are used to construct a comprehensive complete pre-order ranking of green suppliers. Furthermore, geometrical visualization tools such as the GAIA plane, walking weights, and PROMETHEE networks are implemented to provide in-depth insights into the interactions among multiple decision criteria, particularly highlighting the balance between economic and environmental priorities.

The main objectives of this study are:

- To apply Type IV and Type V preference functions in the PROMETHEE method to establish a comprehensive ranking of green suppliers;
- To dynamically select appropriate preference functions based on the nature of the evaluation criteria;
- To utilize geometrical representations (e.g., GAIA plane, walking weights, PROMETHEE networks) to analyze multi-criteria interactions;
- To identify and recognize suppliers that emphasize green practices in supply chain management as part of broader sustainability efforts.

To enhance understanding of the methodological framework, the upcoming section describes the nature and definitions of the preference functions used within PROMETHEE.

7.2 Preference Functions

The PROMETHEE method is particularly suited for decision-making situations that involve multiple, and often conflicting, criteria. Its primary purpose is to establish a preference ranking among the available alternatives. This is achieved by evaluating the differences between alternatives for each criterion using a dedicated preference function. In PROMETHEE, a preference function serves to formalize the degree of deviation between two alternatives with respect to a given criterion.

This section outlines the various types of preference functions employed in PROMETHEE, as these are essential for applying the algorithm. The descriptions are adapted from several key references, including Brans and Vincke [22], Smet and Lidouh [23], and Ozgen *et al.* [24].

Formally, the preference function in PROMETHEE transforms the difference between the performance of alternative a and alternative b on a specific criterion into a value ranging within [0, 1]. A value near zero reflects a state of indifference in the decision maker's judgment, while values closer to one indicate stronger preference. The general categories of preference functions are presented below.

Type I: Usual function

$$p(x) = \begin{cases} 0, & for \quad x \leq 0 \\ 1, & for \quad x > 0 \end{cases}$$

In this type of preference function, indifference between alternatives only happens when $p(a) = p(b)$.

Type II: Quasi function (U-shaped)

$$p(x) = \begin{cases} 0, & for \quad -m \leq x \leq m \\ 1, & for \quad x < -m, x > m \end{cases}$$

If $p(a)$ and $p(b)$ does not exceed m, then a and b are indifferent. In addition, parameter m needs to be found. In type II, it is always used for qualitative criteria.

Type III: Linear preference function

$$p(x) = \begin{cases} 0, x = 0 \\ \frac{x}{m}, -m \le x \le m \\ 1, x > m \\ 1, x < -m \end{cases}$$

The preference intensity increases proportionally and attains strictness at the threshold value *m*. Therefore, the parameter m requires explicit definition.

Type IV: Linear preference and Indifference Area function

$$p(x) = \begin{cases} 0, -q < x < q \\ 0.5, -p < x \le -q, q < x \le p \\ 1, x > p, x < -p \end{cases}$$

Within a certain interval, no distinction is made between alternatives. The Type IV preference function is typically applied when dealing with quantitative criteria.

Type V: Level function

$$\text{Function: } p(x) = \begin{cases} 0, & for \quad -s \le x \le s \\ \frac{x-s}{r-s}, & for \quad s < x \le r, -r \le x < -s \\ 1, & for \quad x > r, x < -r \end{cases}$$

Indifference if the deviation between $p(a)$ and $p(b)$ does not exceed *s*.

Type VI: Gaussian function

$$\text{Function: } p(x) = \begin{cases} 0, & for \quad x = 0 \\ 1 - e^{\frac{x^2}{2\sigma^2}}, & for \quad -\infty < x < +\infty \end{cases}$$

Indifference on the interval (-∞. + ∞).

In the PROMETHEE framework, six preference functions form the foundation, enabling the measurement of score differences between alternatives with respect to each criterion.

7.3 Criteria of Green Suppliers

Evidence from the literature indicates that green supplier selection must be addressed as a MCDM problem, since it requires balancing environmental and economic aspects. For instance, q-rung orthopair fuzzy approaches have been adopted in recent studies to strengthen the decision-making process within green supply chains [25]. Comparable research further confirms that both economic and environmental dimensions are essential when evaluating suppliers [26]. Therefore, determining suitable selection criteria represents a key step in the overall process. This section reviews the criteria most frequently discussed in the green supply chain management literature and explains them in detail.

7.3.1 Cost

When selecting suppliers, cost often emerges as the most influential determinant. Partnering with suitable suppliers contributes to significant cost savings and enhances customer value. Previous research [27] emphasizes that cost is not limited to purchase price alone but also involves transportation, maintenance, energy, inspection, inventory, safety, and holding costs. These elements show that cost can be broken down into several distinct components.

7.3.2 Quality

Ensuring quality is a key managerial responsibility, covering production improvement, goal-setting, and monitoring. Through quality assurance, firms are able to meet customer expectations, make better use of resources, and remain consistent with organizational policies [28]. Within supplier selection, quality has long been regarded as a primary benchmark for assessing performance. Prior studies [29] highlight that this dimension includes aspects such as certification, adherence to standards, and continuous enhancements in quality management methods.

7.3.3 Delivery

Fulfilling customer orders accurately is essential for sustaining competitiveness in today's customer-driven markets. To meet customer expectations, firms must build efficient supply chains supported by reliable suppliers who can deliver the required products or services at the correct time, place, and conditions [30]. This requires solutions to be implemented in real-time. The method of execution of orders consists of two phases. Within the initial section, customers place the order and suppliers deliver the products within the final section. The time between receipts for goods was defined as the time of order performance [31]. The delivery was accepted for the choice of green suppliers and contains the prevalence of demand that reflects the strength of the business association between customer and supplier. Secondly, the result of the purchase requirement fee, which was a potential response from the supplier, was seen as sufficient for purchase deliveries due to the desires of the purchaser at the service level. In conclusion, for the selection of suppliers the period and set-up are accepted as necessary [29].

7.3.4 Services

In the modern competitive business landscape, companies are pressured to deliver products that meet high quality standards while remaining cost-effective. Service-related performance is strongly influenced by factors such as response speed, inventory efficiency, and design flexibility, which collectively determine the overall level of customer service. Supply chains contribute to customer satisfaction by emphasizing objectives like on-time delivery, reduced operational costs, lower waste, rapid adaptability, high productivity, streamlined stock levels, minimized errors and damages, and motivated staff. Among these aspects, quick responsiveness is often regarded as the most decisive element, since firms must continuously adjust to the dynamic and diverse needs of their customers [7].

Service quality has become a fundamental concern in industries that rely heavily on customer interaction. As a result, the evaluation of service often includes responsiveness, stock management, and design capacity as key dimensions. To remain competitive, organizations must identify shifting consumer demands and establish reliable inventory systems capable of handling uncertainties in the marketplace [32]. Moreover, suppliers are expected to enhance service delivery through the development of effective and well-structured distribution channels.

7.3.5 Environmental Management System

In recent years, environmental considerations have become an integral part of procurement practices. Growing awareness of ecological issues, coupled with the adverse effects of industrial production, has led consumers to place greater emphasis on sustainability when evaluating companies. As a result, many buyers now expect their suppliers to implement robust Environmental Management Systems (EMS) [33]. Standards and certifications related to environmental management have therefore emerged as essential evaluation criteria. This aspect is particularly important since customers increasingly demand that suppliers demonstrate effective and responsible application of EMS in their operations [34].

7.3.6 Pollution Control

Pollution control was a crucial factor that needed to be implemented in order to persuade the supplier to choose. More businesses prefer to work with suppliers who have unique values. The supplier's attitude toward pollution will determine how well it cooperates [35]. Solid waste is the solid waste disposed of in the environment and causes pollution. Associated with the negative impact of pollution, solid waste management systems were produced by countries, municipalities, companies and humans. The improper removal of solid waste leads to health, atmosphere, resources, economy, and aesthetics being injured. It was therefore obligatory to control and control waste through certain programs and directives [36]. Pollution control was well accustomed to developing it. The first was solid waste, which refers to solid wastes ready for pollution and which want to be controlled in line with the rules [37]. The second was energy consumption, taking into account the growing energy requirements, but it was expensive for businesses. Programs that meet the criterion of the correct use of energy consumption should therefore be encouraged by the suppliers [38]. The ultimate criterion was to avoid the use of harmful material.

7.3.7 Green Packaging

Supplier selection also depends on the compatibility of production equipment and technological capacity. Advanced machinery allows for the achievement of both high-quality standards and large-scale output. In addition, suppliers are expected to demonstrate strong analytical and development capabilities, including the ability to design new products that align with the company's present as well as future requirements [39]. It is equally important that suppliers continuously enhance their technological capabilities to address evolving customer needs [3].

7.3.8 Technology

The selection of suppliers requires production machinery and technology compatibility. The extremely advanced instrumentation enables top quality and product quantity to be produced. The analytical and development potential as well as the supplier's new product design are also necessary to meet the company's current and future demand [40]. Suppliers should be able to build their technology for the customer's present and future demands [3].

7.3.9 Production Capacity

Capacity was described in the context of production because the highest production rate and production capability were also described. Capacity to raise concerns about all resources and factors affecting a manufacturer's power to offer instruments, work, space, and time in conjunction with a range of shifts. The result of the capacity design was an investment strategy with capacity utilization, which supports optimal policies that attempt and attempt to change, while taking into account the different operating objectives and constraints of the system [41]. Production capacity was the quantity of product the supplier can supply between single units of time [42].

7.3.10 Strategic Alliance

In today's highly dynamic global markets, strategic alliances are essential for competitive success. The term 'Strategic Alliance' was now frequently used to refer to an arrangement between two or more independent businesses to collaborate on a single economic endeavor. Strategic alliances have evolved and spread across companies as a cross-organizational structure. The strategic alliance was mainly based on improving its ambitious positioning, achieving a recent demand approach, building on key capacities, and sharing the opportunity and value of critical development projects [43]. The strategic alliance was that the definitive important criteria within the criteria set to illustrate the vital relationship with suppliers for a short and long time. The objective of this criterion was to determine an important and useful relationship between suppliers and companies in order to boost their competitiveness and also to reduce the value parameter as many processes are complex. To achieve these objectives, the key criterion was divided into several aspects: readiness to exchange information, capacity to distribute both risks and benefits, recognition of shared goals and corporate activities, the ability to establish sustainable partnerships, and finally, the alignment of culture and business policies [29].

This list of criteria is not exhaustive, but it includes the green aspect in the selection. In this research, these criteria are part of the variables in the framework of the decision using the PROMETHEE approach. Details of the experiment are presented in the following section.

7.4 Methodology

This section is concerned with the methodology used for this study. Four subsections are presented which are decision makers, alternatives and criteria, linguistic data collection and evaluation model.

7.4.1 Decision Makers

In this study, two apparel companies were chosen as the subjects where decision makers are invited to make evaluation. These companies are the companies that offer a variety range of natural clothing, design, and services to consumers. Besides, high attention is paid to ensuring every product sold is a truly natural product. This is commonly recognized to be a more environmentally friendly product when compared to synthetics. Natural products are comfy to wear and good for the environment. They are a sustainable resource and can be used without depleting or damaging the environment as they are renewable, biodegradable, and carbon neutral. Two senior managers, one manager, and two supervisors from two companies were identified as decision makers that can provide evaluations about criteria and alternatives of this study. The actual names of the companies are withheld to ensure privacy protection. Detailed descriptions of decision makers are given in Table 7.1.

Table 7.1 Biographical data of decision makers.

Decision maker	Designation	Years of experience	Company
D_1	Senior Manager	12	Marconco Enterprise
D_2	Supervisor	5	Marconco Enterprise
D_3	Senior Manager	6	Bossy Enterprise
D_4	General Manager	10	Bossy Enterprise
D_5	Supervisor	5	Bossy Enterprise

Table 7.2 Five-point Likert scales.

Rating	Weight of criteria
1	Negligible
2	Minor
3	Moderate
4	Significant
5	Crucial

The decision-makers participated in informal interviews that were structured around a questionnaire. This questionnaire consisted of two sections: the first gathered information on the weighting of the criteria, while the second focused on assessing each supplier. All criteria were rated using a five-point Likert scale, as illustrated in Table 7.2.

7.4.2 Alternatives and Criteria

The alternatives considered in this study represent different suppliers. Among them, Supplier A_1, A_2, A_3 and A_4 operates as a fabric manufacturing company. Supplier A_1 which is a fabric manufacturing company. This company offers several types of fabric such as cotton, synthetic, rayon, linen, silk, wool, and others. Supplier A_2 which is a thread manufacturing company. The wide variety of thread like synthetic thread, silk thread and

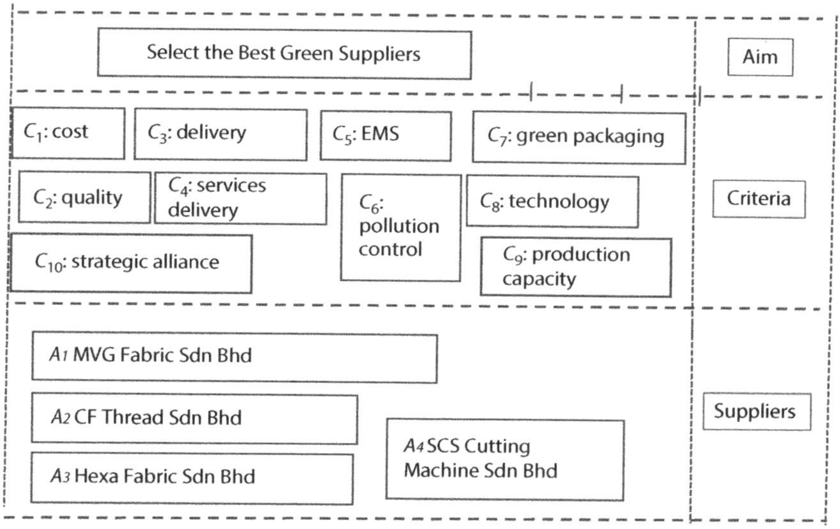

Figure 7.1 Criteria and alternatives of green supplier selection.

organic thread. Supplier A_3, which is a fabric coloring manufacturer. They provide high-quality chemical dyeing and natural dyeing. Finally, supplier A_4 is cutting machine manufacturing company. They provide custom-engineered solutions and innovative technologies that improve production and efficiency by getting the most out of each resource besides reducing the usage of electricity and keeping the environment safe. The actual names of these suppliers are withheld to ensure privacy protection. Besides the alternatives, this study also defines ten criteria. The criteria are C_1: cost, C_2: quality, C_3: delivery, C_4: service, C_5: EMS, C_6: pollution control, C_7: green packaging, C_8: technology, C_9: production capacity, C_{10}: strategic alliance. The hierarchical structure of the decision problem which consists of aim, criteria, and alternatives is shown in Figure 7.1.

7.4.3 Data Collection

In this research, the evaluation data are obtained from semi-structured interview with a group of five decision makers. They provide rating on the importance of criteria using the five-point Likert scale (see Table 7.2). The ratings of criteria are summarized in Table 7.3.

Decision-makers are also tasked with assessing the significance of suppliers based on specific criteria. The supplier ratings for each criterion are summarized in Table 7.4.

Table 7.3 Ratings of criteria.

Criteria	D_1	D_2	D_3	D_4	D_5
C_1	3	4	4	5	4
C_2	2	4	3	5	4
C_3	4	3	5	2	3
C_4	4	4	3	3	5
C_5	3	4	3	3	4
C_6	4	3	4	4	3
C_7	4	2	4	3	4
C_8	3	4	3	2	3
C_9	4	3	3	3	3
C_{10}	4	3	4	3	3

The information in Table 7.3 and Table 7.4 is the input data for the PROMETHEE method. The computational procedures of PROMETHEE method are given in the following section.

7.4.4 Evaluation Model: PROMETHEE Method

The computational procedures of PROMETHEE method begin with evaluation on criteria rather than alternatives. In essence, this evaluation requires numerical data in which relative importance of criteria is provided by decision makers. The computational procedures of PROMETHEE are presented as follows.

Step 1: Define set of criteria $j=\{1,\ldots, s\}$ and a finite alternatives m, in a decision problem.
Step 2: Determine the relative weight of each criterion. These weights reflect their comparative importance, with the requirement that their total must equal 1.
Step 3: Equation (7.1) was used to compute the aggregated decision matrix.

$$R_{ij} = \frac{|X_{ij} - \min(X_{ij})|}{[\max(X_{ij}) - \min(X_{ij})]} \tag{7.1}$$

Table 7.4 Rating of suppliers.

		Decision maker							Decision maker				
Criteria	**Supplier**	D_1	D_2	D_3	D_1	D_2	**Criteria**	**Supplier**	D_1	D_2	D_3	D_1	D_2
C_1	A_1	4	3	4	3	4	C_6	A_1	3	2	3	4	3
	A_2	4	3	2	3	4		A_2	4	5	3	3	4
	A_3	3	4	4	3	3		A_3	5	3	3	3	4
	A_4	3	4	2	5	3		A_4	4	3	3	4	2
C_2	A_1	2	4	3	4	2	C_7	A_1	4	2	3	4	3
	A_2	3	3	4	3	4		A_2	4	4	5	2	3
	A_3	3	4	4	3	3		A_3	3	3	4	4	2
	A_4	4	3	4	3	3		A_4	2	5	4	2	3
C_3	A_1	2	4	4	4	3	C_8	A_1	3	3	5	3	3
	A_2	4	3	5	4	2		A_2	3	3	3	2	3
	A_3	4	4	3	3	2		A_3	4	2	3	4	3
	A_4	3	2	3	4	4		A_4	4	4	2	4	4
C_4	A_1	4	4	2	4	4	C_9	A_1	4	3	3	3	5
	A_2	3	4	3	3	4		A_2	3	4	4	3	3
	A_3	2	3	4	2	3		A_3	2	3	4	4	2
	A_4	4	4	3	2	2		A_4	4	3	3	2	3
C_5	A_1	4	3	4	2	4	C_{10}	A_1	3	2	4	4	4
	A_2	5	4	3	3	4		A_2	4	3	3	2	3
	A_3	4	4	5	3	4		A_3	2	4	2	4	3
	A_4	2	3	2	2	3		A_4	4	3	3	2	3

In this expression, the symbol X_{ij} refers to the assessment given by decision maker where i ranges from 1 to n for criterion where j ranges from 1 to s.

Calculate the average of weight using Equation (7.2).

$$\text{Average weight} = \frac{\sum_{i=0}^{m} C_{ji}}{m} \tag{7.2}$$

and the averaged rating using Equation (7.3).

$$\text{Averaged rating} = \frac{\sum_{i=1}^{m} R_{ji}}{m} \tag{7.3}$$

Step 4: For any pair of alternatives, the deviation relative to each criterion can be written as:

$$d_j(a,b) = m_j(a) - m_j(b) \tag{7.4}$$

In this step, the score gap between alternative a and alternative b is calculated for each criterion considered.

Step 5: The preference function $P_j(a,b) = F_j[d_j(a,b)]$ is defined to map the difference $P_j(a,b)$ between alternatives on a given criterion into a degree of preference between 0 and 1. A smaller value signals indifference, while a larger value indicates a stronger preference. PROMETHEE offers six forms of preference functions, and in this research, the linear and level symmetric types are applied.

Step 6: Calculate the aggregated preference using Equation (7.5)

$$\pi(a,b) = \sum_{k=1}^{n} P(a,b) \times w_k] / \sum_{k=1}^{n} w_k \tag{7.5}$$

where $w_j > 0$ represents the weight given to each condition. The sign $\pi(a,b)$ indicates that out of all the criteria, degree of a n is chosen over b.

IF $\pi(a,b) \approx 0$ indicates a tenuous preference for a over b.

$\pi(a,b) \approx 1$ suggests that a strongly prefers b to b.

Step 7: Attain the preference order.
Pre-orders may be placed in part or in whole during this step. PROMETHEE I can be used to secure a partial pre-order. The computation must move on to a number of additional phases in PROMETHEE II if a complete pre-order is required. The additional steps are listed as follows in PROMETHEE II,

Step 7(a): Each alternative is assessed in terms of two types of outranking flows:

- The leaving flow (also referred to as the positive flow) represents the average strength by which an alternative a^{th} surpasses others:

$$\phi^{-(a)} \tag{7.6}$$

- The entering flow (or negative flow) measures the extent to which the same alternative a^{th} is outperformed by others:

$$\phi^{+(a)} \tag{7.7}$$

Step 7(b): For each alternative, the net flow is obtained by subtracting the entering flow from the leaving flow, and this value acts as the key basis for ranking.

$$\phi(a)=\phi^{+(a)}-\phi^{-(a)} \tag{7.8}$$

Step 7(c): Determine the pre-order of alternatives.
A higher value of the outgoing (leaving) flow combined with a lower incoming (entering) flow indicates a superior performing alternative. These results can be represented either through a partial ranking (PROMETHEE I) or a complete ranking (PROMETHEE II).

In PROMETHEE I, alternative a is considered superior to alternative b when at least one of the following conditions is fulfilled [44–46]:

Alternative a is preferred to outrank alternatives b, a Pb)

$$\begin{aligned} a\,\mathrm{P}b \text{ if} : \Phi^{+}(a) > \Phi^{+}(b) \text{ and } \Phi^{-}(a) < \Phi^{-}(b) \text{ or} \\ \Phi^{+}(a) > \Phi^{+}(\mathrm{b}) \text{ and } \Phi^{-}(a) = \Phi^{-}(\mathrm{b}) \text{ or} \\ \Phi^{+}(a) = \Phi^{+}(\mathrm{b}) \text{ and } \Phi^{-}(a) < \Phi^{-}(\mathrm{b}). \end{aligned}$$

Indifference situation

$$aPb \text{ if}: \Phi^+(a) = \Phi^+(b) \text{ and } \Phi^-(a) = \Phi^-(b)$$

Incomparable situation

$$aRb \text{ if}: \Phi^+(a) > \Phi^+(b) \text{ and } \Phi^-(a) > \Phi^-(b) \text{ or}$$
$$\Phi^+(a) < \Phi^+(\mathrm{b}) \text{ and } \Phi^-(a) < \Phi^-(\mathrm{b})$$

In addition, PROMETHEE II provides a complete pre-order. Outranking based on net flow for each alternative can be found using Equation (7.8). $\Phi(a)$ denotes the net flow. The complete pre-orders of the alternatives can avoid incomparability. In the case where a larger net flow for alternative a as compared to alternative b, means that alternative a outranks alternative b.

7.4.5 Preference Function

In Step 5 of the above computational procedures, preference function must be defined. This function represents the difference between evaluation of an alternative and another alternative with respect to each criterion. This difference is converted into a degree of 0 to 1. In this research two types of symmetrical preference functions are used. The functions are level function (Type IV) and linear preference and indifference area function (Type V). Detailed of these symmetrical functions are explained as below.

i. Type IV: Level Preference Function.
   In this function, the difference is given into three values. It could be 0, $\frac{1}{2}$, or 1.

The graph of the function is shown in Figure 7.2.

For the Type IV preference function, indifference is defined within the interval [-*r*, *r*]. This function is typically applied to quantitative criteria and is characterized by its symmetry with respect to the y-axis.

ii. Type V: Linear Preference and Indifference Area Function
   The difference is given into three values subjected to the values of threshold p. The value of a threshold of indifference is q. This function is presented in Figure 7.3.

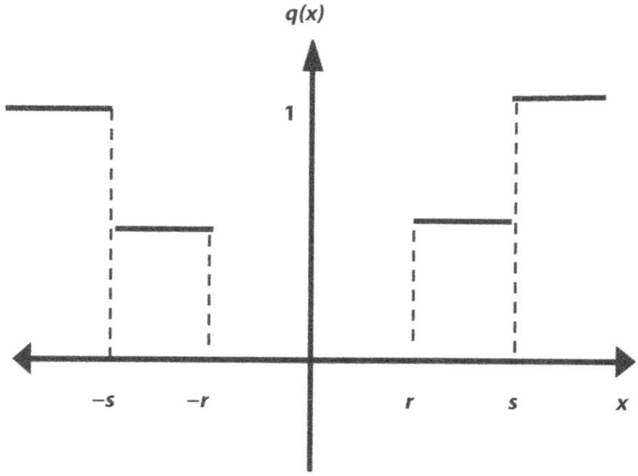

Figure 7.2 Type IV – level function.

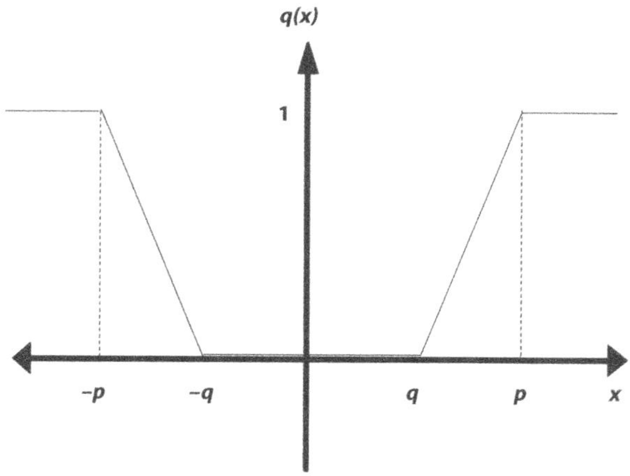

Figure 7.3 Type V – linear preference and indifference area function.

Indifference if the deviation $q(a)$ and $q(b)$ does not exceed q. Similar with Type IV, this preference function is also symmetrical about the y-axis.

The evaluations of criteria against four companies are being used as input data to the PROMETHEE method. Next section explains detailed computational implementation for the case of green supplier selection.

7.5 Implementation

The preference function is used to express the difference between one alternative and another. In the PROMETHEE approach, the linear and level preference functions were selected because they align well with the nature of the evaluation criteria. For example, quantitative measures such as cost and timely delivery are better captured through the linear preference function. On the other hand, qualitative aspects like product quality are more appropriately handled using the level preference function, particularly when the criteria are few and distinct.

To handle the green supplier evaluation, this work adopts the Type V linear preference function incorporating zones of indifference and preference together with the Type IV level preference function. The computational procedures are outlined below.

Step 1: The weights of criteria are computed by considering all the decision maker's opinion. The ratings given by the decision makers need to be normalized into [0, 1] using Equation (7.1). Simple fractions are calculated first.

$$\text{Fraction}, k_i = \frac{x_i}{totalweight}$$

$$\text{For example, } D_1,\ C_1: k_1 = \frac{3-1}{5-1} = 0.5,\ C_2: k_2 = \frac{2-1}{5-1} = 0.25, ..,$$

$$C_{10}: k_{10} = \frac{4-1}{5-1} = 0.75$$

$$C_1: F_1 = \frac{0.5}{0.5+0.25+...+0.75} = 0.08,\ C_2: F_2 = 0.04, ...,\ C_{10}: F_{10} = 0.12$$

The remaining parts of the calculation are iterated similarly. The fraction data are shown in Table 7.5.

Normalized data of each criterion are presented in Table 7.6.

Table 7.5 Fraction of criteria.

Criteria	D_1	D_2	D_3	D_4	D_5
C_1	0.5	0.75	0.75	1	0.75
C_2	0.25	0.75	0.5	1	0.75
C_3	0.75	0.5	1	0.25	0.5
C_4	0.75	0.75	0.5	0.5	1
C_5	0.5	0.75	0.5	0.5	0.75
C_6	0.75	0.5	0.75	0.75	0.5
C_7	0.75	0.25	0.75	0.5	0.75
C_8	0.5	0.75	0.5	0.25	0.5
C_9	0.75	0.5	0.5	0.5	0.5
C_{10}	0.75	0.5	0.75	0.5	0.5

Table 7.6 Normalized data of criteria.

Criteria	D_1	D_2	D_3	D_4	D_5
C_1	0.08	0.125	0.115385	0.173913	0.115385
C_2	0.04	0.125	0.076923	0.173913	0.115385
C_3	0.12	0.083333	0.153846	0.043478	0.076923
C_4	0.12	0.125	0.076923	0.086957	0.153846
C_5	0.08	0.125	0.076923	0.086957	0.115385
C_6	0.12	0.083333	0.115385	0.130435	0.076923
C_7	0.12	0.041667	0.115385	0.086957	0.115385
C_8	0.08	0.125	0.076923	0.043478	0.076923
C_9	0.12	0.083333	0.076923	0.086957	0.076923
C_{10}	0.12	0.083333	0.115385	0.086957	0.076923

Table 7.7 Weight of criteria.

Criteria	Aggregate weight
C_1	0.12193645
C_2	0.10624415
C_3	0.09551616
C_4	0.11254515
C_5	0.09685284
C_6	0.10521516
C_7	0.09587848
C_8	0.08046488
C_9	0.0888272
C_{10}	0.09651951

Step 2: The weight of criteria is calculated using Equation (7.2). The criterion aggregated weights are shown in Table 7.7.

Step 3: Aggregate rating of suppliers
Supplier ratings were obtained using the averaging approach (refer to Equation (7.3)) followed by normalization as shown in Equation (7.1). The assessment results of the four suppliers in relation to the criteria are summarized in Table 7.8.

Step 4: Compute the criterion-wise difference between the two alternatives. In this step, the deviations of A_i with respect to other suppliers are computed. These values denote the differences between two different alternatives and are computed using Equation (7.4). The summarized deviations are presented in Table 7.9.

Step 5: Selection of preference function
The choice of a preference function depends on the nature of the criteria being assessed. For this research, the linear preference function with an

Table 7.8 Evaluation of suppliers based on the defined criteria.

Criteria	A_1	A_2	A_3	A_4
C_1	0.65	0.55	0.6	0.6
C_2	0.5	0.6	0.6	0.6
C_3	0.6	0.65	0.55	0.55
C_4	0.65	0.6	0.45	0.5
C_5	0.6	0.7	0.75	0.35
C_6	0.5	0.7	0.65	0.55
C_7	0.55	0.65	0.55	0.55
C_8	0.6	0.45	0.55	0.65
C_9	0.65	0.6	0.5	0.5
C_{10}	0.6	0.5	0.5	0.5

indifference threshold (Type V) and the level preference function (Type IV) were identified as the most suitable options.

Both linear and level functions incorporate indifference and preference thresholds. The indifference threshold (q) defines the maximum value below which no preference is given to one supplier over another. Conversely, the preference threshold (p) represents the minimum value beyond which full preference is established. Table 7.10 presents the criteria along with the corresponding preference function types and the threshold values.

In this study, the values of the thresholds were defined as $p = 0.1$ and $q = 0.05$.

Table 7.11 presents the value of preference function after considering type of functions and threshold values.

Table 7.9 Difference between two candidate suppliers across the criteria.

Suppliers	Criteria									
	C_1	C_2	C_3	C_4	C_5	C_6	C_7	C_8	C_9	C_{10}
A_1A_2	0.1	-0.1	-0.05	0.05	-0.1	-0.2	-0.1	0.15	0.05	0.1
A_1A_3	0.05	-0.1	0.05	0.2	-0.15	-0.15	0	0.05	0.15	0.1
A_1A_4	0.05	-0.1	0.05	0.15	0.25	-0.05	0	-0.05	0.15	0.1
A_2A_1	-0.1	0.1	0.05	-0.05	0.1	0.2	0.1	-0.15	-0.05	-0.1
A_2A_3	-0.05	0	0.1	0.15	-0.05	0.05	0.1	-0.1	0.1	0
A_2A_4	-0.05	0	0.1	0.1	0.35	0.15	0.1	-0.2	0.1	0
A_3A_1	-0.05	0.1	-0.05	-0.2	0.15	0.15	0	-0.05	-0.15	-0.1
A_3A_2	0.05	0	-0.1	-0.15	0.05	-0.05	-0.1	0.1	-0.1	0
A_3A_4	0	0	0	-0.05	0.4	0.1	0	-0.1	0	0
A_4A_1	-0.05	0.1	-0.05	-0.15	-0.25	0.05	0	0.05	-0.15	-0.1
A_4A_2	0.05	0	-0.1	-0.1	-0.35	-0.15	-0.1	0.2	-0.1	0
A_4A_3	0	0	0	0.05	-0.4	-0.1	0	0.1	0	0

Step 6: Compute the preference index.
The indices are computed using Equation (7.5). For example,

$$\pi(A_1, A_2) = \sum_{j=1}^{10} \begin{matrix} (1*0.1219365 + 0*0.1062441 + 0*0.0955162 + 0*0.1125452 + \\ 0*0.0968528 + 0*0.10521520 + 0*0.0958785 + 1*0.0804649 + \\ 0*0.0888272 + 0.5*0.0965195) \end{matrix}$$
$$= 0.250661$$

Table 7.10 Preference function types and their associated criteria.

Criteria	Type of preference function
C_1	V
C_2	IV
C_3	IV
C_4	IV
C_5	IV
C_6	IV
C_7	IV
C_8	IV
C_9	IV
C_{10}	IV

The preference indices are summarized in Table 7.12.

Step 7: Determine the incoming (negative) and outgoing (positive) outranking flows.

These values are derived from Equation (7.6) for the positive flow and Equation (7.7) for the negative flow. Table 7.13 summarizes the positive outranking values and negative outranking values for suppliers.

Using PROMETHEE I (partial pre-order) method, the partial pre-order of a$P^{(I)}$b is

$A_1P^{(I)}\ A_4$, $A_2P^{(I)}\ A_1$, $A_2P^{(I)}\ A_3$, $A_2P^{(I)}\ A_4$ and $A_3P^{(I)}\ A_4$. This partial pre-order can be depicted in Figure 7.4.

Step 8: Determine the net outranking flow (PROMETHEE II) and complete pre-order.

The net flow values are calculated using Equation (7.8). Table 7.14 presents the net flow values for supplier.

Table 7.11 Value of preference function.

Deviation of suppliers	Criteria									
	C_1	C_2	C_3	C_4	C_5	C_6	C_7	C_8	C_9	C_{10}
A_1A_2	1	0	0	0	0	0	0	1	0	0.5
A_1A_3	0	0	0	1	0	0	0	0	1	0.5
A_1A_4	0	0	0	1	1	0	0	0	1	0.5
A_2A_1	0	0.5	0	0	0.5	1	0.5	0	0	0
A_2A_3	0	0	0.5	1	0	0	0.5	0	0.5	0
A_2A_4	0	0	0.5	0	1	1	0.5	0	0.5	0
A_3A_1	0	0.5	0	0	1	1	0	0	0	0
A_3A_2	0	0	0	0	0.5	0	0	0.5	0	0
A_3A_4	1	0	0	0	1	0.5	0	0	0	0
A_4A_1	0	0.5	0	0	0	0	0	0	0	0
A_4A_2	0	0	0	0	0	0	0	1	0	0
A_4A_3	0	0	0	0	0	0	0	0.5	0	0

Table 7.12 Preference index.

Suppliers	A_1	A_2	A_3	A_4
A_1		0.250661	0.249632	0.346485
A_2	0.2547029		0.252656	0.342179
A_3	0.25519008	0.088659		0.271397
A_4	0.05312207	0.080465	0.040232	

Table 7.13 PROMETHEE I flow.

Suppliers	$\varphi^{+}(A_i)$	$\varphi^{-}(A_i)$
A_1	0.28225938	0.187672
A_2	0.2831793	0.139928
A_3	0.20508194	0.18084
A_4	0.0579398	0.32002

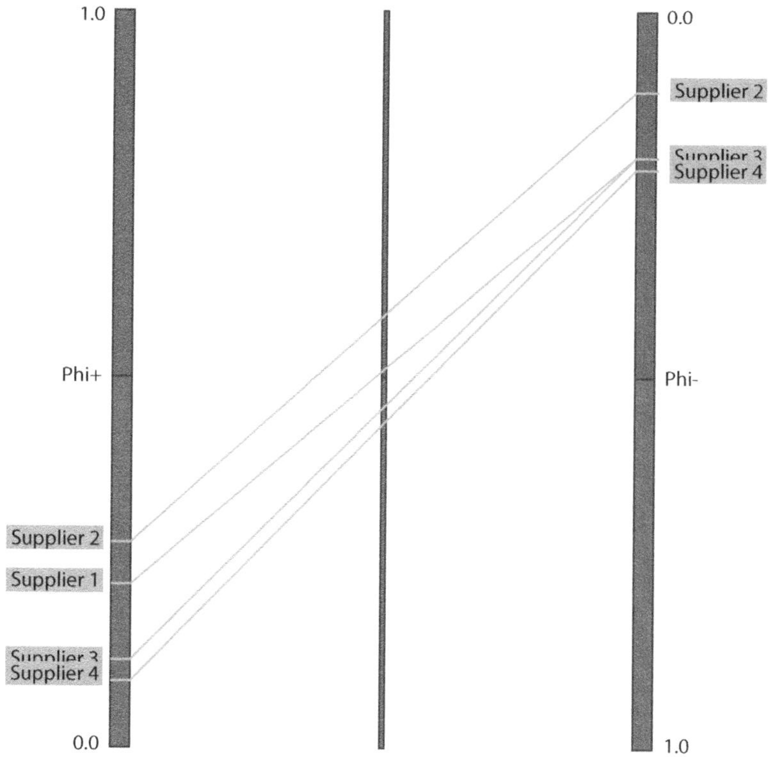

Figure 7.4 PROMETHEE I partial pre-order.

Table 7.14 Net flow values and pre-order of suppliers.

Suppliers	Net flow	Pre-order
A_1	0.0945877	2
A_2	0.14325102	1
A_3	0.02424173	3
A_4	-0.2620805	4

The results indicate that Supplier A_2 a thread manufacturing company, ranks as the top supplier based on the combination of Type IV and Type V preference functions within the PROMETHEE evaluation model. This supplier is followed by A_1, A_3, and A_4. The complete pre-order ranking is visually represented in Figure 7.5.

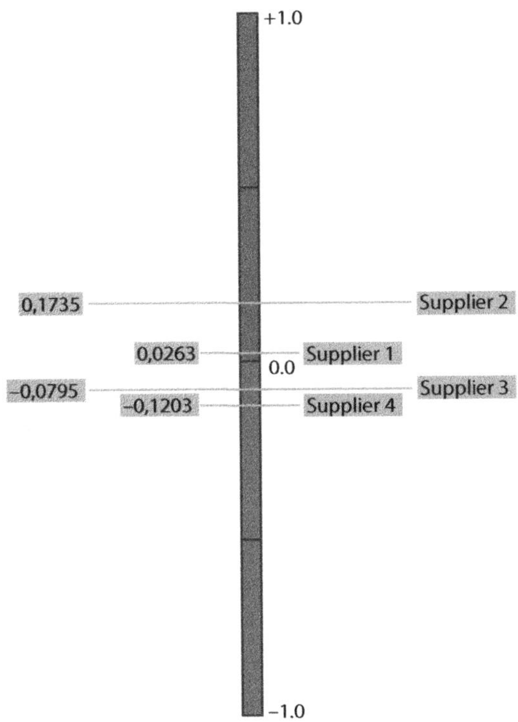

Figure 7.5 PROMETHEE II complete pre-order.

It is evident that Supplier 2 is above all the suppliers of which indicated that this supplier has a cut in practicing green features in manufacturing. Further evidence on the results is presented in the next section.

7.6 Geometrical Representations

Outranking result is used to identify the order of importance of the suppliers. However, this result is somewhat failed to see the performance of suppliers against one benchmark supplier. As to support the complete pre-order results, further geometrical representation analyses are made. The first analysis is the GAIA plane followed by PROMETHEE network and Walking weights to end these analyses. These geometrical representations are useful tools for analyzing conflicts between the criteria. Mareschal and Brans [46] highlight that representing actions and criteria on a two-dimensional plane offers valuable insights to decision makers in analyzing the problem. Such a graphical representation enables them to verify the consistency of preferences and ensures the reliability of the evaluation process.

7.6.1 Graphical Analysis for Interactive Aid (GAIA) Plane

The GAIA plane provides a visual tool that highlights the similarities among suppliers as well as their respective strengths and weaknesses. In this representation, criteria are illustrated as vectors (lines), while the alternatives or suppliers are depicted as points within the plane. Figure 7.6 shows the plane where strengths and weaknesses between them can be interpreted.

The arrangement of criteria within the GAIA plane makes it possible to assess the level of agreement among them and provides deeper insights into the competitive environment. We can see that there are two categories of requirements for green suppliers: the first category includes the production capacity, service, and delivery requirements. They all have the same length, meaning they have similar power of discrimination. The second group of criteria for green suppliers includes green packaging, pollution control, environmental management system, and cost. It can be seen that the line of 'cost' is shorter, which means that the latter has less influence than the former. Supplier A_2 not only secures the top rank but also stands out distinctly from the other suppliers. Its strong performance is attributed to the second category of green supplier requirements, namely green packaging, environmental management programs, pollution control, and cost

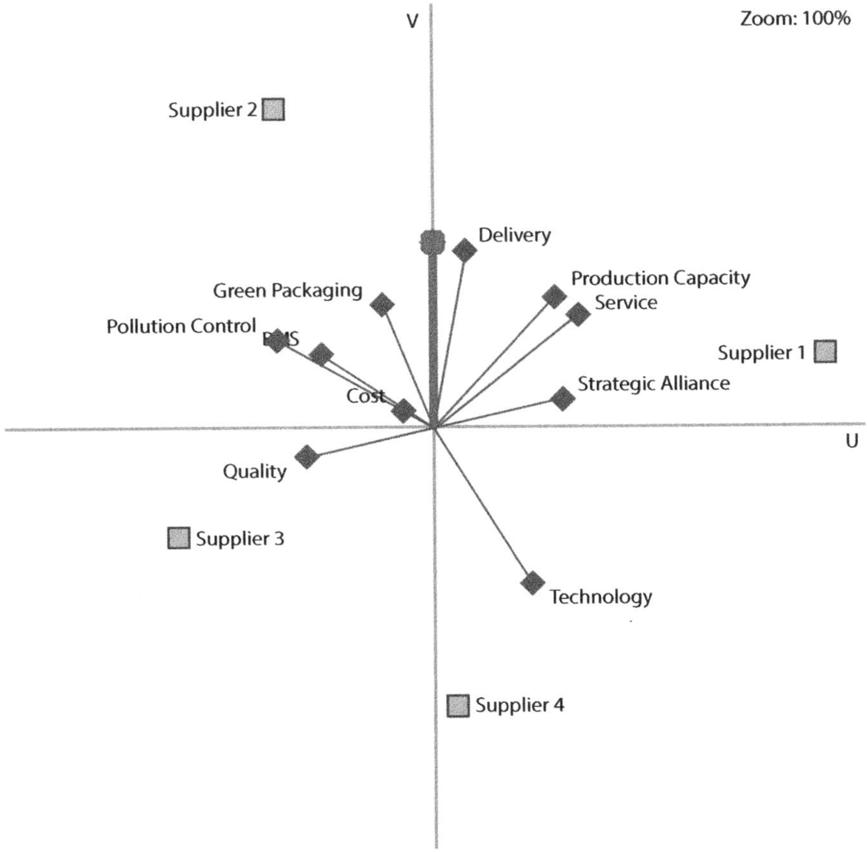

Figure 7.6 GAIA plane.

efficiency. However, it shows weaknesses in strategic alliances and technological capacity. The second-ranked supplier in the pre-order also demonstrates a stable position, performing strongly in all management-related indicators but weaker in climate-related aspects. The most significant drawback for this supplier lies in its lack of product consistency.

7.6.2 PROMETHEE Network

The results can also be shown in the form of a network of which the distance between green suppliers can be visualized and also indicates the direction of preference flow. Figure 7.7 shows the distances between suppliers and also direction of influences.

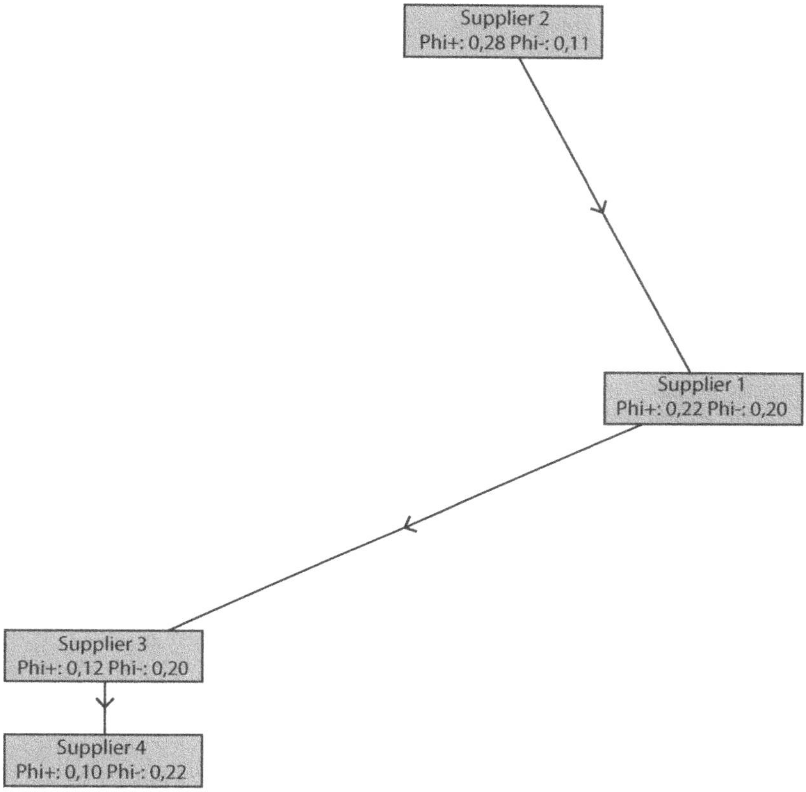

Figure 7.7 PROMETHEE network.

Supplier A_2 is identified as the top-performing supplier, as it exerts influence over the remaining suppliers. It is surprising to see there are not many differences for supplier A_3 and supplier A_4 in terms of their distance. This indicates that these two suppliers shared almost the similar performance.

7.6.3 Walking Weights

Weights of criteria play a significant role and would bring significant impacts to the results. The Walking Weights, a feature to allow weights to be adjusted and would impact the pre-order. Figure 7.8 shows the walking weights of PROMETHEE II.

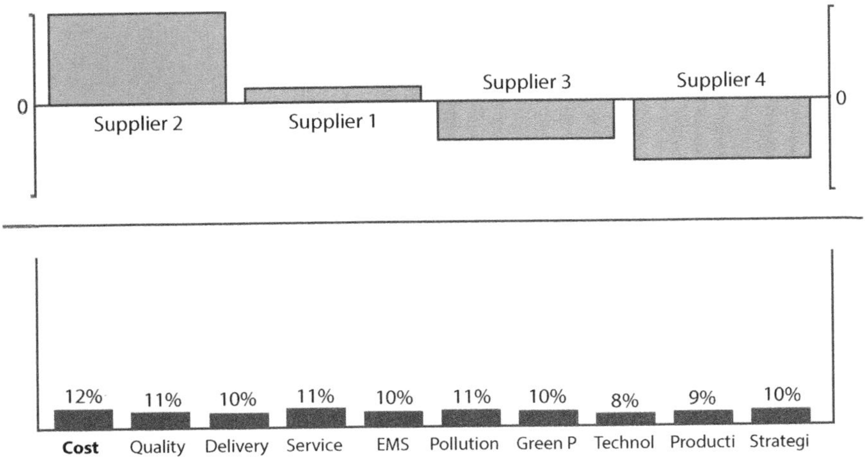

Figure 7.8 Walking weights.

The figure illustrates two charts: the upper chart presents the PROMETHEE II net flow results, while the lower chart displays the weights of the evaluation criteria. The results clearly indicate that supplier A_2 outperforms the others, whereas supplier A_4 consistently remains the lowest in the ranking. Supplier A_2 holds a firmly secured position as the most favorable alternative.

However, this position is no longer secured if changes happen to weights of criteria. Therefore, sensitivity of decision-making is dynamically and proportionately analyzed in this regard. The changes in weight of criterion are checked. In this paper, it is hypothesized that an increase significantly in weight of criterion may contribute to a fundamental change in alternatives pre-orders. The weight of C_9 is now increased by 36%. The use of walking weight shows that the increase of weight of C_9 to 36% does not much modify the alternatives pre-order. Figure 7.9 shows the pre-order of alternatives after the increase of C_9 by 36%.

The pre-order of suppliers has been significantly changed as a result of substantial changes in weight of one of the criteria. Therefore, this result indicates that the pre-order is sensitive against the changes in weight of criteria. The walking weight analysis provides a good sign on the importance criteria that eventually would affect the assessment of alternatives.

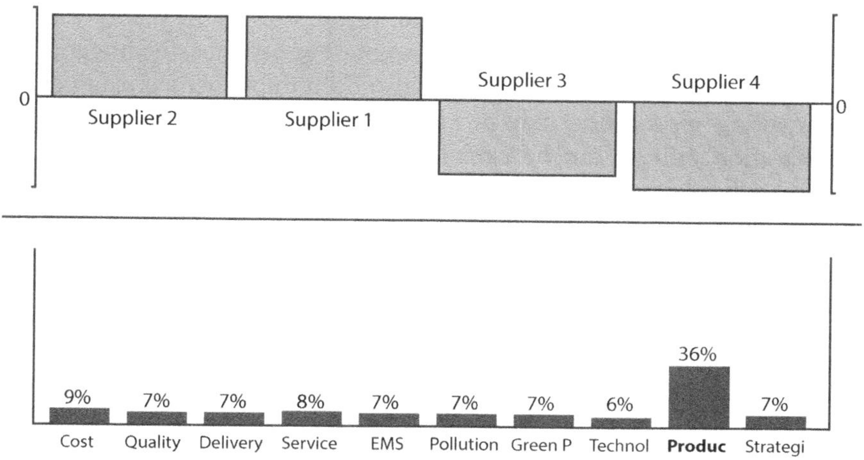

Figure 7.9 Increase of walking weights on Criterion 9.

7.7 Conclusion

Globalization has led many organizations to incur substantial financial losses as a result of fluctuating costs, supply chain interruptions, and quality inconsistencies, which negatively affect brand reputation. To address these challenges, strategic producers increasingly rely on green suppliers, who are essential in reducing the risks associated with both natural and human-induced disruptions, thereby strengthening the resilience of supply chains before and after crises. There is considerable uncertainty on both the supply and demand sides of the supply chain, which can be effectively managed by selecting resilient suppliers. This paper has identified the optimal green supplier, supported by geometrical representations using the PROMETHEE method. The study proposed a set of criteria weights and evaluated supplier performance using a 5-point Likert scale. The linear preference function and level preference function were applied to assess these criteria. The findings indicate that Supplier A_2 is the best choice, based on the PROMETHEE method utilizing both linear and level preference functions. PROMETHEE has demonstrated the comparative advantages of Supplier A_2 over other competitors. In summary, the PROMETHEE evaluation model when paired with appropriate preference functions effectively supports the selection of the best supplier. However, the study is subject to certain limitations, particularly regarding the choice and application of preference functions. A more rigorous investigation into these functions and how they influence outcomes presents an opportunity for future research. Another direction for future work is the incorporation of broader sustainable development concepts. For instance, the integration of green energy elements, which have also been implemented using decision-making approaches, may be valuable to explore [47]. Additionally, the selection criteria can be expanded to encompass a wider range of sustainability dimensions, such as economic, environmental, and social development.

AI disclosure statement: The author confirms that no artificial intelligence (AI)-generated content or AI-assisted writing tools were used in the preparation of this chapter (including summaries and the abstract). All text, analysis, and conclusions are the result of the author's original work.

References

1. Sullivan, K., Thomas, S., Rosano, M., Using industrial ecology and strategic management concepts to pursue the Sustainable Development Goals. *J. Cleaner Prod.*, 174, 237–246, 2018.
2. Moshood, T.D., Nawanir, G., Mahmud, F., Mohamad, F., Ahmad, M.H., Abdul Ghani, A., Kumar, S., Green product innovation: A means towards achieving global sustainable product within biodegradable plastic industry. *J. Cleaner Prod.*, 363, 132506, 2022.
3. Dzikriansyah, M.A., Masudin, I., Zulfikarijah, F., Jihadi, M., Jatmiko, R.D., The role of green supply chain management practices on environmental performance: A case of Indonesian small and medium enterprises. *Cleaner Logist. Supply Chain*, 6, 100100, 2023.
4. Rao, P., Greening the supply chain: a new initiative in South East Asia. *Int. J. Oper. Prod. Manage.*, 22, 6, 632–655, 2002.
5. Sarkis, J., Zhu, Q., Lai, K.H., An organizational theoretic review of green supply chain management literature. *Int. J. Prod. Econ.*, 130, 1, 1–15, 2011.
6. Andalib Ardakani, D., Soltanmohammadi, A., Seuring, S., The impact of customer and supplier collaboration on green supply chain performance. *Benchmarking An Int. J.*, 30, 7, 2248–2274, 2023.
7. Gunasekaran, A., Lai, K., Cheng, T.C.E., Responsive supply chain: a competitive strategy in a networked economy. *Omega*, 36, 4, 549–564, 2008.
8. Luthra, S., Govindan, K., Kannan, D., Mangla, S.K., Garg, C.P., An integrated framework for sustainable supplier selection and evaluation in supply chains. *J. Cleaner Prod.*, 140, 1686–1698, 2017.
9. Bali, O., Kose, E., Gumus, S., Green supplier selection based on IFS and GRA. *Grey Syst. Theory Appl.*, 2013.

10. Ghadikolaei, A.S., Parkouhi, S.V., Saloukolaei, D.D., Extension of a Hybrid MABAC–DANP Method Under Gray Environment for Green Supplier Selection. *Int. J. Inf. Technol. Decis. Making*, 21, 02, 755–788, 2022.
11. Ecer, F., Multi-criteria decision making for green supplier selection using interval type-2 fuzzy AHP: a case study of a home appliance manufacturer. *Oper. Res.*, 22, 1, 199–233, 2022.
12. Celik, E., Yucesan, M., Gul, M., Green supplier selection for textile industry: a case study using BWM-TODIM integration under interval type-2 fuzzy sets. *Environ. Sci. Pollut. Res.*, 28, 45, 64793–64817, 2021.
13. Wei, C., Wu, J., Guo, Y., Wei, G., Green supplier selection based on CODAS method in probabilistic uncertain linguistic environment. *Technol. Econ. Dev. Econ.*, 27, 3, 530–549, 2021.
14. Wei, D., Meng, D., Rong, Y., Liu, Y., Garg, H., Pamucar, D., Fermatean Fuzzy Schweizer–Sklar operators and BWM-entropy-based combined compromise solution approach: an application to green supplier selection. *Entropy*, 24, 6, 776, 2022.
15. Sun, Y. and Cai, Y., A Flexible Decision-Making Method for Green Supplier Selection Integrating TOPSIS and GRA Under the Single-Valued Neutrosophic Environment. *IEEE Access*, 9, 83025–83040, 2021.
16. Brans, J.P., L'ingenierie de la decision, l'laboration d'instruments d'aidea la decision. Colloque sur /'Aidea la Decision. Faculte des Sciences de l'Administration. Universite Laval, 1982.
17. Brans, J.P. and Vincke, P., Note—A Preference Ranking Organisation Method: (The PROMETHEE Method for Multiple Criteria Decision-Making). *Manage. Sci.*, 31, 6, 647–656, 1985.
18. Genç, N., Durna, E., Kacıra, E., The preference of the most appropriate radical-based regeneration process for spent activated carbon by the PROMETHEE approach. *Environ. Sci. Pollut. Res.*, 29, 4, 5240–5255, 2022.
19. Demirel, Y.E., Simsek, E., Ozturk, E., Kitis, M., Selection of priority energy efficiency practices for industrial steam boilers by PROMETHEE decision model. *Energy Effic.*, 14, 8, 1–20, 2021.
20. Agustin, E.S.A.S., Martini, R., Setiyono, B., Evaluating rural tourism competitiveness: Application of PROMETHEE-GAIA method. *Cogent Econ. Finance*, 10, 1, 2054526, 2022.
21. Balali, V., Zahraie, B., Roozbahani, A., A comparison of AHP and PROMETHEE family decision making methods for selection of building structural system. *Am. J. Civ. Eng. Archit.*, 2, 5, 149–159, 2014.
22. Brans, J.P. and Vincke, P., Note A Preference Ranking Organisation Method. *Manage. Sci.*, 31, 6, 647–656, 1985.
23. De Smet, Y. and Lidouh, K., An introduction to multicriteria decision aid: The PROMETHEE and GAIA methods, in: *European Big Data Management and Analytics Summer School*, pp. 150–176, Springer Berlin Heidelberg, Berlin, Heidelberg, 2012.

24. Özgen, A., Tuzkaya, G., Tuzkaya, U.R., Özgen, D., A multi-criteria decision making approach for machine tool selection problem in a fuzzy environment. *Int. J. Comp. Intell. Syst.*, 4, 4, 431–445, 2011.
25. Gurmani, S.H., Garg, H., Chen, H., Tao, Z., Zhang, Z., Optimizing performance evaluation of green supply chain management practices with linguistic q-rung orthopair fuzzy information. *Appl. Soft Comput.*, 113194, 2025.
26. Liang, D., Fu, Y., Garg, H., A novel robustness PROMETHEE method by learning interactive criteria and historical information for blockchain technology-enhanced supplier selection. *Expert Syst. Appl.*, 235, 121107, 2024.
27. Ghodsypour, S.H. and O'Brien, C., The total cost of logistics in supplier selection, under conditions of multiple sourcing, multiple criteria and capacity constraint. *Int. J. Prod. Econ.*, 73, 1, 15–27, 2001.
28. Manning, L., Baines, R.N., Chadd, S.A., Quality assurance models in the food supply chain. *Br. Food J.*, 108, 2, 91–104, 2006.
29. Acar, A.Z., Önden, I., Gürel, O., Evaluation of the parameters of the green supplier selection decision in textile industry. *Fibres Text. East. Eur*, 2016, Available from: http://yadda.icm.edu.pl/baztech/element/bwmeta1.element.baztech-46457f0d-c221-43d5-b53c-0fea3d5414d0.
30. Wisner, J., Tan, K., Leong, G., *Principles of supply chain management: a balanced approach*, Third Edit., Thomson Publication, South-Western, Mason, Ohio, 2009.
31. Bressolles, G. and Lang, G., KPIs for performance measurement of e-fulfillment systems in multi-channel retailing: An exploratory study. *Int. J. Retail Distrib. Manage.*, 48, 1, 35–52, 2020.
32. Hsieh, T.-Y., Lu, S.-T., Tzeng, G.H., Fuzzy MCDM approach for planning and design tenders selection in public office buildings. *Int. J. Project Manage.*, 22, 7, 573–584, 2004.
33. Handfield, R., Walton, S.V., Sroufe, R., Melnyk, S.A., Applying environmental criteria to supplier assessment: A study in the application of the Analytical Hierarchy Process. *Eur. J. Oper. Res.*, 141, 1, 70–87, 2002.
34. Altinoz, C. and Winchester S., C., A Fuzzy Approach to Supplier Selection. *J. Text. Inst. Taylor & Francis Group*, 92, 2, 155–167, 2015, Available from: http://www.tandfonline.com/doi/ abs/10.1080/00405000108659605.
35. Gurel, O., Acar, A.Z., Onden, I., Gumus, I., Determinants of the green supplier selection. *3rd International Conference on Leadership. Technology and Innovation Management*, Istanbul, 2013.
36. Marshall, R.E. and Farahbakhsh, K., Systems approaches to integrated solid waste management in developing countries. *Waste Manage. (Oxford)*, 33, 4, 988–1003, 2013.
37. Gary Teng, S. and Jaramillo, H., A model for evaluation and selection of suppliers in global textile and apparel supply chains. *Int. J. Phys. Distrib. Logist. Manage.*, 35, 7, 503–523, 2005.

38. Chan F., T. and Chan H., K., An AHP for selection of suppliers in the fast changing fashion market. *Int. J. Adv. Manuf. Technol.*, 51, 9–12, 1195–207, 2015, Available from: http://link.springer. com/10.1007/s00170-010-2683-6.
39. Seifollahi, N., Analysis of the Effect of Green Packaging on Attracting and Retaining Environmentally Friendly Customers with the Mediating role of Green Brand Image. *Pollution*, 9, 3, 950–964, 2023.
40. Hashemi, S.H., Karimi, A., Tavana, M., An integrated green supplier selection approach with analytic network process and improved grey relational analysis. *Int. J. Prod. Econ.*, 159, 1, 178–191, 2015.
41. ElMaraghy, H. and Deif, A.M., Dynamic modelling of impact of lean policies on production levelling feasibility. *CIRP Ann.*, 63, 1, 389–392, 2014.
42. Gören, H.G. and Şenocak, A.A., Macbeth Based Taguchi Loss Functions Approach for Green Supplier Selection: A Case Study in Textile Industry. *Tekst. Konfeks.*, 28, 2, 90–97, 2018.
43. Isoraite, M., Importance of strategic alliances in company's activity. *Intellect. Econ.*, 1, 5, 39–46, 2009.
44. Dağdeviren, M., Decision making in equipment selection: an integrated approach with AHP and PROMETHEE. *J. Intell. Manuf.*, 19, 4, 397–406, 2008.
45. Tuzkaya, G., Gülsün, B., Kahraman, C., Özgen, D., An integrated fuzzy multi-criteria decision making methodology for material handling equipment selection problem and an application. *Expert Syst. Appl.*, 37, 4, 2853–2863, 2010.
46. Mareschal, B. and Brans, J.P., Geometrical representations for MCDA. *Eur. J. Oper. Res.*, 34, 1, 69–77, 1988.
47. David, D. and Alamoodi, A., A bibliometric analysis of research on multiple criteria decision making with emphasis on Energy Sector between (2019-2023). *Appl. Data Sci. Anal.*, 2023, 143–149, 2023.

8

Adopting Green Logistics in India: A Comparison of Manufacturing Sectors Using p,q-Quasirung Orthopair Fuzzy Group Decision Analysis

Sanjib Biswas*, Sriparna Guha and Aparajita Sanyal

Amity Business School, Amity University Kolkata, Kolkata, India

Abstract

Over the years, green logistics systems (GLS) have emerged as a crucial solution in the pursuit of reducing carbon footprints and achieving environmental sustainability. While the extant literature shows increasing contributions made by the researchers and practitioners related to GLS, the present chapter makes two value additions: a) discerning key enablers for successfully implementing GLS and b) comparing the manufacturing sectors in India concerning their status related to GLS implementation. The current study proposes a novel p,q – Quasirung Orthopair Fuzzy Number (p,q – QOFN) based group decision framework with the fairly aggregation operator. This work consolidates experts' opinions by utilizing the p,q – QROFS Weighted Fairly Averaging (p,q QOFWFA) method. Then, it uses the COBRAC (comparisons between ranked criteria) method to determine the weights of the enablers. The current work utilizes the CORASO (compromise ranking from alternative solutions) method to determine the aggregated scores of the alternative sectors. For validation of the result, several MCDM models are compared. The stability of the results is tested through the sensitivity analysis.

Keywords: Green logistics system, environmental sustainability, p,q QOFWFA, COBRAC, CORASO

**Corresponding author*: sbiswas1@kol.amity.edu; ORCID: https://orcid.org/0000-0002-9243-2403

Sriparna Guha: ORCID: https://orcid.org/0000-0003-3092-3722

Aparajita Sanya: ORCID: https://orcid.org/0000-0002-9968-5817

Harish Garg (ed.) Decision Support Systems in Smart Computing: Embracing Uncertainty and Challenges, (219–258) © 2026 Scrivener Publishing LLC

8.1 Introduction

Over the last three decades, the logistics management function has garnered significant attention from scholars and practitioners due to its pivotal roles in enhancing operational efficiency, improving service quality, optimizing costs, mobilizing resources, and exceeding customer expectations. The significance of logistics is growing, primarily because of globalization. With the rise of multinational firms (MNCs) engaging in global sourcing, production, and distribution, their supply chains have become increasingly complex to manage [1]. Logistics and supply chain management (LSCM) provides a significant competitive advantage for organizations in the global landscape. Logistics is not a supplementary activity to trade but rather a fundamental activity that forms the foundation and facilitates the movement of the entire trade system, fostering economic growth [2].

The logistics sector in an emerging country like India has been a challenging and rapidly growing area, in line with the country's rapid industrial growth and significant market expansion. The substantial influx of traffic has created favorable conditions for expansion in various aspects of logistics, including transportation, warehousing, freight forwarding, express cargo delivery, container services, and shipping services. The growth trajectory also suggests that the sector is facing increasing demand to deliver the necessary solutions to support future expansion. The robustness of the logistics sector is expected to play a crucial role in determining the rate of future economic expansion [3]. According to a recent market research report [4], the logistics sector in India is projected to grow more than ₹30 trillion by 2029. Given the potential for massive growth driven by technological advancements and the vastness of the market, the logistics sector has been increasingly facing the challenge of addressing climate change and reducing the generation of carbon footprint in line with the country's ambitious target of becoming a net-zero nation by 2070 [5]. As a result, the requirement of greening logistics has emerged as an area of utmost importance.

According to Dzwigol *et al.* [6], green logistics (GL) refers to the practice of integrating environmental concerns into LSCM to enhance the environmental performance of both suppliers and customers. The key concerns of GLS are executing processes to meet customers' needs, optimizing resources, and minimizing waste generation, all while aligning with primary intentions such as limiting carbon emissions and improving energy efficiency [7, 8]. Human society must adopt a low-carbon and environmentally friendly development trajectory despite the role of industrialization in driving societal progress, due to the adverse environmental consequences it has caused. The logistics development must adhere to environmentally sustainable practices. As the world transitions towards a low-carbon and blue economy, green logistics plays an intricate role in mitigating the greenhouse effect and preserving biodiversity and ecological systems [9].

Green logistics embodies three vantage points: the public-private, operational-strategic, and local-to-global spheres of influence. In the earliest view of green logistics, interest groups advocated for government action to mitigate the negative impacts of freight transportation. At the same time, governmental agencies sought ways to gain a deeper understanding of the issue and identify practical solutions [2]. Along with public sector interest, commercial sector involvement in green logistics research has been increasing as companies develop environmental plans for their logistics operations. There has been an expansion of corporate commitment (under the Paris Agreement) to green logistics, shifting from minor operational adjustments to incorporating environmental concepts into strategic planning at both operational and strategic levels. Understanding how logistics impact the weather globally, given that climate change has been a pressing environmental issue [9]. The Indian green logistics industry is projected to have an estimated CAGR of 12.10% by 2032, resulting in a revenue of $194.21 million by that year [10].

It is evident from the above discussions that greening logistics operations has multifaceted benefits and enormous potential to grow in the near future. The government of India is also committed to developing an efficient, robust, and sustainable logistics ecosystem that fosters clean energy use and enhances mobility. Several initiatives have been undertaken [11]. However, substantial advancements are required to implement innovations that guarantee sustainability. Emerging enterprises and eco-entrepreneurs are required to incorporate green logistics into their business frameworks, which suggests opportunities for further research.

The scholarly fraternity has been working on several aspects of green logistics, addressing the challenges of implementation, for example, Derse [12] and Kamewor *et al.* [13]. However, to the best of our knowledge, we found a limited number of studies that have worked on the crucial enablers for executing GLS magnificently. Furthermore, there is a gap in the literature that assesses the readiness of the manufacturing sector in India to implement the GLS from the perspective of the enabling factors. Additionally, there is a scarcity of robust soft computing frameworks for addressing the issue of implementing GLS in the Indian manufacturing sector. These gaps in the literature have motivated us to undertake the current study. We aim to address these research gaps by answering the following research objectives.

a) To identify the key enablers for adopting and practicing green logistics.
b) To develop a robust comparative assessment framework for the manufacturing sectors for examining their readiness to implement GLS.

The present paper is distinguished from the prior studies in several aspects, which are the contributions of this work:

- First, it examines the enabling factors for adopting green logistics while also considering the associated barriers.
- Secondly, it presents a comparative analysis of the manufacturing sectors, given the adoption of green logistics.
- Thirdly, it offers an innovative granular analysis using a soft computing approach for addressing the GLS adoption problem. In this regard, the current study offers a relevant use of the TTF theoretical framework.
- Fourth, the present work develops a novel COBRAC-CORASO framework that utilizes p,q-Quasirung Orthopair Fuzzy Numbers (p,q-QROFNs) for group decision-making.

The present work has several practical significances. The study offers policymakers' and industry leaders' valuable insights into the factors that enable and hinder the adoption of GLS, enabling them to develop more effective and sustainable plans. It also enables sectoral benchmarking, allowing for the comparison of the readiness of different manufacturing sectors, and facilitating the development of tailored interventions. The study also evaluates the industry readiness, helping firms identify areas for improvement in greener practices. This helps logistics managers and operations chiefs make informed decisions on GLS implementation in India. The soft-computing framework employed in this work utilizes a robust uncertainty analysis and the theoretical rigor of the TTF model, which can be applied to assess technology readiness in any other sector or context.

The manuscript proceeds as follows. Section 8.2 provides a brief theoretical background. Section 8.3 discusses some of the related contributions. Section 8.4 outlines the research approach. The findings of the data analysis are exhibited in Section 8.5. Key observations in the context of the present problem and research implications are highlighted in Section 8.6. Section 8.7 provides the concluding summary of the paper and indicates some possibilities for further extensions.

8.2 Theoretical Background

8.2.1 The Task and Technology Fit (TTF) Model

The TTF framework [14] is a widely used theoretical model that explains the alignment of advanced technology adoption with operational functions and its impact on performance. TTF entails three kinds of fits such as a) fitment of the functional requirements (in terms of complexities, interdependencies, and uncertainties): b) fitment of the technology features (accessibility, information management, technology integration, compatibility, and scope of applications): c) Skills and abilities (individual abilities, competencies, skill-sets, training). A higher fit indicates the effective adoption of advanced technologies within the system, thereby improving performance. In the context of green logistics, TTF refers to an organization's ability to adopt green technologies at both the system and individual levels. Various scholars have applied TTF in several contexts, for instance, the adaptation of e-learning systems and its impact on students' satisfaction in higher education [15], the adaptability of blockchain technology in marine bunkering operations [16], societal impacts of supply chain and logistics management driven by advanced technologies [17], the transformation of traditional supply chain management with blockchain technology for improving sharing of environmental information and fostering better governance on real-time [18] among others.

8.2.2 p,q-Quasirung Orthopair Fuzzy Sets

The concept of p,q-QROFS was introduced to incorporate both belongingness and non-belongingness degrees, providing greater flexibility to decision-makers in selecting the range of values [19]. The p,q-QROFS is a generalized version of the q-rung Orthopair fuzzy set [20], Pythagorean Fuzzy Set, PFS [21, 22], and Intuitionistic Fuzzy Set, IFS [23]. Various scholars have increasingly applied the p,q-QROFS in several research problems [24–29]. The following are some of the fundamental definitions, properties, and operations.

Definition 1. Intuitionistic Fuzzy Sets (IFS)
Given the elements x belonging to the universe $\mathcal{U}$, the definition of an IFS [23] is as follows.

$$A_{\mathcal{J}} = \left\{ x, \left\langle \hbar_{\mathcal{J}}(x), \lambda_{\mathcal{J}}(x) \right\rangle \right\} \Big| 0 \le \hbar_{\mathcal{J}}(x) + \lambda_{\mathcal{J}}(x) \le 1 \tag{8.1}$$

In the definition 1, $\hbar_{\mathcal{J}}(x)$ and $\lambda_{\mathcal{J}}(x)$ denote the degrees of belongingness (DoB) and non-belongingness (DoNB), respectively.

Definition 2. q Rung Orthopair Fuzzy Sets (q-ROFS)
If $A_{\mathcal{Q}}$ is a q-ROFS, then it is defined [20, 30, 31] as follows.

$$A_{\mathcal{Q}} = \left\{ x, \left\langle \hbar_{\mathcal{Q}}(x), \lambda_{\mathcal{Q}}(x) \right\rangle \right\} \Big| 0 \le \left(\hbar_{\mathcal{Q}}(x) \right)^q + \left(\lambda_{\mathcal{Q}}(x) \right)^q \le 1 \tag{8.2}$$

By varying the value of the natural integer q, q-ROFS can be simplified to IFS (setting $q = 1$), PFS (setting $q = 2$), and FFSs (setting $q = 3$).

Definition 3. (p,q) Quasirung Orthopair Fuzzy Sets (p,q-QROFS)
Seikh and Mandal [19] introduced the concept of p,q-QROFS and defined it as follows.

$$A_{\mathcal{P}} = \left\{ x, \left\langle \hbar_{\mathcal{P}}(x), \lambda_{\mathcal{P}}(x) \right\rangle \right\} \Big| 0 \le \left(\hbar_{\mathcal{P}}(x) \right)^p + \left(\lambda_{\mathcal{P}}(x) \right)^q \le 1 \tag{8.3}$$

Instead of q-ROFS, p,q-QROFS uses two natural numbers, p and q $(p, q \ge 1;\ p > or = or < q)$ so that it provides a broader scope for selecting DoB and DoNB values.

The degree of ambiguity (DoA) is determined by Equation 8.4.

$$\pi_{\mathcal{P}} = \sqrt[\iota]{1 - \left(\hbar_{\mathcal{P}}(x) \right)^p - \left(\lambda_{\mathcal{P}}(x) \right)^q} \tag{8.4}$$

In Equation 8.4, $\iota = l.c.m(p, q)$ is a small number.

This work hereafter will use $\mathcal{P} = (\hbar, \lambda)$ to denote a (p,q) Quasirung Orthopair Fuzzy Number (p,q-QROFN) for simplified understanding and use without compromising the true definition and meaning of the terms of the p,q-QROFS.

Definition 4. Let $\mathcal{P}=(\hbar,\lambda)$, $\mathcal{P}_1=(\hbar_1,\lambda_1)$ and $\mathcal{P}_2=(\hbar_2,\lambda_2)$ are any three p,q-QROFNs. Then, the following definitions related to operating with the p,q-QROFNs hold good.

i) *If* $\hbar_1 \leq \hbar_2$ and $\lambda_1 \geq \lambda_2$ then $\mathcal{P}_1 \leq \mathcal{P}_2$
ii) $\mathcal{P}_1 \oplus \mathcal{P}_2 = \left(\sqrt[p]{\hbar_1^p + \hbar_2^p - \hbar_1^p \hbar_2^p}, \lambda_1 \lambda_2\right)$
iii) $\mathcal{P}_1 \otimes \mathcal{P}_2 = \left(\hbar_1 \hbar_2, \sqrt[q]{\lambda_1^q + \lambda_2^q - \lambda_1^q \lambda_2^q}\right)$
iv) $\alpha\mathcal{P} = (\sqrt[p]{1-(1-\hbar^p)^\alpha}, \lambda^\alpha)$, where $\alpha(\geq 0) \in \mathbb{R}$
v) $\mathcal{P}^\alpha = (\hbar^\alpha, \sqrt[q]{1-(1-\lambda^q)^\alpha})$
vi) $\mathcal{P}^C = (\lambda, \hbar)$

Definition 5.
The score value of $\mathcal{P}$ is obtained by using Equation 8.5.

$$S(\mathcal{P}) = \frac{1+\hbar^p - \lambda^q}{2}; \ 0 \leq S(\mathcal{P}) \leq 1 \tag{8.5}$$

The accuracy value is obtained by using Equation 8.6.

$$\mathcal{A}(\mathcal{P}) = \hbar^p + \lambda^q; \ 0 \leq \mathcal{A}(\mathcal{P}) \leq 1 \tag{8.6}$$

For the comparison, the following rules are followed

i) If $S(\mathcal{P}_1) < S(\mathcal{P}_2)$ then $\mathcal{P}_1 \prec \mathcal{P}_2$
ii) If $S(\mathcal{P}_1) > S(\mathcal{P}_2)$ then $\mathcal{P}_1 \succ \mathcal{P}_2$
iii) If $S(\mathcal{P}_1) = S(\mathcal{P}_2)$ then

$$\mathcal{A}(\mathcal{P}_1) < \mathcal{A}(\mathcal{P}_2) \Rightarrow \mathcal{P}_1 \prec \mathcal{P}_2$$
$$\mathcal{A}(\mathcal{P}_1) > \mathcal{A}(\mathcal{P}_2) \Rightarrow \mathcal{P}_1 \succ \mathcal{P}_2$$
$$\mathcal{A}(\mathcal{P}_1) = \mathcal{A}(\mathcal{P}_2) \Rightarrow \mathcal{P}_1 = \mathcal{P}_2$$

Definition 6.
The p, q-QROF weighted averaging (p, q-QROFWA) and p, q-QOF weighted geometric (p, q-QROFWG) operators for aggregating the series of n p,q-QOFNs, $\mathcal{P}_j = (\hbar_j, \lambda_j)$; $j = 1, 2 \ldots n$, are derived using Equations 8.7 and 8.8.

$$p,q-QROFWA(\mathcal{P}_1,\mathcal{P}_2,\ldots,\mathcal{P}_n)=\overset{n}{\underset{j=1}{\oplus}}\omega_j\,\mathcal{P}_j=\left(\begin{array}{l}\sqrt[p]{1-\prod_{j=1}^{n}(1-\hbar_j^p)^{\omega_j}},\\ \prod_{j=1}^{n}\lambda_j^{\omega_j}\end{array}\right) \tag{8.7}$$

$$p,q-QROFWG(\mathcal{P}_1,\mathcal{P}_2,\ldots,\mathcal{P}_n)=\overset{n}{\underset{j=1}{\otimes}}\mathcal{P}_j^{\omega_j}=\left(\begin{array}{l}\prod_{j=1}^{n}\hbar_j^{\omega_j},\\ \sqrt[q]{1-\prod_{j=1}^{n}(1-\lambda_j^q)^{\omega_j}}\end{array}\right) \tag{8.8}$$

ω_j is the weight of the p,q-QROFN $\mathcal{P}_j$ such that $\omega_j>0;\sum_{j=1}^{n}\omega_j=1$

Definition 7. Fairly operations

We follow the definitions related to fairly operations on q-ROFNs [32] to provide a generalized definition of fairly operations on p,q-QROFNs as follows.

$$\text{i) } \mathcal{P}_1\underset{f}{\otimes}\mathcal{P}_2=\left\langle\begin{array}{l}\left(\left(\dfrac{\hbar_1^p\hbar_2^p}{\hbar_1^p\hbar_2^p+\lambda_1^q\lambda_2^q}\right)\times\left(1-\left(1-\hbar_1^p-\lambda_1^q\right)\left(1-\hbar_2^p-\lambda_2^q\right)\right)\right)^{\frac{1}{p}},\\ \left(\left(\dfrac{\lambda_1^q\lambda_2^q}{\hbar_1^p\hbar_2^p+\lambda_1^q\lambda_2^q}\right)\times\left(1-\left(1-\hbar_1^p-\lambda_1^q\right)\left(1-\hbar_2^p-\lambda_2^q\right)\right)\right)^{\frac{1}{q}}\end{array}\right\rangle \tag{8.9}$$

ii) $$\beta \underset{f}{\mathcal{P}} = \left\langle \begin{array}{c} \left(\left(\frac{\hbar^{p\beta}}{\hbar^{p\beta} + \lambda^{q\beta}} \right) \times \left(1 - \left(1 - \hbar^{p} - \lambda^{q} \right)^{\beta} \right) \right)^{\frac{1}{p}}, \\ \left(\left(\frac{\lambda^{q\beta}}{\hbar^{p\beta} + \lambda^{q\beta}} \right) \times \left(1 - \left(1 - \hbar^{p} - \lambda^{q} \right)^{\beta} \right) \right)^{\frac{1}{q}} \end{array} \right\rangle \tag{8.10}$$

Definition 8. p,q QROF Weighted Fairly Averaging (p,q QROFWFA)
The aggregation operator, p,q-QROFWFA, is defined using the concept described in Definition 7 by [32] as follows.

$$p,q\ \text{QROFWFA}(\mathcal{P}_1, \mathcal{P}_2, \ldots, \mathcal{P}_n)$$

$$= \left(\begin{array}{c} \left(\frac{\prod_{j=1}^{n} (\hbar_j^{p})^{w_j}}{\prod_{j=1}^{n} (\hbar_j^{p})^{w_j} + \prod_{j=1}^{n} (\lambda_j^{q})^{w_j}} \times \left(1 - \prod_{j=1}^{n} \left(1 - \hbar_j^{p} - \lambda_j^{q} \right)^{w_j} \right) \right)^{\frac{1}{p}}, \\ \left(\frac{\prod_{j=1}^{n} (\lambda_j^{q})^{w_j}}{\prod_{j=1}^{n} (\hbar_j^{p})^{w_j} + \prod_{j=1}^{n} (\lambda_j^{q})^{w_j}} \times \left(1 - \prod_{j=1}^{n} \left(1 - \hbar_j^{p} - \lambda_j^{q} \right)^{w_j} \right) \right)^{\frac{1}{q}} \end{array} \right) \tag{8.11}$$

8.3 Literature Investigation

This section retrospectively examines past contributions to identifying barriers to the adoption of green logistics. Organizations are increasingly prioritizing sustainable practices that correspond with the needs of society, nature, and business. Corporate policies promote sustainable logistical practices, while green knowledge, information awareness, and performance targets are crucial for effective cost management and efficient routing schedules in green logistics [33].

Panghal *et al.* [34] addressed the barriers to adopting GLS in the food sector in India. The authors identified six broad types of barriers, encompassing organizational, statutory and regulatory, customer, supplier, technological, and financial aspects. The work of Chhabra and Singh [35] identified 16 barriers to the adoption of green logistics within the Indian manufacturing sector, emphasizing their significance for sustainability in relation to Industry 4.0 and the Circular Economy. The study of Derse [12] examined the integration of green logistics and reverse logistics, emphasizing sustainability concerns and prioritizing solutions through informed decision-making processes. The author highlighted the impact of financial constraints, regulatory challenges, and stakeholder cooperation on the successful adoption of green logistics. In another study, Kamewor *et al.* [13] conducted a bibliometric and systematic literature analysis to investigate green logistics, focusing on its development, theoretical foundations, and research trends. It analyzes industries such as manufacturing, retail, and transportation, with an emphasis on the transition from voluntary environmental activities to regulation-driven practices. The research highlights the growing importance of digitalization in sustainable logistics.

Olejniczak *et al.* [36] reported an increasing awareness of environmental impacts among businesses and consumers, particularly in the e-commerce sector. Gupta *et al.* [37] advocated for building digital infrastructure and emphasized the importance of innovativeness in fostering green logistics. Moreover, augmenting research and development capacity and cultivating human resources in intelligent technologies can be beneficial. The research by Khayyat *et al.* [38] examined the implementation and utilization of green logistics technology and information systems in Saudi Arabia, focusing on environmental consciousness, corporate ethos, and financial factors. The study identified critical elements, including significant environmental awareness among stakeholders, a supportive organizational culture, and a comprehensive understanding of the benefits of green logistics technologies. However, there is potential for improvement in technological readiness, more defined governmental regulations, financial support, and strong policy backing. The study by Yang *et al.* [39] identified resource and energy utilization, as well as green technology innovation, as the motivating parameters. In contrast, the production procedure, equipment, and environmental coordination were found to be the inducing factors for the quality of green distribution transformer manufacturing and the recognition of experts.

Liu *et al.* [40] introspected the sustainability aspects blended with technological and intra-organizational variables that influence the adoption of GLS within Chinese third-party logistics firms. The findings suggest that institutional pressure is the primary factor influencing the adoption of green technology innovation. The study sheds light on the relationship between a company's longevity and its accumulation of experience and resources, thereby enhancing its ability to adopt green technological breakthroughs. The authors employ an integrated Technology-Organization-Environment (TOE) framework and a diffusion of innovation (DOI) theory-based framework.

The advancement of zero-emission transportation modes is crucial for mitigating climate change and reducing carbon emissions. A substantial expense associated with the development of clean transportation technologies is the primary barrier to implementing zero-emission models [41]. Nikseresht *et al.* [42] emphasized the need for researchers to develop innovative approaches and metrics for evaluating green logistics performance in real-world applications. The work of Starostka-Patyk *et al.* [43] analyzed the environmental effects of logistics from a macro perspective within European Union countries. The authors developed a framework for the Green Logistics Performance Index emphasizing the concerns for the environment and operational efficiency. Scholars [44] also noted that environmental policies, financial resources, dedication to sustainable investments, and public perceptions significantly impact the effectiveness of green logistics.

From the methodological perspective, scholars resorted to multivariate analysis like exploratory factor analysis [34, 38], statistical modeling and hypothesis testing [38], SEM [40, 44], multiple linear regression [33], ANN [40], conceptual analysis through review and synthesis of past studies [13, 42], MCDM techniques like DEMATEL [12, 35], SWARA [12], FUCOM [12], BWM [37, 41]. Past research has also suggested that there are additional prospects for future energy applications using MCDM [45].

Based on the literature review, the following observations can be made. Firstly, we observe that studies focusing on green logistics are available. However, the prior studies mainly focused on identifying the barriers to green logistics and their impact on performance. Some studies conceptually discuss the determinants of implementing green logistics and its benefits. No prior work appears to be visible that identifies the enablers of green logistics. Secondly, the requirement for green logistics is pervasive across all industries. Still, there have been no contributions regarding a comparative analysis of several industries in relation to the adoption of green logistics. Thirdly, uncertainty-based models have been employed in a limited number of studies. For example, Derse [12] used fuzzy sets in their MCDM model. Gupta *et al.* [37] applied the Bayesian best-worst method. Moktadir and Ren [41] developed the Interval Type-2 Trapezoidal

Fuzzy Set (IT2TrFS) Pareto with a generalized IT2TrFS weighted averaging (GIT2TrFSWA) operator-based IT2TrFS-Best-Worst Method (BWM) utilizing lower defuzzification (LD). This necessitates exploring the possibility of developing a robust soft-computing framework. Fourthly, it is also evident that past studies are lacking in using appropriate theoretical lenses to discern the criticalities of green logistics.

8.4 Research Methodology

This section outlines the step-by-step approach for conducting the present research. The steps are delineated below.

Stage 1: Development of the factor rating and crisp decision matrix
The steps under this stage are discussed below.

Step 1.1. Identification of the success factors influencing the implementation of GL
Initially, the factors are identified through a literature review. Then, we consulted the experts to confirm the list of factors (Table 8.1).

Table 8.1 List of factors influencing the successful implementation of GL.

Factors	Description	Supportive references
F1	Awareness of Green Technologies	[12, 33]
F2	Focus on Green	[12, 33]
F3	Structured Environmental Public Policy	[12, 38, 46]
F4	Logistics Innovation	[12, 34–36, 38]
F5	Cost-Effective Technology	[12, 34–36]
F6	Skill Development	[38]
F7	Well-Designed Recovery Network	[36, 38]
F8	Information Sharing	[38]
F9	Employee Involvement	[33]
F10	Incentive for Green	[12]
F11	Public-Company-Govt. Interrelationship	[38]

Table 8.2 List of sectors under comparison.

S/L	Description	Key focus areas
S1	Automobile	Renewable energy-driven transportation (electric vehicles, Hydrogen fuel), eco-friendly packaging
S2	Textile and Apparel	Organic and recyclable materials, water-efficient and hazardous chemical-free process, green transportation
S3	Chemical	Reduction of hazardous materials, sustainable packaging and storage, and waste management
S4	FMCG, Electronics/ Electrical equipment, and Consumer Durables	Biodegradable packaging, recycling, Carbon, and energy-efficient process, waste management
S5	Steel/Metal/ Cement	Carbon and energy-efficient production process, Maritime logistics, waste management
S6	Healthcare and Pharmaceutical	Energy-efficient green storage, hazardous waste management, Recycling

Step 1.2. Identification of the sectors for comparison

This study conducts a comparative analysis of six manufacturing sectors (Table 8.2). The sectors are identified based on technical reports [47–50] and expert discussions.

Step 1.3. Selection of the experts

We approached experienced professionals and decision-makers from various industries, as well as expert scholars from academia, primarily with expertise in logistics and supply chain management. Additionally, we consulted with environmental scientists and experts in financial budgeting and technology management. Table 8.3 provides a summary of the ten experts who took part in this study. The size of the focused group of experts meets the minimum requirement for group decision-making [51, 52].

Table 8.3 Experts' profile.

Expert	Experience group	Area	Sector
E1	10-15 years	LSCM	Industry
E2	15-20 years	LSCM	Academic
E3	15-20 years	Technology management	Industry
E4	10-15 years	Infrastructure	Industry
E5	15-20 years	Finance and Control	Industry
E6	20-25 years	LSCM	Industry
E7	15-20 years	Environmental science	Academic
E8	20-25 years	LSCM	Industry
E9	15-20 years	LSCM	Industry
E10	25+ years	LSCM	Industry

Step 1.4. Collection of responses

A questionnaire was developed in two parts: a) rating of the factors and b) evaluation of the sectors based on various factors. The questionnaire was administered physically. The experts were provided with a five-point linguistic evaluation scale (Table 8.4) to rate the factors and various sectors. The corresponding p,q-QROFN values were taken from the work of [32].

Table 8.4 Linguistic scales and corresponding p,q-QROFNs.

		p,q-QROFN	
Linguistic expression	**Code**	$\hbar$	$\lambda\!\!\!^-$
Very high impact/readiness	5	0.90	0.10
High impact/readiness	4	0.75	0.20
Medium impact/readiness	3	0.50	0.45
Low impact/readiness	2	0.35	0.60
Very low impact/readiness	1	0.10	0.90

Step 1.5. Formulation of the decision matrix and criteria rating matrix

Suppose, $F_j(j=1,2,...,n)$ denotes the enabling factor, $S_i(i=1,2,..,m)$ is the sector under comparison and $E_k(k=1,2,..,g)$ indicates the expert. Let, $\wp_j^{(k)}=\left(\hbar_j^{(k)},\lambda_j^{(k)}\right)$ is the rating of the jth factor by k^{th} expert. Suppose, $\Im_{ij}^{(k)}=\left(\hbar_{ij}^{(k)},\lambda_{ij}^{(k)}\right)$ is the evaluated rating of the ith sector under the effect of jth factor by k^{th} expert. The ratings are done using the codes corresponding to the linguistic expressions given in Table 8.4. The ratings of the factors and evaluations of various sectors influenced by these factors are provided in the supplementary dataset.

Then, we apply p,q QROFWFA aggregation (Equation 8.11) to aggregate the responses of the experts. The aggregated ratings of the jth factor $(j=1,2,..,n)$ and the ith sector $(i=1,2,..,m)$ under the effect of jth factor are given by Equations 8.12 and 8.13.

$$\wp_j=\left(\hbar_j,\lambda_j\right)=p,q\ \text{QROFWFA}(\wp_j^{(1)},\wp_j^{(2)},...,\wp_j^{(g)})$$
$$=\left(\left(\frac{\prod_{k=1}^{g}\left\{(\hbar_j^{(k)})^p\right\}^{\omega_k}}{\prod_{k=1}^{g}\left\{(\hbar_j^{(k)})^p\right\}^{\omega_k}+\prod_{k=1}^{g}\left\{(\lambda_j^{(k)})^q\right\}^{\omega_k}}\times\left(1-\prod_{k=1}^{g}\left(1-(\hbar_j^{(k)})^p-(\lambda_j^{(k)})^q\right)^{\omega_k}\right)\right)^{\frac{1}{p}},\left(\frac{\prod_{k=1}^{g}\left\{(\lambda_j^{(k)})^q\right\}^{\omega_k}}{\prod_{k=1}^{g}\left\{(\hbar_j^{(k)})^p\right\}^{\omega_k}+\prod_{k=1}^{g}\left\{(\lambda_j^{(k)})^q\right\}^{\omega_k}}\times\left(1-\prod_{k=1}^{g}\left(1-(\hbar_j^{(k)})^p-(\lambda_j^{(k)})^q\right)^{\omega_k}\right)\right)^{\frac{1}{q}}\right) \quad (8.12)$$

$$\mathfrak{I}_{ij} = \left(\hbar_{ij}, \lambda_{ij}\right) = p,q \text{ QROFWFA}(\mathfrak{I}_{ij}^{(1)}, \mathfrak{I}_{ij}^{(2)}, \ldots, \mathfrak{I}_{ij}^{(g)})$$

$$= \left(\left(\frac{\prod_{k=1}^{g} \left\{(\hbar_{ij}^{(k)})^p\right\}^{\omega_k}}{\prod_{k=1}^{g} \left\{(\hbar_{ij}^{(k)})^p\right\}^{\omega_k} + \prod_{k=1}^{g} \left\{(\lambda_{ij}^{(k)})^q\right\}^{\omega_k}} \times \left(1 - \prod_{k=1}^{g} \left(1 - (\hbar_{ij}^{(k)})^p - (\lambda_{ij}^{(k)})^q\right)^{\omega_k}\right) \right)^{\frac{1}{p}}, \left(\frac{\prod_{k=1}^{g} \left\{(\lambda_{ij}^{(k)})^q\right\}^{\omega_k}}{\prod_{k=1}^{g} \left\{(\hbar_{ij}^{(k)})^p\right\}^{\omega_k} + \prod_{k=1}^{g} \left\{(\lambda_{ij}^{(k)})^q\right\}^{\omega_k}} \times \left(1 - \prod_{k=1}^{g} \left(1 - (\hbar_{ij}^{(k)})^p - (\lambda_{ij}^{(k)})^q\right)^{\omega_k}\right) \right)^{\frac{1}{q}} \right) \tag{8.13}$$

We assume that all experts are given equal importance, i.e., the weight of every expert, $\omega_k = 1/g$. In this way, we formulate the factor rating and initial decision matrix for evaluating the alternatives as follows.

Factor rating matrix: $\begin{pmatrix} \wp_1 \\ \wp_2 \\ \cdots \\ \wp_n \end{pmatrix}_{1 \times n}$

Initial decision matrix for alternative evaluation: $\begin{pmatrix} \mathfrak{I}_{11} & \cdots & \mathfrak{I}_{1n} \\ \vdots & \ddots & \vdots \\ \mathfrak{I}_{m1} & \cdots & \mathfrak{I}_{mn} \end{pmatrix}_{m \times n}$

It is worth noting that all elements of these matrices are p,q-QROFNs. Then, we normalize the initial decision matrix for alternative evaluation using Equation 8.14.

$$\Phi_{ij} = \begin{cases} \mathfrak{I}_{ij} = (\hbar_{ij}, \lambda_{ij}); j \in B \\ \mathfrak{I}_{ij}{}^{C} = (\lambda_{ij}, \hbar_{ij}); j \in NB \end{cases} \tag{8.14}$$

Now, we apply Equation 8.5 to determine the crisp values of the elements of the factor rating (Equation 8.15) and the initial decision matrix (Equation 8.16) as follows.

$$f_j = S(\wp_j) = \frac{1 + \hbar_j^p - \lambda_j^q}{2} \tag{8.15}$$

$$y_{ij} = S(\Phi_{ij}) = \frac{1 + \hbar_{ij}^p - \lambda_{ij}^q}{2} \tag{8.16}$$

Hence, we obtain the final factor rating and decision matrix, as shown below.

Final factor rating matrix (crisp value): $\begin{pmatrix} f_1 \\ f_2 \\ \cdots \\ f_n \end{pmatrix}_{1\times n}$

Final crisp decision matrix for evaluating the sectors:

$$D = \begin{pmatrix} y_{11} & \cdots & y_{1n} \\ \vdots & \ddots & \vdots \\ y_{m1} & \cdots & y_{mn} \end{pmatrix}_{m\times n}$$

Stage 2: Determination of the factor weights (COBRAC method)

This paper uses the COBRAC method to determine criteria weights. COBRAC offers numerous benefits, including a) improved consistency, b) lesser pairwise comparisons within local intervals, c) a better ability to handle variations in features and size of the criteria set, d) mitigation of subjective bias, and e) providing a more precise and reliable result [53]. The COBRAC method has been applied in various settings (for example, [29]). The procedural steps of the COBRAC method are described below.

Step 2.1. Relative assessment of the factors

The factors are compared based on f_j values and are sorted accordingly. For example, the most influential factor that has the highest f_j is placed in the first position, and subsequently, the other factors are ordered. Let the order be $F_{j(1)} > F_{j(2)} > ...... > F_{j(r)}$, where $F_j(j = 1,2,...,n)$ can be any factor with positional rank $r(1,2,...,n)$.

Step 2.2. Pairwise comparison of the factors

The COBRAC method requires $(n-1)$ pairwise comparisons of the factors to establish their relative contributions. However, COBRAC differs from its counterpart, FUCOM, as the former conducts local pairwise comparisons. For each pair, e.g., $(F_{r-1}, F_r; f_{r-1} > f_r)(r = 2,3,..,n)$, a relative priority value $\zeta_{r-1,r} \in [0,1]$ is obtained to indicate the relative contributions of the members of the local pair being compared. For example, $\zeta_{r-1,r} = 0.70$ implies that the contributions of F_{r-1} and F_r are 70% and 30%, respectively, within the local interval.

Step 2.3. Model formulation for weight calculation

The COBRAC method forms $(n-1)$ relationships among n factors. If ω_j is the weight of the jth factor then the relationships can be expressed as follows:

$$\omega_1 : \omega_2 = \zeta_{1,2} : (1-\zeta_{1,2});$$
$$.....$$
$$\omega_{n-1} : \omega_n = \zeta_{n-1,n} : (1-\zeta_{n-1,n}) \tag{8.17}$$

Applying the transitivity property, we can write

$$\frac{\omega_{n-1}}{\omega_n} - \frac{\zeta_{n-1,n}}{(1-\zeta_{n-1,n})} = 0 \tag{8.18}$$

The condition $\left|\frac{\omega_{n-1}}{\omega_n} - \frac{\zeta_{n-1,n}}{(1-\zeta_{n-1,n})}\right| < 0$ indicates the deviation from the consistency (∂), while condition Equation 8.18 does not hold good in some real-life situations. The underlying objective is to minimize the deviation from the consistency while deriving the factor weights. The following model is formulated to determine the factor weights.

$$\min \max_j \left\{\left|\frac{\omega_{j-1}}{\omega_j} - \frac{\zeta_{j-1,j}}{(1-\zeta_{j-1,j})}\right|\right\}$$
$$s.t.$$
$$\sum_{j=1}^{n} \omega_j = 1; \omega_j \geq 0 \ \forall j \in [0,1] \tag{8.19}$$

Equation 8.18 is then converted into a MILP model (the final model) for deriving the factor weights as follows.

$$\begin{aligned}
&Min\ \partial \\
&s.t. \\
&\left|\frac{\omega_{j-1}}{\omega_j} - \frac{\zeta_{j-1,j}}{(1-\zeta_{j-1,j})}\right| \le \partial, \forall j \in [0,1] \\
&\sum_{j=1}^{n} \omega_j = 1; \omega_j \ge 0 \forall j
\end{aligned} \tag{8.20}$$

Stage 3: Evaluation of the alternatives (CORASO method)

The CORASO method offers benefits such as simplicity in computation, the distinct effect of two extreme reference solutions, and stability in ranking [53]. It has been applied by various scholars (for instance, [54, 55]). The procedural steps are described below.

Step 3.1. Formulation of the decision matrix
Step 3.2. Normalization of the decision matrix
See step 1.5
Step 3.3. Find out the weighted normalized values
The weighted normalized values for the alternatives are calculated as

$$\vartheta_{ij} = y_{ij} w_j \tag{8.21}$$

Step 3.4. Calculate the aggregate values
The aggregate values are calculated as

$$\xi_i = \sum_{j=1}^{n} \vartheta_{ij} \tag{8.22}$$

Step 3.5. Derive the deviations from reference solutions
The CORASO method derives two types of deviations as follows:

$$\psi_i = \frac{\xi_i}{\xi_{i(\max)}} \tag{8.23}$$

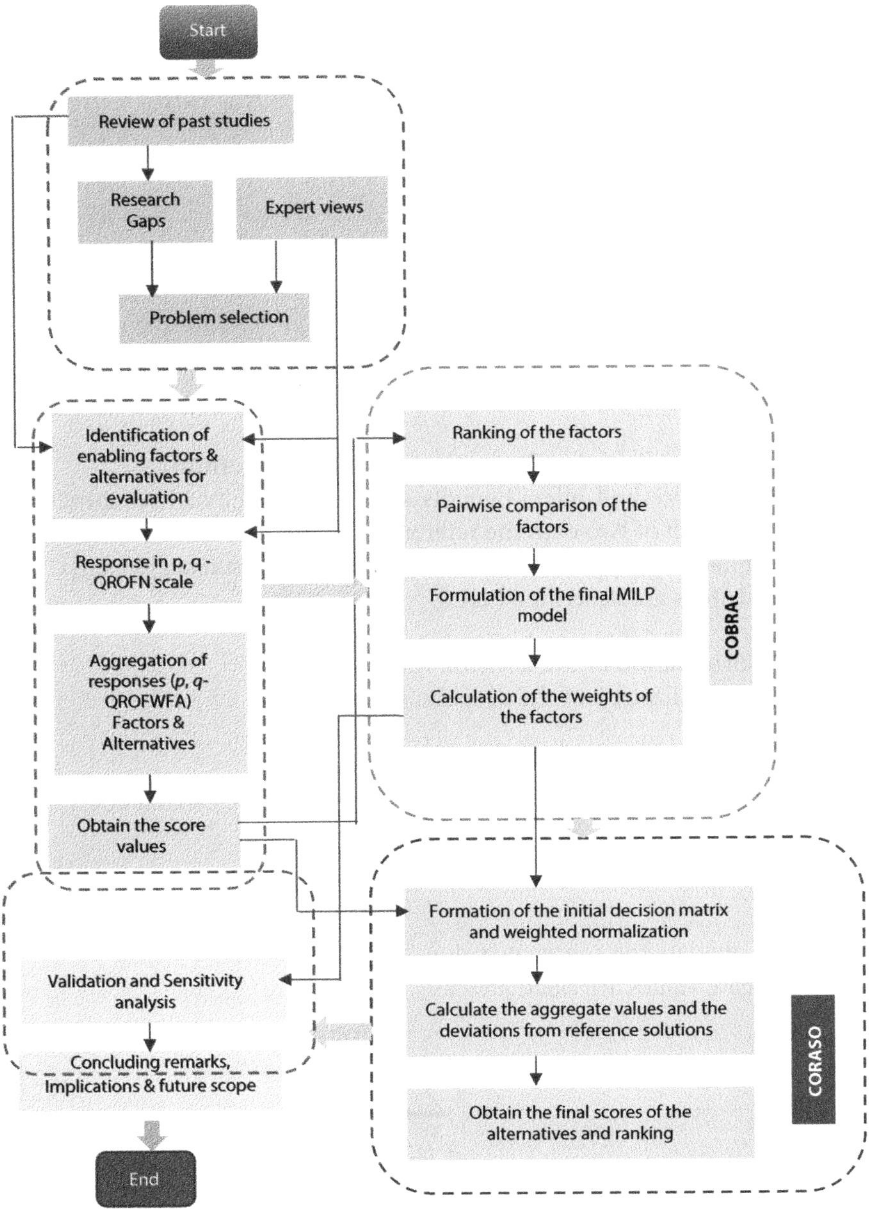

Figure 8.1 Flow chart of the research methodology.

$$\psi_i^* = \frac{\xi_{i(\min)}}{\xi_i} \tag{8.24}$$

Step 3.6. Calculate the final score of the alternatives
The final scores are calculated as follows.

$$\gamma_i = \frac{\psi_i - \psi_i^*}{\psi_i + \psi_i^*} \tag{8.25}$$

Decision: The alternative with a higher final score is ranked first.
The steps of the research methodology are pictorially represented in Figure 8.1.

8.5 Findings

This section highlights notable findings obtained through data analysis. The results can be presented in three stages. First, we demonstrate the construction of the decision matrix for evaluating the alternatives and the rating matrix for the enabling factors. The responses of the experts regarding the importance of the enabling factors and the evaluation of the performance of the alternatives under various factors are recorded in the supplementary file. Then, we apply p,q QROFWFA aggregation (Equations 8.12 and 8.13) to aggregate the responses of the experts.

Example,

$$\wp_1 = (\hbar_1, \bar{\lambda}_1) = p,q\ \text{QROFWFA}(\wp_1^{(1)}, \wp_1^{(2)}, \ldots, \wp_1^{(10)})$$

$$= \left(\left(\frac{\prod_{k=1}^{10} \left\{ (\hbar_1^{(k)})^3 \right\}^{0.1}}{\prod_{k=1}^{10} \left\{ (\hbar_1^{(k)})^3 \right\}^{0.1} + \prod_{k=1}^{10} \left\{ (\bar{\lambda}_1^{(k)})^2 \right\}^{0.1}} \times \left(1 - \prod_{k=1}^{10} \left(1 - (\hbar_1^{(k)})^3 - (\bar{\lambda}_1^{(k)})^2 \right)^{0.1} \right) \right)^{\frac{1}{3}}, \left(\frac{\prod_{k=1}^{10} \left\{ (\bar{\lambda}_1^{(k)})^2 \right\}^{0.1}}{\prod_{k=1}^{10} \left\{ (\hbar_1^{(k)})^3 \right\}^{0.1} + \prod_{k=1}^{10} \left\{ (\bar{\lambda}_1^{(k)})^2 \right\}^{0.1}} \times \left(1 - \prod_{k=1}^{g} \left(1 - (\hbar_1^{(k)})^3 - (\bar{\lambda}_1^{(k)})^2 \right)^{0.1} \right) \right)^{\frac{1}{2}} \right) = (0.6835, 0.3063)$$

Table 8.5 Aggregated rating of the factors (expressed in p,q-QROFNs).

Factors	**F1**		**F2**		**F3**		**F4**	
Aggregated response	0.6825	0.3063	0.5185	0.4973	0.8705	0.1271	0.8301	0.1582
Factors	F5		F6		F7		F8	
Aggregated response	0.8135	0.169	0.6142	0.4094	0.5033	0.5162	0.5908	0.4553
Factors	F9		F10		F11			
Aggregated response	0.2927	0.7583	0.7897	0.259	0.7071	0.4108		

It is worth mentioning that in this study, ten experts took part in the survey, and we assume equal priority, i.e., $k = 1,2,...,10$; $\omega_k = 1/10 = 0.1$. Also, for the initial case, we assume that $p = 3$; $q = 2$ [29]. The p,q-QROFN-based factor rating and alternative evaluation matrix are given in Tables 8.5 and 8.6.

Then, we normalize the initial decision matrix for alternative evaluation (Table 8.6) using Equation 8.14. In this study, all enabling factors are of beneficial type (i.e., the goal is to maximize). Therefore, Table 8.6 will remain as a normalized decision matrix for alternative evaluation.

Next, we proceed to calculate the crisp values of all p,q-QROFNs (given in Tables 8.5 and 8.6) using Equations 8.15 and 8.16. Example,

$$f_1 = S(\wp_1) = \frac{1 + 0.6835^3 - 0.3063^2}{2} = 0.612;$$

$$y_{11} = S(\Phi_{11}) = \frac{1 + 0.8222^3 - 0.1797^2}{2} = 0.762$$

The crisp values are given in Tables 8.7 and 8.8, respectively.

Next, we proceed to stage 2. We utilize the procedural steps of the COBRAC method (Equations 8.17–8.20) to derive the factor weights. Table 8.9 presents the results of pairwise comparisons and calculated weights, as well as the DFC value.

The final model to calculate the weights is given below. It may be noted that COBRAC requires $n - 1 = 10$ pairwise comparisons. The other popular methods like AHP, and BWM would have required $n(n-1)/2 = 55$

Table 8.6 Aggregated rating of the alternatives under the influence of various factors (expressed in p,q-QROFNs).

Factors/ sectors	F1		F2		F3		F4	
S1	0.8222	0.1797	0.8222	0.1797	0.8381	0.1679	0.8190	0.2339
S2	0.6569	0.4302	0.6045	0.5626	0.6045	0.5626	0.4538	0.5896
S3	0.8044	0.1916	0.7866	0.2795	0.8523	0.1563	0.6351	0.4693
S4	0.8589	0.1655	0.8002	0.2489	0.7380	0.3082	0.8291	0.2068
S5	0.6867	0.3511	0.7327	0.3310	0.8291	0.2068	0.6008	0.4977
S6	0.7816	0.2437	0.6514	0.4060	0.8291	0.2068	0.6522	0.3580
Factors/ sectors	**F5**		**F6**		**F7**		**F8**	
S1	0.7324	0.2682	0.8291	0.2068	0.6867	0.3511	0.8300	0.1907
S2	0.7844	0.2032	0.5310	0.5619	0.4844	0.6889	0.6208	0.4352
S3	0.6690	0.3584	0.6993	0.2992	0.8118	0.2206	0.7706	0.2476
S4	0.8301	0.1582	0.8446	0.1930	0.6567	0.5090	0.8589	0.1655
S5	0.5948	0.4813	0.6993	0.2992	0.7327	0.3310	0.6019	0.5222
S6	0.8705	0.1271	0.6867	0.3511	0.6989	0.4269	0.7816	0.2437
Factors/ sectors	**F9**		**F10**		**F11**			
S1	0.7093	0.3199	0.6931	0.3279	0.8523	0.1563		
S2	0.4923	0.5780	0.6690	0.3584	0.6045	0.5626		
S3	0.5647	0.5470	0.5213	0.5244	0.8222	0.1797		
S4	0.7759	0.2841	0.6000	0.4390	0.7380	0.3082		
S5	0.5265	0.5424	0.3656	0.6858	0.7034	0.3430		
S6	0.6084	0.4585	0.7141	0.2976	0.6790	0.3749		

Table 8.7 Crisp rating scores for the enabling factors (factor rating matrix).

Factor	Crisp rating score	Factor	Crisp rating score	Factor	Crisp rating score
F1	0.6120	F5	0.7549	F9	0.2251
F2	0.4461	F6	0.5320	F10	0.7127
F3	0.8217	F7	0.4305	F11	0.5923
F4	0.7735	F8	0.4995		

Table 8.8 Decision matrix for alternative evaluation with crisp data.

Factors/sectors	F1	F2	F3	F4	F5	F6
S1	0.7617	0.7617	0.7802	0.7473	0.6605	0.7636
S2	0.5492	0.4522	0.4522	0.3729	0.7207	0.4170
S3	0.7419	0.7043	0.7973	0.5179	0.5855	0.6262
S4	0.8031	0.7252	0.6535	0.7636	0.7735	0.7827
S5	0.6002	0.6419	0.7636	0.4846	0.4894	0.6262
S6	0.7091	0.5558	0.7636	0.5746	0.8217	0.6002
Factors/sectors	**F7**	**F8**	**F9**	**F10**	**F11**	
S1	0.6002	0.7677	0.6273	0.6127	0.7973	
S2	0.3195	0.5249	0.3926	0.5855	0.4522	
S3	0.7432	0.6982	0.4405	0.4333	0.7617	
S4	0.5121	0.8031	0.6932	0.5116	0.6535	
S5	0.6419	0.4727	0.4259	0.2893	0.6152	
S6	0.5796	0.7091	0.5075	0.6378	0.5863	

Table 8.9 Calculation of factor weights (COBRAC method).

Factor	Crisp rating score	ζ	$1-\zeta$	$\zeta/(1-\zeta)$	Weight (w)
F3	0.8217	0.5151	0.4849	1.0623	0.1284
F4	0.7735	0.5061	0.4939	1.0247	0.1209
F5	0.7549	0.5144	0.4856	1.0591	0.1179
F10	0.7127	0.5380	0.4620	1.1645	0.1114
F1	0.6120	0.5082	0.4918	1.0333	0.0956
F11	0.5923	0.5268	0.4732	1.1133	0.0925
F6	0.5320	0.5158	0.4842	1.0653	0.0831
F8	0.4995	0.5282	0.4718	1.1197	0.0780
F2	0.4461	0.5089	0.4911	1.0362	0.0697
F7	0.4305	0.6567	0.3433	1.9128	0.0673
F9	0.2251				0.0352
	∂	0.0000		Sum	1.0000

and $(2n-3)=19$ pairwise comparisons, respectively. This shows the superiority of the COBRAC method. Also, $\partial = 0.0000$ suggests that the model (Equation 8.26) is consistent and reliable.

$$
\begin{aligned}
&Min\ \partial \\
&s.t. \\
&\left|\frac{w_3}{w_4}-1.0623\right| \le \partial; \left|\frac{w_4}{w_5}-1.0247\right| \le \partial; \left|\frac{w_5}{w_{10}}-1.0591\right| \le \partial; \\
&\left|\frac{w_{10}}{w_1}-1.1645\right| \le \partial; \left|\frac{w_1}{w_{11}}-1.0333\right| \le \partial; \left|\frac{w_{11}}{w_6}-1.1133\right| \le \partial; \\
&\left|\frac{w_6}{w_8}-1.0653\right| \le \partial; \left|\frac{w_8}{w_2}-1.1197\right| \le \partial; \left|\frac{w_2}{w_7}-1.0362\right| \le \partial; \\
&\left|\frac{w_7}{w_9}-1.9128\right| \le \partial; \sum_{j=1}^{10} w_j = 1; w_j \ge 0 \forall j
\end{aligned} \tag{8.26}
$$

Table 8.10 Weighted decision matrix.

Weight	0.0956	0.0697	0.1284	0.1209	0.1179	0.0831	0.0673	0.0780	0.0352	0.1114	0.0925
Factors/ sectors	F1	F2	F3	F4	F5	F6	F7	F8	F9	F10	F11
S1	0.0728	0.0531	0.1002	0.0903	0.0779	0.0635	0.0404	0.0599	0.0221	0.0682	0.0738
S2	0.0525	0.0315	0.0581	0.0451	0.0850	0.0347	0.0215	0.0410	0.0138	0.0652	0.0419
S3	0.0709	0.0491	0.1024	0.0626	0.0691	0.0521	0.0500	0.0545	0.0155	0.0483	0.0705
S4	0.0768	0.0505	0.0839	0.0923	0.0912	0.0651	0.0344	0.0627	0.0244	0.0570	0.0605
S5	0.0574	0.0447	0.0980	0.0586	0.0577	0.0521	0.0432	0.0369	0.0150	0.0322	0.0569
S6	0.0678	0.0387	0.0980	0.0694	0.0969	0.0499	0.0390	0.0553	0.0178	0.0710	0.0543

Table 8.11 Calculation of final score and ranking.

Factors/ sectors	ξ_i	ψ_i	ψ_i^*	γ_i	Rank
S1	0.7221	1	0.6787	0.1914	1
S2	0.4901	0.6787	1	-0.191	6
S3	0.6448	0.8929	0.7601	0.0803	4
S4	0.6988	0.9676	0.7014	0.1595	2
S5	0.5527	0.7654	0.8868	-0.074	5
S6	0.6583	0.9116	0.7446	0.1008	3
Max	0.7221				
Min	0.4901				

Next, we proceed to evaluate the alternatives using the steps of the CORASO method (stage 3). First, we calculate the weighted normalized values using Equation 8.21 (Table 8.10). Example, $\vartheta_{11} = y_{11}w_1 = 0.7611 \times 0.0956 = 0.0728.$

Then, we calculate the aggregate values (Equation 8.22) and derive the deviations (Equation 8.23) and final scores (Equation 8.24) for all alternatives (Table 8.11).

Example,

$$\xi_1 = \sum_{j=1}^{11} \vartheta_{1j} = \vartheta_{11} + \vartheta_{12} + ... + \vartheta_{1(11)} = 0.7221; \psi_1 = \frac{\xi_1}{Max(\xi_1, \xi_2, .., \xi_6)} = \frac{0.7221}{0.7221} = 1$$

$$\psi_1^* = \frac{Min(\xi_1, \xi_2, .., \xi_6)}{\xi_1} = \frac{0.4901}{0.7221} = 0.6787; \gamma_1 = \frac{\psi_1 - \psi_1^*}{\psi_1 + \psi_1^*} = \frac{0.7221 - 0.6787}{0.7221 + 0.6787} = 0.1914$$

8.5.1 Comparison with Other MCDM Models

The MCDM models differ for various reasons, including variations in normalization approaches, the selection of aggregation techniques, the range of values for alternatives under different criteria, the inseparability of alternatives, and others [56–58]. The existing literature recommends comparing several MCDM methods to warrant the reliability of a specific model [59–61]. This study compares the results of the CORASO method with those of several other models, including SAW, RAM, PIV, MABAC,

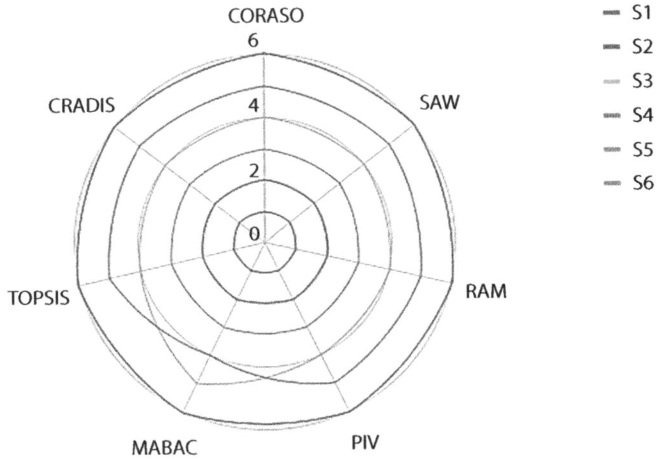

Figure 8.2 Comparison of various MCDM models.

Table 8.12 Result of Spearman's rank correlation test.

Method	SAW	RAM	PIV	MABAC	TOPSIS	CRADIS
CORASO	1.000**	1.000**	1.000**	0.943**	1.000**	1.000**

**p <0.01 (two-tailed)

TOPSIS, and CRADIS (Figure 8.2). Then, we conduct the Spearman's rank correlation test (Table 8.12). The rank correlation coefficients are found to be very high and statistically significant, suggesting the reliability of our approach.

8.5.2 Sensitivity Analysis

One of the cornerstones of a robust MCDM analysis is the stability of the outcome. The stability issues stem from several exceptions in the underlying conditions, such as changes in the criteria weights, variations in the aggregation parameters, the exclusion or inclusion of criteria and alternatives, and many others [62–64]. To assess the stability of the final result, scholars employed sensitivity analysis. This paper examines the sensitivity of the result to the changes in values of two parameters, p and q used in p,q-QROFWFA. With respect to the changing values of p and q

(Table 8.13) we rank the alternatives (Figure 8.3) under various experimental conditions.

The following observations can be made based on the results of sensitivity analysis.

- Sector S3 (Chemical) exhibits considerable sensitivity to changes in p-values while showing minor sensitivity to variations in the q-value. Its performance deteriorates with $p > 8$ but improves when $q > 8$.
- The performance of S5 (Steel/Metal/Cement) marginally improves with $p > 8$ but remains unchanged with the variations in q. It suggests S5 shows a minor sensitivity to p values but remains insensitive to the changes in q.
- Sector S6 (Health and Pharmaceutical) is insensitive to the changes in p but its performance shows a minor dip while increasing q beyond 8.

Table 8.13 Experimental conditions for sensitivity analysis.

Case	p	q	Case	p	q	Case	p	q	Case	p	q	Case	p	q
Initial	3	2	Case 3	5	2	Case 6	9	2	Case 9	3	4	Case 12	3	8
Case 1	2	2	Case 4	6	2	Case 7	10	2	Case 10	3	5	Case 13	3	9
Case 2	4	2	Case 5	8	2	Case 8	3	3	Case 11	3	6	Case 14	3	10

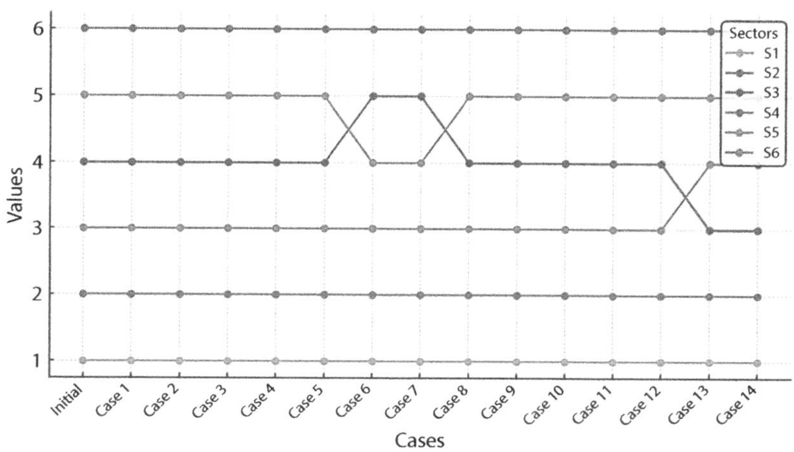

Figure 8.3 Result of sensitivity analysis.

- The top performers, Sectors S1 (Automobiles) and S4 (FMCG and Consumer Durables), and the worst performer, S2 (Textile and Apparel), exhibit complete stability.

Overall, we contend that our model provides a stable result.

8.6 Discussion

The present study provides several significant findings. The ranking of the enabling factors for GL provides valuable insights for decision-making. We notice that Structured Environmental Public Policy (F3) emerges as a dominant enabler (w = 0.1284). The result invokes a holistic ecosystem supported by the government and institutions within the legal, policy, and budgetary framework to promote and enforce sustainable practices. Greenwashing is a matter of concern today. Our findings reinstate the need for a structured policy framework that integrates local and global requirements, addresses global environmental concerns, and drives sustainable development [65]. The finding also highlights the necessity of logistics innovation (F3) (w =0.1209) to enable GL. Recent studies [66] have advocated for the use of advanced digital technologies, such as AI/ML, blockchain, digital twin, GPS/RFID, and the Internet of Things, to ensure transparency, reduce carbon footprint, and optimize service quality. The third crucial enabler is cost-effective technology (F5) (w =0.1179). Again, this underscores the need to develop advanced Indigenous technologies to improve operational efficiency while reducing service costs to an affordable level [13, 67, 68]. Besides these top three drivers, we could also notice that incentives for green (F10) (w = 0.1114) and awareness (F1) (w = 0.0956) hold the fourth and fifth positions. The study by Zhan and Wu [69] argued that performance-linked incentives and subsidies enhance supply chain performance and encourage firms to prioritize environmental protection. Green credit plays a pivotal role in promoting green practices in logistics. However, awareness about the benefits and practices related to green logistics among the stakeholders influences the successful adoption of green practices [38].

The ranking of the sectors reveals that automobiles (S1), and FMCG and consumer durables (S4) remained stable in the top two positions. These two sectors demonstrate strong performance in aspects such as structured environmental public policies (F3) and logistics innovation (F4).

Scholars have advocated for regulatory compliance and agility in embracing technological advancements that substantially influence the adoption of green practices, while green process innovations exert a more pronounced effect on these industries [70, 71]. On the other hand, the textile and apparel industries exhibit poor performance in adopting green logistics practices. The growth of green logistics in these sectors faces numerous constraints, including a lack of cost-effective technology solutions, difficulties in implementing structured environmental policies and regulations, high water usage requirements, inadequate waste management, lack of awareness and knowledge, and limited recycling capabilities [72].

8.6.1 Research Implications

The present study has several implications for managerial decision-making, societal development, and technical advancements.

a) Managerial implications: Organizations must align their commercial strategies with environmental policies to get a competitive edge. Investment in green technology is crucial for enhancing sustainability performance in industries such as steel, chemicals, and textiles. Furthermore, they should enhance their supply chains by developing logistics and recovery networks to improve operational efficiency and mitigate environmental impacts.
b) Social implications: The results clearly indicate that public awareness campaigns can promote environmentally sustainable practices, particularly within the textile sector. Enhancing employee competencies in sustainable practices can facilitate transitions to environmentally friendly operations, promoting job security and ecological responsibility. Collaboration between firms and governments can enhance regulatory compliance and community engagement in sustainability efforts.
c) Technical implications: The essay highlights the importance of innovation in recovery networks, the role of big data and AI in promoting sustainability, and the impact of decarbonization and renewable energy on sectors such as steel and chemicals. It underscores the necessity for structured recovery networks, the integration of big data and

artificial intelligence, and the prioritizing of alternative fuels and carbon capture technologies for sustained environmental advantages. Furthermore, the current work presents an innovative group decision-making model that incorporates imprecise information, which may be further explored in practical applications.

8.7 Conclusion

This work addresses a crucial issue: the adoption of green logistics. The ongoing work identifies the key enabling factors that influence green logistics practices. Grounded on the theoretical foundation of TTF, the current study develops a multi-criteria group decision analysis framework using p,q-QROFN to conduct a comparison of the enablers. This study presents a novel extension of the MCDM models, such as COBRAC and CORASO, utilizing p,q-QROFN Fairly aggregation. Subsequently, the reliability and stability of the hybrid COBRAC and CORASO methods are examined and found to be satisfactory. The development of a novel COBRAC-CORASO framework based on p,q-Quasirung Orthopair Fuzzy Numbers (p,q-QROFNs) for group decision-making offers several advantages, including computational simplicity, flexibility in handling uncertainty analysis, the ability to deal with large decision matrices, and robust outcomes.

The study highlights the urgent need to formulate a structured green policy for effective governance, as well as the requirement for logistics innovation to develop cost-effective and efficient technological solutions. Among the sectors being compared, the Automobile (S1) and FMCG (S4) industries exhibit significant adaptability, whereas the Textile and Apparel (S2) industry continues to encounter ongoing difficulties in adopting sustainable methods. The Chemical (S3) and Steel/Metal/Cement (S5) sectors exhibit moderate responsiveness to environmental requirements, suggesting that strategic investments in green technologies and incentives could enhance their sustainability initiatives.

However, the study could have benefited from incorporating experts from other industries and a greater number of alternatives and attributes to overcome its limitations.

8.7.1 Limitations and Future Scopes

Although the present study advances the literature by proposing an innovative and reliable MCDM framework to identify the key enablers for the adoption of green logistics practices and the readiness of various industries, it also paves the way for further extensions, as summarized below.

a) It is evident from several past contributions that advanced technologies (e.g., digital twin, blockchain, AR/VR, IoT) and analytical methods inspired by AI/ML have the potential to become game changers, helping to implement green logistics practices. However, the present study is silent on their role in enhancing environmental sustainability through green logistics practices. This will be an exciting opportunity for further research.
b) Although the current research has compared various industries based on their readiness to adopt green logistics through the lens of several enabling factors, there is a possibility of investigating the impact of such enablers on firm performance and green logistics practices. A large-scale empirical study may be planned in this regard. In this context, an in-depth sectoral analysis can also be performed.
c) This study has focused solely on the manufacturing sector. In future work, researchers can also consider the relevance of enabling factors and their impact on sustainable logistics practices by service organizations, such as 3PLs, E-commerce service providers, and others.
d) Future work may be planned to explore the barriers to the adoption of green logistics and their enabling factors at various stages of the supply chain, such as inbound, outbound, and last-mile delivery.
e) Future research can also concentrate on multi-modal green logistics networks (including the reverse path) to unveil the critical issues for holistic logistics planning.
f) The current work employs a theoretical framework based on the TTF model. Future plans may also include multiple theoretical lenses in addition to TTF.
g) This work can also be extended further by considering other measures of uncertainty, like various fuzzy numbers and rough sets. The methods used in this research can also be explored in solving several other practical research problems.

Nonetheless, the innovative and rigorous approach to addressing a topical issue is the strength of the current work, which may be of interest to decision-makers and scholars.

Declarations

The authors hereby declare that the present work is an original one. No external funding has been received to carry out this research. Necessary information is provided in the paper and/or made available as a supplementary file. For any further requirements, the authors may be contacted. The paper is free from commercial influence, and the authors are solely responsible for the research outcomes and opinions expressed in this work. No generative AI software is used for data presentation and idea generation. For polishing the write-up and correcting grammatical mistakes, the authors have sought help from the professional software Grammarly.

Authors' Contributions

All authors have equally contributed to conceptualization, research design, data collection and formatting, methodology, software development, formal analysis, validation, writing the original draft, and editing.

AI disclosure statement: The author acknowledges the use of AI-based tools for minor language editing or grammatical correction. However, all intellectual contributions, analyses, and conclusions presented in this chapter are entirely the author's own.

References

1. Banik, A., Taqi, H.M.M., Ali, S.M., Ahmed, S., Garshasbi, M., Kabir, G., Critical success factors for implementing green supply chain management in the electronics industry: an emerging economy case. *Int. J. Logist. Res. Appl.*, *25*, 4–5, 493–520, 2022, https://doi.org/10.1080/13675567.2020.1839029.
2. Asif, M.S., Lau, H., Nakandala, D., Fan, Y., Hurriyet, H., Adoption of green supply chain management practices through collaboration approach in developing countries–From literature review to conceptual framework. *J. Cleaner Prod.*, *276*, 124191, 2020.

3. Singh, P.L., Sindhwani, R., Sharma, B.P., Srivastava, P., Rajpoot, P., Lalit, Kumar, R., Analyse the critical success factor of green manufacturing for achieving sustainability in automotive sector, in: *Recent Trends in Industrial and Production Engineering: Select Proceedings of ICCEMME 2021*, Springer Singapore, pp. 79–94, 2022.
4. IBEF Report, Transforming India's Logistics Sector: Challenges and Opportunities, 2024, Available at: https://www.ibef.org/research/case-study/transforming-india-s-logistics-sector-challenges-and-opportunities (Last accessed on January 22, 2025).
5. PIB Report, Net zero emissions target, 2023, Available at: https://pib.gov.in/PressReleaseIframePage.aspx?PRID=1945472 (Last accessed on January 25, 2025).
6. Dzwigol, H., Trushkina, N., Kwilinski, A., The organizational and economic mechanism of implementing the concept of green logistics. *London Acad. Sci. Bus.*, 4, 2, 41–75, 2021.
7. Menon, R.R. and Ravi, V., Analysis of enablers of sustainable supply chain management in electronics industries: The Indian context. *Cleaner Eng. Technol.*, 5, 100302, 2021, https://doi.org/10.1016/j.clet.2021.100302.
8. Roh, T., Noh, J., Oh, Y., Park, K.S., Structural relationships of a firm's green strategies for environmental performance: The roles of green supply chain management and green marketing innovation. *J. Cleaner Prod.*, *356*, 131877, 2022, https://doi.org/10.1016/j.jclepro.2022.131877.
9. Nayak, K., Singhal, D., Tripathy, S., Mohapatra, B., Evaluation of key enablers of green supply chain management in Indian manufacturing industries: a fuzzy approach. *Int. J. Serv. Oper. Manage.*, *44*, 1, 62–92, 2023, https://doi.org/10.1504/IJSOM.2023.128946.
10. Inkwood Research, 2023, https://www.inkwoodresearch.com/reports/india-green-logistics-market/ (Accessed on January 25, 2025).
11. PIB Report, DPIIT promotes green logistics industry balancing economic growth and environment, 2024, https://pib.gov.in/PressReleasePage.aspx?PRID=2037575 (Last accessed on January 25, 2025).
12. Derse, O., Prioritizing solutions of green Reverse logistics barriers with Fuzzy DEMATEL–FUCOM–SWARA methods. *Ecol. Indic.*, 165, 112198, 2024, https://doi.org/10.1016/j.ecolind.2024.112198.
13. Kamewor, F.T., Kwateng, K.O., Mensah, J., Green logistics practices: A bibliometric and systematic methodological review and future research opportunities. *J. Cleaner Prod.*, 143735, 2024, https://doi.org/10.1016/j.jclepro.2024.143735.
14. Goodhue, D.L. and Thompson, R.L., Task-technology fit and individual performance. *MIS Q.*, 213–236, 1995, https://doi.org/10.2307/249689.
15. Alyoussef, I.Y., E-Learning acceptance: The role of task–technology fit as sustainability in higher education. *Sustainability*, 13, 11, 6450, 2021, https://doi.org/10.3390/su13116450.

16. Mumtaz, U.U., Bergey, P., Letch, N., Assessing the role of blockchain technology for marine bunkering operations–A case study of task technology fit. *Mar. Policy*, 159, 105909, 2024, https://doi.org/10.1016/j.marpol.2023.105909.
17. Sun, X., Kuo, Y.H., Xue, W., Li, Y., Technology-driven logistics and supply chain management for societal impacts. *Transp. Res. Part E Logist. Transp. Rev.*, 185, 103523, 2024, https://doi.org/10.1016/j.tre.2024.103523.
18. Jan, A., Salameh, A.A., Rahman, H.U., Alasiri, M.M., Can blockchain technologies enhance environmental sustainable development goals performance in manufacturing firms? Potential mediation of green supply chain management practices. *Bus. Strategy Environ.*, 33, 3, 2004–2019, 2024, https://doi.org/10.1002/bse.3579.
19. Seikh, M.R. and Mandal, U., Multiple attribute group decision making based on quasirung orthopair fuzzy sets: Application to electric vehicle charging station site selection problem. *Eng. Appl. Artif. Intell.*, 115, 105299, 2022, https://doi.org/10.1016/j.engappai.2022.105299.
20. Yager, R.R., Modeling multi-criteria objective functions using fuzzy measures. *Inf. Fusion*, 29, 105–111, 2016, https://doi.org/10.1016/j.inffus.2015.07.007.
21. Yager, R.R., Pythagorean membership grades in multicriteria decision making. *IEEE Trans. Fuzzy Syst.*, 22, 4, 958–965, 2013, https://doi.org/10.1109/TFUZZ.2013.2278989.
22. Yager, R.R., Properties and applications of Pythagorean fuzzy sets, in: *Imprecision and Uncertainty in information representation and processing: new tools based on intuitionistic fuzzy sets and generalized nets*, pp. 119–136, Springer International Publishing, Cham, 2015.
23. Atanassov, K.T., Intuitionistic fuzzy sets. *Fuzzy Sets Syst.*, 20, 1, 87–96, 1986, https://doi.org/10.1016/S0165-0114(86)80034-3.
24. Rahim, M., Garg, H., Khan, S., Alqahtani, H., Khalifa, H.A.E.W., Group decision-making algorithm with sine trigonometric p, q-quasirung orthopair aggregation operators and their applications. *Alex. Eng. J.*, 78, 530–542, 2023, https://doi.org/10.1016/j.aej.2023.07.051.
25. Ahmad, T., Rahim, M., Yang, J., Alharbi, R., Khalifa, H.A.E.W., Development of p, q– quasirung orthopair fuzzy hamacher aggregation operators and its application in decision-making problems. *Heliyon*, 10, 3, 2024, https://doi.org/10.1016/j.heliyon.2024.e24726.
26. Talib, H.M., Albahri, A.S., Thierry, O.C., Fuzzy decision-making framework for sensitively prioritizing autism patients with moderate emergency level. *Appl. Data Sci. Anal.*, 2023, 16–41, 2023, https://doi.org/10.58496/ADSA/2023/002.
27. Redhu, A. and Kumar, K., Multi-attribute group decision making based on p, q-quasirung orthopair fuzzy Yager prioritized weighted geometric aggregation operator of p, q-quasirung orthopair fuzzy numbers. *Granular Comput.*, 9, 4, 75, 2024, https://doi.org/10.1007/s41066-024-00495-1.
28. Chu, Y.M., Garg, H., Rahim, M., Amin, F., Asiri, A., Ameer, E., Some p, q-cubic quasi-rung orthopair fuzzy operators for multi-attribute

decision-making. *Complex Intell. Syst.*, 10, 1, 87–110, 2024, https://doi.org/10.1007/s40747-023-01092-6.
29. Biswas, S., Pamucar, D., Simic, V., Technology adaptation in sugarcane supply chain based on a novel p, q Quasirung Orthopair Fuzzy decision making framework. *Sci. Rep.*, 14, 1, 26486, 2024, https://doi.org/10.1038/s41598-024-75528-5.
30. Yager, R.R. and Alajlan, N., Approximate reasoning with generalized orthopair fuzzy sets. *Inf. Fusion*, 38, 65–73, 2017, https://doi.org/10.1016/j.inffus.2017.02.005.
31. Yager, R.R., Alajlan, N., Bazi, Y., Aspects of generalized orthopair fuzzy sets. *Int. J. Intell. Syst.*, 33, 11, 2154–2174, 2018, https://doi.org/10.1002/int.22008.
32. Saha, A., Majumder, P., Dutta, D., Debnath, B.K., Multi-attribute decision making using q-rung orthopair fuzzy weighted fairly aggregation operators. *J. Ambient Intell. Hum. Comput.*, 12, 8149–8171, 2021, https://doi.org/10.1007/s12652-020-02585-9.
33. Pillay, K. and Mbhele, T.P., The challenges of green logistics in the Durban road freight industry. *Environ. Econ.*, 6, 1, 64–73, 2015.
34. Panghal, A., P, A., Vern, P., Mor, R.S., Adoption barriers to green logistics in the Indian food industry: A circular economy perspective. *Int. Social Sci. J.*, 74, 252, 519–538, 2024, https://doi.org/10.1111/issj.12466.
35. Chhabra, D. and Kr Singh, R., Analyzing barriers to green logistics in context of Circular Economy and Industry 4.0 in the Indian manufacturing industry. *Int. J. Logist. Res. Appl.*, 27, 11, 1939–1952, 2024, https://doi.org/10.1080/13675567.2022.2134847.
36. Olejniczak, K., Dębicka, A., Zielewicz, J., Urbańska, J., Schab, M., Nowak, S., Green logistics in e-commerce: goals and challenges. *Zesz. Nauk. Politech. Pozn. Organ. Zarządz.*, 18, 1, 127–144, 2023.
37. Gupta, H., Shreshth, K., Kharub, M., Kumar, A., Strategies to overcome challenges to smart sustainable logistics: a Bayesian-based group decision-making approach. *Environ. Dev. Sustainability*, 26, 5, 11743–11770, 2024, https://doi.org/10.1007/s10668-023-03477-6.
38. Khayyat, M., Balfaqih, M., Balfaqih, H., Ismail, M., Challenges and Factors Influencing the Implementation of Green Logistics: A Case Study of Saudi Arabia. *Sustainability*, 16, 13, 5617, 2024, https://doi.org/10.3390/su16135617.
39. Yang, Z., Shang, W.L., Zhang, H., Garg, H., Han, C., Assessing the green distribution transformer manufacturing process using a cloud-based q-rung orthopair fuzzy multi-criteria framework. *Appl. Energy*, 311, 118687, 2022, https://doi.org/10.1016/j.apenergy.2022.118687.
40. Liu, S., Thurasamy, R., Hati, S.R.H., Determinants and Outcomes of Green Technology Innovation Adoption among Third-Party Logistics Firms in China: A SEM-ANN Analysis. *Systems*, 12, 9, 331, 2024, https://doi.org/10.3390/systems12090331.

41. Moktadir, M.A. and Ren, J., Towards green logistics: An innovative decision support model for zero-emission transportation modes development. *Transp. Res. Part E Logist. Transp. Rev.*, 189, 103648, 2024, https://doi.org/10.1016/j.tre.2024.103648.
42. Nikseresht, A., Golmohammadi, D., Zandieh, M., Sustainable green logistics and remanufacturing: a bibliometric analysis and future research directions. *Int. J. Logist. Manage.*, 35, 3, 755–803, 2024, https://doi.org/10.1108/IJLM-03-2023-0085.
43. Starostka-Patyk, M., Bajdor, P., Białas, J., Green logistics performance Index as a benchmarking tool for EU countries environmental sustainability. *Ecol. Indic.*, 158, 111396, 2024, https://doi.org/10.1016/j.ecolind.2023.111396.
44. Youngswaing, W., Jomnonkwao, S., Cheunkamon, E., Ratanavaraha, V., Key factors shaping green logistics in Thailand's auto industry: an application of structural equation modeling. *Logistics*, 8, 1, 17, 2024, https://doi.org/10.3390/logistics8010017.
45. David, D. and Alamoodi, A., A bibliometric analysis of research on multiple criteria decision making with emphasis on Energy Sector between (2019-2023). *Appl. Data Sci. Anal.*, 2023, 143–149, 2023, https://doi.org/10.58496/ADSA/2023/013.
46. Beškovnik, B. and Jakomin, L., Challenges of green logistics in Southeast Europe. *Promet Traffic Transp.*, 22, 2, 147–155, 2010, https://doi.org/10.7307/ptt.v22i2.174.
47. Deloitte, Sustainable supply chains in India, 2023, Available at: https://www.deloitte.com/in/en/about/governance/global-impact-report/sustainable-and-responsible-supply-chain.html (Last accessed on January 22, 2025).
48. FICCI, Sustainable multimodal logistics: A vision and green logistics paradigm, 2024, Available at: https://ficci.in/public/storage/SPDocument/23916/HjutM3qScDsxpQTG5SDa3LZzaqdqvfvHuX4wP5vX.pdf (Last accessed on January 22, 2025).
49. Aayog, N.I.T.I., *Transforming trucking in India: Pathways to zero-emission truck deployment*, Government of India, 2022, Available at: https://www.niti.gov.in/sites/default/files/2023-02/ZETReport09092022.pdf (Last Accessed on January 22, 2025).
50. Aayog, N.I.T.I., *Zero emission vehicles (ZEVs): Towards a policy framework*, Government of India, 2021, Available at: https://e-amrit.niti.gov.in/assets/admin/dist/img/new-fronend-img/report-pdf/EV_report.pdf (Last accessed on January 22, 2025).
51. Kendall, M.G., *Rank correlation methods*, Charles Griffin & Company, 1948.
52. Biswas, S., Exploring the implications of digital marketing for higher education using intuitionistic fuzzy group decision making approach. *BIMTECH Bus. Perspect.*, 2, 1, 33–51, 2021, https://doi.org/10.1177/bsp.2021.2.1.33.
53. Pamucar, D., Simic, V., Görçün, O.F., Küçükönder, H., Selection of the best Big Data platform using COBRAC-ARTASI methodology with adaptive

standardized intervals. *Expert Syst. Appl.*, 239, 122312, 2024, https://doi.org/10.1016/j.eswa.2023.122312.

54. Puška, A., Nedeljković, M., Božanić, D., Štilić, A., Muhsen, Y.R., Evaluation of agricultural drones based on the COmpromise Ranking from Alternative SOlutions (CORASO) methodology. *Eng. Rev.*, 44, 4-SI 2024, 77–90, 2024, https://doi.org/10.30765/er.2653.
55. Tufan, D., Ulutaş, A., Supplier Selection in the Food Sector: An Integrated Approach Using LODECI and CORASO Methods. *Spectr. Decis. Mak. Appl.*, 3, 1, 40–51, 2026, https://doi.org/10.31181/sdmap31202631.
56. Biswas, S., Chatterjee, P., Zavadskas, E.K., PRASIAS: A New Preference Ranking Model for Comparing Organizational Performance under Disruption. *Int. J. Inf. Technol. Decis. Mak.*, 2025a. https://doi.org/10.1142/S0219622025500208.
57. Puška, A., Selection of CRM systems using objective criteria for the needs of small companies. *Int. J. Knowl. Innov. Stud.*, 3, 1, 1–11, 2025, https://doi.org/10.56578/ijkis030101.
58. Rahim, M., Tag Eldin, E.M., Khan, S., Ghamry, N.A., Alanzi, A.M., Khalifa, H.A.E.W., Multi-criteria group decision-making based on dombi aggregation operators under p, q-quasirung orthopair fuzzy sets. *J. Intell. Fuzzy Syst.*, 46, 1, 53–74, 2024, https://doi.org/10.3233/JIFS-233327.
59. Biswas, S. and Pamučar, D.S., Combinative distance based assessment (CODAS) framework using logarithmic normalization for multi-criteria decision making. *Serb. J. Manage.*, 16, 2, 321–340, 2021, https://doi.org/10.5937/sjm16-27758.
60. Biswas, S., Biswas, B., Mitra, K., A novel group decision making model to compare online shopping platforms. *Spectr. Decis. Mak. Appl.*, 2, 1, 1–27, 2025b. https://doi.org/10.31181/sdmap2120259.
61. Garg, H., Ayaz, K., Emam, W., Multi attribute decision-making algorithms using Hamacher Choquet-integral operators with complex intuitionistic fuzzy information. *AIMS Math.*, 9, 12, 35860–35884, 2024.
62. Deveci, M., Gokasar, I., Pamucar, D., Biswas, S., Simic, V., An integrated proximity indexed value and q-rung orthopair fuzzy decision-making model for prioritization of green campus transportation, in: *q-Rung orthopair fuzzy sets: theory and applications*, pp. 303–332, Springer Nature Singapore, Singapore, 2022.
63. Görçün, O.F., Pamucar, D., Biswas, S., The blockchain technology selection in the logistics industry using a novel MCDM framework based on Fermatean fuzzy sets and Dombi aggregation. *Inf. Sci.*, 635, 345–374, 2023, https://doi.org/10.1016/j.ins.2023.03.113.
64. Saqlain, M., Garg, H., Kumam, W., Zulqarnain, R.M., Einstein Aggregation Operator Technique for Linguistic q-Rung Orthopair Fuzzy Hypersoft Set with Application to Sustainable Construction Industry. *IEEE Access*, 2025, https://doi.org/10.1109/ACCESS.2025.3555015.

65. Puppim de Oliveira, J.A. and Qian, H., Perspectives in global environmental governance. *Glob. Public Policy Gov.*, 3, 1, 5–11, 2023, https://doi.org/10.1007/s43508-023-00063-4.
66. Xu, C. and Li, L., The dynamic relationship among green logistics, technological innovation and green economy: Evidence from China. *Heliyon*, 10, 4, e26534, 2024, https://doi.org/10.1016/j.heliyon.2024.e26534.
67. Yang, B. and Wang, Z., Environmental regulation, green technology innovation and green logistics development level of fresh agricultural products. *Int. J. Logist. Res. Appl.*, 1–22, 2024, https://doi.org/10.1080/13675567.2024.2367545.
68. Wang, C., Rahman, M.M., Siddik, A.B., Wen, Z.G., Sobhani, F.A., Exploring the synergy of logistics, finance, and technology on innovation. *Sci. Rep.*, 14, 1, 21918, 2024, https://doi.org/10.1038/s41598-024-72409-9.
69. Zhan, K. and Wu, D., Impact of green credit incentives on operational decisions of green supply chain. *Green Low-Carbon Econ.*, 2024, https://doi.org/10.47852/bonviewGLCE42021699.
70. Kim, H. and Zhang, L., Green Process Innovations in FMCG and Their Impact on Sustainability. *J. Clean. Prod.*, 280, 125–137, 2024.
71. Wang, J., Li, Y., Zhou, P., Green Logistics and Sustainability in the Automotive Sector. *Eur. J. Sustain. Dev.*, 12, 3, 45–62, 2023.
72. García, R., Chen, S., Patel, M., Challenges in Implementing Circular Economy Models in the Textile Industry. *J. Ind. Ecol.*, 29, 1, 34–52, 2025.

9

Distance-Based Consensus in a Fuzzy Soft Group Decision-Making and Its Application on Sustainable Supplier Selection

Soumi Manna[1]*, Tanushree Mitra Basu[2] and Shyamal Kumar Mondal[1]

[1]Department of Applied Mathematics, Vidyasagar University, Midnapore, W.B., India
[2]Department of Applied Mathematics, C.D.O.E, Vidyasagar University, Midnapore, W.B., India

Abstract
In the current phase of research, group decision-making based on fuzzy soft set theory has become a well-accepted strait to the researchers. However, due to diverse backgrounds of the associated decision makers, it is a very difficult task to them to provide similar types of opinions about an alternative, in spite of that, to complete a transparent decision process and to get a quality solution from the problem, opinions of all the decision makers should be taken into consideration. Such type of situation in a problem demands consensus-measuring mechanism for the decision makers. Therefore, in this paper, we have studied a consensus-measuring and reaching approach to consensus threshold in fuzzy soft set-based group decision-making. In this regard, a new algorithmic approach has been proposed for solving fuzzy soft set-based group decision-making problems by utilizing fuzzy distance and fuzzy soft distance *via* three main steps: consensus level measuring step, consensus level increasing step and then, best decision solution selection step. After that, we have demonstrated a case study on sustainable supplier selection problem in a textile industry to show the applicability of our proposed approach. A comprehensive comparative discussion has been illustrated from which it has been proven that, our proposed methodology is more logical and effective than the other existing fuzzy soft set-based group decision-making.

**Corresponding author*: soumimaths13@gmail.com

Harish Garg (ed.) Decision Support Systems in Smart Computing: Embracing Uncertainty and Challenges, (259–304) © 2026 Scrivener Publishing LLC

Keywords: Fuzzy soft set, fuzzy aggregation, group decision-making, comprehensive consensus level, sustainable supplier selection

9.1 Introduction

Uncertainty is an unavoidable plague in science and mathematics. Usually, in classical mathematics, all the constructed models require exact or real data to make a conventional prediction from a problem. But, from the grounds of reality, it is not always possible to serve all the data in real or exact forms because of the issue of uncertainty. Consequently, researchers have paid much more attention on solving problems containing uncertain information. Zadeh's fuzzy set theory [27] is one of the current effective mathematical tools for handling uncertainty by using the notion of membership function. Over the past few decades, many real-life related problems from several fields including, pattern recognition [22], decision-making [28], approximate-reasoning [3], cluster analysis [21], medical science [6], etc. have been concluded by using fuzzy set theory.

However, Molodtsov alluded that, in fuzzy set theory, the membership function of an element may differ from one to another. So, there is an open question about the uniqueness of a membership function which reduces the efficiency of fuzzy set theory in solving problems under uncertainty. Besides, in a particular case, construct of a membership function is very difficult. Molodtsov stated that [20], lack of parameterization may be the reason of these difficulties. Then, to reduce these difficulties, he proposed the idea of soft set theory [20] by using the notion of parameterization. Basically, in a soft set, all the associated alternatives are defined through some considered parameters instead of using a membership function likewise fuzzy set. Consequently, with a very small duration of time, soft set theory has achieved huge popularity to the researchers. Then, several algebraic operations, algebraic structures and fundamental results have been initiated through soft set theory. First, Maji *et al.* [18] engaged in developing some basic algebraic operations including, union, intersection, AND, OR, etc. on soft sets. Then, researchers have introduced several algebraic structures like, soft group [1], soft mapping [19], soft relation [23], etc. on soft set theory. Further, soft set has been applied [18] in solving decision-making problems. In this regard, Çağman and Enginoğlu [5] introduced the notion of soft matrices and some of their properties to handle decision-making problems more easily.

Besides these theoretical developments, several new generalizations of soft set theory have been introduced by using different parameterizations.

Fuzzy soft set [17] is one of the significant generalizations of soft set theory where, soft set theory has been incorporated with fuzzy set theory by considering all the parameters in fuzzy sense i.e., by using fuzzy parameterization. In a fuzzy soft set, the evaluation of an alternative over a parameter is in terms of fuzzy membership where no need to introduce a membership function to define a fuzzy membership of an alternative rather all the evaluations are defined based on the human cognitive system. In solving various types of real-life problems, fuzzy soft sets have been widely used by the researchers. For instance, Roy and Maji [24], Kong *et al.* [14, 15], Feng *et al.* [8], etc. have used fuzzy soft sets in decision-making. Then, Basu *et al.* [4], Li *et al.* [16], Wang *et al.* [26], etc. have used fuzzy soft sets in decision-making in medical science. Moreover, sometimes, in a fuzzy soft set-based decision-making, multiple decision makers have been engaged in evaluating the associated alternatives with respect to some parameters. Based on the existing literature, we have seen that, Roy and Maji [24], Basu *et al.* [4] and Alcantud [2] have addressed such type of multiple observer decision-making problems through fuzzy soft sets and in this regard, they have used different aggregation operators to construct a resultant fuzzy soft set from a multiple numbers of fuzzy soft sets.

Moreover, Saeed *et al.* [25] proposed a new idea of refined fuzzy soft sets where both the membership and nonmembership degrees have been allowed. They have also defined some operations like complement, union, intersection, projection, etc., over this refined fuzzy soft set so that one can use it in solving decision-making problems. Further, Garg and Arora [11] proposed a decision-making approach over group-based generalized intuitionistic fuzzy soft set (GGIFSS) to reduce the single experts preferences influence. Fathima *et al.* [7] also developed a new decision-making approach based on spherical fuzzy soft sets. Garg *et al.* [12] also used spherical fuzzy soft topology in group decision making. Further there are many other decision-making problems [10].

Research Gap: In current fuzzy soft set-based decision-making, researchers have focused on recognizing the best alternative based on the opinions of the decision makers with respect to some selected parameters. In reality, though, the opinions of all the decision-makers regarding an alternative might not be correct, or some of them might hold differing views. Therefore, it is crucial to measure the consensus of a decision maker in order to obtain an exact outcome. Consensus measurement of a decision maker about an alternative means, the determination of the similarity degree of the decision maker with the other decision makers for his/her provided opinion about the alternative. Therefore, prior to choosing the best alternative from a group decision-making process, measuring a decision maker's consensus is crucial because, if there is low disagreement with the others, then the decision maker will get an opportunity to recheck his/her opinion about the alternative before selecting the best decision solution from the problem. But, in all the above existing approaches, researchers did not focus on this issue. So, there is a research gap in solving fuzzy soft set-based group decision-making.

Objectives: The following are the primary goals of this work in order to address this research gap:

- Present an algorithmic approach for handling decisions involving multiple decision makers under fuzzy soft set environment.
- Find out the consensus of the decision makers to determine the similarity in their opinions.
- Make an idea for increasing the consensus of a decision maker, who has less consensus than the considered threshold value.
- Apply the algorithmic approach in real life.

Highlights: From the above discussion, our main contributions can be highlighted as follows:

- We have established a methodological approach for solving fuzzy soft set-based group decision-making problems with the help of fuzzy distance and fuzzy soft distance which mainly contains three major parts.
- In the first part, we have provided Algorithm I by which one can measure the comprehensive consensus level of a decision maker about an alternative in a fuzzy soft set-based group decision-making.
- Then, in the second part, we have discussed Algorithm II where we have given two suggestions by which a decision maker, who has less comprehensive consensus than the considered threshold value, can reformulate his/her primary opinion about the alternative so that, his/her comprehensive consensus level can be increased up to the considered threshold value.
- After that, we have provided two algorithms, Algorithm III and Algorithm IV for selecting the best alternatives.

- A sustainable supplier selection problem of a textile industry has been solved by using our proposed fuzzy soft set-based group approach to show the real-life applicability of our proposed approach.

The outline of the paper is as follows:
Section 9.2 recalls some basic notions which have been utilized in this paper. In Section 9.3, we have provided a new methodological approach to solve fuzzy soft set-based group decision-making problems. Then, in Section 9.4, an experimental analysis regarding the sustainable supplier selection problem of a textile industry has been illustrated and solved by applying our proposed methodological approach. In Section 9.5, we have discussed some comparative analyses to verify the validity and effectiveness of our proposed approach Section 9.6 contains some conclusions of this paper.

9.2 Some Basic Relevant Notions

In this section, we have discussed some basic concepts including, fuzzy soft set (FSS), fuzzy distance, fuzzy soft distance, etc. which are related with our main interpretation.

9.2.1 Fuzzy Set Theory

In 1965, Prof. Zadeh [27] mentioned fuzzy set theory in literature to handle uncertainty by using the idea of membership function.

Definition 1 [27]. Let, X be an initial universe. Then, a fuzzy set A over X is an order pair (X, μ) where, μ is a mapping defined as, $\mu : X \rightarrow [0, 1], \forall x \in X$.

Then, for each $x \in X$, $\mu(x) \in [0, 1]$ is called the membership degree of x.

Now, if, $X = \{x_1; x_2, .., x_M\}$ is an initial universe, then a fuzzy set A over X can be defined as follows:

$$A = \{x_1/\mu(x_1); x_2/\mu(x_2), ..., x_M/\mu(x_M)\}$$

Definition 2 [27]. Let, $A = \{(x, \mu_A(x))|x \in X\}$, be a fuzzy set over the universe X. The complement of A is denoted by A^c and is expressed as,

$$A^c = \{(x, \mu_A^c(x)) \mid x \in X\}$$

where, $\mu_A^c(x) = 1 - \mu_A(x), x \in X$

Definition 3 [13]. Let $A = \{(x, \mu_A(x)) | x \in X\}$ and $B = \{(x, \mu_B(x)) | x \in X\}$ over a fixed universal set X. Then, the Fuzzy Euclidean Distance between A and B is defined as follows:

$$d_{Eu}(A,B)^1 = \left(\frac{1}{n} \sum_{j=1}^{n} \left(\mu_A(x) - \mu_B(x) \right)^2 \right)^{1/2}$$

9.2.2 Soft Set Theory

Soft set theory is a recent mathematical approach to deal with uncertainty by using the idea of parameterization where, initial illustration of an object is performed through some parameters in an approximate manner with the help of human cognitive process.

Definition 4 [20]. A soft set over the universe X can be referred as an order pair, (f, E) where, f is a set-valued map defined as, $f: E \to P(X)$; $P(X)$ is the set of all subsets of i.e., for each $e \in E$, a set of e-approximate elements of X is derived which is expressed as $f(e)$.

So, a soft set is a parameterized family of subsets of an universal set. By using the number 0 and 1, soft set can be illustrated in tabular form.

Example 1. Let, $X = \{b_1, b_2, b_3\}$ be the set of three bags and $E = \{$*Low weight*(e_1), *good design*(e_2), *cheap*(e_3), *good chain quality*$(e_4)\}$ be the set of four corresponding parameters by which we have defined these three bags.

Now, assume that, f is a mapping which represents the 'quality of the three bags' as follows, $f(e_1) = \{b_1, b_2, b_3\}$; $f(e_2) = \{b_1, b_2\}$; $f(e_3) = \{b_2, b_3\}$; $f(e_4) = \{b_1, b_3\}$.

Then, $(f, E) = \{(e_1, \{b_1, b_2, b_3\}), (e_2, \{b_1, b_2\}), (e_3, \{b_2, b_3\}), (e_4, \{b_1, b_3\})\}$ is a soft set over X by which '*quality of the three bags has been expressed over the four considered parameters*'. Tabular form of the soft set (f, E) has been

Table 9.1 Soft set (f, E).

	e_1	e_2	e_3	e_4
b_1	1	1	0	1
b_2	1	1	1	0
b_3	1	0	1	1

given in Table 9.1. In Table 9.1, the entry 1 indicates the *belongingness* of a parameter to a bag and the entry 0 indicates the *not non-belongingness* of a parameter to a bag.

9.2.3 Fuzzy Soft Set Theory

Fuzzy soft set theory is a generalization of the classical soft set theory by using fuzzy set theory where, all the considered parameters are in fuzzy sense.

Definition 5 [4]. Let, X be an initial universal set and E be the corresponding parameter set which are in fuzzy sense. Then, a fuzzy soft set over the set X can be defined as an order pair $(\tilde{f},E)$ where, $\tilde{f}$ is a set-valued map or approximate function depicted as, $\tilde{f}:E\rightarrow\tilde{P}(X), \tilde{P}(X)$ is the set of all fuzzy subsets of the set X. So, for each $e\in E, \tilde{f}(e)$ is a fuzzy set over the set X.

Mathematical illustration of a fuzzy soft set:
If, $X = \{x_1, x_2, .., x_m\}$ be a universal set and $E = \{e_1, e_2, .., e_n\}$ set of some fuzzy parameters. Then, a fuzzy soft set $(\tilde{f},E)$ over X is defined as follows:

$$\begin{aligned}(\tilde{f},E) &= \{(e_1,\tilde{f}(e_1)),(e_2,\tilde{f}(e_2)),..,(e_n,\tilde{f}(e_n))\}\\ &= \{(e_1,(x_1/\tilde{f}_{e_1}(x_1),x_2/\tilde{f}_{e_1}(x_2),..,x_m/\tilde{f}_{e_1}(x_m))),(e_2,(x_1/\tilde{f}_{e_2}(x_1),\\ &\quad x_2/\tilde{f}_{e_2}(x_2),..,x_m/\tilde{f}_{e_2}(x_m))),..,(e_n,(x_1/\tilde{f}_{e_n}(x_1),\\ &\quad x_2/\tilde{f}_{e_n}(x_2),..,x_m/\tilde{f}_{e_n}(x_m)))\}\end{aligned}$$

Here, $\tilde{f}_{e_j}(x_s)$ is the fuzzy-valued rating of an alternative x_s over the parameter e_j, s = 1, 2, ..., m and j = 1, 2, .., n. Tabular form of the fuzzy soft set $(\tilde{f},E)$ has been illustrated in Table 9.2. Now, we have discussed an example as follows.

Example 2. $X = \{d_1, d_2, d_3\}$ is a set of three dresses and $E = \{$*Cheap, Modern, Longevity*$\}$ is the corresponding three parameters which are in fuzzy sense.

Now, consider an approximate function $\tilde{f}$ which describes '*the attractiveness of the dresses*' in fuzzy sense as follows,

$$\begin{aligned}\tilde{f}(Cheap) &= \{(d_1,0.2),(d_2,0.5),(d_3,0.5)\};\\ \tilde{f}(Modern) &= \{(d_1,0.6),(d_2,0.1),(d_3,0.8)\};\\ \tilde{f}(Longevity) &= \{(d_1,0.8),(d_2,0.5),(d_3,0.6)\}.\end{aligned}$$

Table 9.2 Fuzzy soft set $(\tilde{f},E)$.

	e_1	e_2	...	e_n
x_1	$\tilde{f}_{e_1}(x_1)$	$\tilde{f}_{e_2}(x_1)$	...	$\tilde{f}_{e_n}(x_1)$
x_2	$\tilde{f}_{e_1}(x_2)$	$\tilde{f}_{e_2}(x_2)$	...	$\tilde{f}_{e_n}(x_2)$
...	...	...	...	...
x_m	$\tilde{f}_{e_1}(x_m)$	$\tilde{f}_{e_2}(x_m)$		$\tilde{f}_{e_n}(x_m)$

Then, $(\tilde{f},E)=\{(Cheap,\{(d_1,0.2),(d_2,0.5),(d_3,0.5)\}),(Modern,\{(d_1,0.6),(d_2,0.1),(d_3,0.8)\}),(Longevity,\{(d_1,0.8),(d_2,0.5),(d_3,0.6)\})\}$ is a fuzzy soft set over X, which represents '*the attractiveness of the three dresses over the three associated parameters*'. Now, the tabular representation of the fuzzy soft set $(\tilde{f},E)$ has been given in Table 9.3.

Definition 6 [17]. Let, $(\tilde{f},E)$ and $(\tilde{g},E)$ be two fuzzy soft sets over the fixed universe X as follows:

$$(\tilde{f},E)=\{(e_j,\tilde{f}(e_j))\,|\,e_j\in E\}=\{(e_j,(x_s,\tilde{f}_{e_j}(x_s)))\,|\,\forall e_j\in E,x_s\in X\};$$
$$(\tilde{g},E)=\{(e_j,\tilde{g}(e_j))\,|\,e_j\in E\}=\{(e_j,(x_s,\tilde{g}_{e_j}(x_s)))\,|\,\forall e_j\in E,x_s\in X\}.$$

Then, the fuzzy soft union of $(\tilde{f},E)$ and $(\tilde{g},E)$ is denoted by, $(\tilde{f},E)\tilde{\cup}(\tilde{f},E)=(\tilde{h},E)$ where, $\forall e_j\in E,\tilde{h}(e_j)=\tilde{f}(e_j)\cup\tilde{g}(e_j)=max_{s=1}^{m}\{\tilde{f}_{e_j}(x_s),\tilde{g}_{e_j}(x_s)\}$, $\cup$ *is the fuzzy union.*

Table 9.3 Fuzzy soft set $(\tilde{f},E)$.

	Cheap	*Modern*	*Longevity*
d_1	0.2	0.6	0.8
d_2	0.5	0.1	0.5
d_3	0.5	0.8	0.6

Definition 7 [9]. The, Euclidean distance of two fuzzy soft sets $(\tilde{f}, E)$ and $(\tilde{g}, E)$ (as defined above) is as follows:

$$D_{Eu}((\tilde{f}, E), (\tilde{g}, E)) = \frac{1}{n}\sum_{j=1}^{n} d_{Eu}(\tilde{f}(e_j), \tilde{g}(e_j))$$

where, $d_{Eu}(\tilde{f}(e_j), \tilde{g}(e_j)) = \left(\sum_{s=1}^{m} \left(\tilde{f}_{e_j}(x_s) - \tilde{g}_{e_j}(x_s) \right)^2 \right)^{\frac{1}{2}}$.

9.3 Fuzzy Soft Set-Based Group Decision-Making

Basically, fuzzy soft set-based group decision-making problems are humanistic and subjective in nature. Consequently, researchers have used it widely in practice. In a fuzzy soft set-based group decision-making, associated decision alternatives are evaluated by some decision makers with respect to some considered parameters in terms of fuzzy membership. In the existing literature it has been observed that, the researchers Roy and Maji [24], Basu *et al.* [4] and Alcantud [2] applied fuzzy soft sets in solving group decision-making to recognize the best alternative from a real-life problem where multiple decision makers have been involved. But, however, employed decision makers can have diverse opinions about the decision alternatives due to their different choices, different knowledge backgrounds and individual satisfaction levels. So, in that case, there may be an error at the final stage. Then, to deal with such an unworthy situation in a practical group decision-making problem, measuring the consensus of the opinion of an decision maker with the others is an effective issue. Therefore, now we have given a new algorithmic approach for solving fuzzy soft set-based group decision-making problems which exceeds the above difficulty. The main goals of our proposed approach are, to measure the consensus level of the associated decision makers about every alternative and then provide some suggestions to increase the consensus level of a decision maker, who has low consensus with the other decision makers for his/her provided opinion about the alternative, up to the considered threshold value. After that, to recognize the best alternative.

Now, the mathematical illustration of our considered fuzzy soft set-based group decision-making problem has been given in the next subsection.

9.3.1 Mathematical Illustration of the Problem

If we have m options or m alternatives as, $X = \{x_1, x_2, .., x_m\}$ and to define these m alternatives we have considered n parameters $E = \{e_1, e_2, .., e_n\}$ in fuzzy sense. Now, assume that, k decision makers $(D = \{d_1, d_2, .., d_k\})$ are employed to analyze these m alternatives with respect to n parameters through fuzzy soft set theory. Then, k fuzzy soft sets as, $(\tilde{f}^1, E), (\tilde{f}^2, E), .., (\tilde{f}^k, E)$ over X will be obtained for the k decision makers. The lth fuzzy soft set $(\tilde{f}^l, E)$ can be expressed mathematically as follows:

$$
\begin{aligned}
(\tilde{f}^l, E) = \{&(e_1, \{(x_1, \tilde{f}^l_{e_1}(x_1)), (x_2, \tilde{f}^l_{e_1}(x_2)), \ldots, (x_m, \tilde{f}^l_{e_1}(x_m))\}), (e_2, \{(x_1, \tilde{f}^l_{e_2}(x_1)),\\
&(x_2, \tilde{f}^l_{e_2}(x_2)), \ldots, (x_m, \tilde{f}^l_{e_2}(x_m))\}), \ldots, (e_n, \{(x_1, \tilde{f}^l_{e_n}(x_1)),\\
&(x_2, \tilde{f}^l_{e_n}(x_2)), \ldots, (x_m, \tilde{f}^l_{e_n}(x_m))\})\}; l = 1, 2, \ldots, k.
\end{aligned}
$$

These k fuzzy soft sets can be expressed in tabular form as given in Table 9.4.

Table 9.4 Tabular form of k fuzzy soft sets.

	$(\tilde{f}^1, E)$				$(\tilde{f}^2, E)$			
	e_1	e_2	...	e_n	e_1	e_2	...	e_n
x_1	$\tilde{f}^1_{e_1}(x_1)$	$\tilde{f}^1_{e_2}(x_1)$	...	$\tilde{f}^1_{e_n}(x_1)$	$\tilde{f}^2_{e_1}(x_1)$	$\tilde{f}^2_{e_2}(x_1)$	...	$\tilde{f}^2_{e_n}(x_1)$
x_2	$\tilde{f}^1_{e_1}(x_2)$	$\tilde{f}^1_{e_2}(x_2)$	...	$\tilde{f}^l_{e_n}(x_2)$	$\tilde{f}^2_{e_1}(x_2)$	$\tilde{f}^2_{e_2}(x_2)$	...	$\tilde{f}^2_{e_n}(x_2)$
x_m	$\tilde{f}^1_{e_1}(x_m)$	$\tilde{f}^1_{e_2}(x_m)$	...	$\tilde{f}^l_{e_n}(x_m)$	$\tilde{f}^2_{e_1}(x_m)$	$\tilde{f}^2_{e_2}(x_m)$	...	$\tilde{f}^2_{e_n}(x_m)$

	$(\tilde{f}^k, E)$			
	e_1	e_2	...	e_n
..	$\tilde{f}^k_{e_1}(x_1)$	$\tilde{f}^k_{e_2}(x_1)$	...	$\tilde{f}^k_{e_n}(x_1)$
..	$\tilde{f}^k_{e_1}(x_2)$	$\tilde{f}^k_{e_2}(x_2)$	...	$\tilde{f}^k_{e_n}(x_2)$
..	$\tilde{f}^k_{e_1}(x_m)$	$\tilde{f}^k_{e_2}(x_m)$	...	$\tilde{f}^k_{e_n}(x_m)$

9.3.2 Optimality Criteria

Now, in order to solve such type of fuzzy soft group decision-making problems, we will follow the following optimal criteria.

(i) The satisfaction of the optimal decision alternative will be maximum for most of the corresponding parameters over most of the associated decision makers.
(ii) The optimal decision alternative does not have huge difference of satisfaction from one decision maker to other decision makers with respect to each of the considered parameters.
(iii) The optimal decision alternative should have a minimum distance from the ideal decision alternative of this fuzzy soft group decision-making problem.

9.3.3 Solution Framework

In a fuzzy soft group decision-making, all the associated decision makers may have different opinions about the m decision alternatives due to their different choices, different knowledge backgrounds and individual satisfaction levels. So, before recognizing the best decision alternative consensus measuring mechanism for the decision makers is an essential issue from this problem. In this Subsection, we have proposed a solution approach to solve our considered fuzzy soft set-based group decision-making which follows the above-defined optimality criteria. Our proposed methodology consists mainly three parts as given in Figure 9.1. In first part, we have measured the comprehensive consensus level of every decision maker for every alternative over the every associated fuzzy soft set. In second part, we have given two suggestions to the decision makers, who have less comprehensive consensus than the considered threshold value λ for a certain alternative, to reformulate his/her opinion about the alternative so that, his/her comprehensive consensus level about the alternative can be increased up to the considered threshold value λ before selecting the best decision alternative from the problem. In third part, best decision alternative recognition process has been provided. For each of the different parts, we have provided individual algorithms. Algorithm I is for first part (to measure the comprehensive consensus level). Algorithm II is for second part (to increase the comprehensive consensus level). For third part (best alternative selection), we have provided two different algorithms, Algorithm III and Algorithm IV.

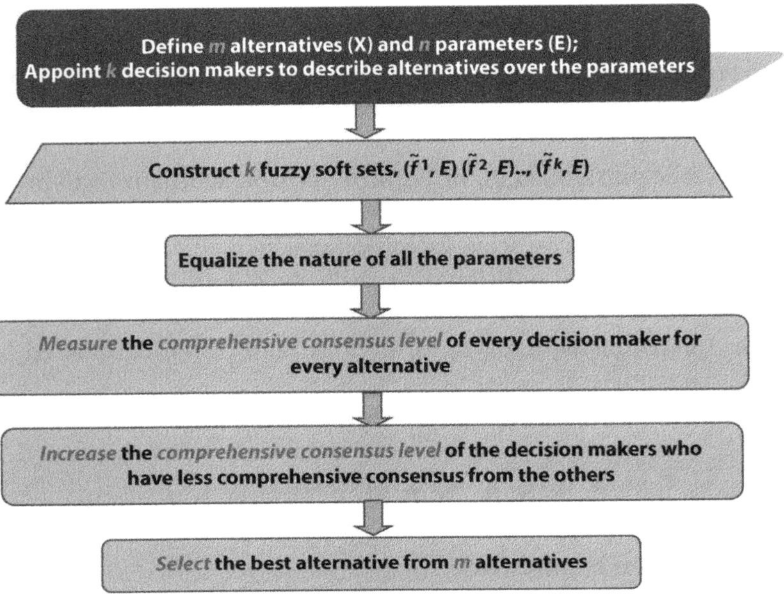

Figure 9.1 Schematic framework of our proposed approach.

9.3.3.1 *Algorithm I (Measurement of Comprehensive Consensus Level)*

Step 1. Input the set of m alternatives, $X = \{x_1, x_2, .., x_m\}$, and the set of n corresponding parameters, $E = \{e_1, e_2, .., e_n\}$. Input k fuzzy soft sets $(\tilde{f}^1, E), (\tilde{f}^2, E), .., (\tilde{f}^k, E)$ which have been given by k decision makers, $D = \{d_1, d_2, .., d_k\}$. Tabular form of the k fuzzy soft sets has been given in Table 9.4.

Step 2. *Equalization of all the decision evaluations.*
In this fuzzy soft group decision-making, considered parameters may have conflicting disposition in practice i.e., some of them may have positive character (positive parameter means, with respect to such kind of parameter, high evaluation of a decision alternative is good) and some of them may have negative character (negative parameter means, with respect to such kind of parameter, low evaluation of a decision alternative is good). Then, to deal with this equivocal situation in a fuzzy soft group decision-making, we have equalized all the corresponding decision evaluations before solving this problem as follows:

- Firstly, we have classified positive parameters (suppose its collection set is A) and negative parameters (suppose its collection set is B) from the set E where, $A \cup B = E$ and $A \cap B = \varphi$.
- Then, we have taken the fuzzy complement (as given in Section 2) of the evaluations of all the decision alternatives with respect to every negative parameter for every associated fuzzy soft set.

Step 3. *Measurement of the consensus level of every pair of decision makers.* The consensus level or closeness level between two decision makers d_l and $d_{l'}$ with respect to their associated fuzzy soft sets $(\tilde{f}^l, \tilde{E})$ and $(f^{l'}, E)$ for an alternative x_s is denoted $\Theta^s(l, l')$ and is derived as follows:

$$\Theta^s(l,l') = 1 - d(\tilde{f}^l(x_s), \tilde{f}^{l'}(x_s)) \tag{9.1}$$

where, d is the fuzzy distance (given in point *(ii)* in Section 9.2.2) and $\tilde{f}^l(x_s)$, $\tilde{f}^{l'}(x_s)$ are the fuzzy approximations of an alternative x_s over all the parameters provided by the experts d_l and $d_{l'}$ as follows:

$$\tilde{f}^l(x_s) = \{(e_1, \tilde{f}^l_{e_1}(x_s)), (e_2, \tilde{f}^l_{e_2}(x_s)), .., (e_n, \tilde{f}^l_{e_n}(x_s))\};$$
$$\tilde{f}^{l'}(x_s) = \{(e_1, \tilde{f}^{l'}_{e_1}(x_s)), (e_2, \tilde{f}^{l'}_{e_2}(x_s)), .., (e_n, \tilde{f}^{l'}_{e_n}(x_s))\}.$$

Step 4. *Derivation of the comprehensive consensus level of a decision maker d_l for an alternative x_s.* The comprehensive consensus level of a decision maker d_l for an alternative x_s with respect to his/her associated fuzzy soft set $(\tilde{f}^l, E)$ is denoted by, $\Theta^s(l)$ and is defined by the following equation:

$$\Theta^s(l) = \sum_{l'=1, l \neq l'}^{k} \frac{\Theta^s(l,l')}{k-1} \tag{9.2}$$

Step 5. Let, λ $(0 < \lambda \leq 1)$ be the threshold value for the comprehensive consensus level of this fuzzy soft set based group decision-making. If, comprehensive consensus level of each of the decision makers for every alternative is greater than or equals to the considered threshold value λ then, we can go to the selection process i.e., if $\Theta^s(l) \geq \lambda$; $\forall s = 1, 2, .., m$; $l = 1, 2, .., k$ then, we will start the selection process to recognize the best decision alternative.

But, if, the comprehensive consensus level of some decision makers for some alternatives is less than the considered threshold value λ then, we will go to the Algorithm II to increase the comprehensive consensus level of these decision makers before selecting the best decision alternative.

9.3.3.2 *Algorithm II (Improvement Process of Comprehensive Consensus Level)*

Suppose that, at T^{th} decision round ($T = 1, 2, 3, ...$), the comprehensive consensus level ($\Theta^s(l)$) of a decision maker d_l for an alternative x_s is less than the considered threshold value λ. Then, to increase the comprehensive consensus level of the decision maker d_l for the alternative x_s at the next decision round ($T + 1$), we will follow the following steps. Suppose, at T^{th} decision round, the primary evaluation of an alternative x_s over a parameter e_j given by the decision maker d_l is $\tilde{f}^{l}_{ej,T}(xs)$.

Step 1. Select the decision maker (d_l) and the associated alternative (x_s) whose corresponding comprehensive consensus level at the Tth decision round is less than the considered threshold value λ.
Step 2. Then, detect the corresponding parameter e_j for which the comprehensive consensus of the decision maker d_l for the alternative x_s is less than the considered threshold value λ as follows:

- First, evaluate the total deviation of a decision maker d_l with the other decision makers for the alternative x_s over the parameter e_j. It can be denoted by $D^s(l)(e_j)$ and can be derived by the following equation:

$$D^s(l)(e_j) = \frac{1}{k-1} \sum_{l \neq l', l'=1}^{k} |\tilde{f}^{l}_{e_j,T}(x_s) - \tilde{f}^{l'}_{e_j,T}(x_s)| \tag{9.3}$$

Suppose, λ' is the threshold value in deriving the total deviation of a decision maker $d_{l'}$.

- Select the parameter (e_j) for which the total deviation of the decision maker d_l for the alternative x_s is greater than the considered threshold value λ', i.e., $D^s(\lambda)(e_j) > \lambda'$.

Step 3. Then, for the next $(T + 1)^{th}$ decision round, apply appropriate suggestion (as provided below) to reformulate the evaluation of the alternative x_s for the decision maker d_l over the parameter e_j.

Step 4. After applying our proposed suggestion at the $(T + 1)^{th}$ decision round, we will check the comprehensive consensus level $(\Theta^s(l))$ of the decision maker d_l for the alternative x_s at this decision round by using Equations 9.1 and 9.2.
Step 5. If, at this decision round, the value of $\Theta^s(l)$ is greater than or equals to the considered threshold value λ, then we will go to the selection process. Otherwise, we have to go to Step 1 of this algorithm and we have to repeat this algorithm again. This process will repeat until the comprehensive consensus level $(\Theta^s(l))$ of every decision maker d_l for every alternative x_s is greater than or equals to the considered threshold value λ.

The suggestions to reformulate the primary evaluation of the expert d_l for x_s alternative over the parameter e_j are as follows:

Suggestion 1.

$$\tilde{f}^{l}_{e_{j,(T+1)}}(x_s) = \gamma\left(\tilde{f}^{l}_{e_{j,T}}(x_s)\right) \;\circledS_\gamma\; (1-\gamma)\left(\bigcup_{l=1}^{k} \tilde{f}^{l}_{e_{j,T}}(x_s)\right).$$

Suggestion 2.

$$\tilde{f}^{l}_{e_{j,(T+1)}}(x_s) = \gamma\left(\tilde{f}^{l}_{e_{j,T}}(x_s)\right) \;\circledS_\gamma\; \tilde{A}\left((\tilde{f}^{1}_{e_{j,T}}(x_s)),(\tilde{f}^{2}_{e_{j,T}}(x_s)),..,(\tilde{f}^{k}_{e_{j,T}}(x_s))\right).$$

where, $\cup$ is the standard fuzzy union, $\tilde{A}$ is the fuzzy aggregation, $\circledS_\gamma$ is the convex linear sum, and γ is the influence factor.

Remark 1: *Suggestion 1* will be preferable for the cases, when the opinion of a decision maker d_l about an alternative x_s over a parameter e_j is smaller than the other decision makers.
Remark 2: *Suggestion 2* will be preferable for the cases, when the opinion of a decision maker d_l about an alternative x_s over a parameter e_j is larger than the other decision makers or when the opinion of a decision maker d_l about an alternative x_s lies between the larger evaluation and smaller evaluation over the opinions of all the decision makers.

9.3.3.3 *Selection Process for Choosing the Best Alternative*

After checking comprehensive consensus every expert for every alternative, now we have evaluated the best decision alternative from m corresponding alternatives for this fuzzy soft set based group decision-making.

Suppose T is the final decision round where, comprehensive consensus level of every decision maker for every alternative is greater than or equals to the considered threshold value λ. At T^{th} decision round, the corresponding k fuzzy soft sets have been given in Table 9.5.

Now, to recognize the best decision alternative based on all the k fuzzy soft sets $(\tilde{f}_{\mathrm{T}}^{1},E),(\tilde{f}_{\mathrm{T}}^{2},E),..,(\tilde{f}_{\mathrm{T}}^{k},E)$ at the final T^{th} decision round, we have provided two algorithms: Algorithm III and Algorithm IV.

- *In Algorithm III,* firstly, we have aggregated k fuzzy soft sets $(\tilde{f}_{\mathrm{T}}^{1},E),(\tilde{f}_{\mathrm{T}}^{2},E),..,(\tilde{f}_{\mathrm{T}}^{k},E)$ by using AND operator to construct a single resultant fuzzy soft set $(\tilde{f}_{\mathrm{T}},E)$. Then, from this resultant fuzzy soft set $(\tilde{f}_{\mathrm{T}},E)$, we have obtained the ranking order of the alternatives to recognize best decision alternative.
- On the other hand, *in Algorithm IV,* firstly, we have derived the ranking indices of every alternative from each of the individual fuzzy soft sets $(\tilde{f}_{\mathrm{T}}^{1},E),(\tilde{f}_{\mathrm{T}}^{2},E),..,(\tilde{f}_{\mathrm{T}}^{k},E)$ and then, we have aggregated these ranking index values over all the k fuzzy soft sets to get overall ranking index of an alternative. After that, we have obtained the ranking order of every alternative to recognize best decision alternative.

Table 9.5 Tabular form of k fuzzy soft sets at final decision round T.

	$(\tilde{f}_{\mathrm{T}}^{1},E)$				$(\tilde{f}_{\mathrm{T}}^{2},E)$			
	e_1	e_2	...	e_n	e_1	e_2	...	e_n
x_1	$\tilde{f}_{e_1,\mathrm{T}}^{1}(x_1)$	$\tilde{f}_{e_2,\mathrm{T}}^{1}(x_1)$	...	$\tilde{f}_{e_n,\mathrm{T}}^{1}(x_1)$	$\tilde{f}_{e_1,\mathrm{T}}^{2}(x_1)$	$\tilde{f}_{e_2,\mathrm{T}}^{2}(x_1)$	...	$\tilde{f}_{e_n,\mathrm{T}}^{2}(x_1)$
x_2	$\tilde{f}_{e_1,\mathrm{T}}^{1}(x_2)$	$\tilde{f}_{e_2,\mathrm{T}}^{1}(x_2)$	...	$\tilde{f}_{e_n,\mathrm{T}}^{l}(x_2)$	$\tilde{f}_{e_1,\mathrm{T}}^{2}(x_2)$	$\tilde{f}_{e_2,\mathrm{T}}^{2}(x_2)$	...	$\tilde{f}_{e_n,\mathrm{T}}^{2}(x_2)$
x_m	$\tilde{f}_{e_1,\mathrm{T}}^{1}(x_m)$	$\tilde{f}_{e_2,\mathrm{T}}^{1}(x_m)$	...	$\tilde{f}_{e_n,\mathrm{T}}^{l}(x_m)$	$\tilde{f}_{e_1,\mathrm{T}}^{2}(x_m)$	$\tilde{f}_{e_2,\mathrm{T}}^{2}(x_m)$	...	$\tilde{f}_{e_n,\mathrm{T}}^{2}(x_m)$

	$(\tilde{f}_{\mathrm{T}}^{k},E)$			
	e_1	e_2	...	e_n
..	$\tilde{f}_{e_1,\mathrm{T}}^{k}(x_1)$	$\tilde{f}_{e_2,\mathrm{T}}^{k}(x_1)$	...	$\tilde{f}_{e_n,\mathrm{T}}^{k}(x_1)$
..	$\tilde{f}_{e_1,\mathrm{T}}^{k}(x_2)$	$\tilde{f}_{e_2,\mathrm{T}}^{k}(x_2)$	...	$\tilde{f}_{e_n,\mathrm{T}}^{k}(x_2)$
..	$\tilde{f}_{e_1,\mathrm{T}}^{k}(x_m)$	$\tilde{f}_{e_2,\mathrm{T}}^{k}(x_m)$	...	$\tilde{f}_{e_n,\mathrm{T}}^{k}(x_m)$

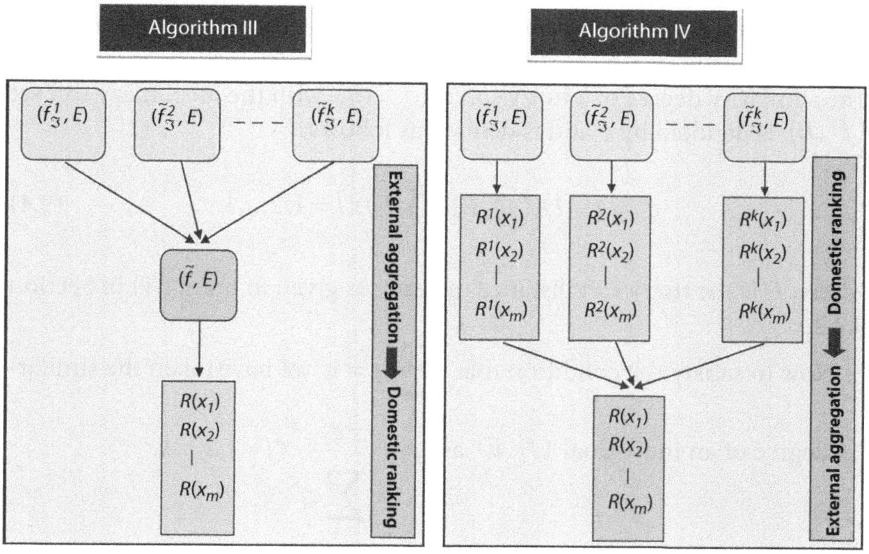

Figure 9.2 Key features of Algorithm III and Algorithm IV.

So, the backgrounds of these two algorithms are little bit different as given in Figure 9.2. Algorithm III is suitable for the problems where, integrated opinion of the decision makers is significant and Algorithm IV is suitable for the problems where, individual opinion of a decision maker is significant. In the following, we have given the detail descriptions of these two algorithms.

Algorithm III

Step 1. ***Construction of the ideal fuzzy soft set.***

Construct the ideal fuzzy soft set $(\tilde{f}^I,E)$ form k fuzzy soft sets $(\tilde{f}_{\mathrm{T}}^1,E),(\tilde{f}_{\mathrm{T}}^2,E),..,(\tilde{f}_{\mathrm{T}}^k,E)$ by using fuzzy soft union operation as follows:

$$(\tilde{f}^I,E)=(\tilde{f}_{\mathrm{T}}^1,E)\cup(\tilde{f}_{\mathrm{T}}^2,E)\cup..\cup(\tilde{f}_{\mathrm{T}}^k,E)$$

where, $\forall e_j \in E$, and $x_s \in X$,

$$\tilde{f}_{e_j}^I(x_s)=\tilde{f}_{e_j,\mathrm{T}}^1(x_s)\bigcup\tilde{f}_{e_j,\mathrm{T}}^2(x_s)\bigcup..\bigcup\tilde{f}_{e_j,\mathrm{T}}^k(x_s)$$
$$=max\{\tilde{f}_{e_j,\mathrm{T}}^1(x_s),\tilde{f}_{e_j,\mathrm{T}}^2(x_s),..,\tilde{f}_{e_j,\mathrm{T}}^k(x_s)\}$$

Step 2. ***Derivation of the similarity degree of an individual*** $(\tilde{f}_{\mathrm{T}}^{l}, E)$ ***with the ideal fuzzy soft set*** $(\tilde{f}^{I}, E)$.
The similarity degree of a fuzzy soft set $(\tilde{f}_{\mathrm{T}}^{l}, E)$ with the ideal fuzzy soft set $(\tilde{f}^{I}, E)$ is denoted by ς_l and is defined as follows:

$$\varsigma_l = 1 - D((\tilde{f}_{\mathrm{T}}^{l}, E)(\tilde{f}^{I}, E)); l = 1, 2, .., k \tag{9.4}$$

where, D is the fuzzy soft distance measure as given in point (*iv*) in Section 9.2.2.

Now to satisfy the condition that $\sum_{l=1}^{k} \varsigma_l = 1$, we have taken the similarity degree of an individual $(\tilde{f}_{\mathrm{T}}^{l}, E)$ as, $\rho_l = \dfrac{\varsigma_l}{\sum_{l=1}^{k} \varsigma_l} \; \forall l = 1, 2, .., k$.

Step 3. ***Construction of the weighted fuzzy soft set*** $(\tilde{f}_{\mathrm{T}\rho}^{l}, E)$ ***from the individual*** $(\tilde{f}_{\mathrm{T}}^{l}, E)$.
Now, construct the weighted fuzzy soft set $(\tilde{f}_{\mathrm{T}\rho}^{l}, E)$ from the individual fuzzy soft set $(\tilde{f}_{\mathrm{T}}^{l}, E)$ by multiplying the corresponding similarity degree ρ_l as follows:

$$\begin{aligned} (\tilde{f}_{\mathrm{T}\rho}^{l}, E) &= \rho_l \times (\tilde{f}_{\mathrm{T}}^{l}, E) \\ &= \{(e_j, (x_s, \rho_l \tilde{f}_{e_j,\mathrm{T}}^{l}(x_s))) \mid \forall e_j \in E, x_s \in X\} \end{aligned} \tag{9.5}$$

Step 4. ***Computation of the resultant fuzzy soft set*** $(\tilde{f}_{\mathrm{T}}, E)$.
By using 'AND' operator, now compute resultant fuzzy soft set $(\tilde{f}_{\mathrm{T}}, E)$ from k fuzzy soft sets $(\tilde{f}_{\mathrm{T}\rho}^{1}, E)$, $(\tilde{f}_{\mathrm{T}\rho}^{2}, E)$,..,$(\tilde{f}_{\mathrm{T}\rho}^{k}, E)$. Tabular form of the resultant fuzzy soft set is given in Table 9.6.

Table 9.6 Resultant fuzzy soft set $(\tilde{f}_{\mathrm{T}}, E)$ at final decision round T.

	e_1	e_2	...	e_n
x_1	$\tilde{f}_{e_1,\mathrm{T}}(x_1)$	$\tilde{f}_{e_2,\mathrm{T}}(x_1)$	...	$\tilde{f}_{e_n,\mathrm{T}}(x_1)$
x_2	$\tilde{f}_{e_1,\mathrm{T}}(x_2)$	$\tilde{f}_{e_2,\mathrm{T}}(x_2)$	...	$\tilde{f}_{e_n,\mathrm{T}}(x_2)$
x_m	$\tilde{f}_{e_1,\mathrm{T}}(x_m)$	$\tilde{f}_{e_2,\mathrm{T}}(x_m)$	...	$\tilde{f}_{e_n,\mathrm{T}}(x_m)$

Step 5. ***Determination of the positive ideal solution and negative ideal solution from the resultant fuzzy soft set.***
Evaluate positive ideal and negative ideal solutions from the resultant fuzzy soft set $(\tilde{f}_{\mathrm{T}}, E)$ as follows:

$$x_{I^+} = \left\{(e_1, max_{s=1}^{m}\tilde{f}_{e_1,\mathrm{T}}(x_s)), (e_2, max_{s=1}^{m}\tilde{f}_{e_2,\mathrm{T}}(x_s)), \ldots, (e_n, max_{s=1}^{m}\tilde{f}_{e_n,\mathrm{T}}(x_s))\right\}$$
$$x_{I^-} = \left\{(e_1, min_{s=1}^{m}\tilde{f}_{e_1,\mathrm{T}}(x_s)), (e_2, min_{s=1}^{m}\tilde{f}_{e_2,\mathrm{T}}(x_s)), \ldots, (e_n, min_{s=1}^{m}\tilde{f}_{e_n,\mathrm{T}}(x_s))\right\}$$

Step 6. ***Derivation of the distance of an alternative x_s from x_{I^+} and x_{I^-}.***
Now, by using fuzzy distance, evaluate the positive $(d(x_s, x_{I^+}))$ and negative distances $(d(x_s, x_{I^-}))$ of an alternative x_s ($s = 1, 2, .., m$) from positive ideal (x_{I^+}) and negative ideal (x_{I^-}) solutions over the resultant fuzzy soft set $(\tilde{f}_{\mathrm{T}}, E)$.

Step 7. ***Determination of the confidence grade of an alternative x_s.***
By using positive distance and negative distance, derive the confidence grade (CG_s) or ranking value ($R(x_s)$) of the alternative x_s as follows:

$$R(x_s) = CG_s = \frac{d(x_s, x_{I^+})}{d(x_s, x_{I^-}) + d(x_s, x_{I^+})} \tag{9.6}$$

Step 8. ***Selection of the best alternative.***
The alternative having minimum confidence grade or ranking value is the best decision alternative among the corresponding m alternatives for this fuzzy soft set-based group decision-making problem.

If, the best decision alternative is not unique i.e., suppose if, x_{m1}, x_{m2},.., x_{mM} have the same confidence grade where, m_1, m_2, .., $m_M \in \{1, 2, .., m\}$, then we will go to the next steps.

Step 8.1 Evaluate the total fluctuation rate $FG_{s'}$ of an alternative $x_{s'}$; $s' = m_1, m_2, .., m_M$ with respect to every pair of parameters as follows:

$$FG_{s'} = \sum_{j=1, j\neq j'}^{n} \left|\tilde{f}_{e_j,\mathrm{T}}(x_{s'}) - \tilde{f}_{e_{j'},\mathrm{T}}(x_{s'})\right|$$

Step 8.2 From the set of alternatives, who have same confidence grade at Step 8, recognize the best decision alternative based on their minimum fluctuation rate i.e.,

$$Best\ decision\ alternative = min_{s'=m_1}^{m_M} FG_{s'} \tag{9.7}$$

If, the best decision alternative is not unique, then we will select any one of them.

Algorithm IV

Step 1. ***Construction of the ideal fuzzy soft set.***
Construct the ideal fuzzy soft set $(\tilde{f}^I, E)$ likewise Step 1 of Algorithm III.

Step 2. ***Derivation of the similarity degree of an individual*** $(\tilde{f}_{\mathrm{T}}^l, E)$ ***with the ideal*** $(\tilde{f}^I, E)$.
By using Equation 9.4, derive the similarity degree ρ_l of an individual fuzzy soft set $(\tilde{f}_{\mathrm{T}}^l, E)$ with the ideal fuzzy soft set $(\tilde{f}^I, E)$.

Step 3. ***Construction of the weighted fuzzy soft set*** $(\tilde{f}_{\mathrm{T}\rho}^l, E)$ ***from an individual*** $(\tilde{f}_{\mathrm{T}}^l, E)$.
Now, construct the weighted fuzzy soft set $(\tilde{f}_{\mathrm{T}\rho}^l, E)$ from an individual fuzzy soft set $(\tilde{f}_{\mathrm{T}}^l, E)$ by using Equation 9.5.

Step 4. ***Determination of the positive ideal and negative ideal solutions from an individual*** $(\tilde{f}_{\mathrm{T}\rho}^l, E)$.
The positive ideal $(I^+(\tilde{f}_{\mathrm{T}\rho}^l))$ and negative ideal $(I^-(\tilde{f}_{\mathrm{T}\rho}^l))$ solutions from a weighted fuzzy soft set $(\tilde{f}_{\mathrm{T}\rho}^l, E)$ are as follows: $\forall l = 1, 2, .., k$,

$$\begin{aligned}
I^+(\tilde{f}_{\mathrm{T}\rho}^l) &= \left\{\cup_{s=1}^m \tilde{f}_{e_1,\mathrm{T}_\rho}^l(x_s), \cup_{s=1}^m \tilde{f}_{e_2,\mathrm{T}_\rho}^l(x_s), .., \cup_{s=1}^m \tilde{f}_{e_n,\mathrm{T}_\rho}^l(x_s)\right\} \\
&= \left\{max_{s=1}^m \tilde{f}_{e_1,\mathrm{T}_\rho}^l(x_s), max_{s=1}^m \tilde{f}_{e_2,\mathrm{T}_\rho}^l(x_s), .., max_{s=1}^m \tilde{f}_{e_n,\mathrm{T}_\rho}^l(x_s)\right\} \\
I^-(\tilde{f}_{\mathrm{T}\rho}^l) &= \left\{\cap_{s=1}^m \tilde{f}_{e_1,\mathrm{T}_\rho}^l(x_s), \cap_{s=1}^m \tilde{f}_{e_2,\mathrm{T}_\rho}^l(x_s), .., \cap_{s=1}^m \tilde{f}_{e_n,\mathrm{T}_\rho}^l(x_s)\right\} \\
&= \left\{min_{s=1}^m \tilde{f}_{e_1,\mathrm{T}_\rho}^l(x_s), min_{s=1}^m \tilde{f}_{e_2,\mathrm{T}_\rho}^l(x_s), .., min_{s=1}^m \tilde{f}_{e_n,\mathrm{T}_\rho}^l(x_s)\right\}
\end{aligned}$$

Step 5. ***Derivation of the distance of an alternative*** x_s.
By utilizing fuzzy distance, derive the positive distance $d^l(x_s, I^+(\tilde{f}_{\mathrm{T}\rho}^l))$ and negative distance $d^l(x_s, I^-(\tilde{f}_{\mathrm{T}\rho}^l))$ of an alternative x_s from the positive ideal solution and negative ideal solution over a weighted fuzzy soft set $(\tilde{f}_{\mathrm{T}\rho}^l, E)$. In Table 9.7 and Table 9.8, these values have been presented.

Step 6. ***Determination of the confidence grade of an alternative*** x_s ***over a weighted fuzzy soft set*** $(\tilde{f}_{\mathrm{T}\rho}^l, E)$.
Now, we have evaluated the confidence grade of an alternative x_s over a weighted fuzzy soft set $(\tilde{f}_{\mathrm{T}\rho}^l, E)$ by the following equation. In Table 9.9, these values have been presented.

Table 9.7 Positive distances of the alternatives.

	$(\tilde{f}^1_{T\rho},E)$	$(\tilde{f}^2_{T\rho},E)$	...	$(\tilde{f}^k_{T\rho},E)$
x_1	$d^1(x_1,I^+(\tilde{f}^l_{T\rho}))$	$d^2(x_1,I^+(\tilde{f}^l_{T\rho}))$	...	$d^k(x_1,I^+(\tilde{f}^l_{T\rho}))$
x_2	$d^1(x_2,I^+(\tilde{f}^l_{T\rho}))$	$d^2(x_2,I^+(\tilde{f}^l_{T\rho}))$	...	$d^k(x_2,I^+(\tilde{f}^l_{T\rho}))$
x_m	$d^1(x_m,I^+(\tilde{f}^l_{T\rho}))$	$d^2(x_2,I^+(\tilde{f}^l_{T\rho}))$	...	$d^k(x_m,I^+(\tilde{f}^l_{T\rho}))$

Table 9.8 Negative distances of the alternatives.

	$(\tilde{f}^1_{T\rho},E)$	$(\tilde{f}^2_{T\rho},E)$	...	$(\tilde{f}^k_{T\rho},E)$
x_1	$d^1(x_1,I^-(\tilde{f}^l_{T\rho}))$	$d^2(x_1,I^-(\tilde{f}^l_{T\rho}))$	...	$d^k(x_1,I^-(\tilde{f}^l_{T\rho}))$
x_2	$d^1(x_2,I^-(\tilde{f}^l_{T\rho}))$	$d^2(x_2,I^-(\tilde{f}^l_{T\rho}))$	...	$d^k(x_2,I^-(\tilde{f}^l_{T\rho}))$
x_m	$d^1(x_m,I^-(\tilde{f}^l_{T\rho}))$	$d^2(x_2,I^-(\tilde{f}^l_{T\rho}))$	...	$d^k(x_m,I^-(\tilde{f}^l_{T\rho}))$

$$CG^l_s = \frac{d^l(x_s,I^+(\tilde{f}^l_{T\rho}))}{d^l(x_s,I^+(\tilde{f}^l_{T\rho}))+d^l(x_s,I^-(\tilde{f}^l_{T\rho}))} \tag{9.8}$$

Step 7. Construction of the ranking value of an alternative x_s.
Now, the ranking value of an alternative x_s over all the k weighted fuzzy soft sets $(\tilde{f}^1_{T\rho},E),(\tilde{f}^2_{T\rho},E),..,(\tilde{f}^k_{T\rho},E)$ is as follows:

$$R^{CG}(x_s) = \frac{1}{k}\sum_{l=1}^{k} CG^l_s \; ; s=1,2,\ldots,m \tag{9.9}$$

Table 9.9 Confidence grades of the alternatives.

	$(\tilde{f}^1_{T\rho},E)$	$(\tilde{f}^2_{T\rho},E)$	...	$(\tilde{f}^k_{T\rho},E)$
x_1	CG^1_1	CG^2_1	...	CG^k_1
x_2	CG^1_2	CG^2_2	...	CG^k_2
x_m	CG^1_m	CG^2_m	...	CG^k_m

Step 8. *Selection of the best alternative.*
The alternative having minimum ranking value among m corresponding alternatives is the best decision alternative for this fuzzy soft set-based group decision-making problem.

If, the best decision alternative is not unique i.e., suppose if x_{m1}, x_{m2},.., x_{mM} have the same ranking value where, $m_1, m_2, .., m_M \in \{1, 2, .., m\}$, then we will go to the next steps.

Step 8.1 Determine the possibility index $PI_{s'}$ of an alternative $x_{s'}; s' = m_1, m_2, \ldots, m_M$ as a best decision alternative over all the decision makers as follows:

$$PI_{s'} = \frac{n(x_{s'})}{k}$$

where, $n(x_{s'})$ is the number of decision makers who have recognized $x_{s'}$ as the best alternative.

Based on the possibility index, the best decision alternative will be that alternative that has maximum possibility index among the other alternatives. i.e., select the alternative that have been recognized as the best decision alternative by the maximum number of decision makers.

If, in case, the best decision alternative is not unique, then we have to select any one of them.

Example 3. Let us consider that, $X = \{x_1, x_2, x_3, x_4\}$ be a universal set containing four alternatives and $E = \{e_1, e_2, e_3, e_4\}$ be the corresponding parameter set containing four fuzzy parameters each of which is in positive sense. Now consider three fuzzy soft sets $(\tilde{f}^1, E)$, $(\tilde{f}^2, E)$ and $(\tilde{f}^3, E)$ over X given by three decision makers $D = \{d_1, d_2, d_3\}$ as given in Tables 9.10, 9.11, and 9.12.

Solution: Throughout the solution, for deriving fuzzy distance and fuzzy soft distance, we have used Euclidean distance as given in Section 9.2.

Table 9.10 FSS $(\tilde{f}^1, E)$ (Example 3).

	e_1	e_2	e_3
x_1	0.8	0.6	0.1
x_2	0.6	0.6	0.7
x_3	0.5	0.4	0.8

Table 9.11 FSS $(\tilde{f}^2, E)$ (Example 3).

	e_1	e_2	e_3
x_1	0.1	0.4	0.7
x_2	0.6	0.5	0.6
x_3	0.6	0.4	0.2

Table 9.12 FSS $(\tilde{f}^3, E)$ (Example 3).

	e_1	e_2	e_3
x_1	0.7	0.4	0.6
x_2	0.5	0.4	0.7
x_3	0.6	0.5	0.3

Algorithm I (Measurement of comprehensive consensus level of a decision maker for every alternative)
Let, the threshold value for comprehensive consensus level be, $\lambda = 0.80$.

Step 1. Three fuzzy soft sets have been given in Tables 9.10, 9.11 and 9.12.
Step 2. Since, every parameter is positive in nature therefore, we do not need the equalization process.
Steps 3, 4. Now, by using Equations 9.1 and 9.2, comprehensive consensus level of the decision makers for every alternative is as follows:

$$\Theta^1(1) = \mathbf{0.51},\ \Theta^2(1) = 0.89,\ \Theta^3(1) = \mathbf{0.78};$$

$$\Theta^1(2) = \mathbf{0.54},\ \Theta^2(2) = 0.90,\ \Theta^3(2) = 0.84;$$

$$\Theta^1(3) = \mathbf{0.68},\ \Theta^2(3) = 0.88,\ \Theta^3(3) = 0.86;$$

From the above values it has been observed that, the comprehensive consensus level of the decision makers d_1, d_2 and d_3 for the alternative x_1 is less than the considered threshold value ($\lambda = 0.8$). Moreover, the comprehensive consensus level of the decision maker d_1 for the alternative x_3

is less than the considered threshold value ($\lambda = 0.8$). Therefore, according to our approach, we have to go to the Algorithm II to reformulate the evaluations of the alternatives so that, the comprehensive consensus level of all the decision makers for every alternative can reach to the considered threshold value.

Algorithm II (To increase the comprehensive consensus level)
In Algorithm II, we will derive the total deviation of a decision maker with the other decision makers for the corresponding alternative over each of the parameters. It has been considered that, the threshold value for the total deviation of a decision maker for this fuzzy soft set based group decision-making is 0.4.

Step 1. Here, the decision makers d_1, d_2 and d_3 have less comprehensive consensus for the alternative x_1 and also for the alternative x_3, d_3 decision maker has the less comprehensive consensus level.
Step 2. Then, by using Equation 9.3, the total deviation of the decision makers d_1, d_2 and d_3 for the alternative x_1 with respect to every parameter is as follows:

$$D^1(1)(e_1) = 0.4; D^1(1)(e_2) = 0.2; D^1(1)(e_3) = \mathbf{0.55}.$$

$$D^1(2)(e_1) = \mathbf{0.65}; D^1(2)(e_2) = 0.1; D^1(1)(e_3) = 0.35.$$

$$D^1(3)(e_1) = 0.35; D^1(3)(e_2) = 0.1; D^1(3)(e_3) = 0.3.$$

Similarly, the total deviation of the decision maker d_3 for the alternative x_1 with respect to every parameter is as follows:

$$D^3(1)(e_1) = 0.1; D^3(1)(e_2) = 0.05; D^3(1)(e_3) = \mathbf{0.55}.$$

From the above results it has been observed that, the total deviation of the alternative x_1 with respect to the parameter e_3 for the decision maker d_1 and the total deviation of the same alternative x_1 with respect to the parameter e_1 for the decision maker d_2 are greater than the considered threshold value ($\lambda' = 0.4$). Besides, the total deviation of the alternative x_3 with respect to the parameter e_3 for the decision maker d_1 is greater than the considered threshold value ($\lambda' = 0.4$). Therefore, they need a reformulation.

Step 3. Now, we have reformulated the primary evaluations (at $T = 0$ decision round) by using our proposed suggestions for $T = 1$ decision round.

- From, the primary tables (Table 9.10, Table 9.11, and Table 9.12), we have seen that, at $T = 0$, $\tilde{f}^{1}_{e_3,0}\ (x_1) = 0.1$. i.e., the primary evaluation of the alternative x_1 with respect to the parameter e_3 given by the decision maker d_1 is smallest than the other decision makers so, here *Suggestion 1* is appropriate.
- Again, evaluation of the alternative x_1 with respect to the parameter e_3 given by the decision maker d_2 is smallest than the other decision makers, so here also *Suggestion 1* is appropriate.
- But, the evaluation of the alternative x_3 with respect to the parameter e_3 given by the decision maker d_1 is highest than the decision makers. Therefore, in that case, *Suggestion 2* is appropriate.

Now, by applying these suggestions on the evaluations of the Tables 9.10, 9.11, 9.12 i.e., at $T = 0$ decision round, the new reformulated fuzzy soft sets at $T = 1$ decision round take the form as given in Table 9.13, Table 9.14, and Table 9.15.

Step 4. Then, by using Equations 9.1 and 9.2, we have derived the comprehensive consensus level of the decision makers whose comprehensive consensus level at the $T = 0$ decision round was less than the considered threshold value. At $T = 1$ decision round, comprehensive consensus level of the decision makers are as follows:

Table 9.13 FSS (f_1^1, E) (Example 3) (at T=1).

	e_1	e_2	e_3
x_1	0.8	0.6	0.4
x_2	0.6	0.6	0.7
x_3	0.5	0.4	0.62

Table 9.14 FSS (f_1^2, E) (Example 3) (at T=1).

	e_1	e_2	e_3
x_1	0.45	0.4	0.9
x_2	0.6	0.5	0.6
x_3	0.6	0.4	0.2

Table 9.15 FSS (f_1^3, E) (Example 3) (at T=1).

	e_1	e_2	e_3
x_1	0.7	0.4	0.6
x_2	0.5	0.4	0.7
x_3	0.6	0.5	0.3

$$\Theta^1(1) = 0.80;\ \Theta^1(2) = 0.80;\ \Theta^3(1) = 0.80.$$

Step 5. Since, each of the above comprehensive consensus levels of the decision makers is equal to the considered threshold value $\lambda = 0.8$, so now we can go to the selection step.

Selection of the best decision alternative. By using Algorithm III:
Step 1. Now, the ideal fuzzy soft set corresponding to the three fuzzy soft sets $(\tilde{f}_1^1, E)$, $(\tilde{f}_1^2, E)$ and $(\tilde{f}_1^3, E)$ at the final $T = 1$ decision round, has been given Table 9.16.

Table 9.16 Ideal fuzzy soft set $(\tilde{f}^I, E)$ (Example 3).

	e_1	e_2	e_3
x_1	0.8	0.6	0.7
x_2	0.6	0.6	0.7
x_3	0.6	0.5	0.62

Step 2. Now, the similarity degree of each the individuals $(\tilde{f}_1^1, E)$, $(\tilde{f}_1^2, E)$ and $(\tilde{f}_1^3, E)$ with the ideal fuzzy soft set is as follows: $\rho_1 = 0.35$; $\rho_2 = 0.31$; $\rho_3 = 0.34$.
Step 3. Three weighted fuzzy soft sets from each of the individuals $(\tilde{f}_1^1, E)$, $(\tilde{f}_1^2, E)$ and $(\tilde{f}_1^3, E)$ (given in Tables 9.13, 9.14, and 9.15) have been given in Tables 9.17, 9.18, and 9.19.
Step 4. Then, by using AND operator, the resultant fuzzy soft set from the three weighted fuzzy soft sets $(\tilde{f}_{1\rho}^1, E)$, $(\tilde{f}_{1\rho}^2, E)$ and $(\tilde{f}_{1\rho}^3, E)$ has been given in Table 9.20.

Table 9.17 Weighted FSS $(\tilde{f}_{1\rho}^1, E)$ (Example 3).

	e_1	e_2	e_3
x_1	0.8	0.6	0.4
x_2	0.6	0.6	0.7
x_3	0.5	0.4	0.62

Table 9.18 Weighted FSS $(\tilde{f}_{1\rho}^2, E)$ (Example 3).

	e_1	e_2	e_3
x_1	0.45	0.4	0.9
x_2	0.6	0.5	0.6
x_3	0.6	0.4	0.2

Table 9.19 Weighted FSS $(\tilde{f}_{1\rho}^3, E)$ (Example 3).

	e_1	e_2	e_3
x_1	0.7	0.4	0.6
x_2	0.5	0.4	0.7
x_3	0.6	0.5	0.3

Table 9.20 Resultant fuzzy soft set $(\tilde{f}_1, E)$ (Example 3).

	e_1	e_2	e_3
x_1	0.8	0.6	0.7
x_2	0.6	0.6	0.7
x_3	0.6	0.5	0.62

Step 5. Now, based on the resultant fuzzy soft set $(\tilde{f}_1, E)$, positive ideal and negative ideal solutions are as follows: $x_{I^+} = \{0.18, 0.14, 0.19\}; x_{I^-} = \{0.14, 0.12, 0.09\}$.
Steps 6, 7. After that, by using Equation 9.6, confidence grade or ranking value of the alternatives is as follows: $CG(x_1) = 0.57$; $CG(x_2) = 0.09$; $CG(x_3) = 0.72$.
Step 8. So, we have seen that, by using Algorithm III, best alternative for this group decision-making is, x_2.

By using Algorithm IV:
Step 1. The ideal fuzzy soft set has been given Table 9.16.
Step 2. Now, the similarity degree of each the individuals $(\tilde{f}_1^1, E)$, $(\tilde{f}_1^2, E)$ and $(\tilde{f}_1^3, E)$ with the ideal fuzzy soft set is as follows: $\rho_1 = 0.35$; $\rho_2 = 0.31$; $\rho_3 = 0.34$.
Step 3. Then, the three corresponding weighted fuzzy soft sets $(\tilde{f}_{1\rho}^1, E)$, $(\tilde{f}_{1\rho}^2, E)$ and $(\tilde{f}_{1\rho}^3, E)$ have been given in Tables 9.17, 9.18, and 9.19.
Step 4. Now, the positive ideal and negative ideal solutions for each of the weights fuzzy soft sets are as follows:

$$I^+(\tilde{f}_{1\rho}^1) = \{0.28, 0.21, 0.24\}; I^+(\tilde{f}_{1\rho}^2) = \{0.19, 0.16, 0.22\}; I^+(\tilde{f}_{1\rho}^3) = \{0.24, 0.17, 0.24\};$$
$$I^-(\tilde{f}_{1\rho}^1) = \{0.18, 0.14, 0.14\}; I^-(\tilde{f}_{1\rho}^2) = \{0.14, 0.12, 0.06\}; I^-(\tilde{f}_{1\rho}^3) = \{0.17, 0.14, 0.10\};$$

Steps 5, 6. Then, by using Equation 9.8, the confidence grade of the alternatives based on each of the weighted fuzzy soft sets is as follows:

$$CG^1(x_1) = 0.45; CG^2(x_1) = 0.28; CG^3(x_1) = 0.29;$$

$$CG^1(x_2) = 0.36; CG^2(x_2) = 0.17; CG^3(x_2) = 0.35;$$

$$CG^1(x_3) = 0.61; CG^2(x_3) = 0.77; CG^3(x_3) = 0.77.$$

Step 7. After that, by using Equation 9.9, the ranking values of the alternatives are as follows:

$$\tilde{R}^{CG}(x_1)=0.34;\tilde{R}^{CG}(x_2)=0.29;\tilde{R}^{CG}(x_3)=0.72.$$

Step 8. Hence, the best alternative is, x_2.
So, we have seen that, by using Algorithm IV, the best decision alternative is x_2.

Hence, overall it can be concluded that, x_2 is the best alternative among three alternatives for this fuzzy soft set-based group decision-making.

Example 4. Now, we have considered another example. Let, $(\tilde{f}^1,E)$, $(\tilde{f}^2,E)$ and $(\tilde{f}^3,E)$ be three fuzzy soft sets given by three decision makers $D=\{d_1, d_2, d_3\}$ over a universal set $X=\{x_1, x_2, x_3, x_4\}$ as given in Tables 9.21, 9.22, and 9.23 where, $E=\{e_1, e_2, e_3, e_4\}$ be the set of corresponding parameters and e_1, e_2, e_4 are the positive parameters whereas, e_3 is the negative parameter. Now, we will select the best decision alternative from the set of four alternatives.

Table 9.21 FSS $(\tilde{f}^1,E)$ (Example 4).

	e_1	e_2	e_3	e_4
x_1	0.6	0.7	0.5	0.7
x_2	0.7	0.5	0.8	0.3
x_3	0.2	0.1	0.5	0.5
x_4	0.3	0.3	0.6	0.8

Table 9.22 FSS $(\tilde{f}^2,E)$ (Example 4).

	e_1	e_2	e_3	e_4
x_1	0.8	0.6	0.6	0.2
x_2	0.6	0.5	0.8	0.4
x_3	0.3	0.1	0.6	0.6
x_4	0.3	0.4	0.5	0.7

Table 9.23 FSS $(\tilde{f}^3, E)$ (Example 4).

	e_1	e_2	e_3	e_4
x_1	0.7	0.6	0.7	0.8
x_2	0.6	0.4	0.7	0.3
x_3	0.2	0.1	0.6	0.5
x_4	0.3	0.5	0.4	0.7

Solution: Algorithm I: Measurement of comprehensive consensus level of the decision makers for every alternative
Let the threshold value for comprehensive consensus level be, $\lambda = 0.70$.

Steps 1, 2. Since, e_3 is negative parameter therefore, by using Definition 2 in Section 9.2, equalized value of all the decision evaluations has been given in Tables 9.24, 9.25, and 9.26.

Table 9.24 FSS $(\tilde{f}^1, E)$ after equalization (Example 4).

	e_1	e_2	e_3	e_4
x_1	0.6	0.7	0.5	0.3
x_2	0.7	0.5	0.2	0.3
x_3	0.2	0.1	0.5	0.5
x_4	0.3	0.3	0.4	0.8

Table 9.25 FSS $(\tilde{f}^2, E)$ after equalization (Example 4).

	e_1	e_2	e_3	e_4
x_1	0.8	0.6	0.4	0.2
x_2	0.6	0.5	0.2	0.4
x_3	0.3	0.1	0.4	0.6
x_4	0.3	0.4	0.5	0.7

Table 9.26 FSS $(\tilde{f}^3, E)$ after equalization (Example 4).

	e_1	e_2	e_3	e_4
x_1	0.7	0.6	0.3	0.2
x_2	0.6	0.4	0.3	0.3
x_3	0.2	0.1	0.4	0.5
x_4	0.3	0.5	0.6	0.7

Steps 3, 4. Comprehensive consensus level of the decision makers for every alternative is as follows:

$$\Theta^1(1) = 0.87,\ \Theta^2(1) = 0.92,\ \Theta^3(1) = 0.93;\ \Theta^4(1) = 0.88.$$

$$\Theta^1(2) = 0.90,\ \Theta^2(2) = 0.92,\ \Theta^3(2) = 0.92;\ \Theta^4(2) = 0.92.$$

$$\Theta^1(3) = 0.90,\ \Theta^2(3) = 0.91,\ \Theta^3(3) = 0.94;\ \Theta^4(3) = 0.90.$$

Since, the comprehensive consensus of all the decision makers for every alternative is greater than the considered threshold value ($\lambda = 0.7$) so, we will go to the selection step.

Selection of the best alternative. By using Algorithm III:
The confidence grades or ranking values of the alternatives are, $CG(x_1) = 0.44$; $CG(x_2) = 0.48$; $CG(x_3) = 0.65$; $CG(x_4) = 0.42$.

So, by using Algorithm III, ranking order of the alternatives is, $x_4 > x_1 > x_2 > x_3$.

By using Algorithm IV:
The ranking values of the alternatives are, $\tilde{R}^{CG}(x_1) = 0.42$; $\tilde{R}^{CG}(x_2) = 0.49$; $\tilde{R}^{CG}(x_3) = 0.67$; $\tilde{R}^{CG}(x_4) = 0.44$.

So, by using Algorithm IV, ranking order of the alternatives is, $x_1 > x_4 > x_2 > x_3$.

Hence, we have seen that, through Algorithm III, the best decision alternative is x_4 and through Algorithm IV, the best decision alternative is x_1.

9.4 A Case Study on Sustainable Supplier Selection in a Textile Industry

In the recent years, companies have paid attention on sustainable supplier selection in order to maintain environmental and social legislation additionally with their economic development. Therefore, they have incorporated sustainability-related parameters for best supplier selection so that, environmental, economic and social aspects can be served simultaneously. The textile and fashion industry is one of the foremost industrial sectors that have to adopt with the changing of era. In the global economic development of a country, this industry plays a significant role. But, nowadays, people are more interested in using sustainable products to maintain natural resources and to clean our planet. Therefore, textile industries have focused to follow the following agendas to order to maintain the sustainability in producing and selling their products.

- Use of recyclable and biodegradable materials in producing and packing garments instead of unsafe chemical materials and pesticides.
- Use of renewable energy to power machines in manufacturing the products.
- To reduce carbon emissions as well as greenhouse gas emissions during manufacturing of products.
- To manage the hazardous waste materials.
- To improve overall environmental footprint of textiles.
- To make sure the workers safety and health.
- To make sure good social conditions of the workers.

A supply chain of a textile industry contains basically three parts: supplier, manufacturer and customer as given in Figure 9.3. In this system, supplier selection problem is an emergent issue to enhance the competitive ground of the industry. Accordingly, sustainable supplier selection of a textile industry is an urgent problem in a textile supply chain management system. Now, in this section, we have illustrated a real case study in

Figure 9.3 Supply chain of a textile industry.

recognizing best sustainable supplier of a textile industry which is located in Kolkata in the state West Bengal in India.

Considered sustainable criteria

Now, we have considered some sustainable criteria to select best sustainable supplier of a textile industry such as, cost, on-time delivery, quality, emission of dangerous gas, projects for environment, management of hazardous waste, public disclosure, philanthropy, certification, etc. These criteria can be categorized into three types: economic, environmental and social as given in Figure 9.4. Based on these considered criteria, now we have selected the best sustainable supplier from a set of four suppliers for a textile and fashion industry. A group of three decision makers has been appointed to complete this selection process. Now assume that, the opinions of the decision makers about the suppliers over the considered criteria have been expressed by fuzzy soft sets. Now, in the following, we have illustrated this decision-making problem mathematically.

Mathematical formulation of the case study

Example 5. Let, $X = \{S_1, s_2, S_3, S_4\}$ be the set of four suppliers, which has been considered as a universal set and $E = \{$*Cost*(e_1), *On time delivery*(e_2), *Quality*(e_3), *Emission of dangerous gas*(e_4), *Projects for environment*(e_5), *Management of hazardous waste*(e_6), *Public disclosure*(e_7), *Philanthropy*(e_8), *Certification*$(e_9)\}$ be a set of nine sustainable supplier selection criteria based on which based supplier will be selected. $D = \{d_1, d_2, d_3\}$ is a set of

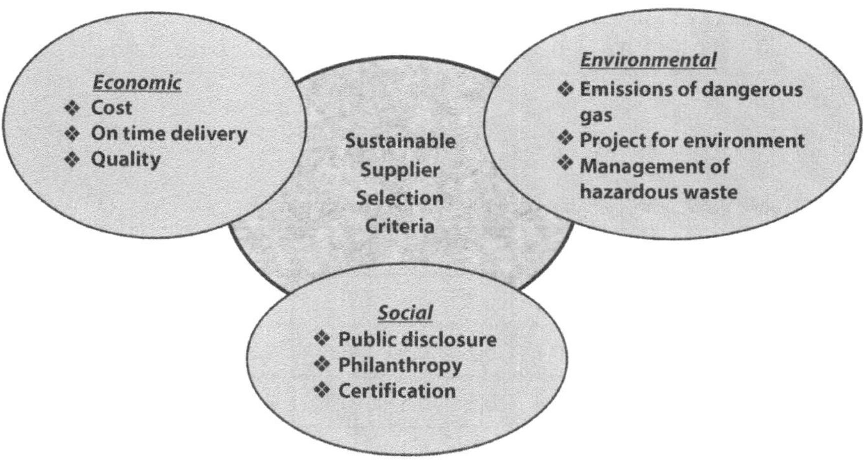

Figure 9.4 Criteria for sustainable supplier selection.

three decision makers who have been appointed to complete this selection process. Now, the assessment of the four suppliers by the three decision makers has been given in three fuzzy soft sets $(\tilde{f}^1, E)$, $(\tilde{f}^2, E)$, $(\tilde{f}^3, E)$ as given in Tables 9.27, 9.28 and 9.29. Here, among the nine considered parameters, cost (e_1) and Emission of dangerous gas (e_4) are two negative parameters and rest of the others are positive parameters.

Table 9.27 FSS $(\tilde{f}^1, E)$ provided by d_1 (Example 5).

	e_1	e_2	e_3	e_4	e_5	e_6	e_7	e_8	e_9
S_1	0.2	0.6	1	0.2	0.6	0.3	0.9	0.1	0.5
S_2	0.4	0.2	0.9	0.4	0.6	0.7	0.1	0.2	0.4
S_3	0.9	0.4	0.5	0.5	0.3	0.2	0.6	0.1	0.4
S_4	0.4	0.7	0.1	0.9	0.4	0.5	0.6	0.2	0.1

Table 9.28 FSS $(\tilde{f}^2, E)$ provided by d_2 (Example 5).

	e_1	e_2	e_3	e_4	e_5	e_6	e_7	e_8	e_9
S_1	0.3	0.4	0.9	0.1	0.5	0.4	0.8	0.2	0.6
S_2	0.5	0.2	0.8	0.3	0.7	0.8	0.1	0.3	0.4
S_3	0.8	0.5	0.3	0.6	0.3	0.2	0.5	0.1	0.3
S_4	0.3	0.6	0.3	0.9	0.4	0.4	0.7	0.3	0.1

Table 9.29 FSS $(\tilde{f}^3, E)$ provided by d_3 (Example 5).

	e_1	e_2	e_3	e_4	e_5	e_6	e_7	e_8	e_9
S_1	0.4	0.4	0.8	0.2	0.5	0.3	1	0.2	0.4
S_2	0.5	0.2	0.7	0.2	0.5	0.6	0.2	0.4	0.4
S_3	0.8	0.3	0.4	0.5	0.4	0.3	0.5	0.2	0.3
S_4	0.4	0.6	0.2	0.8	0.4	0.5	0.7	0.1	0.1

Solution: Now, we will recognize the best sustainable supplier by using our proposed fuzzy soft set-based group decision-making approach. As the fuzzy distance and fuzzy soft distance, here we have used the Euclidean distance (given in Section 9.2).

Measurement of comprehensive consensus level of a decision maker. By using Algorithm I:

Let us assume that, the threshold value of the comprehensive consensus level for this decision-making problem is, $\lambda = 0.8$.

Steps 1, 2. Since, e_1 and e_4 are the two negative parameters then, to equalize all the evaluations, we have taken fuzzy complement of the evaluations of all the alternatives with respect to each of the e_1 and e_4 parameters. Results have been given in Tables 9.30, 9.31 and 9.32.

Steps 3,4. The comprehensive consensus level of the decision makers for the alternatives is as follows:

$$\Theta^1(1) = 0.88;\ \Theta^1(2) = 0.88;\ \Theta^1(3) = 0.88.$$

$$\Theta^2(1) = 0.90;\ \Theta^2(2) = 0.92;\ \Theta^2(3) = 0.90.$$

$$\Theta^3(1) = 0.91;\ \Theta^3(2) = 0.90;\ \Theta^3(3) = 0.91.$$

$$\Theta^4(1) = 0.91;\ \Theta^4(2) = 0.91;\ \Theta^4(3) = 0.92.$$

Step 5. Since, each $\Theta^l(s) \geq \lambda(= 0.8)$ (*threshold value*); $s = 1, 2, 3, 4$, $l = 1, 2, 3$ therefore, we will directly go to the Selection step.

Table 9.30 FSS $(\tilde{f}^1, E)$ after equalization (Example 5).

	e_1	e_2	e_3	e_4	e_5	e_6	e_7	e_8	e_9
S_1	0.8	0.6	1	0.8	0.6	0.3	0.9	0.1	0.5
S_2	0.6	0.2	0.9	0.6	0.6	0.7	0.1	0.2	0.4
S_3	0.1	0.4	0.5	0.5	0.3	0.2	0.6	0.1	0.4
S_4	0.6	0.7	0.1	0.1	0.4	0.5	0.6	0.2	0.1

Table 9.31 FSS $(\tilde{f}^2, E)$ after equalization (Example 5).

	e_1	e_2	e_3	e_4	e_5	e_6	e_7	e_8	e_9
S_1	0.7	0.4	0.9	0.9	0.5	0.4	0.8	0.2	0.6
S_2	0.5	0.2	0.8	0.7	0.7	0.8	0.1	0.3	0.4
S_3	0.2	0.5	0.3	0.4	0.3	0.2	0.5	0.1	0.3
S_4	0.7	0.6	0.3	0.1	0.4	0.4	0.7	0.3	0.1

Table 9.32 FSS $(\tilde{f}^3, E)$ after equalization (Example 5).

	e_1	e_2	e_3	e_4	e_5	e_6	e_7	e_8	e_9
S_1	0.6	0.4	0.8	0.8	0.5	0.3	1	0.2	0.4
S_2	0.5	0.2	0.7	0.8	0.5	0.6	0.2	0.4	0.4
S_3	0.2	0.3	0.4	0.5	0.4	0.3	0.5	0.2	0.3
S_4	0.6	0.6	0.2	0.2	0.4	0.5	0.7	0.1	0.1

Table 9.33 Ideal fuzzy soft set $(\tilde{f}^I, E)$ (Example 5).

	e_1	e_2	e_3	e_4	e_5	e_6	e_7	e_8	e_9
S_1	0.8	0.6	1	0.9	0.6	0.4	1	0.2	0.6
S_2	0.6	0.2	0.9	0.8	0.7	0.8	0.2	0.4	0.4
S_3	0.2	0.5	0.5	0.5	0.4	0.3	0.6	0.2	0.4
S_4	0.7	0.7	0.3	0.2	0.4	0.5	0.7	0.3	0.1

Selection process.
By using Algorithm III:
Step 1. The ideal fuzzy soft set $(\tilde{f}^I, E)$ based on the three fuzzy soft sets $(\tilde{f}^1, E)$, $(\tilde{f}^2, E)$, $(\tilde{f}^3, E)$ has been given in Table 9.33.
Step 2. The similarity degree of each of the fuzzy soft sets $(\tilde{f}^1, E)$, $(\tilde{f}^2, E)$ and $(\tilde{f}^3, E)$ with the ideal fuzzy soft set are, $\rho_1 = 0.34$; $\rho_2 = 0.33$; $\rho_3 = 0.33$.
Step 3. Now, the weighted fuzzy soft sets from the three corresponding fuzzy soft sets $(\tilde{f}^1, E)$, $(\tilde{f}^2, E)$ and $(\tilde{f}^3, E)$ have been given in Tables 9.34, 9.35, and 9.36.

Table 9.34 Weighted FSS $(\tilde{f}_\rho^1, E)$ (Example 5).

	e_1	e_2	e_3	e_4	e_5	e_6	e_7	e_8	e_9
S_1	0.272	0.204	0.340	0.272	0.204	0.102	0.306	0.034	0.170
S_2	0.204	0.068	0.306	0.204	0.204	0.238	0.034	0.068	0.136
S_3	0.034	0.136	0.170	0.170	0.102	0.068	0.204	0.034	0.136
S_4	0.204	0.238	0.034	0.034	0.136	0.170	0.204	0.068	0.034

Table 9.35 Weighted FSS $(\tilde{f}_\rho^2, E)$ (Example 5).

	e_1	e_2	e_3	e_4	e_5	e_6	e_7	e_8	e_9
S_1	0.231	0.132	0.297	0.297	0.165	0.132	0.264	0.066	0.198
S_2	0.165	0.066	0.264	0.231	0.231	0.264	0.033	0.099	0.132
S_3	0.066	0.165	0.099	0.132	0.099	0.066	0.165	0.033	0.099
S_4	0.231	0.198	0.099	0.033	0.132	0.132	0.231	0.099	0.033

Table 9.36 Weighted FSS $(\tilde{f}_\rho^3, E)$ (Example 5).

	e_1	e_2	e_3	e_4	e_5	e_6	e_7	e_8	e_9
S_1	0.198	0.132	0.264	0.264	0.165	0.099	0.330	0.066	0.132
S_2	0.165	0.066	0.231	0.264	0.165	0.198	0.066	0.132	0.132
S_3	0.066	0.099	0.132	0.165	0.132	0.099	0.165	0.066	0.099
S_4	0.198	0.198	0.066	0.066	0.132	0.165	0.231	0.033	0.033

Step 4. Resultant fuzzy soft set (using AND operator) has been given in Table 9.37.

Step 5. Now, the positive ideal and negative ideal solutions based on Table 9.37 are as follows:

$$x_{I^+} = \{0.198, 0.198, 0.264, 0.264, 0.165, 0.198, 0.264, 0.068, 0.132\};$$

$$x_{I^-} = \{0.034, 0.066, 0.034, 0.033, 0.099, 0.066, 0.033, 0.033, 0.033\}.$$

Table 9.37 Resultant fuzzy soft set $(\tilde{f}, E)$ (Example 5).

	e_1	e_2	e_3	e_4	e_5	e_6	e_7	e_8	e_9
S_1	0.198	0.132	0.264	0.264	0.165	0.099	0.264	0.034	0.132
S_2	0.165	0.066	0.231	0.204	0.165	0.198	0.033	0.068	0.132
S_3	0.034	0.099	0.099	0.132	0.099	0.066	0.165	0.033	0.099
S_4	0.198	0.198	0.034	0.033	0.132	0.132	0.204	0.033	0.033

Steps 6, 7. Then, by using Equation 9.6, the confidence grades of the alternatives are as follows:

$$CG_S 1 = 0.2142;\ CG_S 2 = 0.4461;\ CG_S 3 = 0.6386;\ CG_S 4 = 0.5584.$$

Step 8. So, the ranking order of the alternatives is, $S_1 > S_2 > S_4 > S_3$. Hence, by using Algorithm III, S_1 is the best decision alternative.

By using Algorithm IV:

Step 1, Step 2 and Step 3 are same as Algorithm III. Three weighted fuzzy soft sets have been given in Tables 9.34, 9.35, and 9.36.

Step 4. Now, positive ideal and negative ideal solutions for every weighted fuzzy soft set are as follows:

$$I^{+}(\tilde{f}_{\rho}^{1}) = \{0.272, 0.238, 0.340, 0.272, 0.204, 0.238, 0.306, 0.068, 0.170\};$$

$$I^{+}(\tilde{f}_{\rho}^{2}) = \{0.034, 0.068, 0.034, 0.034, 0.102, 0.068, 0.034, 0.034, 0.034\};$$

$$I^{+}(\tilde{f}_{\rho}^{3}) = \{0.231, 0.198, 0.297, 0.297, 0.231, 0.264, 0.264, 0.099, 0.198\};$$

$$I^{-}(\tilde{f}_{\rho}^{1}) = \{0.066, 0.066, 0.099, 0.033, 0.099, 0.066, 0.033, 0.033, 0.033\};$$

$$I^{-}(\tilde{f}_{\rho}^{2}) = \{0.198, 0.198, 0.264, 0.264, 0.165, 0.198, 0.330, 0.132, 0.132\};$$

$$I^{-}(\tilde{f}_{\rho}^{3}) = \{0.066, 0.066, 0.066, 0.066, 0.132, 0.099, 0.066, 0.033, 0.033\}.$$

Steps 5, 6, 7. Then, by using Equations 9.8 and 9.9, the ranking values of the alternatives are as follows:

$$\tilde{R}^{CG}(S_1) = 0.2328; \tilde{R}^{CG}(S_2) = 0.4698; \tilde{R}^{CG}(S_3) = 0.6327;$$
$$\tilde{R}^{CG}(S_4) = 0.5716.$$

Step 8. So, the ranking order of the alternatives is, $S_1 > S_2 > S_4 > S_3$. Hence, by using Algorithm IV, S_1 is the best decision alternative.

Thus, from the above results we have seen that, by using Algorithm III and Algorithm IV, supplier S_1 is best. So, overall it can be concluded that, S_1 is the best sustainable supplier for this textile industry.

9.5 Comparative Discussion

Now, in this section, we have discussed the validity and effectiveness of our proposed fuzzy soft set-based group decision-making approach.

Validity of Our Proposed Approach

In our methodology, before selecting the best decision alternative, we have measured the consensus of a decision maker with the other associated decision makers for his/her provided description about an alternative and then, some suggestions have been provided to reformulate the description of a decision maker who have less consensus from the considered threshold value about an alternative so that, the consensus of the decision maker can be increased up to the requisite value for the decision-making problem. After that, final decision has been taken. This is the key idea of our proposed approach.

Now, from the existing studies we have seen that, in the references such as, [24] (Roy and Maji's approach), [4] (Basu *et al.* approach), [2] (Alcantud's approach), etc., some algorithms have been found by which fuzzy soft set-based group decision-making problems can be dealt. But, in these existing approaches, researchers were not concerned with measuring the consensus of a decision maker with other associated decision makers but rather they were concerned only with the best final decision selection. Therefore, in our methodology, an additional consensus-measuring part has been added. Now, to verify the validity of our proposed approach firstly, we have derived the best decision alternative by our proposed approach without performing the additional consensus measuring and increasing step.

Final ranking of the associated alternatives based on Examples 3, 4 and 5 has been given in Tables 9.38, 9.39, and 9.40 respectively. From these tables we have seen that, in Examples 3 and 5, best decision alternative is same for each of the methods including our proposed approach (without measuring consensus). So, from these resulting values it can be concluded that, our proposed approach is valid.

Table 9.38 Final ranking order of the alternatives based on Example 3.

Methods	Ranking order of the alternatives	Best decision alternative
Our approach through Algorithm III (except consensus step)	$x_2 > x_3 > x_1$	x_2
Our approach through Algorithm IV (except consensus step)	$x_2 > x_3 > x_1$	x_2
By Roy and Maji's approach [24]	$x_2 > x_3 > x_1$	x_2
By Basu *et al.* approach [4]	$x_2 > x_3 > x_1$	x_2
By Alcantud's approach [2]	$x_2 > x_3 > x_1$	x_2

Table 9.39 Final ranking order of the alternatives based on Example 4.

Methods	Ranking order of the alternatives	Best decision alternative
Our approach through Algorithm III (except consensus step)	$x_1 > x_4 > x_2 > x_3$	x_4
Our approach through Algorithm IV (except consensus step)	$x_1 > x_2 > x_4 > x_3$	x_1
By Roy and Maji's approach [24]	$x_1 = x_4 > x_2 = x_3$	x_1, x_4
By Basu *et al.* approach [4]	$x_1 = x_2 = x_3 = x_4$	x_1, x_2, x_3, x_4
By Alcantud's approach [2]	$x_1 > x_4 > x_2 > x_3$	x_1

Table 9.40 Final ranking order of the alternatives based on Example 5.

Methods	Ranking order of the suppliers	Best sustainable supplier
Our approach through Algorithm III (except consensus step)	$S_1 > S_2 > S_3 > S_4$	S_1
Our approach through Algorithm IV (except consensus step)	$S_1 > S_2 > S_3 > S_4$	S_1
By Roy and Maji's approach [24]	$S_1 > S_2 > S_4 > S_3$	S_1
By Basu *et al.* approach [4]	$S_1 > S_2 > S_4 > S_3$	S_1
By Alcantud's approach [2]	$S_1 > S_2 > S_4 > S_3$	S_1

Effectiveness of Our Proposed Approach

Now, we have illustrated the effectiveness of our proposed fuzzy soft set-based group decision-making approach.

- **For Example 3.** From Example 3 we have seen that, there was an inconsistency in some evaluations of the alternatives and therefore, we have performed consensus level increasing step. After increasing consensus, final results have been given below:

Through Algorithm III, best alternative is x_2. Through Algorithm IV, best alternative is x_2.

Now, by comparing these results with the Table 9.38, we have observed that, the final decision alternative is same as x_2 for both the cases of 'with consensus' and 'without consensus'.

Though, in this example, for both the cases, results are same, however, for other examples, there may be different results for 'with consensus' and 'without consensus'.

- **For Example 4:** Since, in Example 4, comprehensive consensus level of each of the decision makers for every alternative is greater than the considered threshold value therefore, in this example, we do not need to perform the consensus level increasing step. Again, from Table 9.39, it is observed that, through our proposed Algorithm III, x_4 is the best alternative and through our proposed Algorithm IV, x_1 is the best alternative. Actually, the background of these two algorithms is slightly different. In Algorithm III, firstly we have performed an external aggregation and then we have derived the ranking indices of the alternatives on the other hand, in Algorithm IV, firstly we have derived the ranking indices of the alternatives for each of the individual fuzzy soft sets and then we have performed an aggregation on the ranking index values of the alternatives over all the associated fuzzy soft sets. So, when individual decision of a decision maker is more important than the integrated value then, Algorithm IV is more useful than Algorithm III. Because, in that case, by using our proposed Algorithm IV, we can get the best decision alternative based on the opinion of an individual decision maker.

- **For Example 5:**
  In this example also, the comprehensive consensus level of each of the decision makers for every alternative is greater than the considered threshold value therefore, in this example no need to perform the consensus level increasing step.

So, from the above discussions, the main advantages of our proposed approach can be summarized as follows:

(i) In our proposed algorithm, there is a lot of emphasis on measuring consensus of the decision makers for every alternative which is not found in the existing approaches. Therefore, by our proposed approach we can get more accurate results than the existing approaches [2, 4, 24].

(ii) Moreover, in the best alternative selection part of our proposed algorithm, we have provided two different algorithms, Algorithm III and Algorithm IV where, Algorithm III is suitable for the problems where, integrated opinion of all the decision makers is required on the other hand, Algorithm IV is more better for the problems where, individual opinion of a decision maker is required. So, by our proposed approach, we can select the algorithm for selecting the best decision alternative according to the needs of a problem.

Thus, from the overall illustration it can be concluded that, our proposed approach is more useful and effective than the other existing approaches.

9.6 Conclusion

In this paper, we have used fuzzy soft set theory in solving group decision-making problems where consensus measure of the decision makers pays more attention.

Major Findings
Our major findings in this paper are as follows:

- A stepwise algorithmic approach has been proposed to determine the best alternative from some associated alternatives

based on a group of decision makers opinions over some fuzzy parameters.
- Our proposed methodology contains mainly three main parts.
- In first part, we have derived the consensus of a decision maker with the other decision makers for his/her provided opinion about every alternative.
- In second part, we have increased the consensus of a decision maker, who had less consensus at the first part.
- Finally, at third part, we have selected the best decision alternative.
- Moreover, in this paper we have solved a problem regarding the sustainable supplier selection of textile industry by using our proposed approach which shows a real-life applicability of our proposed approach.

Advantages
The main advantages of our proposed approach are,

- In a real-life related problem, if one decision maker may provide an incorrect opinion about an alternative then by our proposed approach, he/she will get a chance to reformulate his/her opinion before selecting the best alternative. This is the main advantage of our proposed approach.
- Further, in the selection step of our proposed approach we have provided two different algorithms for selecting the best alternative where, one is appropriate, when overall opinion of all the decision makers is necessary and another one is appropriate, when individual opinion of a decision maker is necessary. So, by selecting perfect algorithm according to the requirements of a problem, we will get more errors less results. This is an another advantage of our proposed approach.

Limitations

This proposed approach can only applied for the decision making problems where all the corresponding parameters are in fuzzy sense. If in a problem, all the parameters are in other uncertain situations like intuitionistic fuzzy, neutrosophic, complex fuzzy etc. one cannot apply this algorithm directly.

Future Research Work

As a further research, one can extend our proposed approach to solve other types of soft sets like, intuitionistic fuzzy soft sets, linguistic valued soft sets, neutrosophic soft sets, etc. Moreover, our proposed approach can be applied to other real-life related problems for instance, in disease diagnosis, in company manager selection, in game theory, etc.

9.7 Acknowledgement

This work is supported by the Department of Science and Technology (DST), New Delhi, India, through the letter No. DST/INSPIRE/03/2014/003326.

AI disclosure statement: The author acknowledges the use of AI-based tools for minor language editing or grammatical correction. However, all intellectual contributions, analyses, and conclusions presented in this chapter are entirely the author's own.

References

1. Aktas, H. and Çagman, N., Soft sets and Soft groups. *Inf. Sci.*, 177, 13, 2726–2735, 2007.
2. Alcantud, J.C.R., A novel algorithm for fuzzy soft set based decision making from multiob- server input parameter data set. *Inf. Fusion*, 29, 142–148, 2016.
3. Baldwin, J.F., A new approach to approximate reasoning using a fuzzy logic. *Fuzzy Sets Syst.*, 2, 4, 309–325, 1979.
4. Basu, T.M., Mahapatra, N.K., Mondal, S.K., A balanced solution of a fuzzy soft set based decision making problem in medical science. *Appl. Soft Comput.*, 12, 10, 3260–3275, 2012.
5. Çagman, N., Enginoğlu, S., Soft matrix theory and its decision making. *Comput. Math. Appl.*, 59, 10, 3308–3314, 2010.
6. Djatna, T., Hardhienata, M.K.D., Masruriyah, A.F.N., An intuitionistic fuzzy diagnosis ana- lytics for stroke disease. *J. Big Data*, 5, 35, 2018.
7. Fathima Perveen, P.A., John, S.J., Babitha, K.V., Spherical Fuzzy Soft Sets, in: *Decision Making with Spherical Fuzzy Sets,*. Studies in Fuzziness and Soft Computing, vol. 392, C. Kahraman, and F. Kutlu Gndogdu, (Eds.), Springer, Cham, 2021.

8. Feng, F., Jun, Y.B., Liu, X., Li, L., An adjustable approach to fuzzy soft set based decision making. *J. Comput. Appl. Math.*, 234, 1, 10–20, 2010.
9. Feng, Q. and Zheng, W., New similarity measures of fuzzy soft sets based on distance measures. *Ann. Fuzzy Math. Inf.*, 7, 4, 669–686, 2014.
10. Garg, H., Agarwal, N., Tripathi, A., Generalized intuitionistic fuzzy entropy measure of order a and degree and its applications to multi-criteria decision making problem. *Int. J. Fuzzy. Syst. Appl.*, 6, 1, 86107, 2017.
11. Garg, H. and Arora, R., Generalized and group-based generalized intuitionistic fuzzy soft sets with applications in decision-making. *Appl. Intell.*, 48, 343356, 2018, https://doi.org/10.1007/s10489-017-0981-5.
12. Garg, H., Perveen, P.A.F., John, S.J., Perez-Dominguez, L., Spherical Fuzzy Soft Topology and Its Application in Group DecisionMaking Problems. *Math. Probl. Eng.*, 2022, 1007133, 2022.
13. Kacprzyk, J., *Multistage Fuzzy Control*, Wiley, Chichester, 1997.
14. Kong, Z., Gao, L., Wang, L., Comment on A fuzzy soft set theoretic approach to deccision making problems. *J. Comput. Appl. Math.*, 223, 2, 540–542, 2009.
15. Kong, Z., Wang, L., Wu, Z., Application of fuzzy soft set in decision making problems based on grey theory. *J. Comput. Appl. Math.*, 236, 6, 1521–1530, 2011.
16. Li, Z., Wen, G., Xie, N., An approach to fuzzy soft sets in decision making based on grey relational analysis and Dempster-Shafer theory of evidence: An application in medical diagnosis. *Artif. Intell. Med.*, 2015, http://dx.doi.org/10.1016/j.artmed.2015.05.002.
17. Maji, P.K., Biswas, R., Roy, A.R., Fuzzy soft sets. *J. Fuzzy Math.*, 9, 3, 589–602, 2001.
18. Maji, P.K., Roy, A.R., Biswas, R., Soft Set Theory. *Comput. Math. Appl.*, 45, 555–562, 2003.
19. Majumdar, P. and Samanta, S.K., On soft mappings. *Comput. Math. Appl.*, 60, 2666–2672, 2010.
20. Molodsov, D., Soft Set Theory-First results. *Comput. Math. Appl.*, 37, 19–31, 1999.
21. Pham, D.L. and Prince, J., An adaptive fuzzy c-means algorithm for image segmentation in the presence of intensity inhomogeneities. *Pattern Recogn. Lett.*, 20, 57–68, 1998.
22. Pedrycz, W., Fuzzy sets in pattern recognition: Methodology and methods. *Pattern Recognit.*, 23, 12, 121–146, 1990.
23. Qin, K., Liu, Q., Xu, Y., Redefined soft relations and soft functions. *Int. J. Comput. Intell. Syst.*, 8, 5, 819–828, 2015.
24. Roy, A.R. and Maji, P.K., A fuzzy soft set theoretic approach to decision making problems. *J. Comput. Appl. Math.*, 203, 2, 412–418, 2007.

25. Saeed, M., Saif Ud Din, I., Tariq, I., Garg, H., Refined Fuzzy Soft Sets: Properties, Set- Theoretic Operations and Axiomatic Results. *J. Comput. Cognit. Eng.*, 3, 1, 24–33, 2023, https://doi.org/10.47852/bonviewJCCE3202847.
26. Wang, J., Hu, Y., Xiao, F., Deng., X., Deng, Y., A novel method to use fuzzy soft sets in decision making based on ambiguity measure and Dempster-Shafer theory of evidence: An application in medical diagnosis. *Artif. Intell. Med.*, 69, 1–11, 2016.
27. Zadeh, L.A., Fuzzy Sets. *Inf. Control*, 8, 338–353, 1965.
28. Zhang, N. and Wei, G., Extension of VIKOR method for decision making problem based on hesitant fuzzy set. *Appl. Math. Modell.*, 37, 7, 4938–4947, 2013.

Part III

SUSTAINABLE DEVELOPMENT AND ENVIRONMENTAL DECISION-MAKING

10

A HyF-VIKOR Method for Sustainable Transportation *via* a Novel Distance Measure

Palash Dutta* **and Alakananda Konwar**

Department of Mathematics, Dibrugarh University, Dibrugarh, India

Abstract

Rapid urban growth, industrialization, and depletion of fossil fuels have rapidly increased the demand in sustainable transportation. Sustainable transportation is essential for addressing environmental issues, enhancing economic resilience, and promoting social justice for the advancement of future generations. Yet, uncertainty and hesitancy over decision information regarding sustainable transportation are not effectively portrayed in the existing literature. While fuzzy sets and their traditional extensions have effectively demonstrated practical issues on sustainable transportation but their inability to handle optimistic and pessimistic grades independently as well as lack of precision in uncertainty representation are crucial limitations. Motivated to address this problem, this research introduces the VIekriterijumsko KOmpromisno Rangiranje (VIKOR) – Multi Criteria Decision Making (MCDM) technique, which is supported by a novel distance measure within Hyperbolic Fuzzy Set (HyFS) framework. HyFS offers greater adaptability and reliability through permitting the independent assignment of optimism and pessimism degrees. This novel distance measure efficaciously encounters all the axiomatic definitions and fundamental properties of a distance measure on HyFS while demonstrating its superiority and reliability through a comparative analysis against the existing distance measures. Further, we employ this proposed methodology on sustainable transportation MCDM problems and perform a comparative analysis with the existing MCDM methods for its validation and robustness. The experimental results illustrate that the proposed MCDM methodology based on the proposed distance measure can efficaciously address practical decision-making

**Corresponding author*: palash.dtt@gmail.com

Harish Garg (ed.) Decision Support Systems in Smart Computing: Embracing Uncertainty and Challenges, (307–350) © 2026 Scrivener Publishing LLC

problems in Hyperbolic Fuzzy (HyF) environment and correspondingly possess higher consistency in comparison to the existing MCDM methods.

Keywords: Hyperbolic fuzzy sets, distance measure, VIKOR, sustainable transportation, MCDM

10.1 Introduction

Real-life situations often involve uncertainty created by a lack of understanding, ambiguity, practical information, inaccuracies, and so on. Zadeh [1] introduced the concept of Fuzzy Set theory (FST) to handle such uncertainty whereby encouraging decision-making closer to human reasoning and is appropriate for a variety of applications where straightforward, binary logic might not adequately represent the complexity of situations. A membership function is used in FST to express the uncertain information related to the decision problem. However, in the majority of instances, human intuition in real-life problems involves a preference degree, a non-preference degree, and a hesitating degree. Atanassov [2] developed Intuitionistic Fuzzy Set Theory (IFST) to comprehend these intricate uncertain circumstances with membership degree, non-membership degree, and hesitation degree such that the sum of the membership, non-membership, and hesitancy degree equals one. Despite its efficiency, however, certain uncertain data in some real-life problems may violate the limitations of IFST. For such situations, Yager [3] developed an extension of IFST, called Pythagorean Fuzzy Set Theory (PFST), where the sum of the squares of the membership degree, non-membership degree, and hesitancy degree must be equal to one. Thus, PFST provides a more comprehensive framework for capturing uncertainty in numerous real-life applications. However, Yager [4] introduced the Q-rung orthopair fuzzy set theory (Q-ROFST) and Senapati & Yager [5] introduced the Fermatean fuzzy set theory (FFST) to better understand complex uncertain situations in a more comprehensive way and allow a higher flexibility in choosing membership and non-membership grades whenever PFST meets limitations. The Fermatean Fuzzy Set (FFS) is a specific instance of the Q-ROFS with $q = 3$, where the total of the cubic power of the membership and non-membership degrees is limited to one. Greater the area of membership and non-membership grade of FFS and Q-ROFS $(q > 3)$, higher is the effectuality in real-world problems such as decision-making, pattern recognition, etc., as compared to Intuitionistic fuzzy sets (IFS) and Pythagorean fuzzy sets (PFS). Although the non-standard fuzzy sets including IFS, PFS, FFS, and Q-ROFS represent proficiently the uncertain information in various decision-making scenarios but however in certain real-life situations it is a universal intuition to choose full membership and partial non-membership (or vice versa). The ability to independently assign membership and non-membership is crucial for the decision-makers to achieve their objectives in real-world decision-making. For instance, during the COVID-19 epidemic, multiple treatments have uncertain long-term effects even though effectively eradicate the illness. Subsequently is crucial to look at the long-term impacts of COVID-19 as well as the immediate and long-term consequences of the vaccination. Although there is a dearth of real long-haul data, we are starting to learn about COVID-19 "long-haulers" people who experience problems long after they first recover such as fatigue, hacking, joint pain, and other symptoms that can be persistent. Additionally, there may also be concerns that serious problems might result from the lung damage caused by the infection. Antibody-based COVID-19 vaccinations were the developments in the fight against the COVID-19 pandemic. In this case, an optimistic degree of one and a pessimistic degree of (0,1) can be employed to independently portray the short-term and long-term impacts of COVID-19 vaccinations on human health. IFS, PFS, FFS, and Q-ROFS are unable to manage these kinds of perplexing circumstances. To analyze such complex paradoxical real-life scenarios, Dutta and Borah [6] created a novel non-standard fuzzy set called Hyperbolic Fuzzy Set (HyFS) organized with an optimistic degree and a pessimistic degree in the range [0,1] such that both optimistic and pessimistic degrees are independent of one another. HyFSs exhibit numerous benefits over other fuzzy set extensions while handling complex and uncertain information. Their flexibility, ability to express, reliability, and computational efficiency make them an advantageous tool for numerous decision-making applications implementing uncertainties. The graphical representation of membership and non-membership grades of IFS, PFS, FFS, Q-ROFS, and HyFS is displayed in Figure 10.1. Table 10.1 presents the structural comparison of an IFS, PFS, FFS, Q-ROFS, and HyFS.

In present times, rapid urbanization, industrialization, rise in population, and climate change have tremendously increased the requirement for sustainable transportation. Sustainable transportation is a necessity for addressing environmental challenges, conserving fossil fuels, mitigating health risks, and enhancing the social and economy of a society. Electric vehicles play a substantial part in sustainable transportation by lowering emissions, mitigating the consumption of resources, and boosting productivity, accepting advanced green technology while simultaneously integrating with broader environmental and social concerns. The increasing integration of renewable energy sources, like solar, wind,

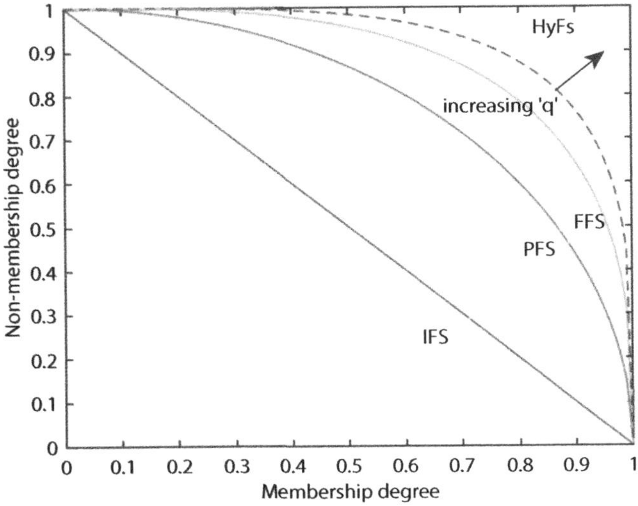

Figure 10.1 Membership and non-membership grades of IFS, PFS, FFS, and HyFS.

Table 10.1 Structural presentation of IFS, PFS, FFS, Q-ROFS, and HyFS.

IFS	PFS	FFS	Q-ROFS	HyFS
$0 \le \zeta + \eta \le 1$	$0 \le \zeta^2 + \eta^2 \le 1$	$0 \le \zeta^2 + \eta^2 \le 1$	$0 \le \zeta^q + \eta^q \le 1$	$0 \le \zeta \le 1; 0 \le \eta \le 1$
$\pi = 1 - (\zeta + \eta)$	$\pi = \sqrt{1 - (\zeta^2 + \eta^2)}$	$\pi = \sqrt[3]{1 - (\zeta^3 + \eta^3)}$	$\pi = \sqrt[q]{1 - (\zeta^q + \eta^q)}$	No hesitancy
$\zeta + \eta + \pi = 1$	$\zeta^2 + \eta^2 + \pi^2 = 1$	$\zeta^3 + \eta^3 + \pi^3 = 1$	$\zeta^q + \eta^q + \pi^q = 1$	$\zeta\eta = 1$

and hydropower, into the electrical grid additionally adds to the environmental advantages of electric vehicles by lowering their reliance on fossil fuels for power with the goals of ecological safeguarding and a healthier planet. Determining an effective Electric Vehicle Charging Station (EVCS) site requires thoughtful decision-making due to its impacts on availability, productivity, cost-effectiveness, and sustainability. In order to avoid insufficient utilization, network stress, and discomfort for electric vehicle users, optimal charging station selection is achieved through a data-driven and MCDM method that addresses uncertain decision-making. The primary objective of this study is to determine an efficient EVCS site for promoting sustainable transportation. In light of this, we design a novel HyF- VIekriterijumsko KOmpromisno Rangiranje (VIKOR) Multi-Criteria Decision Making (MCDM) method supported by a novel distance measure for choosing an optimal EVCS alternative site in an uncertain environment.

The HyF-VIKOR approach to EVCS site selection addresses several more complex and highly uncertain technical, environmental, social, and economic factors, enhancing its efficiency and accessibility. Furthermore, the newly developed HyF distance measure implemented in the proposed HyF-VIKOR method enhances the decision-making process and delivers more reliable and consistent outcomes regarding EVCS site selection by overcoming the shortcomings of some prominent distance measures from the literature.

To meet the objectives, the remaining section of the study is structured as follows:

Section 10.2 contains a review of the existing literature related to this study. Section 10.3 comprises the preliminaries on fuzzy sets and their extensions. Section 10.4 introduces a novel HyF distance measure and discusses its properties in the HyF framework. Also, this section delivers some noteworthy existing distance measures on IFS, PFS, FFS, and Q-ROFS and further we conduct a superiority check of our proposed distance measure over those existing ones related in this study. In section 10.5, we present a novel HyF-VIKOR MCDM method supported by the proposed HyF distance measure from the previous section. Following in section 10.6, we utilize the novel HyF-VIKOR MCDM in a case study on EVCS site selection to determine the optimal EVCS and perform a comparative analysis check of our proposed methodology with some existing MCDM methods to showcase its reliability and consistency. Additionally, we conducted a Spearmen Rank Correlation test between our proposed method and the encompassed MCDM in this study to check the robustness of the proposed HyF MCDM method. Finally, the conclusion and future studies of this article are presented in section 10.7.

10.2 Literature Review

A literature review is a crucial component of a research study. This study presents a concise literature review on distance measures, the VIKOR MCDM method, and the existing decision-making procedures on EVCS site selection.

10.2.1 Distance Measure

In decision-making, a distance measure assesses the closeness or divergence between alternatives depending on particular criteria. In the past few decades, various distance measures based on decision-making approaches have been developed to control fuzziness in real-life situations. Szmidt & Kacprzyk [7] contributed normalized Euclidean and Hamming distance measures in IFS. Grzegorzewski [8] defined IFS distance based on Hausdorff metric. Consequently, Wang & Xin [9]; Park *et al.* [10] proposed distance measures on IFS with their implementation in pattern recognition problems. Furthermore, Ngan *et al.* [11] developed the H-max distance measure of IFS in decision-making; Mahanta & Panda [12] proposed a distance measure in IFS with its applications in medical diagnosis and pattern recognition; Followed by, the introduction of PFS (Yager [3]) has encouraged researchers to develop numerous distance measures on PFS. Xiao & Ding [13] presented the normalized Euclidean and Hamming distance measures in PFS and utilized them in the field of medical diagnosis; Mahanta & Panda [14] established the distance measure over PFS along with its potential applications in pattern identification and medical diagnosis. The introduction of Q-ROFS by Yager [4], encouraged Du [15] the creation of Minkowski-type distance measures such as Hamming, Euclidean, and Chebyshev for Q-ROFS. Hussain *et al.* [16] offered a Q-ROFS distance measure based on the Hausdroff metric and applications in pattern recognition, whereas Peng *et al.* [17] produced a Q-ROFS distance measure and employed it for selecting a mobile edge caching technique. Furthermore, owing to the significant adaptability of decision makers within the FF environment, as well as its ability to cope with complicated, uncertain scenarios, researchers have devised numerous distance measures such as Senapati & Yager [5] introduced the Euclidean distance measure for FFSs; Ganie [18] created four distance measures over FFS that depend on the t-conorm and offered its application in pattern analysis; Deng & Wang [19] proposed two novel distance measures on FFS relying on the triangular divergence and the Hellinger distance, respectively, with applications in pattern recognition and medical diagnosis.

10.2.2 Application of the VIKOR Method

Opricovic [20] initially developed the VIKOR method to solve decision-making problems with multiple and conflicting criteria. The main objective of the VIKOR method is to assign ratings and evaluate a variety of alternatives. It also identifies compromise solutions for problems with conflicting criteria, which may assist decision-makers in arriving at a final selection. According to Opricovic & Tzeng [21], the compromise solution is an achievable option that is the most similar to the ideal. Opricovic [22] extended the VIKOR method to a fuzzy environment for determining a compromise solution based on diverse criteria. In present times, researchers successfully employed the VIKOR method to diverse multi and inconsistent criteria decision-making problems. Suh *et al.* [23] developed a novel fuzzy VIKOR model for addressing the problem of mobile service quality evaluation. Krishankumar *et al.* [24] explored a VIKOR method based on transformation procedures and applied it to address a staff selection problem in an IFS scenario. Zhou & Chen [25] extended the VIKOR technique in the Pythagorean Fuzzy context and offered its application in the selection of blockchain technology solutions. Demir *et al.* [26] integrated the Analytic Hierarchy Process (AHP) and VIKOR techniques in PFSs to access rail transportation in Turkey. Gul [27] introduces the VIKOR method in the FFS context with applications in the COVID-19 laboratory selection problem. Arya & Kumar [28] developed VIKOR for Q-rung orthopair fuzzy information measures and their application in the selection of medical consumption products. Unver *et al.* [29] extended VIKOR method in intuitionistic fuzzy valued neutrosophic value setting based on an information measure for MCDM. Garg *et al.* [30] conducted VIKOR approach for bi-level multi-criteria nonlinear fractional programming problems with entropy measure for energy awareness in wireless sensor network architecture. Khan *et al.* [31] conducted a selection of software Reliability Growth Models by employing VIKOR Method in Q-ROFSs. Besides, Gul *et al.* [32] and Mardani *et al.* [33] provided a systemic literature review on the VIKOR method along with its application.

10.2.3 Electric Vehicle Charging Site (EVCS) Selection

Electric Vehicles are a key pillar towards sustainable transportation in the present world. Proper evaluation of EVCS sites is essential for smooth accessibility, compatibility, and operation of electric vehicles together with sustainability perspectives. In this study, we review some noteworthy research works on EVCS selection from the literature. Guo & Zhao [34] determined the optimal site selection of electric vehicle charging stations by using fuzzy TOPSIS based on a sustainability perspective. Guler & Yomralioglu [35] selected a suitable location for the electric vehicle fast charging station with fuzzy AHP methods and using GIS technology. Seikh & Mandal [36] studied on application of the electric vehicle charging station site selection problem under the TOPSIS method in p, q–quasirung Orthopair fuzzy sets (p,q-QOFS). Karaşan *et al.* [37] selected the location of electric vehicle charging stations in Turkey under a fuzzy MCDM method. Cui *et al.* [38] conducted optimal siting of EVCSs in China by employing the VIKOR approach in PFS. Rani & Mishra [39] developed the Einstein aggregation operators-based MULTIMOORA method for EVCS selection in Bihar, India.

Wu *et al.* [40] performed an intuitionistic decision framework for electric vehicle charging station site selection for residential communities in Beijing.

10.2.4 Motivation of the Study

The primary reasons that motivated us to conduct this research study are listed below:

i. Distance measures are vital tools in the ranking of fuzzy sets. Although, in recent years researchers have developed numerous distance measures in the literature but the existing distance measures such as Szmidt & Kacprzyk [7], Grzegorzewski [8], Wang & Xin [9], Park *et al.*, [10], Ngan *et al.* [11], Mahanta & Panda [12], Xiao & Ding [13], Mahanta and Panda [14], Du [15], Hussain *et al.* [16], Peng *et al.* [17], Ganie [18], Deng and Wang [19] have exhibited drawbacks in certain fuzzy scenarios. This motivated us to introduce a novel distance measure in the HyF setting which can capture higher uncertainty and complex imprecise real-life situations without information loss. Also, this novel HyF distance measure successfully overcomes the limitations of those existing distance measures while producing precise and consistent outcomes.
ii. The VIKOR MCDM technique ranks and chooses alternatives in a decision with conflicting criteria. This method delivers a comprehensive and compromise response to complex decision-making situations. This encourages us to develop a VIKOR method within a HyF framework that can successfully generate reliable and efficient rankings in numerous complex real-life decision-making applications.
iii. The majority of the former research on EVCS site selection in the literature is carried out in IFS, PFS, Q-ROFS, and FFS frameworks which have severe limitations in portraying complex and independent uncertainties inherited in human judgment. However, choosing an EVCS site involves considering a variety of conflicting factors, thereby increasing the complexity as well as the uncertainty of identifying an appropriate and reliable EVCS location. Also, there does not exist any previous work on a selection of EVCS sites in a HyF setting. This inspired us to carry out an application on

EVCS in the HyF environment which offers decision experts to structure complex uncertainty and allot independent as well as total belongingness and non-belongingness degrees to uncertain decisions of human judgment. In this study, the optimal selection of an EVCS site is carried out under our proposed VIKOR MCDM method based on the novel distance measure in a HyF environment.

10.2.5 Objectives of the Study

The key objectives of this research study are outlined below:

- A new HyF distance measure with flexible parameters is constructed that meets the desired axioms of a distance metric to efficiently rank HyFSs.
- VIKOR MCDM method is extended to the HyF framework to produce a more reliable ranking of alternatives in decision-making scenarios.
- Employment of the proposed HyF-VIKOR approach based on the novel distance measure to an application of EVCS site selection for achieving sustainable transportation goals.

10.3 Preliminaries

This section offers a brief outline of FS, IFS, PFS, Q-ROFS, FFS, and, HyFS as well as displays the basic operational laws of HyFS.

Definition 1 [1]
On a finite universe of discourse W, a fuzzy set (FS) E on W is specified as $E=\{\langle w, \zeta_F(w): w \in \mathrm{W}\rangle\}$ such that, $\zeta_F(w): \mathrm{W} \rightarrow [0,1]$ represents the membership function of the element $w \in \mathrm{W}$ to E.

Definition 2 [2]
On a finite universe of discourse W, an Intuitionistic Fuzzy Set (IFS), $I=\{\langle w, \zeta_I(w), \eta_I(w): w \in \mathrm{W}\rangle\}$ is defined by a membership function $\zeta_I(w): \mathrm{W} \rightarrow [0,1]$ and a non-membership function $\eta_I: \mathrm{W} \rightarrow [0,1]$ of the element $w \in \mathrm{W}$ to the set I, such that $0 \le \zeta_I(w)+\eta_I(w) \le 1$ and $\pi_I(\mathrm{w})=1-\zeta_I(w)-\eta_I(w)$ signifies the hesitancy degree of the element $w \in \mathrm{W}$ to the set I.

Definition 3 [3]
On a finite universe of discourse W, a Pythagorean Fuzzy Set (PFS), $P=\{\langle w,\zeta_P(w),\eta_P(w): w\in \mathrm{W}\rangle\}$ is defined by a membership degree $\zeta_P(w): \mathrm{W}\rightarrow[0,1]$ and a non-membership function $\eta_P: \mathrm{W}\rightarrow[0,1]$ of the element $w\in \mathrm{W}$ to the set P, such that $0\leq\zeta_P^2(w)+\eta_P^2(w)\leq 1$ and $\pi_{\mathrm{P}}(\mathrm{w})=\sqrt{1-\zeta_P^2(w)-\eta_P^2(w)}$, represents the hesitancy degree of the element $w\in \mathrm{W}$ to the set P.

Definition 4 [4]
On a finite universe of discourse W, a Q-Rung Orthopair Fuzzy, $Q=\{\langle w,\zeta_Q(w),\eta_Q(w): w\in \mathrm{W}\rangle\}$ is defined by a membership degree $\zeta_Q(w)$: $\mathrm{W}\rightarrow[0,1]$ and a non-membership function $\eta_Q: \mathrm{W}\rightarrow[0,1]$ of the element $w\in \mathrm{W}$ to the set Q, such that $0\leq\zeta_Q^q(w)+\eta_Q^q(w)\leq 1$ and $\pi_{\mathrm{Q}}(\mathrm{w})=\sqrt{1-\zeta_Q^q(w)-\eta_Q^q(w)}$ represents the hesitancy degree of the element $w\in \mathrm{W}$ to the set Q.

Definition 5 [5]
On a finite universe of discourse W, a Fermatean Fuzzy Set (FFS), $F=\{\langle w,\zeta_F(w),\eta_F(w): w\in \mathrm{W}\rangle\}$ is defined by a membership degree $\zeta_F(w): \mathrm{W}\rightarrow[0,1]$ and a non-membership function $\eta_F(w): \mathrm{W}\rightarrow[0,1]$ of the element $w\in \mathrm{W}$ to the set F, such that $0\leq\zeta_F^3(w)+\eta_F^3(w)\leq 1$ and $\pi_{\mathrm{F}}(\mathrm{w})=\sqrt{1-\zeta_F^3(w)-\eta_F^3(w)}$ represents the hesitancy degree of the element $w\in \mathrm{W}$ to the set F.

Definition 6 [6]
On a finite universe of discourse W, a Hyperbolic fuzzy set, $'\mathrm{H}=\{(w,\zeta_H(w),\eta_H(\mathrm{w})): w\in W\}$, on W is characterized by an optimistic degree $\zeta_{\mathrm{H}}(w)$: $\mathrm{W}\rightarrow[0,1]$ and a pessimistic degree $\eta_{'\mathrm{H}}(\mathrm{w})$: $\mathrm{W}\rightarrow[0,1]$ of $\mathrm{w}\in W$ such that the optimistic and pessimistic degrees are independent of each other with the property $0\leq(\zeta_{\mathrm{H}}(w))(\eta_{'\mathrm{H}}(\mathrm{w}))\leq 1$ for all $w\in \mathrm{W}$. We signify a hyperbolic fuzzy set on a finite universe of discourse W as *HyFS(W)*.

Definition 7: The Operational Laws on HyFS [6]
For any three $'\mathrm{H}=\{(w,\zeta_H(w),\eta_H(\mathrm{w})): w\in W\}$, $'\mathrm{H}_1=\{(w,\zeta_{'\mathrm{H}_1}(w),\eta_{'\mathrm{H}_1}(\mathrm{w})): w\in W\}$, $'\mathrm{H}_2=\{(w,\zeta_{'\mathrm{H}_2}(w),\eta_{'\mathrm{H}_2}(\mathrm{w})): w\in W\}\in HyFS(W)$, the fundamental set operations are defined as follows:

i. $'\mathrm{H}^c=\{(w,1-\zeta_{'\mathrm{H}}(w),1-\eta_{'\mathrm{H}}(\mathrm{w})): \mathrm{w}\in \mathrm{W}\}$
ii. $('\mathrm{H}^{c^c})^c='\mathrm{H}^c$

iii. $'\mathrm{H}_1 \subseteq {'\mathrm{H}_2}$ if and only if $\zeta_{'\mathrm{H}_1}(w) \le \zeta_{'\mathrm{H}_2}(w)$ and $\eta_{'\mathrm{H}_1}(\mathrm{w}) \ge \eta_{'\mathrm{H}_2}(\mathrm{w})$
iv. $'\mathrm{H}_1 = {'\mathrm{H}_2}$ if and only if $\zeta_{'\mathrm{H}_1}(w) \subseteq \zeta_{'\mathrm{H}_2}(w)$ and $\eta_{'\mathrm{H}_1}(\mathrm{w}) \supseteq \eta_{'\mathrm{H}_2}(\mathrm{w})$
v. $'\mathrm{H}_1 \wedge {'\mathrm{H}_2} = \left\{\left(w, \min\left(\zeta_{'\mathrm{H}_1}(w), \zeta_{'\mathrm{H}_2}(w)\right), \max\left(\eta_{'\mathrm{H}_1}(\mathrm{w}), \eta_{'\mathrm{H}_2}(\mathrm{w})\right)\right) : \mathrm{w} \in \mathrm{W}\right\}$
vi. $\mathrm{H'}_1 \vee \mathrm{H'}_2 = \left\{\left(w, \max\left(\zeta_{'\mathrm{H}_1}(w), \zeta_{'\mathrm{H}_2}(w)\right), \min\left(\eta_{'\mathrm{H}_1}(\mathrm{w}), \eta_{'\mathrm{H}_2}(\mathrm{w})\right)\right) : \mathrm{w} \in \mathrm{W}\right\}$

Definition 8 [6]
For a $'\mathrm{H} \in HyFS(W)$, the score $S('\mathrm{H})$ and accuracy function $A('\mathrm{H})$ is defined respectively as

$$S('\mathrm{H}) = 2\zeta_{'\mathrm{H}}(w) - \zeta_{'\mathrm{H}}(w)\eta_{'\mathrm{H}}(\mathrm{w}), \text{ where } S('\mathrm{H}) \in [0,2]$$
$$A('\mathrm{H}) = 2\zeta_{'\mathrm{H}}(w) - \zeta_{'\mathrm{H}}(w)\eta_{'\mathrm{H}}(\mathrm{w}), \text{ where } A('\mathrm{H}) \in [0,2]$$

10.4 A Novel HyF Distance Measure

Distance measure plays a significant role in assessing the similarity and dissimilarity of uncertain information in diverse decision-making environments. This section highlights some of the existing notable distance measures. Also, we introduce a novel distance measure on HyFS and establish several properties and theorems associated with the novel distance measure. Further, the proposed distance measure is compared with the existing distance measures to showcase its superiority and reliability over the existing distance measures.

10.4.1 Existing Distance Measures

In the literature, researchers across the world have developed various distance measures to quantify ambiguous information. In this sub-section, we discuss some previously established distance measures on IFS, PFS, FFS, and Q-ROFS from the literature. Consider, $'\mathrm{H}_1 = \{(w_i, \zeta_{'\mathrm{H}_1}(w_i), \eta_{'\mathrm{H}_1}(\mathrm{w}_i)): w_i \in W\}, {'\mathrm{H}_2} = \{(w_i, \zeta_{'\mathrm{H}_2}(w_i), \eta_{'\mathrm{H}_2}(\mathrm{w}_i)): w_i \in W\} \in HyFS(W)$, where $W = \{w_i : i = 1,2,3\ldots,n\}$ then clearly $'\mathrm{H}_1, {'\mathrm{H}_2}$ are also IFS, PFS, FFS, and Q-ROFS. Table 10.2 displays the existing distance measures between $'\mathrm{H}_1$ and $'\mathrm{H}_2$ as follows

Table 10.2 Existing distance measures.

Researchers	Distance measures
Schimdt & Kacprzyk [7]	$d^1_{ISK}('\mathrm{H}_1,'\mathrm{H}_2)=\sqrt{\frac{1}{2n}\sum_{i=1}^{n}\left[\begin{array}{c}\left(\zeta_{'\mathrm{H}_1}(w_i)-\zeta_{'\mathrm{H}_2}(w_i)\right)^2+\left(\eta_{'\mathrm{H}_1}(w_i)-\eta_{'\mathrm{H}_2}(w_i)\right)^2+\\(\pi_1(w_i)-\pi_2(w_i))^2\end{array}\right]}$ $d^2_{ISK}('\mathrm{H}_1,'\mathrm{H}_2)=\frac{1}{2n}\sum_{i=1}^{n}\left(\begin{array}{c}\lvert\zeta_{'\mathrm{H}_1}(w_i)-\zeta_{'\mathrm{H}_2}(w_i)\rvert+\lvert\eta_{'\mathrm{H}_1}(w_i)-\eta_{'\mathrm{H}_2}(w_i)\rvert\\+\lvert\pi_1(w_i)-\pi_2(w_i)\rvert\end{array}\right)$
Grzegorzwski [8]	$d_{IG}('\mathrm{H}_1,'\mathrm{H}_2)=\frac{1}{n}\sum_{i=1}^{n}max\left(\lvert\zeta_{'\mathrm{H}_1}(w_i)-\zeta_{'\mathrm{H}_2}(w_i)\rvert,\lvert\eta_{'\mathrm{H}_1}(w_i)-\eta_{'\mathrm{H}_2}(w_i)\rvert\right)$
Wang & Xin [9]	$d_{IWX}('\mathrm{H}_1,'\mathrm{H}_2)=\frac{1}{n}\sum_{i=1}^{n}\left(\frac{\left(\lvert\zeta_{'\mathrm{H}_1}(w_i)-\zeta_{'\mathrm{H}_2}(w_i)\rvert+\lvert\eta_{'\mathrm{H}_1}(w_i)-\eta_{'\mathrm{H}_2}(w_i)\rvert\right)}{4}+\frac{max\left(\lvert\zeta_{'\mathrm{H}_1}(w_i)-\zeta_{'\mathrm{H}_2}(w_i)\rvert,\lvert\eta_{'\mathrm{H}_1}(w_i)-\eta_{'\mathrm{H}_2}(w_i)\rvert\right)}{2}\right)$
Park *et al.* [10]	$d_{IPA}('\mathrm{H}_1,'\mathrm{H}_2)=\frac{1}{4n}\sum_{i=1}^{n}\left(\begin{array}{c}\lvert\zeta_{'\mathrm{H}_1}(w_i)-\zeta_{'\mathrm{H}_2}(w_i)\rvert+\lvert\eta_{'\mathrm{H}_1}(w_i)-\eta_{'\mathrm{H}_2}(w_i)\rvert+\lvert\pi_1(w_i)-\pi_2(w_i)\rvert+\\2max\left(\lvert\zeta_{'\mathrm{H}_1}(w_i)-\zeta_{'\mathrm{H}_2}(w_i)\rvert,\lvert\eta_{'\mathrm{H}_1}(w_i)-\eta_{'\mathrm{H}_2}(w_i)\rvert,\lvert\pi_1(w_i)-\pi_2(w_i)\rvert\right)\end{array}\right)$

(*Continued*)

Table 10.2 Existing distance measures. (*Continued*)

Researchers	Distance measures
Ngan *et al.* [11]	$d^1_{ING}('H_1,'H_2)=\frac{1}{3n}\sum_{i=1}^{n}\left(\left\vert\zeta_{H_1}(w_i)-\zeta_{H_2}(w_i)\right\vert+\left\vert\eta_{H_1}(w_i)-\eta_{H_2}(w_i)\right\vert+\left\vert\max\left(\zeta_{H_1}(w_i),\zeta_{H_2}(w_i)\right)-\max\left(\eta_{H_1}(w_i),\eta_{H_2}(w_i)\right)\right\vert\right)$ $d^2_{ING}('H_1,'H_2)=\frac{1}{n}\sum_{i=1}^{n}\left(\frac{\left\vert\zeta_{H_1}(w_i)-\zeta_{H_2}(w_i)\right\vert+\left\vert\eta_{H_1}(w_i)-\eta_{H_2}(w_i)\right\vert}{4}+\frac{\left\vert\max\left(\zeta_{H_1}(w_i),\eta_{H_2}(w_i)\right)-\max\left(\zeta_{H_2}(w_i),\eta_{H_1}(w_i)\right)\right\vert}{2}\right)$
Mahanta & Panda [12]	$d_{IMP}('H_1,'H_2)=\frac{1}{n}\sum_{i=1}^{n}\left(\frac{\left\vert\zeta_{H_1}(w_i)-\eta_{H_2}(w_i)\right\vert+\left\vert\eta_{H_1}(w_i)-\eta_{H_2}(w_i)\right\vert}{\zeta_{H_1}(w_i)+\eta_{H_2}(w_i)+\eta_{H_1}(w_i)+\eta_{H_2}(w_i)}\right)$
Xiao & Ding [13]	$d^1_{PXD}('H_1,'H_2)=\sqrt{\frac{1}{2n}\sum_{i=1}^{n}\left[\left(\zeta^2_{H_1}(w_i)-\eta^2_{H_2}(w_i)\right)^2+\left(\eta^2_{H_1}(w_i)-\eta^2_{H_2}(w_i)\right)^2+(\pi_1^2(w_i)-\pi_2^2(w_i))^2\right]}$ $d^2_{PXD}('H_1,'H_2)=\frac{1}{2n}\sum_{i=1}^{n}\left(\left\vert\left(\zeta^2_{H_1}(w_i)-\eta^2_{H_2}(w_i)\right)\right\vert+\left\vert\left(\eta^2_{H_1}(w_i)-\eta^2_{H_2}(w_i)\right)\right\vert+\left\vert(\pi_1^2(w_i)-\pi_2^2(w_i))\right\vert\right)$
Mahanta & Panda [14]	$d_{PMP}('H_1,'H_2)=\frac{1}{n}\sum_{i=1}^{n}\frac{\left\vert\zeta^2_{H_1}(w_i)-\eta^2_{H_2}(w_i)\right\vert+\left\vert\eta^2_{H_1}(w_i)-\eta^2_{H_2}(w_i)\right\vert}{\zeta^2_{H_1}(w_i)+\eta^2_{H_2}(w_i)+\eta^2_{H_1}(w_i)+\eta^2_{H_2}(w_i)}$

(*Continued*)

Table 10.2 Existing distance measures. (*Continued*)

Researchers	Distance measures
Senapati & Yager [5]	$d^1_{FSY}('H_1,'H_2)=\sqrt{\frac{1}{2n}\sum_{i=1}^{n}\left[\left(\zeta^3_{'H_1}(w_i)-\eta^3_{'H_2}(w_i)\right)^2+\left(\eta^3_{'H_1}(w_i)-\eta^3_{'H_2}(w_i)\right)^2+(\pi^3_1(w_i)-\pi^3_2(w_i))^2\right]}$ $d^2_{FSY}('H_1,'H_2)=\frac{1}{2n}\sum_{i=1}^{n}\left(\left\|\left(\zeta^3_{'H_1}(w_i)-\eta^3_{'H_2}(w_i)\right)\right\|+\left\|\eta^3_{'H_1}(w_i)-\eta^3_{'H_2}(w_i)\right\|+\|(\pi^3_1(w_i)-\pi^3_2(w_i))\|\right)$
Ganie [18]	$d^1_{FG}('H_1,'H_2)=\frac{1}{n}\sum_{i=1}^{n}\left[\left\|\zeta^3_{'H_1}(w_i)-\eta^3_{'H_2}(w_i)\right\|+\left\|\left(\eta^3_{'H_1}(w_i)-\eta^3_{'H_2}(w_i)\right)\right\|-\frac{2\left\|\left(\zeta^3_{'H_1}(w_i)-\eta^3_{'H_2}(w_i)\right)\right\|\left\|\left(\eta^3_{'H_1}(w_i)-\eta^3_{'H_2}(w_i)\right)\right\|}{1-\left\|\left(\zeta^3_{'H_1}(w_i)-\eta^3_{'H_2}(w_i)\right)\right\|\left\|\left(\eta^3_{'H_1}(w_i)-\eta^3_{'H_2}(w_i)\right)\right\|}\right]$ $d^2_{FG}('H_1,'H_2)=\frac{1}{n}\sum_{i=1}^{n}\left[\left(\left\|\left(\zeta^3_{'H_1}(w_i)-\eta^3_{'H_2}(w_i)\right)\right\|+\left\|\eta^3_{'H_1}(w_i)-\eta^3_{'H_2}(w_i)\right\|-\left\|\left(\zeta^3_{'H_1}(w\ )-\eta^3_{'H_2}(w\ )\right)\right\|\left\|\eta^3_{'H_1}(w_i)-\eta^3_{'H_2}(w_i)\right\|\right)\right]$ $d^3_{FG}('H_1,'H_2)=\frac{1}{n}\sum_{i=1}^{n}\left[min\left(1,\left\|\left(\zeta^3_{'H_1}(w_i)-\eta^3_{'H_2}(w_i)\right)\right\|+\left\|\eta^3_{'H_1}(w_i)-\eta^3_{'H_2}(w_i)\right\|\right)\right]$ $d^4_{FG}\left('H_1,'H_2\right)=\frac{1}{n}\sum_{i=1}^{n}\left[\frac{\left\|\zeta^3_{'H_1}(w_i)-\eta^3_{'H_2}(w_i)\right\|+\left\|\eta^3_{'H_1}(w_i)-\eta^3_{'H_2}(w_i)\right\|}{1+\left\|\left(\zeta^3_{'H_1}(w_i)-\eta^3_{'H_2}(w_i)\right)\right\|\left\|\eta^3_{'H_1}(w_i)-\eta^3_{'H_2}(w_i)\right\|}\right]$

(*Continued*)

Table 10.2 Existing distance measures. (*Continued*)

Researchers	Distance measures
Deng & Wang [19]	$d^1_{FDW}('H_1,'H_2)=\sqrt{\frac{1}{2n}\sum_{i=1}^{n}\left[\left(\sqrt{\zeta^3_{'H_1}(w_i)}-\sqrt{\zeta^3_{'H_2}(w_i)}\right)^2+\left(\sqrt{\eta^3_{'H_1}(w_i)}-\sqrt{\eta^3_{'H_2}(w_i)}\right)^2\right]}$ $d^2_{FDW}('H_1,'H_2)=\sqrt{\frac{1}{2n}\sum_{i=1}^{n}\left[\frac{\left(\sqrt{\zeta^3_{'H_1}(w_i)}-\sqrt{\zeta^3_{'H_2}(w_i)}\right)^2}{\zeta^3_{'H_1}(w_i)+\eta^3_{'H_2}(w_i)}+\frac{\left(\sqrt{\eta^3_{'H_1}(w_i)}-\sqrt{\eta^3_{'H_2}(w_i)}\right)^2}{\eta^3_{'H_1}(w_i)+\eta^3_{'H_2}(w_i)}\right]}$
Du [15]	$d^1_{QD}('H_1,'H_2)=\frac{1}{2n}\sum_{i=1}^{n}\left(\left\|(\zeta_{'H_1}(w_i))^q-(\zeta_{'H_2}(w_i))^q\right\|+\left\|(\eta_{'H_1}(w_i))^q-(\eta_{'H_2}(w_i))^q\right\|\right)$ $d^2_{QD}('H_1,'H_2)=\left[\frac{1}{2n}\sum_{i=1}^{n}\left\{\left((\zeta_{'H_1}(w_i))^q-(\zeta_{'H_2}(w_i))^q\right)^2+\left((\eta_{'H_1}(w_i))^q-(\eta_{'H_2}(w_i))^q\right)^2\right\}\right]^{\frac{1}{2}}$ $d^3_{QD}('H_1,'H_2)=\frac{1}{n}\sum_{i=1}^{n}max\left(\left\|(\zeta_{'H_1}(w_i))^q-(\zeta_{'H_2}(w_i))^q\right\|,\left\|(\eta_{'H_1}(w_i))^q-(\eta_{'H_2}(w_i))^q\right\|\right)$

(*Continued*)

Table 10.2 Existing distance measures. (*Continued*)

Researchers	**Distance measures**
Peng *et al.* [17]	$d_{QPe}('H_1,'H_2)=\frac{1}{2n}\sum_{i=1}^{n}\left(\begin{array}{c}\left(\zeta_{'H_1}(w_i)-\zeta_{'H_2}(w_i)\right)^2\\+\left\{\left(1-\left(\eta_{'H_1}(w_i)\right)^q\right)^{\frac{1}{q}}-\left(1-\left(\eta_{'H_2}(w_i)\right)^q\right)^{\frac{1}{q}}\right\}^2\end{array}\right)$
Hussain *et al.* [16]	$d_{QH}('H_1,'H_2)=\frac{1}{n}\sum_{i=1}^{n}max\left(\begin{array}{c}\left\|\left(\zeta_{'H_1}(w_i)\right)^q-\left(\zeta_{'H_2}(w_i)\right)^q\right\|,\\\left\|\left(1-\left(\eta_{'H_1}(w_i)\right)^q\right)-\left(1-\left(\eta_{'H_2}(w_i)\right)^q\right)\right\|\end{array}\right)$

10.4.2 Proposed Novel Distance Measure on HyFSs

In this sub-section, a novel distance measure on HyFSs is constructed on the concept of differences of optimistic and pessimistic degrees between two HyFSs along with the cross-evaluation of the optimistic and pessimistic degrees between them. The implementation of the cross-evaluation factor in the proposed Hyperbolic fuzzy distance measure empowers decision-makers to precisely evaluate human judgments while gathering accurate information without information loss in diverse uncertain decision-making situations. Followed, the fundamental properties and propositions for the proposed distance measure are also discussed in this sub-section.

Definition 9: Given a finite universe of discourse $W = \{w_i : i = 1,2,3\ldots,n\}$, let $'H_1 = \{(w_i, \zeta_{'H_1}(w_i), \eta_{'H_1}(w_i)) : w_i \in W\}$, $'H_2 = \{(w_i, \zeta_{'H_2}(w_i), \eta_{'H_2}(w_i)) : w_i \in W\}$ be two HyFSs then we define the novel distance between $'H_1$ and $'H_2$ as

$$D_{HyPA}('H_1,'H_2) = \left[\frac{1}{3n}\sum_{i=1}^{n}\left(\left(\frac{|\zeta_{'H_1}(w_i) - \zeta_{'H_2}(w_i)|}{\zeta_{'H_2}(w_i) + \zeta_{'H_2}(w_i)}\right)^2 + \left(\frac{|\eta_{'H_1}(w_i) - \eta_{'H_2}(w_i)|}{\eta_{'H_1}(w_i) + \eta_{'H_2}(w_i)}\right)^2 + |(\zeta_{'H_1}(w_i)\eta_{'H_2}(w_i) - \eta_{'H_1}(w_i)\zeta_{'H_2}(w_i)|^2\right)\right]^{\frac{1}{2}}$$

where, $'n'$ is the number of pairs of HyFSs.

Lemma 1: Let $g:[0,1]\times[0,1] \to \mathbb{R}$ be a real-valued function defined by $g(x,y) = \left(\left(\frac{|a-x|}{(a+x)}\right)^2 + \left(\frac{|b-y|}{(b+y)}\right)^2\right)$ where $a,b \in [0,1]$ and $a+b \leq 1$, then it satisfies the following axioms

i. $g(x,y)$ is increasing function of x and decreasing function of y under the condition $a \leq x \leq 1$ and $0 \leq y \leq b$

ii. $g(x,y)$ is decreasing function of x and increasing function of x under the condition $0 \leq x \leq a$ and $b \leq y \leq 1$

iii. If $a \leq x_1 \leq x_2 \leq 1$ and $0 \leq y_2 \leq y_1 \leq b$, then $g(x_2,y_2) \geq g(x_1,y_1)$. And if $0 \leq x_1 \leq x_2 \leq a$ and $b \leq y_2 \leq y_1 \leq 1$, then $g(x_2,y_2) \leq g(x_1,y_1)$

Proof: The proof of the lemma is as follows

i. Let $a \le x \le 1$ and $0 \le y \le b$, then $|a-x| = x-a > 0$ and $|b-y| = b-y > 0$

Now, $$\frac{\partial}{\partial x}\left[\left(\frac{|a-x|}{(a+x)}\right)^2 + \left(\frac{|b-y|}{(b+y)}\right)^2\right] = \frac{\partial}{\partial x}\left[\left(\frac{x-a}{(a+x)}\right)^2 + \left(\frac{b-y}{(b+y)}\right)^2\right]$$

$$= \frac{1}{(x+a)^4}[(x+a)^2 2(x-a) - (x-a)^2 2(x+a).1] = \frac{4a(x-a)}{(x+a)^3} > 0$$

$$\frac{\partial}{\partial y}\left[\left(\frac{|a-x|}{(a+x)}\right)^2 + \left(\frac{|b-y|}{(b+y)}\right)^2\right] = \frac{\partial}{\partial y}\left[\left(\frac{x-a}{(a+x)}\right)^2 + \left(\frac{b-y}{(b+y)}\right)^2\right]$$

$$= \frac{-1}{(y+b)^4}[(b+y)^2 2(b-y) - (b-y)^2 2(b+y).1] = \frac{-4b(b-y)}{(y+b)^3} < 0$$

Hence, $g(x, y)$ is increasing function of x and decreasing function of y under the condition $a \le x \le 1$ and $0 \le y \le b$

ii. Let condition $0 \le x \le a$ and $b \le y \le 1$, then $|a-x| = a-x > 0$ and $|b-y| = y-b > 0$

Now, $$\frac{\partial}{\partial x}\left[\left(\frac{|a-x|}{(a+x)}\right)^2 + \left(\frac{|b-y|}{(b+y)}\right)^2\right] = \frac{\partial}{\partial x}\left[\left(\frac{a-x \lim_{\delta x \to 0}}{(a+x)}\right)^2 + \left(\frac{y-b}{(b+y)}\right)^2\right]$$

$$= \frac{1}{(x+a)^4}[(x+a)^2 2(a-x)(-1) - (a-x)^2 2(x+a).1] = \frac{-4a(a-x)}{(x+a)^3} < 0$$

$$\frac{\partial}{\partial y}\left[\left(\frac{|a-x|}{(a+x)}\right)^2 + \left(\frac{|b-y|}{(b+y)}\right)^2\right] = \frac{\partial}{\partial y}\left[\left(\frac{a-x}{(a+x)}\right)^2 + \left(\frac{y-b}{(b+y)}\right)^2\right]$$

$$= \frac{1}{(y+b)^4}[(b+y)^2 2(y-b) - (y-b)^2 2(b+y).1] = \frac{4b(y-b)}{(y+b)^3} > 0$$

Hence, $g(x, y)$ is increasing function of x and decreasing function of y under the condition $0 \le x \le a$ and $b \le y \le 1$

iii. Let $a \le x_1 \le x_2 \le 1$ and $0 \le y_2 \le y_1 \le b$, then by point i. from the above lemma we obtain $g(x_2, y_2) \ge g(x_1, y_2) \ge g(x_1, y_1) \Rightarrow g(x_2, y_2) \ge g(x_1, y_1)$. Again let $0 \le x_1 \le x_2 \le a$ and $b \le y_2 \le y_1 \le 1$, then by point ii. from the above lemma we get $g(x_2, y_2) \le g(x_1, y_2) \le g(x_1, y_1)$. Hence, $g(x_2, y_2) \le g(x_1, y_1)$

Corollary 1: If $0 \le a_1 \le a_2 \le a_3 \le 1$ and $0 \le b_3 \le b_2 \le b_1 \le 1$, then

$$\left[\left(\frac{|a_1 - a_3|}{a_1 + a_3}\right)^2 + \left(\frac{|b_1 - b_3|}{b_1 + b_3}\right)^2\right] \ge \left[\left(\frac{|a_i - a_{i+1}|}{a_i + a_{i+1}}\right)^2 + \left(\frac{|b_i - b_{i+1}|}{b_i + b_{i+1}}\right)^2\right] i = 1,2$$

Proof: Taking $a = a_1$ and $b = b_1$, then $a, b \in [0,1]$. Thus from the previous Lemma 1, it is clear that $g(a_3, b_3) \ge g(a_2, b_3) \ge g(a_2, b_2) \Rightarrow g(a_3, b_3) \ge g(a_2, b_2)$. Thus, it follows that,

$$\left[\left(\frac{|a_1 - a_3|}{a_1 + a_3}\right)^2 + \left(\frac{|b_1 - b_3|}{b_1 + b_3}\right)^2\right] \ge \left[\left(\frac{|a_1 - a_2|}{a_1 + a_2}\right)^2 + \left(\frac{|b_1 - b_2|}{b_1 + b_2}\right)^2\right] \quad (10.1)$$

Taking $a = a_3$ and $b = b_3$, then $a, b \in [0,1]$. Thus from the previous Lemma 1, it is clear that $g(a_1, b_1) \ge g(a_2, b_1) \ge g(a_2, b_2) \Rightarrow g(a_1, b_1) \ge g(a_2, b_2)$. Thus, it follows that,

$$\left[\left(\frac{|a_3 - a_1|}{a_3 + a_1}\right)^2 + \left(\frac{|b_3 - b_1|}{b_3 + b_1}\right)^2\right] \ge \left[\left(\frac{|a_3 - a_2|}{a_3 + a_2}\right)^2 + \left(\frac{|b_3 - b_2|}{b_3 + b_2}\right)^2\right] \quad (10.2)$$

Combining the above inequalities (10.1) and (10.2), the outcome follows as

$$\left[\left(\frac{|a_1 - a_3|}{a_1 + a_3}\right)^2 + \left(\frac{|b_1 - b_3|}{b_1 + b_3}\right)^2\right] \ge \left[\left(\frac{|a_i - a_{i+1}|}{a_i + a_{i+1}}\right)^2 + \left(\frac{|b_i - b_{i+1}|}{b_i + b_{i+1}}\right)^2\right] i = 1,2$$

Definition 10

Let $'\mathrm{H}_1 = \{(w_i, \zeta_{\mathrm{H}_1}(w_i), \eta_{\mathrm{H}_1}(\mathrm{w_i})) : w_i \in W\}$, $'\mathrm{H}_2 = \{(w_i, \zeta_{\mathrm{H}_2}(w_i), \eta_{\mathrm{H}_2}(\mathrm{w_i})) : w_i \in W\}$ and $'\mathrm{H}_3 = \{(w_i, \zeta_{\mathrm{H}_3}(w_i), \eta_{\mathrm{H}_3}(\mathrm{w_i})) : w_i \in W\}$, be three HyFSs on a finite universe of discourse $W = \{w_i : i = 1, 2, 3 \ldots, n\}$.

Then the novel FF distance measure $\mathrm{D_{HyPA}}$, satisfies the following properties:

i. $P_1 : 0 \le \mathrm{D_{HyPA}}('\mathrm{H}_1, '\mathrm{H}_2) \le 1$

ii. $P_2 : D_{HyPA}('H_1, 'H_2) = 0$ *if and only if* $F_1 = F_2$
iii. $P_3 : D_{HyPA}('H_1, 'H_2) = D_{HyPA}('H_1, 'H_2)$
iv. P_4: *For* $'H_1 \subseteq 'H_2 \subseteq 'H_3$, *then* $D_{HyPA}('H_1, 'H_2) \leq D_{HyPA}('H_1, 'H_3)$ and $D_{HyPA}('H_2, 'H_3) \leq D_{HyPA}('H_1, 'H_3)$

Proof (P_1): Since, $'H_1$, $'H_2$ and $'H_3$ are HyFSs, then clearly $0 \leq D_{HyPA}('H_1, 'H_2) \leq 1$
Proof (P_2): Let, $D_{HyPA}('H_1, 'H_2) = 0$, then for all $i = 1, 2, \ldots, n$ we have,

$$\frac{1}{3}\left[\left(\frac{|\zeta_{'H_1}(w_i) - \zeta_{'H_2}(w_i)|}{\zeta_{'H_2}(w_i) + \zeta_{'H_2}(w_i)}\right)^2 + \left(\frac{|\eta_{'H_1}(w_i) - \eta_{'H_2}(w_i)|}{\eta_{'H_1}(w_i) + \eta_{'H_2}(w_i)}\right)^2 + |(\zeta_{'H_1}(w_i)\eta_{'H_2}(w_i) - \eta_{'H_1}(w_i)\zeta_{'H_2}(w_i)|^2\right] = 0$$

$$\Leftrightarrow \zeta_{'H_1}(w_i) = \zeta_{'H_1}(w_i) \text{ and } \eta_{'H_1}(w_i) = \eta_{'H_2}(w_i)$$

$$\Leftrightarrow 'H_1 = 'H_2$$

Proof (P_3): Clearly, it is obvious that $D_{HyPA}('H_1, 'H_2) = D_{HyPA}('H_1, 'H_2)$
Proof (P_4): Consider, $'H_1 \subseteq 'H_2 \subseteq 'H_3$
Then, for all $i = 1, 2, \ldots, n$ we have,

$$0 \leq \zeta_{'H_1}(w_i) \leq \zeta_{'H_2}(w_i) \leq \zeta_{'H_3}(w_i) \leq 1 \text{ and } 0 \geq \eta_{'H_1}(w_i) \geq \eta_{'H_2}(w_i) \geq \eta_{'H_3}(w_i) \geq 1$$

Clearly from Corollary 1 we obtain,

$$\left[\left(\frac{|\zeta_{'H_1}(w_i) - \zeta_{'H_3}(w_i)|}{\zeta_{'H_1}(w_i) + \zeta_{'H_3}(w_i)}\right)^2 + \left(\frac{|\eta_{'H_1}(w_i) - \eta_{'H_3}(w_i)|}{\eta_{'H_1}(w_i) + \eta_{'H_3}(w_i)}\right)^2\right] \geq \left[\left(\frac{|\zeta_{'H_1}(w_i) - \zeta_{'H_2}(w_i)|}{\zeta_{'H_1}(w_i) + \zeta_{'H_2}(w_i)}\right)^2 + \left(\frac{|\eta_{'H_1}(w_i) - \eta_{'H_2}(w_i)|}{\eta_{'H_1}(w_i) + \eta_{'H_2}(w_i)}\right)^2\right] \tag{10.3}$$

Also, $\zeta_{'H_1}(w_i)\eta_{'H_3}(w_i) \leq \zeta_{'H_1}(w_i)\eta_{'H_2}(w_i) \leq \zeta_{'H_2}(w_i)\eta_{'H_1}(w_i) \leq \zeta_{'H_3}(w_i)\eta_{'H_1}(w_i)$

$$\Rightarrow |(\zeta_{'H_2}(w_i)\eta_{'H_1}(w_i)) - (\zeta_{'H_1}(w_i)\eta_{'H_2}(w_i))| \leq |(\zeta_{'H_3}(w_i)\eta_{'H_1}(w_i)) - (\zeta_{'H_1}(w_i)\eta_{'H_3}(w_i))| \tag{10.4}$$

Adding (10.3), (10.4) and multiplying with $\frac{1}{3}$ on both sides of the inequality for all $i = 1, 2, \ldots, n$ we attain,

$$\frac{1}{3}\left[\left(\frac{|\zeta_{'H_1}(w_i) - \zeta_{'H_2}(w_i)|}{\zeta_{'H_2}(w_i) + \zeta_{'H_2}(w_i)}\right)^2 + \left(\frac{|\eta_{'H_1}(w_i) - \eta_{'H_2}(w_i)|}{\eta_{'H_1}(w_i) + \eta_{'H_2}(w_i)}\right)^2 + |(\zeta_{'H_1}(w_i)\eta_{'H_2}(w_i) - \eta_{'H_1}(w_i)\zeta_{'H_2}(w_i)|^2\right] \le$$
$$\frac{1}{3}\left[\left(\frac{|\zeta_{'H_1}(w_i) - \zeta_{'H_3}(w_i)|}{\zeta_{'H_3}(w_i) + \zeta_{'H_3}(w_i)}\right)^2 + \left(\frac{|\eta_{'H_1}(w_i) - \eta_{'H_3}(w_i)|}{\eta_{'H_1}(w_i) + \eta_{'H_3}(w_i)}\right)^2 + |(\zeta_{'H_1}(w_i)\eta_{'H_3}(w_i) - \eta_{'H_1}(w_i)\zeta_{'H_3}(w_i)|^2\right] \tag{10.5}$$

Now taking summation for all $i = 1, 2, 3 \ldots n$ and prefacing the factor $\frac{1}{n}$ on both sides of the inequality (10.5) gives, $D_{HyPA}('H_1, 'H_2) \le D_{HyPA}('H_1, 'H_3)$

In a similar manner, we can show, $D_{HyPA}('H_2, 'H_3) \le D_{HyPA}('H_1, 'H_3)$

Figure 10.2, Figure 10.3, and Figure 10.4 represent the nonlinear characteristics of the proposed distance measure.

Proposition 1 For $'H = <\zeta_{'H}, \eta_{'H}>, 'H^c = <1-\zeta_{'H}, 1-\eta_{'H}>$, then

$$D_{HyPA}('H, 'H^c) = \left[\frac{1}{3}((|2\zeta_{'H} - 1|)^2 + (|2\eta_{'H} - 1|)^2 + |(\zeta_{'H} - \eta_{'H})(1 - \zeta_{'H} - \eta_{'H})|^2)\right]^{\frac{1}{2}}$$

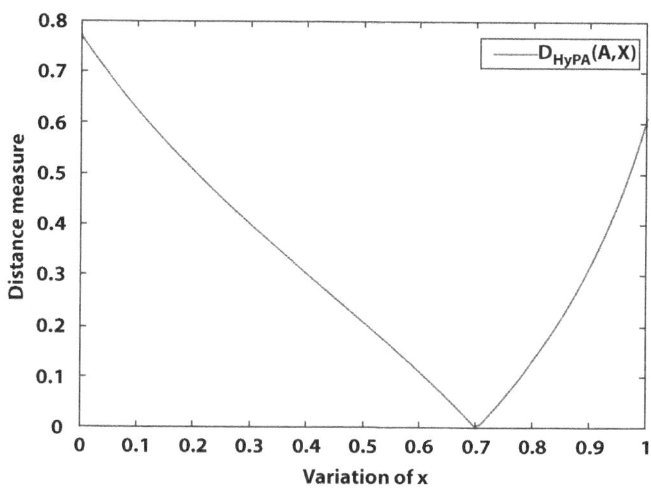

Figure 10.2 Proposed distance measure between A = (0.7, 0.3) and X = (x,1-x).

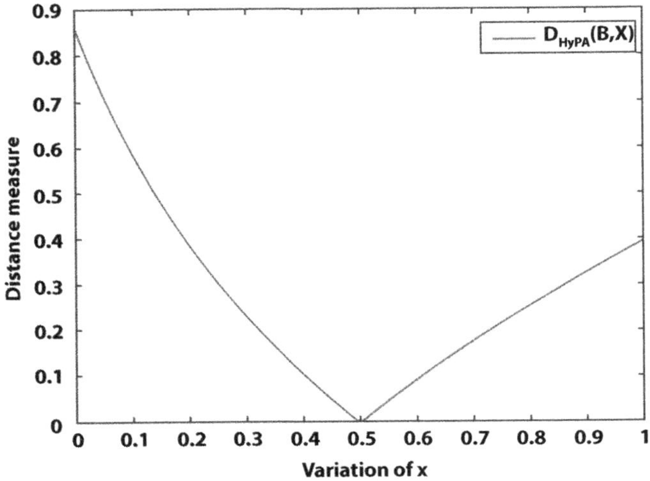

Figure 10.3 Proposed distance measure between B = (0.5,0.5) and X = (x,1-x).

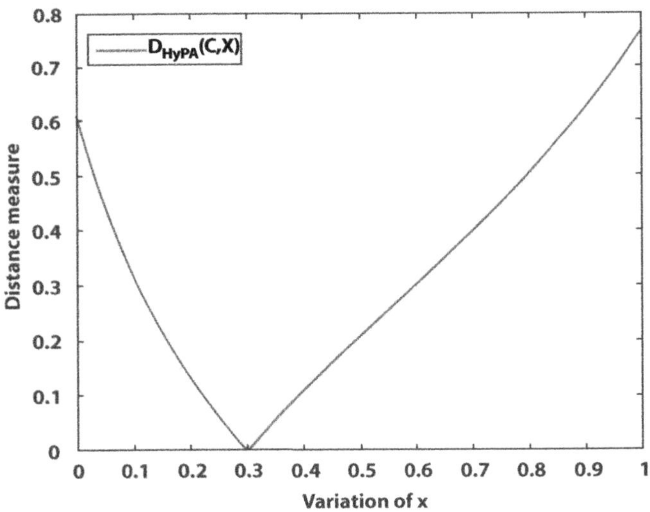

Figure 10.4 Proposed distance measure between C = (0.3,0.7) and X = (x,1-x).

Graphically the distance of $D_{HyPA}('H,'H^c)$ is presented in Figure 10.5.

Proposition 2 For $'H_1 =< \zeta_{'H}, \zeta_{'H} >, 'H_2 =< \eta_{'H}, 1-\eta_{'H} >$ *and* $'H_2^c =< 1-\eta_{'H}, \eta_{'H} >$, then

$$D_{HyPA}('H_1,'H_2) = \left[\frac{1}{3}\left(\left(\frac{|\zeta_{'H} - \eta_{'H}|}{\zeta_{'H} + \eta_{'H}}\right)^2 + \left(\frac{|\zeta_{'H} - 1 + \eta_{'H}|}{\zeta_{'H} + 1 - \eta_{'H}}\right)^2 + |2\zeta_{'H}\eta_{'H} - \zeta_{'H}|^2\right)\right]^{\frac{1}{2}}$$
$$= D_{HyPA}('H_1,'H_2^c)$$

Graphically the distance of $D_{HyPA}('H_1,'H_2) = D_{HyPA}('H_1,'H_2^c)$ is presented in Figure 10.6.

Proposition 3 For $'H_1 =< \zeta_{'H}, 1-\zeta_{'H} >, 'H_2 =< \eta_{'H}, 1-\eta_{'H} >$, then

$$D_{HyPA}('H_1,'H_2) = \left[\frac{1}{3}\left(\left(\frac{|\zeta_{'H} - \eta_{'H}|}{\zeta_{'H} + \eta_{'H}}\right)^2 + \left(\frac{|\zeta_{'H} - \eta_{'H}|}{2 - \zeta_{'H} - \eta_{'H}}\right)^2 + |\zeta_{'H} - \eta_{'H}|^2\right)\right]^{\frac{1}{2}}$$

Graphically the distance of $D_{HyPA}('H_1,'H_2)$ is presented in Figure 10.7.

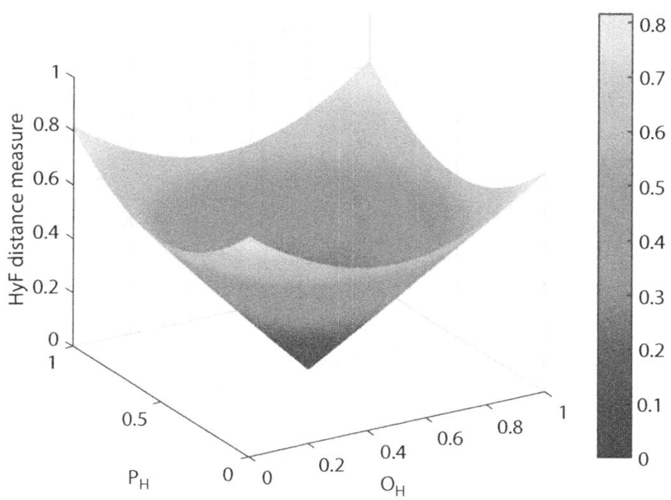

Figure 10.5 Graphical representation of proposition 1.

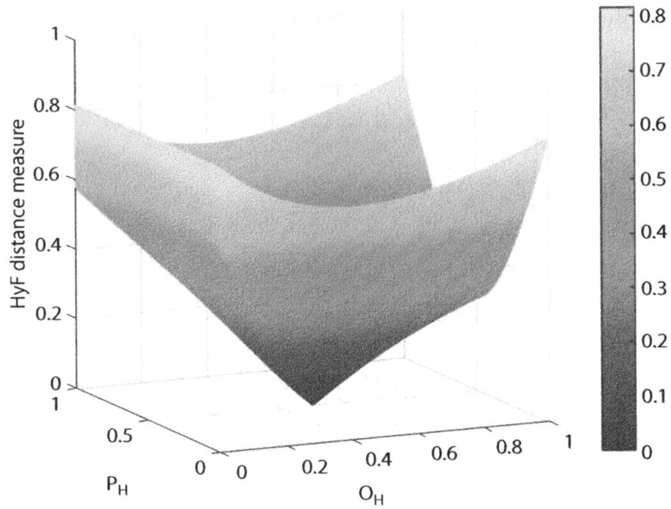

Figure 10.6 Graphical representation of proposition 2.

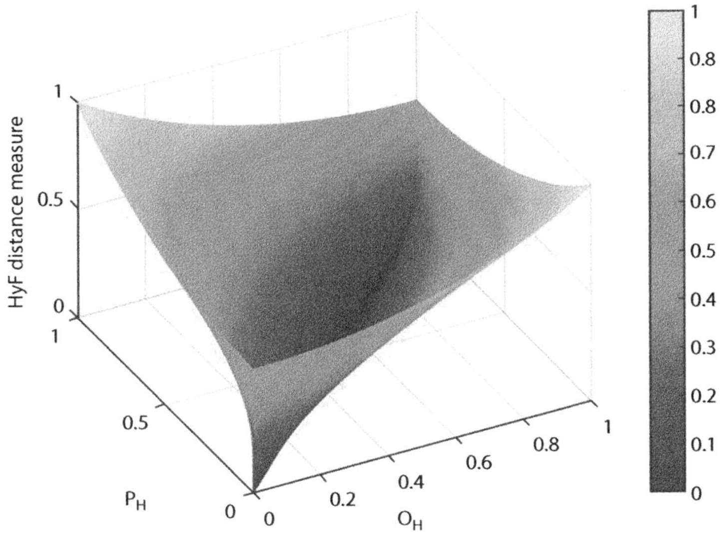

Figure 10.7 Graphical representation of proposition 3.

10.4.3 Comparative Study

In this section, we compare the proposed HyF distance measure with the other existing distance measures as demonstrated in Section 10.2.1 from the literature. This comparative analysis showcases the superiority and

Table 10.3 Comparison of distance measures between various distinct pairs of fuzzy sets.

Distance measure	Event 1	Event 2	Event 3	Event 4	Event 5	Event 6	Event 7
$'H_1$ $'H_2$	(0.3,0.3) (0.4,0.4)	(0.3,0.4) (0.4,0.3)	(0.4,0.3) (0.4,0.4)	(1,0) (0,1)	(0.4,0.2) (0.5,0.3)	(0.4,0.2) (0.5,0.2)	(1,1) (0.5,0.5)
$d^1_{ISK}('H_1,'H_2)$ **Schimdt & Kacprzyk [7]**	**0.1732**	**0.1000**	**0.1000**	1	**0.1732**	**0.1000**	Not reasonable
$d^2_{ISK}('H_1,'H_2)$ **Schimdt & Kacprzyk [7]**	**0.0200**	**0.1000**	**0.1000**	1	**0.2000**	**0.1000**	Not reasonable
$d_{IG}('H_1,'H_2)$ **Grzegorzwski [8]**	**0.1000**	**0.1000**	**0.1000**	1	**0.1000**	**0.1000**	Not reasonable
$d_{IWX}('H_1,'H_2)$ **Wang & Xin [9]**	**0.1000**	**0.1000**	**0.0750**	1	**0.1000**	**0.0750**	Not reasonable
$d_{IPA}('H_1,'H_2)$ **Park *et al.* [10]**	**0.1500**	**0.0750**	**0.0750**	1	**0.1500**	**0.0750**	Not reasonable
$d^1_{ING}('H_1,'H_2)$ **Ngan *et al.* [11]**	**0.0666**	**0.1000**	0.0333	1	**0.1000**	**0.0666**	Not reasonable

(*Continued*)

Table 10.3 Comparison of distance measures between various distinct pairs of fuzzy sets. (*Continued*)

Distance measure	Event 1	Event 2	Event 3	Event 4	Event 5	Event 6	Event 7
$d^2_{ING}('H_1,'H_2)$ **Ngan *et al.* [11]**	0.0500	**0.1000**	0.0250	1	**0.1000**	0.075	Not reasonable
$d_{IMP}('H_1,'H_2)$ **Mahanta & Panda [12]**	**0.1428**	**0.1428**	0.0666	1	**0.1428**	0.0769	Not reasonable
$d^1_{PXD}('H_1,'H_2)$ **Xiao & Ding [12]**	0.1100	0.0700	0.0608	1	0.1118	0.0806	Not reasonable
$d^2_{PXD}('H_1,'H_2)$ **Xiao & Ding [13]**	**0.1300**	0.0700	0.0600	1	**0.1300**	0.0800	Not reasonable
$d_{PMP}('H_1,'H_2)$ **Mahanta & Panda [14]**	**0.2800**	**0.2800**	0.1228	1	0.2593	0.1836	Not reasonable
$d^1_{FSY}('H_1,'H_2)$ **Senapati & Yager [5]**	0.0541	0.037	0.0294	1	0.0601	0.0505	Not reasonable
$d^2_{FSY}('H_1,'H_2)$ **Senapati & Yager [5]**	0.065	0.037	0.028	1	0.068	0.0490	Not reasonable

(*Continued*)

Table 10.3 Comparison of distance measures between various distinct pairs of fuzzy sets. (*Continued*)

Distance measure	**Event 1**	**Event 2**	**Event 3**	**Event 4**	**Event 5**	**Event 6**	**Event 7**
$d^1_{FG}('H_1,'H_2)$ **Ganie [18]**	**0.0714**	**0.0714**	0.037	1	0.0777	0.0610	Not reasonable
$d^2_{FG}('H_1,'H_2)$ **Ganie [18]**	**0.0726**	**0.0726**	0.037	1	0.0788	0.0610	Not reasonable
$d^3_{FG}('H_1,'H_2)$ **Ganie [18]**	**0.074**	**0.074**	0.037	1	0.0800	0.0610	Not reasonable
$d^4_{FG}('H_1,'H_2)$ **Ganie [18]**	**0.0738**	**0.0738**	0.037	1	0.0799	0.0610	Not reasonable
$d^1_{FDW}('H_1,'H_2)$ **Deng & Wang [19]**	**0.0078**	**0.0078**	0.00393	1	0.0078	0.0050	Not reasonable
$d^2_{FDW}('H_1,'H_2)$ **Deng & Wang [19]**	**0.0863**	**0.0863**	0.04319	1	0.1068	0.0267	Not reasonable
$d^1_{QD}('H_1,'H_2)$ **Du [15]**	**0.0078**	**0.0078**	0.0055	1	0.0149	0.0149	Not reasonable

(*Continued*)

Table 10.3 Comparison of distance measures between various distinct pairs of fuzzy sets. *(Continued)*

Distance measure	Event 1	Event 2	Event 3	Event 4	Event 5	Event 6	Event 7
$d_{QD}^2({}'\mathrm{H}_1, {}'\mathrm{H}_2)$ **Du [15]**	**0.0078**	**0.0078**	0.0539	1	0.1115	0.0605	Not reasonable
$d_{QD}^3({}'\mathrm{H}_1, {}'\mathrm{H}_2)$ **Du [15]**	**0.0078**	**0.0078**	0.0078	1	**0.0210**	**0.0210**	Not reasonable
$d_{QPe}({}'\mathrm{H}_1, {}'\mathrm{H}_2)$ **Peng *et al.*, [17]**	**0.0050**	**0.0050**	1.2E-06	1	**0.0050**	**0.0050**	Not reasonable
$d_{QH}({}'\mathrm{H}_1, {}'\mathrm{H}_2)$ **Hussain *et al.* [16]**	**0.0078**	**0.0078**	0	1	**0.0210**	**0.0210**	Not reasonable
$d_{HyPA}({}'\mathrm{H}_1, {}'\mathrm{H}_2)$ **(Proposed)**	0.1166	0.1234	0.0856	1	0.1325	0.0652	0.2722

consistency of the proposed HyF distance measure. In this regard, we adopted 7 pairs of HyFSs from [6] to verify the superiority of the present approach, as shown in the following Table 10.3. Evidently, Table 10.3 presents seven pairs of non-identical pairs of HyFSs that also behave as IFS, PFS, FFS, and Q-ROFS.

In Table 10.3, the **highlighted** bold values represent the contradictory situations for different fuzzy set pairs based on the various existing distance measures included in this study. From Table 10.3, we observe that distance measures *viz* $\boldsymbol{d^1_{ISK}}$, $\boldsymbol{d^2_{ISK}}$, produces identical values for event 2, event 3, and event 6, and for event 1 and event 5, which is a contradiction. Again, the distance measure $\boldsymbol{d_{IG}}$ is inefficient as it evaluates a value of 0.1 for Events 1,2,3,5,6 and 7. Yet again the distance measure $\boldsymbol{d_{IPA}}$ assesses identical value of 0.0750 for events 2,3 and 6 and also assesses the same value of 0.1500 for events 1 and 5. In a similar manner, the distance measure $\boldsymbol{d^1_{ING}}$, cannot distinguish between events 1 and 6 as well as between events 2 and 7. The distance measure $\boldsymbol{d^2_{ING}}$, also fails to provide accuracy as it gives similar values for events 2 and 5. The distance measure $\boldsymbol{d_{IMP}}$ gives alike values for events 1,2,5. The distance measures $\boldsymbol{d_{PMP}}$ evaluate similar values for events 1 and 7 while, d^2_{PXD} contradicts events 1 and 5. The distance measures $d^1_{FG}, d^2_{FG}, d^3_{FG}, d^4_{FG}$, d^1_{FDW}, $\boldsymbol{d^2_{FDW}}$, $d^1_{QD}, d^2_{QD}, d^3_{QD}, d_{QPe}, d_{QH}$ evaluate identical values for the events 1 and 2. Moreover, events 5 and 6 are undistinguishable under the distance measures d^3_{QD}, d_{QPe} and d_{QH}. Further, all the existing distance measures except the proposed distance measure in this study fail to provide a precise output for event 7. However, our proposed novel HyF distance measure captures such human intuitions with reliability and efficacy. Thus, Table 10.3 showcases the novel proposed FF distance measure $ꝺ_{PA}$, does not have such a discrepancy and is considered superior to the existing ones.

10.5 Hyperbolic Fuzzy VIKOR Method

In this section, we extend the traditional VIKOR [20] method to the HyF environment based on the proposed HyF distance measure. The VIKOR ranking tool identifies optimal alternatives by balancing group utility and individual regret toward achieving the ideal outcome. The VIKOR approach within the HyF framework encourages decision-makers to represent greater uncertainty that would produce highly suitable and reliable outputs in diverse practical decision-making issues. The procedure of the VIKOR approach under the HyF framework is presented as follows:

Step 1. Problem Description: Suppose a set of decision-makers $\{e_1, e_2, \ldots e_k\}$ assesses the set of alternatives $\{A_1, A, \ldots A_m\}$ based on the criteria set $\{C_1, C_2, \ldots C_n\}$. Let, every decision-maker $e_r, r = 1,2,\ldots,k$ constructs a decision matrix $Y^r = \left[y_{pq}^r\right], r = 1,2,\ldots,k,\ p = 1,2,\ldots,m, q = 1,2,\ldots,n$ for each alternative $A_p, p = 1,2,\ldots,m$ in relation to a criterion C_q under HyF environment such that d_{pq}^i represents the judgment of ith decision maker on the alternative a_p with reference to the criteria C_q.

Step 2. Compute the aggregated HyF decision matrix.
To determine the aggregated HyF decision matrix, we define a HyF Weighted Aggregation Operator (HyFWGO). Utilizing this HyFWGO, every individual decision matrix is combined with a group decision matrix to obtain the aggregated HyF decision matrix, $A = \left(y_{pq}\right)_{m\times n}$, where

$$\begin{aligned} y_{pq} &= \left(\zeta_{pq}, \eta_{pq}\right) = \text{HyFWGO}\left(y_{pq}^{(1)}, y_{pq}^{(2)}, \ldots, y_{pq}^{(k)}\right) \\ &= \left(\prod_{r=1}^{k} \zeta_{pq}^{u_r}, \prod_{r=1}^{k} \eta_{pq}^{u_r}\right), p = 1,2,\ldots,m, q = 1,2,\ldots,n \end{aligned} \tag{10.6}$$

and $u_r > 0, r = 1,2,\ldots,k$ represents the weight of each individual decision matrix such that $\sum_{r=1}^{k} u_r = 1$ is satisfied.

Step 3. Determining the positive and negative ideal solutions:
In this step, the HyF positive ideal solution (HyPIS) δ_q^+ and the HyF negative ideal solution (HyNIS) δ_q^- for all criteria $C_q, q = 1,2,\ldots,n$ are determined where,

$$\delta_q^+ = \left(\zeta_q^+, \eta_q^+\right) = \begin{cases} \max\limits_p y_{pq}, \ \textit{for benefit criteria} \\ \min\limits_p y_{pq}, \ \textit{for cost criteria} \end{cases} \tag{10.7}$$

and

$$\delta_q^- = \left(\zeta_q^-, \eta_q^-\right) = \begin{cases} \min\limits_p y_{pq}, \ \textit{for benefit criteria} \\ \max\limits_p y_{pq}, \ \textit{for cost criteria} \end{cases} \tag{10.8}$$

Step 4. Calculate the group utility, individual regret, and compromise measure.

In the current method, the group utility S_p, individual regret R_p and compromise measure Q_p of each alternative A_p, $p = 1,2,\ldots,m$ are computed by employing the proposed HyF distance measure from definition 9 and are presented as follows

$$S_p = \sum_{q=1}^{n} u_q \frac{D_{HyPA}(\delta_q^+, y_{pq})}{D_{HyPA}(\delta_q^+, \delta_q^-)} \quad (10.9)$$

$$R_p = \max_{1 \le q \le n}\left(u_q \frac{D_{HyPA}(\delta_q^+, y_{pq})}{D_{HyPA}(\delta_q^+, \delta_q^-)} \right) \quad (10.10)$$

$$Q_p = \Psi \frac{S_p - S^+}{S^- - S^+} + (1-\Psi)\frac{R_p - R^+}{R^- - R^+} \quad (10.11)$$

Where, u_q is the weight of C_q criteria such that $\sum_{q=1}^{n} u_q = 1$. $S^+ = \min_p S_p$, $S^- = \max_p S_p$, $R^+ = \min_p R_p$, $R^- = \max_p R_p$ and Ψ is the weight of the maximum group utility, while $(1-\Psi)$ is the weight of the individual regret.

Step 5. Ranking the alternatives.

Based on the decreasing values of S_p, R_p and Q_p, the alternatives are ranked. The alternative with the minimum value of Q_p is denoted as the most desirable choice.

Step 6. Determine the compromise solution.

For the individuality of the required result, the alternative $A^{(1)}$ with the minimum Q_p value overall $p = 1,2,\ldots,m$, is considered to be the compromise solution, whenever the following conditions are fulfilled

(C1) Acceptable advantage:

$$Q(A^{(2)}) - Q(A^{(1)}) \ge \frac{1}{m-1},$$

where $A^{(1)}$ and $A^{(2)}$ represents the alternatives with the initial and subsequent positions in the order of preference list, respectively, and m is the number of options.

(C2) Adequate stability: The option $A^{(1)}$ must also be ranked best by S_p *and* R_p. The compromise solution is stable within an MCDM procedure, which can be selected with "voting by majority rule ($\Psi > 0.5$)" or by consensus " ($\Psi \approx 0.5$)", or "by veto ($\Psi < 0.5$)".

The following two conditions are implemented to the set of ultimate compromise solutions in the case one of these above conditions is not satisfied:

i. If (C1) is not satisfied, then the set of ultimate compromise solutions consists of the alternatives $A^{(1)}$ and $A^{(2)}$.
ii. If (C2) is not satisfied, then the set of ultimate compromise solutions consists of the alternatives $A^{(1)}, A^{(2)}, \ldots, A^{(t)}$ such that

$$Q\left(A^{(2)}\right) - Q\left(A^{(1)}\right) < \frac{1}{m-1},$$

Where 't' is the largest 'i'. This indicates that the alternatives $A^{(1)}, A^{(2)}, \ldots, A^{(t)}$ are in closeness.

10.6 Application in Sustainable Transportation

This section describes an application for the selection of Electric Vehicle Charging Station (EVCS) sites for Sustainable Transportation by deploying the introduced HyF-VIKOR MCDM approach from the previous Section 10.5. Further, this section covers a comparative analysis of the proposed technique with the existing Fermatean Fuzzy (FF)-Technique for Order Preference by Similarity to Ideal Solution (TOPSIS) [5], FF-Additive Ratio Assessment (ARAS) [27] and FF- Simple Additive Weighting (SAW) [27] methods to check the validity and reliability of our proposed approach.

10.6.1 Case Study on Electric Vehicle Charging Station Site Selection

Urbanization, industrialization, and growing populations are among the primary causes of the pressing demand for sustainable transportation. Sustainable transportation is essential for mitigating climate change, reducing pollution, boosting public health, and encouraging economic and social stability. Shifting to sustainable solutions, particularly adopting electric vehicles rather than fossil fuel vehicles, may significantly decrease carbon emissions, consequently supporting sustainable transportation. The rapid economic development in Shanghai city of China drastically increases the vehicle demand. Consequently, operating electric vehicles is particularly beneficial and thereby the requirement of an Electric Vehicle Charging Station (EVCS) is crucial to lowering carbon pollution while promoting sustainability. Determining the optimal site for EVCS in diverse real-life situations is a complex task owing to numerous uncertain and conflicting social, economic, and environmental criteria which influence the selection of the best ECVS. In this section, we employ the introduced HyF VIKOR MCDM method to a case study on the determination of optimal EVCS site selection in Shanghai, China [38]. VIKOR techniques in the HyF framework are advantageous in their nature through capturing complex uncertainty in diverse sustainability criteria and allowing decision makers to have extreme freedom to portray imprecision human judgment to determine the utmost optimal site for EVCS based on various social, economic, environmental, and technical factors. The authors [38] considered four sites located in Minghang district (A_1), Jiading district (A_2), Baoshan district (A_3), and Pudong district (A_4) as the alternative sites for the construction of an EVCS in Shanghai, China. An expert committee consisting of five decision makers denoted as $\{e_1, e_2, e_{3,} e_4, e_5\}$ has been formed to conduct the assessment and select the most suitable site for the EVCS. These decision-makers are experts in the areas of engineering, economy, environment, electrical power systems, and transportation systems with relative weights of 0.15, 0.20, 0.25, 0.25, 0.15. The optimal ECVS site is determined by the five decision experts based on economic, social, environmental, and engineering feasibility factors, which are broadly divided into 'Construction cost (C_1)', 'Operation and maintenance cost (C_2)', 'Investment payoff period (C_3)', 'Service Capability (C_4)', 'Attitude of local residents (C_5)', 'Capacity expansion in future (C_6)', 'Ecological environmental influence (C_7)', 'Energy saving benefits (C_8)', 'Fine particles emission reduction (C_9)', 'Distance from the substation (C_{10})', 'Convenience of transportation (C_{11})', 'Availability of resources (C_{12})'. The researchers specified $C_3, C_4, C_6, C_8, C_9, C_{11}, C_{12}$ as benefit criteria with weights $0.0752, 0.0968, 0.1245, 0.1144, 0.0968, 0.0538, 0.0353$ respectively while $C_1, C_2, C_5, C_7, C_{10}$ with weights $0.0353, 0.0538, 0.1144, 0.1245, 0.0752$ respectively. The procedure stages to employ the derived HyF VIKOR approach to identify the ideal EVCS in this case study are as follows:

Step 1-2: The linguistic terms in Table 10.4 are utilized to convert the linguistic decision matrix on EVCS in Table 10.5 to the HyF performance matrix in Table 10.6. Utilizing Equation 10.6, the five individual decision matrices are aggregated into a group decision matrix.
Step 3: The HyF positive ideal solution (HyPIS) δ_q^+ and the HyF negative ideal solution (HyNIS) δ_q^- for all the twelve criteria are determined by implementing Equations 10.7 and 10.8, as follows.

$$\delta_q^+ = \left(\zeta_q^+, \eta_q^+\right) = \left\{ \begin{matrix} (0.708, 0.286), (0.650, 0.350), (0.824, 0.170), (0.850, 0.150), \\ (0.534, 0.423), (0.824, 0.170), (0.500, 0.450), (0.764, 0.232), \\ (0.795, 0.185), (0.150, 0.850), (0.609, 0.373), (0.699, 0.255) \end{matrix} \right\}$$

Table 10.4 Linguistic terms for rating the alternatives.

Linguistic terms	**HyFs**
Very Low (VL)	(0.15,0.85)
Low (L)	(0.25,0.75)
Moderately Low (ML)	(0.35,0.65)
Medium (M)	(0.50,0.45)
Moderately High (MH)	(0.65,0.75)
High (H)	(0.75,0.25)
Very High (VH)	(0.85,0.15)

Table 10.5 Linguistic evaluated information of the EVCS alternatives based on the criteria.

Alternatives	Des	Criteria											
		C_1	C_2	C_3	C_4	C_5	C_6	C_7	C_8	C_9	C_{10}	C_{11}	C_{12}
A_1	e_1	H	H	H	H	H	H	M	H	H	L	M	MH
	e_2	VH	H	H	H	H	H	MH	H	MH	L	M	MH
	e_3	H	MH	H	H	H	MH	M	H	H	ML	M	M
	e_4	VH	H	H	MH	MH	H	M	H	H	L	M	H
	e_5	VH	MH	H	H	H	H	M	H	MH	L	M	MH
A_2	e_1	H	MH	H	VH	M	H	M	MH	M	ML	ML	M
	e_2	VH	H	H	VH	MH	H	M	MH	M	ML	ML	M
	e_3	H	MH	VH	VH	M	H	M	M	ML	L	M	M
	e_4	VH	MH	MH	VH	M	H	MH	MH	M	ML	ML	M
	e_5	H	H	H	VH	MH	H	M	M	M	ML	ML	M
A_3	e_1	MH	MH	VH	H	M	VH	M	H	VH	L	MH	H
	e_2	H	MH	VH	VH	M	VH	M	VH	MH	L	MH	H
	e_3	H	MH	VH	VH	MH	VH	MH	H	VH	L	MH	VH
	e_4	MH	MH	H	VH	MH	VH	M	H	VH	VL	M	M
	e_5	H	MH	VH	H	M	VH	M	VH	VH	L	MH	H
A_4	e_1	VH	H	VH	H	H	M	MH	H	M	VL	M	MH
	e_2	VH	MH	VH	H	VH	M	M	H	M	VL	M	MH
	e_3	VH	H	H	H	H	MH	M	H	M	VL	MH	H
	e_4	VH	H	VH	VH	H	M	M	H	M	VL	M	MH
	e_5	VH	H	VH	H	MH	M	MH	VH	M	VL	M	H

Table 10.6 The aggregated decision matrix of the EVCS alternatives based on the criteria.

Alternatives	C_1	C_2	C_3	C_4	C_5	C_6	C_7	C_8	C_9	C_{10}	C_{11}	C_{12}
A_1	(0.808,0.184)	(0.708,0.337)	(0.750,0.250)	(0.747,0.239)	(0.723,0.272)	(0.724,0.272)	(0.527,0.428)	(0.750,0.250)	(0.713,0.281)	(0.272,0.724)	(0.500,0.450)	(0.645,0.326)
A_2	(0.793,0.1198)	(0.683,0.311)	(0.747,0.2939)	(0.850,0.150)	(0.548,0.412)	(0.750,0.350)	(0.534,0.423)	(0.585,0.387)	(0.457,0.492)	(0.322,0.674)	(0.383,0.593)	(0.500,0.450)
A_3	(0.708,0.28)	(0.650,0.350)	(0.798,0.194)	(0.774,0.220)	(0.534,0.423)	(0.824,0.170)	(0.500,0.450)	(0.764,0.232)	(0.795,0.185)	(0.220,0.774)	(0.609,0.373)	(0.699,0.255)
A_4	(0.85,0.15)	(0.728,0.282)	(0.824,0.170)	(0.774,0.220)	(0.753,0.237)	(0.534,0.423)	(0.541,0.417)	(0.764,0.232)	(0.500,0.450)	(0.150,0.850)	(0.534,0.423)	(0.688,0.306)

$$\delta_q^- = \left(\zeta_q^-, \eta_q^-\right) = \left\{ \begin{array}{l} (0.850,0.150), (0.729,0.282), (0.750, 0.250), (0.747,0.239), \\ (0.753,0.237), (0.534,0.423), (0.541,0.417), (0.585,0.387), \\ (0.457,0.493), (0.322,0.674), (0.383,0.593), (0.500,0.450) \end{array} \right\}$$

Step 4: Employing the proposed HyF distance measure from definition 9 to Equations 10.9 and 10.10, the group utility S_p, individual regret R_p of each alternative A_p, $p = 1,2,\ldots,m$ are computed. Following this, the compromise measure Q_p are computed *via* Equation 10.11, such that $\Psi = 0.5$ and the outputs are displayed in Table 10.7.

Step 5: The rankings of the four EVCS sites are generated based on the values of S, R, and Q, as listed in Table 10.7. The minimum value of Q_p denotes the optimal alternative for EVCS selection. Clearly, Table 10.7 indicates that A_3 is the best option accessible, followed by A_1, A_2 and A_4.

Table 10.7 Results on HyF-VIKOR method.

Alternatives	S_p	R_p	Q_p
A_1	0.532	0.097	0.652
A_2	0.621	0.114	0.905
A_3	0.115	0.071	0
A_4	0.622	0.125	1
Ranking order	$A_3 > A_1 > A_2 > A_4$	$A_3 > A_1 > A_2 > A_4$	$A_3 > A_1 > A_2 > A_4$

10.6.2 Comparative Analysis and Discussion

In this section, we compare the ranking results of the EVCS alternatives under the proposed HyF-VIKOR methodology based on the novel HyF distance measure with the three prominent existing MCDM methods such as FF-TOPSIS [5], FF-ARAS [27] and FF-SAW [27] to demonstrate the effectiveness and stability of the proposed MCDM approach. Table 10.8 presents a summary of the ranking results of the four EVCS alternative sites achieved through our proposed HyF-VIKOR approach and the MCDM techniques mentioned above. Referring to the table's outcomes, the top two ECVS alternatives generated by the suggested method synchronize with the other three MCDM techniques; that is, alternative site A_3 is the best alternative site for ECVS under all MCDM, followed by the alternative site A_1. Furthermore, Table 10.8 findings demonstrate that the EVCS ranking results obtained using our suggested method and FF-TOPSIS approach [5] reflect each other identically. Figure 10.8 shows the graphical comparison of the ranking order of the EVCS sites.

Moreover, we examine the Spearman's Rank Correlation Coefficient of the EVCS alternatives ranking in accordance with the suggested

Table 10.8 The comparative study of ECVS alternative sites ranking order.

MCDM approaches	**Ranking order**
FF-TOPSIS [5]	$A_3 > A_1 > A_2 > A_4$
FF-ARAS [27]	$A_3 > A_1 > A_4 > A_2$
FF-SAW [27]	$A_3 > A_1 > A_2 > A_2$
HyF-VIKOR (proposed)	$A_3 > A_1 > A_2 > A_4$

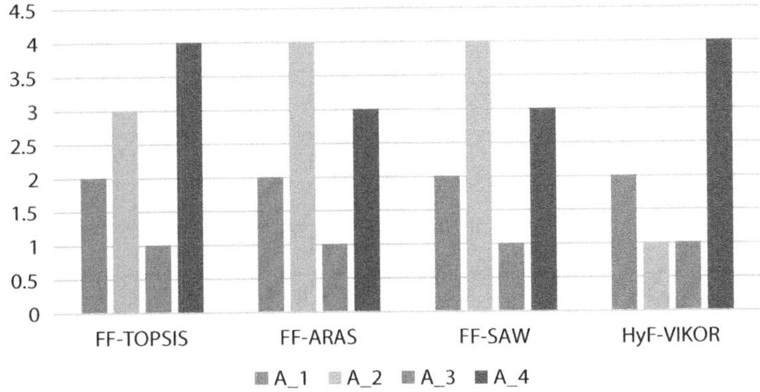

Figure 10.8 Graphical comparison of the EVCS sites ranking order.

HyF-VIKOR methodology with the FF-TOPSIS, FF-ARAS, and FF-SAW methods to assess the robustness of the suggested HyF-VIKOR technique.

Spearman Correlation Coefficient is given as:

$$R_s = 1 - \frac{\sum_{i=1}^{n} f_i^2}{l(l^2 - 1)} \tag{10.12}$$

where R_s denotes the Spearman's rank correlation coefficient, f_i is the difference between the two ranks of each observation, and l is the number of observations. The statistical significance of the variation in the ranking of MCDM approaches is investigated by employing Spearman's Rank Correlation Coefficient. Spearman's Rank Correlation Coefficient is evaluated by utilizing the formula in Equation 10.12. Table 10.9 presents the Spearman's Rank Correlation Coefficient of the ECVS alternatives ranking order between our proposed method and the existing FF-TOPSIS, FF-ARAS, and FF-SAW MCDM methods is 0.978, which is regarded as a high positive correlation. This validates that our proposed approach is

Table 10.9 Spearman's rank correlation coefficient of the EVCS sites ranking order.

MCDM methods	FF-TOPSIS [5]	FF-ARAS [27]	FF-SAW [27]
HyF-VIKOR	1	0.967	0.967

statistically feasible and compatible. Henceforth, the presented comparison analysis validates the reliability and stability of our proposed HyF-VIKOR model. The advantages of the current HyF-VIKOR MCDM model relative to some other existing MCDM methodologies are discussed below:

i. The proposed HyF-VIKOR MCDM methodology based on the novel distance measure is unique from the existing FF-TOPSIS [5], FF-ARAS [27], and FF-SAW [27] methods in the context of HyF framework. This novel MCDM technique under the HyF environment offers decision experts the freedom to portray greater uncertainty through assigning higher membership degrees as large as total membership grades and total non-membership grades simultaneously without the loss of information in numerous real-life decision-making problems.
ii. The proposed HyF-VIKOR method successfully identifies the best compromise alternative in decision-making challenges with conflicting criteria.

VIKOR outperforms in choosing an alternative that succeeds in one criterion but fails in another by balancing the closest to the ideal and reducing worst-case outcomes to provide a compromise solution. Furthermore, the proposed HyF-VIKOR technique within the HyF distance measure is enhanced to produce more accurate decision output in a variety of real-world applications and boosts the efficiency of the MCDM model owing to the superiority of this novel HyF distance measure and its ability to overcome the drawbacks of the existing distance measures.

Furthermore, the merits of the proposed work are highlighted below.

i. This proposed work presents a new distance measure in the HyF context that can capture complex imprecise real-life scenarios and greater degrees of uncertainty without losing information. Additionally, a comparative analysis with some of the notable existing distance measures demonstrates the superiority of the novel proposed HyF distance measure by effectively overcoming the drawbacks of the current ones while delivering accurate and reliable results.
ii. The present research is the initial effort to propose a HyF-VIKOR MCDM approach measure based on the new HyF distance measure. This method effectively governs

complicated and higher-order uncertainty by merging the advantages of the VIKOR method with the flexibility of the HyF framework. Moreover, the novel distance measure employed in this method enhances the decision-making process to yield reliable, stable, and precise rankings in diverse real-life decision-making applications. Furthermore, this proposed method excels the existing FF-TOPSIS [5], FF-ARAS [27], and FF-SAW [27] methods in terms of HyF framework and the HyF distance measure implemented to this approach. This highlights the consistency and robustness of this MCDM method, thereby contributing as a potential tool for decision analysis in fluctuating and uncertain circumstances.

iii. For the first time in this study, ECVS selection decisions are made within the HyF framework utilizing the proposed distance-based HyF-VIKOR approach. A comparison among the ranking outcomes for ECVS alternatives adopting the proposed approach and FF-TOPSIS [5], FF-ARAS [27], and FF-SAW [27] validates the method's robustness and consistency.

10.7 Conclusion and Future Studies

The mounting impacts of resource depletion, pollution, urbanization, and climate change have significantly accelerated the requirement for sustainable transportation. It focuses primarily on improving economic benefits, conserving natural resources, minimizing environmental impact, and encouraging an equitable society while improving effectiveness and ensuring fair access to transportation. Electric vehicle plays a vital role in sustainable transportation. The optimal location of EV charging stations is critical for the widespread adoption of electric vehicles, thereby lowering environmental pollution, preserving natural resources, and offering both social and economic advantages. Moreover, identifying the appropriate site for EVCSs is a complex MCDM problem resulting from the inclusion of multiple uncertain and imprecise criteria. This study proposes a VIKOR approach supported by a novel distance measure for the best location of EVCSs in a Hyperbolic fuzzy context. This novel HyF distance measure successfully evaluates complex real-life uncertain information without information loss. Also, the superiority and reliability of the recently constructed HyF distance measure over some prominent existing distance measures from the literature are examined in this present study through exploring various significant specific fuzzy profiles. Further, implementation of the proposed HyF-VIKOR approach to examine an ideal ECVS in Shanghai city of China produces A_3 as the optimal location site for the establishment of EVCS. The stability and feasibility of our proposed hybrid technique are further validated through a comparison analysis of the proposed HyF-VIKOR approach with the existing MCDM approaches *via* FF-TOPSIS [5], FF ARAS [27], FF-SAW [27]. Additionally, the Spearmen Correlation Coefficient of the ranking order of the ECVS alternative sites between the proposed MCDM approach and the existing MCDM techniques to check the robustness of our hybrid MCDM. Thus, the HyF-VIKOR MCDM based on the novel HyF distance measure successfully captures large uncertain human judgments while offering greater resilience and consistency in comparison to multiple existing MCDMs. This study is unique from others with its capability to address complex uncertain decision-making situations.

The major findings in this research study include the development of a novel HyF distance measure and its incorporation into the VIKOR MCDM approach in the HyF framework. In addition, the proposed HyF-VIKOR approach is applied to a decision-making problem of ECVS site selection. In this study, the VIKOR method incorporated under the novel distance measure in the HyF environment permits decision-makers to portray complex higher-degree uncertainties while producing reliable and consistent outcomes in diverse real-world decision-making applications.

The present study is limited in the evaluation criteria weights used in decision-making applications. Subjective weights generated by expert judgments, alongside objective weights calculated from the performance matrix, are critical components of multi-criteria decision-making processes, as they serve complementary roles in accurately conveying the relative importance of evaluation criteria. This study does not evaluate subjective and objective criterion weights, nor does it include the integration of both subjective and objective weighting methods to generate combined criteria weights. The omission of this criterion weighting consideration may limit the proposed model's applicability and accuracy in specific application environments.

In future research, it is a meaningful topic to integrate both subjective and objective weight calculation methods into the proposed HyF-VIKOR approach to determine criteria weights. Also, we will implement our novel MCDM approach to numerous decision-making domains such as the selection of suppliers, solid waste disposal techniques, renewable energy, and several other real-world MCDM situations that inherit uncertainty.

AI disclosure statement: The author acknowledges the use of AI-based tools for minor language editing or grammatical correction. However, all intellectual contributions, analyses, and conclusions presented in this chapter are entirely the author's own.

References

1. Zadeh, L.A., I. Introduction, and U. S. Navy. *Fuzzy Sets*, 353, 338–353, 1965.
2. Atanassov, K.T., Intuitionistic fuzzy sets. *Fuzzy Sets Syst.*, 20, 1, 87–96, 1986, doi: 10.1016/S0165-0114(86)80034-3.
3. Yager, R.R., Pythagorean fuzzy subsets, in: *2013 joint IFSA world congress and NAFIPS annual meeting (IFSA/NAFIPS)*, 2013, June, IEEE, pp. 57–61.
4. Yager, R.R., Generalized orthopair fuzzy sets. *IEEE transactions on fuzzy systems*, 25, 5, 1222–1230, 2016.
5. Senapati, T. and Yager, R.R., Fermatean fuzzy sets. Journal of ambient intelligence and humanized computing, 11, 2, 663–674, 2020.
6. Dutta, P. and Borah, G., Construction of hyperbolic fuzzy set and its applications in diverse COVID-19 associated problems. *New Math. Nat. Comput.*, *19*, 01, 217–288, 2023.
7. Szmidt, E. and Kacprzyk, J., Distances between intuitionistic fuzzy sets. *Fuzzy Sets Syst.*, *114*, 3, 505–518, 2000.
8. Grzegorzewski, P., Distances between intuitionistic fuzzy sets and/or interval-valued fuzzy sets based on the Hausdorff metric. *Fuzzy sets and systems*, 148, 2, 319-328, 2004.
9. Wang, W. and Xin, X., Distance measure between intuitionistic fuzzy sets. *Pattern recognition letters*, 26, 13, 2063–2069, 2005.
10. Park, J.H., Lim, K.M., Kwun, Y.C., Distance measure between intuitionistic fuzzy sets and its application to pattern recognition. *J. Korean Inst. Intell. Syst.*, *19*, 4, 556–561, 2009.
11. Ngan, R.T., Son, L.H., Cuong, B.C., Ali, M., H-max distance measure of intuitionistic fuzzy sets in decision making. *Appl. Soft Comput.*, 69, 393–425, Aug. 2018, doi: 10.1016/J.ASOC.2018.04.036.
12. Mahanta, J. and Panda, S., A novel distance measure for intuitionistic fuzzy sets with diverse applications. *Int. J. Intell. Syst.*, 36, 2, 615–627, 2021.
13. Xiao, F. and Ding, W., Divergence measure of Pythagorean fuzzy sets and its application in medical diagnosis. *Appl. Soft Comput.*, *79*, 254–267, 2019.

14. Mahanta, J. and Panda, S., Distance measure for Pythagorean fuzzy sets with varied applications. *Neural Comput. Appl.*, 33, 24, 17161–17171, 2021, doi: 10.1007/s00521-021-06308-9.
15. Du, W.S., Minkowski-type distance measures for generalized orthopair fuzzy sets. *Int. J. Intell. Syst.*, 33, 802–817. 47, 2018.
16. Hussain, Z., Abbas, S., Yang, M.S., Distances and similarity measures of q-rung orthopair fuzzy sets based on the Hausdorff metric with the construction of orthopair fuzzy TODIM. *Symmetry*, 14, 11, 2467, 2022.
17. Peng, X., Huang, H., Luo, Z., q-Rung orthopair fuzzy decision-making framework for integrating mobile edge caching scheme preferences. *Int. J. Intell. Syst.*, 36, 5, 2229–2266, 2021.
18. Ganie, A.H., Multicriteria decision-making based on distance measures and knowledge measures of Fermatean fuzzy sets. *Granular Comput.*, 8, 2016, 2022, doi: 10.1007/s41066-021-00309-8.
19. Deng, Z. and Wang, J., New distance measure for Fermatean fuzzy sets and its application. *Int. J. Intell. Syst., 37*, 3, 1903–1930, 2022.
20. Opricovic, S., Multicriteria optimization of civil engineering systems. *Fac. Civ. Eng. Belgrade, 2*, 1, 5–21, 1998.
21. Opricovic, S. and Tzeng, G.H., Compromise solution by MCDM methods: A comparative analysis of VIKOR and TOPSIS. *Eur. J. Oper. Res., 156*, 2, 445–455, 2004.
22. Opricovic, S., A fuzzy compromise solution for multicriteria problems. *Int. J. Uncertainty Fuzziness Knowledge Based Syst., 15*, 03, 363–380, 2007.
23. Suh, Y., Park, Y., Kang, D., Evaluating mobile services using integrated weighting approach and fuzzy VIKOR. *PLoS One*, 14, e0222312. 57, 2019.
24. Krishankumar, R., Premaladha, J., Ravichandran, K.S., Sekar, K.R., Manikandan, R., Gao, X.Z., A novel extension to VIKOR method under intuitionistic fuzzy context for solving personnel selection problem. *Soft Comput.*, 24, 1063–1081, 2020, [CrossRef].
25. Zhou, F. and Chen, T.Y., An extended Pythagorean fuzzy VIKOR method with risk preference and a novel generalized distance measure for multicriteria decision-making problems. *Neural Comput. Appl.*, 33, 18, 11821–11844, 2021.
26. Demir, E., Ak, M.F., Sarı, K., Pythagorean fuzzy based AHP-VIKOR integration to assess rail transportation systems in Turkey. *Int. J. Fuzzy Syst., 25*, 2, 620–632, 2023.
27. Gül, S., Fermatean fuzzy set extensions of SAW, ARAS, and VIKOR with applications in COVID-19 testing laboratory selection problem. *Expert Syst., 38*, 8, e12769, 2021.
28. Arya, V. and Kumar, S., Extended TODIM method based on VIKOR for q-rung orthopair fuzzy information measures and their application in MAGDM problem of medical consumption products. *Int. J. Intell. Syst., 36*, 11, 6837–6870, 2021.

29. Unver, M., Olgun, M., Garg, H., An information measure based extended VIKOR method in intuitionistic fuzzy valued neutrosophic value setting for multi-criteria group decision making. *Scientia Iranica*, 29, 3, 1141–1154, 2022.
30. Garg, H., Thanh, D.N.H., Rizk-Allah, R.M., VIKOR approach for bi-level multi-criteria nonlinear fractional programming problems: new insights. *Kybernetes, 52*, 10, 4375–4400, 2023.
31. Khan, F.M., Munir, A., Albaity, M., Nadeem, M., Mahmood, T., Software reliability growth model selection by using VIKOR method based on q-rung orthopair fuzzy entropy and divergence measures. 12, 86572–86582, 2024.
32. Gul, M., Celik, E., Aydin, N., Taskin Gumus, A., Guneri, A.F., A state of the art literature review of VIKOR and its fuzzy extensions on applications. *Appl. Soft Comput.*, 46, 60–89, 2016.
33. Mardani, Zavadskas, E.K., Govindan, K., Senin, A.A., Jusoh, A., VIKOR technique: A systematic review of the state of the art literature on methodologies and applications. *Sustainability*, 8, 1, 1–38, 2016.
34. Guo, S. and Zhao, H., Optimal site selection of electric vehicle charging station by using fuzzy TOPSIS based on sustainability perspective. *Appl. Energy, 158*, 390–402, 2015.
35. Guler, D. and Yomralioglu, T., Suitable location selection for the electric vehicle fast charging station with AHP and fuzzy AHP methods using GIS. *Ann. GIS, 26*, 2, 169–189, 2020.
36. Seikh, M.R. and Mandal, U., Multiple attribute group decision making based on quasirung orthopair fuzzy sets: Application to electric vehicle charging station site selection problem. *Eng. Appl. Artif. Intell., 115*, 105299, 2022.
37. Karaşan, A., Kaya, I., Erdoğan, M., Location selection of electric vehicles charging stations by using a fuzzy MCDM method: a case study in Turkey. *Neural Comput. Appl., 32*, 4553–4574, 2020.
38. Cui, F.B., You, X.Y., Shi, H., Liu, H.C., Optimal siting of electric vehicle charging stations using Pythagorean fuzzy VIKOR approach. *Math. Probl. Eng., 2018*, 1, 9262067, 2018.
39. Rani, P. and Mishra, A.R., Fermatean fuzzy Einstein aggregation operators-based MULTIMOORA method for electric vehicle charging station selection. *Expert Syst. Appl., 182*, 115267, 2021.
40. Wu, Y., Xie, C., Xu, C., Li, F., A decision framework for electric vehicle charging station site selection for residential communities under an intuitionistic fuzzy environment: A case of Beijing. *Energies, 10*, 9, 1270, 2017.

11

Developing an Uncertainty-Based Sustainable Innovation Adoption Modeling Framework

Ankur Kumar[1], Deepti Aggrawal[2], Ompal Singh[1] and Adarsh Anand[1*]

[1]*Department of Operational Research, University of Delhi, Delhi, India*
[2]*University School of Management and Entrepreneurship, Delhi Technological University, Delhi, India*

Abstract
Within the marketing literature, mathematical models have been shown to be effective in both depicting and predicting the adoption of new products in the market. A vast group of these models has assumed the deterministic nature of the models; however, if the potential market size is large and the product has been on the market for a longer period, the process of adoption is likely to be stochastic. Thus, a stochastic process with a continuous state space would better represent it. This chapter introduces a generalized innovation diffusion modeling framework that incorporates uncertainty into the adoption process. A stochastic differential equation-based mathematical model is then formulated and presented. The applicability and accuracy of the proposed modeling framework are demonstrated using sales data of Apple iPhone (DS-I) and ACER PC (DS-II). Mean-squared error and predictive validity were used to validate the model. It has been demonstrated that SDE-based innovation diffusion models show better results than their counterparts for sales prediction.

Keywords**:** Sustainable innovation, SDE, modeling, uncertainty

**Corresponding author*: adarsh.anand86@gmail.com

Harish Garg (ed.) Decision Support Systems in Smart Computing: Embracing Uncertainty and Challenges, (351–376) © 2026 Scrivener Publishing LLC

11.1 Introduction

In this dynamic, technologically advanced world, we find new products day by day. Thus, customers' preferences for products change significantly. Hence, companies need to innovate their products to sustain themselves in the market [2, 14, 29]. Companies that fail to innovate and adapt their products become obsolete and even lose market share [12, 19, 27] as was found in the most famous company, Nokia. Nokia dominated the market in the mobile phone industry in the early 2000s because of its durability, good features and reliable devices over other companies like Samsung, apple, etc. As time progressed, other rival companies were in a race to advance their mobile phones and embrace the smartphone revolution, but Nokia was rigid with its Symbian operating system and underestimated the potential of the touchscreen and app ecosystem. Thus, failure to adapt to industry trends and innovate was a critical factor in losing their huge market share and becoming obsolete in the market. Although Nokia adopted Windows phones lately, by that time, other companies like Samsung and Apple had already captured significant market share. Nowadays, companies innovate and implement their products in a way that minimizes negative environmental impacts promotes resource efficiency and enhances long-term societal well-being, which is known as Sustainable innovation adoption [30, 33]. Basically, how any innovation will spread in the market and the process of adoption are interpreted in innovation diffusion theory. Diffusion theory explains how a new idea or product is accepted into a social system over time [39]. There are four key elements of the diffusion process, namely, innovation, communication channel, social system and time [38]. Innovation is defined as the process of changing or improving existing products so that it can deliver more value and meet evolving customer needs more effectively [18]. Communication channels refer to the pathways or mechanisms through which information about innovation flows within a social system [22]. These communication channels play a vital role as they influence how fast and effectively an innovation spreads in the social system. The social system mainly consists of groups of individuals or societies who share common beliefs and culture and are the potential adopters of innovation [37]. Finally, time relates to how quickly an innovation spreads amongst the members of the social system [1]. On the basis of the timing of the adoption of innovation, Everett Rogers categorizes the adopters into five categories (Innovators, Early adopters, Early majority, Late majority and Laggards) [9].

Diffusion theory plays a significant role in further study of innovation adoption modeling. However, there is a formidable risk involved in the development and diffusion of new products in the market. Thus, the marketer needs to have proper market analysis and should involve scientific decision-making. Mathematical models proved to be successful aspect in this type of scenario. Basically, diffusion models are used to give predictions about the timing of the adoption of technological products so that marketers can have a better interpretation of the perception and buying behavior of customers [20]. The most prominent and widely used diffusion model is Bass's [8] model. The basic premise of the Bass model is that the dissemination of innovative products in social system is basically propagated through two communication channels, i.e. Media and interpersonal communication channels [32]. Bass [8] gives the notion of potential adopters as 'Innovators' if they buy the product with the influence of mass media and 'Imitators' if they adopt the product under the influence of the word-of-mouth effect. Also, the classical model made the assumption that the adoption of a product occurs instantaneously, which means potential buyers will adopt the product as soon as they get information about the product, but this is not valid in practical scenarios [36]. There exists a considerable time lag between when the potential buyer becomes aware of the product and the final adoption of the product [24]. Rogers [34], in his diffusion theory work, claims that an individual goes through five stages before making a final decision about confirming the product. These five stages are Knowledge, Persuasion, Evaluation, Implementation and Confirmation.

Also, in the Bass [8] model, there is no such place given to uncertainty conditions with respect to diffusion and adoption of products. Bass considered randomness to diffusion path to be constant over time. But this is not true in practical scenarios, for example, customers go through several mental stages in the decision-making process to adopt the product and the decision-making process of individuals is influenced by many factors such as income factors, social influence factors, preference factors, etc. Variations in these factors can introduce randomness to the adoption process. Another example is customers becoming aware of the new products through mass communication and word-of-mouth effects. However, the impact of mass-communication channels such as advertisements, print media, social media, etc., can vary across different demographic groups because an ad campaign may resonate strongly with one segment of the population while failing to engage another, leading to unpredictable outcomes. In the case of word-of-mouth effect, some individuals may be highly influential, spreading positive feedback, while others can provide negative word of mouth that leads to uncertainty in the adoption process. Also, due to technological advancement and cultural and regional differences, the diffusion of a product is subject to stochasticity. But here in this chapter, the authors presented a generalized innovation diffusion modeling framework while inculcating the uncertainty in the adoption process. A stochastic differential equation-based mathematical model is formulated.

Objective of the Work:

- To propose a generalized innovation diffusion modeling framework that incorporates stochasticity into the adoption process.
- To showcase the drawbacks of classical deterministic diffusion models and encounter these drawbacks by integrating stochastic elements to better reflect real-world market conditions and adoption behavior.
- To propose various multiple stochastic innovation diffusion models using different adoption distribution functions and showcase a comparison between these stochastic models with existing deterministic innovation diffusion models (IDMs).

The structure of the remaining sections of this chapter is outlined as follows: Section 11.2 provides a comprehensive literature review related to the proposed framework, offering insights into previous research and foundational concepts. Section 11.3 denotes the proposed methodology of framework. Section 11.4 presents the estimated parameter values for all models and validates them using goodness-of-fit criteria to ensure accuracy and reliability. Section 11.5 offers an in-depth discussion of the results obtained from the proposed models, analyzing their implications and significance. Section 11.6 highlights the managerial implications, demonstrating the practical relevance of the findings in decision-making processes. Section 11.7 concludes the chapter with a summary of key findings, followed by Sections 11.8 and 11.9 with limitations and future scope, respectively. Lastly, list of references supporting the research is attached.

11.2 Literature Review

In marketing management literature, diffusion models are often used to predict and analyze how new products are disseminated into the population.

These models help marketers make strategic decisions about product launches, promotions and pricing [32]. One of the most widely used and innovative diffusion models is the Bass [8] model. The Bass diffusion model is a widely used framework to predict the sales of technological products over time. Bass categorizes the adopters into two distinct categories, namely, "Innovators and Imitators". The adoption curve in the Bass [8] model typically follows the S-shape curve. Bass's model considered several assumptions for the appropriate diffusion process of consumer durable products. But in the past, several researchers have attempted to extend bass model assumptions and his framework to accommodate different aspects of the diffusion process [11, 26].

Bass model and many other diffusion models have assumed the deterministic nature of the model; however, when the potential adopter population is large (e.g., a country or millions of people), factors that affect the adoption process like cultural preferences, regional income differences, make it hard to predict adoption deterministically. Therefore, the stochastic model allows researchers to account for these uncertain, rapidly changing factors in diffusion processes. Eliashberg and Chatterjee [15] were the first to introduce stochastic processes into innovation diffusion modeling. In their diffusion modeling framework, they allow diffusion parameters (e.g., innovation and imitation coefficients) to vary stochastically. This makes their study more dynamic and realistic framework. Giovanis and Skiadas [16] further contributed to the study of stochastic diffusion by applying Ito's type of stochastic differential equation (SDE) to model electricity consumption in Greece and the United States. In their diffusion modeling framework, they combined stochastic processes with the logistic growth model, introducing uncertainty into the modeling of electricity consumption. Gutiérrez *et al.* [17] introduced a mathematical model known as the Gompertz stochastic diffusion model to analyze natural gas consumption trends in Spain. The Gompertz model is widely used to describe growth processes, particularly those that exhibit a slow start, followed by rapid growth, and eventually plateauing over time. By incorporating stochastic (random) elements into the model, the researchers accounted for uncertainties and fluctuations in gas consumption due to external factors such as economic changes, policy regulations, and market dynamics. This approach provided a more realistic representation of how natural gas consumption evolved over time in Spain. Researchers have previously expanded the Bass diffusion theory by incorporating stochastic elements. Boswijk and Franses [10] enhanced the Bass diffusion model by introducing a stochastic error term. This addition helps account for random variations and uncertainties in the adoption process, making the model more adaptable to real-world data. By incorporating stochastic elements, their approach improves the accuracy and reliability of parameter estimation, ensuring that the model better captures fluctuations in consumer adoption behavior. Singh *et al.* [35] enhanced the diffusion process by introducing a stochastic approach, meaning they incorporated elements of randomness into the way adoption occurs over time. Instead of assuming a fixed or predictable adoption rate, their model accounts for uncertainties and variations in consumer behavior, external influences, and market conditions. Negahban and Smith [28] forecasted the demand for recently introduced products using the Bass diffusion model. Their study focused on the uncertainties that arise in the production process, particularly how variations in manufacturing capacity, resource availability, and other supply-side factors affect product launch timing and sales strategies. By incorporating a stochastic supply constraint, they accounted for randomness in production, which can lead to delays or fluctuations in product availability. This approach helps businesses develop more flexible and adaptive sales plans, ensuring that supply limitations are realistically considered when forecasting demand and planning market entry strategies. Anand *et al.* [7] further developed the Bass diffusion model by addressing two key aspects: changing market size and variations in the adoption rate over time. Unlike the traditional model, which assumes a fixed potential market, their approach considers that the number of potential adopters can expand or contract due to factors like population growth, economic conditions, or shifts in consumer preferences. Additionally, they incorporated irregular fluctuations in adoption rates, acknowledging that external influences—such as sudden technological advancements, competitor actions, or marketing campaigns—can cause unpredictable changes in how quickly people adopt a new product or innovation. By making these modifications, their model provides a more realistic and adaptable representation of how innovations spread in dynamic and uncertain market environments. The summary of the key contributions of prior studies on stochastic diffusion modeling is shown in Table 11.1 below.

Although incorporating stochastic (random) elements into diffusion models is crucial for accurately representing how new products spread in the market, there has been limited research on this topic [36]. Specifically, only a few studies have explored the fundamental structural and conceptual assumptions that form the basis of these models in a stochastic setting. Here, in this chapter, the authors introduced a comprehensive innovation diffusion modeling framework that integrates uncertainty into the adoption process. To achieve this, they presented a mathematical model based

Table 11.1 A literature review table summarizing the prior research on stochastic diffusion modeling.

Study	Key features
Eliashberg & Chatterjee [15]	Allowed diffusion parameters (innovation & imitation coefficients) to vary stochastically
Giovanis & Skiadas [16]	Combined stochastic processes with the logistic growth model
Gutiérrez *et al.* [17]	Incorporated stochastic elements to account for uncertainties in consumption
Boswijk & Franses [10]	Improved accuracy of parameter estimation by accounting for random variations
Singh *et al.* [35]	Accounted for uncertainties in consumer behavior and external influences
Negahban & Smith [28]	Considered randomness in production, affecting product launch and sales
Anand *et al.* [7]	Addressed market expansion/contraction and irregular adoption fluctuations
Proposed Modeling Framework	Introduced a comprehensive innovation diffusion modeling framework that integrates uncertainty into the adoption process.

on stochastic differential equations, which allows for the incorporation of random variations and unpredictable fluctuations in adoption patterns. This approach enhances the realism of the diffusion process by accounting for external influences, market dynamics, and behavioral uncertainties that may impact the rate at which innovations are adopted over time.

11.3 Proposed Methodology

The proposed framework uses the various methodologies steps, which are listed as follows:

1. In the beginning, authors start with the innovation diffusion theory and, after that, discuss the drawbacks of classical

models, particularly their failure to account for uncertainty in the adoption process.

2. The authors explore multiple distribution functions F(t) to generalize various existing innovation diffusion models (IDMs).
3. After that, authors incorporate stochastic elements into the adoption process and by using different functional forms for F(t), propose several stochastic innovation diffusion models (SIDMs), each reflecting a particular adoption behavior.
4. Then, the authors validate these models by using real sales data.
5. Also, authors compare the performance of the proposed stochastic innovation diffusion models (SIDMs) over the traditional IDMs and demonstrate the superior predictive accuracy and realism of SIDMs over the classical deterministic models.

11.3.1 Notation and Assumptions

This proposed framework uses a certain notation, which is as follows:

$N(t)$: Cumulative number of adopters by time 't'
m : Potential market size
b : Constant adoption rate during the diffusion phase
S : A fixed positive value that quantifies the extent of irregular fluctuation in adoptions.
k : Shape parameter of Weibull distribution
μ : Mean of normal distribution
σ : Standard deviation of normal distribution
θ : Shape parameter of Gamma distribution
c : Scale parameter of Gamma distribution
β : Learning parameter of the logistic distribution function

This proposed framework is based on a certain set of assumptions, which are as follows:

1. The innovation has a very low rate of rejection.
2. There is no variation in the adoptive population.
3. Adopters are only allowed to adopt once, i.e., repeat purchases are not permitted.

4. Both internal and external influence parameters remain constant.
5. The process of adoption follows stochastically with a continuously varying state space.

11.3.2 Modeling Framework

The Bass Model, introduced in 1969 by [8], is a fundamental mathematical framework designed to forecast the sales and adoption of new products in the market. This model provides insights into how innovations spread among consumers over time, considering two primary factors: innovators and imitators. Innovators are the early adopters who embrace the product independently, while imitators are influenced by the decisions of those who have already adopted the product [25]. Since its introduction, many studies in marketing and diffusion theory have been built upon the Bass Model. Researchers have expanded upon Bass's original work, modifying and refining the model to account for different market conditions, technological advancements, and consumer behavior patterns. As noted by [21] and [3], the sales rate equation can also be written as follows:

$$\frac{dN(t)}{dt} = h(t)\left(m - N(t)\right) \tag{11.1}$$

where $h(t) = \dfrac{f(t)}{1 - F(t)}$ denotes the hazard rate function [40] or the rate of adoption at any time 't' where $f(t)$ denotes the p.d.f. of time to adoption and $F(t)$ denotes the c.d.f. of time to adoption. The following is the result of solving Equation (11.1):

$$N(t) = m.F(t) \tag{11.2}$$

The innovation diffusion model's unified approach framework is provided by Equation (11.2) [23]. A comprehensive mathematical framework that brings together all existing diffusion models into a single unified structure would offer significant benefits in understanding the diffusion process more thoroughly. By integrating various models under one overarching methodology, researchers would be able to analyze the diffusion dynamics with greater clarity and consistency. This unification would not only enhance theoretical understanding but also provide a standardized approach to studying how innovations, ideas, or technologies spread within a population over time. As a result, the development of a unification methodology has become a crucial area of focus in the field of innovation diffusion modeling, as it seeks to establish a common ground for different theoretical perspectives and empirical applications.

Drawing from the literature, researchers explore various distribution functions for F(t) in Equation (11.2) [23]. Here the authors provide a summary of different existing innovation diffusion models in Table 11.2, highlighting how mathematical models can be utilized to develop diverse diffusion frameworks.

11.3.3 Need and Requirement of Modeling Under a Stochastic Environment

As soon as a new product hits the market, the size of the potential customer base plays a crucial role in determining its adoption pattern. If the market size is large, meaning there are a vast number of potential buyers, the rate at which new customers adopt the product will follow a different pattern compared to a smaller market. For example, smartphones have a large market size because nearly everyone across various demographics and regions uses them. Additionally, the length of a product's life cycle also affects the adoption process. If a product remains relevant and in demand for an extended period, the rate of adoption tends to slow down over time. For instance, automobiles have a long life cycle since they remain useful for many years, and newer versions are introduced gradually rather than experiencing immediate mass adoption. As time progresses, the adoption process tends to occur in smaller increments relative to the overall potential customer base. This means that while there may still be new adopters, their numbers grow at a decreasing rate compared to the total number of potential users. In such cases, the adoption process exhibits characteristics of a stochastic process with a continuous state space. A stochastic process is one where outcomes are influenced by probability and randomness, meaning the adoption of the product does not follow a strictly predictable pattern but rather fluctuates based on various external conditions. As a result, to build a diffusion model that incorporates stochastic elements, the adoption rate is assumed to be influenced by both internal and external random factors. This introduces uncertainty into its behavior. To account for this randomness, a stochastic component is added to the adoption rate, making it subject to unpredictable variations i.e.

$$h(t) = \frac{f(t)}{1-F(t)} + '\mathit{noise}' \tag{11.3}$$

The term "noise" in this context refers to the variations or fluctuations in the rate at which adoption occurs. These fluctuations are not fixed or predictable in a precise manner, meaning they do not follow a strict, deterministic pattern. Instead, the behavior of this noise can only be understood in terms of probability, making it a stochastic process. To mathematically describe this randomness, the Wiener process is employed. The Wiener process, also known as Brownian motion, is a fundamental concept in probability theory and stochastic processes. It is often used to model random variations in various fields, including finance, physics, and engineering. By applying the principles of the Wiener process, the noise term can be represented in a way that captures its probabilistic nature, allowing for a more structured understanding of the fluctuations in the rate of adoption and mathematically it can be expressed as [31]:

$$h(t) = \frac{f(t)}{1-F(t)} + s\omega(t) \tag{11.4}$$

Where $\omega(t)$ represents a random variable identified as standard Gaussian white noise, and 's' is a positive constant that quantifies the intensity of the irregular fluctuations. On replacing the expression for the random adoption rate in Equation (11.1), the resulting stochastic differential equation (S.D.E) is:

$$\frac{dN(t)}{dt} = \frac{f(t)}{1-F(t)}(m - N(t)) + s\omega(t)(m - N(t)) \tag{11.5}$$

The variable $\omega(t)$ is determined as the derivative of a one-dimensional Wiener process and it can be represented as:

$$\frac{dW(t)}{dt} = \omega(t) \tag{11.6}$$

On utilizing the expression from Equation (11.6) and applying Itô stochastic calculus, the S.D.E. (5) may take the form as [7, 35]:

$$dN(t) = \left(\frac{f(t)}{1-F(t)} \frac{1}{2} s^2\right)(m - N(t))dt + s(m - N(t))dW(t) \tag{11.7}$$

On utilizing the Itô formula, Equation (11.7) can be solved under the initial condition N(0) = 0, resulting in a cumulative demand function which can be represented as:

$$N(t) = m\left[1-(1-F(t))e^{-sW(t)}\right] \tag{11.8}$$

The expected number of adopters may be written as follows if F(t) represents the adoption distribution function:

$$\overline{N}(t) = E\left[N(t)\right] = m\left[1-(1-F(t))e^{\frac{s^2 t}{2}}\right] \tag{11.9}$$

This Equation (11.9) depicts the mean value function or total number of adoption of new products while inculcating fluctuation patterns in its adoption behavior.

By utilizing various distribution functions for F(t) (the adoption distribution function), the authors proposed different Stochastic Innovation Diffusion Models (SIDM). Table 11.3 provides a summary of the mean value functions corresponding to these distribution functions in the adoption process.

11.4 Data Analysis

The authors used sales data from two different consumer durables, Apple iPhone (DS-I) and the ACER PC (DS-II) to estimate the models, in order to verify the validity and practicality of the proposed framework. The Apple iPhone (DS-I) quarterly sales data covers the period 2007Q3 to 2018Q1 (43 data points) [23], while the ACER PC (DS-II) quarterly sales data covers the period 2009 to 2017 (36 data points) [5]. For both datasets, sales are reported in millions of units.

Here in this chapter, the statistical software SPSS (Statistical Package for Social Sciences) was utilized by the authors to estimate the parameters of the models. Beyond just estimating parameters, the goodness-of-fit criteria play a crucial role in determining how well the proposed models align with the observed data. These criteria assess the accuracy and reliability of the models, ensuring they effectively represent real-world patterns. A strong goodness-of-fit score indicates that the model closely follows the data,

Table 11.2 Innovation diffusion models.

IDM-1	$N(t) = m.(1 - e^{-bt})$ [13]
IDM-2	$N(t) = m\{1 - (1 + bt).e^{-bt}\}$ [6]
IDM-3	$N(t) = m\{1 - e^{-bt^k}\}$ [23]
IDM-4	$N(t) = m\{1 - (1 - \phi(t,u,\sigma))\}$ [23]
IDM-5	$N(t) = m\{1 - (1 - \Gamma(t,\theta,c))\}$ [4]
IDM-6	$N(t) = \frac{m.(1 - e^{-bt})}{1 + \beta e^{-bt}}$ [21]

Table 11.3 Proposed stochastic innovation diffusion models.

SIDM-1	$\overline{N}(t) = m.\left\{1 - (e^{-bt}).e^{\frac{s^2 t}{2}}\right\}$
SIDM-2	$\overline{N}(t) = m\left\{1 - ((1 + bt)e^{-bt}).e^{\frac{s^2 t}{2}}\right\}$
SIDM-3	$\overline{N}(t) = m\left\{1 - e^{(-bt^k + \frac{s^2 t}{2})}\right\}$
SIDM-4	$\overline{N}(t) = m\left\{1 - (1 - \phi(t,u,\sigma))e^{\frac{s^2 t}{2}}\right\}$
SIDM-5	$\overline{N}(t) = m\left\{1 - (1 - \Gamma(t,\theta,c))e^{\frac{s^2 t}{2}}\right\}$
SIDM-6	$\overline{N}(t) = m\left\{1 - \left(\frac{(1 + \beta)e^{-bt}}{1 + \beta e^{-bt}}\right)e^{\frac{s^2 t}{2}}\right\}$

enhancing its credibility and usefulness for predictions or decision-making. Based on a number of comparison criteria, the innovation diffusion models (IDM-1 to IDM-6) (given in Table 11.2 above) and the proposed stochastic innovation diffusion models (SIDM-1 to SIDM-6) covered in Table 11.3 above are validated. These criteria include Mean Square Error (M.S.E.), Bias, Variation, Coefficient of Determination (R2), and Root Mean Square Prediction Error (R.M.S.P.E.) [23]. Tables 11.4 and 11.5 below display the estimated parameter results and comparison criteria for both IDMs and SIDMs models in both data sets (DS-I and DS-II).

Table 11.4 Comparison of estimated parameters results and criteria of goodness of fit for data set-I.

Model	**Model parameter estimation results**	**R^2**	**Bias**	**Variation**	**Mean square error**	**Root mean square prediction error**
IDM-1	$m = 1776.918$ $b = 0.016$	0.717	70.10	257.20	49,870.92	266.58
SIDM-1	$m = 2598.681$ $b = 0.015$ $s = 0.110$	0.747	70.09	246.33	44,529.5	256.109
IDM-2	$m = 3013.104$ $b = 0.030$	0.931	45.128	136.828	12,176.88	144.078
SIDM-2	$m = 3322.13$ $b = 0.007$ $s = 0.006$	0.984	25.08	70.04	2905.37	74.40
IDM-3	$m = 1415.585$ $b = 0.018$ $k = 1.049$	0.707	69.20	259.99	51,658.82	269.04

(Continued)

Table 11.4 Comparison of estimated parameters results and criteria of goodness of fit for data set-I. (*Continued*)

Model	Model parameter estimation results	R^2	Bias	Variation	Mean square error	Root mean square prediction error
SIDM-3	$m = 2488.852$ $b = 0.010$ $k = 0.997$ $s = 0.002$	0.744	63.192	241.7	45,080.55	249.824
IDM-4	$m = 1758.105$ $\mu = 34.865$ $\sigma = 12.492$	0.998	1.78	10.31	94.41	10.46
SIDM-4	$m = 1496.230$ $\mu = 34.00$ $\sigma = 12.402$ $s = 0.078$	0.999	1.773	10.190	92.001	10.343
IDM-5	$m = 2907.835$ $\theta = 0.890$ $c = 0.007$	0.716	71.72	258.939	50,058.78	268.68
SIDM-5	$m = 1450.047$ $\theta = 0.820$ $c = 0.011$ $s = 0.113$	0.740	72.882	251.565	45,878.05	261.90
IDM-6	$m = 1702.328$ $b = 0.134$ $\beta = 96.223$	0.909	59.23	123.78	6873.54	137.221
SIDM-6	$m = 1523.87$ $b = 0.113$ $\beta = 85.43$ $s = 0.107$	0.927	32.65	82.85	3465.765	89.051

Table 11.5 Comparison of estimated parameters results and criteria of goodness of fit for data set-II.

Model	Model parameter estimation results	R^2	Bias	Variation	Mean square error	Root mean square prediction error
IDM-1	$m = 272.32$ $b = 0.023$	0.702	76.54	289.15	53,632.14	299.108
SIDM-1	$m = 270.43$ $b = 0.018$ $s = 0.045$	0.891	60.61	257.11	41,832.27	264.157
IDM-2	$m = 285.76$ $b = 0.021$	0.921	54.36	153.76	14,234.54	163.086
SIDM-2	$m = 281.65$ $b = 0.098$ $s = 0.011$	0.982	37.76	82.44	3032.23	90.676
IDM-3	$m = 278.4$ $b = 0.029$ $k = 1.123$	0.734	61.547	248.87	47,269.64	256.367
SIDM-3	$m = 281.43$ $b = 0.032$ $k = 0.983$ $s = 0.016$	0.876	47.374	202.53	40,456.89	207.996
IDM-4	$m = 271.76$ $\mu = 43.732$ $\sigma = 15.32$	0.995	7.62	15.787	100.43	17.529
SIDM-4	$m = 279.14$ $\mu = 48.88$ $\sigma = 14.11$ $s = 0.037$	0.998	3.44	11.996	95.654	12.479
IDM-5	$m = 291.65$ $\theta = 0.743$ $c = 0.004$	0.783	69.13	249.732	46,123.54	259.123

(Continued)

Table 11.5 Comparison of estimated parameters results and criteria of goodness of fit for data set-II. (*Continued*)

Model	Model parameter estimation results	R^2	Bias	Variation	Mean square error	Root mean square prediction error
SIDM-5	$m = 285.52$ $\theta = 0.678$ $c = 0.034$ $s = 0.138$	0.810	64.62	242.152	41,632.27	250.625
IDM-6	$m = 277.02$ $b = 0.116$ $\beta = 85.172$	0.912	52.45	112.54	6116.21	124.162
SIDM-6	$m = 281.98$ $b = 0.102$ $\beta = 92.76$ $s = 0.110$	0.938	30.21	78.32	3032.32	83.944

Also, the goodness of fit curves for the proposed stochastic innovation diffusion models (SIDMs) for Data Set-I and Data Set-II, respectively, are depicted in Figures 11.1 and 11.2. As can be seen from the figures, there is a

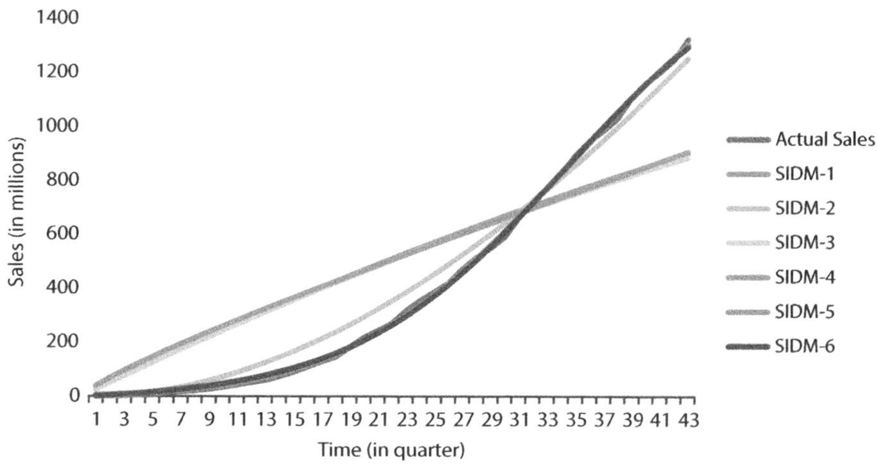

Figure 11.1 Curve of goodness of fit for data set-I.

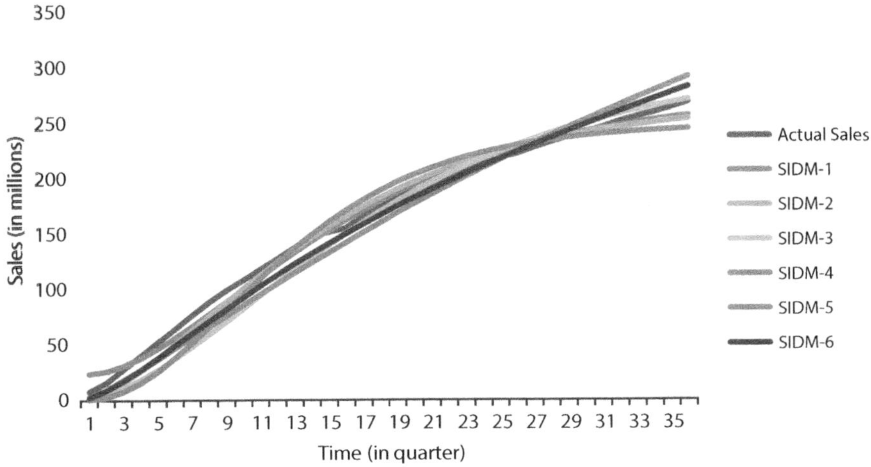

Figure 11.2 Curve of goodness of fit for DS-II.

clear visual comparison between the actual data points and the anticipated values. This indicates that the predictive model closely aligns with the real data, suggesting high accuracy and reliability in its estimations.

11.5 Discussion

The authors of this study conducted a comparative analysis of their newly proposed Stochastic Innovation Diffusion Models (SIMDs) against the existing Innovation Diffusion Models (IDMs). This evaluation was performed for two different datasets, referred to as DS-I and DS-II. The objective of this comparison was to assess the accuracy and reliability of both models based on estimated parameter values and the Goodness of Fit criteria. The results, as presented in Table 11.4, demonstrate that the proposed SIMDs outperform the existing IDMs in terms of model fit for DS-I. This conclusion is drawn from the observation that the coefficient of determination (R^2) for SIMDs is higher compared to the conventional IDMs, while other statistical measures such as Bias, Variation, Mean Square Error (MSE), and Root Mean Square Prediction Error (RMSPE) are lower. These indicators suggest that the SIMDs provide a more precise and reliable representation of the diffusion process for this dataset. A similar trend is observed in Table 11.5, where the results for DS-II are presented. Once again, the proposed SIMDs demonstrate superior performance over the conventional IDMs. The higher R^2 values and the lower values for Bias,

Variation, MSE, and RMSPE reinforce the conclusion that the SIMDs offer a better statistical fit for the second dataset as well.

This study highlights the significance of incorporating stochasticity into innovation diffusion modeling. Unlike previous models that largely ignored the role of uncertainty, the proposed SIMDs recognize and integrate stochastic elements, making them more realistic and applicable in real-world competitive scenarios. In highly dynamic markets where uncertainties play a crucial role in innovation diffusion, the inclusion of stochastic factors enhances model accuracy and predictive capability. The findings suggest that traditional deterministic models may not fully capture the complexities of real-world innovation spread, and therefore, stochastic modeling presents a more effective approach for understanding and forecasting the diffusion of new technologies or ideas.

11.6 Managerial Implications

The findings and framework presented in this research have significant managerial implications, particularly for decision-makers involved in product innovation, marketing strategy, and business forecasting. The application of mathematical models, especially stochastic differential equations (SDEs), to predict product adoption patterns provides businesses with a refined toolset to enhance their strategic planning and execution. Managers often rely on deterministic models to predict market behavior and adoption patterns. However, these models may fall short when dealing with real-world complexities, such as uncertainties in consumer behavior, technological advancements, and macroeconomic shifts. The proposed stochastic model allows managers to incorporate these uncertainties into their forecasting, leading to more robust and realistic predictions. This enhanced forecasting capability can enable businesses to better allocate resources, set achievable sales targets, and plan for contingencies. Product adoption is not a linear process; it is influenced by several external and internal factors, including marketing efforts, word-of-mouth effects, competition, and regulatory environments. By leveraging the SDE-based model, managers can design more effective product launch strategies. For instance, they can identify optimal timing for introducing a product to the market, assess the impact of different marketing intensities, and adjust promotional efforts dynamically as adoption patterns evolve.

Marketing and promotional budgets are often constrained, requiring managers to make data-driven decisions regarding where to invest their resources. The stochastic approach helps in determining which market segments are more likely to adopt a product at different stages of its life-cycle. This insight enables businesses to allocate marketing budgets efficiently, ensuring that resources are directed towards customer segments with the highest likelihood of conversion. Products with long life cycles require sustained marketing efforts and strategic decision-making over extended periods. Traditional models may fail to account for long-term uncertainties, but the stochastic approach ensures that businesses remain agile in responding to unforeseen market changes. This approach helps companies maintain their market presence and sustain profitability in the long run. Global businesses face additional complexities due to variations in consumer behavior, cultural influences, and economic conditions across different regions. The stochastic diffusion model offers a flexible approach to understanding these variations, allowing businesses to tailor their market entry and expansion strategies for different geographical areas. By incorporating local uncertainties into adoption predictions, businesses can make more effective internationalization decisions.

Merits and Benefits of Work

- The proposed modeling framework addresses uncertain variations in consumer behavior and marketing dynamics, which makes the diffusion adoption modeling more realistic and applicable to a real business environment.
- By incorporating stochasticity through a stochastic differential equation, the model provides businesses with deeper insights for planning marketing strategies.
- These models have been validated on real-life datasets, which makes it have more practical utility across different product categories.

11.7 Conclusion

Mathematical modeling plays a crucial role in forecasting the sales of newly introduced products in the market. One of the most well-known and widely used models in this domain is the Bass Diffusion Model [8], which provides a foundational framework for understanding how innovations are adopted over time. Over the years, several researchers have extended and modified the Bass Model to incorporate additional factors that reflect the complexities of real-world market conditions. These modifications have aimed to improve the model's applicability by accounting for various influences on consumer behavior and market dynamics. One key limitation of classical innovation diffusion models, including the Bass Model, is that they often operate under deterministic assumptions. This means they do not adequately consider the role of uncertainty and randomness in the adoption process of new products. However, in today's highly competitive and dynamic market environment, consumer adoption behavior is inherently uncertain and can be influenced by numerous unpredictable factors, such as changing economic conditions, social influence, market trends, and external disruptions. Ignoring this uncertainty can lead to inaccurate predictions and less effective strategic decision-making for businesses.

In this study, the authors emphasize the importance of stochasticity (uncertainty) in innovation diffusion modeling. They propose a new stochastic diffusion modeling framework, which incorporates random variations in the adoption process, making the model more realistic and applicable to actual market conditions. To validate the effectiveness of their proposed approach, they compare their stochastic innovation diffusion models (SIMDs) with existing deterministic innovation diffusion models (IDMs). The comparison is conducted by evaluating estimated parameter values and using the goodness-of-fit criteria to measure how well each model represents the observed data. The results of their analysis indicate that the stochastic diffusion models provide a significantly better fit to the given datasets compared to traditional deterministic models. Specifically, the stochastic models exhibit higher R^2 values and lower errors, such as Bias, Variation, Mean Square Error (MSE), and Root Mean Square Prediction Error (RMSPE), thereby demonstrating their superior predictive capability. This highlights the crucial role of stochasticity in diffusion modeling and suggests that models that account for uncertainty provide more reliable insights into consumer adoption patterns. Given these findings, it is evident that uncertainty cannot be ignored when modeling the diffusion and adoption behavior of consumers in the market. Businesses and researchers must incorporate stochastic elements in their predictive frameworks to enhance accuracy and better reflect real-world dynamics. The study underscores that in the ever-evolving and unpredictable marketplace, embracing uncertainty through stochastic modeling leads to more robust and insightful innovation diffusion analysis.

11.8 Limitations

- The proposed framework assumes no variation in the adoptive population and only allows single-time adoption, which oversimplifies real consumer behavior where repeat purchases are very common.

- This modeling framework does not include the dynamic impact of competitive marketing strategies and pricing campaign policy.
- In this proposed methodology, the internal and external influence parameters (e.g., media and word-of-mouth effects) are assumed constant, while in practice, these factors can evolve significantly over time.

11.9 Future Scope

The proposed innovation diffusion framework opens several avenues for future research and practical applications. First, the proposed models assume homogeneous adopter behavior, which can be further extended by incorporating heterogeneous adopter groups to capture varying risk preferences, demographics, or socio-economic factors. Second, the inclusion of dynamic market conditions, such as fluctuating competition, evolving technology, and changing consumer sentiment, can further enhance the realism of the model. Third, while the study uses real sales data for validation, future work can explore multi-product diffusion scenarios or analyze cross-category influence effects. The model may also be extended to incorporate supply-side uncertainties like production constraints and logistic delays. Moreover, the environmental and sustainability impact of innovations, especially in green technologies, can be integrated into the modeling framework to guide eco-conscious adoption strategies. Lastly, adapting the framework for use in emerging markets, where data irregularities and cultural factors play a significant role, could help refine global diffusion forecasting. These extensions would significantly enhance the model's versatility and its application in strategic marketing, innovation management, and policy formulation.

AI disclosure statement: The author acknowledges the use of AI-based tools for minor language editing or grammatical correction. However, all intellectual contributions, analyses, and conclusions presented in this chapter are entirely the author's own.

References

1. Aggarwal, R., Singh, O., Anand, A., Kapur, P.K., Modeling innovation adoption incorporating time lag between awareness and adoption process. *Int. J. Syst. Assur. Eng. Manag.*, *10*, 83–90, 2019.
2. Aggrawal, D., Anand, A., Kumar, H., Singht, O., Singh, I., Multi-stage multi-generation based product adoption: An analysis using numerical methods. *Nonlinear Stud.*, *31*, 2, 2024.
3. Anand, A., Agarwal, M., Aggrawal, D., Singh, O., Unified approach for modeling innovation adoption and optimal model selection for the diffusion process. *J. Adv. Manag. Res.*, *13*, 2, 154–178, 2016.
4. Anand, A., Irshad, M.S., Dwivedi, Y.K., Modeling view count dynamics for YouTube videos: a multimodal perspective. *Kybernetes*, *51*, 10, 2964–2986, 2022.
5. Anand, A., Kumati, A., Singh, O., Chopra, R., Potential adopter domain dependent innovation diffusion models. *Math. Eng. Sci. Aerosp. (MESA)*, *15*, 2, 2024.
6. Anand, A., Singh, O., Agarwal, M., Aggarwal, R., Modeling adoption process based on awareness and motivation of consumers, in: *Proceedings of 3rd international conference on reliability, infocom technologies and optimization*, pp. 1–6, IEEE, 2014, October.
7. Anand, A., Singhal, S., Singh, O., Revisiting dynamic potential adopter diffusion models under the influence of irregular fluctuations in adoption rate, in: *Handbook of Research on Promoting Business Process Improvement Through Inventory Control Techniques*, pp. 499–519, IGI Global, Scientific Publishing, Hershey, 2018.
8. Bass, F.M., A new product growth for model consumer durables. *Manage. Sci.*, *15*, 5, 215–227, 1969.
9. Boora, S., Process of Diffusion and Adoption in Innovation. *Agric. Ext.*, *69*, 55, 2022.
10. Boswijk, H.P. and Franses, P.H., On the econometrics of the Bass diffusion model. *J. Bus. Econ. Stat.*, 23, 3, 255–268, 2005.
11. Chandrasekaran, D. and Tellis, G.J., A critical review of marketing research on diffusion of new products. *Rev. Mark. Res.*, 39–80, 2017.
12. Christensen, C.M., *The innovator's dilemma: when new technologies cause great firms to fail*, Harvard Business Review Press, Boston, 2015.
13. Coleman, J., Kartz, E., Menzel, H., *Medical Innovation*, BobbsMerrill, New York, 1996.
14. Cooper, R.G., Perspective: The innovation dilemma: How to innovate when the market is mature. *J. Prod. Innovation Manage.*, *28*, s1, 2–27, 2011.
15. Eliashberg, J. and Chatterjee, R., Stochastic issues in innovation diffusion models, in: *Innovation Diffusion Models of New Product*, V. Mahajan and Y. Wind (Eds.), pp. 151–203, Ballinger Publishing Company, Cambridge, MA, 1986.

16. Giovanis, A.N. and Skiadas, C.H., A stochastic logistic innovation diffusion model studying the electricity consumption in Greece and the United States. *Technol. Forecasting Social Change*, 61, 3, 235–246, 1999.
17. Gutiérrez, R., Nafidi, A., Sánchez, R.G., Forecasting total natural-gas consumption in Spain by using the stochastic Gompertz innovation diffusion model. *Appl. Energy*, 80, 2, 115–124, 2005.
18. Kahn, K.B., Understanding innovation. *Bus. Horiz.*, *61*, 3, 453–460, 2018.
19. Kanter, R.M., Innovation: The classic traps. *Harv. Bus. Rev.*, *84*, 11, 72, 2006.
20. Kapur, P.K., Panwar, S., Singh, O., Modeling two-dimensional technology diffusion process under dynamic adoption rate. *J. Model. Manag.*, *14*, 3, 717–737, 2019.
21. Kapur, P.K., Bardhan, A.K., Jha, P.C., An alternative formulation of innovation difusion model and its extension. *Proc. Math. Inform. Theory: Recent Top. Appl.*, 23, 1, 17–23, 2004.
22. Kocsis, G. and Kun, F., Competition of information channels in the spreading of innovations. *Phys. Rev. E—Stat. Nonlinear Soft Matter Phys.*, *84*, 2, 026111, 2011.
23. Kumar, A., Singh, O., Anand, A., Kapur, P.K., Studying innovation adoption using different distribution functions. *Int. J. Syst. Assur. Eng. Manag.*, *15*, 5, 1900–1907, 2024.
24. Kumar, A., Singh, O., Anand, A., Bisht, M., Singh, G., A Waterfall Approach to Study Innovation Adoption Process, in: *2023 4th International Conference on Computation, Automation and Knowledge Management (ICCAKM)*, pp. 01–06, IEEE, 2023, December.
25. Massiani, J. and Gohs, A., The choice of Bass model coefficients to forecast diffusion for innovative products: An empirical investigation for new automotive technologies. *Res. Transp. Econ.*, *50*, 17–28, 2015.
26. Meade, N. and Islam, T., Modelling and forecasting the diffusion of innovation–A 25-year review. *Int. J. Forecast.*, 22, 3, 519–545, 2006.
27. Morris, L., Business model innovation the strategy of business breakthroughs. *Int. J. Innov. Sci.*, *1*, 4, 191–204, 2009.
28. Negahban, A. and Smith, J.S., Production-sales policies for new product diffusion under stochastic supply, in: *Proceedings of the Sixth International Conference on Advances in System Simulation*, International Academy, Research, and Industry Association (IARIA), Red Hook, NY, pp. 197–202, 2014.
29. Nidumolu, R., Prahalad, C.K., Rangaswami, M.R., Why sustainability is now the key driver of innovation. *Harv. Bus. Rev.*, *87*, 9, 56–64, 2009.
30. Noppers, E.H., Keizer, K., Bolderdijk, J.W., Steg, L., The adoption of sustainable innovations: Driven by symbolic and environmental motives. *Glob. Environ. Change*, *25*, 52–62, 2014.
31. Øksendal, B., Stochastic differential equations, in: *Stochastic differential equations*, pp. 65–84, Springer, Berlin Heidelberg, 2003.

32. Peres, R., Muller, E., Mahajan, V., Innovation diffusion and new product growth models: A critical review and research directions. *Int. J. Res. Mark.*, *27*, 2, 91–106, 2010.
33. Rizzo, G., Migliore, G., Schifani, G., Vecchio, R., Key factors influencing farmers' adoption of sustainable innovations: a systematic literature review and research agenda. *Org. Agric.*, *14*, 1, 57–84, 2024.
34. Rogers, E.M., *Diffusion of innovations*, 5th ed., Free Press, New York, 2003.
35. Singh, O., Anand, A., Kapur, P.K., Aggrawal, D., Consumer behaviour-based innovation diffusion modelling using stochastic differential equation incorporating change in adoption rate. *Int. J. Technol. Mark.*, 7, 4, 346–360, 2012.
36. Singhal, S., Anand, A., Singh, O., SDE based generalized innovation diffusion modeling. *Int. J. Math. Eng. Manag. Sci.*, *4*, 3, 697, 2019.
37. Tolba, A.H. and Mourad, M., Individual and cultural factors affecting diffusion of innovation. *J. Int. Bus. Cult. Stud.*, *5*, 1, 2011.
38. Turnbull, P.W. and Meenaghan, A., Diffusion of innovation and opinion leadership. *Eur. J. Mark.*, *14*, 1, 3–33, 1980.
39. Wani, T.A. and Ali, S.W., Innovation diffusion theory. *J. Gen. Manag. Res.*, *3*, 2, 101–118, 2015.
40. Aggrawal, N., Arora, A., Anand, A., Modeling and characterizing viewers of You Tube videos. *Int. J. Syst. Assur. Eng. Manag.*, 9, 539–546, 2018.

12

Clustering India's Polluted Cities Using Novel Logarithmic Measures for Hesitant Fuzzy Sets

Rahul Thakur[1]*, S.C. Malik[1] and Masum Raj[2]

[1]*Department of Statistics, Maharshi Dayanand University, Rohtak, Haryana, India*
[2]*Department of Mathematics, Institute of Applied Sciences and Humanities, G.L.A. University, Mathura, U.P., India*

Abstract

Logarithmic-based distance and similarity measures for hesitant fuzzy sets (HFS) are introduced as an extension of fuzzy set theory to address uncertainty in decision-making. Traditional measures often face limitations such as sensitivity to scale, complexity and the curse of dimensionality, reducing their effectiveness in practical applications. To overcome these limitations, the logarithmic distance and similarity measures are proposed which are sensitive to small variations and improve uncertainty handling. The properties of the proposed measures such as boundedness, symmetry, and strong reflexivity are validated. A comparative analysis with some existing measures is done which underscores the superiority of the proposed measure. These measures are applied to perform the clustering analysis of most polluted cities using air quality data. The analysis reveals how cities are clustered based on similar pollution profiles and diverge as the confidence level increases. The findings help in understanding the pollution patterns across different cities which can help the air quality management and policy planning.

Keywords: Hesitant fuzzy sets (HFSs), distance measure, similarity measure, air quality data, decision-making, clustering analysis

**Corresponding author*: thakurrahul3394@gmail.com

Harish Garg (ed.) Decision Support Systems in Smart Computing: Embracing Uncertainty and Challenges, (377–412) © 2026 Scrivener Publishing LLC

12.1 Introduction

Uncertainty is an inherent characteristic of many real-world problems which require mathematical frameworks to model and analyze imprecise information. In 1965, Zadeh [1] introduced the concept of Fuzzy Sets (FSs) to address such uncertainty in real-world applications. FSs have been widely applied in areas such as decision-making, approximate reasoning and fuzzy control to deal with imprecise or vague information. However, the practical implementation of fuzzy sets often faces challenges particularly when defining precise membership functions due to the complexity or lack of clarity in the available information. To overcome these limitations, various extensions of fuzzy set theory have been proposed each adding a new dimension to handle uncertainty more effectively. Later, FSs were extended for various applications including Atanassov's Intuitionistic Fuzzy Sets (IFSs) [2] and type-2 FSs [3]. Mathematically, IFS is equivalent to Interval-Valued Fuzzy Sets (IVFSs) and incorporates membership, non-membership, and hesitant functions to describe vagueness and uncertainty. Type-2 FS and its extension to type-n FSs [4] treat the membership function as an FS and make IFS which includes crisp interval values i.e. a special case of type-2 FSs. These extensions aim to comprehensively describe the degree of uncertainty through the general membership degree. However, in realistic situations, decision-makers often face challenges such as time pressure, problem complexity, limited information processing capabilities and insufficient knowledge of the public domain and available information. These factors prevent them from providing exact evaluations of decision parameters in MADM problems. Consequently, the preference information provided by experts or decision-makers may be incomplete or imprecise. A more recent and promising extension is the HFS introduced by Torra [5] and further developed by Torra and Narukawa [6]. HFS allows for a set of possible values for the membership degree making it a powerful tool for situations where decision-makers hesitate or are uncertain about their judgments. For instance, consider a scenario where a team of evaluators is assessing the suitability of an alternative, say (y), for inclusion in a set (B). The evaluators might express varying degrees of confidence, hesitating among the values 0.2, 0.4, and 0.7. This uncertainty can be captured by a hesitant fuzzy element (HFE) {0.2, 0.4, 0.7}. The HFE {0.2, 0.4, 0.7} more accurately reflects the evaluators' hesitance compared to a single crisp value such as 0.4, an interval like [0.2, 0.7], or an intuitionistic fuzzy pair like (0.4, 0.5). This is because the membership is not represented by a range or midpoint but by the distinct set of possible values that represent the hesitance of the evaluators [7]. This unique characteristic of HFS makes them particularly valuable in decision-making and evaluation processes as it effectively reflects human hesitation and subjective uncertainty [8–10]. The growing interest in HFS has encouraged numerous studies focusing on its applications to develop suitable measures for HFSs to facilitate evaluation and comparison. Among these, the similarity and distance measures are crucial for assessing the similarity and distance between two HFSs. The study of these measures in HFS theory has been extensively pursued leading to many theoretical and practical advancements. Xu and Xia [7] proposed a range of hesitant fuzzy & ordered distance measures and studied their applications into various scientific domains such as pattern recognition and clustering analysis. Thereafter, Farhadinia [11, 12] explored the connections between entropy, similarity measures, and distance measures for HFSs and extended these measures to interval-valued HFSs. Peng *et al.* [13] introduced the generalized hesitant fuzzy synergetic weighted distance measure and applied it to multi-criteria decision making. Zhang and Xu [14] explored new distance and similarity measures for HFSs and utilized them in clustering analysis. Zeng *et al.* [15] introduced several novel distance and similarity measures for HFSs demonstrating their effectiveness in pattern recognition. Rezaei and Rezaei [16] enhanced these measures by incorporating the variation range as a hesitance degree which significantly improves their effectiveness in clustering applications. Their comparative analysis confirmed the superiority of the proposed measures in terms of accuracy and applicability. Liao *et al.* [17] proposed cosine-based similarity and distance measure tailored to decision-making problems. Gupta and Kumar [18] addressed the limitations of existing distance-based similarity measures in solving problems related to medical, clustering, and pattern recognition, and demonstrated their effectiveness through multiple examples and comparisons. Singha *et al.* [19] proposed modifications to an existing distance measure on HFSs to address real-life situations that the previous measure could not handle. Their study validated the proposed measure through practical examples, highlighting its effectiveness in multi-criteria decision-making problems. Rahim *et al.* [20] paper investigates cosine similarity and Euclidean distance measures for Quasirung Orthopair Fuzzy Sets (QOFSs), addressing their properties and presenting a method to ensure adherence to similarity axioms. A practical example is provided to demonstrate the efficacy of the proposed approach in decision-making. Gupta *et al.* [21] proposed distance and similarity measures for hesitant bi-fuzzy sets (HBFS) in both continuous and discrete environments, incorporating weighted measures to reflect factor importance. The proposed approach is applied to renewable energy system selection and decision-making, with a comparative study highlighting its superiority in pattern recognition. Boulaarasa *et al.* [22] provided a new distance measure for Dual Hesitant Fuzzy Sets (DHFS) and weighted dual hesitant fuzzy sets (WDHFS) for uncertainty handling in fuzzy environments. The measure's effectiveness is demonstrated in medical diagnosis and decision-making, with a comparative analysis showcasing its advantages over existing methods. Thakur *et al.* [23] proposed a new Correlation Coefficient (CC) and Weighted Correlation Coefficient (WCC) measures for Probabilistic Single-Valued Neutrosophic Hesitant Fuzzy Sets (PSVNHFSs), focusing on decision-making under uncertainty, hesitation, and probabilistic elements. The measures are applied to supply chain management, highlighting their effectiveness in ranking suppliers based on attribute weights and decision-makers' risk preferences. Garg *et al.* [24] proposed a new dual hesitant fuzzy correlation coefficient (DHFCC) and solved an engineering cost management problem by a decision-making algorithm. Kaur and Garg [25] introduced an innovative algorithm for autonomous vehicle parking using a newly proposed adjustable probabilistic neutrosophic hesitant fuzzy set (Ad-PNHFS). Liao *et al.* [26] proposed Gained and Lost Dominance Score (GLDS) method for multi-attribute group decision-making (MAGDM) in a PHF environment using the principles of Cumulative Prospect Theory (CPT).

12.1.1 Motivation

The following limitations of the existing measures can be seen:

a) Many traditional distance measures, such as Manhattan and Euclidean distances, may not provide intuitive interpretations when applied to HFs. Their geometric nature may not capture the uncertainty and vagueness inherent in such sets, making it challenging to derive meaningful insights.
b) Several existing measures may be sensitive to the scale of the input data. For instance, the Euclidean distance is heavily influenced by the magnitude of the values which can lead to misleading results when different features are on varying scales unless proper normalization is performed.
c) In high-dimensional spaces, many distance measures (e.g., Hamming distance) can suffer from the "curse of

dimensionality." As dimensions increase, distances between points may become less meaningful reducing the effectiveness of these measures in distinguishing between data points.

d) Many distance measures assume symmetry. However, in applications involving HFSs, the relationships may not be symmetric, leading to potential misinterpretation of distances.
e) Some existing measures may struggle with cases where certain membership or non-membership values are zero or undefined. This limitation can lead to undefined distances or distortions in the analysis when such values are present in the data.
f) Existing measures might oversimplify the relationships between HFSs by relying on linear or fixed weighting mechanisms. This can neglect complex interactions and dependencies that could be better captured through more sophisticated approaches, such as the proposed logarithmic measure.

12.1.2 Major Contributions

The major contributions of the study are:

- Introduced new logarithmic-based distance and similarity measures for HFS to enhance decision-making under uncertainty.
- Overcame drawbacks found in the existing measures such as sensitivity to scale, computational complexity and the curse of dimensionality.
- Demonstrated key mathematical properties of the proposed measures such as boundedness, symmetry and strong reflexivity.
- Applied the proposed measures to cluster the most polluted cities in India based on air quality data which reveals meaningful pollution patterns and aiding in environmental policy planning.

The rest of the paper is structured as follows: Section 12.2 covers basic definitions and some existing similarity and distance measures for HFSs along with their drawbacks. In Section 12.3, we proposed improved Logarithmic similarity and distance measures for HFSs along with their properties. The comparative analysis of the proposed measures with some existing measures also has been done in Section 12.4. The clustering algorithm using HFSs is provided in Section 12.5. The proposed measures are applied to assess air quality in India, using real-world data to cluster regions based on pollution severity in Section 12.6. Some Merits of the proposed work are given in Section 12.7. The last section concludes the paper summary with its findings and potential directions for future research.

12.2 Preliminaries

Definition 2.1 [1]: Let $X = \{x_1, x_2, \ldots, x_p\}$ be a finite universe of discourse. A Fuzzy Set ($\mathcal{E}$) for $x_m \in X$ is defined as

$$\mathcal{E} = \{(x_m, \mu_{\mathcal{E}}(x_m) \,|\, x_m \in X\};\ m = 1,2,\ldots,p \tag{12.1}$$

where $\mu_{\mathcal{E}}(x_m)$ is the membership value of x such that $0 \leq \mu_{\mathcal{E}}(x_m) \leq 1$.

Definition 2.2 [5]: A hesitant fuzzy set $\hbar$ on X is a function that, when applied to X, returns a subset between [0,1]. It can be expressed as

$$\hbar = \{(x_m, \varphi_{\hbar}(x_m) \,|\, x_m \in X\};\ m = 1,2,\ldots,p \tag{12.2}$$

where $\pi_{\hbar}(x_m)$ is a hesitant fuzzy element (HFE) having values between [0,1].

Definition 2.3 [5]: Let $\varphi_{\hbar}, \varphi_{\hbar_1}$, and $\varphi_{\hbar_2}$ are three hesitant fuzzy elements, the different operations on these fuzzy elements can be defined as:

a) Lower bound: $\varphi_{\hbar}^{-}(x_m) = \min \varphi_{\hbar}(x_m)$;
b) Upper bound: $\varphi_{\hbar}^{+}(x_m) = \max \varphi_{\hbar}(x_m)$;

c) $\varphi'_{\hbar}(x_m) = \cup_{\gamma \in \varphi_{\hbar}}\{1-\gamma\}$;
d) $\varphi_{\hbar_1} \cup \varphi_{\hbar_2} = \{\gamma \in \varphi_{\hbar_1} \cup \varphi_{\hbar_2} | \geq \max(\varphi^-_{\hbar_1}, \varphi^-_{\hbar_2})\}$;
e) $\varphi_{\hbar_1} \cap \varphi_{\hbar_2} = \{\gamma \in \varphi_{\hbar_1} \cap \varphi_{\hbar_2} | \leq \min(\varphi^+_{\hbar_1}, \varphi^+_{\hbar_2})\}$;

Later Xu and Xia [7] defined the operations (d) and (e) as

f) $\varphi_{\hbar_1} \cup \varphi_{\hbar_2} = \cup_{\gamma_1 \in \varphi_{\hbar_1}, \gamma_2 \in \varphi_{\hbar_2}} \max(\gamma_1, \gamma_2)$;
g) $\varphi_{\hbar_1} \cap \varphi_{\hbar_2} = \cup_{\gamma_1 \in \varphi_{\hbar_1}, \gamma_2 \in \varphi_{\hbar_2}} \min(\gamma_1, \gamma_2)$;

Definition 2.4 [6]: Let $\varphi_{\hbar}, \varphi_{\hbar_1}$, and $\varphi_{\hbar_2}$ be three hesitant fuzzy elements and δ be any positive real number then

a) $\varphi^{\delta}_{\hbar} = \cup_{\gamma \in \varphi_{\hbar}}\{\gamma^{\delta}\}$;
b) $\delta\varphi_{\hbar} = \cup_{(\gamma \in \varphi_{\hbar})}\{1-(1-\gamma)^{\delta}\}$;
c) $\varphi_{\hbar_1} \oplus \varphi_{\hbar_2} = \cup_{\gamma_1 \in \varphi_{\hbar_1}, \gamma_2 \in \varphi_{\hbar_2}}\{\gamma_1 + \gamma_2 - \gamma_1\gamma_2\}$
d) $\varphi_{\hbar_1} \otimes \varphi_{\hbar_2} = \cup_{\gamma_1 \in \varphi_{\hbar_1}, \gamma_2 \in \varphi_{\hbar_2}}\{\gamma_1\gamma_2\}$

For the HFE $\varphi_{\hbar_i}$ $(i = 1,2,\ldots,n)$ Liao *et al.* [17] extended (c) and (d) in definition (2.4) as:

e) $\oplus^n_{i=1}\varphi_{\hbar_i} = \cup_{\gamma_i \in \varphi_{\hbar_i}}\{1 - \Pi^n_{i=1}(1-\gamma_i\}$
f) $\otimes^n_{i=1}\varphi_{\hbar_i} = \cup_{\gamma_i \in \varphi_{\hbar_i}}\{\Pi^n_{i=1}\gamma_i\}$

The number of elements in different HFSs may be different. Let $\ell_{\varphi_{\hbar}(x_m)}$ is the number of *HFEs*.

Theorem 2.1 [7]: If $\varphi_{\hbar_1}$ and $\varphi_{\hbar_2}$ are two HFEs, then

$$\ell_{\varphi_{\hbar_1} \oplus \varphi_{\hbar_2}} = \ell_{\varphi_{\hbar_1}} \times \ell_{\varphi_{\hbar_2}} \text{ and}$$

$$\ell_{\varphi_{\hbar_1} \otimes \varphi_{\hbar_2}} = \ell_{\varphi_{\hbar_1}} \times \ell_{\varphi_{\hbar_2}}$$

Its generalization for 'n' different HFEs also holds i.e.

$$\ell_{\oplus^n_{i=1}\varphi_{\hbar_i}} = \Pi^n_{i=1}\ell_{\varphi_{\hbar_i}} \text{ and}$$

$$\ell_{\otimes^n_{i=1}\varphi_{\hbar_i}} = \Pi^n_{i=1}\ell_{\varphi_{\hbar_i}}$$

After performing the operations described above, it is evident that the length of the resulting HFE expands, leading to greater computational complexity. A new approach was recommended to shorten the derived HFE during its handling to moderate this. The updated operational rules from Definition 2.4 are outlined as follows:

a) $\varphi_{\hbar}^{\delta} = \left\{\left(\varphi_{\hbar}^{q(k)}\right)^{\delta}; \forall\, k = 1,2,\ldots, s\right\}$

b) $\delta\varphi_{\hbar} = \left\{1 - \left(1 - \varphi_{\hbar}^{q(k)}\right)^{\delta}; \forall\, k = 1,2,\ldots, s\right\}$

c) $\varphi_{\hbar_1} \oplus \varphi_{\hbar_2} = \left\{\varphi_{\hbar_1}^{q(k)} + \varphi_{\hbar_2}^{q(k)} - \varphi_{\hbar_1}^{q(k)}\varphi_{\hbar_2}^{q(k)}; \forall\, k = 1,2,\ldots, s\right\}$

d) $\varphi_{\hbar_1} \otimes \varphi_{\hbar_2} = \left\{\varphi_{\hbar_1}^{q(k)}\varphi_{\hbar_2}^{q(k)}; \forall\, k = 1,2,\ldots, s\right\}$

e) $\oplus_{i=1}^{n}\varphi_{\hbar_i} = \left\{1-\prod_{i=1}^{n}\left(1-\varphi_{\hbar_i}^{q(k)}\right); \forall\, k = 1,2,\ldots, s\right\}$

f) $\otimes_{i=1}^{n}\varphi_{\hbar_i} = \left\{\prod_{i=1}^{n}\varphi_{\hbar_i}^{q(k)}; \forall\, k = 1,2,\ldots, s\right\}$

where $q(k)$ is the minimum kth value in $\varphi_{\hbar_1}$.

Definition 2.5 [7]: Let $\hbar_1, \hbar_2$, and $\hbar_3$ are three HFSs then the distance measure between HFSs must satisfy the following conditions:

a) $0 \le \bar{d}(\hbar_1, \hbar_2) \le 1$ (Boundedness)
b) $\bar{d}(\hbar_1, \hbar_2) = \bar{d}(\hbar_2, \hbar_1)$ (Symmetry or Commutativity)
c) $\bar{d}(\hbar_1, \hbar_2) = 0$ if and only if $\hbar_1 = \hbar_2$ (Strong Reflexivity)
d) If $\hbar_1 \subseteq \hbar_2 \subseteq \hbar_3$, then $\bar{d}(\hbar_1, \hbar_3) \ge \bar{d}(\hbar_1, \hbar_2)$ and $\bar{d}(\hbar_1, \hbar_3) \ge \bar{d}(\hbar_2, \hbar_3)$ (Triangle inequality)

Definition 2.6 [7]: Let $\hbar_1, \hbar_2$, and $\hbar_3$ are three HFSs then the similarity measure between HFSs must satisfy the following conditions:

a) $0 \le \bar{s}(\hbar_1, \hbar_2) \le 1$ (Boundedness)
b) $\bar{s}(\hbar_1, \hbar_2) = \bar{s}(\mathcal{H}_2, \mathcal{H}_1)$ (Symmetry or Commutativity)
c) $\bar{s}(\hbar_1, \hbar_2) = 1$ if and only if $\hbar_1 = \hbar_2$ (Strong Reflexivity)
d) If $\hbar_1 \subseteq \hbar_2 \subseteq \hbar_3$, then $\bar{s}(\hbar_1, \hbar_3) \le \bar{s}(\hbar_1, \hbar_2)$ and $\bar{s}(\hbar_1, \hbar_3) \le \bar{s}(\hbar_2, \hbar_3)$ (Triangle inequality).

From definitions (2.5) and (2.6), it is noted that $\bar{s}(\hbar_1, \hbar_2) = 1 - \bar{d}(\hbar_1, \hbar_2)$.

Various authors studied the similarity and distance measure for HFSs some of which are:

Measure	Mathematical formula	Authors
Manhattan Distance	$\bar{d}_{man}(\hbar_1,\hbar_2)=\frac{1}{\ell_{x_m}}\sum_{k=1}^{\ell_{x_m}}\left\lvert\varphi_{\hbar_1}^{q(k)}(x_m)-\varphi_{\hbar_2}^{q(k)}(x_m)\right\rvert$	Xu and Xia [7]
Hesitant Normalized Hamming Distance	$\bar{d}_{hnh}(\hbar_1,\hbar_2)=\frac{1}{p}\sum_{m=1}^{p}\left[\frac{1}{\ell_{x_m}}\sum_{k=1}^{\ell_{x_m}}\left\lvert\varphi_{\hbar_1}^{q(k)}(x_m)-\varphi_{\hbar_2}^{q(k)}(x_m)\right\rvert\right]$	Xu and Xia [7]
Hesitant Normalized Euclidean Distance	$\bar{d}_{hne}(\hbar_1,\hbar_2)=\left[\frac{1}{p}\sum_{m=1}^{p}\frac{1}{\ell_{x_m}}\sum_{k=1}^{\ell_{x_m}}\left\lvert\varphi_{\hbar_1}^{q(k)}(x_m)-\varphi_{\hbar_2}^{q(k)}(x_m)\right\rvert^{2}\right]^{0.5}$	
Generalized Hesitant Normalized Distance	$\bar{d}_{ghn}(\hbar_1,\hbar_2)=\left[\frac{1}{p}\sum_{m=1}^{p}\frac{1}{\ell_{x_m}}\sum_{k=1}^{\ell_{x_m}}\left\lvert\varphi_{\hbar_1}^{q(k)}(x_m)-\varphi_{\hbar_2}^{q(k)}(x_m)\right\rvert^{\gamma}\right]^{\frac{1}{\gamma}}$	

(Continued)

(*Continued*)

Measure	Mathematical formula	Authors
Hesitant Normalized Hamming-Hausdorff distance	$\bar{d}_{hnhh}(\hbar_1,\hbar_2)=\frac{1}{p}\sum_{m=1}^{p}\max_k\left\|\varphi_{\hbar_1}^{q(k)}(x_m)-\varphi_{\hbar_2}^{q(k)}(x_m)\right\|$	Xu and Xia [7]
Hesitant Normalized Euclidean-Hausdorff distance	$\bar{d}_{hneh}(\hbar_1,\hbar_2)=\left[\frac{1}{p}\sum_{m=1}^{p}\max_k\left\|\varphi_{\hbar_1}^{q(k)}(x_m)-\varphi_{\hbar_2}^{q(k)}(x_m)\right\|^2\right]^{0.5}$	
Hybrid Hesitant Normalized Hamming Distance	$\bar{d}_{hhnh}(\hbar_1,\hbar_2)=\frac{1}{2p}\sum_{m=1}^{p}\left[\frac{1}{\ell_{x_m}}\sum_{k=1}^{\ell_{x_m}}\left\|\varphi_{\hbar_1}^{q(k)}(x_m)-\varphi_{\hbar_2}^{q(k)}(x_m)\right\|+\max_k\left\|\varphi_{\hbar_1}^{q(k)}(x_m)-\varphi_{\hbar_2}^{q(k)}(x_m)\right\|\right]$	
Hybrid Hesitant Normalized Euclidean Distance	$\bar{d}_{hhne}(\hbar_1,\hbar_2)=\left(\frac{1}{2p}\sum_{m=1}^{p}\left[\frac{1}{\ell_{x_m}}\sum_{k=1}^{\ell_{x_m}}\left\|\varphi_{\hbar_1}^{q(k)}(x_m)-\varphi_{\hbar_2}^{q(k)}(x_m)\right\|^2+\max_k\left\|\varphi_{\hbar_1}^{q(k)}(x_m)-\varphi_{\hbar_2}^{q(k)}(x_m)\right\|\right]\right)^{\frac{1}{2}}$	

(*Continued*)

(*Continued*)

Measure	Mathematical formula	Authors
Normalized Hamming Distance	$\bar{d}_{hhd}(\hbar_1,\hbar_2)=\frac{1}{p}\sum_{m=1}^{p}\left[\frac{1}{1+\ell_{x_m}}\left(\lvert\rho_{\hbar_1}(x_m)-\rho_{\hbar_2}(x_m)\rvert+\sum_{k=1}^{\ell_{x_m}}\lvert\varphi_{\hbar_1}^{q(k)}(x_m)-\varphi_{\hbar_2}^{q(k)}(x_m)\rvert\right)\right]$ where $\rho_{\mathcal{H}_1}(x_m)=1-\frac{1}{\ell_{x_m}}$	Zeng *et al.* [15]
Euclidean Hamming Distance	$\bar{d}_{ehd}(\hbar_1,\hbar_2)=\frac{1}{p}\sum_{m=1}^{p}\left[\frac{1}{1+\ell_{x_m}}\left(\lvert\rho_{\hbar_1}(x_m)-\rho_{\hbar_2}(x_m)\rvert^2+\sum_{k=1}^{\ell_{x_m}}\lvert\varphi_{\hbar_1}^{q(k)}(x_m)-\varphi_{\hbar_2}^{q(k)}(x_m)\rvert\right)\right]^{0.5}$	
Generalized Hamming Distance	$\bar{d}_{ghd}(\hbar_1,\hbar_2)=\frac{1}{p}\sum_{m=1}^{p}\left[\frac{1}{1+\ell_{x_m}}\left(\lvert\rho_{\hbar_1}(x_m)-\rho_{\hbar_2}(x_m)\rvert^{\gamma}+\sum_{k=1}^{\ell_{x_m}}\lvert\varphi_{\hbar_1}^{q(k)}(x_m)-\varphi_{\hbar_2}^{q(k)}(x_m)\rvert^{\gamma}\right)\right]^{\frac{1}{\gamma}}$	

(*Continued*)

(*Continued*)

Measure	Mathematical formula	Authors
New Hesitant Normalized Hamming distance	$\bar{d}_{nhnh}(\hbar_1,\hbar_2)=\frac{1}{p}\sum_{m=1}^{p}\left[\frac{1}{2+\ell_{x_m}}\left(\lvert\varpi(\pi_{\hbar_1}(x_m)-\varpi(\pi_{\hbar_2}(x_m)\rvert+\lvert\rho_{\hbar_1}(x_m)-\rho_{\hbar_2}(x_m)\rvert+\sum_{k=1}^{\ell x_m}\lvert\varphi_{\hbar_1}^{q(k)}(x_m)-\varphi_{\hbar_2}^{q(k)}(x_m)\rvert\right)\right]$	Rezaei and Rezaei [16]
New Hesitant Normalized Euclidean Distance	$\bar{d}_{nhne}(\hbar_1,\hbar_2)=\frac{1}{p}\sum_{m=1}^{p}\left[\frac{1}{2+\ell_{x_m}}\left(\lvert\varpi(\pi_{\hbar_1}(x_m)-\varpi(\pi_{\hbar_2}(x_m)\rvert^2+\lvert\rho_{\hbar_1}(x_m)-\rho_{\hbar_2}(x_m)\rvert^2+\sum_{k=1}^{\ell x_m}\lvert\varphi_{\hbar_1}^{q(k)}(x_m)-\varphi_{\hbar_2}^{q(k)}(x_m)\rvert\right)\right]^{1/2}$	
New Hesitant Normalized Minkowski Distance	$\bar{d}_{nhnm}(\hbar_1,\hbar_2)=\frac{1}{p}\sum_{m=1}^{p}\left[\frac{1}{2+\ell_{x_m}}\left(\lvert\varpi(\pi_{\hbar_1}(x_m)-\varpi(\pi_{\hbar_2}(x_m)\rvert^{\gamma}+\lvert\rho_{\hbar_1}(x_m)-\rho_{\hbar_2}(x_m)\rvert^{\gamma}+\sum_{k=1}^{\ell x_m}\lvert\varphi_{\hbar_1}^{q(k)}(x_m)-\varphi_{\hbar_2}^{q(k)}(x_m)\rvert\right)\right]^{1/\gamma}$	

(*Continued*)

(*Continued*)

Measure	Mathematical formula	Authors
HF Distance Measure	$\bar{d}_{hfd}(\hbar_1,\hbar_2)=1-\frac{1}{p}\sum_{m=1}^{p}\left[\frac{1}{\ell_{x_m}}\sum_{k=1}^{\ell_{x_m}}\left(\frac{1}{1+\left\lvert\varphi_{\hbar_1}^{q(k)}(x_m)-\varphi_{\hbar_2}^{q(k)}(x_m)\right\rvert}\right)\right]$	Gupta and Kumar [18]
Normalized HF Distance Measure	$\bar{d}_{nhfd}(\hbar_1,\hbar_2)=1-\frac{1}{p}\sum_{m=1}^{p}\left[\frac{1}{\ell_{x_m}}\sum_{k=1}^{\ell_{x_m}}\left(\frac{1}{1+\left\lvert\varphi_{\hbar_1}^{q(k)}(x_m)-\varphi_{\hbar_2}^{q(k)}(x_m)\right\rvert}\right)^{2}\right]^{1/2}$	
Generalized HF Distance Measure	$\bar{d}_{ghfd}(\hbar_1,\hbar_2)=1-\frac{1}{p}\sum_{m=1}^{p}\left[\frac{1}{\ell_{x_m}}\sum_{k=1}^{\ell_{x_m}}\left(\frac{1}{1+\left\lvert\varphi_{\hbar_1}^{q(k)}(x_m)-\varphi_{\hbar_2}^{q(k)}(x_m)\right\rvert}\right)^{\gamma}\right]^{1/\gamma}$	

12.3 Proposed Distance and Similarity Measures for HFSs

In the previous section, some existing measures were studied and found that there is a lack of sensitivity, leading to identical values across different cases or generating inconsistent and impractical results. To overcome these limitations, we have introduced a new logarithmic-based distance and similarity measure that provides greater sensitivity to small differences and uncertainty. The measures are defined as follows:

12.3.1 Proposed Distance Measure

$$\bar{d}(\hbar_1, \hbar_2) = \frac{1}{2\ell_{x_m}} \sum_{m=1}^{\ell_{x_m}} \left(\varphi_{\hbar_1}(x_m) \log \frac{2\varphi_{\hbar_1}(x_m)}{\varphi_{\hbar_1}(x_m) + \varphi_{\hbar_2}(x_m)} + \varphi_{\hbar_2}(x_m) \log \frac{2\varphi_{\hbar_2}(x_m)}{\varphi_{\hbar_1}(x_m) + \varphi_{\hbar_2}(x_m)} \right) \tag{12.4}$$

Now, we will check the validity of the proposed measure:

Theorem 3.1: Let $\hbar_1$, $\hbar_2$, and $\hbar_3$ are three HFSs then the distance measure between HFSs must satisfy the following conditions:

i) $0 \le \bar{d}(\hbar_1, \hbar_2) \le 1$ (Boundedness)
ii) $\bar{d}(\hbar_1, \hbar_2) = \bar{d}(\hbar_2, \hbar_1)$ (Symmetry or Commutativity)
iii) $\bar{d}(\hbar_1, \hbar_2) = 0$ if and only if $\hbar_1 = \hbar_2$. (Strong Reflexivity)
iv) If $\hbar_1 \subseteq \hbar_2 \subseteq \hbar_3$, then $\bar{d}(\hbar_1, \hbar_3) \ge \bar{d}(\hbar_1, \hbar_2)$ and $\bar{d}(\hbar_1, \hbar_3) \ge \bar{d}(\hbar_2, \hbar_3)$ (Triangle inequality)

Proof: i) Since $\varphi_{\hbar_1}(x_m)$ and $\varphi_{\hbar_2}(x_m)$ are the hesitancy degree which lies between 0 and 1. Also, log(x) is negative for $x \in (0,1)$ so each of the terms in $\bar{d}(\hbar_1, \hbar_2)$ within the sum is positive or zero. Which implies that $0 \le \bar{d}(\hbar_1, \hbar_2) \le 1$.

ii) The measure is symmetric since the terms involving $\varphi_{\hbar_1}(x_m)$ and $\varphi_{\hbar_2}(x_m)$ appears in symmetric form in the measure $\bar{d}(\hbar_1, \hbar_2)$ Swapping $\hbar_1$ to $\hbar_2$ does not change the value of $\bar{d}(\hbar_1, \hbar_2)$ as $\varphi_{\hbar_1}(x_m) \log \dfrac{2\varphi_{\hbar_1}(x_m)}{\varphi_{\hbar_1}(x_m) + \varphi_{\hbar_2}(x_m)}$

is symmetric with respect to $\varphi_{\hbar_1}(x_m)$ and $\varphi_{\hbar_2}(x_m)$. Therefore, the measure satisfies the symmetric condition.

iii) if $\hbar_1 = \hbar_2$ then $\varphi_{\hbar_1}(x_m)$ and $\varphi_{\hbar_2}(x_m)$ so,

$$\bar{d}(\hbar_1, \hbar_2) = \frac{1}{2\ell_{x_m}} \sum_{m=1}^{\ell_{x_m}} \left(\varphi_{\hbar_1}(x_m) \log \frac{2\varphi_{\hbar_1}(x_m)}{\varphi_{\hbar_1}(x_m) + \varphi_{\hbar_2}(x_m)} + \varphi_{\hbar_2}(x_m) \log \frac{2\varphi_{\hbar_2}(x_m)}{\varphi_{\hbar_1}(x_m) + \varphi_{\hbar_2}(x_m)} \right)$$

$\bar{d}(\hbar_1, \hbar_2) = 0$ which means that the HFSs $\hbar_1$ and $\hbar_2$ are identical.

iv) If $\hbar_1 \subseteq \hbar_2 \subseteq \hbar_3$, then $\varphi_{\hbar_1}(x_m) \subseteq \varphi_{\hbar_2}(x_m) \subseteq \varphi_{\hbar_3}(x_m)$ so

$$\left(\varphi_{\hbar_1}(x_m) \log \frac{2\varphi_{\hbar_1}(x_m)}{\varphi_{\hbar_1}(x_m) + \varphi_{\hbar_3}(x_m)} + \varphi_{\hbar_2}(x_m) \log \frac{2\varphi_{\hbar_3}(x_m)}{\varphi_{\hbar_1}(x_m) + \varphi_{\hbar_3}(x_m)} \right) \geq$$

$$\left(\varphi_{\hbar_1}(x_m) \log \frac{2\varphi_{\hbar_1}(x_m)}{\varphi_{\hbar_1}(x_m) + \varphi_{\hbar_2}(x_m)} + \varphi_{\hbar_3}(x_m) \log \frac{2\varphi_{\hbar_2}(x_m)}{\varphi_{\hbar_1}(x_m) + \varphi_{\hbar_2}(x_m)} \right)$$

$$= \bar{d}(\hbar_1, \hbar_3) \geq \bar{d}(\hbar_1, \hbar_2)$$

Similarly,

$$\left(\varphi_{\hbar_1}(x_m) \log \frac{2\varphi_{\hbar_1}(x_m)}{\varphi_{\hbar_1}(x_m) + \varphi_{\hbar_3}(x_m)} + \varphi_{\hbar_2}(x_m) \log \frac{2\varphi_{\hbar_3}(x_m)}{\varphi_{\hbar_1}(x_m) + \varphi_{\hbar_3}(x_m)} \right) \geq$$

$$\left(\varphi_{\hbar_2}(x_m) \log \frac{2\varphi_{\hbar_1}(x_m)}{\varphi_{\hbar_2}(x_m) + \varphi_{\hbar_3}(x_m)} + \varphi_{\hbar_3}(x_m) \log \frac{2\varphi_{\hbar_3}(x_m)}{\varphi_{\hbar_2}(x_m) + \varphi_{\hbar_3}(x_m)} \right)$$

$$= \bar{d}(\hbar_1, \hbar_3) \geq \bar{d}(\hbar_2, \hbar_3) \text{ (Hence Proved)}$$

Figure 12.1 represents the surface plot of the distance measure with respective of different values. The surface plot of the measure clearly depicts that the distance between itself is zero and the distance values between two distinct values are positive in nature and bounded between the values 0 and 1. This proves that the suggested measure holds all the properties graphically also.

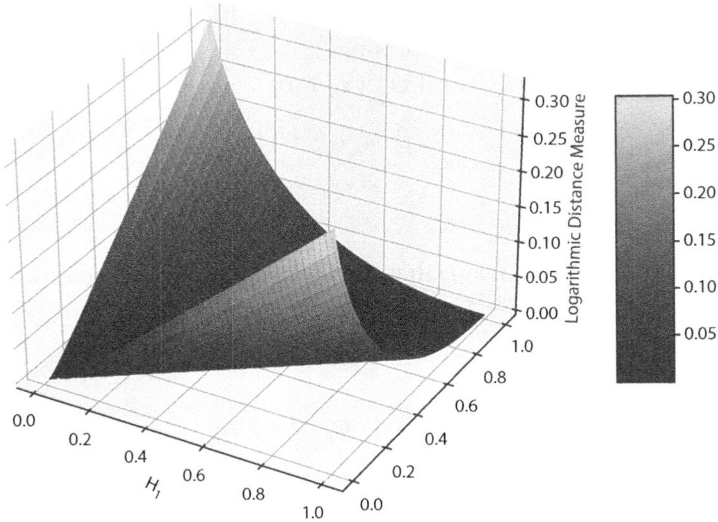

Figure 12.1 Surface plot of proposed distance measure for hesitant fuzzy sets.

12.3.2 Proposed Similarity Measure

We know that $\bar{s}(h_1, h_2) = 1 - \bar{d}(h_1, h_2)$,so

$$\bar{s}(h_1,h_2)=1-\frac{1}{2\ell_{x_m}}\sum_{m=1}^{\ell_{x_m}}\left(\varphi_{h_1}(x_m)\log\frac{2\varphi_{h_1}(x_m)}{\varphi_{h_1}(x_m)+\varphi_{h_2}(x_m)}+\varphi_{h_2}(x_m)\log\frac{2\varphi_{h_2}(x_m)}{\varphi_{h_1}(x_m)+\varphi_{h_2}(x_m)}\right) \quad (12.5)$$

Now, we will check the validity of the proposed measure:

Theorem 3.2: Let h_1, h_2, and h_3 are three HFSs then the similarity measure between HFSs must satisfy the following conditions:

a) $0 \leq \bar{s}(h_1,h_2) \leq 1$ (Boundedness)
b) $\bar{s}(h_1,h_2) = \bar{s}(\mathcal{H}_2,\mathcal{H}_1)$ (Symmetry or Commutativity)
c) $\bar{s}(h_1,h_2) = 1$ if and only if $h_1 = h_2$ (Strong Reflexivity)
d) If $h_1 \subseteq h_2 \subseteq h_3$, then $\bar{s}(h_1,h_3) \leq \bar{s}(h_1,h_2)$ and $\bar{s}(h_1,h_3) \leq \bar{s}$ (h_2,h_3) (Triangle inequality).

Proof: i) Since $\varphi_{h_1}(x_m)$ and $\varphi_{h_2}(x_m)$ are the hesitancy degree which lies between 0 and 1. Also, log(x) is negative for $x \in (0,1)$ so each of the terms in $\bar{s}(\hbar_1,\hbar_2)$ within the sum is positive or zero. Which implies that $0 \leq \bar{s}(\hbar_1,\hbar_2) \leq 1$.

ii) The measure is symmetric since the terms involving $\varphi_{\hbar_1}(x_m)$ and $\varphi_{\hbar_2}(x_m)$ appears in symmetric form in the measure $\bar{s}(\hbar_1,\hbar_2)$. Swapping $\hbar_1$ to $\hbar_2$ does not change the value of $\bar{s}(\hbar_1,\hbar_2)$ as $\varphi_{\hbar_1}(x_m)\log\frac{2\varphi_{\hbar_1}(x_m)}{\varphi_{\hbar_1}(x_m)+\varphi_{\hbar_2}(x_m)}$ is symmetric with respect to $\varphi_{\hbar_1}(x_m)$ and $\varphi_{\hbar_2}(x_m)$. Therefore, the measure satisfies the symmetric condition.

iii) if $\hbar_1 = \hbar_2$ then $\varphi_{\hbar_1}(x_m) = \varphi_{\hbar_2}(x_m)$ so,

$$\bar{s}(\hbar_1,\hbar_2) = 1 - \frac{1}{2\ell_{x_m}}\sum_{m=1}^{\ell_{x_m}}\left(\varphi_{\hbar_1}(x_m)\log\frac{2\varphi_{\hbar_1}(x_m)}{\varphi_{\hbar_1}(x_m)+\varphi_{\hbar_2}(x_m)} + \varphi_{\hbar_2}(x_m)\log\frac{2\varphi_{\hbar_2}(x_m)}{\varphi_{\hbar_1}(x_m)+\varphi_{\hbar_2}(x_m)}\right) \tag{12.6}$$

$\bar{s}(\hbar_1,\hbar_1) = 1$ which means that the HFSs $\hbar_1$ and $\hbar_2$ are identical.

iv) If $\hbar_1 \subseteq \hbar_2 \subseteq \hbar_3$ then $\varphi_{\hbar_1}(x_m) \subseteq \varphi_{\hbar_2}(x_m) \subseteq \varphi_{\hbar_3}(x_m)$ so

$$1 - \left(\varphi_{\hbar_1}(x_m)\log\frac{2\varphi_{\hbar_1}(x_m)}{\varphi_{\hbar_1}(x_m)+\varphi_{\hbar_3}(x_m)} + \varphi_{\hbar_2}(x_m)\log\frac{2\varphi_{\hbar_3}(x_m)}{\varphi_{\hbar_1}(x_m)+\varphi_{\hbar_3}(x_m)}\right) \leq$$

$$1 - \left(\varphi_{\hbar_1}(x_m)\log\frac{2\varphi_{\hbar_1}(x_m)}{\varphi_{\hbar_1}(x_m)+\varphi_{\hbar_2}(x_m)} + \varphi_{\hbar_2}(x_m)\log\frac{2\varphi_{\hbar_2}(x_m)}{\varphi_{\hbar_1}(x_m)+\varphi_{\hbar_2}(x_m)}\right)$$

$$= \bar{s}(\hbar_1, \hbar_3) \leq \bar{s}(\hbar_1, \hbar_2)$$

Similarly,

$$1 - \left(\varphi_{\hbar_1}(x_m)\log\frac{2\varphi_{\hbar_1}(x_m)}{\varphi_{\hbar_1}(x_m)+\varphi_{\hbar_3}(x_m)} + \varphi_{\hbar_2}(x_m)\log\frac{2\varphi_{\hbar_3}(x_m)}{\varphi_{\hbar_1}(x_m)+\varphi_{\hbar_3}(x_m)}\right) \leq$$

$$1 - \left(\varphi_{\hbar_2}(x_m)\log\frac{2\varphi_{\hbar_2}(x_m)}{\varphi_{\hbar_2}(x_m)+\varphi_{\hbar_3}(x_m)} + \varphi_{\hbar_3}(x_m)\log\frac{2\varphi_{\hbar_3}(x_m)}{\varphi_{\hbar_2}(x_m)+\varphi_{\hbar_3}(x_m)}\right)$$

$= \bar{s}(\hbar_1, \hbar_3) \leq \bar{s}(\hbar_2, \hbar_3)$ (Hence Proved)

Figure 12.2 illustrates the surface plot of similarity measure with varying values of HFSs. The plot demonstrates that the similarity between identical elements of sets is one, while the similarity between distinct elements of sets is both positive and confined within the range of 0 to 1.

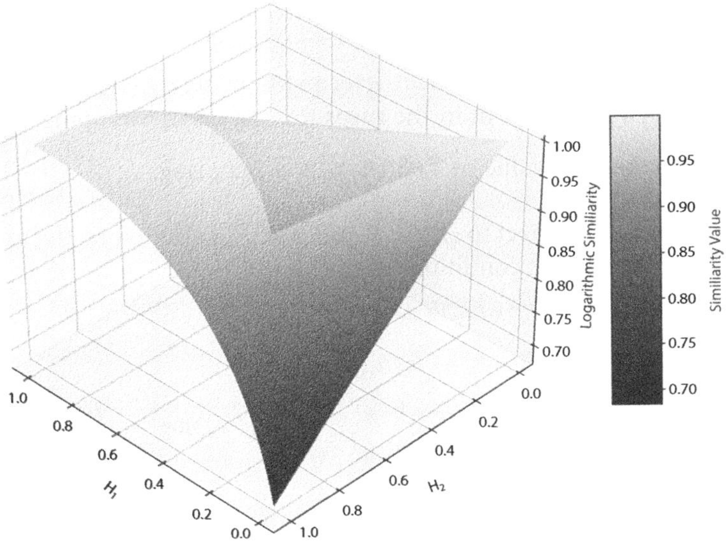

Figure 12.2 Surface plot of proposed similarity measure for hesitant fuzzy sets.

12.4 Comparative Analysis

In an investment decision-making process, the risk level is influenced by the three factors i.e. Economic stability (τ_1), Market volatility (τ_2), Company performance (τ_3). Let $X^* = (\{\tau_1, \tau_2, \tau_3\} | \tau_1 = \tau_2 = \tau_3 = 0)$ denotes the ideal investment with minimal risk. The risk associated with any given investment is assessed using HFSs $\hbar_1 \hbar_2$, and $\hbar_3$ where the membership degree reflects how closely the investment aligns with a low-risk profile. Since there may be hesitation in evaluating risks (e.g., based on different analysts' opinions), the membership value may fluctuate between several values. Thus, we use HFSs to represent the risk profile. Let us take an example of an investment with the following three-factor risk values (0.2,0.4,0.3). Some analysts think this investment carries low risk (values close to X^*), while others believe it is moderately risky. Thus, with the help of HFSs, we can represent this risk profile more accurately. Let us now consider three existing investments denoted in the form of HFSs: $\hbar_1 = \{y_1, 0.80, 0.90, 0.95\}$, $\hbar_2 = \{y_1, 0.50, 0.53, 0.60\}$ and $\hbar_3 = \{y_1, 0.1, 0.15, 0.25\}$. Now, we are asked to recognize a new investment $\mathcal{F} = \{y_1, 0.65, 0.70, 0.75\}$, which has an unknown risk pattern. To allocate this new investment to either $\hbar_1$ (low risk),$\hbar_2$ (moderate risk) and $\hbar_3$ (High risk), the similarity measures are derived using proposed and existing similarity measures. The values computed using various measures reflect the degree of closeness and are given below:

Table 12.1 Ranking of investments based on some existing and proposed similarity measures.

Similarity measure	**$(\hbar_1,\mathcal{F})$**	**$(\hbar_2,\mathcal{F})$**	**$(\hbar_3,\mathcal{F})$**	**Ranking**
$\bar{\mathcal{S}}_{man}$	0.817	0.843	0.467	$\hbar_2 > \hbar_1 > \hbar_3$
$\bar{\mathcal{S}}_{hnh}$	0.817	0.843	0.467	$\hbar_2 > \hbar_1 > \hbar_3$
$\bar{\mathcal{S}}_{hne}$	0.815	0.843	0.466	$\hbar_2 > \hbar_1 > \hbar_3$
$\bar{\mathcal{S}}_{ghn}(\gamma = 6)$	0.810	0.842	0.464	$\hbar_2 > \hbar_1 > \hbar_3$
$\bar{\mathcal{S}}_{ghn}(\gamma = 10)$	0.807	0.841	0.463	$\hbar_2 > \hbar_1 > \hbar_3$
$\bar{\mathcal{S}}_{hnhh}$	0.817	0.843	0.467	$\hbar_2 > \hbar_1 > \hbar_3$
$\bar{\mathcal{S}}_{hneh}$	0.966	0.975	0.715	$\hbar_2 > \hbar_1 > \hbar_3$
$\bar{\mathcal{S}}_{hhnh}$	0.878	0.896	0.644	$\hbar_2 > \hbar_1 > \hbar_3$
$\bar{\mathcal{S}}_{hhne}$	0.873	0.883	0.771	$\hbar_2 > \hbar_1 > \hbar_3$
$\bar{\mathcal{S}}_{hhd}$	0.954	0.961	0.867	$\hbar_2 > \hbar_1 > \hbar_3$
$\bar{\mathcal{S}}_{ehd}$	0.876	0.886	0.789	$\hbar_2 > \hbar_1 > \hbar_3$
$\bar{\mathcal{S}}_{ghd}(\gamma = 6)$	0.761	0.767	0.714	$\hbar_2 > \hbar_1 > \hbar_3$
$\bar{\mathcal{S}}_{ghd}(\gamma = 10)$	0.727	0.731	0.696	$\hbar_2 > \hbar_1 > \hbar_3$
$\bar{\mathcal{S}}_{nhnh}$	0.950	0.959	0.860	$\hbar_2 > \hbar_1 > \hbar_3$
$\bar{\mathcal{S}}_{nhne}$	0.886	0.895	0.797	$\hbar_2 > \hbar_1 > \hbar_3$
$\bar{\mathcal{S}}_{nhnm}(\gamma = 6)$	0.769	0.775	0.724	$\hbar_2 > \hbar_1 > \hbar_3$
$\bar{\mathcal{S}}_{nhnm}(\gamma = 10)$	0.733	0.737	0.703	$\hbar_2 > \hbar_1 > \hbar_3$
$\bar{\mathcal{S}}_{hfd}$	0.845	0.865	0.652	$\hbar_2 > \hbar_1 > \hbar_3$
$\bar{\mathcal{S}}_{nhfd}$	0.846	0.865	0.652	$\hbar_2 > \hbar_1 > \hbar_3$
Proposed	**0.995**	**0.995**	**0.909**	$\hbar_2 > \hbar_1 > \hbar_3$

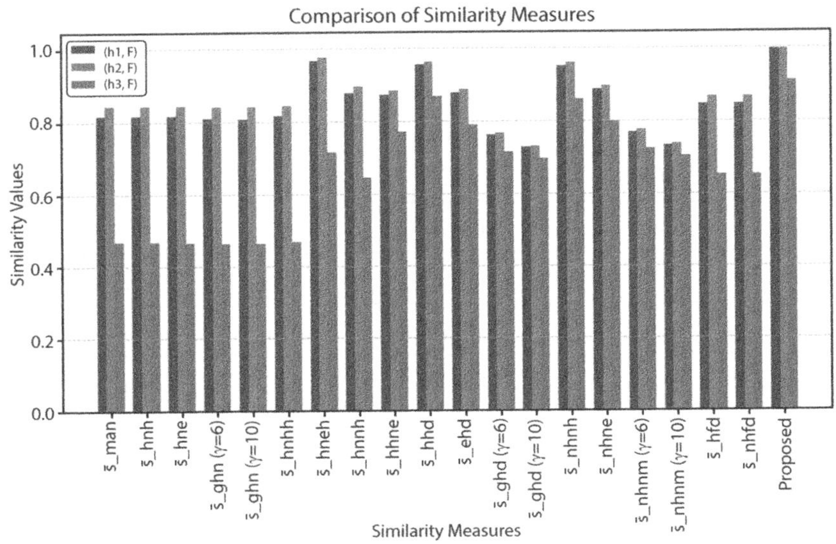

Figure 12.3 Bar plot for the comparison between proposed and existing similarity measures.

It can be seen from Table 12.1 and Figure 12.3 that all measures consistently rank $\mathcal{h}_2$ (moderate risk) higher than $\mathcal{h}_1$ (low risk) and $\mathcal{h}_3$ (high risk) which indicates that the new investment $\mathcal{F}$ is more aligned with moderate risk profiles. The proposed measure yields the highest similarity values i.e. 0.9947 to $(\mathcal{h}_1,\mathcal{F})$, 0.9950 to $(\mathcal{h}_2,\mathcal{F})$ and 0.9085 to $(\mathcal{h}_3,\mathcal{F})$ which is due to the improved sensitivity to small variations. Hence the proposed measure is more effective in capturing the similarity between HFSs given the consistency in rankings and the strong similarity scores, it is recommended to classify the new investment $\mathcal{F}$ as moderate risk, aligning with the characteristics of $\mathcal{h}_2$.

12.5 Clustering Analysis

Clustering is a widely used unsupervised machine learning technique that aims to group a set of objects or data points into clusters based on their similarity. The main goal is to ensure that objects within the same cluster are more similar to each other than to those in other clusters. These are applied in various areas such as Healthcare, economics, image processing and resource management for extracting meaningful patterns and insights from data.

12.5.1 Clustering Algorithm for Hesitant Fuzzy Sets

Let $\wp = (\mathcal{P}_{ij})_{m*m}$ be a HF similarity relation (matrix), where $\mathcal{P}_{ij} = \mathcal{P}(\hbar_i, \hbar_j); i, j = 1,2,\ldots,m$ denotes the similarity measure of HFSs $\hbar_i$ *and* $\hbar_j$ and satisfies all the conditions given in Theorem 3.2. The algorithm for applying the clustering analysis on HFSs is given below:

Step 1: Convert data into HFSs based on pre-defined intervals (e.g., Low, Medium, High). These intervals are used to map each data point to multiple membership values. These intervals assign hesitant membership degrees between 0 and 1 based on where the data falls. Each data point is then represented by a set of possible membership values across different fuzzy categories, capturing uncertainty or hesitation in its classification.
Step 2: Calculate the similarity measure of HFSs and construct the hesitant fuzzy similarity matrix. Let $\{\hbar_1, \hbar_2, \ldots, \hbar_m\}$ be a set of HFSs on $X = \{x_1, x_2, \ldots, x_p\}$. We calculate the similarity measure of the HFSs and establish the HF similarity matrix $\wp = (\mathcal{P}_{ij})_{m*m}$ where $\mathcal{P}_{ij} = \mathcal{P}(\hbar_i, \hbar_j)$.
Step 3: Calculate the HF equivalence matrix. Perform the composition of the HF similarity matrix $\wp$ by $\wp \to \wp^2 \to \wp^4 \to \cdots \to \wp^{2^k} \to \cdots$ as where $\wp^{2^k}$ is called the HF equivalence matrix.
Step 4: Construct a τ – cutting matrix $\wp_\tau = (\mathcal{P}_{ij}^{\tau})_{m*m}$ for a given level of confidence $\tau \in [0,1]$, where $\mathcal{P}_{ij}^{\tau}$ is defined as

$$\mathcal{P}_{ij}^{\tau} = \begin{cases} 0, & if\ \mathcal{P}_{ij} < \tau \\ 1, & if\ \mathcal{P}_{ij} \geq \tau \end{cases} ; i, j = 1,2,\ldots,m \tag{12.9}$$

Step 5: Now, we can classify the similarity measure between each HFS using the principle if all the elements of the ith line (Column) in $\wp_\tau$ are the same as the corresponding elements of the jth line (Column) in $\wp_\tau$, then the , then the HFSs $\hbar_i$ *and* $\hbar_j$ are the same type, known by this clustering principle, the whole 'm' HFSs $\hbar_i$,(i = 1, 2, · · · , m) can be classified.

12.6 Application in Air Pollution Analysis

Air pollution is a major environmental concern in India, particularly in urban and industrial regions where high emissions from vehicles, industries and construction activities contribute to deteriorating air quality. This study utilizes real air quality data to classify cities i.e. Byrnihat (u_1), Delhi (u_2), Gurugram(u_3), Faridabad (u_4), Sri Ganganagar (u_5), Greater Noida (u_6), Muzaffarnagar (u_7), Durgapur (u_8), Asansol (u_9), and Ghaziabad (u_{10}), based on their pollution levels. By grouping cities with similar pollution patterns, targeted air quality management strategies and emission control measures can be implemented. The analysis is based on air quality data collected from multiple cities across India in 2024. The cities included in the study were selected based on their high pollution levels and significant public health impacts. The data of seven attributes i.e. Average PM2.5 concentration (in $\mu g/m^3$) (R_1), Average PM10 concentration (in $\mu g/m^3$) (R_2), NO_2 levels (in $\mu g/m^3$) (R_3), SO_2 levels (in $\mu g/m^3$) (R_4) and Ozone levels (in $\mu g/m^3$) (R_5). The data is shown in Table 12.2.

Step 1: Assign hesitant membership degrees between 0 and 1 to the data given in Table 12.2 based on AQI Categorization given in Table A1 as an appendix. Each data point is then represented by a set of possible membership values across different fuzzy categories as given below in Table 12.3.

Table 12.2 Air quality data for selected Indian cities in 2024.

	R_1	R_2	R_3	R_4	R_5
u_1	128.15	212.9	27.6	16.8	22.97
u_2	99.86	198.45	62.72	26.51	22.11
u_3	105.31	198.09	18.28	4.21	39.46
u_4	86.22	176.8	25	9.93	12.45
u_5	86.77	235.86	44.99	5.47	36.38
u_6	81.49	206.37	42.96	13.59	40.19
u_7	83.91	170.6	23.5	17.81	38.07
u_8	97.53	164.58	10.88	6.03	45.26
u_9	61.18	108.9	21.21	4.84	24.73
u_{10}	76.74	197	51.6	11.9	28.8

Table 12.3 Air quality data for selected Indian cities in terms of hesitant fuzzy set.

	R_1	R_2	R_3	R_4	R_5
u_1	(0.70,0.72)	(0.46,0.48)	(0.19,0.22)	(0.13,0.16)	(0.13,0.15)
u_2	(0.54,0.57)	(0.40,0.43)	(0.36,0.39)	(0.19,0.21)	(0.14,0.16)
u_3	(0.59,0.62)	(0.40,0.42)	(0.14,0.16)	(0.04,0.06)	(0.24,0.26)
u_4	(0.47,0.50)	(0.36,0.39)	(0.18,0.20)	(0.06,0.09)	(0.08,0.10)
u_5	(0.46,0.49)	(0.47,0.49)	(0.34,0.35)	(0.03,0.04)	(0.20,0.23)
u_6	(0.45,0.47)	(0.42,0.45)	(0.32,0.33)	(0.09,0.11)	(0.24,0.26)
u_7	(0.46,0.49)	(0.39,0.42)	(0.17,0.19)	(0.13,0.15)	(0.25,0.28)
u_8	(0.53,0.56)	(0.36,0.39)	(0.08.0.09)	(0.03,0.05)	(0.30,0.32)
u_9	(0.35,0.37)	(0.35,0.37)	(0.16,0.18)	(0.02,0.05)	(0.15,0.16)
u_{10}	(0.41,0.43)	(0.40,0.43)	(0.36,0.39)	(0.08,0.10)	(0.18,0.20)

Step 2: The hesitant fuzzy similarity matrix using Equation (12.5) is

$$\wp = \begin{bmatrix} 1 & 0.9959 & 0.9949 & 0.9956 & 0.9914 & 0.9938 & 0.9954 & 0.9893 & 0.9895 & 0.9925 \\ 0.9959 & 1 & 0.9888 & 0.9928 & 0.9924 & 0.9964 & 0.9940 & 0.9813 & 0.9871 & 0.9967 \\ 0.9949 & 0.9888 & 1 & 0.9948 & 0.9947 & 0.9948 & 0.9968 & 0.9985 & 0.9953 & 0.9923 \\ 0.9956 & 0.9928 & 0.9948 & 1 & 0.9937 & 0.9938 & 0.9944 & 0.9908 & 0.9973 & 0.9947 \\ 0.9914 & 0.9924 & 0.9947 & 0.9937 & 1 & 0.9981 & 0.9934 & 0.9898 & 0.9947 & 0.9982 \\ 0.9938 & 0.9964 & 0.9948 & 0.9938 & 0.9981 & 1 & 0.9975 & 0.9902 & 0.9936 & 0.9993 \\ 0.9954 & 0.9940 & 0.9968 & 0.9944 & 0.9934 & 0.9975 & 1 & 0.9948 & 0.9940 & 0.9952 \\ 0.9893 & 0.9813 & 0.9985 & 0.9908 & 0.9898 & 0.9902 & 0.9948 & 1 & 0.9940 & 0.9867 \\ 0.9895 & 0.9871 & 0.9953 & 0.9973 & 0.9947 & 0.9936 & 0.9940 & 0.940 & 1 & 0.9941 \\ 0.9925 & 0.9967 & 0.9923 & 0.9947 & 0.9982 & 0.9993 & 0.9952 & 0.9867 & 0.9941 & 1 \end{bmatrix}$$

Step 3: Calculate hesitant fuzzy equivalence matrix: Next, we verify if matrix $\wp$ is the equivalent similarity matrix. To do this, we compute the following powers of matrix $\wp$ as shown below:

$$
\wp^{2} = \wp \, o \wp = \begin{bmatrix}
1 & 0.9846 & 0.9943 & 0.9948 & 0.9912 & 0.9861 & 0.9905 & 0.9861 & 0.9855 & 0.9970 \\
0.9846 & 1 & 0.9846 & 0.9846 & 0.9846 & 0.9846 & 0.9846 & 0.9769 & 0.9846 & 0.9846 \\
0.9943 & 0.9846 & 1 & 0.9943 & 0.9912 & 0.9861 & 0.9905 & 0.9861 & 0.9855 & 0.9943 \\
0.9948 & 0.9846 & 0.9943 & 1 & 0.9912 & 0.9861 & 0.9905 & 0.9861 & 0.9855 & 0.9948 \\
0.9912 & 0.9846 & 0.9912 & 0.9912 & 1 & 0.9861 & 0.9905 & 0.9861 & 0.9855 & 0.9912 \\
0.9861 & 0.9846 & 0.9861 & 0.9861 & 0.9861 & 1 & 0.9861 & 0.9885 & 0.9855 & 0.9861 \\
0.9905 & 0.9846 & 0.9905 & 0.9905 & 0.9905 & 0.9861 & 1 & 0.9861 & 0.9855 & 0.9905 \\
0.9861 & 0.9769 & 0.9961 & 0.9861 & 0.9861 & 0.9885 & 0.9861 & 1 & 0.9812 & 0.9861 \\
0.9855 & 0.9846 & 0.9855 & 0.9855 & 0.9855 & 0.9885 & 0.9855 & 0.9812 & 1 & 0.9855 \\
0.9970 & 0.9846 & 0.9948 & 0.9948 & 0.9912 & 0.9861 & 0.9861 & 0.9861 & 0.9855 & 1
\end{bmatrix}
$$

$$
\wp^{4} = \wp^{2} \, o \, \wp^{2} = \begin{bmatrix}
1 & 0.9959 & 0.9959 & 0.9956 & 0.9959 & 0.9959 & 0.9959 & 0.9959 & 0.9956 & 0.9959 \\
0.9959 & 1 & 0.9967 & 0.9856 & 0.9967 & 0.9967 & 0.9967 & 0.9967 & 0.9956 & 0.9967 \\
0.9959 & 0.9967 & 1 & 0.9956 & 0.9968 & 0.9968 & 0.9968 & 0.9985 & 0.9954 & 0.9968 \\
0.9956 & 0.9956 & 0.9956 & 1 & 0.9956 & 0.9956 & 0.9956 & 0.9954 & 0.9973 & 0.9956 \\
0.9959 & 0.9967 & 0.9968 & 0.9956 & 1 & 0.9982 & 0.9975 & 0.9968 & 0.9956 & 0.9982 \\
0.9859 & 0.9967 & 0.9968 & 0.9956 & 0.9982 & 1 & 0.9975 & 0.9968 & 0.9956 & 0.9993 \\
0.9959 & 0.9967 & 0.9968 & 0.9956 & 0.9975 & 0.9975 & 1 & 0.9968 & 0.9956 & 0.9975 \\
0.9859 & 0.9967 & 0.9985 & 0.9954 & 0.9968 & 0.9968 & 0.9968 & 1 & 0.9954 & 0.9968 \\
0.9856 & 0.9956 & 0.9954 & 0.9973 & 0.9956 & 0.9956 & 0.9956 & 0.9954 & 1 & 0.9956 \\
0.9959 & 0.9967 & 0.9968 & 0.9956 & 0.9982 & 0.9993 & 0.9975 & 0.9968 & 0.9956 & 1
\end{bmatrix}
$$

$$
\wp^{8} = \wp^{4} \, o \, \wp^{4} = \begin{bmatrix}
1 & 0.9959 & 0.9959 & 0.9956 & 0.9959 & 0.9959 & 0.9959 & 0.9959 & 0.9956 & 0.9959 \\
0.9959 & 1 & 0.9967 & 0.9856 & 0.9967 & 0.9967 & 0.9967 & 0.9967 & 0.9956 & 0.9967 \\
0.9959 & 0.9967 & 1 & 0.9956 & 0.9968 & 0.9968 & 0.9968 & 0.9985 & 0.9956 & 0.9968 \\
0.9956 & 0.9956 & 0.9956 & 1 & 0.9956 & 0.9956 & 0.9956 & 0.9956 & 0.9973 & 0.9956 \\
0.9959 & 0.9967 & 0.9968 & 0.9956 & 1 & 0.9982 & 0.9975 & 0.9968 & 0.9956 & 0.9982 \\
0.9859 & 0.9967 & 0.9968 & 0.9956 & 0.9982 & 1 & 0.9975 & 0.9968 & 0.9956 & 0.9993 \\
0.9959 & 0.9967 & 0.9968 & 0.9956 & 0.9975 & 0.9975 & 1 & 0.9968 & 0.9956 & 0.9975 \\
0.9859 & 0.9967 & 0.9985 & 0.9956 & 0.9968 & 0.9968 & 0.9968 & 1 & 0.9956 & 0.9968 \\
0.9856 & 0.9956 & 0.9956 & 0.9973 & 0.9956 & 0.9956 & 0.9956 & 0.9956 & 1 & 0.9956 \\
0.9959 & 0.9967 & 0.9968 & 0.9956 & 0.9982 & 0.9993 & 0.9975 & 0.9968 & 0.9956 & 1
\end{bmatrix}
$$

$$
\wp^{16} = \wp^{8} \, o \, \wp^{8} = \begin{bmatrix}
1 & 0.9959 & 0.9959 & 0.9956 & 0.9959 & 0.9959 & 0.9959 & 0.9959 & 0.9956 & 0.9959 \\
0.9959 & 1 & 0.9967 & 0.9856 & 0.9967 & 0.9967 & 0.9967 & 0.9967 & 0.9956 & 0.9967 \\
0.9959 & 0.9967 & 1 & 0.9956 & 0.9968 & 0.9968 & 0.9968 & 0.9985 & 0.9956 & 0.9968 \\
0.9956 & 0.9956 & 0.9956 & 1 & 0.9956 & 0.9956 & 0.9956 & 0.9956 & 0.9973 & 0.9956 \\
0.9959 & 0.9967 & 0.9968 & 0.9956 & 1 & 0.9982 & 0.9975 & 0.9968 & 0.9956 & 0.9982 \\
0.9859 & 0.9967 & 0.9968 & 0.9956 & 0.9982 & 1 & 0.9975 & 0.9968 & 0.9956 & 0.9993 \\
0.9959 & 0.9967 & 0.9968 & 0.9956 & 0.9975 & 0.9975 & 1 & 0.9968 & 0.9956 & 0.9975 \\
0.9859 & 0.9967 & 0.9985 & 0.9956 & 0.9968 & 0.9968 & 0.9968 & 1 & 0.9956 & 0.9968 \\
0.9856 & 0.9956 & 0.9956 & 0.9973 & 0.9956 & 0.9956 & 0.9956 & 0.9956 & 1 & 0.9956 \\
0.9959 & 0.9967 & 0.9968 & 0.9956 & 0.9982 & 0.9993 & 0.9975 & 0.9968 & 0.9956 & 1
\end{bmatrix}
$$

It is evident that similarity matrices $\wp^{16}$ and $\wp^{8}$ are identical. Therefore, matrix $\wp^{8}$ is the equivalent similarity matrix.

Step 4: Construct a $\tau -$ cutting matrix $\wp_{\tau} = \left(\mathcal{P}_{ij}^{\tau}\right)_{m*m}$ for a given level of confidence $\tau \epsilon [0,1]$ using Equation (12.9). Different values of τ will lead to different $\tau -$ cutting matrices. The possible $\tau -$ cutting matrices are as follows:

1. For $0 < \tau \leq 0.9956$

$$\mathcal{P}_{ij}^{\tau} = \begin{bmatrix} 1 & 1 & 1 & 1 & 1 & 1 & 1 & 1 & 1 & 1 \\ 1 & 1 & 1 & 1 & 1 & 1 & 1 & 1 & 1 & 1 \\ 1 & 1 & 1 & 1 & 1 & 1 & 1 & 1 & 1 & 1 \\ 1 & 1 & 1 & 1 & 1 & 1 & 1 & 1 & 1 & 1 \\ 1 & 1 & 1 & 1 & 1 & 1 & 1 & 1 & 1 & 1 \\ 1 & 1 & 1 & 1 & 1 & 1 & 1 & 1 & 1 & 1 \\ 1 & 1 & 1 & 1 & 1 & 1 & 1 & 1 & 1 & 1 \\ 1 & 1 & 1 & 1 & 1 & 1 & 1 & 1 & 1 & 1 \\ 1 & 1 & 1 & 1 & 1 & 1 & 1 & 1 & 1 & 1 \\ 1 & 1 & 1 & 1 & 1 & 1 & 1 & 1 & 1 & 1 \end{bmatrix}$$

2. For $0.9956 < \tau \leq 0.9959$

$$\mathcal{P}_{ij}^{\tau} = \begin{bmatrix} 1 & 1 & 1 & 0 & 1 & 1 & 1 & 1 & 0 & 1 \\ 1 & 1 & 1 & 0 & 1 & 1 & 1 & 1 & 0 & 1 \\ 1 & 1 & 1 & 0 & 1 & 1 & 1 & 1 & 0 & 1 \\ 0 & 0 & 0 & 1 & 0 & 0 & 0 & 0 & 1 & 0 \\ 1 & 1 & 1 & 0 & 1 & 1 & 1 & 1 & 0 & 1 \\ 1 & 1 & 1 & 0 & 1 & 1 & 1 & 1 & 0 & 1 \\ 1 & 1 & 1 & 0 & 1 & 1 & 1 & 1 & 0 & 1 \\ 1 & 1 & 1 & 0 & 1 & 1 & 1 & 1 & 0 & 1 \\ 0 & 0 & 0 & 1 & 0 & 0 & 0 & 0 & 1 & 0 \\ 1 & 1 & 1 & 0 & 1 & 1 & 1 & 1 & 0 & 1 \end{bmatrix}$$

3. For $0.9959 < \tau \leq 0.9967$

$$\mathcal{P}_{ij}^{\tau} = \begin{bmatrix} 1 & 0 & 0 & 0 & 0 & 0 & 0 & 0 & 0 & 0 \\ 0 & 1 & 1 & 0 & 1 & 1 & 1 & 1 & 0 & 1 \\ 0 & 1 & 1 & 0 & 1 & 1 & 1 & 1 & 0 & 1 \\ 0 & 0 & 0 & 1 & 0 & 0 & 0 & 0 & 1 & 0 \\ 0 & 1 & 1 & 0 & 1 & 1 & 1 & 1 & 0 & 1 \\ 0 & 1 & 1 & 0 & 1 & 1 & 1 & 1 & 0 & 1 \\ 0 & 1 & 1 & 0 & 1 & 1 & 1 & 1 & 0 & 1 \\ 0 & 1 & 1 & 0 & 1 & 1 & 1 & 1 & 0 & 1 \\ 0 & 0 & 0 & 1 & 0 & 0 & 0 & 0 & 1 & 0 \\ 0 & 1 & 1 & 0 & 1 & 1 & 1 & 1 & 0 & 1 \end{bmatrix}$$

4. For $0.9967 < \tau \leq 0.9968$

$$\mathcal{P}_{ij}^{\tau} = \begin{bmatrix} 1 & 0 & 0 & 0 & 0 & 0 & 0 & 0 & 0 & 0 \\ 0 & 1 & 0 & 0 & 0 & 0 & 0 & 0 & 0 & 0 \\ 0 & 0 & 1 & 0 & 1 & 1 & 1 & 1 & 0 & 1 \\ 0 & 0 & 0 & 1 & 0 & 0 & 0 & 0 & 1 & 0 \\ 0 & 0 & 1 & 0 & 1 & 1 & 1 & 1 & 0 & 1 \\ 0 & 0 & 1 & 0 & 1 & 1 & 1 & 1 & 0 & 1 \\ 0 & 0 & 1 & 0 & 1 & 1 & 1 & 1 & 0 & 1 \\ 0 & 0 & 1 & 0 & 1 & 1 & 1 & 1 & 0 & 1 \\ 0 & 0 & 0 & 1 & 0 & 0 & 0 & 0 & 1 & 0 \\ 0 & 0 & 1 & 0 & 1 & 1 & 1 & 1 & 0 & 1 \end{bmatrix}$$

5. For $0.9968 < \tau \leq 0.9973$

$$\mathscr{P}_{ij}^{\tau} = \begin{bmatrix} 1 & 0 & 0 & 0 & 0 & 0 & 0 & 0 & 0 & 0 \\ 0 & 1 & 0 & 0 & 0 & 0 & 0 & 0 & 0 & 0 \\ 0 & 0 & 1 & 0 & 0 & 0 & 1 & 1 & 0 & 1 \\ 0 & 0 & 0 & 1 & 0 & 0 & 0 & 0 & 1 & 0 \\ 0 & 0 & 0 & 0 & 1 & 1 & 1 & 0 & 0 & 1 \\ 0 & 0 & 0 & 0 & 1 & 1 & 1 & 0 & 0 & 1 \\ 0 & 0 & 0 & 0 & 1 & 1 & 1 & 0 & 0 & 1 \\ 0 & 0 & 1 & 0 & 0 & 0 & 1 & 1 & 0 & 0 \\ 0 & 0 & 0 & 1 & 0 & 0 & 0 & 0 & 1 & 0 \\ 0 & 0 & 0 & 0 & 1 & 1 & 1 & 0 & 0 & 1 \end{bmatrix}$$

6. For $0.9973 < \tau \leq 0.9975$

$$\mathscr{P}_{ij}^{\tau} = \begin{bmatrix} 1 & 0 & 0 & 0 & 0 & 0 & 0 & 0 & 0 & 0 \\ 0 & 1 & 0 & 0 & 0 & 0 & 0 & 0 & 0 & 0 \\ 0 & 0 & 1 & 0 & 0 & 0 & 0 & 1 & 0 & 0 \\ 0 & 0 & 0 & 1 & 0 & 0 & 0 & 0 & 0 & 0 \\ 0 & 0 & 0 & 0 & 1 & 1 & 1 & 0 & 0 & 1 \\ 0 & 0 & 0 & 0 & 1 & 1 & 1 & 0 & 0 & 1 \\ 0 & 0 & 0 & 0 & 1 & 1 & 1 & 0 & 0 & 1 \\ 0 & 0 & 1 & 0 & 0 & 0 & 0 & 1 & 0 & 0 \\ 0 & 0 & 0 & 0 & 0 & 0 & 0 & 0 & 1 & 0 \\ 0 & 0 & 0 & 0 & 1 & 1 & 1 & 0 & 0 & 1 \end{bmatrix}$$

7. For $0.9975 < \tau \leq 0.9982$

$$\mathcal{P}_{ij}^{\tau} = \begin{bmatrix} 1 & 0 & 0 & 0 & 0 & 0 & 0 & 0 & 0 & 0 \\ 0 & 1 & 0 & 0 & 0 & 0 & 0 & 0 & 0 & 0 \\ 0 & 0 & 1 & 0 & 0 & 0 & 0 & 1 & 0 & 0 \\ 0 & 0 & 0 & 1 & 0 & 0 & 0 & 0 & 0 & 0 \\ 0 & 0 & 0 & 0 & 1 & 1 & 0 & 0 & 0 & 1 \\ 0 & 0 & 0 & 0 & 1 & 1 & 0 & 0 & 0 & 1 \\ 0 & 0 & 0 & 0 & 0 & 0 & 1 & 0 & 0 & 0 \\ 0 & 0 & 1 & 0 & 0 & 0 & 0 & 1 & 0 & 0 \\ 0 & 0 & 0 & 0 & 0 & 0 & 0 & 0 & 1 & 0 \\ 0 & 0 & 0 & 0 & 1 & 1 & 0 & 0 & 0 & 1 \end{bmatrix}$$

8. For $0.9982 < \tau \leq 0.9985$

$$\mathcal{P}_{ij}^{\tau} = \begin{bmatrix} 1 & 0 & 0 & 0 & 0 & 0 & 0 & 0 & 0 & 0 \\ 0 & 1 & 0 & 0 & 0 & 0 & 0 & 0 & 0 & 0 \\ 0 & 0 & 1 & 0 & 0 & 0 & 0 & 1 & 0 & 0 \\ 0 & 0 & 0 & 1 & 0 & 0 & 0 & 0 & 0 & 0 \\ 0 & 0 & 0 & 0 & 1 & 0 & 0 & 0 & 0 & 0 \\ 0 & 0 & 0 & 0 & 0 & 1 & 0 & 0 & 0 & 1 \\ 0 & 0 & 0 & 0 & 0 & 0 & 1 & 0 & 0 & 0 \\ 0 & 0 & 1 & 0 & 0 & 0 & 0 & 1 & 0 & 0 \\ 0 & 0 & 0 & 0 & 0 & 0 & 0 & 0 & 1 & 0 \\ 0 & 0 & 0 & 0 & 0 & 1 & 0 & 0 & 0 & 1 \end{bmatrix}$$

9. For $0.9985 < \tau \leq 0.9993$

$$\mathcal{P}_{ij}^{\tau} = \begin{bmatrix} 1 & 0 & 0 & 0 & 0 & 0 & 0 & 0 & 0 & 0 \\ 0 & 1 & 0 & 0 & 0 & 0 & 0 & 0 & 0 & 0 \\ 0 & 0 & 1 & 0 & 0 & 0 & 0 & 0 & 0 & 0 \\ 0 & 0 & 0 & 1 & 0 & 0 & 0 & 0 & 0 & 0 \\ 0 & 0 & 0 & 0 & 1 & 0 & 0 & 0 & 0 & 0 \\ 0 & 0 & 0 & 0 & 0 & 1 & 0 & 0 & 0 & 1 \\ 0 & 0 & 0 & 0 & 0 & 0 & 1 & 0 & 0 & 0 \\ 0 & 0 & 0 & 0 & 0 & 0 & 0 & 1 & 0 & 0 \\ 0 & 0 & 0 & 0 & 0 & 0 & 0 & 0 & 1 & 0 \\ 0 & 0 & 0 & 0 & 0 & 1 & 0 & 0 & 0 & 1 \end{bmatrix}$$

10. For $0.9993 < \tau \leq 1.00$

$$\mathcal{P}_{ij}^{\tau} = \begin{bmatrix} 1 & 0 & 0 & 0 & 0 & 0 & 0 & 0 & 0 & 1 \\ 0 & 1 & 0 & 0 & 0 & 0 & 0 & 0 & 0 & 0 \\ 0 & 0 & 1 & 0 & 0 & 0 & 0 & 0 & 0 & 0 \\ 0 & 0 & 0 & 1 & 0 & 0 & 0 & 0 & 0 & 0 \\ 0 & 0 & 0 & 0 & 1 & 0 & 0 & 0 & 0 & 0 \\ 0 & 0 & 0 & 0 & 0 & 1 & 0 & 0 & 0 & 0 \\ 0 & 0 & 0 & 0 & 0 & 0 & 1 & 0 & 0 & 0 \\ 0 & 0 & 0 & 0 & 0 & 0 & 0 & 1 & 0 & 0 \\ 0 & 0 & 0 & 0 & 0 & 0 & 0 & 0 & 1 & 0 \\ 0 & 0 & 0 & 0 & 0 & 0 & 0 & 0 & 0 & 1 \end{bmatrix}$$

Step 5: For various confidence levels τ, the corresponding clusters are presented in the Table 12.4 below.

The following points could be drawn from the table:

a) For $0 < \tau \leq 0.9956$, all ten cities are grouped together into one large cluster. This suggests that, at this level of granularity, the cities exhibit broadly similar air pollution characteristics across all pollutants.

Table 12.4 Clusters corresponding to different confidence levels.

Sr. no.	Level of confidence	Clusters
1.	$0 < \tau \leq 0.9956$	$\{u_1, u_2, u_3, u_4, u_5, u_6, u_7, u_8, u_9, u_{10}\}$
2.	$0.9956 < \tau \leq 0.9959$	$\{u_1, u_2, u_3, u_5, u_6, u_7, u_8, u_{10}\}\{u_4, u_9\}$
3.	$0.9959 < \tau \leq 0.9967$	$\{u_1\}, \{u_2, u_3, u_5, u_6, u_7, u_8, u_{10}\}\{u_4, u_9\}$
4.	$0.9967 < \tau \leq 0.9968$	$\{u_1\}, \{u_2\}, \{u_3, u_5, u_6, u_7, u_8, u_{10}\}\{u_4, u_9\}$
5.	$0.9968 < \tau \leq 0.9973$	$\{u_1\}, \{u_2\}, \{u_3, u_8\}, \{u_4, u_9\}\{u_5, u_6, u_7, u_{10}\}$
6.	$0.9973 < \tau \leq 0.9975$	$\{u_1\}, \{u_2\}\{u_4\}, \{u_9\}\{u_3, u_8\}\{u_5, u_6, u_7, u_{10}\}$
7.	$0.9975 < \tau \leq 0.9982$	$\{u_1\}, \{u_2\}, \{u_4\}, \{u_7\}, \{u_9\}, \{u_3, u_8\}, \{u_5, u_6, u_{10}\}$
8.	$0.9982 < \tau \leq 0.9985$	$\{u_1\}, \{u_2\}, \{u_4\}, \{u_5\}, \{u_7\}, \{u_9\}, \{u_3, u_8\}, \{u_6, u_{10}\}$
9.	$0.9985 < \tau \leq 0.9993$	$\{u_1\}, \{u_2\}, \{u_4\}, \{u_5\}, \{u_7\}, \{u_9\}, \{u_3\}, \{u_8\}, \{u_6, u_{10}\}$
10.	$0.9993 < \tau \leq 1.00$	$\{u_1\}, \{u_2\}, \{u_4\}, \{u_5\}, \{u_7\}, \{u_9\}, \{u_3\}, \{u_8\}, \{u_6\}, \{u_{10}\}$

b) At $0.9956 < \tau \leq 0.9959$ confidence level, Faridabad and Asansol separates from the main cluster. This indicates that these two cities have distinct pollution patterns compared to the other. It may be due to unique industrial emissions or geographical factors affecting air quality.

c) For $0.9959 < \tau \leq 0.9967$, Byrnihat forms its own cluster suggesting that its pollution characteristics diverge significantly from rest.

d) At $0.9967 < \tau \leq 0.9968$, Delhi also forms separate cluster which shows its distinct pollution profile likely influenced by extreme vehicular emissions and industrial activities.

e) For $0.9968 < \tau \leq 0.9973$, Durgapur and Gurugram distinct from the larger group. Meanwhile, Greater Noida, Sri Ganganagar, Ghaziabad and Muzaffarnagar remain clustered together due to similar air quality trends in these cities.

f) At $0.9973 < \tau \leq 0.9975$, Faridabad and Asansol each form individual clusters which implies that their pollution levels are distinct from each other and the rest of the cities.

g) For $0.9975 < \tau \leq 0.9982$, Muzaffarnagar also separates from the large cluster due to the fact that its air pollution characteristics are significantly different from other cities.

h) At $0.9982 < \tau \leq 0.9985$, Sri Ganganagar forms its own cluster which indicates that its pollution profile is now distinctly separate from the rest.

i) For $0.9985 < \tau \leq 0.9993$, Gurugram and Durgapur split into their own clusters which show unique pollution trends for these cities.

j) At the highest confidence level i.e. $0.9993 < \tau \leq 1.00$, each city is now in its own individual cluster. This final stage indicates that at this level of precision, all ten cities exhibit sufficiently unique air pollution patterns, with no significant overlap in their pollution characteristics.

12.7 Merits of the Proposed Work

In this paper, logarithmic-based distance and similarity measures are proposed which have the following advantages:

a) It overcomes the disadvantages of the existing measures such as sensitivity to small variations.

b) The proposed measure has less sensitivity to scale differences and allays the curse of dimensionality.

c) The proposed measures are mathematically proven to validate the essential properties of boundedness, symmetry and strong reflexivity.

d) The comparative analysis of the proposed measures shows that the measure effectively captures the similarity between HFSs and provides consistent rankings and strong similarity scores in decision-making scenarios.

e) The proposed measures are applied in clustering analysis of air-polluted cities, providing valuable insights for environmental policy and strategic planning.

12.8 Conclusion

In this paper, we proposed novel logarithmic-based distance and similarity measures for HFSs to overcome the limitations of existing measures. Theoretical validation confirms that the proposed measures satisfy key properties such as boundedness, symmetry, and strong reflexivity.

Comparative evaluations demonstrated that the logarithmic similarity measure captures the similarity between HFSs more effectively, providing consistent rankings and higher discrimination in decision-making contexts. The practical application to air pollution data illustrates the utility of these measures in grouping cities based on pollution levels, where uncertainty and variations in air quality data are significant. By providing greater sensitivity to smaller differences and offering better interpretability, the proposed measures present a valuable addition to decision-making scenarios where uncertainty is inherent.

Major findings include the successful theoretical validation of these measures and their application in clustering India's most polluted cities. The results of the application show how the proposed similarity measures could discriminate polluted cities according to differences in air quality data at various confidence levels.

Future work could be the adaptation of proposed measures to other multi-criteria decision-making problems such as healthcare, finance and manufacturing, extending the measures to other types of fuzzy sets such as interval valued hesitant fuzzy sets or neutrosophic hesitant fuzzy sets and exploring the use of machine learning algorithms in association with these measures for pattern recognition and predictive analytics under fuzzy environment.

12.9 Declarations

Data availability: The research data supporting the results of our manuscript have been obtained from the Central Pollution Control Board (CPCB), Government of India. The full dataset is publicly available and can be accessed at the following URL: https://cpcb.nic.in/index.php.

AI disclosure statement: The author confirms that no artificial intelligence (AI)-generated content or AI-assisted writing tools were used in the preparation of this chapter (including summaries and the abstract). All text, analysis, and conclusions are the result of the author's original work.

References

1. Zadeh, L.A., Fuzzy sets. *Inf. Control*, 8, 3, 338–353, 1965, doi: 10.1016/S0019-9958(65)90241-X.
2. Atanassov, K.T., Intuitionistic fuzzy sets. *Fuzzy Sets Syst.*, 20, 1, 87–96, Aug. 1986, doi: 10.1016/S0165-0114(86)80034-3.
3. Zadeh, L.A., The concept of a linguistic variable and its application to approximate reasoning—I. *Inf. Sci. (N. Y.)*, 8, 3, 199–249, Jan. 1975, doi: 10.1016/0020-0255(75)90036-5.
4. Miyamoto, S., Remarks on basics of fuzzy sets and fuzzy multisets. *Fuzzy Sets Syst.*, 156, 3, 427–431, Dec. 2005, doi: 10.1016/J.FSS.2005.05.040.
5. Torra, V., Hesitant fuzzy sets. *Int. J. Intell. Syst.*, 25, 6, 529–539, Jun. 2010, doi: 10.1002/INT.20418.
6. Torra, V. and Narukawa, Y., On hesitant fuzzy sets and decision. *IEEE International Conference on Fuzzy Systems*, pp. 1378–1382, 2009, doi: 10.1109/FUZZY.2009.5276884.
7. Xu, Z. and Xia, M., Distance and similarity measures for hesitant fuzzy sets. *Inf. Sci.—Informatics Computer Science, Intelligent Systems, Applications: An International Journal*, 181, 11, 2128–2138, Jun. 2011, doi: 10.1016/J.INS.2011.01.028.
8. Rodríguez, R.M., Martínez, L., Torra, V., Xu, Z.S., Herrera, F., Hesitant Fuzzy Sets: State of the Art and Future Directions. *Int. J. Intell. Syst.*, 29, 6, 495–524, Jun. 2014, doi: 10.1002/INT.21654.
9. Zhang, X. and Xu, Z., Hesitant fuzzy QUALIFLEX approach with a signed distance-based comparison method for multiple criteria decision analysis. *Expert Syst. Appl.*, 42, 2, 873–884, Feb. 2015, doi: 10.1016/J.ESWA.2014.08.056.
10. Zhang, X. and Xu, Z., The TODIM analysis approach based on novel measured functions under hesitant fuzzy environment. *Knowl. Based Syst.*, 61, 48–58, May 2014, doi: 10.1016/J.KNOSYS.2014.02.006.
11. Farhadinia, B., Information measures for hesitant fuzzy sets and interval-valued hesitant fuzzy sets. *Inf. Sci. (N. Y.)*, 240, 129–144, Aug. 2013, doi: 10.1016/J.INS.2013.03.034.
12. Farhadinia, B., Distance and similarity measures for higher order hesitant fuzzy sets. *Knowl. Based Syst.*, 55, 43–48, Jan. 2014, doi: 10.1016/J.KNOSYS.2013.10.008.
13. Peng, D.H., Gao, C.Y., Gao, Z.F., Generalized hesitant fuzzy synergetic weighted distance measures and their application to multiple criteria decision-making. *Appl. Math. Modell.*, 37, 8, 5837–5850, Apr. 2013, doi: 10.1016/J.APM.2012.11.016.
14. Zhang, X. and Xu, Z., Novel distance and similarity measures on hesitant fuzzy sets with applications to clustering analysis. *J. Intell. Fuzzy Syst.*, 28, 5, 2279–2296, Jan. 2015, doi: 10.3233/IFS-141511.

15. Zeng, W., Li, D., Yin, Q., Distance and similarity measures between hesitant fuzzy sets and their application in pattern recognition. *Pattern Recognit. Lett.*, 84, 267–271, Dec. 2016, doi: 10.1016/J.PATREC.2016.11.001.
16. Rezaei, K. and Rezaei, H., New distance and similarity measures for hesitant fuzzy sets and their application in hierarchical clustering. *J. Intell. Fuzzy Syst.*, 39, 3, 4349–4360, Jan. 2020, doi: 10.3233/JIFS-200364.
17. Liao, H., Xu, Z., Zeng, X.J., Novel correlation coefficients between hesitant fuzzy sets and their application in decision making. *Knowl. Based Syst.*, 82, 115–127, Jul. 2015, doi: 10.1016/J.KNOSYS.2015.02.020.
18. Gupta, R. and Kumar, S., Novel similarity measure between hesitant fuzzy set and their applications in pattern recognition and clustering analysis. *J. Eng. Appl. Sci.*, 71, 1, 1–26, Dec. 2024, doi: 10.1186/S44147-023-00329-Y/TABLES/12.
19. Singha, B., Sen, M., Sinha, N., Modified distance measure on hesitant fuzzy sets and its application in multi-criteria decision making problem. *OPSEARCH*, 57, 2, 584–602, Jun. 2020, doi: 10.1007/S12597-019-00431-X/TABLES/6.
20. Rahim, M., Abosuliman, S.S., Alroobaea, R., Shah, K., Abdeljawad, T., Cosine similarity and distance measures for p,q– quasirung orthopair fuzzy sets: Applications in investment decision-making. *Heliyon*, 10, 11, e32107, Jun. 2024, doi: 10.1016/J.HELIYON.2024.E32107.
21. Gupta, S., Joshi, D.K., Awasthi, N., Pant, M., Prasad Joshi, B., Chaube, S., Distance and similarity measures of Hesitant bi-fuzzy set and its applications in renewable energy systems. *Math. Comput. Simul*, 219, 321–336, May 2024, doi: 10.1016/J.MATCOM.2023.12.021.
22. Boulaaras, S., Mostafa, G.E., Jan, R., Mekawy, I., Applications of distance measure between dual hesitant fuzzy sets in medical diagnosis and weighted dual hesitant fuzzy sets in making decision. *Sci. Rep.*, 14, 1, 1–14, Oct. 2024, doi: 10.1038/s41598-024-75687-5.
23. Thakur, R., Raj, M., Malik, S.C., Correlation Coefficient Measures for Probabilistic Single Valued Neutrosophic Hesitant Fuzzy Sets and its Application in Supply Chain Management. *J. Fuzzy Ext. Appl.*, Jan. 2025, doi: 10.22105/JFEA.2025.475283.1602.
24. Garg, H., Sun, Y., Liu, X., Dual hesitant fuzzy Correlation coefficient-based decision-making algorithm and its applications to Engineering Cost Management problems. *Eng. Appl. Artif. Intell.*, 126, 107170, Nov. 2023, doi: 10.1016/J.ENGAPPAI.2023.107170.
25. Kaur, G. and Garg, H., A novel algorithm for autonomous parking vehicles using adjustable probabilistic neutrosophic hesitant fuzzy set features. *Expert Syst. Appl.*, 226, 120101, Sep. 2023, doi: 10.1016/J.ESWA.2023.120101.

26. Liao, N., Cai, Q., Garg, H., Wei, G., Xu, X., Novel Gained and Lost Dominance Score Method Based on Cumulative Prospect Theory for Group Decision-Making Problems in Probabilistic Hesitant Fuzzy Environment. *Int. J. Fuzzy Syst.*, 25, 4, 1414–1428, Jun. 2023, doi: 10.1007/S40815-022-01440-7/FIGURES/4.

Appendix

Table A1 Air quality index (AQI) categorization based on pollutant concentrations.

	PM2.5	**PM10**	**NO_2**	**SO_2**	**O_3**
Good	0–30	0–50	0–21	0–20	0–25
Satisfactory	30–60	50–100	22–43	20–40	26–51
Moderate	60–90	100–250	44–96	40–80	52–86
Poor	90–120	250–250	97–149	80–380	87–106
Very Poor	120–250	350–430	150–213	380–800	107–381
Severe	250–380	430–700	214–750	800–1600	382–450

Part IV

SMART CITIES, INFRASTRUCTURE, AND URBAN SYSTEMS

13

Linear Diophantine MEREC-COPRAS Technique in Smart Parking Systems

K. Jeevitha[1,2], J. Vimala[3*] and Muhammed Riaz[4]

[1]Center for Computational Biology, SRM Institute of Science and Technology, Ramapuram, Chennai, India
[2]Center for Research, Easwari Engineering College, Ramapuram, Chennai, India
[3]Department of Mathematics, Alagappa University, Karaikudi, Tamil Nadu, India
[4]Department of Mathematics, University of the Punjab, Lahore, Pakistan

Abstract
In the context of Linear Diophantine Fuzzy Sets (LDFS), this chapter introduces a novel hybrid decision-making technique that combines the Complex Proportional Assessment (COPRAS) approach and the Methods Based on the Removal Effects of Criteria (MEREC). Linear Diophantine Fuzzy Sets offer a complex mathematical framework that extends the capabilities of conventional fuzzy sets by reducing their inherent limitations. The MEREC method calculates unbiased criteria weights, while the COPRAS technique ranks alternatives based on their impacts and performance. The objective of this research is to present a comprehensive and efficient method for making decisions by combining the advantages of MEREC and COPRAS and demonstrating their cooperation inside the LDF framework. The effectiveness of the proposed hybrid MCDM technique is validated by providing an example that shows how it may be used to solve real-world problems. Additionally, a comprehensive analysis of a smart parking system is presented, where the method is applied to identify the ideal parking spot according to specified criteria. The results demonstrate the effectiveness and reliability of the proposed method in managing challenging decision-making scenarios, highlighting its potential for additional applications in a variety of domains.

***Keywords*:** Linear diophantine fuzzy set, MEREC, COPRAS, parking system, MCDM

**Corresponding author*: vimaljey@alagappauniversity.ac.in

Harish Garg (ed.) Decision Support Systems in Smart Computing: Embracing Uncertainty and Challenges, (415–434) © 2026 Scrivener Publishing LLC

13.1 Introduction

Multiple Criteria Decision Making (MCDM) has become a crucial field of study in many engineering and industrial fields because of its capacity to manage difficult decision-making situations with competing criteria. The study [17] provides a thorough analysis of the growing integration of MCDM approaches into software engineering procedures. It emphasizes how decisions about software development frequently require balancing trade-offs between risk, time, money, and quality. Methods like VIKOR, the Analytic Hierarchy Process (AHP), the Technique for Order Preference by Similarity to Ideal Solution (TOPSIS), Complex Proportional Assessment (COPRAS) approach and the Methods Based on the Removal Effects of Criteria (MEREC) are frequently used in software selection, risk management, and needs prioritization. David Emmanuel [19] reveals a surge in publications related to hybrid MCDM approaches that combine fuzzy logic, entropy, and optimization techniques to better capture uncertainty and stakeholder preferences.

The challenge of making optimal decisions in situations involving uncertain data, whether due to ignorance or errors, has led to the adoption of theoretical tools like fuzzy set theory [27] and its derivatives. The level of membership is insufficient to handle every situation, notwithstanding the overwhelming reaction. An intuitionistic fuzzy set (IFS) associated with non-membership grades was created by Atannosov [14]. As a generalization of IFS, Yager then presented the new theory of Pythagorean fuzzy sets (PFS) [20] with q-rung orthopair fuzzy sets (q-ROFS) [21]. The grade scores of these commonly available fuzzy sets are constrained, and thus are unable to depict specific issues.

The LDFS [16], as a groundbreaking extension of fuzzy theory, overcomes the previous limitations associated with previous approaches by incorporating reference parameters. Aiyared Iampam [10] employed several Einstein aggregation techniques to address MCDM problems using LDFS, enabling the determination of optimal solutions and the derivation of ranking insights. Saya Ayub [24] further linked algebraic properties with LDF relationships through decision-making techniques. Expanding the scope of LDFS, Riaz [9] proposed the idea of soft rough sets in material handling equipment. Additionally, Riaz [23] formulated aggregation operators based on LDF numbers to prioritize and select logistics providers. To address medical challenges, the similarity measure for LDMFS was applied in the prediction of preeclampsia [25]. Riaz [13] also developed Frank aggregation operators for interval-valued LDFNs. Vimala [18] elaborated on the attributes and applications of LDFS while formulating the MARCOS method for this framework. Farid [12] introduced prioritized linear Diophantine fuzzy

Einstein operators for practical applications. Kannan *et al.* [40] presented an LDFS clustering approach by leveraging the LDF correlation coefficient. To solve supplier selection issues, Petchimuthu [11] used IVLDF data and its aggregation operators. Also, Tehreem *et al.* [41] developed the prioritized aggregation operators based on Schweizer-Sklar t-norm for linear Diophantine fuzzy sets, which demonstrates practical applicability in green sustainable chain management. Palanikumar *et al.* [22] propose a decision framework that leverages q-rung complex Diophantine neutrosophic sets to fuse sensor data for robotic applications. Several studies have significantly contributed to the development of LDF theory, including similarity measures for decision-making problems [38], algebraic foundations of LDFS [15], and advanced spherical Linear Diophantine fuzzy soft rough set models for multi-criteria decision making [26].

The COPRAS approach was presented by Zavadskas and Kaklauskas [28] and was used to compare possibilities and determine which option was better [29]. This method can be applied to optimize criteria in a multi-factor evaluation [30]. Options are systematically rated and evaluated using the COPRAS technique according to their level of relevance and utility [31]. The foundation of this approach is linear normalization, which transforms several criteria into a common scale to enable direct comparison. Additionally, it allows decision-makers to express and include their priorities and preferences into the analysis by including the relative relevance [32]. This approach is frequently used in situations where decisions have uncertain results [33]. As a popular method for combining several aspects to make judgments, it has experienced several developments. Vahdani and Mousavi [34] proposed a novel COPRAS method that uses interval values to demonstrate the robot selection problem. Turanoglu Bekar and Cakmakci [35] developed a decision support system for improving maintenance performance by evaluating total productive maintenance (TPM) solutions using the COPRAS technique in conjunction with grey numbers theory. Mishra and Rani [36] introduced an adaptation of COPRAS technique in hesitant fuzzy sets to assess quality of the service. In order to select a green supplier, Kumari and Mishra [37] illustrated the application of intuitionistic fuzzy sets in multicriteria decision making. The study [2, 39] advances the state of MCDM by proposing a sophisticated hybrid model.

Method based on removal effects of criteria (MEREC) can be used to determine the objective weight of the criteria [8]. By employing the decision matrix to determine the weight of the criterion, these approaches do away with the need for expert evaluation. These methods often use the differences in how well various options perform across each criterion to determine the weights. The criteria that exhibit a higher degree of variance are assigned higher weights. But when deciding how much weight to give each criterion, the MEREC technique takes into account how its removal will affect the alternatives' total performance. A criterion is given more weight in the MEREC approach if eliminating it has a bigger effect on the alternatives' overall performance. In addition to assigning a weight to each criterion, this viewpoint might assist DMs in removing some factors from the decision-making process. The MEREC technique is one of the most effective ways for defining objective criterion weights which was established by Keshavarz *et al.* [1]. The integrated MEREC approach on a Fermatean fuzzy framework was introduced by Rani *et al.* [4]. A hybrid IF-MEREC-RS-DNMA technique was proposed by Hezam *et al.* [5] for assessing alternative fuel cars with an emphasis on sustainability.

Smart parking systems play a crucial role in smart city initiatives, tackling the persistent challenge of finding suitable parking spaces in densely populated urban areas, particularly near hospitals, workplaces, and shopping centers. While IoT technologies provide drivers with parking availability and road condition updates, the overwhelming information often leads to confusion and unorganized parking, contributing to traffic congestion, pollution, and wasted time. Effective parking management requires consideration of multiple factors, such as traffic conditions, parking availability, walking distance, cost, and the drivers' physical condition. This study proposes a novel approach to smart parking management using Multi-Criteria Decision-Making (MCDM) methods, specifically MEREC-COPRAS, to determine the optimal parking space. A significant contribution of this research is introducing and testing a new evaluation tool to analyze the performance of MCDM methods, offering a practical and innovative solution to improve parking systems in urban areas.

13.1.1 Motivation and Contribution of this Study

Effective decision-making frequently entails inaccurate data and ambiguity in complex contexts. Conventional fuzzy set methods have trouble managing this kind of ambiguity. This research is driven by the need to create a hybrid MCDM approach that is more resilient and adaptable in order to improve the precision, flexibility, and dependability of choices made in practical applications, such choosing the best parking spots.

The contributions of this study are presented as follows:

1. It presented a hybrid MCDM approach that combines the Linear Diophantine Fuzzy framework with the MEREC and COPRAS approaches.

2. It addressed the drawbacks of conventional fuzzy sets by utilizing the LDF framework, offering a more adaptable and effective method of managing uncertainty in decision-making.
3. The study improved the dependability of the decision-making process by using the MEREC approach to objectively enumerate the weights for criteria.
4. In order to rank the options in the LDF environment accurately and proportionately, it used the COPRAS approach.
5. In order to demonstrate the method's potential for practical applications, this research conducted a case study to apply it in choosing the best parking spots.

13.1.2 Research Gap

Despite significant advancements in multi-criteria decision-making (MCDM) methods and fuzzy set theories, challenges remain in effectively handling uncertainty and ensuring objective and reliable decision outcomes. While various hybrid MCDM approaches have been proposed, the integration of objective weighting methods with advanced fuzzy frameworks is still limited. In particular, although the Linear Diophantine Fuzzy (LDF) framework offers enhanced flexibility through its reference parameter and relaxed membership space, there has been no prior attempt to combine it with a hybrid MCDM approach that leverages both the MEREC method and the COPRAS method. This gap in the literature motivates the present study, which aims to develop and demonstrate novel LDF-MEREC-COPRAS algorithm that addresses this limitation and offers a more robust decision-making tool.

The rest of this research is structured as follows: The Preliminaries are presented in Section 13.2, which also gives the background information on MEREC, COPRAS, and LDF sets. In Section 13.3, the suggested LDF-MEREC-COPRAS method is presented, and a thorough numerical case study illustrates how to use it. The study is concluded in Section 13.4 with a summary of the results and recommendations for possible future research directions.

13.2 Preliminaries

This section provides the basic concepts and definitions. Let H is taken as a universal set throughout this paper.

Definition 2.1. [27] The fuzzy set P is characterized as

$$P = \{(\delta_i, \mu(\delta_i)) : \delta_i \in H\}$$

where μ is a mapping from a universal set to [0,1].

Definition 2.2. [14] The intuitionistic fuzzy set I is structured as

$$I = \{(\delta_i, \mu(\delta_i), v(\delta_i)) : \delta_i \in H\}$$

where μ and $v \in [0,1]$ and represent membership and non-membership degrees of the elements in universal set.

Definition 2.3. [16] A LDFS V on Δ is a structure symbolized as:

$$V = \{(\delta_i, (\mu_V(\delta_i), v_V(\delta_i)), (\alpha_V(\delta_i), \beta_V(\delta_i))) : \delta_i \in H\}$$

where, $\mu_V(\delta_i), v_V(\delta_i), \alpha_V(\delta_i), \beta_V(\delta_i) \in [0, 1]$ are degrees of satisfaction, dissatisfaction and their reference parameters respectively. These grades satisfy the condition $0 \le \alpha_V(\delta_i)\mu_V(\delta_i) + \beta_V(\delta_i)v_V(\delta_i) \le 1$ for all $\delta_i \in H$ with $0 \le \alpha_V(\delta_i) + \beta_V(\delta_i) \le 1$.

The term $(\mu_V, v_V), (\alpha_V, \beta_V)$ is referred as Linear Diophantine Fuzzy Number(LDFN).

Definition 2.4. [16] Consider two LDFN $D_1 = (\mu_{D_1}, v_{D_1}),(\alpha_{D_1}, \beta_{D_1})$ and $D_2 = (\mu_{D_2}, v_{D_2}),(\alpha_{D_2}, \beta_{D_2})$. The arithmetic operations between D_1 and D_2 are summarized as follows:

1. $D_1 \cup D_2 = ((max\{\mu_{D_1}, \mu_{D_2}\}, min\{v_{D_1}, v_{D_2}\}),(max\{\alpha_{D_1}, \alpha_{D_2}\}, min\{\beta_{D_1}, \beta_{D_2}))$
2. $D_1 \cap D_2 = ((min\{\mu_{D_1}, \mu_{D_2}\}, max\{v_{D_1}, v_{D_2}\}),(min\{\alpha_{D_1}, \alpha_{D_2}\}, max\{\beta_{D_1}, \beta_{D_2})).$
3. $D_1^c = ((v_{D_1}, \mu_{D_1}),(\beta_{D_1}, \alpha_{D_1}))$
4. $D_1 \oplus D_2 = ((\mu_{D_1} + \mu_{D_2} - \mu_{D_1}\mu_H, v_{D_1}, v_{D_2}),(\alpha_{D_1} + \alpha_{D_2} - \alpha_{D_1}\alpha_H, \beta_{D_1}, \beta_{D_2}))$
5. $D_1 \otimes D_2 = ((\mu_{D_1}\mu_{D_2}), v_{D_1} + v_{D_2} - v_{D_1}v_{D_2}, (\alpha_{D_1}\alpha_{D_2}, \beta_{D_1} + \beta_{D_2} - \beta_{D_1}\beta_{D_2}))$
6. $\sigma D_1 = ((1-(1-\mu_{D_1}^{\sigma}),(v_{D_1})^{\sigma}),(1-(1-\alpha_{D_1})^{\sigma},(\beta_{D_1})^{\sigma}))$, where σ is non-zero positive real number.
7. $D_1^{\sigma} = (((\mu_{D_1})^{\sigma}, 1-(1-v_{D_1})^{\sigma}),((\alpha_{D_1})^{\sigma}, 1-(1-\beta_{D_1})^{\sigma}))$

Definition 2.5. [16] Let D = $(\mu_D, \nu_D), (\alpha_D, \beta_D)$ be the LDFN over H. Then the Score function(Δ) of D is computed as

$$\Delta(D) = \frac{1}{2}[(\mu_D - \nu_D) + (\alpha_D - \beta_D)]$$

13.3 Proposed Hybrid LDF-MEREC-COPRAS Approach

This section comprises the LDF-MEREC-COPRAS algorithm and its numerical application in smart parking system.

13.3.1 Algorithmic Workflow of LDF-MEREC-COPRAS

The workflow of LDF-MEREC-COPRAS is constructed as follows:

Step 1: Constructing a decision matrix: The first step is to create the decision matrix using the data from the decision makers, as indicated by equation.

$$L = [l_{ij}] = \begin{bmatrix} l_{11} & l_{12} & \cdots & l_{1n} \\ l_{21} & l_{22} & \cdots & l_{2n} \\ l_{m1} & l_{m2} & \cdots & l_{mn} \end{bmatrix}$$

where $l_{ij} = \left((\mu_{l_{ij}}, \nu_{l_{ij}}), (\alpha_{l_{ij}}, \beta_{l_{ij}})\right)$ is the decision matrix element for the ith alternative in the jth criterion.

Step 2: Compute the weight of the criteria using MEREC-Method as follows:

Step 2.1: Create a LDF Decision matrix, where an element g_{rj} is a LDF value given by r^{th} decision maker (r=1,2,...,p) for j^{th} criteria (j=1,2,3,...n).

$$G = [g_{rj}] = \begin{bmatrix} g_{11} & g_{12} & \cdots & g_{1n} \\ g_{21} & g_{22} & \cdots & g_{2n} \\ g_{p1} & g_{p2} & \cdots & g_{pn} \end{bmatrix}$$

where $g_{rj} = ((\mu_{g_{rj}}, v_{g_{rj}}), (\alpha_{g_{rj}}, \beta_{g_{rj}}))$

Step 2.2: Determine the matrix of scores.

$$Y = [y_{ij}]$$

where $y_{rj} = \frac{1}{2}[(\mu_{g_{rj}} - v_{g_{rj}}) + (\alpha_{g_{rj}} - \beta_{g_{rj}})]$

Step 2.3: Compute the Overall Performance of the Alternatives using the following formula:

$$Q_r = \frac{1}{n}\sum_{j=1}^{n} ln(1 - g_{rj})$$

(r = 1,2,3,…,p)

Step 2.4: Enumerate the Performance of the Alternative by Removing Each Criterion using the following formula:

$$Q_{rj} = \frac{1}{n}\sum_{k=1, k/=j}^{n} ln(1 - g_{rk})$$

(r = 1,2,3,…,p) and (j = 1,2,3,…,n)

Step 2.5: Determine the Total Absolute Deviation

$$s_j = \sum_{r=1}^{p} |Q_{rj} - Q_r|$$

Step 2.6: Calculate the Weight of Criteria

$$\Omega_j = \frac{s_j}{\sum_{k=1}^{n} s_k}$$

Step 3: Utilizing the weights (Ω_j) determined in the preceding step, compute the weighted decision matrix.

$$L^{\Omega} = [l_{ij} * \Omega] = \begin{bmatrix} l_{11} * \Omega & l_{12} * \Omega & \dots & l_{1n} * \Omega \\ l_{21} * \Omega & l_{22} * \Omega & \dots & l_{2n} * \Omega \\ l_{m1} * \Omega & l_{m2} * \Omega & \dots & l_{mn} * \Omega \end{bmatrix}$$

where $l_{ij} * \Omega_j = ((1-(1-\mu_{l_{ij}}^{\Omega j}), (v_{l_{ij}})^{\Omega j}), (1-(1-\alpha_{l_{ij}})^{\Omega j}, (\beta_{l_{ij}})^{\Omega j}))$.

Step 4: Calculate the minimizing and maximizing indices as below:

$$\Pi_i = \bigoplus_{j \in BC} l_{ij} * \Omega_j$$

$$\Upsilon_i = \bigoplus_{j \in CC} l_{ij} * \Omega_j$$

Step 5: Compute the relative significance value.

$$\rho_i = \Delta(\Pi_i) + \frac{\sum_{i=1}^{m} \Delta(\Upsilon_i)}{\Delta(\Upsilon_i) \sum_{i=1}^{m} \frac{1}{\Delta(\Upsilon_i)}}$$

where Δ is a score function for LDF values.

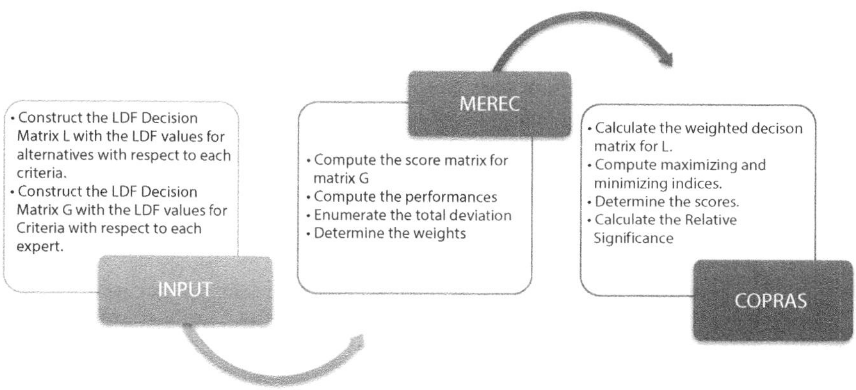

Figure 13.1 LDF-MEREC-COPRAS algorithmic flow.

Step 6: Sort the alternatives in descending order as the higher value is the most optimal.

In the Figure 13.1, the algorithm is graphically represented.

13.3.2 An Illustrative Example

The selection of parking lots for vehicles in a smart parking system is a critical aspect of modern urban planning aimed at enhancing efficiency and user convenience. Smart parking systems leverage advanced technologies such as IoT sensors, real-time data analytics, and mobile applications to identify and allocate optimal parking spaces. The selection of parking slots is influenced by several key factors, each playing a significant role in ensuring convenience, efficiency, and user satisfaction:

- **Size and Space:** Parking systems must recommend spots that are appropriate for particular vehicle sizes since inadequate space can make maneuvering difficult and increase the chance of damage to automobiles.
- **Distance:** An important consideration is how close the motorist is to their destination. Convenience is increased when parking spaces are closer to the destination (such as a hospital, retail mall, or place of employment). When closer slots aren't accessible, though, trade-offs might have to be made, necessitating a balance between availability and expense.
- **Cost:** Decisions are heavily influenced by the cost of parking. Particularly for longer trips, such those at work or public transport hubs, drivers frequently favor less expensive solutions. In metropolitan regions, dynamic pricing systems can influence choices by charging more for slots that are in great demand and offering discounts for less convenient locations.
- **Waiting Duration:** Prolonged wait times to reserve a parking space lower customer satisfaction and exacerbate traffic jams. When it comes to entry, exit, or slot allocation, drivers prefer parking systems or places with short wait periods. Waiting time can be decreased with the use of queue management systems and real-time slot availability information.
- **Accessibility:** An important consideration is the possibility of securing a spot, particularly in crowded locations during peak hours. Decision-making can be greatly improved by systems that offer real-time information on slot occupancy and availability. High availability promotes effective parking operations and lessens driver annoyance.

The efficiency of parking systems is determined by all of these elements combined. To accommodate a range of user needs, a well-designed parking management system must strike a balance between size, distance, cost, waiting time, and availability. Parking systems can optimize slot selection, enhance traffic flow, lessen their impact on the environment, and offer a smooth user experience by combining real-time monitoring, user preferences, and dynamic criterion evaluation.

Let $\{\varphi_1, \varphi_2, \varphi_3, \varphi_4, \varphi_5\}$ be the set of parking slots and $\{\psi_1, \psi_2, \psi_3, \psi_4, \psi_5\}$ be the parameters contribute for choosing best parking slot. Let $\{E_1, E_2, E_3, E_4, E_5\}$ be the set of experts.

13.3.3 Computational Workflow

Calculation of Weight by the MEREC Method

(1) Define the LDF matrix for the criteria $\{\psi_1, \psi_2, \psi_3, \psi_4, \psi_5\}$, where the LDF values were given by the experts $\{E_1, E_2, E_3, E_4, E_5\}$.

$$G=[g_{ij}]=\begin{bmatrix} (0.6,0.5),(0.2,0.7) & (0.5,0.7),(0.4,0.5) & (0.8,0.3),(0.6,0.4) & (0.7,0.5),(0.5,0.5) & (0.7,0.5),(0.5,0.4) \\ (0.7,0.2),(0.2,0.7) & (0.5,0.4),(0.4,0.5) & (0.7,0.6),(0.6,0.4) & (0.4,0.6),(0.5,0.5) & (0.6,0.4),(0.5,0.4) \\ (0.7,0.3),(0.2,0.7) & (0.7,0.6),(0.4,0.5) & (0.9,0.3),(0.6,0.4) & (0.8,0.3),(0.5,0.5) & (0.5,0.6),(0.5,0.4) \\ (0.9,0.2),(0.2,0.7) & (0.4,0.6),(0.4,0.5) & (0.8,0.4),(0.6,0.4) & (0.7,0.6),(0.5,0.5) & (0.4,0.7),(0.5,0.4) \\ (0.5,0.7),(0.2,0.7) & (0.8,0.4),(0.4,0.5) & (0.6,0.5),(0.6,0.4) & (0.9,0.3),(0.5,0.5) & (0.3,0.8),(0.5,0.4) \end{bmatrix}$$

(2) The Score matrix is computed as below:

$$Y=\begin{bmatrix} -0.2 & -0.15 & 0.35 & 0.1 & 0.15 \\ 0 & 0 & 0.15 & -0.1 & 0.15 \\ -0.05 & 0 & 0.4 & 0.25 & 0 \\ 0.1 & -0.1 & -0.15 & 0.3 & 0.05 \\ -0.35 & 0.15 & 0.15 & 0.3 & -0.2 \end{bmatrix}$$

(3) The Overall Performance of the Alternatives is calculated as

$$Q_1 = -0.075315772$$

$$Q_2 = -0.045945536$$

$$Q_3 = -0.149943506$$

$$Q_4 = -0.055651326$$

$$Q_5 = -0.039857331$$

(4) The Performance of the Alternative by Removing Each Criterion is computed as

$$[Q_{ij}] = \begin{bmatrix} -0.139725105 & -0.129085201 & 0.013551014 & -0.067804587 & -0.053514983 \\ -0.05743192 & -0.05743192 & -0.016802187 & -0.081259465 & -0.016802187 \\ -0.199626924 & -0.187429383 & -0.059722977 & -0.115508865 & -0.187429383 \\ -0.043224029 & -0.104504644 & 0.019604578 & -0.056740834 & -0.093391703 \\ -0.124847812 & -0.009191931 & -0.009191931 & 0.039347073 & -0.095402053 \end{bmatrix}$$

(5) The total deviations are calculated as

$$S_1 = 0.222996912,\ S_2 = 0.182260406,\ S_3 = 0.314151968,$$
$$S_4 = 0.157553668,\ S_5 = 0.181715113$$

(6) The weights of the criterion are enumerated as

$$\Omega_1 = 0.210637132,\ \Omega_2 = 0.172158479,\ \Omega_3 = 0.296739847,$$
$$\Omega_4 = 0.148821131,\ \Omega_5 = 0.171643409$$

Ranking of Alternatives by COPRAS Method

(1) Construct the LDF matrix with rows as alternatives $\{\varphi_1, \varphi_2, \varphi_3, \varphi_4, \varphi_5\}$ and the column as $\{\psi_1, \psi_2, \psi_3, \psi_4, \psi_5\}$.

$$L = \begin{bmatrix} (0.72,0.29),(0.93,0.04) & (0.89,0.20),(0.90,0.08) & (0.74,0.40),(0.69,0.22) & (0.63,0.35),(0.86,0.12) & (0.73,0.14),(0.81,0.11) \\ (0.84,0.20),(0.90,0.08) & (0.76,0.30),(0.86,0.12) & (0.84,0.30),(0.9,0.10) & (0.52,0.49),(0.81,0.12) & (0.83,0.46),(0.75,0.12) \\ (0.65,0.49),(0.86,0.09) & (0.62,0.48),(0.8,0.17) & (0.78,0.29),(0.85,0.14) & (0.63,0.40),(0.81,0.13) & (0.92,0.16),(0.9,0.10) \\ (0.85,0.24),(0.89,0.10) & (0.54,0.60),(0.7,0.22) & (0.73,0.40),(0.82,0.13) & (0.72,0.19),(0.84,0.11) & (0.84,0.21),(0.89,0.11) \\ (0.76,0.25),(0.84,0.09) & (0.69,0.39),(0.43,0.55) & (0.69,0.34),(0.72,0.24) & (0.86,0.15),(0.90,0.07) & (0.69,0.40),(0.74,0.16) \end{bmatrix}$$

(2) The weighted Decision matrix L^* is determined with the weights

$$\Omega_1 = 0.210637132,\ \Omega_2 = 0.172158479,\ \Omega_3 = 0.296739847,$$
$$\Omega_4 = 0.148821131,\ \Omega_5 = 0.171643409$$

$$L^{\Omega} = \begin{bmatrix} (0.235,0.770),(0.429,0.508) & (0.316,0.758),(0.327,0.647) & (0.330,0.762),(0.294,0.638) & (0.137,0.855),(0.253,0.729) & (0.201,0.713),(0.248,0.685) \\ (0.320,0.712),(0.384,0.587) & (0.218,0.813),(0.287,0.694) & (0.419,0.699),(0.495,0.505) & (0.103,0.899),(0.219,0.729) & (0.262,0.875),(0.212,0.695) \\ (0.198,0.860),(0.339,0.602) & (0.153,0.881),(0.242,0.737) & (0.362,0.692),(0.430,0.558) & (0.137,0.872),(0.219,0.738) & (0.352,0.731),(0.326,0.673) \\ (0.329,0.740),(0.372,0.616) & (0.125,0.916),(0.187,0.770) & (0.322,0.762),(0.399,0.546) & (0.173,0.781),(0.239,0.720) & (0.270,0.765),(0.315,0.685) \\ (0.260,0.747),(0.320,0.602) & (0.183,0.850),(0.092,0.902) & (0.293,0.726),(0.314,0.655) & (0.254,0.754),(0.290,0.673) & (0.182,0.854),(0.206,0.730) \end{bmatrix}$$

(3) The maximizing indices are enumerated as

$$\Pi_1 = (0.340, 0.659), (0.574, 0.370)$$

$$\Pi_2 =(0.390, 0.641), (0.519, 0.428)$$

$$\Pi_3 =(0.309, 0.751), (0.484, 0.444)$$

$$\Pi_4 =(0.445, 0.578), (0.522, 0.443)$$

$$\Pi_5 =(0.447, 0.563), (0.517, 0.405)$$

The minimizing indices are enumerated as

$$\Upsilon_1 = (0.634, 0.412), (0.643, 0.283)$$

$$\Upsilon_2 =(0.665, 0.498), (0.716, 0.244)$$

$$\Upsilon_3 =(0.650, 0.446), (0.709, 0.277)$$

$$\Upsilon_4 =(0.567, 0.534), (0.665, 0.288)$$

$$\Upsilon_5 =(0.528, 0.528), (0.506, 0.431)$$

(4) The score of the Π_i and Υ_i is calculated as

$$\Delta(\Pi_1)= -0.058,\ \Delta(\Pi_2)=-0.080,$$

$$\Delta(\Pi_3)=-0.201,\ \Delta(\Pi_4)=-0.027,$$

$$\Delta(\Pi_5)=-0.002,\ \Delta(\Upsilon_1) = 0.290,$$

$$\Delta(\Upsilon_2) = 0.320,\ \Delta(\Upsilon_3) = 0.318,$$

$$\Delta(\Upsilon_4) = 0.205, \Delta(\Upsilon_5) = 0.037$$

(5) The relative significance values are computed as

$$\rho_1 = 0.040, \rho_2 = 0.009, \rho_3 = -0.112, \rho_4 = 0.111, \rho_5 = 0.755.$$

(6) The alternatives are ranked as follows:

$$\varphi_5 > \varphi_4 > \varphi_1 > \varphi_2 > \varphi_3$$

Result and Discussion: By the results, the parking slot φ_5 is the most suitable slot (Refer Figure 13.2). By incorporating MCDM methods like the Linear Diophantine MEREC-COPRAS approach, these systems evaluate various factors such as proximity to the destination, cost, space availability, and security. This ensures not only the optimal utilization of parking resources but also a reduction in traffic congestion and fuel wastage caused by prolonged searches for parking. Such intelligent systems provide a seamless and user-friendly experience, contributing to smarter and more sustainable urban mobility solutions.

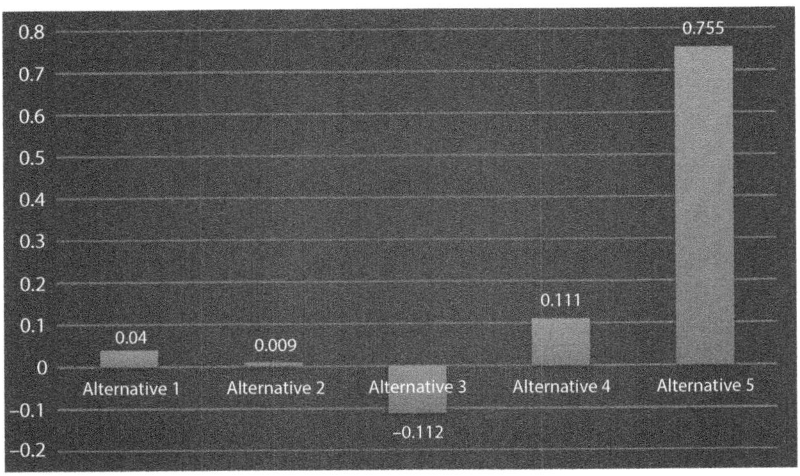

Figure 13.2 Ranking of alternatives.

13.3.4 Comparative Analysis

The suggested hybrid LDF-MEREC-COPRAS strategy outperforms other fuzzy-based MCDM techniques in a variety of ways, demonstrated by an extensive comparison. Fuzzy TOPSIS, Fuzzy VIKOR, and Fuzzy COPRAS are examples of traditional fuzzy algorithms that mainly take into account membership values, neglecting non-membership variables that are just as significant in real-world decision-making. On the other hand, our suggested approach successfully integrates both membership and non-membership elements using the linear Diophantine fuzzy framework, guaranteeing a more thorough and precise depiction of uncertainty. Additionally, while handling non-membership values, intuitionistic fuzzy set (IFS)-based techniques such as IFS-TOPSIS, IFS-VIKOR, IFS-COPRAS, and IFS-based aggregation operators frequently fall short of upholding the necessary requirement that the sum of membership and non-membership degrees not exceed 1. IFS models become unreliable when this requirement is violated, but our suggested model is still strong and mathematically valid. The definitions of reference parameters, which are essential in intricate decision-making contexts, are also absent from more sophisticated fuzzy extensions like Pythagorean fuzzy sets [2, 6] and fermatean fuzzy sets [7]. Furthermore, newer LDF-based models like LDF-MARCOS, LDF-CODAS, LDF-TOPSIS, and LDF-VIKOR rely on decision makers' subjectively assigned weights rather than offering a methodical way to determine weights. By incorporating the MEREC technique, which impartially and accurately determines the weights of criteria based on redundancy and contribution, our approach overcomes this restriction. The suggested hybrid model, which combines the advantages of the LDF framework with MEREC and COPRAS, improves computational reliability and decision correctness, making it a more effective and efficient tool for resolving challenging MCDM issues.

13.3.5 Merits of this Study

The following are the merits of the proposed method:

1. A reference parameter is incorporated into the Linear Diophantine Fuzzy (LDF) framework, allowing for more flexible and realistic modeling of uncertainty by relaxing the range of membership space.
2. In comparison to traditional MCDM techniques, the hybrid application of MEREC and COPRAS provides better

performance by guaranteeing both objective weighing of criteria and efficient ranking of alternatives.

3. The suggested framework makes it possible to make decisions in situations with imprecise or ambiguous facts with more accuracy and dependability.

13.4 Conclusion

This work introduces an innovative approach that blends MCDM methodologies, specifically MEREC-COPRAS, in order to locate the most appropriate parking places, thereby addressing the major difficulties of smart parking in urban contexts. The suggested framework ensures an exhaustive and user-centered parking management system by taking into account a variety of parameters, including traffic conditions, parking availability, walking distance, cost, and the physical state of the driver. The new assessment tool for MCDM techniques is being developed and tested, which will further improve the solution's applicability and resilience. This creative method not only makes parking selection easier, but it also helps to cut down on pollution, traffic, and resource waste, opening the door for more intelligent and environmentally friendly urban transportation solutions. Our next challenge is to implement new hybrid approaches in the LDF framework, such as CRITIC-TOPSIS, DEMATEL-VIKOR, MABAC, and EDAS.

13.5 Acknowledgments

The chapter has been written with the financial support of RUSA-Phase 2.0(F 24-51/2014-U).

AI disclosure statement: The author confirms that no artificial intelligence (AI)-generated content or AI-assisted writing tools were used in the preparation of this chapter (including summaries and the abstract). All text, analysis, and conclusions are the result of the author's original work.

Bibliography

1. Keshavarz-Ghorabaee, M., Amiri, M., Zavadskas, E.K., Turskis, Antucheviciene, J., Determination of objective weights using a new method

based on the removal effects of criteria (MEREC). *Symmetry*, 13, 4, 525, 2021, https://doi.org/10.3390/sym13040525.

2. Biswas, A. and Sarkar, B., Pythagorean fuzzy TOPSIS for multicriteria group decision-making with unknown weight information through entropy measure. *Int. J. Intell. Syst.*, 34, 6, 11081128, 2019.
3. Ozdemir, Y. and Gl, M., Measuring development levels of NUTS-2 regions in Turkey based on capabilities approach and multi-criteria decision-making. *Comput. Ind. Eng.*, 128, 150169, 2019.
4. Rani, P., Mishra, A.R., Saha, A., Hezam, I.M., Pamucar, D., Fermatean fuzzy Heronian mean operators and MEREC-based additive ratio assessment method: an application to food waste treatment technology selection. *Int. J. Intell. Syst.*, 37, 3, 26122647, 2022.
5. Hezam, I.M., Mishra, A.R., Rani, P., Cavallaro, F., Saha, A., Ali, J., Streimikiene, D., A hybrid intuitionistic fuzzy-MEREC-RS DNMA method for assessing the alternative fuel vehicles with sustainability perspectives. *Sustainability*, 14, 9, 5463, 2022, https://doi.org/10.3390/su14095463.
6. Chaurasiya, R. and Jain, D., Hybrid MCDM method on Pythagorean fuzzy set and its application. *Decis. Mak. Appl. Manag. Eng.*, 6, 1, 379398, 2022.
7. Mishra, A.R., Chen, S.M., Rani, P., Multicriteria decision making based on novel score function of Fermatean fuzzy numbers, the CRITIC method, and the GLDS method. *Inf. Sci.*, 623, 915931, 2023.
8. Mishra, A.R., Saha, A., Rani, P., Hezam, I.M., Shrivastava, R., Smarandache, F., An integrated decision support framework using single-valued-MEREC-MULTIMOORA for low carbon tourism strategy assessment. *IEEE Access*, 10, 2441124432, 2022, https://doi.org/10.1109/ACCESS.2022.3155171.
9. Riaz, M., Hashmi, M., Kalsoom, H., Pamucar, D., Chu, M., Linear Diophantine fuzzy soft rough sets for the selection of sustainable material handling equipment. *Symmetry*, 12, 1215, 2020, https://doi.org/10.3390/sym12101215.
10. Iampan, A., Garcia, G.S., Riaz, M., Farid, H.M.A., Chinram, R., Linear Diophantine fuzzy Einstein aggregation operators for multi-criteria decision-making problems. *J. Math.*, Article ID 131, 2021, https://doi.org/10.1155/2021/6742319.
11. Petchimuthu, S., Riaz, M., Kamaci, H., Correlation coefficient measures and aggregation operators on interval-valued linear Diophantine fuzzy sets and their applications. *Comput. Appl. Math.*, 41, 409430, 2022.
12. Farid, H.M.A., Riaz, M., Khan, M.J., Kumam, P., Sitthithakerngkiet, K., Sustainable thermal power equipment supplier selection by Einstein prioritized linear Diophantine fuzzy aggregation operators. *AIMS Math.*, 7, 1120111242, 2022.
13. Riaz, M., Farid, H.M., Wang, W., Pamucar, D., Interval-valued linear Diophantine fuzzy Frank aggregation operators with multi-criteria decision-making. *Mathematics*, 10, 1811, 2022, https://doi.org/10.3390/math10101811.
14. Atanassov, K.T., Intuitionistic fuzzy sets. *Fuzzy Set Syst.*, 20, 1, 8796, 1986.

15. Kamaci, H., Linear Diophantine fuzzy algebraic structures. *J. Ambient Intell. Hum. Comput.*, 12, 1035310373, 2021.
16. Riaz, M. and Hashmi, M.R., Linear Diophantine fuzzy set and its applications towards multi-attribute decision-making problems. *J. Intell. Fuzzy Syst.*, 37, 54175439, 2019.
17. Mohmmed, S., Oleiwi, A., Asman, T., Saleh, H., Mahmood, A., Avci, I., Survey of MCDM-based software engineering methods. *Babylonian J. Math.*, 13, 1318, 2024, https://doi.org/10.58496/BJM/2024/002.
18. Jayakumar, V., Kannan, J., Kausar, N., Deveci, M., Wen, X., Multicriteria group decision making for prioritizing IoT risk factors with linear Diophantine fuzzy sets and MARCOS method. *Granular Comput.*, 9, 3, 2024, May, https://doi.org/10.1007/s41066-024-00480-8.
19. David Emmanuel, D. and Alamoodi, A., A bibliometric analysis of research on multiple criteria decision making with emphasis on energy sector between 20192023. *Appl. Data Sci. Anal.*, 143–149, 2023, https://doi.org/10.58496/ADSA/2023/013.
20. Yager, R.R., Pythagorean membership grades in multicriteria decision making. *IEEE Trans. Fuzzy Syst.*, 22, 4, 958965, 2014.
21. Yager, R.R., Generalized orthopair fuzzy sets. *IEEE Trans. Fuzzy Syst.*, 25, 5, 12221230, 2017.
22. Palanikumar, M., Kausar, N., Garg, H., Kadry, S., Kim, J., Robotic sensor based on score and accuracy values in q-rung complex Diophantine neutrosophic normal set with an aggregation operation. *Alexandria Eng. J.*, 77, 149164, 2023, https://doi.org/10.1016/j.aej.2023.06.064.
23. Riaz, M., Farid, H.M.A., Aslam, M., Pamucar, D., Bozanic, D., Novel approach for third-party reverse logistic provider selection process under linear Diophantine fuzzy prioritized aggregation operators. *Symmetry*, 13, 1152, 2021, https://doi.org/10.3390/sym13071152.
24. Ayub, S., Shabir, M., Riaz, M., Aslam, M., Chinram, R., Linear Diophantine fuzzy relations and their algebraic properties with decision making. *Symmetry*, 13, 6, 945, 2021, https://doi.org/10.3390/sym13060945.
25. Kannan, J., Jayakumar, V., Kausar, N., *et al.*, Enhancing decision-making with linear Diophantine multi-fuzzy set: application of novel information measures in medical and engineering fields. *Sci. Rep.*, 14, 28537, 2024, https://doi.org/10.1038/s41598-024-79725-0.
26. Hashmi, M.R., Tehrim, S.T., Riaz, M., Pamucar, D., Cirovic, G., Spherical linear Diophantine fuzzy soft rough sets with multi-criteria decision making. *Axioms*, 10, 185, 2021, https://doi.org/10.3390/axioms10070185.
27. Zadeh, L.A., Fuzzy sets. *Inf. Control*, 8, 3, 338353, 1965.
28. Zavadskas, E.K., Kaklauskas, A., Šarka, S., The new method of multicriteria evaluation of projects. *Technol. Econ. Dev. Econ.*, 1, 3, 131139, 1996, Available from etalpykla.

29. Zavadskas, E.K., Kaklauskas, A., Vilutiene, T., Multicriteria evaluation of apartment blocks maintenance contractors: Lithuanian case study. *Int. J. Strateg. Prop. Manag.*, 13, 4, 319338, 2009, https://doi.org/10.3846/1648-715X.2009.13.319-338.
30. Podvezko, V., The comparative analysis of MCDA methods SAW and COPRAS. *Eng. Econ.*, 22, 2, 134146, 2011, https://doi.org/10.5755/j01.ee.22.2.310.
31. Kaklauskas, A., Zavadskas, E.K., Naimaviciene, J., *et al.*, Model for a complex analysis of intelligent built environment. *Autom. Constr.*, 19, 3, 326340, 2010, https://doi.org/10.1016/j.autcon.2009.12.006.
32. Zavadskas, E.K., Turskis, Kildiene, S., State of art surveys of overviews on MCDM/MADM methods. *Technol. Econ. Dev. Econ.*, 20, 1, 165179, 2014, https://doi.org/10.3846/20294913.2014.892037.
33. Ghorabaee, M.K., Amiri, M., Sadaghiani, J.S., *et al.*, Multiple criteria group decision-making for supplier selection based on COPRAS method with interval type-2 fuzzy sets. *Int. J. Adv. Manuf. Technol.*, 75, 5, 11151130, 2014, https://doi.org/10.1007/s00170-014-6142-7.
34. Vahdani, B., Mousavi, S.M., Tavakkoli-Moghaddam, R., *et al.*, Robot selection by a multiple criteria complex proportional assessment method under an interval-valued fuzzy environment. *Int. J. Adv. Manuf. Technol.*, 73, 5, 687697, 2014, https://doi.org/10.1007/s00170-014-5849-9.
35. Bekar, E.T., Cakmakci, M., Kahraman, C., Fuzzy COPRAS method for performance measurement in total productive maintenance: a comparative analysis. *J. Bus. Econ. Manag.*, 17, 5, 663684, 2016, https://doi.org/10.3846/16111699.2016.1202314.
36. Mishra, A.R., Rani, P., Pardasani, K.R., Multiple-criteria decision-making for service quality selection based on Shapley COPRAS method under hesitant fuzzy sets. *Granular Comput.*, 4, 3, 435449, 2019, https://doi.org/10.1007/s41066-018-0103-8.
37. Kumari, R. and Mishra, A.R., Multi-criteria COPRAS method based on parametric measures for intuitionistic fuzzy sets: application of green supplier selection. *Iran. J. Sci. Technol. Trans. Electr. Eng.*, 44, 4, 16451662, 2020, https://doi.org/10.1007/s40998-020-00312-w.
38. Mohammad, M.M.S., Abdullah, S., Al-Shomrani, M.M., Some linear Diophantine fuzzy similarity measures and their application in decision-making problem. *IEEE Access*, 10, 2985929877, 2022, https://doi.org/10.1109/ACCESS.2022.3151684.
39. Gao, K., Liu, T., Rong, Y., Simic, V., Garg, H., Senapati, T., A novel BWM-entropy-COPRAS group decision framework with spherical fuzzy information for digital supply chain partner selection. *Complex Intell. Syst.*, 10, 69837008, 2024, https://doi.org/10.1007/s40747-024-01500-5.

40. Kannan, J., Jayakumar, V., Saeed, M., Alballa, T., Khalifa, H.A.E.-W., Gomaa, H.G., Linear Diophantine fuzzy clustering algorithm based on correlation coefficient and analysis on logistic efficiency of food products. *IEEE Access*, 2024, https://doi.org/10.1109/ACCESS.2024.3371986.
41. Tehreem, A., Harish, G., Xiaodi, L., Walim, E., Prioritized aggregation operators based on Schweizer-Sklar t-norm for linear Diophantine fuzzy sets and their application in green sustainable chain. *Alex. Eng. J.*, 82, 587–600, 2023, 10.1016/j.aej.2023.09.033.

14

Synergizing Hexagonal Fuzzy Numbers and Fuzzy Graph-Based Weighting Mechanisms in Advanced WASPAS for Parking Lot Selection

Kishor C and Jagadeeswari Murugan*

Department of Mathematics, School of Advanced Sciences, Vellore Institute of Technology, Vellore, Tamil Nadu, India

Abstract

The selection of parking lot is a decision influenced by factors such as cost, location, and security, helping to determine the most convenient choice. This work proposes a fuzzy weighted aggregated sum product assessment (WASPAS) approach for identifying the optimal parking lot, utilizing LR representation of hexagonal fuzzy numbers to encapsulate imprecise and uncertain data. The fuzzy graph-based method is utilized to ascertain the criteria's weights by modeling the interrelations and impacts among various parameters. The suggested approach integrates the fuzzy weighted sum and fuzzy weighted product models, utilizing the weights obtained from the fuzzy graph to modify the ratings for each alternative parking facility. This facilitates a more precise evaluation of alternatives in situations where the given data is ambiguous or imprecise. This method efficiently captures the interactions among the criteria by combining fuzzy graphs, so offering a flexible framework for evaluating parking lots. This study indicates that the fuzzy graph-based fuzzy WASPAS method offers a resilient and adaptable decision-making method for parking lot selection, addressing ambiguity in the interactions among criteria. This method provides an effective solution for identifying the optimal parking facility based on several ambiguous criteria, hence improving the decision-making process in transportation and urban planning.

Keywords: LR hexagonal fuzzy number, fuzzy WASPAS, criteria weighting, parking lot evaluation, fuzzy graph

**Corresponding author*: jagadeeswari.m@vit.ac.in

Harish Garg (ed.) Decision Support Systems in Smart Computing: Embracing Uncertainty and Challenges, (435–468) © 2026 Scrivener Publishing LLC

14.1 Introduction

In the present world, the increasing use of personal vehicles is leading to significant challenges in parking availability in major cities, particularly during peak hours. Parking lots serve a key role in urban infrastructure by providing defined locations for vehicle storage, promoting orderly traffic circulation, and minimizing congestion. Efficient parking management is vital for promoting urban mobility, lowering fuel use, and improving overall transportation efficiency. With fast urbanization and an increasing number of vehicles, the demand for well-planned parking solutions has grown dramatically. Poor parking infrastructure can lead to traffic congestion, increased travel times, greater pollution levels, and inconvenience for commuters. Thus, maximizing the selection of parking lots is a crucial task in urban planning and transportation systems. A wide range of sensors installed in the parking area facilitates the identification of available parking spaces, with information readily accessible to users *via* the internet. Selecting the best parking lot is a complex multi-criteria decision-making (MCDM) problem which considers cost, availability, location, security, environmental impact, and so on as criteria. Based on people's needs, they'll prioritize these variables differently. A lot of traditional MCDM procedures presume all relevant data is exact and well-defined, but the real-world parking selection scenarios are often unclear. Variable parking costs, security perceptions, and availability provide issues that typical deterministic approaches cannot address. A well-established framework for MCDM helps make decisions with competing criteria. Many MCDM methods let decision-makers rank alternatives based on various parameters. However, conventional methods generally assume that choice criteria are independent and assign precise numerical values, which may not be realistic in practice. To solve these issues, fuzzy set theory has emerged as a valuable tool in decision-making processes by allowing for the representation of imprecise and uncertain data. Fuzzy logic provides a mathematical foundation to quantify subjective assessments, making it particularly beneficial in parking lot selection. Among several fuzzy-based approaches, the Weighted aggregated sum product assessment (WASPAS) method has gained importance due to its ability to integrate both additive and multiplicative decision models. However, classic fuzzy WASPAS methods rely on subjective expert judgments or fixed weight assignment procedures, which may not sufficiently capture the interdependencies among decision criteria.

14.1.1 Literature Review

Fuzzy set theory [1], introduced by Zadeh, laid the groundwork for handling uncertainty, which was later extended to fuzzy graphs [2] by Rosenfeld and applied to clustering [3] by Yeh and Bang. Aliniai *et al.* [4] utilized GIS-based MCDM methods for sustainable parking site selection. The application of fuzzy MCDM expanded with Turskis *et al.* [5] who evaluated EU infrastructure. In 2021, Chakraborty *et al.* [6] and Nayagam and Murugan [7] introduced hexagonal fuzzy numbers and approximations for improved decision modeling, while Demir *et al.* [8] addressed parking site selection in Istanbul. Amari *et al.* [9] emphasized health-based criteria in parking lot decisions, and Gazi *et al.* [10] proposed a hexagonal fuzzy MCDM model for restaurant location ranking. Kaur and Garg [11] applied neutrosophic hesitant fuzzy sets to autonomous parking, while Ali *et al.* [12] explored fuzzy graph clustering in dynamical systems.

14.1.2 Research Gap

Despite having tremendous advanced approaches in fuzzy MCDM, many present methodologies typically fall short in properly addressing the multidimensional uncertainty inherent in real-world decisions. Asymmetry and imprecise judgments are difficult to capture by triangular or trapezoidal fuzzy numbers. Inter-criteria interactions are sometimes simplified using fixed weights or basic aggregation methods, which fail to reflect genuine dependencies between characteristics like cost, distance, and security. Although fuzzy graphs provide a valuable tool for modeling such interrelationships, their integration with advanced fuzzy aggregation approaches remains underdeveloped. Furthermore, the WASPAS method, while fast in merging additive and multiplicative models has been rarely modified to accommodate criteria specified through LR-based hexagonal fuzzy numbers or to apply fuzzy graph-derived weights. This highlights a major research gap in building a robust, uncertainty-resilient, and structurally informed fuzzy decision-making framework that synergistically blends LR hexagonal fuzzy numbers, fuzzy graphs, and the WASPAS approach for complex urban planning challenges.

14.1.3 Motivation

This study is motivated to improve decision-making approach in parking lot selection, where data is sometimes unclear in which variables like cost, distance, and security are interconnected. LR representation of hexagonal fuzzy numbers offers a more flexible and accurate technique to model such imprecise information compared to other fuzzy numbers. Along with this fuzzy graph efficiently captures the dependencies among criteria, which provides more accurate weight assignment. While incorporating these into the WASPAS method, the suggested strategy offers a robust and adaptive framework for picking the ideal parking facility under uncertainty which combines additive and multiplicative evaluation.

14.1.4 Research Objectives and Novelty

- To formulate an advanced fuzzy WASPAS model incorporating LR representation of hexagonal fuzzy numbers.
- Fuzzy graphs can be used to derive criteria weights, which capture the structural dependencies among criteria.
- To develop an integrated approach that uses induced LR hexagonal fuzzy numbers in both the weighted sum and weighted product models of WASPAS.
- To demonstrate the applicability of the proposed method in evaluating parking lot options under multiple ambiguous criteria.

The remainder of this paper is organized as follows. In, Section 14.2 the essential preliminaries related to fuzzy set theory and MCDM frameworks are presented, Section 14.3 introduces the concept of LR hexagonal fuzzy numbers which highlights their structure and mathematical formulation. In Section 14.4, a set of ranking measures based on score functions is proposed for effectively comparing LR generalized hexagonal fuzzy numbers. Section 14.5 details the development of the fuzzy WASPAS method integrated with LR hexagonal fuzzy numbers, where the weights of the criteria are derived using a fuzzy graph-based approach to capture the inter-dependencies among criteria. Section 14.6 applies the proposed methodology to a real-life parking lot selection case study. Section 14.7 discusses the outcomes, proving the method's efficacy, and Section 14.8 closes with major discoveries, limits, and future study.

14.2 Preliminaries

This section provides essential concepts and definitions required for the proposed fuzzy WASPAS approach. It includes an overview of fuzzy set theory, hexagonal fuzzy numbers, fuzzy graphs, ranking measures for hexagonal fuzzy numbers. These fundamental concepts serve as the foundation for developing the decision-making framework in this study.

Definition 14.2.1. (Fuzzy set) [1] A fuzzy set N, on a universal set U is defined as a set of ordered pairs $N = \{(u, \sigma_N(u)) | u \in U\}$, where $\sigma_N(u)$ is the membership function for N and for every element u in U, takes value from 0 to 1.

Definition 14.2.2. (Support of N) [1] The *support* of a fuzzy set N is the set of all points $u \in U$ such that $\sigma_N(u) > 0$, that is $Support(N) = \{u | \sigma_N(u) > 0\}$.

Definition 14.2.3. (τ -cut of N) [1] The τ *-cut* of a fuzzy set N is defined as $N^\tau = \{u | \sigma_N(u) \geq \tau\}$, where $\tau \in [0, 1]$.

Definition 14.2.4. (Fuzzy number) [13] A *fuzzy number* N is a type of fuzzy set, defined over the real number line $\mathbb{R}$, where its membership is partial retained, ensuring the existence of some $u_0 \in U$, such that $\sigma_N(u_0) = 1$. The membership function defined in $[a, b]$ is given as

$$\sigma_{\mathcal{N}}(u) = \begin{cases} h_1(u) & \text{if } u \in [-\infty, a] \\ 1 & \text{if } u \in [a, b] \\ h_2(u) & \text{if } u \in [b, \infty] \end{cases}$$

where h_1 is a continuous monotonic increasing function and h_2 is a continuous monotonic decreasing function and $\sigma_N(u) = 0$ for all $u \notin [a, b]$.

Definition 14.2.5. (Generalized hexagonal fuzzy number) [7] A fuzzy number $N = (n_1, n_2, n_3, n_4, n_5, n_6; h, h_L, h_R)$ defined on R is known to be *Generalized hexagonal fuzzy number (GHexFN)*, if its membership function is defined as

$$\mathcal{N}(x) = \begin{cases} h_L\left(\dfrac{x - n_1}{n_2 - n_1}\right) & \text{if } x \in [n_1, n_2] \\ h_L + (h - h_L)\left(\dfrac{x - n_2}{n_3 - n_2}\right) & \text{if } x \in [n_2, n_3] \\ h & \text{if } x \in [n_3, n_4] \\ h_R + (h - h_R)\left(\dfrac{n_5 - x}{n_5 - n_4}\right) & \text{if } x \in [n_4, n_5] \\ h_R\left(\dfrac{n_6 - x}{n_6 - n_5}\right) & \text{if } x \in [n_5, n_6] \\ 0 & \textit{otherwise} \end{cases} \quad (14.1)$$

where $n_1 \leq n_2 \leq n_3 \leq n_4 \leq n_5 \leq n_6 \in R$; h, h_L, $h_R \in [0, 1]$ and $h_L \leq h$, $h_R \leq h$ with the restrictions $h_L(n_3 - n_2) \neq (h - h_L)(n_2 - n_1)$ and $h_R(n_5 - n_4) \neq (h - h_R)(n_6 - n_5)$, equivalently, $h_L(n_3 - n_1) \neq h(n_2 - n_1)$ and $h_R(n_6 - n_4) \neq h(n_6 - n_5)$. If $h = 1$, then the *GHexFN* is said to be *HexFN*.

Definition 14.2.6. (Midpoint score) [7] The *midpoint score* (M) of the *GHexFN* $N = (n_1, n_2, n_3, n_4, n_5, n_6; h, h_L, h_R)$ is defined as $M(N) = h\frac{(n_3 + n_4)}{2}$

Definition 14.2.7. (Span score) [7] The *span* (S) of the *GHexFN* $N = (n_1, n_2, n_3, n_4, n_5, n_6; h, h_L, h_R)$ is defined as $S(N) = h\frac{(n_4 - n_3)}{2}$

Definition 14.2.8. (Left dissimilitude) [7] The *left dissimilitude* (LD) score of the *GHexFN* $N = (n_1, n_2, n_3, n_4, n_5, n_6; h, h_L, h_R)$ is defined as $LD(N) = \frac{h_L(n_3 - n_1) - h(n_2 - n_1)}{4}$

Definition 14.2.9. (Left aggregation) [7] The *left aggregation* (LA) score of the *GHexFN* $N = (n_1, n_2, n_3, n_4, n_5, n_6; h, h_L, h_R)$ is defined as $LA(N) = \frac{h_L(n_3 - n_1) + h(n_2 - n_1)}{4}$

Definition 14.2.10. (Right dissimilitude) [7] The *right dissimilitude* (RD) score of the *GHexFN* $N = (n_1, n_2, n_3, n_4, n_5, n_6; h, h_L, h_R)$ is defined as $RD(N) = \frac{h_R(n_6 - n_4) - h(n_6 - n_5)}{4}$

Definition 14.2.11. (Right aggregation) [7] The *right aggregation* (RA) score of the *GHexFN* $N = (n_1, n_2, n_3, n_4, n_5, n_6; h, h_L, h_R)$ is defined as $RA(N) = \frac{h_L(n_6 - n_4) + h(n_6 - n_5)}{4}$

The definition 14.2.6, 14.2.7, 14.2.8, 14.2.9, 14.2.10, 14.2.11 are the ranking measures for hexagonal fuzzy numbers.

Definition 14.2.12. (Fuzzy Graphs) [14] A *fuzzy graph* $G = (V, \sigma, \mu)$ is a ordered triplet, where V is a non-empty vertex set with $\sigma: V \rightarrow [0, 1]$ represents vertex membership and $\mu: V \times V \rightarrow [0, 1]$ represents edge membership with condition $\mu(C_1, C_2) \leq min[\sigma(C_1), \sigma(C_2)]$, where $C_i \in V$. The fuzzy graph can also be mentioned as $G = (\sigma, \mu)$

Definition 14.2.13. (Degree of the node) [14] The *degree of node* $C \in V$, of the fuzzy graph G is defined by

$$\mathbf{d}(C) = \sum \mu(C, C_i)$$

$\forall C_i \in V - \{C\}$, where $\mu(C, C_i)$ is the edge membership. The total degree is defined as $\mathcal{TD} = \sum_i \mathbf{d}(C_i)$.

14.3 Concepts of LR Hexagonal Fuzzy Number

LR generalized hexagonal fuzzy numbers give a structured representation of uncertainty by extending traditional fuzzy numbers with six key parameters. These numbers incorporate left and right membership functions to depict progressive transitions in uncertain data. To facilitate computational applications, it is required to develop operations such as addition, scalar multiplication, and division. Additionally, weighted aggregation techniques play a crucial role in combining multiple fuzzy values while preserving their inherent. This section officially defines LR generalized hexagonal fuzzy numbers and investigates their essential arithmetic features, and introduces weighted aggregation method to boost their application in decision-making and optimization situations.

Definition 14.3.1. (LR representation of *GHexFN*) A LR fuzzy number N $= (m, n : s_1, s_2, s_3, s_4; s, s_L, s_R)$ defined on R is said to be *LR generalized hexagonal fuzzy number (LR-GHexFN)* with the membership function defined as

$$\mathcal{N}(x) = \begin{cases} s_L\left(\dfrac{(x-m)+(s_1+s_2)}{s_1}\right) & \text{if } x \in [m-s_2-s_1, m-s_2] \\ s_L + (s-s_L)\left(\dfrac{(x-m)+s_2}{s_2}\right) & \text{if } x \in [m-s_2, m] \\ s & \text{if } x \in [m,n] \\ s_R + (s-s_R)\left(\dfrac{(n-x)+s_3}{s_3}\right) & \text{if } x \in [n, n+s_3] \\ s_R\left(\dfrac{(n-x)+(s_3+s_4)}{s_4}\right) & \text{if } x \in [n+s_3, n+s_3+s_4] \\ 0 & \textit{otherwise} \end{cases} \tag{14.2}$$

where $m - s_2 - s_1 \leq m - s_2 \leq m \leq n \leq n + s_3 \leq n + s_3 + s_4$, $s_L \leq s$, $s_R \leq s$ with restrictions $s_L(s_2) \neq (s - s_L)(s_1)$ and $s_R(s_3) \neq (s - s_R)(s_4)$, equivalently $s_L(s_1 + s_2) \neq s(s_1)$ and $s_R(s_3 + s_4) \neq s(s_4)$. If $s = 1$, then the *LR-GHexFN* becomes *LR-HexFN*. The *LR-GHexFN* can be represented as *GHexFN* as N = $(m - s_2$

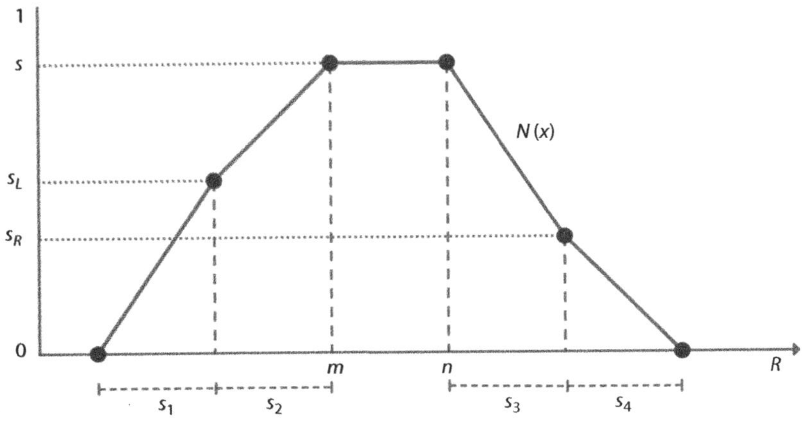

Figure 14.1 LR G-HexFN.

$- s_1, m - s_2, m, n, n + s_3, n + s_3 + s_4; s, s_L, s_R$). The LR-GHexFN is given in the Figure 14.1.

14.3.1 Significance of LR Hexagonal Fuzzy Numbers

Hexagonal fuzzy numbers in LR form, offer a more expressive and flexible framework that represents uncertainty compared to standard fuzzy numbers like triangular or trapezoidal kinds. The six-parameters in hexagonal fuzzy number provide a better depiction of asymmetric and nuanced evaluations, which is beneficial in real-world decision-making situations. Hexagonal fuzzy numbers can successfully model expert judgments and linguistic assessments by capturing gradual transitions and different degrees of confidence. Real-world data, whether acquired from expert surveys or fluctuating measurements, can be smoothly translated into hexagonal fuzzy numbers to reflect the inherent vagueness and ambiguity. Although these numbers offer slightly higher computational complexity due to their richer structure, but the increased computing effort is justified by the large gain in decision accuracy, resilience. The approximation of hexagonal fuzzy numbers [7] reduces the loss of information. Thus, adopting hexagonal fuzzy numbers boosts the quality of fuzzy decision-making models without incurring prohibitive computing loads, making them a feasible alternative for complicated issues like parking lot selection under uncertainty.

Remark 14.3.1. In this remark we study about Generalized pentagonal fuzzy number, Generalized trapezoidal fuzzy number, Generalized triangular fuzzy number, Generalized interval fuzzy number, Generalized single point fuzzy number with the representation of *LR-GHexFN*.

1. A *LR-Generalized pentagonal fuzzy number (LR-GPnFN)* is a special case of *LR-GHexFN* when $m = n$, and it can be expressed as $\mathrm{N} = (m, m : s_1, s_2, s_3, s_4; s, s_L, s_R)$.
2. A *LR-Generalized trapezoidal fuzzy number (LR-GTpFN)* is considered as *LR-GHexFN* with the conditions $m \neq n$, $s_L(s_1 + s_2) = s(s_1)$ and $s_R(s_3 + s_4) = s(s_4)$. A *LR-GTpFN* can be viewed as *LR-GHexFN* by the following cases
   (a) $\mathrm{N} = (m, n : s_1, 0, 0, s_4; s, s, s)$ with vertices $((m, s), (n, s), (s_1, 0), (s_2, s), (s_3, s), (s_4, 0))$
   (b) $\mathrm{N} = (m, n : 0, s_2, 0, s_4; s, 0, s)$ with vertices $((m, s), (n, s), (s_1, 0), (s_2, 0), (s_3, s), (s_4, 0))$
   (c) $\mathrm{N} = (m, n : s_1, 0, s_3, 0; s, s, 0)$ with vertices $((m, s), (n, s), (s_1, 0), (s_2, s), (s_3, 0), (s_4, 0))$
   (d) $\mathrm{N} = (m, n : 0, s_2, s_3, 0; s, 0, 0)$ with vertices $((m, s), (n, s), (s_1, 0), (s_2, 0), (s_3, 0), (s_4, 0))$
3. A *LR-Generalized triangular fuzzy number (LR-GTrFN)* is a *LR-GTrFN* with $m = n$ and it can be expressed as $\mathrm{N} = (m, m : s_1, 0, 0, s_4; s, s, s)$ with vertices $((m, s), (n, s), (s_1, 0), (s_2, s), (s_3, s), (s_4, 0))$.
4. A *LR-Generalized interval fuzzy number (LR-GInFN)* is a *LR-GHexFN* with $m \neq n$, $s_1 = s_2 = s_3 = s_4 = 0$, and it can be expressed as $\mathrm{N} = (m, n : 0, 0, 0, 0; s, s, s)$.
5. A *LR-Generalized single point fuzzy number (LR-GSpFN)* is a *LR-GInFN* with $m = n$, and it can be expressed in *LR-GHexFN* as $\mathrm{N} = (m, m : 0, 0, 0, 0; s, s, s)$.

LR-GHexFN arithmetic operations are better than standard fuzzy arithmetic because they use asymmetric left and right shape functions. These operations maintain mathematical consistency while retaining the ambiguous characteristics of data.

Definition 14.3.2. (*Addition*) Let $\mathrm{N}_1 = (m_1, n_1 : s_1, s_2, s_3, s_4; s, s_L, s_R)$ and $\mathrm{N}_2 = (m_2, n_2 : r_1, r_2, r_3, r_4; r, r_L, r_R)$ are the two *LR-GHexFNs*, then the addition of two *LR-GHexFNs* is defined as

$$N_1 + N_2 = (m_1 + m_2, n_1 + n_2 : s_1 + r_1, s_2 + r_2, s_3 + r_3, s_4 + r_4; t, t_L, t_R) \tag{14.3}$$

where $t = s + r - sr$, $t_L = s_L + r_L - s_L r_L$, $t_R = s_R + r_R - s_R r_R$ and the membership function is given as

$$(\mathcal{N}_1 + \mathcal{N}_2)(x) = \begin{cases} t_L\left(\dfrac{x-(m_1+m_2)+(s_1+s_2+r_1+r_2)}{s_1+r_1}\right), & \text{if } x \in [(m_1+m_2-s_1-s_2-r_1-r_2),(m_1+m_2-s_2-r_2)] \\ t_L+(t-t_L)\left(\dfrac{x-(m_1+m_2)+s_2+r_2}{s_2+r_2}\right), & \text{if } x \in [(m_1+m_2-s_2-r_2),(m_1+m_2)] \\ t, & \text{if } x \in [(m_1+m_2),(n_1+n_2)] \\ t_R+(t-t_R)\left(\dfrac{s_3+r_3+(n_1+n_2)-x}{s_3+r_3}\right), & \text{if } x \in [(n_1+n_2),(n_1+n_2+s_3+r_3)] \\ t_R\left(\dfrac{s_3+s_4+r_3+r_4+(n_1+n_2)-x}{s_4+r_4}\right), & \text{if } x \in [(n_1+n_2+s_3+r_3),(n_1+n_2+s_3+s_4+r_3+r_4)] \\ 0, & \textit{otherwise} \end{cases}$$

Definition 14.3.3. (*Scalar Multiplication*) Let N be any *LR-GHexFN*, then the scalar multiplication of N with $\lambda \geq 0$ is defined as

$$\lambda N = (\lambda m, \lambda n : \lambda s_1, \lambda s_2, \lambda s_3, \lambda s_4; s, s_L, s_R) \tag{14.4}$$

Definition 14.3.4. (*Division*) Let $N_1 = (m_1, n_1 : s_1, s_2, s_3, s_4; s, s_L, s_R)$ and $N_2 = (m_2, n_2 : r_1, r_2, r_3, r_4; r, r_L, r_R)$ are the two *LR-GHexFNs*, if $N_1,N_2 > 0$, then the division of two *LR-GHexFNs* is defined as

$$N_1/N_2 = \left(\frac{m_1}{n_2}, \frac{n_1}{m_2} : \frac{(m_1-s_2)r_4+(n_2+r_3)s_1}{(n_2+r_3)(n_2+r_3+r_4)}, \frac{m_1 r_3+s_2 n_2}{n_2(n_2+r_3)}, \frac{s_3 m_2+n_1 r_2}{m_2(m_2-r_2)}, \frac{(m_2-r_2)s_4+(n_1+s_3)r_1}{(m_2-r_2)(m_2-r_2-r_1)}; t, t_L, t_R\right) \tag{14.5}$$

where $t = sr$, $t_L = s_L r_R$, $t_R = s_R r_L$ and the membership function is given as

$$(\mathcal{N}_1/\mathcal{N}_2)(x)=\begin{cases} t_L\left(\dfrac{x-(m_1-s_2-s_1/n_2+r_3+r_4)}{(m_1-s_2/n_2+r_3)-(m_1-s_2-s_1/n_2+r_3+r_4)}\right), \\ \quad \text{if } x\in[(m_1-s_2-s_1/n_2+r_3+r_4),(m_1-s_2/n_2+r_3)] \\ t_L+(t-t_L)\left(\dfrac{x-(m_1-s_2/n_2+r_3}{(m_1/n_2)-(m_1-s_2/n_2+r_3)}\right), \\ \quad \text{if } x\in[(m_1-s_2/n_2+r_3),(m_1/n_2)] \\ t, \\ \quad \text{if } x\in[(m_1/m_2),(n_1/n_2)] \\ t_R+(t-t_R)\left(\dfrac{(n_1+s_3/m_2-r_2)-x}{(n_1+s_3/m_2-r_2)-(n_1/m_2)}\right), \\ \quad \text{if } x\in[(n_1/n_2),(n_1+s_3/m_2-r_2)] \\ t_R\left(\dfrac{(n_1+s_3+s_4/m_2-r_2-r_1)-x}{(n_1+s_3+s_4/m_2-r_2-r_1)-(n_1+s_3/m_2-r_2)}\right), \\ \quad \text{if } x\in[(n_1+s_3/m_2-r_2),(n_1+s_3+s_4/m_2-r_2-r_1)] \\ 0, \\ \quad \textit{otherwise} \end{cases}$$

Definition 14.3.5. (Weighted Aggregation) Let the *LR generalized hexagonal fuzzy number* be $N_j = (m_j, n_j : s_{1j}, s_{2j}, s_{3j}, s_{4j}; s_j, s_L j, s_R j)$ $j = 1, 2, \ldots n$. Let $w_j \in [0, 1]$ for $j = 1, 2, \ldots n$ with $\Sigma_j w_j = 1$ be the weights of N_j.

- F_w is the weighted aggregation operator which is defined as

$$\begin{aligned}\mathcal{F}_w(\mathcal{N}_1,\mathcal{N}_2,\ldots,\mathcal{N}_n) &= \sum_j w_j\mathcal{N}_j = (\sum_j w_j m_j, \sum_j w_j n_j : \\ &\sum_j w_j s_{1j}, \sum_j w_j s_{2j}, \\ &\sum_j w_j s_{3j}, \sum_j w_j s_{4j}; 1-\prod_j(1-s_j), 1-\prod_j(1-s_{L_j}), \\ &1-\prod_j(1-s_{R_j}))\end{aligned} \tag{14.6}$$

- G_w is the weighted multiplicative aggregation operator which is defined as

$$\mathcal{G}_w(\mathcal{N}_1,\mathcal{N}_2,\ldots,\mathcal{N}_n)=\prod_j \mathcal{N}_j^{w_j}=(\prod_j m_j^{w_j},\prod_j n_j^{w_j}:$$
$$\prod_j (m_j-s_{2j}-s_{1j})^{w_j}-\prod_j (m_j-s_{2j})^{w_j}$$
$$\prod_j (m_j)^{w_j}-\prod_j (m_j-s_{2j})^{w_j},\prod_j (n_j-s_{3j})^{w_j}-\prod_j (n_j)^{w_j},$$
$$\prod_j (n_j-s_{3j}+s_{4j})^{w_j}-\prod_j (n_j-s_{3j})^{w_j};\prod_j s_j,\prod_j s_{L_j},\prod_j s_{R_j}) \tag{14.7}$$

14.4 Ranking Measures for *LR-GHexFNs* Using Score Functions

To compare *LR-GHexFNs*, ranking measures are used to convert fuzzy values into crisp representations. This section defines different ranking measures and presents a systematic ranking procedure to ensure accurate and reliable decision-making.

Definition 14.4.1. (Midpoint score) The *midpoint score* (*MPS*) of the *LR-GHexFN* N = $(m, n : s_1, s_2, s_3, s_4; s, s_L, s_R)$ is defined as

$$MPS(\mathrm{N})=s\frac{(m+n)}{2} \tag{14.8}$$

Remark 14.4.1. Consider two *LR-GHexFNs* $\mathrm{N}_1 = (m_1, n_1 : s_1, s_2, s_3, s_4; s, s_L, s_R)$ and $\mathrm{N}_2 = (m_2, n_2 : r_1, r_2, r_3, r_4; r, r_L, r_R)$. If $MPS(\mathrm{N}_1) > MPS(\mathrm{N}_2)$ ($MPS(\mathrm{N}_1) < MPS(\mathrm{N}_2)$), then $\mathrm{N}_1 > \mathrm{N}_2$ ($\mathrm{N}_1 < \mathrm{N}_2$).

Example 14.4.1. Let N_1 = (0.60, 0.80 : 0.20, 0.20, 0.20, 0.20; 0.80, 0.40, 0.50) and N_2 = (0.30, 0.35 : 0.05, 0.05, 0.05, 0.05; 0.50, 0.30, 0.60) be the two *LR-GHexFNs* with ranking measures $MPS(\mathrm{N}_1) = 0.56$, $MPS(\mathrm{N}_2) = 0.1625$. Since $MPS(\mathrm{N}_1) > MPS(\mathrm{N}_2)$, it follows that $\mathrm{N}_1 > \mathrm{N}_2$.

Example 14.4.2. Let N_1 = (0.30, 0.50 : 0.20, 0.20, 0.20, 0.20; 0.20, 0.15, 0.10) and N_2 = (0.10, 0.30 : 0.05, 0.05, 0.05, 0.05; 0.40, 0.30, 0.20) be the two *LR-GHexFNs* with ranking measures $MPS(\mathrm{N}_1) = 0.44$, $MPS(\mathrm{N}_2) = 0.08$. Here $MPS(\mathrm{N}_1) = MPS(\mathrm{N}_2)$, but $\mathrm{N}_1 \neq \mathrm{N}_2$.

The ranking measure gives equal values, but the *LR-GHexFNs* are not equal. Thus, another ranking measure is required to rank *LR-GHexFNs*. Hence the new measure named *span* is developed in the upcoming definition.

Definition 14.4.2. (Span) The *span* (*SP*) of the *LR-GHexFN* $N = (m, n : s_1, s_2, s_3, s_4; s, s_L, s_R)$ is defined as

$$SP(N) = s\frac{(n-m)}{2} \tag{14.9}$$

Remark 14.4.2. Consider two *LR-GHexFNs* $N_1 = (m_1, n_1 : s_1, s_2, s_3, s_4; s, s_L, s_R)$ and $N_2 = (m_2, n_2 : r_1, r_2, r_3, r_4; r, r_L, r_R)$. If $MPS(N_1) = MPS(N_2)$, $SP(N_1) > SP(N_2)$ ($SP(N_1) < SP(N_2)$), then $N_1 > N_2$ ($N_1 < N_2$).

Example 14.4.3. Let $N_1 = (0.30, 0.50 : 0.15, 0.10, 0.25, 0.15; 0.20, 0.15, 0.05)$ and $N_2 = (0.10, 0.30 : 0.02, 0.05, 0.10, 0.05; 0.40, 0.15, 0.25)$ be the two *LR-GHexFNs* with ranking measures $MPS(N_1) = MPS(N_1) = 0.08$, $SP(N_1) = 0.02$, $SP(N_2) = 0.04$. Since $SP(N_1) < SP(N_2)$, it follows that $N_1 < N_2$.

Note 14.4.1. Consider two *LR-GHexFNs* $N_1 = (m_1, n_1 : s_1, s_2, s_3, s_4; s, s_L, s_R)$ and $N_2 = (m_2, n_2 : r_1, r_2, r_3, r_4; r, r_L, r_R)$.

If $MPS(N_1) < MPS(N_2)$, it follows that $N_1 < N_2$.
If $MPS(N_1) > MPS(N_2)$, it follows that $N_1 > N_2$.
If $MPS(N_1) = MPS(N_2)$, it follows
- If $SP(N_1) < SP(N_2)$, it follows that $N_1 < N_2$.
- If $SP(N_1) > SP(N_2)$, it follows that $N_1 > N_2$.
- If $SP(N_1) = SP(N_2)$, it follows
  - If $s < r$, it follows that $N_1 < N_2$.
  - If $s > r$, it follows that $N_1 > N_2$.

Example 14.4.4. Let $N_1 = (1.20, 1.60 : 0.92, 0.20, 0.20, 0.20; 0.35, 0.27, 0.20)$ and $N_2 = (0.60, 0.80 : 0.20, 0.20, 0.10, 0.30; 0.70, 0.30, 0.15)$ be the two *LR-GHexFNs* with ranking measures $MPS(N_1) = MPS(N_2) = 0.49$, $SP(N_1) = SP(N_2) = 0.07$, and $s < r$ therefore $N_1 < N_2$.

Note 14.4.2. If $MPS(N_1) = MPS(N_2)$, $SP(N_1) = SP(N_2)$, $s = r$, it does not necessarily mean that $N_1 = N_2$. This is evident from the following example.

Example 14.4.5. Let $N_1 = (0.30, 0.50 : 0.15, 0.10, 0.25, 0.15; 0.20, 0.10, 0.06)$ and $N_2 = (0.30, 0.50 : 0.02, 0.25, 0.05, 0.05; 0.20, 0.15, 0.30)$ be the two *LR-GHexFNs* with ranking measures $MPS(N_1) = MPS(N_2) = 0.08$, $SP(N_1) = SP(N_2) = 0.02$ and $s = r$, but $N_1 \neq N_2$.

The ranking measure gives equal values, but the *LR-GHexFNs* are not equal. Thus, another ranking measure is required to rank *LR-GHexFNs*. Hence the new measure named *left slope variation* is developed in the upcoming definition.

Definition 14.4.3. (Left slope variation) The *left slope variation* score (*LSV*) of the LR-GHexFN $N = (m, n : s_1, s_2, s_3, s_4; s, s_L, s_R)$ is defined as

$$LSV(N) = \frac{s_L(s_1 + s_2) - s(s_1)}{4} \tag{14.10}$$

Remark 14.4.3. Consider two *LR-GHexFNs* $N_1 = (m_1, n_1 : s_1, s_2, s_3, s_4; s, s_L, s_R)$ and $N_2 = (m_2, n_2 : r_1, r_2, r_3, r_4; r, r_L, r_R)$. If $MPS(N_1) = MPS(N_2)$, $SP(N_1) = SP(N_2)$, $s = r$, and $LSV(N_1) > LSV(N_2)$ ($LSV(N_1) < LSV(N_2)$), then $N_1 > N_2$ ($N_1 < N_2$).

Example 14.4.6. Let $N_1 = (0.60, 0.90 : 0.05, 0.50, 0.22, 0.03; 0.40, 0.22, 0.35)$ and $N_2 = (0.60, 0.90 : 0.48, 0.10, 0.80, 0.30; 0.40, 0.22, 0.25)$ be the two *LR-GHexFNs* with ranking measures $MPS(N_1) = MPS(N_2) = 0.30$, $SP(N_1) = SP(N_2) = 0.06$ and $LSV(N_1) = 0.02525 > LSV(N_2) = -0.0161$, therefore $N_1 > N_2$.

Note 14.4.3. Consider two *LR-GHexFNs* $N_1 = (m_1, n_1 : s_1, s_2, s_3, s_4; s, s_L, s_R)$ and $N_2 = (m_2, n_2 : r_1, r_2, r_3, r_4; r, r_L, r_R)$.

If $LSV(N_1) < LSV(N_2)$, it follows that $N_1 < N_2$.
If $LSV(N_1) > LSV(N_2)$, it follows that $N_1 > N_2$.
If $LSV(N_1) = LSV(N_2)$, it follows
- If $s_L < r_L$, it follows that $N_1 < N_2$.
- If $s_L > r_L$, it follows that $N_1 > N_2$.

Example 14.4.7. Let $N_1 = (0.60, 0.90 : 0.05, 0.50, 0.22, 0.03; 0.70, 0.30, 0.45)$ and $N_2 = (0.60, 0.90 : 0.10, 0.40, 0.10, 1; 0.70, 0.40, 0.60)$ be the two *LR-GHexFNs* with ranking measures $MPS(N_1) = MPS(N_2) = 0.525$, $SP(N_1) = SP(N_2) = 0.105$ and $LSV(N_1) = LSV(N_2) = 0.0325$, $s_L < r_L$, therefore $N_1 < N_2$.

Note 14.4.4. If $MPS(N_1) = MPS(N_2)$, $SP(N_1) = SP(N_2)$, $s = r$, $LSV(N_1) = LSV(N_2)$, $s_L = r_L$, it does not necessarily mean that $N_1 = N_2$. This is evident from the following example.

Example 14.4.8. Let $N_1 = (0.60, 0.90 : 0.05, 0.50, 0.22, 0.03; 0.40, 0.22, 0.45)$ and $N_2 = (0.60, 0.90 : 0.05, 0.50, 0.10, 1; 0.40, 0.22, 0.25)$ be the two *LR-GHexFNs* with ranking measures $MPS(N_1) = MPS(N_2) = 0.30$, $SP(N_1)$

$= SP\,(N_2) = 0.06$ and $LSV\,(N_1) = LSV\,(N_2) = 0.02525$, $s_L = r_L = 0.22$ but $N_1 \neq N_2$.

The ranking measure gives equal values, but the *LR-GHexFNs* are not equal. Thus, another ranking measure is required to rank *LR-GHexFNs*. Hence the new measure named *left inclination aggregation* is developed in the upcoming definition.

Definition 14.4.4. (Left inclination aggregation) The *left inclination aggregation* score (*LIA*) of the LR-GHexFN $N = (m, n : s_1, s_2, s_3, s_4; s, s_L, s_R)$ is defined as

$$LIA(N) = \frac{s_L(s_1 + s_2) + s(s_1)}{4} \tag{14.11}$$

Remark 14.4.4. Consider two *LR-GHexFNs* $N_1 = (m_1, n_1 : s_1, s_2, s_3, s_4; s, s_L, s_R)$ and $N_2 = (m_2, n_2 : r_1, r_2, r_3, r_4; r, r_L, r_R)$. If $MPS(N_1) = MPS(N_2)$, $SP\,(N_1) = SP\,(N_2)$, $LSV\,(N_1) = LSV\,(N_2)$, $s = r$, $s_L = r_L$, $LIA(N_1) > LIA(N_2)$ ($LIA(N_1) < LIA(N_2)$), then $N_1 > N_2$ ($N_1 < N_2$).

Example 14.4.9. Let $N_1 = (0.60, 0.90 : 0.05, 0.50, 0.22, 0.03; 0.40, 0.22, 0.35)$ and $N_2 = (0.60, 0.90 : 0.08, 0.50, 0.22, 0.88; 0.40, 0.22, 0.25)$ be the two *LR-GHexFNs* with ranking measures $MPS(N_1) = MPS(N_2) = 0.30$, $SP\,(N_1) = SP\,(N_2) = 0.06$ and $LSV\,(N_1) = LSV\,(N_2) = 0.02525$, $s_L = r_L = 0.22$, $LIA(N_1) = 0.03525 < LIA(N_2) = 0.0399$, therefore $N_1 < N_2$.

Note 14.4.5. Consider two *LR-GHexFNs* $N_1 = (m_1, n_1 : s_1, s_2, s_3, s_4; s, s_L, s_R)$ and $N_2 = (m_2, n_2 : r_1, r_2, r_3, r_4; r, r_L, r_R)$.

If $LSV\,(N_1) < LSV\,(N_2)$, it follows that $N_1 < N_2$.
If $LSV\,(N_1) > LSV\,(N_2)$, it follows that $N_1 > N_2$.
If $LSV\,(N_1) = LSV\,(N_2)$, it follows
  If $s_L < r_L$, it follows that $N_1 < N_2$.
  If $s_L > r_L$, it follows that $N_1 > N_2$.
    If $s_L = r_L$, it follows
    If $LIA(N_1) < LIA(N_2)$, it follows that $N_1 < N_2$.
    If $LIA(N_1) > LIA(N_2)$, it follows that $N_1 > N_2$.

Note 14.4.6. If $MPS(N_1) = MPS(N_2)$, $SP\,(N_1) = SP\,(N_2)$, $s = r$, $LSV\,(N_1) = LSV\,(N_2)$, $s_L = r_L$, $LIA(N_1) = LIA(N_2)$ it does not necessarily mean that $N_1 = N_2$. This is evident from the following example.

Example 14.4.10. Let N_1 = (0.60, 0.90 : 0.05, 0.50, 0.22, 0.03; 0.40, 0.22, 0.25) and N_2 = (0.60, 0.90 : 0.05, 0.50, 0.22, 0.88; 0.40, 0.22, 0.20) be the two *LR-GHexFNs* with ranking measures $MPS(N_1) = MPS(N_2) = 0.30$, $SP(N_1) = SP(N_2) = 0.06$, $s = r = 0.40$, $LSV(N_1) = LSV(N_2) = 0.02525$, $s_L = r_L = 0.22$, $LIA(N_1) = LIA(N_2) = 0.03525$, but $N_1 \neq N_2$.

The ranking measure gives equal values, but the *LR-GHexFNs* are not equal. Thus, another ranking measure is required to rank *LR-GHexFNs*. Hence the new measure named *right slope variation* is developed in the upcoming definition.

Definition 14.4.5. (Right slope variation) The *right slope variation* score (*RSV*) of the LR-GHexFN $N = (m, n : s_1, s_2, s_3, s_4; s, s_L, s_R)$ is defined as

$$RSV(N) = \frac{s_R(s_3 + s_4) - s(s_4)}{4} \tag{14.12}$$

Remark 14.4.5. Consider two *LR-GHexFNs* $N_1 = (m_1, n_1 : s_1, s_2, s_3, s_4; s, s_L, s_R)$ and $N_2 = (m_2, n_2 : r_1, r_2, r_3, r_4; r, r_L, r_R)$. If $MPS(N_1) = MPS(N_2)$, $SP(N_1) = SP(N_2)$, $s = r$, $LSV(N_1) = LSV(N_2)$, $s_L = r_L$, $LIA(N_1) = LIA(N_2)$, and $RSV(N_1) > RSV(N_2)$ ($RSV(N_1) < RSV(N_2)$), then $N_1 > N_2$ ($N_1 < N_2$).

Example 14.4.11. Let N_1 = (0.60, 0.90 : 0.05, 0.50, 0.22, 0.03; 0.40, 0.22, 0.35) and N_2 = (0.60, 0.90 : 0.05, 0.50, 0.80, 0.30; 0.40, 0.22, 0.25) be the two *LR-GHexFNs* with ranking measures $MPS(N_1) = MPS(N_2) = 0.30$, $SP(N_1) = SP(N_2) = 0.06$, $s = r = 0.40$, $LSV(N_1) = LSV(N_2) = 0.02525$, $s_L = r_L = 0.22$, $LIA(N_1) = LIA(N_2) = 0.03525$ and $RSV(N_1) = 0.018875 < RSV(N_2) = 0.03875$, therefore $N_1 < N_2$.

Note 14.4.7. Consider two *LR-GHexFNs* $N_1 = (m_1, n_1 : s_1, s_2, s_3, s_4; s, s_L, s_R)$ and $N_2 = (m_2, n_2 : r_1, r_2, r_3, r_4; r, r_L, r_R)$.

If $RSV(N_1) < RSV(N_2)$, it follows that $N_1 < N_2$.
If $RSV(N_1) > RSV(N_2)$, it follows that $N_1 > N_2$.
If $RSV(N_1) = RSV(N_2)$, it follows that
  If $s_R < r_R$, it follows that $N_1 < N_2$.
  If $s_R > r_R$, it follows that $N_1 > N_2$.

Example 14.4.12. Let N_1 = (0.60, 0.90 : 0.05, 0.50, 0.22, 0.03; 0.70, 0.22, 0.35) and N_2 = (0.60, 0.90 : 0.05, 0.50, 0.145, 0.03; 0.70, 0.22, 0.50) be the two *LR-GHexFNs* with ranking measures $MPS(N_1) = MPS(N_2) = 0.525$, $SP(N_1) = SP(N_2) = 0.105$, $s = r = 0.70$, $LSV(N_1) = LSV(N_2) = 0.0215$, $LIA(N_1)$

$= LIA(\mathrm{N}_2) = 0.039$, $RSV(\mathrm{N}_1) = RSV(\mathrm{N}_2) = 0.016625$, and $s_R < r_R$, therefore $\mathrm{N}_1 < \mathrm{N}_2$.

Note 14.4.8. If $MPS(\mathrm{N}_1) = MPS(\mathrm{N}_2)$, $SP(\mathrm{N}_1) = SP(\mathrm{N}_2)$, $s = r$, $LSV(\mathrm{N}_1) = LSV(\mathrm{N}_2)$, $s_L = r_L$, $LIA(\mathrm{N}_1) = LIA(\mathrm{N}_2)$, $RSV(\mathrm{N}_1) = RSV(\mathrm{N}_2)$, $s_R = r_R$, it does not necessarily mean that $\mathrm{N}_1 = \mathrm{N}_2$. This is evident from the following example.

Example 14.4.13. Let $\mathrm{N}_1 = (0.60, 0.90 : 0.05, 0.50, 0.22, 0.03; 0.70, 0.22, 0.35)$ and $\mathrm{N}_2 = (0.60, 0.90 : 0.05, 0.50, 0.27, 0.08; 0.70, 0.22, 0.35)$ be the two *LR-GHexFNs* with ranking measures $MPS(\mathrm{N}_1) = MPS(\mathrm{N}_2) = 0.525$, $SP(\mathrm{N}_1) = SP(\mathrm{N}_2) = 0.105$, $s = r = 0.70$, $LSV(\mathrm{N}_1) = LSV(\mathrm{N}_2) = 0.0215$, $LIA(\mathrm{N}_1) = LIA(\mathrm{N}_2) = 0.039$, $RSV(\mathrm{N}_1) = RSV(\mathrm{N}_2) = 0.016625$, $s_R = r_R$, but $\mathrm{N}_1 \neq \mathrm{N}_2$.

The ranking measure gives equal values, but the *LR-GHexFNs* are not equal. Thus, another ranking measure is required to rank *LR-GHexFNs*. Hence the new measure named *right inclination aggregation* is developed in the upcoming definition.

Definition 4.6. (Right inclination aggregation) The *right inclination aggregation* score (*RIA*) of the *LR-GHexFN* $\mathrm{N} = (m, n : s_1, s_2, s_3, s_4; s, s_L, s_R)$ is defined as

$$RIA(\mathrm{N}) = \frac{s_R(s_3 + s_4) + s(s_4)}{4} \tag{14.13}$$

Remark 14.4.6. Consider two *LR-GHexFNs* $\mathrm{N}_1 = (m_1, n_1 : s_1, s_2, s_3, s_4; s, s_L, s_R)$ and $\mathrm{N}_2 = (m_2, n_2 : r_1, r_2, r_3, r_4; r, r_L, r_R)$. If $MPS(\mathrm{N}_1) = MPS(\mathrm{N}_2)$, $SP(\mathrm{N}_1) = SP(\mathrm{N}_2)$, $s = r$, $LSV(\mathrm{N}_1) = LSV(\mathrm{N}_2)$, $s_L = r_L$, $LIA(\mathrm{N}_1) = LIA(\mathrm{N}_2)$, $RSV(\mathrm{N}_1) = RSV(\mathrm{N}_2)$, $s_R = r_R$, and $RIA(\mathrm{N}_1) > RIA(\mathrm{N}_2)$ ($RIA(\mathrm{N}_1) < \mathrm{RIA}(\mathrm{N}_2)$), then $\mathrm{N}_1 > \mathrm{N}_2$ ($\mathrm{N}_1 < \mathrm{N}_2$).

Example 14.4.14. Let $\mathrm{N}_1 = (0.60, 0.90 : 0.05, 0.50, 0.22, 0.03; 0.70, 0.22, 0.35)$ and $\mathrm{N}_2 = (0.60, 0.90, 0.05, 0.50, 0.27, 0.08; 0.70, 0.22, 0.35)$ be the two *LR-GHexFNs* with ranking measures $MPS(\mathrm{N}_1) = MPS(\mathrm{N}_2) = 0.525$, $SP(\mathrm{N}_1) = SP(\mathrm{N}_2) = 0.105$, $s = r = 0.70$, $LSV(\mathrm{N}_1) = LSV(\mathrm{N}_2) = 0.0215$, $s_L = r_L = 0.22$, $LIA(\mathrm{N}_1) = LIA(\mathrm{N}_2) = 0.039$, $RSV(\mathrm{N}_1) = RSV(\mathrm{N}_2) = 0.016625$, $s_R = r_R = 0.35$, $RIA(\mathrm{N}_1) = 0.027125 < \mathrm{RIA}(\mathrm{N}_2) = 0.044625$ therefore $\mathrm{N}_1 < \mathrm{N}_2$.

Note 14.4.9. Consider two *LR-GHexFNs* $\mathrm{N}_1 = (m_1, n_1 : s_1, s_2, s_3, s_4; s, s_L, s_R)$ and $\mathrm{N}_2 = (m_2, n_2 : r_1, r_2, r_3, r_4; r, r_L, r_R)$.

If $RSV(\mathrm{N}_1) < \mathrm{RSV}(\mathrm{N}_2)$, it follows that $\mathrm{N}_1 < \mathrm{N}_2$.
If $RSV(\mathrm{N}_1) > RSV(\mathrm{N}_2)$, it follows that $\mathrm{N}_1 > \mathrm{N}_2$.
If $RSV(\mathrm{N}_1) = RSV(\mathrm{N}_2)$, it follows

If $s_R < r_R$, it follows that $N_1 < N_2$.
If $s_R > r_R$, it follows that $N_1 > N_2$.
If $s_R = r_R$, it follows
If $RIA(N_1) < RIA(N_2)$, it follows that $N_1 < N_2$.
If $RIA(N_1) > RIA(N_2)$, it follows that $N_1 > N_2$.
If $RIA(N_1) = RIA(N_2)$, it results in $N_1 = N_2$

Note 14.4.10. If $MPS(N_1) = MPS(N_2)$, $SP(N_1) = SP(N_2)$, $s = r$, $LSV(N_1) = LSV(N_2)$, $s_L = r_L$, $LIA(N_1) = LIA(N_2)$, $RSV(N_1) = RSV(N_2)$, $s_R = r_R$, $RIA(N_1) = RIA(N_2)$, it means that $N_1 = N_2$. This is evident from the following example.
Example 14.4.15. Let N_1 = (0.60, 0.90 : 0.05, 0.50, 0.22, 0.03; 0.70, 0.22, 0.35) and N_2 = (0.60, 0.90, 0.05, 0.50, 0.22, 0.03; 0.70, 0.22, 0.35) be the two *LR-GHexFNs* with ranking measures $MPS(N_1) = MPS(N_2) = 0.525$, $SP(N_1) = SP(N_2) = 0.105$, $s = r = 0.70$, $LSV(N_1) = LSV(N_2) = 0.0215$, $s_L = r_L = 0.22$, $LIA(N_1) = LIA(N_2) = 0.039$, $RSV(N_1) = RSV(N_2) = 0.016625$, $s_R = r_R = 0.35$, $RIA(N_1) = RIA(N_2) = 0.027125$ therefore $N_1 = N_2$.

The following theorem shows the total ordering of the *LR-GHexFNs*.

Theorem 14.4.1. Let the ranking measures *MPS,SP,LSV,LIA,RSV,RIA* are equal for the two *LR-GHexFNs* $N_1 = (m_1, n_1 : s_1, s_2, s_3, s_4; s, s_L, s_R)$ and $N_2 = (m_2, n_2 : r_1, r_2, r_3, r_4; r, r_L, r_R)$ along with $s = r$, $s_L = r_L$ $s_R = r_R$, then $N_1 = N_2$ ($m_1 = m_2$, $n_1 = n_2$, $s_1 = r_1$, $s_2 = r_2$, $s_3 = r_3$, $s_4 = r_4$).
Proof. Let $N_1 = (m_1, n_1 : s_1, s_2, s_3, s_4; s, s_L, s_R)$ and $N_2 = (m_2, n_2 : r_1, r_2, r_3, r_4; r, r_L, r_R)$ be the two *LR-GHexFNs*. Given that $s = r$, $s_L = r_L$ $s_R = r_R$, $MPS(N_1) = MPS(N_2)$,$SP(N_1) = SP(N_2)$,$LSV(N_1) = LSV(N_2)$,$LIA(N_1) = RIA(N_2)$,$RIA(N_1) = RIA(N_2)$ $RIA(N_1) = RIA(N_2)$.

To prove : $m_1 = m_2$, $n_1 = n_2$, $s_1 = r_1$, $s_2 = r_2$, $s_3 = r_3$, $s_4 = r_4$ ($N_1 = N_2$)
Using Equation (14.8) and Equation (14.9),
$MPS(N_1) + SP(N_1) = MPS(N_2) + SP(N_2)$, gives $sm_1 = rm_2$
Since $s = r$, we get $m_1 = m_2$
$MPS(N_1) - SP(N_1) = MPS(N_2) - SP(N_2)$, gives $sn_1 = rn_2$
Since $s = r$, we get $n_1 = n_2$
Using Equation (14.10) and Equation (14.11),
$LSV(N_1) - LIA(N_1) = LSV(N_2) - LIA(N_2)$, gives $s(s_1) = r(r_1)$
Since $s = r$, we get $s_1 = r_1$
$LSV(N_1) + LIA(N_1) = LSV(N_2) + LIA(N_2)$, gives $s_L(s_1 + s_2) = r_L(r_1 + r_2)$
Since $s_L = r_L$ and $s_1 = r_1$, we get $s_2 = r_2$
Using Equation (14.12) and Equation (14.13),
$RSV(N_1) - RIA(N_1) = RSV(N_2) - RIA(N_2)$, gives $s(s_4) = r(r_4)$
Since $s = r$, we get $s_4 = r_4$

$RSV(N_1) + RIA(N_1) = RSV(N_2) + RIA(N_2)$, gives $s_R(s_3 + s_4) = r_R(r_3 + r_4)$
Since $s_R = r_R$ and $s_4 = r_4$, we get $s_3 = r_3$
From the above, we get $m_1 = m_2$, $n_1 = n_2$, $s_1 = r_1$, $s_2 = r_2$, $s_3 = r_3$, $s_4 = r_4$. Therefore $N_1 = N_2$.

A ranking approach for the full class of *LR-GHexFN* is formulated in this subsection using the previously defined score functions.

Comparison of two LR-GHexFNs

For any two LR-GHexFNs $N_1 = (m_1, n_1 : s_1, s_2, s_3, s_4; s, s_L, s_R)$ and $N_2 = (m_2, n_2 : r_1, r_2, r_3, r_4; r, r_L, r_R)$,
If $MPS(N_1) < MPS(N_2)$, it follows that $N_1 < N_2$.
If $MPS(N_1) > MPS(N_2)$, it follows that $N_1 > N_2$.
If $MPS(N_1) = MPS(N_2)$, it follows
  If $SP(N_1) < SP(N_2)$, it follows that $N_1 < N_2$.
  If $SP(N_1) > SP(N_2)$, it follows that $N_1 > N_2$.
  If $SP(N_1) = SP(N_2)$, it follows
    If $s < r$, it follows that $N_1 < N_2$.
    If $s > r$, it follows that $N_1 > N_2$.
    If $s = r$, it follows
      If $LSV(N_1) < LSV(N_2)$, it follows that $N_1 < N_2$.
      If $LSV(N_1) > LSV(N_2)$, it follows that $N_1 > N_2$.
      If $LSV(N_1) = LSV(N_2)$, it follows
        If $s_L < r_L$, it follows that $N_1 < N_2$.
        If $s_L > r_L$, it follows that $N_1 > N_2$.
        If $s_L = r_L$, it follows
          If $LIA(N_1) < LIA(N_2)$, it follows that $N_1 < N_2$.
          If $LIA(N_1) > LIA(N_2)$, it follows that $N_1 > N_2$.
          If $LIA(N_1) = LIA(N_2)$, it follows
            If $RSV(N_1) < RSV(N_2)$, it follows that $N_1 < N_2$.
            If $RSV(N_1) > RSV(N_2)$, it follows that $N_1 > N_2$.
            If $RSV(N_1) = RSV(N_2)$, it follows
              If $s_R < r_R$, it follows that $N_1 < N_2$.
              If $s_R > r_R$, it follows that $N_1 > N_2$.
              If $s_R = r_R$, it follows
                If $RIA(N_1) < RIA(N_2)$, it follows that $N_1 < N_2$.
                If $RIA(N_1) > RIA(N_2)$, it follows that $N_1 > N_2$.
                If $RIA(N_1) = RIA(N_2)$, it results in $N_1 = N_2$

14.5 Fuzzy WASPAS Method with *LR-HexFN*

Fuzzy Weighted Aggregated Sum Product Assessment is one of the Fuzzy Multi-criteria decision-making methods (MCDM). In the field of MCDM, the main purpose is to select the best alternative from a predefined set of choices. These choices are analyzed based on several criteria, which are the basis for evaluation and comparison. In this, we have m alternatives and n criteria and the set of alternatives is defined as $X = \{X_1, X_2, ...X_m\}$ and the set of criteria is defined as $C = \{C_1, C_2, ...C_n\}$. By examining the alternatives using the criteria, this method helps to select the best alternative.

14.5.1 Weight Determination Through Fuzzy Graphs

In the fuzzy graph, the set of nodes is the set of criteria, where the edges between the nodes are the criteria interaction weights which give us the edge membership value. The set of criteria is finite hence the set of nodes is also finite. In this fuzzy graph, consider the vertex membership as 1 for all nodes, i.e. $\sigma(C_i) = 1, \forall i = 1, 2, ...n$.

The *degree of the node* is $\mathbf{d}(\mathcal{C}) = \sum \mu(\mathcal{C},\mathcal{C}_i), \forall C_i \in V - \{C\}$ and the *total degree* T D is defined as $\mathcal{TD} = \sum_i \mathbf{d}(\mathcal{C}_i)$.

Definition 14.5.1. (Fuzzy Decision Weight) The *fuzzy decision weight* of the nodes is defined as

$$w(C) = \frac{\mathbf{d}(C)}{TD} \tag{14.14}$$

14.5.2 Fuzzy WASPAS Approach with LR Hexagonal Fuzzy Numbers

1. Convert the linguistic decision matrix to fuzzy decision matrix by converting the qualitative linguistic terms to their corresponding LR hexagonal fuzzy numbers.
2. Let $DM = [u_{ij}]_{m\times n}$ be the fuzzy decision matrix, where u_{ij} is the LR hexagonal fuzzy number, i.e., $u_{ij} = (l_{ij}, m_{ij}, n_{ij}, r_{ij}, s_{ij}, t_{ij}; 1, h_{L_{ij}}, h_{R_{ij}})$.

$$\mathcal{DM} = \begin{bmatrix} u_{11} & u_{12} & \cdots & u_{1n} \\ u_{21} & u_{22} & \cdots & u_{2n} \\ \vdots & \vdots & \ddots & \vdots \\ u_{m1} & u_{m2} & \cdots & u_{mn} \end{bmatrix}$$

Here, each entry is a LR hexagonal fuzzy number.

3. Now, convert the fuzzy decision matrix into normalized decision matrix which is denoted as $N_D = [v_{ij}]_{m\times n}$
   - For Beneficial criteria

$$v_{ij} = \frac{u_{ij}}{max(u_{ij})} \tag{14.15}$$

   for $i = 1, 2, 3, ...m$
   - For Non-beneficial criteria

$$v_{ij} = \frac{min(u_{ij})}{(u_{ij})} \tag{14.16}$$

   for $i = 1, 2, 3, ...m$

   Here, the maximum and minimum of the LR hexagonal fuzzy numbers are calculated using the ranking measures and the division of two *LR-HexFNs* is done using Definition 14.3.4.

4. Using Definition 14.5.1, calculate the weight of the criteria that satisfies the condition $\sum_j w_j = 1, j = 1, 2, \ldots n.$
5. From the Definition 14.3.5, find the weighted arithmetic average operator which is known as fuzzy weighted sum model denoted as

$$\begin{aligned}\Omega_1(X_i) &= \sum_{j=1}^{n} w_j v_{ij} \\ &= (\sum_j w_j m_j, \sum_j w_j n_j : \sum_j w_j s_{1j}, \sum_j w_j s_{2j}, \sum_j w_j s_{3j}, \sum_j w_j s_{4j}; \\ &\quad 1-\prod_j (1-s_j), 1-\prod_j (1-s_{L_j}), 1-\prod_j (1-s_{R_j}))\end{aligned} \tag{14.17}$$

6. From the Definition 14.3.5, find the weighted geometric average operator which is known as fuzzy weighted product model denoted as

$$\begin{aligned}\Omega_2(X_i) &= \prod_{j=1}^{n}(v_{ij})^{wj} \\ &= \Big(\prod_j m_j^{w_j}, \prod_j n_j^{w_j} : \prod_j (m_j - s_{2j} - s_{1j})^{w_j} - \prod_j (m_j - s_{2j})^{w_j}, \\ &\prod_j (m_j)^{w_j} - \prod_j (m_j - s_{2j})^{w_j}, \prod_j (n_j + s_{3j})^{w_j} - \prod_j (n_j)^{w_j}, \\ &\prod_j (n_j + s_{3j} + s_{4j})^{w_j} - \prod_j (n_j + s_{3j})^{w_j}; \prod_j s_j, \prod_j s_{L_j}, \prod_j s_{R_j}\Big)\end{aligned} \tag{14.18}$$

7. After finding the fuzzy weighted sum model and fuzzy weighted product model, calculate the aggregated value (Ω) for each alternative.

$$\Omega(X_i) = \lambda\Omega_1(X_i) + (1 - \lambda)\Omega_2(X_i) \tag{14.19}$$

where λ is the real number in [0, 1]

8. Using ranking measures, compare the *LR-HexFN*, and the larger the values gives better alternative.

With this method, the best alternative is selected based on the given criteria.

14.5.3 Flow Chart Representation of Fuzzy WASPAS Approach

A flowchart representation is employed in Figure 14.2 to offer a clear and structured depiction of the Fuzzy WASPAS approach. This flowchart outlines each stage in sequence, facilitating a complete understanding of the integration of fuzzy logic into the WASPAS approach for enhanced decision analysis.

The proposed method holds the following merits:

- LR hexagonal fuzzy numbers help to model asymmetric and imprecise data effectively.
- Fuzzy graphs derive the weights of criteria based on their interrelationships.
- Enhances the WASPAS method by integrating LR hexagonal fuzzy numbers and fuzzy graphs.
- Treats the real-world complexity in parking lot selection using imprecise and interconnected criteria.

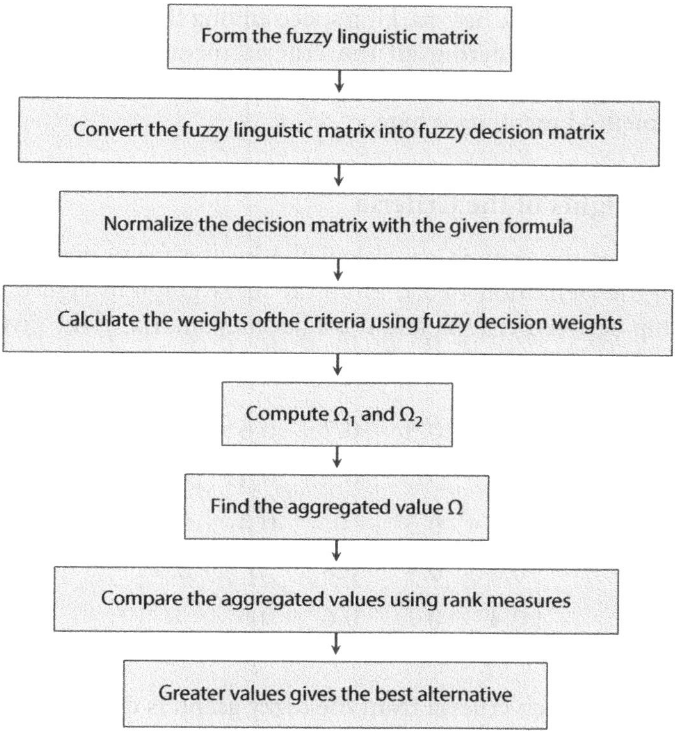

Figure 14.2 Flowchart representation of the fuzzy WASPAS approach using LR hexagonal fuzzy numbers.

- This approach offers a flexibility to other uncertain decision-making situations.
- Supports intelligent and uncertainty-aware urban planning and infrastructure decisions.

14.6 Real-Life Application

The linguistic terms used in this application are Extremely Inconvenient (EI), Unsatisfactory (US), Moderate (M), Satisfactory (S), Very Convenient (VC). $X = \{X_1, X_2, X_3, X_4, X_5\}$ are the set of alternatives and the set of criteria includes parking space availability, parking fee, security level, ease of access, traffic congestion around the parking lot is denoted by the set $C = \{C_1, C_2, C_3, C_4, C_5\}$, where C_1 – parking space availability, C_2 – parking fee, C_3 – security level, C_4 – ease of access, C_5 – traffic congestion around the lot.

The aim is to find the best parking space among the given parking space availability with considering all the criteria mentioned. To commence with, we need to find the criteria weights and compute the best parking lot using the method mentioned here.

14.6.1 Weights of the Criteria

The weights of the criteria are calculated by the fuzzy decision weight defined in the Definition 14.5.1. From the fuzzy graph in Figure 14.3, the relationship between criteria and the adjacency matrix of the given fuzzy graph is

$$\begin{bmatrix} 0 & 0.3 & 0.7 & 0.6 & 0.4 \\ 0.3 & 0 & 0.5 & 0.4 & 0.7 \\ 0.7 & 0.5 & 0 & 0.8 & 0.6 \\ 0.6 & 0.4 & 0.8 & 0 & 0.5 \\ 0.4 & 0.7 & 0.6 & 0.5 & 0 \end{bmatrix}$$

The degree of each criteria from the fuzzy graph is $\mathbf{d}(C)_1 = 2.0$, $\mathbf{d}(C)_2 = 1.9$, $\mathbf{d}(C)_3 = 2.6$, $\mathbf{d}(C)_4 = 2.3$, $\mathbf{d}(C)_5 = 2.2$, and the total degree is $T\,D = 11$. The weights of the criteria are calculated using Equation (14.14).

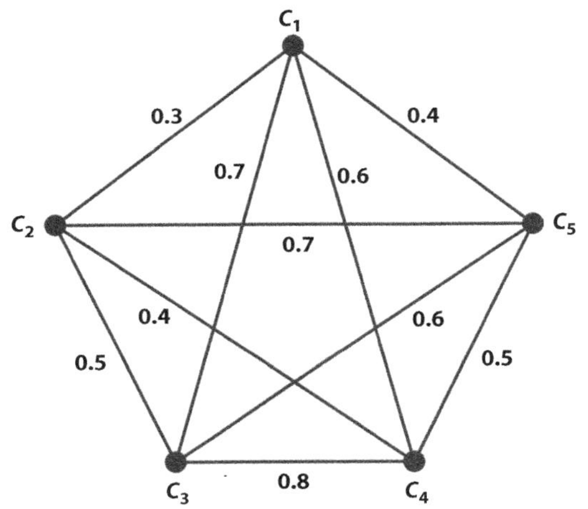

Figure 14.3 Relationship between criteria.

Table 14.1 Fuzzy decision weights.

Weights	Fuzzy decision weights
w_1	0.1818
w_2	0.1727
w_3	0.2364
w_4	0.2091
w_5	0.2000

$w(C_1)=\frac{2.0}{11}=0.1818$, $w(C_2)=\frac{1.9}{11}=0.1727$, $w(C_3)=\frac{2.6}{11}=0.2364$, $w(C_4)=\frac{2.3}{11}=0.2091$, $w(C_1)=\frac{2.2}{11}=0.2000$. The calculated fuzzy decision weights are given in Table 14.1.

14.6.2 *LR-HexFN* in Fuzzy WASPAS

The corresponding LR-hexagonal fuzzy number for the fuzzy linguistic term is given in Table 14.2.

Followed by this the fuzzy linguistic decision matrix is given in Table 14.3.

Using Table 14.2 and Table 14.3 the LR hexagonal fuzzy decision matrix is framed and given in Table 14.4.

Among the five criteria, C_1,C_3,C_4 are beneficial criteria and C_2,C_5 are non-beneficial criteria.

Table 14.2 LR-HexFN for fuzzy linguistic term.

Fuzzy linguistic terms	LR-HexFN
Extremely Inconvenient (EI)	(6,8:2,2,2,2;1,0.60,0.70)
Unsatisfactory (US)	(10,12:2,6,2,2;1,0.65,0.75)
Moderate (M)	(12,14:2,6,4,2;1,0.70,0.60)
Satisfactory (S)	(16,18:2,8,4,6;1,0.55,0.80)
Very Convenient (VC)	(18,20:2,8,6,4;1,0.75,0.50)

Table 14.3 Fuzzy linguistic matrix.

Alternative/criteria	C_1	C_2	C_3	C_4	C_5
X_1	M	VC	S	US	EI
X_2	US	S	VC	M	M
X_3	S	US	S	VC	US
X_4	VC	EI	M	S	S
X_5	EI	M	US	US	VC

Table 14.4 LR hexagonal fuzzy decision matrix.

A/C	C_1	C_2	C_3
X_1	(12,14:2,6,4,2;1,0.70,0.60)	(18,20:2,8,6,4;1,0.75,0.50)	(16,18:2,8,4,6;1,0.55,0.80)
X_2	(10,12:2,6,2,2;1,0.65,0.75)	(16,18:2,8,4,6;1,0.55,0.80)	(18,20:2,8,6,4;1,0.75,0.50)
X_3	(16,18:2,8,4,6;1,0.55,0.80)	(10,12:2,6,2,2;1,0.65,0.75)	(16,18:2,8,4,6;1,0.55,0.80)
X_4	(18,20:2,8,6,4;1,0.75,0.50)	(6,8:2,2,2,2;1,0.60,0.70)	(12,14:2,6,4,2;1,0.70,0.60)
X_5	(6,8:2,2,2,2;1,0.60,0.70)	(12,14:2,6,4,2;1,0.70,0.60)	(10,12:2,6,2,2;1,0.65,0.75)

A/C	C_4	C_5
X_1	(10,12:2,6,2,2;1,0.65,0.75)	(6,8:2,2,2,2;1,0.60,0.70)
X_2	(12,14:2,6,4,2;1,0.70,0.60)	(12,14:2,6,4,2;1,0.70,0.60)
X_3	(18,20:2,8,6,4;1,0.75,0.50)	(10,12:2,6,2,2;1,0.65,0.75)
X_4	(16,18:2,8,4,6;1,0.55,0.80)	(16,18:2,8,4,6;1,0.55,0.80)
X_5	(10,12:2,6,2,2;1,0.65,0.75)	(18,20:2,8,6,4;1,0.75,0.50)

To find the *minimum* and *maximum LR-HexFNs*, the ranking measures are used.

For beneficial criteria, In C_1, the scores of each element of the column is $MPS((12, 14 : 2, 6, 4, 2; 1, 0.70, 0.60)) = 13$, $MPS((10, 12 : 2, 6, 2, 2; 1, 0.65, 0.75)) = 11$, $MPS((16, 18 : 2, 8, 4, 6; 1, 0.55, 0.80)) = 17$, $MPS((18, 20 : 2, 8, 6, 4; 1, 0.75, 0.50)) = 19$, $MPS((6, 8 : 2, 2, 2, 2; 1, 0.60, 0.70)) = 7$, and the *max LR-HexFN* is (18, 20 : 2, 8, 6, 4; 1, 0.75, 0.50), since it has the greatest *MPS* value. Now using Equation (14.15), the normalized value is calculated.

$$
\begin{aligned}
v_{11} &= \frac{u_{11}}{max(u_{i1})} \\
&= \frac{(12,14:2,6,4,2;1,0.70,0.60)}{(18,20:2,8,6,4;1,0.75,0.50)} \\
&= (\frac{12}{20},\frac{14}{18}:\frac{(12-6)4+(20+6)2}{(20+6)(20+6+4)},\frac{12(6)+6(20)}{20(20+6)}, \\
&\quad \frac{4(18)+14(8)}{18(18-8)},\frac{(18-8)2+(14+4)2}{(18-8)(18-8-2)};(1)(1),(0.70)(0.75),(0.60)(0.50)) \\
&= (0.6000,0.7778:0.0975,0.3692,1.0222,0.7000;1,0.525,0.3)
\end{aligned}
$$

Similarly, the normalized value for all the elements of beneficial criteria in the matrix is calculated by identifying the *max LR-HexFN* for each column of beneficial criteria.

For non-beneficial criteria, the *min LR-HexFN* is identified by the ranking measures. In C_5, the scores of each element of the column is *MPS*((6, 8 : 2, 2, 2, 2; 1, 0.60, 0.70)) = 7, *MPS*((12, 14 : 2, 6, 4, 2; 1, 0.70, 0.60)) = 13, *MPS*((10, 12 : 2, 6, 2, 2; 1, 0.65, 0.75)) = 11, *MPS*((16, 18 : 2, 8, 4, 6; 1, 0.55, 0.80)) = 17, *MPS*((18, 20 : 2, 8, 6, 4; 1, 0.75, 0.50)) = 19, and the *min LR-HexFN* is (6, 8 : 2, 2, 2, 2; 1, 0.60, 0.70), since it has least *MPS* value.

Now using Equation (14.16), the normalized value is calculated.

$$
\begin{aligned}
v_{15} &= \frac{min(u_{i5})}{u_{15}} \\
&= \frac{(6,8:2,2,2,2;1,0.60,0.70)}{(6,8:2,2,2,2;1,0.60,0.70)} \\
&= (0.7500,1.3333:0.2333,0.3500,1.1667,3.5000;1,0.36,0.49)
\end{aligned}
$$

Similarly, the normalized value for all the elements of non-beneficial criteria in the matrix is calculated by identifying the *min LR-HexFN* for each column of non-beneficial criteria.

The normalized value for all the elements in the fuzzy decision matrix is calculated and the normalized fuzzy decision matrix is given in Table 14.5.

Table 14.5 Normalized fuzzy decision matrix.

A/C	C_1	C_2
X_1	(0.6000,0.7778:0.0975,0.3692,1.0222,0.7000;1,0.525,0.3)	(0.3000,0.4444:0.0871,0.1462,0.5556,0.5000;1,0.45,0.35)
X_2	(0.5000,0.6667:0.0871,0.3462,0.7333,0.6000;1,0.4875,0.375)	(0.3333,0.5000:0.0985,0.1515,0.7500,0.7500;1,0.33,0.56)
X_3	(0.8000,1.0000:0.1077,0.4923,1.2000,0.8000;1,0.4125,0.4)	(0.5000,0.8000:0.1607,0.2143,1.7000,3.5000;1,0.39,0.525)
X_4	(0.9000,1.1111:0.1179,0.5154,1.4889,1.1500;1,0.5625,0.25)	(0.7500,1.3333:0.2333,0.3500,1.1667,3.5000;1,0.36,0.49)
X_5	(0.3000,0.4444:0.0871,0.1462,0.5556,0.5000;1,0.45,0.35)	(0.4286,0.6667:0.1222,0.2064,1.0000,1.3333;1,0.42,0.42)

A/C	C_3	C_4
X_1	(0.8000,1.0000:0.1077,0.4923,1.2000,0.8000;1,0.4125,0.4)	(0.5000,0.6667:0.0871,0.3462,0.7333,0.6000;1,0.4875,0.375)
X_2	(0.9000,1.1111:0.1179,0.5154,1.4889,1.1500;1,0.5625,0.25)	(0.6000,0.7778:0.0975,0.3692,1.0222,0.7000;1,0.525,0.3)
X_3	(0.8000,1.0000:0.1077,0.4923,1.2000,0.8000;1,0.4125,0.4)	(0.9000,1.1111:0.1179,0.5154,1.4889,1.1500;1,0.5625,0.25)
X_4	(0.6000,0.7778:0.0975,0.3692,1.0222,0.7000;1,0.525,0.3)	(0.8000,1.0000:0.1077,0.4923,1.2000,0.8000;1,0.4125,0.4)
X_5	(0.5000,0.6667:0.0871,0.3462,0.7333,0.6000;1,0.4875,0.375)	(0.5000,0.6667:0.0871,0.3462,0.7333,0.6000;1,0.4875,0.375)

A/C	C_5
X_1	(0.7500,1.3333:0.2333,0.3500,1.1667,3.5000;1,0.36,0.49)
X_2	(0.4286,0.6667:0.1222,0.2064,1.0000,1.3333;1,0.42,0.42)
X_3	(0.5000,0.8000:0.1607,0.2143,1.7000,3.5000;1,0.39,0.525)
X_4	(0.3333,0.5000:0.0985,0.1515,0.7500,0.7500;1,0.33,0.56)
X_5	(0.3000,0.4444:0.0871,0.1462,0.5556,0.5000;1,0.45,0.35)

Using Equations (14.17) and (14.18), the weighted aggregation $\Omega_1(X_i)$ and $\Omega_2(X_i)$ are calculated and given in Table 14.6 and Table 14.7.

The aggregated value for each alternative is calculated by $\Omega(\mathcal{X}_i) = \lambda\Omega_1(\mathcal{X}_i) + (1-\lambda)\Omega_2(\mathcal{X}_i)$. For $\lambda = 0.5$, $\Omega(\mathcal{X}_i) = (0.5)\Omega_1(\mathcal{X}_i) + (0.5)\Omega_2(\mathcal{X}_i)$, the aggregated value for $\lambda = 0.5$ is given in Table 14.8.

Now, the $MPS(X_i)$ is calculated and the ranking is given in Table 14.9.

Table 14.6 Fuzzy WSM.

$\Omega_1(X_i)$	FWSM
X_1	(0.6046,0.8606:0.1231,0.3512,0.9522,1.2282;1,0.9497,0.9130)
X_2	(0.5724,0.7662:0.1056,0.3294,1.0286,0.9235;1,0.9586,0.9163)
X_3	(0.7091,0.9487:0.1296,0.3935,1.4468,1.8794;1,0.9438,0.9391)
X_4	(0.6689,0.9252:0.1270,0.3746,1.1148,1.2963;1,0.9476,0.9293)
X_5	(0.4113,0.5818:0.0931,0.2457,0.7115,0.6885;1,0.9539,0.9043)

Table 14.7 Fuzzy WPM.

$\Omega_2(X_i)$	FWPM
X_1	(0.5735,0.8082:0.1184,0.3373,0.9196,0.9894;1,0.0171,0.0077)
X_2	(0.5396,0.7392:0.1099,0.3092,0.9952,0.9022;1,0.02,0.0066)
X_3	(0.6882,0.9407:0.1353,0.3746,1.4487,1.6805;1,0.0146,0.011)
X_4	(0.6338,0.8788:0.1263,0.3518,1.0959,1.1355;1,0.0145,0.0082)
X_5	(0.4006,0.5710:0.0924,0.2367,0.6979,0.6530;1,0.0202,0.0072)

Table 14.8 Fuzzy aggregated value for $\lambda = 0.5$.

Alternative	Fuzzy WASPAS
X_1	(0.5891,0.8344:0.1207,0.3443,0.9359,1.1088;1,0.9506,0.9137)
X_2	(0.5560,0.7527:0.1077,0.3193,1.0119,0.9129;1,0.9594,0.9169)
X_3	(0.6987,0.9447:0.1324,0.3841,1.4478,1.7799;1,0.9446,0.9398)
X_4	(0.6514,0.9020:0.1267,0.3632,1.1054,1.2159;1,0.9484,0.9299)
X_5	(0.4060,0.5764:0.0928,0.2412,0.7047,0.6708;1,0.9548,0.9050)

Table 14.9 Midpoint score.

Alternative	$MPS(X_i)$	Rank
X_1	0.7118	3
X_2	0.6544	4
X_3	0.8217	1
X_4	0.7849	2
X_5	0.4934	5

14.7 Results and Discussion

The ranking results obtained in Table 14.9 for $\lambda = 0.5$ indicates that among the five evaluated parking lots X_1, X_2, X_3, X_4, X_5, X_3 is the most optimal choice with the highest aggregated value of 0.8217. Table 14.10 shows the ranking results remain consistent across different λ values, with X_3 consistently achieving the highest score, confirming its robustness as the optimal choice. The variations in midpoint scores for other λ values highlight the

Table 14.10 Midpoint scores for different values of λ.

Alternative	$\lambda = 0.0$	$\lambda = 0.1$	$\lambda = 0.2$	$\lambda = 0.3$	$\lambda = 0.4$
X_1	0.6909	0.6950	0.6992	0.7034	0.7076
X_2	0.6394	0.6424	0.6454	0.6484	0.6514
X_3	0.8145	0.8159	0.8174	0.8188	0.8203
X_4	0.7563	0.7604	0.7645	0.7685	0.7726
X_5	0.4858	0.4869	0.4880	0.4890	0.4901

Alternative	$\lambda = 0.6$	$\lambda = 0.7$	$\lambda = 0.8$	$\lambda = 0.9$	$\lambda = 1.0$
X_1	0.7159	0.7201	0.7243	0.7285	0.7326
X_2	0.6574	0.6604	0.6633	0.6663	0.6693
X_3	0.8231	0.8246	0.8260	0.8275	0.8289
X_4	0.7808	0.7849	0.7889	0.7930	0.7971
X_5	0.4923	0.4934	0.4944	0.4955	0.4966

sensitivity of ranking to decision-maker preferences, demonstrating the flexibility of the proposed Fuzzy WASPAS approach in adapting to different weighting scenarios.

A comparative study is carried out with the well-known multi-criteria decision-making (MCDM) approaches, such as Weighted product model (WPM), WASPAS, TOPSIS, and SAW, in order to verify the efficacy of the suggested approach. The final scores for each alternative were given in Table 14.11. From the graph given in the Figure 14.4, it is clear that the suggested approach consistently performs better than the current approaches across

Table 14.11 Comparison of scores of alternatives by different MCDM methods.

	WPM	TOPSIS	SAW	WASPAS	Proposed method
X_1	0.6524	0.5050	0.6933	0.6729	0.7118
X_2	0.6306	0.5204	0.6683	0.6494	0.6544
X_3	0.8029	0.7484	0.8117	0.8073	0.8217
X_4	0.7239	0.5686	0.7587	0.7413	0.7849
X_5	0.4338	0.1726	0.4417	0.4378	0.4934

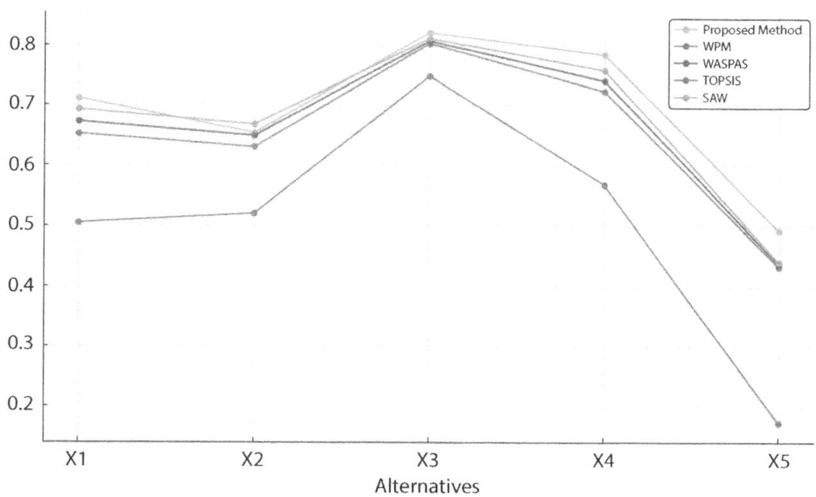

Figure 14.4 Comparison of the proposed method with existing MCDM techniques.

the alternatives. These results show the proposed approach's resilience and flexibility in selection of parking lots.

14.8 Conclusion and Future Work

This study proposed an advanced decision-making framework for optimal parking lot selection by integrating the LR representation of hexagonal fuzzy numbers with a fuzzy graph-based weighting mechanism in the WASPAS method. The key finding of this research is that the synergistic use of LR hexagonal fuzzy numbers that allows for more precise modeling of uncertainty and asymmetry in subjective evaluations, while fuzzy graphs effectively capture interdependencies among criteria to derive meaningful weights. For future research, the method can be extended to incorporate dynamic or real-time data, enabling adaptive decision-making in smart parking systems. Further studies could also explore the use of hybrid fuzzy numbers or type-2 fuzzy sets for handling higher degree of uncertainty.

Acknowledgment

The authors extend their gratitude to VIT Faculty SEED grant (RGEMS) for their invaluable support and to Vellore Institute of Technology Vellore, Tamil Nadu, India, for funding this research.

AI disclosure statement: The author acknowledges the use of AI-based tools for minor language editing or grammatical correction. However, all intellectual contributions, analyses, and conclusions presented in this chapter are entirely the author's own.

Bibliography

1. Zadeh, L.A., Fuzzy sets. *Inf. Control*, 8, 3, 338–353, 1965.
2. Rosenfeld, A., Fuzzy graphs, in: *Fuzzy sets and their applications to cognitive and decision processes*, pp. 77–95, Academic Press, New York, 1975.
3. Yeh, C.-T. and Chu, H.-M., Approximations by lr-type fuzzy numbers. *Fuzzy Sets Syst.*, 257, 23–40, 2014.
4. Aliniai, K., Yarahmadi, A., Zarin, J.Z., Yarahmadi, H., Lak, S.B., Parking lot site selection: An opening gate towards sustainable gis-based urban traffic management. *J. Indian Soc. Remote Sens.*, 43, 801–813, 2015.

5. Turskis, Z., Goranin, N., Nurusheva, A., Boranbayev, S., A fuzzy waspas-based approach to determine critical information infrastructures of EU sustainable development. *Sustainability*, 11, 2, 424, 2019.
6. Chakraborty, A., Maity, S., Jain, S., Mondal, S.P., Alam, S., Hexagonal fuzzy number and its distinctive representation, ranking, defuzzification technique and application in production inventory management problem. *Granular Comput.*, 6, 507–521, 2021.
7. Nayagam, V.L.G. and Murugan, J., Hexagonal fuzzy approximation of fuzzy numbers and its applications in mcdm. *Complex Intell. Syst.*, 7, 3, 1459–1487, 2021.
8. Demir, S., Basaraner, M., Gumus, A.T., Selection of suitable parking lot sites in megacities: A case study for four districts of istanbul. *Land Use Policy*, 111, 105731, 2021.
9. Amari, A., Moussaid, L., Tallal, S., New parking lot selection approach based on the multi-criteria decision making (mcdm) methods: health criteria. *Sustainability*, 15, 2, 938, 2023.
10. Gazi, K.H., Mondal, S.P., Chatterjee, B., Ghorui, N., Ghosh, A., De, D., A new synergistic strategy for ranking restaurant locations: A decision-making approach based on the hexagonal fuzzy numbers. *RAIRO Oper. Res.*, 57, 2, 571–608, 2023.
11. Kaur, G. and Garg, H., A novel algorithm for autonomous parking vehicles using adjustable probabilistic neutrosophic hesitant fuzzy set features. *Expert Syst. Appl.*, 226, 120101, 2023.
12. Ali, A.H., *et al.*, Fuzzy graph modeling and clustering analysis of nonlinear dynamical systems. *Babylonian J. Math.*, 2023, 18–22, 2023.
13. Kumar, R., Khepar, J., Yadav, K., Kareri, E., Alotaibi, S.D., Viriyasitavat, W., Gulati, K., Kotecha, K., Dhiman, G., A systematic review on generalized fuzzy numbers and its applications: past, present and future. *Arch. Comput. Methods Eng.*, 29, 7, 5213–5236, 2022.
14. Mordeson, J.N. and Chang-Shyh, P., Operations on fuzzy graphs. *Inf. Sci.*, 79, 3-4, 159–170, 1994.
15. Turskis, Z., Zavadskas, E.K., Antuchevičiene, J., Kosareva, N., A hybrid model based on fuzzy ahp and fuzzy waspas for construction site selection, 2015.
16. Kizielewicz, B. and Bączkiewicz, A., Comparison of fuzzy topsis, fuzzy vikor, fuzzy waspas and fuzzy mmoora methods in the housing selection problem. *Procedia Comput. Sci.*, 192, 4578–4591, 2021.
17. Mishra, A.R. and Rani, P., Multi-criteria healthcare waste disposal location selection based on fermatean fuzzy waspas method. *Complex Intell. Syst.*, 7, 5, 2469–2484, 2021.
18. Kutlu Gundogdu, F. and Kahraman, C., Extension of waspas with spherical fuzzy sets. *Informatica*, 30, 2, 269–292, 2019.
19. Rajarajeswari, P., Sudha, A.S., Karthika, R., A new operation on hexagonal fuzzy number. *Int. J. Fuzzy Log. Syst.*, 3, 3, 15–26, 2013.

20. Karthikeyan, N., *et al.*, A proposed method to solve transportation problem by generalized pentagonal and hexagonal fuzzy numbers. *Int. J. Aquat. Sci.*, 12, 2, 1499–1509, 2021.
21. Kane, L., Diakite, M., Kane, S., Bado, H., Diawara, D., Fully fuzzy transportation problems with pentagonal and hexagonal fuzzy numbers. *J. Appl. Res. Ind. Eng.*, 8, 3, 251–269, 2021.
22. Ghadle, K., Pathade, P., *et al.*, Optimal solution of balanced and unbalanced fuzzy transportation problem using hexagonal fuzzy numbers. *Int. J. Math. Res.*, 5, 2, 131–137, 2016.
23. He, R., Ma, C., Li, Y., Site selection of public parking lot in the new district. *Int. J. Wireless Mobile Comput.*, 8, 2, 147–152, 2015.
24. Kazazi Darani, S., Akbari Eslami, A., Jabbari, M., Asefi, H., Parking lot site selection using a fuzzy ahp-topsis framework in Tuyserkan, Iran. *J. Urban Plann. Dev.*, 144, 3, 04018022, 2018.
25. Ayyildiz, E. and Erdogan, M., A fermatean fuzzy swara-topsis methodology based on scor model for autonomous vehicle parking lot selection. *Appl. Soft Comput.*, 166, 112198, 2024.
26. Farzanmanesh, R., Naeeni, A.G., Abdullah, A.M., Parking site selection management using fuzzy logic and multi criteria decision making. *EnvironmentAsia*, 3, 3, 109–116, 2010.
27. Prabakar, P., Sajith, L., Sivagami, K., Kavindra, A., Muruganandam, L., Chakraborty, S., Production of mwcnts from plastic wastes: Method selection through multi-criteria decision-making techniques. *J. Taiwan Inst. Chem. Eng.*, 169, 106000, 2025.
28. Kishor, C., Murugan, J., Thiruvenkadam, S., Raju, J., Ra, I.-H., Selection of gubbins for wind turbine blades using fuzzy waspas method, in: *2024 Joint 13th International Conference on Soft Computing and Intelligent Systems and 25th International Symposium on Advanced Intelligent Systems (SCIS&ISIS)*, IEEE, pp. 1–6, 2024.
29. Al-Hawary, T., Complete fuzzy graphs. *Int. J. Math. Comb.*, 4, 26, 2011.
30. Zhou, J., Yang, F., Wang, K., Fuzzy arithmetic on lr fuzzy numbers with applications to fuzzy programming. *J. Intell. Fuzzy Syst.*, 30, 1, 71–87, 2016.
31. Stefanini, L. and Sorini, L., Fuzzy arithmetic with parametric lr fuzzy numbers, in: *IFSA/EUSFLAT Conf.*, pp. 600–605, 2009.
32. Saneifard, R., Ranking lr fuzzy numbers with weighted averaging based on levels, 2009.
33. Veeramani, C., Duraisamy, C., Sumathi, M., A note on ranking of lr fuzzy numbers. *Opsearch*, 50, 282–296, 2013.

15

Dissemination Index in Fuzzy Graph Networks

Parvathy Gnana Sambandam[1]*, Sundareswaran Raman[1], Shanmugapriya Marayanagaraj[1] and Said Broumi[2]

[1]*Department of Mathematics, Sri Sivasubramaniya Nadar College of Engineering, Kalavakkam, Chennai, India*
[2]*Laboratory of Information Processing, Faculty of Science Ben M'Sik, University of Hassan II, Casablanca, Morocco*

Abstract
This chapter introduces a novel framework for analyzing information flow in fuzzy graph networks through the concept of dissemination. A new parameter, the dissemination index, is proposed to measure the effectiveness of information spread within a fuzzy graph. Optimal disseminating sequences are identified, and dissemination indices are computed for various standard fuzzy graphs. The dissemination gap, defined as the difference between the maximum and minimum dissemination indices, is analyzed to assess the uniformity and efficiency of information flow. The proposed model is applied to a smart hospital emergency alert system, ensuring prompt and reliable communication between critical nodes. Modeling the hospital as a fuzzy graph network enables efficient dissemination of alerts for rapid emergency response.

Keywords: Fuzzy graph dissemination, dissemination index, disseminating sequence, dissemination gap, smart hospital alert system

15.1 Introduction

In many real-world scenarios, such as social media influence, emergency alert systems, disease transmission, and sensor-based anomaly detection,

**Corresponding author*: parvathyg@ssn.edu.in

Harish Garg (ed.) Decision Support Systems in Smart Computing: Embracing Uncertainty and Challenges, (469–492) © 2026 Scrivener Publishing LLC

information spreads gradually through a network rather than instantaneously. This process of information propagation involves not only source nodes that initiate the spread, but also intermediate nodes that help carry the information further. Recognizing these distinct roles, this work introduces two types of nodes in the information dissemination process: disseminators, which begin the spread and propagators, which receive and forward information to other nodes. The idea of modeling such information flow in networks was originally formalized through the concept of graph burning [8], which simulates the sequential activation of nodes to represent the spread of information [4, 5, 8].

Motivated by the limitations of traditional crisp graph models, recent research has shifted toward fuzzy graph networks, which offer a more realistic representation of systems characterized by uncertainty and partial relationships. The foundational theory of fuzzy graphs was established in 1975 by [21, 22] and later expanded through the introduction of strong arcs [7], which describe the strength and robustness of interactions between nodes.

In this chapter, a new parameter called the *dissemination index* is introduced. This index identifies the most efficient combination of source nodes (disseminators) and the minimum number of rounds (phases) required to spread information across the entire fuzzy network. The model also introduces the concept of a *dissemination gap*, defined as difference between the maximum and minimum dissemination indices among possible configurations. This helps measure how uniformly and efficiently information can spread across the system.

A Key motivation behind this work is the growing need for reliable and fast information flow in smart hospital environments. In situations where emergency alerts must be communicated between ICU monitors, nurse stations, operating rooms, emergency units and delay or failure in communication can have serious consequences for patient safety. By representing these hospital components as nodes within a fuzzy network, the proposed dissemination framework aims to improve how alerts are spread, ultimately supporting faster response times and more dependable outcomes. The relevance of fuzzy graph models in such setting is further supported by recent research. For example, in [20], a linear Diophantine fuzzy graph was used to extend the operational life of wireless charging sensor networks through a mobile robot that manages both power and communication efficiently. Similarly [11] introduced a bipartite fuzzy graph approach based on probabilistic dual hesitant values to help screen travelers during the COVID-19 pandemic, highlighting the importance of uncertainty-aware models in health and safety applications.

These studies clearly highlight the increasing importance of fuzzy graph-based models for handling information flow in uncertain and dynamic environments. Inspired by such real-world applications, especially in health and safety systems, this work aims to create a suitable framework for applying the dissemination index in smart hospital settings. By modeling key components such as ICU monitors, nurse stations and emergency rooms as nodes in a fuzzy network, the propose approach seeks to improve the speed and reliability of emergency communications, ultimately enhancing patient care and response times.

15.1.1 Literature Survey

Fuzzy graph theory has seen steady development since its inception by [21, 22], who introduced fuzzy graphs as a way to model uncertainty in networks, especially within cognitive and decision-making processes. His foundational contributions set the stage for much of the later research in fuzzy graph theory. Building upon this, [6] provided early critical observations on the structure and properties of fuzzy graphs, helping to distinguish their behavior from that of classical graphs. [7] later introduced the concept of strong arcs, which became a key element in analyzing connectivity and strength in fuzzy relationships.

[14–16] contributed extensively to the theoretical development of fuzzy graphs. Their work covered fuzzy hypergraphs [14], cycles and cocycles [16] and specialized structures such as fuzzy trees and cycles [15], offering a clear understanding of structural nuances in fuzzy systems. Their collaborations led to further exploration of advanced topics [17], culminating in comprehensive treatments of fuzzy graph theory in book form [26].

The structural elements of fuzzy graphs were also explored in depth by [25], who classified types of arcs and elaborated on their roles in shaping graph behavior. Their joint survey [27] provided a thorough overview of the field's development, highlighting key trends and open problems. [28] focused on completed fuzzy graphs, extending the framework to explore completeness and total connectivity in fuzzy structures. Together these studies reflect a rich and evolving theoretical landscape. They demonstrate how foundational insights have been expanded through detailed examinations of structure, connectivity and control, making fuzzy graph theory a versatile tool for modeling uncertainty in complex systems.

Domination in fuzzy graphs plays a vital role in ensuring that all nodes are effectively influenced or reached, making it a robust framework for comprehensive information dissemination. The foundational idea was introduced by [23], who defined domination using effective edges to capture influence in uncertain environments. This foundational work was further developed in [24], where additional properties and characterizations of fuzzy domination were explored. [19] extended this by studying domination and arc domination using strong arcs. [12] introduced the concept of the strong domination number in fuzzy graphs by utilizing the membership values of strong arcs and determined this parameter for structures such as complete and complete bipartite fuzzy graphs. Further, [13] proposed the strong arc domination number, examined it for fuzzy cycles and trees, and explored its relationship with arc covering. These studies underline the growing role of domination parameters in modeling influence and information spread in fuzzy networks.

Graph burning is a discrete-time process that models the spread of information or influence in a network, making it highly relevant for studying information dissemination. In each round, an unburned node is chosen as a new ignition point, while previously burned nodes continue to ignite their neighbors. The process ends when all nodes in the graph are burned. The burning number refers to the minimum number of steps needed to achieve this complete spread. This concept was formally introduced by [8] as a framework for modeling social contagion. Their subsequent work [9] focused on the strategies for efficient burning and examined the computational aspects of the problem. [4] later proved that determining the burning number is NP-hard, and further provided tight bounds for specific classed of graphs [5], highlighting the relationship between graph structure and dissemination efficiency. More recently, [3] refined these bounds and deepened the understanding of the problem's computational difficulty. In addition, [18] explored the k-burning number problem establishing its APX-hardness and suggesting approximation techniques for practical applications. [30] contributed by characterizing Q-graphs based on their burning numbers, demonstrating how structural graph properties can influence the pattern of information speed. Collectively, these contributions establish graph burning as an insightful and applicable model for analyzing and optimizing information dissemination in various types of networks.

15.1.2 Why Graph Burning Offers a More Realistic Framework for Information Propagation

For instance, in a public emergency communication system, multiple official agencies issue alerts simultaneously in different regions. These messages are then picked up by local authorities, media outlets and digital platforms, who further transmit the alerts to communities and individuals. This layered transmission ensures broader and more efficient coverage within a short time.

Traditional fuzzy domination-based models focus only on identifying a minimal set of dominating nodes that cover all other nodes in one step. They do not model how the information actually propagates through the network over time, nor do they account for the supporting role of intermediate nodes. As a result, such models can underestimate the complexity and delay of real dissemination processes.

In contrast, the graph burning model inherently incorporates both disseminators and propagators. It reflects how information spreads progressively over multiple steps and captures the influence of each node over time. This metric is more practical and informative when modeling real-time or sequential dissemination scenarios, making graph burning a stronger and more realistic framework for information propagation.

15.1.3 Motivation and Proposed Method

In real-life situations, information spreads gradually from one node to another with the help of intermediate nodes, following a cooperative process. However, traditional information propagation parameters like domination in fuzzy graphs focus mainly on identifying key nodes that can "cover" the entire network, without accounting for the cooperative role of intermediate nodes in sustaining the spread. Therefore, this step-by-step cooperative spreading process is not captured by traditional information dissemination models, making them less suitable for modeling real-world information dissemination.

To bridge this gap, a propagation-based framework is introduced in fuzzy graphs, which reflects how information gradually spreads through both source nodes and intermediate nodes. This approach identifies a disseminating sequence, a set of nodes that actively initiate and sustain the spread and introduces a dissemination index to quantify the minimum total strength required to ensure the entire network is reached effectively. Unlike traditional propagation models, it effectively reflects the cooperative and stepwise nature of real-world information dissemination.

15.1.4 Objective of the Proposed Method

- ➢ To introduce a propagation-based framework in fuzzy graphs that models information dissemination through both source (disseminator) and intermediate (propagator) nodes.

- To define and utilize a disseminating sequence that captures the step-by-step spread of information across the fuzzy graph network.
- To establish the dissemination index as a new parameter for quantifying the minimum total membership strength needed to ensure complete information reaches across the network.
- To identify the minimum set of disseminators that can achieve complete network coverage in the least number of phases, with their combined membership values representing the overall efficiency of the fuzzy graph's dissemination process.

15.2 Dissemination Index

In a fuzzy graph $G = (V, \sigma, \mu)$, the dissemination process defines how nodes influence or connect with one another *via* α-strong arcs [8]. By focusing on α-strong arcs, the dissemination process ensures that the spread of influence or data occurs through reliable paths, thereby improving the robustness and efficiency of the network. In the process of information propagation within a network, certain nodes play distinct roles to ensure efficient dissemination. The *disseminator* is a node that initiates the spread of information across the network. It actively takes responsibility for acquainting other nodes with the information, serving as the primary source of dissemination. A *propagator* is a node that receives information from a disseminator (or another propagator) and further transmits it to other nodes, helping sustain and extend the information flow throughout the network.

The dissemination process in a fuzzy graph differs from other network propagation mechanisms in that both the disseminator and propagator nodes play significant roles in spreading information throughout the network. Unlike traditional methods the propagator nodes also help by keeping the information moving and reaching more parts of the network. Therefore, the objective is to identify the minimum set of disseminators with the least number of phases (rounds) in the fuzzy graph, where the sum of their membership value defines the dissemination index of the graph, representing the overall strength and effectiveness of its information dissemination capability. The proposed definitions for this study are as follows,

Definition 1: Two nodes $u, v \in V(G)$ of a fuzzy graph $G = (V, \sigma, \mu)$ are said to disseminate each other, if there exists a α-strong arc between them. If u disseminates v, then the node u is referred to as a disseminator, and the node v is referred to as a propagator.

Definition 2: A sequence $\mathfrak{D}_{\mathcal{S}} \subseteq V(G)$ is a disseminating sequence if for every $V(G) \setminus \mathfrak{D}_{\mathcal{S}}$, there exists $u_i \in \mathfrak{D}_{\mathcal{S}}$ such that the union of their α-strong neighborhoods satisfies $\cup N_{\mathcal{S}}[u_i] = V(G)$. Each member of $\mathfrak{D}_{\mathcal{S}}$ is called as a disseminator or source node.

Definition 3: Let $G = (V, \sigma, \mu)$ be a fuzzy graph, and let $\mathfrak{D}_{\mathcal{S}} \subseteq V(G)$ be a disseminating sequence. The disseminating index of a fuzzy graph G, denoted by $\mathfrak{D}_{\mathfrak{l}}(G)$, is defined as the minimum total membership value of the disseminators, given by $\mathfrak{D}_{\mathfrak{l}}(G) = min\left(\sum_{v_i \in \mathfrak{D}_{\mathcal{S}}} \sigma(v_i)\right)$.

Remark 1: The term disseminating sequence is used for the set $\mathfrak{D}_{\mathcal{S}} \subseteq V(G)$, since the order of the nodes within the set is significant and cannot be interchanged.

Example 1: Consider the fuzzy graph shown in Figure 15.1, where all arcs are α-strong arcs. Initially, select $\boldsymbol{v_3}$ as the disseminator in Phase 1. The set of nodes disseminated by $\boldsymbol{v_3}$ in Phase 2 is $\boldsymbol{N_{\mathcal{S}}(v_3) = \{v_2, v_4, v_5, v_6, v_7, v_8\}}$. Since in every phase there must be a disseminator, choose $\boldsymbol{v_1}$ as the disseminator in Phase 2. Consequently, the set of disseminators is $\boldsymbol{\mathfrak{D}_{\mathcal{S}}(G) = \{v_3, v_1\}}$. Thus, the dissemination process completes within two phases. The dissemination Index is $\boldsymbol{\mathfrak{D}_{\mathfrak{l}}(G) = 0.8 + 0.7 = 1.5}$. Now, consider interchanging the order of $\boldsymbol{\mathfrak{D}_{\mathcal{S}}(G) = \{v_3, v_1\}}$, meaning $\boldsymbol{v_1}$ acts as the disseminator in Phase 1. In this case, the set of nodes disseminated by $\boldsymbol{v_1}$

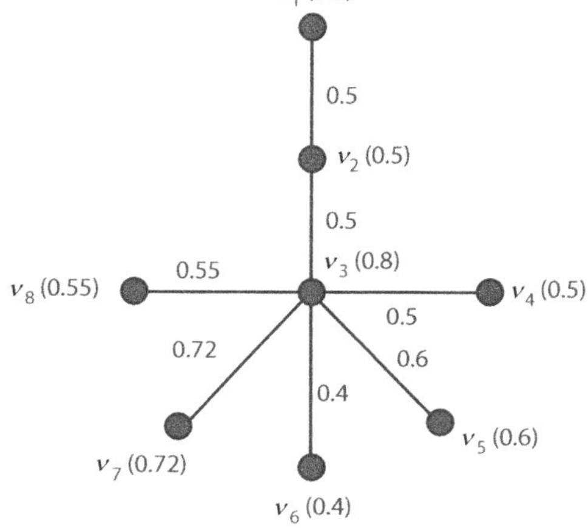

Figure 15.1 Graph G showing non-interchangeable node order in dissemination.

in Phase 2 is $N_{\mathscr{B}}(v_1)=\{v_2\}$. Next, if v_3 is selected as the disseminator in Phase 2, then the nodes $\{v_4, v_5, v_6, v_7, v_8\}$ become propagators requiring further dissemination in Phase 3. One of these propagators must then act as the disseminator in Phase 3 say v_5. Hence, under this changed order, dissemination would require three phases instead of two. This contradicts the objective of minimizing the number of phases required for complete dissemination. Therefore, it is concluded that maintaining the original order of the dissemination sequence plays a crucial role in achieving optimal dissemination in a fuzzy graph.

Throughout the manuscript, strong arc represents α-strong arc.

15.2.1 Dissemination Process for a Fuzzy Graph

To disseminate the entire fuzzy graph G within h phases, the following steps are followed:

Initialization: Set $\mathfrak{D}_{\mathscr{B}}(G)=\phi$

Step 1: Consider the fuzzy graph $G=(V,\sigma,\mu)$ and identify all α-strong arcs.

Step 2: Preferably select the node with the maximum α-strong neighborhood degree and the least membership grade.

If multiple nodes satisfy these conditions, choose the one with the minimum eccentricity.

Let K^* be the collection of nodes with maximum α-strong neighborhood degree and the least membership grade. i.e., Let $K^* = \{v_1^*, v_2^*, \ldots, v_h^*\}$.

Step 3: For $1 \le i \le h$

Select a node $v_i^* \in V(G)$ as the disseminator in phase i.

Step 4: If $N_{\mathscr{B}}(v_i^*) \neq \phi$, proceed to Step 4; otherwise, include v_i in $\mathfrak{D}_{\mathscr{B}}(G)$.

Step 5: In phase $i+1$:

The Propagator nodes in $N_{\mathscr{B}}(v_i)$ are disseminated by the disseminator v_i of Phase i.

Choose a new disseminator say v_{i+1} either from $N_{\&}(v_i^*)$ or $V(G)-N_{\mathscr{B}}[v_i^*]$

Step 6: Do Step 4 and Step 5 until all nodes are disseminated.

Step 7: End For

Step 8: $\mathfrak{D}_{I}(G)=min\left(\sum_{v_i\in\mathfrak{D}_{\&}}\sigma(v_i)\right)$

Example 2:

Table 15.1 illustrates the identification of strong arcs. It is transparent that (v, w) and (w, z) are not strong arcs, whereas all the other arcs are strong. Therefore, the nodes v and w cannot mutually disseminate information. In the same way, w cannot disseminate z.

The disseminating sequences of Figure 15.2 are as follows:

$$\mathfrak{D}_{\mathcal{B}}(G) = \left(v(0.4), w(0.6), z(0.4)\right), \mathfrak{D}_{\mathcal{B}}(G) = \left(u(1), x(0.3), z(0.4)\right)$$

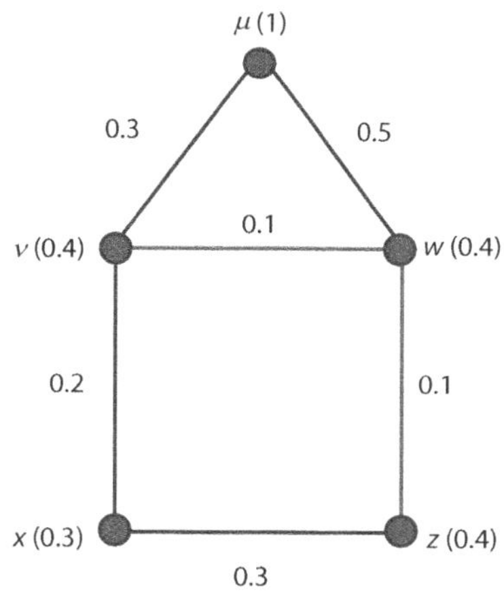

Figure 15.2 Illustration of dissemination process.

Table 15.1 Identification of strong arcs.

Arcs	Weight of arcs	$CONN_{G-(x,y)}(x, y)$	Strong arc/non-strong arc
(u, v)	0.3	0.1	Strong arc
(u, w)	0.5	0.1	Strong arc
(v, w)	0.1	0.3	Not Strong arc
(v, x)	0.2	0.1	Strong arc
(w, z)	0.1	0.2	Not Strong arc
(x, z)	0.3	0.1	Strong arc

$$\mathfrak{D}_{\mathscr{g}}(G) = (z(0.4), u(1), v(0.4)),\ \mathfrak{D}_{\mathscr{g}}(G) = (x(0.3), u(1), w(0.6)),$$
$$\mathfrak{D}_{\mathscr{g}}(G) = (w(0.6), x(0.3), z(0.4)),\ \mathfrak{D}_{\mathscr{g}}(G) = (z(0.4), v(0.4), w(0.6))$$

$$\mathfrak{D}_{\mathfrak{l}}(G) = \wedge((0.4+0.6+0.4),(1+0.3+0.4),(0.4+1+0.4),(0.3+1+0.6),(0.6+0.3+0.4),\ (0.4+0.4+0.6))$$
$$= \wedge(1.4, 1.7, 1.8, 1.9, 1.3, 1.4) = 1.3$$

Hence, the disseminating index of the fuzzy graph in Figure 15.1 is $\mathfrak{D}_{\mathfrak{l}}(G) = 1.3$.

Proposition 1: Let G be a connected fuzzy graph G with two nodes, then $\mathfrak{D}_{\mathfrak{l}}(G) = \mathrm{p}$.

The dissemination index of the G with two nodes is p since the edge is the strong arc (choosing both vertices in both phases).

Aside from the aforementioned, the fuzzy graph with isolated nodes also has the dissemination index as p, which prompted the following theorem.

Theorem 1: Let G be a fuzzy graph of order p. Then $\mathfrak{D}_{\mathfrak{l}}(G) = \mathrm{p}$ if and only if every node of G is isolated.

Proof: As every node in the fuzzy graph G: (V, σ, μ) is isolated, it is very clear that $\mathfrak{D}_{\mathfrak{l}}(G) = \mathrm{p}$. Conversely let $\mathfrak{D}_{\mathfrak{l}}(G) = \mathrm{p}$. To prove every node of G is isolated. By contrary, let u be a non-isolated node of G. Then there exists an arc say (u, v). Since G is connected and $u, v \in V(G)$, by Proposition 1 $\mathfrak{D}_{\mathfrak{l}}(G) = \mathrm{p}$. Now, let u be a non-isolated node with strong neighbours say $N_s(u) = \{v, t\}$. Therefore, $(\sigma(u), \sigma(v))$ or $(\sigma(u), \sigma(t))$ is the disseminating sequence. Hence $\mathfrak{D}_{\mathfrak{l}}(G) < p$, which is a contradiction. Hence every node of G is isolated.

Theorem 2: If G: (V, σ, μ) is a complete fuzzy graph, then $\mathfrak{D}_{\mathfrak{l}}(G) = \wedge\{\sigma(u) + \sigma(v); u, v \in V(G)\}$.

Proof: Each and every node is connected to each other, and all of the arcs are strong arcs as G is a complete fuzzy graph. Therefore, $\mathfrak{D}_{\mathscr{g}}(G) = (\sigma(u), \sigma(v))$ is a disseminating sequence for each $u, v \in V(G)$. Hence, $\mathfrak{D}_{\mathfrak{l}}(G) = \wedge\{\sigma(u) + \sigma(v); u, v \in V(G)\}$.

Theorem 3: Let G be a strong fuzzy graph with $|\sigma^*| = n$, then $\mathfrak{D}_{\mathfrak{l}}(G) = \min_{\mathfrak{D}_{\mathscr{g}} \subseteq V(G)} \{\sum_{v_i \in \mathfrak{D}_{\mathscr{g}}} \sigma(v_i)\}$.

Proof: G is a strong fuzzy graph, implying all the arcs of G are strong arcs. Let $v_1, v_2, \ldots, v_n$ be the vertices of G. Choose a node $v_i \in V(G), 1 \le i \le \hbar$ as the disseminator in phase i with maximum strong neighborhood degree, then in phase $i+1$, $N_{\mathscr{B}}(v_i)$ nodes are disseminated by v_i of phase i. Also, choose a disseminator v_{i+1} in phase $i+1$ from $V(G)\{v_1, v_2, \ldots v_i\}$. Assume v_{i+1} as new v_i and repeat the process until all the nodes of $V(G)$ are disseminated. Eventually, $\cup_{i=1}^{\hbar} N_{\mathscr{B}}[v_i] = V(G)$. Therefore, the disseminating sequence $\mathfrak{D}_{\mathscr{B}}(G) = \{\sigma(v_1), \sigma(v_2), \ldots, \sigma(v_{\hbar})\}$ sequential order as in the phases.

Hence, $\mathfrak{D}_{\mathfrak{f}}(G) = \min_{\mathfrak{D}_{\mathscr{B}} \subseteq V(G)} \{\sum_{v_i \in \mathfrak{D}_{\mathscr{B}}} \sigma(v_i)\}$.

Proposition 2: If $G:(V, \sigma, \mu)$ is a fuzzy cycle such that G^* is a cycle with $|\sigma^*| = n$, $n \geq 3$. Then, $s\mathfrak{D}_{\mathfrak{f}}(G) = \min_{\mathfrak{D}_{\mathscr{B}} \subseteq V(G)} \left[\sum_{i=1}^{\left\lceil n^{\frac{1}{2}} \right\rceil} \sigma(\alpha_i), \alpha_i \in \mathfrak{D}_{\mathscr{B}} \right]$.

Proof: As G is a fuzzy cycle. All arcs of G are strong arcs. As G^* is a cycle with $|\sigma^*| = n$. By the method of induction, $\left\lceil n^{\frac{1}{2}} \right\rceil$ disseminators from G^*. Then, the minimum value of the sum of the membership values of the $\left\lceil n^{\frac{1}{2}} \right\rceil$ disseminators prove the result.

Remark 2: Proposition 2 holds good if G^* is a path for a fuzzy graph $G:(V, \sigma, \mu)$.

Theorem 4: If G: (V, σ, μ) is a complete bipartite fuzzy graph with partite sets V_1 and V_2, Then, either one of the following holds:

(i) $\mathfrak{D}_{\mathfrak{f}}(G) = \wedge\{\sigma(\alpha) + \sigma(\beta) + \sigma(\omega)\}$
(ii) $\mathfrak{D}_{\mathfrak{f}}(G) = \wedge\{\sigma(\alpha) + \sigma(\beta)\}$

Proof: All the arcs of G are strong as it is a complete bipartite fuzzy graph. The proof is very obvious if $|V_1| = |V_2| = 1$ and the condition (ii) holds.

Case (i): Let $|V_1| = |V_2| = 2$, then there exist two possibilities:

(i) $|V_1|_s < |V_2|_s$
(ii) $|V_1|_s > |V_2|_s$
(iii) $|V_1|_s = |V_2|_s$

Subcase(i): Let $|V_1|_s < |V_2|_s$, choose $\wedge_{\alpha \in V_1} \sigma(\alpha)$ in the first phase. $N_s(\alpha)$ nodes are disseminated in the second phase, where $|N_s(\alpha)| = |V_2|$ and choose $\beta \in V_1$ in the same phase (since, $|V_1|_s < |V_2|_s$, and if $\beta \in V_2$, then the node $V_1 - \wedge_{\alpha \in V_1} \sigma(\alpha)$ is disseminated in the third phase. Therefore, $\wedge(\sigma(\alpha)+\sigma(\beta)+\sigma(\omega)) > \wedge(\sigma(\alpha)+\sigma(\beta))$. So, choose β from V_1). Therefore, $\mathfrak{D}_{\mathcal{g}}(G) = \{\sigma(\alpha), \sigma(\beta)\}, \alpha, \beta \in V_1$. Hence (ii) holds.
Subcase(ii): Let $|V_2|_s < |V_1|_s$, choose $\wedge_{\alpha \in V_2} \sigma(\alpha)$ in the first phase. $N_s(\alpha)$ nodes are disseminated in the second phase, where $|N_s(\alpha)| = |V_1|$ and choose $\beta \in V_2$ in the same phase (since, $|V_2|_s < |V_1|_s$, and if $\beta \in V_1$, then the node $V_2 - \wedge_{\alpha \in V_2} \sigma(\alpha)$ is disseminated in the third phase and so $\wedge(\sigma(\alpha)+\sigma(\beta)+\sigma(\omega)) > \wedge(\sigma(\alpha)+\sigma(\beta))$. Therefore, choose β from V_2). Therefore, $\mathfrak{D}_{\mathcal{g}}(G) = \{\sigma(\alpha), \sigma(\beta)\}, \alpha, \beta \in V_2$. Hence (ii) holds.
Subcase(iii): Let $|V_1|_s = |V_2|_s$, Choose a node α, in the first phase either from V_1 or V_2. Therefore, in phase two, α disseminates $N_s(\alpha) = V(G) - V_1$ if $\alpha \in V_1$ or $N_s(\alpha) = V(G) - V_2$ if $\alpha \in V_2$, since all the nodes of V_1 of $V(G)$ are adjacent to V_2 of $V(G)$ and conversely. Now,

$$V(G) - \Lambda\{\sigma(\alpha)\} - N_s(\alpha) \tag{15.1}$$

nodes are left non-disseminated in the second phase.

If $\alpha \in V_1$ in (1), then $V_1 - \Lambda\sigma(\alpha)$ is left non-disseminated. That is., only one node is about to disseminate. So, choose $\beta \in V_1$ in the second phase (since, $|V_1|_s = |V_2|_s$, and if $\beta \in V_2$, then the node $V_1 - \wedge_{\alpha \in V_1} \sigma(\alpha)$ is disseminated in the third phase and so $\wedge(\sigma(\alpha)+\sigma(\beta)+\sigma(\omega)) > \wedge(\sigma(\alpha)+\sigma(\beta))$. Therefore, choose β from V_1). Thus, $\mathfrak{D}_{\mathcal{g}}(G) = \{\sigma(\alpha), \sigma(\beta)\}, \alpha, \beta \in V_1$. Hence (ii) holds.

If $\alpha \in V_2$ in (1), then $V_2 - \Lambda\sigma(\alpha)$ is left non-disseminated. That is., only one node is about to disseminate. So, choose $\beta \in V_2$ in the second phase (since, $|V_1|_s = |V_2|_s$, and if $\beta \in V_1$, then the node $V_2 - \wedge_{\alpha \in V_2} \sigma(\alpha)$ is disseminated in the third phase and so $\wedge(\sigma(\alpha)+\sigma(\beta)+\sigma(\omega)) > \wedge(\sigma(\alpha)+\sigma(\beta))$. Therefore, choose β from V_2). Thus, $\mathfrak{D}_{\mathcal{g}}(G) = \{\sigma(\alpha), \sigma(\beta)\}, \alpha, \beta \in V_2$. Hence (ii) holds.

Case (ii): Let $|V_1| = 2$ and $|V_2| > 2$ then there exist two cases:
Subcase(i): Let $|V_1|_s = |V_1|$ and $|V_1|_s > |V_2|_s$, choose $\wedge_{\alpha \in V_2} \sigma(\alpha)$ in the first phase. Now $N_s(\alpha)$ nodes are disseminated by α. That is., nodes of V_1 are entirely disseminated in the second phase. Thus, $V_2 - \wedge_{\alpha \in V_2} \sigma(\alpha)$ are left non-disseminated. Therefore, choose $\beta \in V_2$ such that $\sigma(\beta) \geq \sigma(\alpha)$ in the second phase. Now, any node in V_1 disseminates the $V_2 - \{\sigma(\alpha)\} - \sigma(\beta)$ in the third phase. Even though all nodes of $V(G)$ are disseminated, choose

a node $\omega \in V_2$ in the third phase (since, $|V_1|_s > |V_2|_s$ and by the definition of disseminating sequence) such that $\sigma(\omega) \geq \sigma(\beta) \geq \sigma(\alpha)$. Hence, $\{\sigma(\alpha), \sigma(\beta), \sigma(\omega)\}$, $\alpha, \beta, \omega \in V_2$. Therefore (i) holds.

Subcase(ii): Let $|V_1|_s < |V_2|_s$ and assume the membership grade of each node in V_1 is less than the membership grade of V_2. Choose $\wedge_{\alpha \in V_1} \sigma(\alpha)$ in the first phase. Now, $N_s(\alpha)$ nodes are disseminated by α. That is., nodes of V_2 are entirely disseminated in the second phase. Thus, $V_1 - \wedge_{\alpha \in V_1} \sigma(\alpha)$ are left non-disseminated. Thus, choose $\beta \in V_1$ such that $\sigma(\beta) \geq \sigma(\alpha)$ in the second phase. Hence $\{\sigma(\alpha), \sigma(\beta)\}$, $\alpha, \beta \in V_1$. Therefore (ii) holds.

Case (iii): Let $|V_2| = 2$ and $|V_1| > 2$ then there exist two cases:

Subcase(i): Let $|V_2|_s = |V_2|$ and $|V_2|_s < |V_1|_s$, choose $\wedge_{\alpha \in V_1} \sigma(\alpha)$ in the first phase. Now $N_s(\alpha)$ nodes are disseminated by α. That is, nodes of V_2 are entirely disseminated in the second phase. Thus, $V_1 - \wedge_{\alpha \in V_1} \sigma(\alpha)$ are left non-disseminate. Therefore, choose $\beta \in V_1$ such that $\sigma(\beta) \geq \sigma(\alpha)$ in the second phase. Now, any node in V_2 disseminates the $V_1 - \{\sigma(\alpha)\} - \sigma(\beta)$ in the third phase. Even though all nodes of $V(G)$ are disseminated, choose a node $\omega \in V_1$ in the third phase (since, $|V_2|_s > |V_1|_s$ and by the definition of disseminating sequence) such that $\sigma(\omega) \geq \sigma(\beta) \geq \sigma(\alpha)$. Hence, $\{\sigma(\alpha), \sigma(\beta), \sigma(\omega)\}$, $\alpha, \beta, \omega \in V_1$. Therefore (i) holds.

Subcase(ii): Let $|V_2|_s < |V_1|_s$ and assume the membership grade of each node in V_2 is less than the membership grade of V_1. Choose $\wedge_{\alpha \in V_2} \sigma(\alpha)$ in the first phase. Now, $N_s(\alpha)$ nodes are disseminated by α. That is, nodes of V_1 are completely disseminated in the second phase. Thus, $V_2 - \wedge_{\alpha \in V_2} \sigma(\alpha)$ are left non-disseminated. Thus, choose $\beta \in V_2$ such that $\sigma(\beta) \geq \sigma(\alpha)$ in the second phase. Hence $\{\sigma(\alpha), \sigma(\beta)\}$, $\alpha, \beta \in V_2$. Therefore (ii) holds.

Case(iv): Let $|V_1| = |V_2| \geq 3$ and let $|V_1|_s < |V_2|_s$ and assume the membership grade of each node in V_1 is less than the membership grade of V_2.

Choose $\wedge(\sigma(\alpha))$, $\alpha \in V_1$ in the first phase. Thus, $N_s(\alpha)$ nodes are disseminated. i.e., $V(G) \setminus V_1$ nodes are disseminated in the second phase and choose a node $\sigma(\beta), \sigma(\beta) \geq \sigma(\alpha), \beta \in V_1$ in the same phase. Now, $V_1 - \{\sigma(\alpha)\} - \sigma(\beta)$ nodes are left non-disseminated. Choose a node ω such that $\sigma(\omega) \geq \sigma(\beta) \geq \sigma(\alpha), \omega \in V_1$ in the third phase. As $V(G) - V_1$ nodes are adjacent with $V_1 - \{\sigma(\alpha)\} - \sigma(\beta)$, each node of $V_1 - \{\sigma(\alpha)\} - \sigma(\beta)$ are disseminated in the third phase. Thus, $\mathfrak{D}_{\mathcal{S}}(G) = \sigma(\alpha), \sigma(\beta), \sigma(\omega)$, where $\alpha, \beta, \omega \in V_1$. Hence (i) holds.

Case (v): Let $|V_1| = |V_2| \geq 3$ and let $|V_2|_s < |V_1|_s$ and assume the membership grade of each node in V_2 is less than the membership grade of V_1.

Choose $\sigma(\alpha)$, $\alpha \in V_2$ in the first phase. Thus, $N_s(\alpha)$ nodes are disseminated. i.e., $V(G)-V_2$ nodes are disseminated in the second phase and choose $\sigma(\beta), \sigma(\beta) \geq \sigma(\alpha), \beta \in V_2$ in the same phase. Now, $V_2-\{\sigma(\alpha)\}-\sigma(\beta)$ nodes are left non-disseminated. Choose $\sigma(\omega)$ such that $\sigma(\omega) \geq \sigma(\beta) \geq \sigma(\alpha)$ in the third phase. As $V(G)-V_2$ nodes are adjacent with $V_2-\{\sigma(\alpha)\}-\sigma(\beta)$, each node of $V_2-\{\sigma(\alpha)\}-\sigma(\beta)$ are disseminated in the third phase. Thus, $\mathfrak{D}_{\mathcal{S}}(G)=\sigma(\alpha),\sigma(\beta),\sigma(\omega)$, where $\alpha,\beta,\omega \in V_2$. Hence (i) holds.

Case (vi): Let $|V_1|=|V_2|\geq 3$ and let $|V_1|_s=|V_2|_s$ and assume that the minimum membership value exists for both the partite sets V_1 and V_2.

Choose a node α, in the first phase either from V_1 or V_2. Therefore, in phase two, α disseminates $N_s(\alpha)=V(G)-V_1$ if $\alpha \in V_1$ or $N_s(\alpha)=V(G)-V_2$ if $\alpha \in V_2$, since all the nodes of V_1 of $V(G)$ are adjacent to V_2 of $V(G)$ and conversely. Now,

$$V(G)-\Lambda\{\sigma(\alpha)\}-N_s(\alpha) \tag{15.2}$$

nodes are left non-disseminated in the second phase.

Subcase (i): If $\alpha \in V_1$ in Equation (15.2), then choose $\beta \in N_s(\alpha)$ such that $\sigma(\beta) \geq \sigma(\alpha)$ in the second phase, that is $\beta \in V_2$. Thus, $N_s(\beta)=V_1-\{\Lambda(\sigma(\alpha))\}$ nodes are disseminated and choose a node $\omega \in V_1-\{\Lambda\{\sigma(\alpha)\}$ in the third phase such that $\sigma(\omega) \geq \sigma(\beta) \geq \sigma(\alpha)$. Therefore, $\mathfrak{D}_{\mathcal{S}}(G)=\sigma(\alpha),\sigma(\beta),\sigma(\omega)$, where $\alpha,\omega \in V_1$ and $\beta \in V_2$ is the optimum disseminating sequence.
Subcase (ii): If $\alpha \in V_2$ in Equation (15.1), then choose $\beta \in N_s(\alpha)$ such that $\sigma(\beta) \geq \sigma(\alpha)$ in the second phase, that is $\beta \in V_1$. Thus, $N_s(\beta)=V_2-\{\Lambda(\sigma(\alpha))\}$ nodes are disseminated and choose a node $\omega \in V_2-\{\Lambda\{\sigma(\alpha)\}$ in the third phase such that $\sigma(\omega) \geq \sigma(\beta) \geq \sigma(\alpha)$. Therefore, $\mathfrak{D}_{\mathcal{S}}(G)=\sigma(\alpha),\sigma(\beta),\sigma(\omega)$, where $\alpha,\omega \in V_2$ and $\beta \in V_1$ is the optimum disseminating sequence.
Corollary 1: Let $|V_1|=1$ and $|V_2|=n$ in Theorem 3.4. Then G^*, the underlying crisp graph is a star graph $K_{1,n}$.
Proof: Let G^* be the star graph of the underlying fuzzy graph G in theorem 3.4 with $|V_1|=1$ and $|V_2|=n$.
Case (i): Let $|V_1|_s<|V_2|_s$. Choose $\alpha \in V_1$ in the first phase, then $|N_s(\alpha)|=|V_2|=n$ nodes are disseminated by α in the second phase. Therefore, choose $\wedge_{\beta \in V_2}\sigma(\beta)$ in the second phase. Hence $\mathfrak{D}_{\mathcal{S}}(G)=\{\sigma(\alpha),\sigma(\beta)\}, \alpha \in V_1$ and $\beta \in V_2$, $\mathfrak{D}_{\mathfrak{l}}(G)=\sigma(\alpha)+\wedge_{\beta \in V_2}\sigma(\beta)$, $\alpha \in V_1$.

Case (ii): Let $|V_1|_s > |V_2|_s$. Choose $\wedge_{\alpha \in V_2} \sigma(\alpha)$ in the first phase, then $|N_s(\alpha)| = |V_1| = 1$ say $\tau \in V_1$ node is disseminated in the second phase. Thus, $V_2 - \wedge_{\alpha \in V_2} \sigma(\alpha)$ are left non-disseminated. Choose $\beta \in V_2$ such that $\sigma(\beta) \geq \sigma(\alpha)$ in the second phase (since, $|V_1|_s > |V_2|_s$). Now, $V_2 - \Lambda\{\sigma(\alpha)\} - \Lambda\sigma(\beta)$ are about to disseminate. Thus, choose $\omega \in V_2$ such that $\sigma(\omega) \geq \sigma(\beta) \geq \sigma(\alpha)$ in the third phase and the nodes except $V_2 - \{\sigma(\alpha)\} - \{\sigma(\beta)\} - \{\sigma(\omega)\}$ are disseminated by $\tau \in V_1$ in the same phase. Hence, $\mathfrak{D}_{\mathcal{S}}(G) = \{\sigma(\alpha), \sigma(\beta), \sigma(\omega)\}$ where $\alpha, \beta, \omega \in V_2$ and $\mathfrak{D}_{\mathfrak{l}}(G) = \wedge(\sigma(\alpha) + \sigma(\beta) + \sigma(\omega))$.

Case (iii): Let $|V_1|_s = |V_2|_s$

Subcase (i): Let $|V_1| = 1$ and $|V_2| = 2$. Choose $\wedge_{\alpha \in V_2} \sigma(\alpha)$ as the disseminator in the first phase. Therefore, $N_s(\alpha) = \tau$, $\tau \in V_1$ is disseminated in the second phase. Thus, $V_2 - \wedge_{\alpha \in V_2} \sigma(\alpha) = \beta$ (say) is chosen as the disseminator in the second phase. Thus, $\mathfrak{D}_{\mathcal{S}}(G) = \{\sigma(\alpha), \sigma(\beta)\}$, where $\alpha, \beta \in V_2$. Hence, $\mathfrak{D}_{\mathfrak{l}}(G) = \sigma(\alpha) + \sigma(\beta)$.

Subcase (ii): Let $|V_1| = 1$ and $|V_2| > 2$. Choose $\wedge_{\alpha \in V_2} \sigma(\alpha)$ as the disseminator in the first phase. Therefore, $N_s(\alpha) = \tau$, $\tau \in V_1$ is disseminated in the second phase. Thus, $V_2 - \wedge_{\alpha \in V_2} \sigma(\alpha)$ nodes are left non-disseminated. Choose $\beta \in V_2$ (since, $|V_1|_s = |V_2|_s$) such that $\sigma(\beta) \geq \sigma(\alpha)$ in the second phase. Thus, choose $\omega \in V_2$ such that $\sigma(\omega) \geq \sigma(\beta) \geq \sigma(\alpha)$ in the third phase and the nodes except $V_2 - \{\sigma(\alpha)\} - \{\sigma(\beta)\} - \{\sigma(\omega)\}$ are disseminated by $\tau \in V_1$ in the same phase. Hence, $\mathfrak{D}_{\mathcal{S}}(G) = \{\sigma(\alpha), \sigma(\beta), \sigma(\omega)\}$ where $\alpha, \beta, \omega \in V_2$ and $\mathfrak{D}_{\mathfrak{l}}(G) = \wedge(\sigma(\alpha) + \sigma(\beta) + \sigma(\omega))$.

Theorem 5: Let $G: (V, \sigma, \mu)$ be a non-trivial fuzzy graph of order p, then $\wedge(\sigma(u) + \sigma(v)) \leq \mathfrak{D}_{\mathfrak{l}}(G) \leq p$

Proof: Case (i): Let G be a connected fuzzy graph with nodes u and v. Since G is connected, u and v are strong neighbours. Therefore, u and v disseminate mutually. Hence, by the definition of dissemination $\mathfrak{D}_{\mathcal{S}}(G) = (\sigma(u), \sigma(v))$ with $\mathfrak{D}_{\mathfrak{l}}(G) = (\sigma(u) + \sigma(v)) = p$.

Case (ii): Let G be a connected fuzzy graph with nodes u, v and w and if $N_s(u) = (v, w)$ it is obvious to see that $\mathfrak{D}_{\mathfrak{l}}(G) = \wedge(\sigma(u) + \sigma(v), \sigma(u) + \sigma(w)) < p$. Also, if extending G to n nodes. It is clear that $\mathfrak{D}_{\mathfrak{l}}(G) < p$.

Case (iii): Let G be a fuzzy graph with all nodes isolated, then by Theorem 1 $\mathfrak{D}_{\mathcal{S}}(G) = p$. Hence, by the above cases $\wedge(\sigma(u) + \sigma(v)) \leq \mathfrak{D}_{\mathfrak{l}}(G) \leq p$.

15.3 Dissemination Gap in Fuzzy Graph

Drawing inspiration from the well-dominated and well-covered graph frameworks studied in classical graph theory [1, 2, 10, 29], a new parameter called the dissemination gap is introduced.

Definition 4: A disseminating sequence $\mathfrak{D}_{\mathscr{B}}$ is called minimal if no proper subsequence is a disseminating sequence.

Definition 5: The maximum disseminating index of a minimal disseminating sequence is called upper disseminating index and is denoted by $\widetilde{\mathfrak{D}_{\mathfrak{l}}}(G)$.

Example 3: Consider the fuzzy graph shown in Figure 15.3. In this fuzzy graph, the arcs $(v_1, v_2), (v_2, v_3)$ and (v_3, v_4) are identified as strong arcs. However, node v_1 cannot disseminate information the nodes v_3 and v_4 and vice versa. This is due to the arcs (v_1, v_3) and (v_1, v_4) are not strong arcs.

The possible minimal disseminating sequences for Figure 15.3:

1. $\mathfrak{D}_{\mathscr{B}}(G) = (v_2(1), v_4(0.4))$
2. $\mathfrak{D}_{\mathscr{B}}(G) = (v_3(0.9), v_1(1))$
3. $\mathfrak{D}_{\mathscr{B}}(G) = \left(v_1(1), v_3(0.9), v_4(0.4)\right)$
4. $\mathfrak{D}_{\mathscr{B}}(G) = (v_4(0.4), v_2(1), v_1(1))$

Therefore, $\mathfrak{D}_{\mathfrak{l}}(G) = \wedge(1+0.4, 0.9+1) = 1.4$ and $\widetilde{\mathfrak{D}_{\mathfrak{l}}}(G) = \vee\{1+0.4, 0.9+1, 1+0.9+0.4, 0.4+1+1\} = 2.4$.

Definition 6: The disseminating gap $\delta_{\mathscr{B}}$ of a fuzzy graph G is the difference between the upper disseminating index and the disseminating index of G. i.e. $\delta_{\mathscr{B}}(G) = \widetilde{\mathfrak{D}_{\mathfrak{l}}}(G) - \mathfrak{D}_{\mathfrak{l}}(G)$.

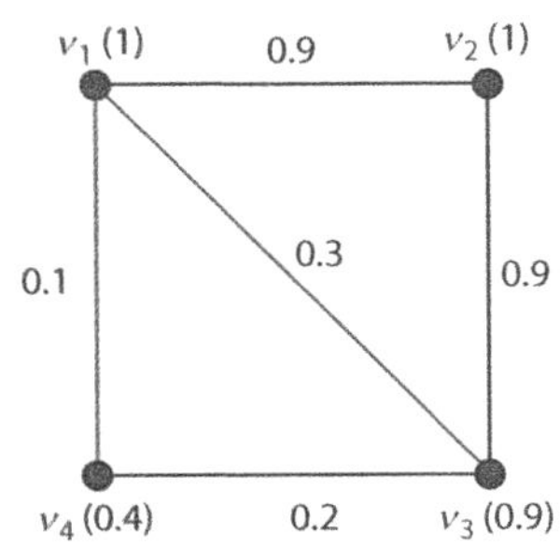

Figure 15.3 Illustration of minimal disseminating sequence.

Definition 7: A fuzzy graph G is said to be well-disseminated graph if its dissemination gap $\delta_{\mathscr{B}}(G)=0$. Similarly, G is considered almost well-disseminated if $\delta_{\mathscr{B}}(G)=1$.

$\delta_{\mathscr{B}}(G)=0$ indicates that there is no dissemination loss, that is the graph G is well-disseminated.

$\delta_{\mathscr{B}}(G)=1$ indicates that there exists a gap between the potential and actual information flow due to weak connections.

Example 4: Consider the strong fuzzy graph in Figure 15.4. The disseminating sequences are (v_1, v_3), (v_2, v_4), (v_1, v_2) and (v_3, v_4) which are minimum and minimal disseminating sequences. Therefore, $\mathfrak{D}_{\mathfrak{l}}(G)=1.4$ and $\widetilde{\mathfrak{D}_{\mathfrak{l}}}(G)=1.4$. Thus, $\delta_{\mathscr{B}}(G)=\widetilde{\mathfrak{D}_{\mathfrak{l}}}(G)-\mathfrak{D}_{\mathfrak{l}}(G)=0$. Hence, the strong fuzzy graph in Figure 15.4 is a well-disseminated graph.

Example 5: Consider Figure 15.3 in which $\mathfrak{D}_{\mathfrak{l}}(G)=1.4$ and $\widetilde{\mathfrak{D}_{\mathfrak{l}}}(G)=2.4$ such that $\delta_{\mathscr{B}}(G)=\widetilde{\mathfrak{D}_{\mathfrak{l}}}(G)-\mathfrak{D}_{\mathfrak{l}}(G)=1$.

Theorem 6: A disseminating sequence with minimum disseminators in a fuzzy graph is always minimal disseminating sequence.

Proof: Let $\mathfrak{D}_{\mathscr{B}}=\{v_1, v_2, \ldots, v_k\}$ is a disseminating sequence with minimum number of disseminators in a fuzzy graph. Assume contrary that $\mathfrak{D}_{\mathscr{B}}$ is not a minimal disseminating sequence. This means there exists at least node $v_i \in \mathfrak{D}_{\mathscr{B}}$ such that if we remove it, the remaining sequence $\mathfrak{D}'_{\mathscr{B}}=\mathfrak{D}_{\mathscr{B}}-\{v_i\}$ is still a valid disseminating sequence. However, this implies that $\mathfrak{D}'_{\mathscr{B}}$ has fewer disseminators than $\mathfrak{D}_{\mathscr{B}}$, which contradicts the original assumption that $\mathfrak{D}_{\mathscr{B}}$ already had the minimum number of disseminators. Therefore, it is concluded that any disseminating sequence with the minimum number of disseminators must also be minimal.

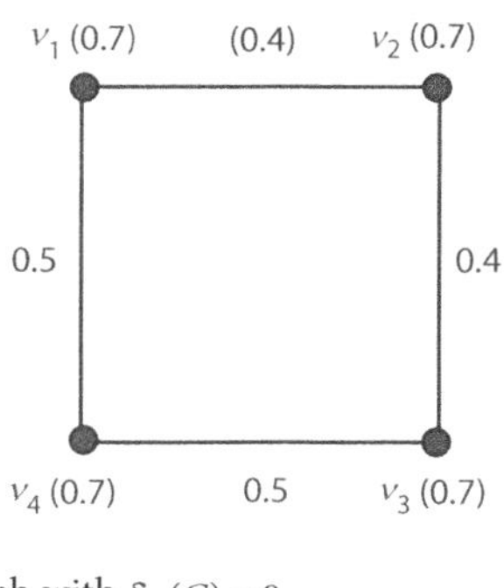

Figure 15.4 Strong fuzzy graph with $\delta_{\mathscr{B}}(G)=0$.

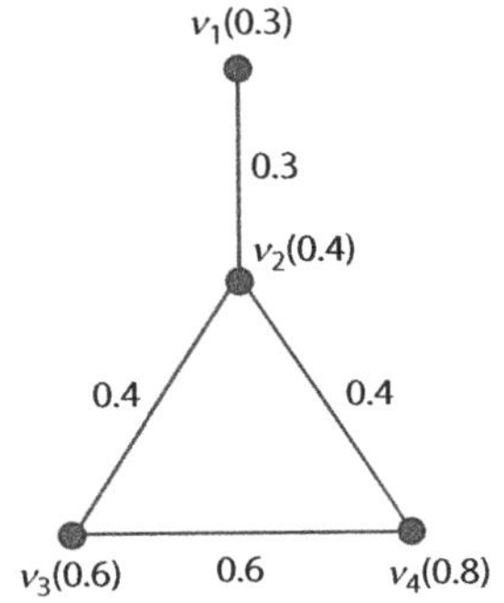

Figure 15.5 Complete fuzzy graph.

A counterexample for Theorem 6 is as follows, Consider the complete fuzzy graph G illustrated in Figure 15.5 where all arcs are strong. The disseminating sequences $(v_2(0.4), v_1(0.3), (v_2(0.4), v_3(0.6)), (v_2(0.4), v_4(0.8)), (v_3(0.6), v_1(0.3))$ and $(v_4(0.8), v_1(0.3))$ are minimal disseminating sequences with two disseminators, whereas $(v_1(0.3), v_3(0.6), v_4(0.8))$ is also a minimal disseminating sequence but with three disseminators. This motivated the following remark.

Remark 3: A minimal disseminating sequence in a fuzzy graph does not necessarily contain the minimum number of disseminators.

Remark 4: If $\mathfrak{D}_{\mathscr{B}}$ is the minimal disseminating sequence with minimum disseminators of a fuzzy graph G, then $V - \mathfrak{D}_{\mathscr{B}}$ is a disseminating sequence. The Proof of this statement is quite obvious.

Theorem 7: A Strong fuzzy graph $\boldsymbol{G}$ is said to be well-disseminated if $\sigma(\boldsymbol{v}) = \text{constant}$, for all $\boldsymbol{v} \in \boldsymbol{V}(\boldsymbol{G})$.

Proof: Since $\boldsymbol{G}$ is strong fuzzy graph, all arcs are strong. As $\boldsymbol{G}$ is also well-disseminated, then by definition, $\delta_{\mathscr{B}}(\boldsymbol{G}) = \boldsymbol{0}$, which implies $\widetilde{\mathfrak{D}}_{\mathfrak{l}}(\boldsymbol{G}) - \mathfrak{D}_{\mathfrak{l}}(\boldsymbol{G}) = \boldsymbol{0}$. This means that the maximum dissemination index and minimum dissemination index are equal. Consequently, the number of disseminators in the maximum dissemination sequence and the minimum dissemination sequence must be the same. As a result, the total membership value of the disseminators in both the sequences is equal. This condition can hold if $\sigma(\boldsymbol{v})$ is constant for all vertices $\boldsymbol{v} \in \boldsymbol{V}(\boldsymbol{G})$. Hence, $\sigma(\boldsymbol{v}) = \text{constant}$, for all $\boldsymbol{v} \in \boldsymbol{V}(\boldsymbol{G})$.

15.4 Application of Dissemination Index in Smart Hospital Emergency Alert System

In a smart hospital, various departments and medical devices are connected *via* an IoT-based communication network. Each node represents a department or system involved in emergency management, such as patient monitoring, alert broadcasting and nurse dispatch. Due to interference, device failures and access restrictions, communication links between nodes (departments) are uncertain and vary in strength. This dynamic nature of connectivity poses a challenge in ensuring that critical alerts (e.g., emergency broadcasts, equipment malfunctions, patient distress signals) are reliably disseminated to all necessary units. Table 15.2 lists the nodes, associated labels and their descriptions.

Let $G=(V,\sigma,\mu)$ be a fuzzy graph modeling of the hospital communication network as shown in the Figure 15.6, where:

- V represents hospital departments or subsystems,
- $\sigma(v_i)$ denotes the functional reliability or availability of node v_i,

Table 15.2 Node description.

Node	Label	Description
$v_1(1)$	Emergency Response Hub	Central controller for emergency broadcasts
$v_2(0.98)$	ICU Monitoring System	Critical care monitoring and alerts
$v_3(0.77)$	General Ward Sensors	Monitors patient vitals in general wards
$v_4(0.89)$	Nurse Station A	Handles alerts and dispatch in zone A
$v_5(0.5)$	Nurse Station B	Handles alerts and dispatch in zone B
$v_6(0.88)$	Surgical Theatre	Operation room – secure, limited communication
$v_7(0.9)$	Pharmacy	Medicine dispatch and emergency drug alerts
$v_8(0.5)$	Security and Access Control	Controls facility access during emergencies

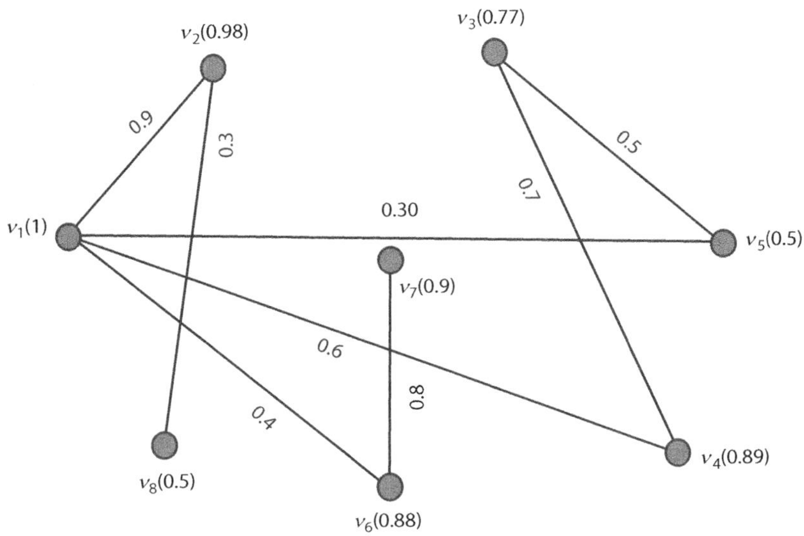

Figure 15.6 Fuzzy graph model of a smart hospital emergency alert system.

Table 15.3 Fuzzy arcs between nodes.

From	To	Arc weight $\mu(e)$	Description
v_1	v_2	0.95	Strong arc
v_1	v_4	0.60	Strong arc
v_1	v_5	0.30	Non-Strong arc
v_1	v_6	0.40	Strong arc
v_4	v_3	0.70	Strong arc
v_5	v_3	0.50	Strong arc
v_2	v_8	0.30	Strong arc
v_6	v_7	0.80	Strong arc

- $\mu(e_{i,j})$ is the strength of communication between nodes v_i and v_j as listed in Table 15.3.

The goal is to identify a disseminating sequence $\mathfrak{D}_{\mathscr{B}} \subseteq V(G)$, such that every node in $V \setminus \mathfrak{D}_{\mathscr{B}}$, the propagators can receive emergency information *via* strong arcs from some $v_i \in \mathfrak{D}_8$, and to minimize the total dissemination cost represented by the dissemination index. Using the proposed Algorithm 15.2.1, {v1,v5,v8} is the representative minimum disseminators to alert the entire system in three phases with dissemination index 2.

15.5 Conclusion

The introduction of dissemination in fuzzy networks opens up a promising avenue for both theoretical exploration and real-world applications. In this chapter, a new parameter, the dissemination index was proposed to quantify the efficiency of information spread in fuzzy graphs. Methods for identifying optimal disseminating sequences and calculating their corresponding indices were established for several standard graph classes. The concept of a dissemination gap, representing the difference between ideal and actual dissemination performance, was also introduced as a tool for evaluating and improving network efficiency.

This framework demonstrates particular relevance in time-sensitive systems such as smart hospital emergency networks, where reliable and rapid communication among medical units is essential. Looking ahead, future research will focus on refining upper and lower bounds for the dissemination index, uncovering new structural properties and extending the model to include and edge-based dissemination index offering a deeper understanding of how information flows through the links in fuzzy networks.

AI disclosure statement: The author acknowledges the use of AI-based tools for minor language editing or grammatical correction. However, all intellectual contributions, analyses, and conclusions presented in this chapter are entirely the author's own.

References

1. Alizadeh, H. and Gözüpek, D., Almost well-dominated bipartite graphs with minimum degree at least two. *RAIRO Oper. Res.*, 55, S1633–S1646, 2021.
2. Anderson, S.E., Kuenzel, K., Rall, D.F., On well-dominated graphs. *Graphs Comb.*, 37, 151–655, 2021.
3. Antony, D., Das, A., Gosavi, S., Jacob, D., Kulamarva, S., Graph Burning: Bounds and Hardness, arXiv preprint arXiv:2402.18984, 2024.
4. Bessy, S., Bonato, A., Janssen, J., Rautenbach, D., Roshanbin, E., Burning a graph is hard. *Discrete Appl. Math.*, 232, 73–87, 2017.

5. Bessy, S., Bonato, A., Janssen, J., Rautenbach, D., Roshanbin, E., Bounds on the burning number. *Discrete Appl. Math.*, 235, 16–22, 2018.
6. Bhattacharya, P., Some remarks on fuzzy graphs. *Pattern Recognit. Lett.*, 297–302, 1987.
7. Bhutani, and Rosenfeld, A., Strong arcs in fuzzy graphs. *Inf. Sci.*, 152, 319–322, 2003.
8. Bonato, A., Janssen, J., Roshanbin, E., Burning a graph as a model of social contagion, in: *Lecture Notes in Computer Science*, vol. 8882, pp. 13–22, Springer, Cham, 2014.
9. Bonato, A., Janssen, J., Roshanbin, E., How to burn a graph. *Internet Math.*, 12, 85–100, 2016.
10. Finbow, B., Hartnell, A., Nowakowski, R., Well-dominated graphs: A collection of well-Covered Ones. *Ar. Comb.*, 25, 5–10, 1988.
11. Garg, H. and Kaur, G., Algorithms for Screening Travelers During Covid-19 Outbreak Using Probabilistic Dual Hesitant Values Based on Bipartite Graph Theory. *Appl. Comput. Math.*, 20, 1, 22–48, 2021.
12. Manjusha, O.T. and Sunitha, M.S., Strong Domination in Fuzzy Graphs. *Fuzzy Inf. Eng.*, 7, 3, 369–377, 2015.
13. Manjusha, O.T., Arc Domination in Fuzzy Graphs using Strong Arcs. *Malaya J. Math.*, 9, 789–796, 2021.
14. Moderson, J.N. and Nair, P.S., *Fuzzy Graphs and Fuzzy Hypergraphs*, Physica – Verlag, Heidelberg, Germany, 2000.
15. Moderson, J.N., Fuzzy cycles and fuzzy trees. *J. Fuzzy Math.*, 10, 1, 189–202, 2002.
16. Moderson, J.N. and Nair, P.S., Cycles and cocycles of fuzzy graphs. *Inf. Sci. (Ny)*, 90, 39–49, 1996.
17. Moderson, J.N. and Mathew, S., *Advanced Topics in Fuzzy Graph Theory*, Studies in Fuzziness and Soft Computing, vol. 375, Springer Nature (Book), Cham, 2019.
18. Mondal, D., Rajasingh, A.J., Parthiban, N., Rajasingh, I., APX-hardness and approximation for the k-burning number problem. *Theor. Comput. Sci.*, 932, 21–30, 2022.
19. Nagoorgani, A. and Chandrasekaran, V.T., Domination in Fuzzy Graph. *Adv. Fuzzy Sets Syst.*, 1, 1, 17–26, 2006.
20. Prakash, K., Parimala, M., Garg, H., Lifetime Prolongation of a Wireless Charging Sensor Network using a Mobile Robot *via* Linear Diophantine Fuzzy Graph Environment. *Complex Intell. Syst.*, 8, 2419–2434, 2022.
21. Rosenfeld, A., Fuzzy graphs, in: *Fuzzy Sets and their Application to Cognitive and Decision Processes*, pp. 75–95, Academic Press, New York, 1975.
22. Rosenfeld, A., Fuzzy graphs. *IEEE Trans. Syst. Man Cybern.*, 5, 1–7, 1975.
23. Somasundaram, A. and Somasundaram, S., Domination in Fuzzy Graphs – I. *Pattern Recognit. Lett.*, 19, 787–791, 1998.
24. Somasundaram, A., Domination in fuzzy graphs-II. *J. Fuzzy Math.*, 13, 2, 281–288, 2005.

25. Mathew, S. and Sunitha, M.S., Types of arcs in a fuzzy graph. *Inf. Sci.*, 179, 11, 1760–1768, 2009.
26. Mathew, S., Moderson, J.N., Malik, D.S., *Fuzzy Graph Theory*, Studies in Fuzziness and Soft Computing, vol. 363, Springer Nature (Book), Cham, 2018.
27. Sunitha, M.S. and Mathew, S., Fuzzy Graph Theory: A Survey. *Ann. Pure Appl. Math.*, 4, 92–110, 2013.
28. Al-Hawary, T., Complete Fuzzy Graphs. *Int. J. Math. Comb.*, 4, 26–34, 2011.
29. Topp, J. and Volkmann, L., Well covered and well dominated block graphs and uni-cyclic graphs. *Math. Pannon.*, 1, 2, 55–66, 1990.
30. Li, Y., Wu, J., Qin, X., Wei., L., Characterization of Q graph by the burning number. *AIMS Math.*, 9, 2, 2024.

Part V

HEALTHCARE AND MEDICAL APPLICATIONS

16

A Novel Approach for Evaluating Complicated Pregnancies *via* Picture Fuzzy Distance Analysis

Chukwudi Obinna Nwokoro[1*], Paul Augustine Ejegwa[2], Felix C.C. Wekere[3], Nneka Gabriel Job[4], Kelechi Cynthia Nwokoro[4] and Faith-Michael Uzoka[5]

[1]Department of Informaiton and Communication Technology, Abia State University, Uturu, Abia State, Nigeria
[2]Department of Mathematics, Joseph Sarwuan Tarka University, Makurdi, Nigeria
[3]Department of Obstetrics and Gynaecology, Rivers State University (RSUTH), Rivers State, Nigieria
[4]Department of Paediatrics, University of Port-Harcourt Teaching Hospital, Rivers State, Nigeria
[5]Department of Mathematics and Computing, Mount Royal University, Calgary, Canada

Abstract
Women in their reproductive years face numerous uncertainties during and after pregnancy, including, maternal conditions such as preeclampsia, genetic disorders, and labor complications like dystocia, uterine rupture, and excessive postpartum bleeding. In addition, they may encounter urinary tract infections, bacterial vaginosis, sexually transmitted infections, preterm birth risks, gestational diabetes, intrauterine growth restriction (IUGR), and complications related to shared placental circulation. To address these complexities, Picture Fuzzy Sets (PFSs) were introduced to offer a robust framework for modeling and managing such uncertainties. This study utilizes locally obtained datasets to propose a new distance measure for PFSs that incorporates the positive, neutral, and negative degrees, resulting in more stable outcomes for maternal health scenarios. Specifically, the proposed distance measure yielded consistent values for maternal patients; who show improved stability compared to measures suggested by other researchers. In real-world settings, fertile individuals may encounter significant health challenges; however, with close monitoring and proper medical treatment, a full-term

**Corresponding author*: nwokoro.chukwudi@nbu.edu.ng

Harish Garg (ed.) Decision Support Systems in Smart Computing: Embracing Uncertainty and Challenges, (495–530) © 2026 Scrivener Publishing LLC

pregnancy is achievable, highlighting the effectiveness of the proposed distance measure. We introduce a new weight to the distance measures which gives reduced spatial metrics, refines sensitivity, and prioritizes critical outcomes like preterm birth and miscarriage, particularly for patients, M1 (0.0517), M2 (0.0584), M3 (0.0331), M4 (0.0221), and M5 (0.0699). It provides valuable insights to physicians for improved maternal healthcare management. Future research could explore advanced fuzzy methodologies, such as q-rung ortho-pair fuzzy sets and other sophisticated extensions, to further refine maternal risk assessment and enhance predictive accuracy.

***Keywords*:** Maternal health, pregnancy uncertainties, picture fuzzy sets (PFSs), risk assessment and distance measures

16.1 Introduction

16.1.1 Background of the Study

The health and well-being of women of childbearing age continue to be a significant concern for both healthcare professionals and others. It encourages everyone to overcome their circumstances and achieve success, especially for unborn children, ensuring their comfort during pregnancy and after birth. World Health Organization (WHO) [1] pointed out the significance of ensuring that fertile-aged women experience comfort and proper care during pregnancy to maintain focus and safety in both mental and physical states. This inclusive support helps reduce complications, such as preeclampsia/eclampsia [2], gestational diabetes [3], preeclampsia [2, 4], placenta previa [5], placental abruption [6] and postpartum hemorrhage [7]. WHO [8], further recommends regular antenatal check-ups to monitor health, prevent infections, and address conditions among others such as anemia and obstetric cholestasis, which can meaningfully enhance relief and improve outcomes for both mother and baby. In the same vein, United Nations Children's Fund (UNCF) [9] offers procedures for managing physical distresses common in the first, second and third trimester, including symptoms such as acid reflux, sleep difficulties, nausea, fatigue, breast tenderness, hormonal changes, Noticeable fetal growth, and the mother may feel the baby move (quickening), back pain, swelling, and Braxton Hicks contractions. Therefore, recommended self-care measures such as using supportive pillows, engaging in modest exercise, eating a balanced diet, and seeking appropriate medical care attention. Based on these uncertainties surrounding gestation experiences and outcomes, deploying tools like fuzzy sets can help address these complexities by modeling and managing variations in maternal vitality factors.

Zadeh [10] introduced fuzzy set theory to handle uncertain issues, with bounding of [0, 1] which represents membership degree (MD) of the function in a set. It further denotes partial membership, unlike the traditional crisp set where a member belongs to a set which is strictly zero or one. One major challenge is integrating the non-membership degree of a given set, which led Atanassov [11, 12] to introduce Intuitionistic Fuzzy Sets (IFS). These sets aim to utilize both membership and non-membership degrees in a way that subtracting the membership degree may not necessarily correspond to the non-membership degree. The intuitionistic fuzzy hesitation is achieved by subtracting the membership degree from the sum of the membership and non-membership degrees, effectively managing ambiguity. This approach has been applied across various fields, including tropical disease management, predicting academic performance, voting outcomes, rechargeable energy systems, and pattern recognition [13–20]. There is no doubt that the widespread use of IFS is beneficial in addressing vagueness and overcoming some of the limitations of fuzzy sets. However, it may struggle with handling multiple inputs, computational tasks, and decision-making, particularly when the sum of the membership and non-membership degrees exceeds one.

16.1.2 Literature Review

In 2014, Smarandache [21] introduced the concept of Picture Fuzzy Sets (PFS) as an extension of intuitionistic fuzzy sets to address additional layers of vagueness and uncertainty in datasets. Unlike intuitionistic fuzzy sets, which account for only membership and non-membership, Picture Fuzzy Sets incorporate a third parameter to represent neutrality or indecision. This added dimension enables PFS to manage more complex decision-making and ambiguity by assigning each element in the dataset a positive membership, negative membership, neutrality, and rejection value, facilitating a more balanced and nuanced strategic choice. Undoubtedly, numerous studies have been directed toward utilizing Picture Fuzzy Sets (PFS). Zhao *et al.* [22] have made significant contributions by implementing dynamic PFS in distance measures and applying parametric similarity measures to improve multi-attribute decision-making processes. Duong and Thao [23] proposed a dissimilarity measure for PFSs in multi-criteria decision-making (MCDM). Van Dinh *et al.* [24] further explored PFS by implementing distance and dissimilarity measures, while Dinh and Thao [25] built upon this work. Palash Dutta [26] applied PFSs to diagnose tropical diseases, showcasing their use in healthcare. Van Pham [27] integrated entropy and distance measures into decision support systems, while Cuong *et al.* [28] utilized logic operators on PFSs for inference processing.

Riaz *et al.* [29] introduced bipolar PFS operators with novel distance measures for MCDM. Singh and. Ahmed and Dai suggested a multi-expert TOPSIS approach with PFS similarity measures. At the same time, Mahmood *et al.* [30] used cosine functions to compare TOPSIS and similarity measures for picture hesitant fuzzy sets in strategic decision-making. Cao [31] adopted PFSs to propose a new TOPSIS method for ranking determinants in mobile multimedia healthcare service adoption. Khalil *et al.* [32] developed interval-valued PFSs and applied them to decision-making scenarios, Zhu and Zhe [33] combined picture fuzzy sets and interval-valued picture sets and Devi *et al.* [34] used dimensionality reduction methods to improve environmental decision-making with PFSs. In 2018 Wei [35] introduced practical similarity measures for PFSs; offering hope for their real-world applications, Garg *et al.* [36] proposed an operator PF Schweizer using a symmetric mean [37–40], Finally, Peng and Dai [41] proposed an algorithm for PFS multiple attribute decision-making that incorporated new distance measures, providing a practical solution to improve the decision-making process.

Distance measures are crucial for quantifying similarity or dissimilarity between sets in picture fuzzy sets, particularly by accounting for their positive membership, negative membership, neutrality, and rejection degrees. Various researchers have widely adopted this approach to enhance the accuracy and robustness of analyses across diverse applications. Zhao *et al.* [42] implemented a distance measure in picture fuzzy sets (PFS) but did not address the relationship among various distance measures. Son [43] applied picture distance measures to improve clustering in decision-making, failed to compare the effectiveness of different clustering techniques. Dutta [44] applied PFS in medical diagnosis but could not consider weighting the symptoms in terms of predictive value. Dinh and Thao [25] explored similarity measures within multiple attribute decision-making without advancing new methods, while Sahu *et al.* [45] integrated picture fuzzy sets and rough set theory for career selection among students, maintaining the original set theories without modification. Guleria and Bajaj [46] introduced a probabilistic distance measure for PFS in classification but noted its limitations and recommended further extensions. Zhu *et al.* [33] proposed a new PFS distance measure for pattern recognition and medical diagnosis nevertheless highlighting the need for additional methods. Dinh *et al.* [25] applied distance and dissimilarity measures in PFS without a practical application, while Son [43] explored analogousness measures in picture distance however did not apply them to complex problems. Khan *et al.* [47] used distance measures in complex PFS for medical diagnosis and pattern recognition then suggested exploring additional methods. Ganie [48, 49] applied a PFS distance measure for pattern recognition but saw the need to enhance existing techniques.

Similarly, Khan *et al.* [50] used similarity and bi-parametric distance measures in PFS for medical diagnosis without advancing the method. Jan *et al.* [51] developed distance and similarity measures in PFS for building materials with a multi-attribute approach in decision-making but did not employ a novel technique. Kumar [52] applied a PFS distance measure in medical diagnosis without proposing a new metric. Luo and Zhang [53] introduced a new similarity measure in PFS, though they identified certain inconsistencies when differentiating between fuzzy information. Adak *et al.*, [54] used PFS distance measures to improve multi-criteria decision-making but did not adopt alternative techniques. Verma and Rohtagi [55] introduced a novel similarity measure for PFS in pattern recognition and medical diagnosis, recommending future applications in other fields.

16.1.3 Motivation and Contributions

Few studies have specifically focused on medical diagnosis; to my knowledge, no research has applied picture fuzzy sets (PFSs) to pregnancy outcomes thus far. It is essential to acknowledge that women of childbearing age can face various complications during pregnancy, delivery and postpartum. Despite these challenges, some mothers may experience such complications and still return to a state of normalcy, where their condition's degree of neutrality might be considered close to zero. Furthermore, not every mother encounters these complications, and the natural progression of childbirth represents a subset of maternal outcomes that may not be sufficiently captured by intuitionistic fuzzy sets (IFS). The objectives of this work are as follows:

a) introduce a new picture fuzzy distance function for PFS;
b) implement the proposed PFS on maternal data;
c) compare its performance with existing methods proposed by other researchers.

The structure of the paper is as follows: Section 16.2 provides foundational knowledge of PFS and the theoretical development of the proposed PFS. Section 16.3 details its implementation on the maternal dataset. Section 16.4 presents and discusses the results, comparing them with existing distance measures. Finally, Section 16.5 concludes the study and suggests directions for future research.

16.2 Preliminaries

Definition 1 [28]. Let $X=\{x_1,x_2,\ldots,x_n\}$ be a universe of discourse (UOD). A fuzzy set (FS) in X is defined as follows (16.1):

$$A=\{\langle x,\varepsilon_A(x)\rangle \mid \mathrm{x}\in \mathrm{X}\}, \tag{16.1}$$

where $\varepsilon_A(x)\in[0,1]$ illustrate the positive membership. For each $x\in X$, we have, $0\leq\varepsilon_A(x)\leq 1, \forall\, x\in X$. Therefore, $\zeta_A(x)=1-\varepsilon_A(x)$ where $\zeta_A(x)\colon X\to[0,1]$ connote the negative membership associated with $\mathrm{x}\in\mathrm{X}$.

Definition 2 [24, 28]. Let $X=\{x_1,x_2,\ldots,x_n\}$ be a universe of discourse (UOD). An intuitionistic fuzzy set (IFS) in X is defined as follows (16.2):

$$A=\{\langle x,\varepsilon_A(x),\zeta_A(x)\rangle| \mathrm{x}\in \mathrm{X}\}, \tag{16.2}$$

where $\varepsilon_A(x),\zeta A(x)\in[0,1]$ illustrate the positive membership. For each $x\in X$, we have, $0\leq\varepsilon_A(x)+\zeta_A(x)\leq 1$, for all $x\in X$, and $\xi_A(x)=1-\varepsilon_A(x)-\zeta_A(x)$ where $\xi_A(x)\colon X\to[0,1]$ connotes the neutral membership associated with $\mathrm{x}\in\mathrm{X}$.

16.2.1 Picture Fuzzy Sets

In the context of a Picture Fuzzy Set (PFS), each element is characterized by membership, non-membership, and neutrality degrees, all within the interval [0, 1], with the sum not exceeding 1.

Definition 3 [28]. Let A be a PFS on the UOD X, and defined as (16.3):

$$A=\{\langle x,\varepsilon_A(x),\ \zeta_A(x),\xi_A(x)\rangle| \mathrm{x}\in \mathrm{X}\}, \tag{16.3}$$

where $\varepsilon_A(x)$, $\zeta_A(x)$, $\xi_A(x)\in[0,1]$ are positive membership, negative membership, and neutral membership degrees of x in A, respectively, and $0\leq\varepsilon_A(x)+\zeta_A(x)+\xi_A(x)\leq 1, \forall\, x\in X$, where the refusal membership degree $\psi_A(x)$ of x in A is defined as follows (16.4):

$$\psi_A(x) = 1 - \varepsilon_A(x) - \zeta_A(x) - \xi_A(x). \tag{16.4}$$

Definition 4 [28]. Supposing $A, B,$ and C are PFSs in X. Then, the distance function between the PFSs is a function φ: $PFS(X) \times PFS(X) \rightarrow [0,1]$ such that;

a. $0 \leq \varphi(A,B) \leq 1$ (boundedness),
b. $\varphi(A,A) = 0,\ \varphi(B,B) = 0,$ and $\varphi(C,C) = 0$ (reflexivity),
c. $\varphi(A,B) = \varphi(B,A)$ (Symmetry),
d. $\varphi(A,C) + \varphi(C,B) \geq \varphi(A,B)$ (triangle inequality).

16.2.2 Proposed Picture Fuzzy Distance Measure

One hallmark of the recommended PF distance measure in this paper, we introduced the weight (ω_i) which was not estimated rather calculated from the maternal dataset.

Let PFSs A, B in UOD $X = \{x_1, x_2, \ldots, x_n\}$ be defined as follows:

$$A = \{\langle x_i, \varepsilon_A(x_i) - \zeta_A(x_i) - \xi_A(x_i)\rangle \mid x_i \in X\} \text{ and}$$
$$B = \{\langle x_i, \varepsilon_B(x_i) - \zeta_B(x_i) - \xi_B(x_i)\rangle \mid x_i \in X\}.$$

The new distance approach between PFSs and its weighted form are (16.5) and (16.6):

$$\varphi(A, B) = \sqrt[p]{\frac{1}{4n} \sum_{i=1}^{n} \begin{bmatrix} |\varepsilon_A(x_i) - \varepsilon_B(x_i)|^p + |\zeta_A(x_i) - \zeta_B(x_i)|^p \\ + |\xi_A(x_i) - \xi_B(x_i)|^p + |\psi_A(x_i) - \psi_B(x_i)|^p \end{bmatrix}}, \tag{16.5}$$

$$\varphi^{\omega}(A, B) = \sqrt[p]{\frac{1}{4} \sum_{i=1}^{n} \omega_i \begin{bmatrix} |\varepsilon_A(x_i) - \varepsilon_B(x_i)|^p + |\zeta_A(x_i) - \zeta_B(x_i)|^p \\ + |\xi_A(x_i) - \xi_B(x_i)|^p + |\psi_A(x_i) - \psi_B(x_i)|^p \end{bmatrix}} \tag{16.6}$$

where p is a natural number such that $p \leq 2$ and $a = \dfrac{\varepsilon_A{}^4 + \zeta_A{}^4 + \xi_A{}^4 + \psi_A{}^4}{4} + \dfrac{\varepsilon_B{}^4 + \zeta_B{}^4 + \xi_B{}^4 + \psi_B{}^4}{4}$ $b = \sum_{i=1}^{n}$

$\left[\frac{\varepsilon_A{}^4+\zeta_A{}^4+\xi_A{}^4+\psi_A{}^4}{4}+\frac{\varepsilon_B{}^4+\zeta_B{}^4+\xi_B{}^4+\psi_B{}^4}{4}\right]$, $w_i=\frac{a}{b}$ for $w_i \in [0,1]$ and $\sum_{i=1}^{n} w_i=1$.

If $p=1$, then $\varphi(A,B)$ and $\varphi^{\omega}(A,B)$ become picture fuzzy Hamming distance functions (16.7) and (16.8):

$$\varphi(A,B)=\frac{1}{4n}\sum_{i=1}^{n}\left[\begin{array}{c}|\varepsilon_A(x_i)-\varepsilon_B(x_i)|^p+|\zeta_A(x_i)-\zeta_B(x_i)|^p\\+|\xi_A(x_i)-\xi_B(x_i)|^p+|\psi_A(x_i)-\psi_B(x_i)|^p\end{array}\right], \tag{16.7}$$

$$\varphi^{\omega}(A,B)=\frac{1}{4}\sum_{i=1}^{n}\omega_i\left[\begin{array}{c}|\varepsilon_A(x_i)-\varepsilon_B(x_i)|^p+|\zeta_A(x_i)-\zeta_B(x_i)|^p\\+|\xi_A(x_i)-\xi_B(x_i)|^p+|\psi_A(x_i)-\psi_B(x_i)|^p\end{array}\right]. \tag{16.8}$$

If $p=2$, then $\varphi(A,B)$ and $\varphi^{\omega}(A,B)$ become picture fuzzy Euclidean distance functions (16.9) and (16.10):

$$\varphi(A,B)=\sqrt{\frac{1}{4n}\sum_{i=1}^{n}\left[\begin{array}{c}(\varepsilon_A(x_i)-\varepsilon_B(x_i))^2+(\zeta_A(x_i)-\zeta_B(x_i))^2\\+(\xi_A(x_i)-\xi_B(x_i))^2+(\psi_A(x_i)-\psi_B(x_i))^2\end{array}\right]}, \tag{16.9}$$

$$\varphi^{\omega}(A,B)=\sqrt{\frac{1}{4}\sum_{i=1}^{n}\omega_i\left[\begin{array}{c}(\varepsilon_A(x_i)-\varepsilon_B(x_i))^2+(\zeta_A(x_i)-\zeta_B(x_i))^2\\+(\xi_A(x_i)-\xi_B(x_i))^2+(\psi_A(x_i)-\psi_B(x_i))^2\end{array}\right]}. \tag{16.10}$$

Now, we discuss the properties of the new distance method and its weighted form as follows:

Theorem 1. Suppose A and B are *PFS* in $X=\{x_1,x_2,\ldots,x_n\}$. Then, $\varphi(A,B)$ and $\varphi^{\omega}(A,B)$ satisfy boundedness property, reflexive property, symmetry property and separable property.

Proof. To begin with, we verify boundedness property, reflexive property, symmetry property, and separable property for $\varphi(A, B)$. Now, we show boundedness property for $\varphi(A, B)$. From the properties of the graded functions of A and B, we have

$$0 \leq \varepsilon_A(x_i) \leq 1, 0 \leq \zeta_A(x_i) \leq 1, 0 \leq \xi_A(x_i) \leq 1, 0 \leq \psi_A(x_i) \leq 1.$$

Thus, we get

$$\begin{gathered} 0 \leq \varepsilon_A(x_i) - \varepsilon_B(x_i) \leq 1, 0 \leq \zeta_A(x_i) - \zeta_B(x_i) \leq 1, \\ 0 \leq \xi_A(x_i) - \xi_B(x_i) \leq 1, 0 \leq \psi_A(x_i) - \psi_B(x_i) \leq 1. \end{gathered}$$

For $p = 1$, we get

$$\begin{gathered} 0 \leq |\varepsilon_A(x_i) - \varepsilon_B(x_i)| \leq 1, 0 \leq |\zeta_A(x_i) - \zeta_B(x_i)| \leq 1, \\ 0 \leq |\xi_A(x_i) - \xi_B(x_i)| \leq 1, 0 \leq |\psi_A(x_i) - \psi_B(x_i)| \leq 1. \end{gathered}$$

In addition, we have

$$0 \leq \sum_{i=1}^{n} \begin{pmatrix} |\varepsilon_A(x_i) - \varepsilon_B(x_i)| + |\zeta_A(x_i) - \zeta_B(x_i)| \\ + |\xi_A(x_i) - \xi_B(x_i)| + |\psi_A(x_i) - \psi_B(x_i)| \end{pmatrix} \leq 1.$$

Hence, $0 \leq \varphi(A, B) \leq 1$, which proves boundedness.
Similarly, for $p = 2$ we have

$$\begin{gathered} 0 \leq \left(\varepsilon_A(x_i) - \varepsilon_B(x_i)\right)^2 \leq 1, 0 \leq \left(\zeta_A(x_i) - \zeta_B(x_i)\right)^2 \leq 1, \\ 0 \leq \left(\xi_A(x_i) - \xi_B(x_i)\right)^2 \leq 1, 0 \leq \left(\psi_A(x_i) - \psi_B(x_i)\right)^2 \leq 1, \end{gathered}$$

which implies that

$$0 \leq \sum_{i=1}^{n} \begin{pmatrix} \left(\varepsilon_A(x_i) - \varepsilon_B(x_i)\right)^2 + \left(\zeta_A(x_i) - \zeta_B(x_i)\right)^2 \\ + \left(\xi_A(x_i) - \xi_B(x_i)\right)^2 + \left(\psi_A(x_i) - \psi_B(x_i)\right)^2 \end{pmatrix} \leq 1,$$

which also proves boundedness. The proof of boundedness of $\varphi^{\omega}(A, B)$ is similar.

Next, we need to validate that $\varphi(A, A) = 0$ and $\varphi(B, B) = 0$. For $p = 1$, we have

$$\varphi(A, A) = \frac{1}{4n} \sum_{i=1}^{n} \begin{bmatrix} |\varepsilon_A(x_i) - \varepsilon_A(x_i)| + |\zeta_A(x_i) - \zeta_A(x_i)| \\ + |\xi_A(x_i) - \xi_A(x_i)| + |\psi_A(x_i) - \psi_A(x_i)| \end{bmatrix} = 0,$$

$$\varphi(B, B) = \frac{1}{4n} \sum_{i=1}^{n} \begin{bmatrix} |\varepsilon_B(x_i) - \varepsilon_B(x_i)| + |\zeta_B(x_i) - \zeta_B(x_i)| \\ + |\xi_B(x_i) - \xi_B(x_i)| + |\psi_B(x_i) - \psi_B(x_i)| \end{bmatrix} = 0,$$

as desired.

Similarly for $p = 2$, we have

$$\varphi(A, A) = \sqrt{\frac{1}{4n} \sum_{i=1}^{n} \begin{bmatrix} (\varepsilon_A(x_i) - \varepsilon_A(x_i))^2 + (\zeta_A(x_i) - \zeta_A(x_i))^2 \\ + (\xi_A(x_i) - \xi_A(x_i))^2 + (\psi_A(x_i) - \psi_A(x_i))^2 \end{bmatrix}} = 0,$$

$$\varphi(B, B) = \sqrt{\frac{1}{4n} \sum_{i=1}^{n} \begin{bmatrix} (\varepsilon_B(x_i) - \varepsilon_B(x_i))^2 + (\zeta_B(x_i) - \zeta_B(x_i))^2 \\ + (\xi_B(x_i) - \xi_B(x_i))^2 + (\psi_B(x_i) - \psi_B(x_i))^2 \end{bmatrix}} = 0,$$

as expected. Similarly, $\varphi^{\omega}(A, A) = 0$ and $\varphi^{\omega}(B, B)$. Hence, the reflexive property holds.

The symmetry property holds for $p = 1$ since

$$\begin{aligned}
\varphi(A, B) &= \frac{1}{4n} \sum_{i=1}^{n} \begin{bmatrix} |\varepsilon_A(x_i) - \varepsilon_B(x_i)| + |\zeta_A(x_i) - \zeta_B(x_i)| \\ + |\xi_A(x_i) - \xi_B(x_i)| + |\psi_A(x_i) - \psi_B(x_i)| \end{bmatrix} \\
&= \frac{1}{4n} \sum_{i=1}^{n} \begin{bmatrix} |-(\varepsilon_B(x_i) - \varepsilon_A(x_i))| + |-(\zeta_B(x_i) - \zeta_A(x_i))| \\ + |-(\xi_B(x_i) - \xi_A(x_i))| + |-(\psi_B(x_i) - \psi_A(x_i))| \end{bmatrix} \\
&= \frac{1}{4n} \sum_{i=1}^{n} \begin{bmatrix} |\varepsilon_B(x_i) - \varepsilon_A(x_i)| + |\zeta_B(x_i) - \zeta_A(x_i)| \\ + |\xi_B(x_i) - \xi_A(x_i)| + |\psi_B(x_i) - \psi_A(x_i)| \end{bmatrix} = \varphi(B, A).
\end{aligned}$$

Similarly, for $p = 2$ we get

$$\varphi(A,B)=\sqrt{\frac{1}{4n}\sum_{i=1}^{n}\begin{bmatrix}\left(\varepsilon_A(x_i)-\varepsilon_B(x_i)\right)^2+\left(\zeta_A(x_i)-\zeta_B(x_i)\right)^2\\+\left(\xi_A(x_i)-\xi_B(x_i)\right)^2+\left(\psi_A(x_i)-\psi_B(x_i)\right)^2\end{bmatrix}}$$

$$=\sqrt{\frac{1}{4n}\sum_{i=1}^{n}\begin{bmatrix}(-[\varepsilon_B(x_i)-\varepsilon_A(x_i)])^2+(-[\zeta_B(x_i)-\zeta_A(x_i)])^2\\+(-[\xi_B(x_i)-\xi_A(x_i)])^2+(-[\psi_B(x_i)-\psi_A(x_i)])^2\end{bmatrix}}$$

$$=\sqrt{\frac{1}{4n}\sum_{i=1}^{n}\begin{bmatrix}\left(\varepsilon_B(x_i)-\varepsilon_A(x_i)\right)^2+\left(\zeta_B(x_i)-\zeta_A(x_i)\right)^2\\+\left(\xi_B(x_i)-\xi_A(x_i)\right)^2+\left(\psi_B(x_i)-\psi_A(x_i)\right)^2\end{bmatrix}}=\varphi(B,A).$$

In the same way, $\varphi^{\omega}(A,A)$ satisfies the symmetry property.

Finally, we verify the separable property. Suppose $\varphi(A,B)=0$ for $p=1$, then

$$\frac{1}{4n}\sum_{i=1}^{n}\begin{bmatrix}|\varepsilon_A(x_i)-\varepsilon_B(x_i)|+|\zeta_A(x_i)-\zeta_B(x_i)|\\+|\xi_A(x_i)-\xi_B(x_i)|+|\psi_A(x_i)-\psi_B(x_i)|\end{bmatrix}=0,$$

which implies that $\begin{bmatrix}|\varepsilon_A(x_i)-\varepsilon_B(x_i)|+|\zeta_A(x_i)-\zeta_B(x_i)|\\+|\xi_A(x_i)-\xi_B(x_i)|+|\psi_A(x_i)-\psi_B(x_i)|\end{bmatrix}=0.$ Thus,

$\varepsilon_A(x_i)=\varepsilon_B(x_i)$, $\zeta_A(x_i)=\zeta_B(x_i)$, $\xi_A(x_i)=\xi_B(x_i)$, and $\psi_A(x_i)=\psi_B(x_i)$. Hence, $A=B$.

Conversely, if $A=B$ then $\varepsilon_A(x_i)=\varepsilon_B(x_i)$, $\zeta_A(x_i)=\zeta_B(x_i)$, $\xi_A(x_i)=\xi_B(x_i)$, and $\psi_A(x_i)=\psi_B(x_i)$.

Thus, $\frac{1}{4n}\sum_{i=1}^{n}\begin{bmatrix}|\varepsilon_A(x_i)-\varepsilon_B(x_i)|+|\zeta_A(x_i)-\zeta_B(x_i)|\\+|\xi_A(x_i)-\xi_B(x_i)|+|\psi_A(x_i)-\psi_B(x_i)|\end{bmatrix}=0$, which implies that $\varphi(A,B)=0$.

Now, we prove for $p=2$. Suppose $\varphi(A,B)=0$, then we have

$$\sqrt{\frac{1}{4n}\sum_{i=1}^{n}\begin{bmatrix}\left(\varepsilon_A(x_i)-\varepsilon_B(x_i)\right)^2+\left(\zeta_A(x_i)-\zeta_B(x_i)\right)^2\\+\left(\xi_A(x_i)-\xi_B(x_i)\right)^2+\left(\psi_A(x_i)-\psi_B(x_i)\right)^2\end{bmatrix}}=0,$$

which follows that $\begin{bmatrix} \left(\varepsilon_A(x_i)-\varepsilon_B(x_i)\right)^2+\left(\zeta_A(x_i)-\zeta_B(x_i)\right)^2 \\ +\left(\xi_A(x_i)-\xi_B(x_i)\right)^2+\left(\psi_A(x_i)-\psi_B(x_i)\right)^2 \end{bmatrix}=0$. Thus, $\varepsilon_A(x_i)=\varepsilon_B(x_i)$, $\zeta_A(x_i)=\zeta_B(x_i)$, $\xi_A(x_i)=\xi_B(x_i)$, and $\psi_A(x_i)=\psi_B(x_i)$. Hence, $A=B$.

Conversely, if $A=B$, then it is straightforward that $\varphi(A,B)=0$. Therefore, the separable property holds.

In the same way, $\varphi^{\omega}(A,A)$ satisfies the separable property.

16.2.2.1 *Merits of the Proposed Measure*

The novel distance measure introduced within the Picture Fuzzy Set (PFS) framework offers meaningful insights for evaluating maternal health risks more effectively. Key advantages include:

a) Capturing positive, neutral, and negative membership degrees for a comprehensive representation of uncertainty.
b) Integrating outcome weighting helps to reduce bias and prioritizes critical risks associated with mothers within the bearing age range.
c) Verifying the locally generated clinical data, then relating the outcome to practical relevance to support physician's decision-making

16.2.3 Established Distance Measures

The existing distance measuring methods under PFSs developed by Singh *et al.* [56] Zhao *et al.* [42], Dutta [57], and, Dinh and Thao [25] are presented as (16.11) (16.12) (16.13), and (16.14):

a. Singh *et al.* [56]

$$\varphi_{Se}(A,B)=\sqrt{\frac{1}{4n}\sum_{i=1}^{n}\max_{1\le i\le n}\begin{bmatrix}|\varepsilon_A(x_i)-\varepsilon_B(x_i)|^2,|\zeta_A(x_i)-\zeta_B(x_i)|^2, \\ |\xi_A(x_i)-\xi_B(x_i)|^2,|\psi_A(x_i)-\psi_B(x_i)|^2\end{bmatrix}} \tag{16.11}$$

b. Zhao *et al.* [42]

$$\varphi_{Ze}(A,B)=\sqrt[p]{\frac{1}{3}\sum_{i=1}^{n}w_i\left[\begin{array}{c}|\varepsilon_A(x_i)-\varepsilon_B(x_i)|^p+|\zeta_A(x_i)-\zeta_B(x_i)|^p\\+|\xi_A(x_i)-\xi_B(x_i)|^p\end{array}\right]} \tag{16.12}$$

c. Dutta [57]

$$\varphi_{Du}(A,B)\frac{1}{3n}\sum_{i=1}^{n}\left(\begin{array}{c}|\varepsilon_A(x_i)-\varepsilon_B(x_i)|^2+|\zeta_A(x_i)-\zeta_B(x_i)|^2\\+|\xi_A(x_i)-\xi_B(x_i)|^2\end{array}\right) \tag{16.13}$$

d. Dinh and Thao [25]

$$\varphi_{DT}(A,B)=\frac{1}{n}\sum_{i=1}^{n}\max_{1\le i\le n}\left[\begin{array}{c}|\varepsilon_A(x_i)-\varepsilon_B(x_i)|^2,|\zeta_A(x_i)-\zeta_B(x_i)|^2,\\|\xi_A(x_i)-\xi_B(x_i)|^2,|\psi_A(x_i)-\psi_B(x_i)|^2\end{array}\right] \tag{16.14}$$

16.3 Maternal Outcomes Analysis Based on Picture Fuzzy Distance Measures

The data utilized in this study were sourced from our previous research employing intuitionistic fuzzy methods to enhance maternal outcomes [3, 7]. The dataset was collected from both private and tertiary healthcare facilities within the Niger Delta region of Nigeria. Over 2,000 patients were included in the study, with 15 input features encompassing Maternal Blood Pressure (MBP), Maternal Weight (MW), Hemoglobin Level (HL), Packed Cell Volume (PCV), Pulse Rate (PR), Mode of Delivery (MOD), Malaria Frequency (MP), Hepatitis B (HB), Diabetes Status (DM), Herbal Ingestion (HI), Respiratory Disorder (RD), Maternal Age (MA), Ascorbic Acid Level (ACC), Preeclampsia (PREE), and Antenatal Booking (AB). The corresponding seven output features were Miscarriage, Preterm Contraction, Stillbirth, Placenta Previa, Urinary Tract Infection (UTI), Full-Term Delivery, and Mortality. Ethical clearance was

Table 16.1 Maternal and diagnosis.

Maternal outcome and diagnosis															
	MBPM	MW	HL	PCVL	PR	MOD	MP	HB	DM	HI	RD	MA	ACC	PREE	AB
M1	(0.4,0.5,0.05)	(0.4,0.5,0.05)	(0.4,0.5,0.05)	(0.4,0.5,0.05)	(0.4,0.5,0.05)	(0.4,0.5,0.05)	(0.4,0.5,0.05)	(0.4,0.5,0.05)	(0.4,0.5,0.05)	(0.4,0.5,0.05)	(0.4,0.5,0.05)	(0.4,0.5,0.05)	(0.4,0.5,0.05)	(0.4,0.5,0.05)	(0.4,0.5,0.05)
M2	(0.4,0.5,0.25)	(0.4,0.5,0.25)	(0.4,0.5,0.25)	(0.4,0.5,0.25)	(0.4,0.5,0.25)	(0.4,0.5,0.25)	(0.4,0.5,0.25)	(0.4,0.5,0.25)	(0.4,0.5,0.25)	(0.4,0.5,0.25)	(0.4,0.5,0.25)	(0.4,0.5,0.25)	(0.4,0.5,0.25)	(0.4,0.5,0.25)	(0.4,0.5,0.25)
M3	(0.4,0.1,0.25)	(0.4,0.1,0.25)	(0.4,0.1,0.25)	(0.4,0.1,0.25)	(0.4,0.1,0.25)	(0.4,0.1,0.25)	(0.4,0.1,0.25)	(0.4,0.1,0.25)	(0.4,0.1,0.25)	(0.4,0.1,0.25)	(0.4,0.1,0.25)	(0.4,0.1,0.25)	(0.4,0.1,0.25)	(0.4,0.1,0.25)	(0.4,0.1,0.25)
M4	(0.4,0.2,0.2)	(0.4,0.2,0.2)	(0.4,0.2,0.2)	(0.4,0.2,0.2)	(0.4,0.2,0.2)	(0.4,0.2,0.2)	(0.4,0.2,0.2)	(0.4,0.2,0.2)	(0.4,0.2,0.2)	(0.4,0.2,0.2)	(0.4,0.2,0.2)	(0.4,0.2,0.2)	(0.4,0.2,0.2)	(0.4,0.2,0.2)	(0.4,0.2,0.2)
M5	(0.2,0.7,0.05)	(0.2,0.7,0.05)	(0.2,0.7,0.05)	(0.2,0.7,0.05)	(0.2,0.7,0.05)	(0.2,0.7,0.05)	(0.2,0.7,0.05)	(0.2,0.7,0.05)	(0.2,0.7,0.05)	(0.2,0.7,0.05)	(0.2,0.7,0.05)	(0.2,0.7,0.05)	(0.2,0.7,0.05)	(0.2,0.7,0.05)	(0.2,0.7,0.05)

Table 16.2 Outcome and diagnosis.

	MBPM	MW	HL	PCVL	PR	MOD	MP	HB	DM	HI	RD	MA	ACC	PREE	AB
Miscarriage	(0.2, 0.3, 0.25)	(0.2, 0.3, 0.25)	(0.2, 0.3, 0.25)	(0.2, 0.3, 0.25)	(0.2, 0.3, 0.25)	(0.2, 0.3, 0.25)	(0.2, 0.3, 0.25)	(0.2, 0.3, 0.25)	(0.2, 0.3, 0.25)	(0.2, 0.3, 0.25)	(0.2, 0.3, 0.25)	(0.2, 0.3, 0.25)	(0.2, 0.3, 0.25)	(0.2, 0.3, 0.25)	(0.2, 0.3, 0.25)
Pre-term	(0.3, 0.2, 0.25)	(0.3, 0.2, 0.25)	(0.3, 0.2, 0.25)	(0.3, 0.2, 0.25)	(0.3, 0.2, 0.25)	(0.3, 0.2, 0.25)	(0.3, 0.2, 0.25)	(0.3, 0.2, 0.25)	(0.3, 0.2, 0.25)	(0.3, 0.2, 0.25)	(0.3, 0.2, 0.25)	(0.3, 0.2, 0.25)	(0.3, 0.2, 0.25)	(0.3, 0.2, 0.25)	(0.3, 0.2, 0.25)
Still Birth	(0.3, 0.2, 0.25)	(0.3, 0.2, 0.25)	(0.3, 0.2, 0.25)	(0.3, 0.2, 0.25)	(0.3, 0.2, 0.25)	(0.3, 0.2, 0.25)	(0.3, 0.2, 0.25)	(0.3, 0.2, 0.25)	(0.3, 0.2, 0.25)	(0.3, 0.2, 0.25)	(0.3, 0.2, 0.25)	(0.3, 0.2, 0.25)	(0.3, 0.2, 0.25)	(0.3, 0.2, 0.25)	(0.3, 0.2, 0.25)
Placentae Previa	(0.2, 0.6, 0.1)	(0.2, 0.6, 0.1)	(0.2, 0.6, 0.1)	(0.2, 0.6, 0.1)	(0.2, 0.6, 0.1)	(0.2, 0.6, 0.1)	(0.2, 0.6, 0.1)	(0.2, 0.6, 0.1)	(0.2, 0.6, 0.1)	(0.2, 0.6, 0.1)	(0.2, 0.6, 0.1)	(0.2, 0.6, 0.1)	(0.2, 0.6, 0.1)	(0.2, 0.6, 0.1)	(0.2, 0.6, 0.1)
UTI	(0.2, 0.7, 0.05)	(0.2, 0.7, 0.05)	(0.2, 0.7, 0.05)	(0.2, 0.7, 0.05)	(0.2, 0.7, 0.05)	(0.2, 0.7, 0.05)	(0.2, 0.7, 0.05)	(0.2, 0.7, 0.05)	(0.2, 0.7, 0.05)	(0.2, 0.7, 0.05)	(0.2, 0.7, 0.05)	(0.2, 0.7, 0.05)	(0.2, 0.7, 0.05)	(0.2, 0.7, 0.05)	(0.2, 0.7, 0.05)
Full-Term	(0.2, 0.8, 0.0)	(0.2, 0.8, 0.0)	(0.2, 0.8, 0.0)	(0.2, 0.8, 0.0)	(0.2, 0.8, 0.0)	(0.2, 0.8, 0.0)	(0.2, 0.8, 0.0)	(0.2, 0.8, 0.0)	(0.2, 0.8, 0.0)	(0.2, 0.8, 0.0)	(0.2, 0.8, 0.0)	(0.2, 0.8, 0.0)	(0.2, 0.8, 0.0)	(0.2, 0.8, 0.0)	(0.2, 0.8, 0.0)
Mortality	(0.1, 0.0, 0.45)	(0.1, 0.0, 0.45)	(0.1, 0.0, 0.45)	(0.1, 0.0, 0.45)	(0.1, 0.0, 0.45)	(0.1, 0.0, 0.45)	(0.1, 0.0, 0.45)	(0.1, 0.0, 0.45)	(0.1, 0.0, 0.45)	(0.1, 0.0, 0.45)	(0.1, 0.0, 0.45)	(0.1, 0.0, 0.45)	(0.1, 0.0, 0.45)	(0.1, 0.0, 0.45)	(0.1, 0.0, 0.45)

obtained from all participating health facilities, and patient confidentiality was rigorously maintained throughout the study.

Let $M = \{M_1, M_2, M_3, M_4, M_5\}$, be the set of maternal patients, and

$$D = \{MBP, MOD, MW, HL, PCV, PR, MP, HC, DM, HI, RD, MA, ACC, PREE, AB\},$$

be the set of symptoms obtained during antenatal clinic. The associated maternal outcomes may include risks such as miscarriage, preterm labor (contractions), stillbirth, placenta previa, urinary tract infection (UTI), full-term delivery, and mortality. These risks are detailed in the data presented in Table 16.1 and Table 16.2, as follows:

1. Table 16.1 presents maternal patients and diagnoses based on expert knowledge using picture fuzzy relations.
2. Table 16.2 displays maternal outcomes and diagnoses represented through Picture Fuzzy Sets (PFS).

Table 16.1 and Table 16.2 utilize the Picture Fuzzy Set (PFS) framework, characterized by four key parameters: membership degree, non-membership degree, neutral membership degree, and hesitation degree. This model is valuable in scenarios where patients present with ambiguous or mixed symptoms, positive, negative, or neutral, making it challenging for physicians to pinpoint the exact diagnosis. Such complexities often necessitate careful deliberation regarding the most appropriate management and treatment strategies. There is no doubt that adopting PFS provides a structured approach to handling uncertainty, ensuring a more accurate and nuanced assessment of the patient's condition.

16.4 Result and Discussion

The new distance method and its weighted form are applied to the medical data in Tables 16.1 and 16.2 to obtain the distances of the maternal outcomes and the pregnant women. The distance results are shown in Tables 16.3 and 16.4 respectively.

Based on the results in Tables 16.3 and 16.4, the weighted distance calculations indicate that using p=1 provides smoother and more balanced assessments of the relationships between maternal conditions and outcomes. At the same time, p=2 offers greater precision and sharper

Table 16.3 Distances of the maternal outcomes and the pregnant women (p= 1).

Outcome	Miscarriage	Pre-term	Still birth	Placentae previa	UTI	Full-term	Mortality
M1	0.1730	0.1667	0.1602	0.1387	0.1387	0.1534	0.2447
M2	0.1430	0.1348	0.1430	0.1507	0.1651	0.1906	0.2286
M3	0.1280	0.1045	0.1129	0.1811	0.2002	0.2176	0.1539
M4	0.1065	0.0805	0.0900	0.1507	0.1708	0.1889	0.1660
M5	0.2727	0.3124	0.3198	0.1804	0.1524	0.2045	0.3476

Table 16.4 Distances of the maternal outcomes and the pregnant women (p= 2).

Outcome	Miscarriage	Pre-term	Still birth	Placentae previa	UTI	Full-term	Mortality
M1	0.0746	0.0781	0.0774	0.0517	0.0594	0.0753	0.1520
M2	0.0612	0.0674	0.0682	0.0584	0.0738	0.0941	0.1352
M3	0.0548	0.0331	0.0394	0.1071	0.1280	0.1497	0.0721
M4	0.0413	0.0221	0.0270	0.0825	0.1011	0.1208	0.0810
M5	0.1494	0.1836	0.1904	0.0699	0.0762	0.0976	0.2496

differentiation, making it more appropriate for datasets requiring detailed analysis and a focus on variability. Furthermore, Table 16.4 suggests that patients categorized under M1 and M2 are at risk for miscarriage, preterm birth, or stillbirth, highlighting the close interrelation among these adverse pregnancy outcomes. Miscarriage, defined as the spontaneous loss of pregnancy before 20 weeks of gestation, shares several risk factors with preterm birth and stillbirth. Preterm birth, which occurs when a baby is born before 37 weeks, can lead to neonatal morbidity and mortality [43–45], and if complications are severe, it may result in stillbirth. This progression underscores the potential severity of these conditions, as M3, M4, and M5 exhibit increased values, indicating a higher likelihood of stillbirth in these categories.

The underlying causes of these outcomes often involve a combination of maternal, placental, and fetal factors, with common risk factors include advanced maternal age [46–48], previous pregnancy loss [64, 65], maternal infections [66], chronic health conditions [67], placental abnormalities

[68, 69], and lifestyle factors such as smoking and drug use [42, 55, 56]. Persisting issues like intrauterine infections or genetic abnormalities [73, 74], if unresolved, can contribute to complications later in pregnancy, potentially leading to preterm birth or stillbirth.

Intrauterine infections are particularly significant, as their timing and severity can influence whether they cause miscarriage, preterm labor, or stillbirth. These infections may induce inflammation and the premature rupture of membranes, increasing the risk across all three outcomes. A crucial pathophysiological connection exists among these conditions, often centered on uteroplacental insufficiency reduced blood flow to the placenta that can restrict fetal growth, heightening the risk of preterm birth or stillbirth.

According to Tiruneh *et al.* [75] and Soobryan *et al.* [76], regarding maternal health conditions, hypertension and pre-eclampsia can diminish blood flow to the placenta, increasing the risk of preterm birth and stillbirth. Women with unmanaged hypertension face a greater likelihood of experiencing a miscarriage and preterm labor, as hypertension can impair placental function, leading to complications that may ultimately result in stillbirth. Maternal infections such as bacterial vaginosis, Chlamydia, or Group B Streptococcus are associated with preterm birth and miscarriage due to their role in causing inflammation and premature membrane rupture.

Placental complications, such as placenta previa (where the placenta covers the cervix) [77], significantly raise the risk of preterm labor. If not appropriately managed, these complications may lead to fetal loss [78]. Thus, meticulous management of chronic conditions like hypertension and diabetes is critical in reducing the chances of complications that could progress to preterm birth or stillbirth [79], particularly in cases represented by M3, M4, and M5. These groups demonstrate a higher risk, indicating the need for vigilant monitoring to prevent severe outcomes like stillbirth.

16.4.1 Sensitivity Analysis

To assess the effectiveness of the proposed method, computations are required for both weighted and unweighted scenarios are required when $p=1$ and $p=2$. Table 16.4 provides a detailed comparison of the results in both cases.

Table 16.5 summarizes the adjusted and unadjusted distance outputs in relation to maternal outcomes. We observed lower distance measures for both adjusted and unadjusted cases, indicating higher similarity between maternal conditions. Specifically, patients M1 and M2 are more likely to

Table 16.5 Comparative results for weighted and unweighted between patients and maternal outcome.

Condition pair	Unweighted distance (p=1)	Weighted distance (p=1)	Unweighted distance (p=2)	Weighted distance (p=2)
M1 - Miscarriage	0.4183	0.1730	0.1803	0.0746
M1 - Preterm	0.4031	0.1667	0.1887	0.0781
M1 - Stillbirth	0.3873	0.1602	0.1871	0.0774
M1 - Placentae Previa	0.3354	0.1387	0.1250	0.0517
M1 - UTI	0.3354	0.1387	0.1436	0.0594
M1 - Full-Term	0.3708	0.1534	0.1820	0.0753
M1 - Mortality	0.5916	0.2447	0.3674	0.1520
M2 - Miscarriage	0.3354	0.1430	0.1436	0.0612
M2 - Preterm	0.3162	0.1348	0.1581	0.0674
M2 - Stillbirth	0.3354	0.1430	0.1601	0.0682
M2 - Placentae Previa	0.3536	0.1507	0.1369	0.0584
M2 - UTI	0.3873	0.1651	0.1732	0.0738
M2 - Full-Term	0.4472	0.1906	0.2208	0.0941
M2 - Mortality	0.5362	0.2286	0.3172	0.1352
M3 - Miscarriage	0.3354	0.1280	0.1436	0.0548
M3 - Preterm	0.2739	0.1045	0.0866	0.0331
M3 - Stillbirth	0.2958	0.1129	0.1031	0.0394
M3 - Placentae Previa	0.4743	0.1811	0.2806	0.1071
M3 - UTI	0.5244	0.2002	0.3354	0.1280
M3 - Full-Term	0.5701	0.2176	0.3921	0.1497
M3 - Mortality	0.4031	0.1539	0.1887	0.0721
M4 - Miscarriage	0.2958	0.1065	0.1146	0.0413
M4 - Preterm	0.2236	0.0805	0.0612	0.0221

(Continued)

Table 16.5 Comparative results for weighted and unweighted between patients and maternal outcome. (*Continued*)

Condition pair	Unweighted distance (p=1)	Weighted distance (p=1)	Unweighted distance (p=2)	Weighted distance (p=2)
M4 - Stillbirth	0.2500	0.0900	0.0750	0.0270
M4 - Placentae Previa	0.4183	0.1507	0.2291	0.0825
M4 - UTI	0.4743	0.1708	0.2806	0.1011
M4 - Full-Term	0.5244	0.1889	0.3354	0.1208
M4 - Mortality	0.4610	0.1660	0.2250	0.0810
M5 - Miscarriage	0.4472	0.2727	0.2449	0.1494
M5 - Preterm	0.5123	0.3124	0.3010	0.1836
M5 - Stillbirth	0.5244	0.3198	0.3123	0.1904
M5 - Placentae Previa	0.2958	0.1804	0.1146	0.0699
M5 - UTI	0.2500	0.1524	0.1250	0.0762
M5 - Full-Term	0.3354	0.2045	0.1601	0.0976
M5 - Mortality	0.5701	0.3476	0.4093	0.2496

experience miscarriage or preterm outcomes. Additionally, patient M4 consistently exhibited the lowest distances, suggesting a higher likelihood of preterm or stillbirth, making it highly sensitive. In contrast, patient M5 showed higher distances, particularly for miscarriage and mortality, indicating lower sensitivity to these outcomes. Overall, the adjusted distances were consistently more minor than the unadjusted distances, highlighting the impact of the weight values. To provide a more precise visual representation of these findings, a radar graphs were used to depict the results for each of the patients as seen in Figure 16.1.

We adopted a radial plot for its ability to visually compare multidimensional data, revealing patterns, relationships, and sensitivities across input variables. The distinct shapes of the radar chart for each maternal condition highlight varying sensitivity levels to specific outcomes. Larger areas along particular axes (outcomes) indicate heightened sensitivity for those

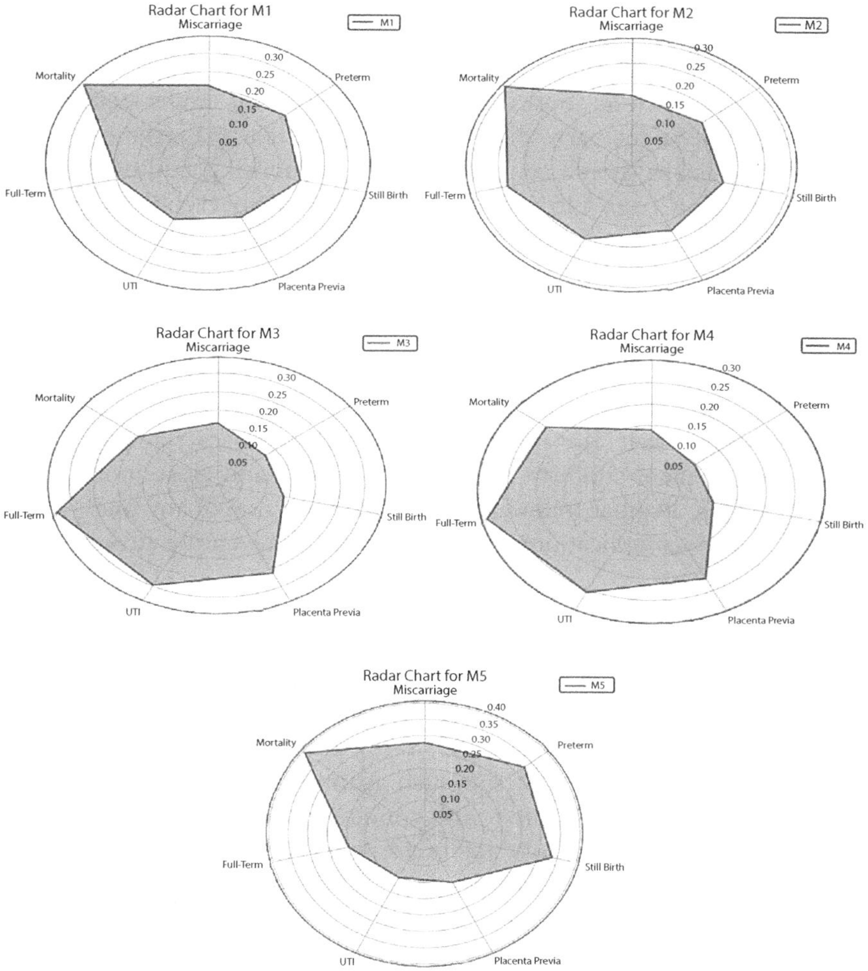

Figure 16.1 Radial plot between maternal patients and outcomes.

outcomes in particular conditions. For instance, the spikes observed for patients M3 and M4 towards outcomes like placenta previa and mortality suggest a strong correlation with these severe risks. Patient M2 displays a balanced risk profile with relatively lower sensitivity towards critical outcomes such as mortality, whereas patient M5 demonstrates broader sensitivity across outcomes like miscarriage and preterm birth, signaling risks spanning multiple dimensions.

16.4.1.1 Medical Implications and Recommendations

a. **Patients M3 and M5:** Their strong sensitivity to severe outcomes such as mortality and placenta previa underscores the need for early diagnosis and proactive management. Physicians should consider frequent monitoring, additional imaging (e.g., ultrasound), and targeted interventions to mitigate these risks.
b. **Patients M1 and M2:** These patients show moderate sensitivity to outcomes like UTIs and preterm birth, which are often preventable. Proactive measures, including infection control, adequate hydration, and timely administration of antibiotics, should be prioritized to minimize the risks.
c. **Patient M4:** The observed sensitivity to miscarriage and subsequent stillbirth calls for continuous and close monitoring. Regular follow-ups and early detection of any unexpected complications will be essential in preventing adverse outcomes.

If these sensitivities and risks are not addressed, the potential for severe maternal and neonatal complications increases, underscoring the importance of targeted medical management based on the identified patterns.

Table 16.4 reveals that patient M1 faces the highest risk of mortality, likely driven by underlying factors such as maternal infections, placental issues, or unmanaged chronic health conditions. In contrast, patient M4 showcases the lowest distance for preterm birth, indicating the highest sensitivity to this outcome and an urgent need for preventive measures. Patient M2, with better outcomes for full-term births and miscarriage, suggests that timely and close medical supervision could transform a high-risk scenario into a successful full-term birth. For further clarity, Table 16.4 is captured in a heatmap in Figure 16.2.

To address these findings, patient M1 requires comprehensive diagnostic testing to identify potential risks and targeted interventions, including nutritional support, infection control, and stress management. Regular fetal and maternal monitoring should be prioritized to prevent complications. For patient M4, preventive measures such as corticosteroid administration, frequent ultrasounds, and lifestyle modifications like reduced physical activity are critical to mitigating the risk of preterm birth. Patient M2 would benefit from continued prenatal care, nutritional supplements, and education to ensure a favorable outcome. Patient M3, who may be at risk of placenta previa and mortality, requires close monitoring with

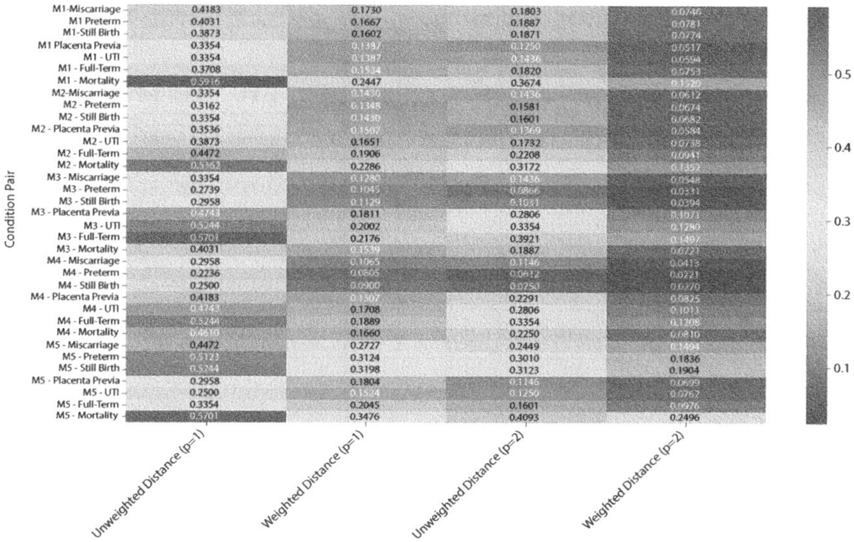

Figure 16.2 Heatmap of distances for maternal conditions and outcomes.

regular check-ups to address potential underlying health issues, such as hypertension or diabetes, which could exacerbate these risks. Proactive treatment, which includes using safe antibiotics and measures to promote hydration and hygiene, is essential to minimize the likelihood of recurrent infections and associated complications. Undoubtedly, these strategies collectively highlight the importance of early detection and personalized care plans in enhancing maternal and neonatal outcomes.

The ratios consistently range between 0.1 and 0.7 across the board, highlighting the significant impact of weighting in reducing distance values. Overall, the weighted metrics enhance the analysis by refining comparisons and narrowing the disparities between maternal conditions and outcomes, reflecting the prioritization of specific parameters.

16.4.2 Comparative Result

Here, we evaluate the existing methods of distance measure under PFSs developed Singh *et al.* [56] Zhao *et al.* [42], Dutta [57], and, Dinh and Thao [25] and compare the outcomes with the new method. The results of the computation are shown in Table 16.6.

From Tables 16.6–16.9 present the results of the existing methods under the defined evaluation conditions. In contrast, the proposed method, as shown in Table 16.10, provides more precise and consistent results

Table 16.6 Dutta [57] distance measure.

Outcome	Miscarriage	Pre-term	Still birth	Placentae previa	UTI	Full-term	Mortality
M1	**0.0350**	**0.0325**	**0.0325**	0.0550	0.0650	0.0800	0.0750
M2	**0.0250**	**0.0200**	**0.0200**	0.0450	0.0550	0.0750	0.0850
M3	0.0500	**0.0475**	0.0475	0.0700	0.0800	0.1000	0.1100
M4	0.0400	**0.0375**	0.0375	0.0600	0.0700	0.0900	0.0950
M5	0.0650	**0.0625**	0.0625	0.0850	0.0950	0.1100	0.1200

Table 16.7 Dinh and Thao [25] distance measure.

Outcome	Miscarriage	Pre-term	Still birth	Placentae previa	UTI	Full-Ttrm	Mortality
M1	**0.0400**	0.0900	0.0900	0.0400	0.0400	0.0900	0.2500
M2	**0.0400**	0.0900	0.0900	0.0400	0.0400	0.0900	0.2500
M3	0.0400	**0.0100**	**0.0100**	0.2500	0.3600	0.4900	0.0900
M4	0.0400	**0.0100**	**0.0100**	0.1600	0.2500	0.3600	0.0900
M5	0.1600	0.2500	0.2500	0.0100	**0.0000**	0.0100	0.4900

Table 16.8 Singh *et al.* [56] distance measure.

Outcome	Miscarriage	Pre-term	Still birth	Placentae previa	UTI	Full-term	Mortality
M1	**0.0500**	0.0750	0.0750	0.0500	0.0500	0.0750	0.1250
M2	**0.0500**	0.0750	0.0750	0.0500	0.0500	0.0750	0.1250
M3	0.0500	**0.0250**	**0.0250**	0.1250	0.1500	0.1750	0.0750
M4	0.0500	**0.0250**	**0.0250**	0.1000	0.1250	0.1500	0.0750
M5	0.1000	0.1250	0.1250	0.0250	**0.0000**	0.0250	0.1750

Table 16.9 Zhao *et al.* [42] distance measure.

Outcome	Miscarriage	Pre-term	Still birth	Placentae previa	UTI	Full-term	Mortality
M1	0.4972	0.4725	**0.4586**	0.4778	0.4736	0.4862	0.5095
M2	0.5141	0.4847	**0.4731**	0.4875	0.4910	0.5047	0.5231
M3	0.5239	0.4965	**0.4893**	0.4979	0.5032	0.5159	0.5348
M4	0.5098	0.4816	**0.4743**	0.4841	0.4892	0.4953	0.5182
M5	0.5689	0.5581	**0.5500**	0.5587	0.5601	0.5742	0.5832

Table 16.10 New method distance measure.

Outcome	Miscarriage	Pre-term	Still birth	Placentae previa	UTI	Full-term	Mortality
M1	0.0746	0.0781	0.0774	**0.0517**	0.0594	0.0753	0.1520
M2	0.0612	0.0674	0.0682	**0.0584**	0.0738	0.0941	0.1352
M3	0.0548	**0.0331**	0.0394	0.1071	0.1280	0.1497	0.0721
M4	0.0413	**0.0221**	0.0270	0.0825	0.1011	0.1208	0.0810
M5	0.1494	0.1836	0.1904	**0.0699**	0.0762	0.0976	0.2496

compared to these approaches, while incorporating all the defining properties and parameters of PFSs. The data in Table 16.10 indicates that the new distance measure exhibits consistent patterns across datasets M1 to M5, with M1 consistently yielding the lowest values and M5 the highest. This pattern suggests a correlation between the escalation of maternal risk factors and the increase in values for adverse pregnancy outcomes. For instance, the relatively low values in M1 imply minimal risks, while the progressively higher values from M1 to M5 highlight increasing risks as maternal complications intensify. Notably, the outcomes for full-term and preterm birth exhibit minimal fluctuation across datasets, indicating relatively stable outcomes for most patients. However, M5 demonstrates the highest values across multiple categories, particularly for mortality, underscoring the need for urgent and comprehensive medical intervention for patients in this group. This observation aligns with current research indicating that elevated maternal risk factors often translate to heightened adverse outcomes [64–68].

While patients in lower-risk categories (M1 and M2) generally present fewer complications, ongoing monitoring remains crucial to detect any subtle changes that could indicate emerging risks. Conversely, those in higher-risk categories, particularly M5, should be prioritized for intensive medical supervision, given the increased probability of severe outcomes. Effective risk stratification and proactive management are essential for minimizing complications and improving maternal and neonatal health [83].

Similarly, Dinh and Thao [25] reveal that datasets M1 and M2 display comparable values across all outcomes, indicating a consistent risk profile. For instance, both datasets show moderate values of 0.0900 for Preterm Birth and Stillbirth, suggesting a stable yet moderate risk level for these conditions. Key observations from this method include the notably low-risk profile for preterm birth and stillbirth in M3, which have values of 0.0100. However, M3 also presents a significant risk for Placenta Previa (0.2500) and Mortality (0.0900). In contrast, dataset M5 is characterized by alarmingly high values, with Preterm Birth at 0.2500 and Mortality at 0.4900, making it the highest-risk dataset for these adverse outcomes.

Based on this analysis, physician recommendations suggest that patients represented by M3 should receive focused attention on managing high-risk conditions such as placenta previa and mortality. Meanwhile, patients in the M5 category, given their elevated risks for preterm birth and mortality, should be prioritized for immediate and intensive care interventions to reduce potential complications.

The Singh *et al.* [56] method demonstrates that datasets M1 and M2 have nearly identical values across all outcomes, indicating a similar risk profile. For example, both datasets share a Miscarriage value of 0.0500, suggesting comparable risks for early pregnancy loss. M3 presents elevated dangers in certain areas, such as placenta previa (0.1250) and Urinary Tract Infections (UTI) (0.1500), suggesting increased vulnerability to these conditions. On the other hand, M5 shows relatively low values for placenta previa and full-term outcomes yet exhibits significantly higher values for Mortality, indicating a critical need to monitor for potentially fatal complications. These observations align with findings that indicate certain risk factors such as maternal health conditions [58–62], infection [70–72], and pregnancy complications [80–82] can influence adverse pregnancy outcomes [63–65]. Continuous monitoring and appropriate management of these factors are crucial to improving maternal and neonatal health outcomes [84–86].

The Zhao *et al.* [42] distance measure results demonstrate a consistent and gradual increase in values across datasets M1 to M5, highlighting its capacity to capture cumulative complexity and variability in the data. Outcomes such as "mortality" consistently exhibit the highest values, emphasizing the method's heightened sensitivity to critical conditions, while outcomes like "miscarriage," "pre-term," and "stillbirth" show stable patterns, reflecting its consistent accuracy in less variable conditions. The measure notably becomes more adept at distinguishing subtle complexities in "full-term" outcomes, traditionally considered less complicated, with values rising from 0.4862 in M1 to 0.5742 in M5. Similarly, intermediate outcomes like "UTI" and "placentae previa" demonstrate steady increases. However, the minimal value observed across these datasets suggests that a majority of patients may experience a stillbirth outcome, potentially introducing some bias into the method. The significant causes of stillbirth include maternal health conditions such as hypertension, diabetes, and infections; fetal factors like congenital abnormalities and infections; placental complications such as insufficiency and abruption; umbilical cord issues; labor complications; and, in some cases, unexplained factors.

The line graph provides a comprehensive visualization of the distance values for various maternal and neonatal outcomes across five different distance measurement methods Singh *et al.* [56] Zhao *et al.* [42], Dutta [57], and, Dinh and Thao [25], and the new method. Each line represents a specific maternal outcome, Miscarriage, Preterm, Stillbirth, placenta previa, UTI, Full-Term, and Mortality plotted for datasets M1 to M5.

Figure 16.3 clearly highlights how the distance values for each outcome shift as we move from M1 to M5. The methods proposed by Dutta [57], Dinh and Thao [25], Singh *et al.* [56], and Zhao *et al.* [42] serve as valuable baselines, with Dutta [57] exhibiting consistency, Dinh and Thao [25] reflecting sharp fluctuations, Singh *et al.* showing moderate variation, and Zhao *et al.* [42] demonstrating stability. However, the new method, particularly across patients M1, M2, M3, M4, and M5, stands out due to its superior sensitivity and discriminative power, especially in addressing complex outcomes such as mortality, stillbirth, and pre-term conditions. Additionally, the new method emphasizes the importance of closely monitoring full-term patients who may experience complications, even though they are not typically considered at high risk, to ensure optimal outcomes. This approach significantly enhances diagnostic precision and decision-making processes, offering healthcare professionals a robust tool for managing maternal and neonatal health more effectively.

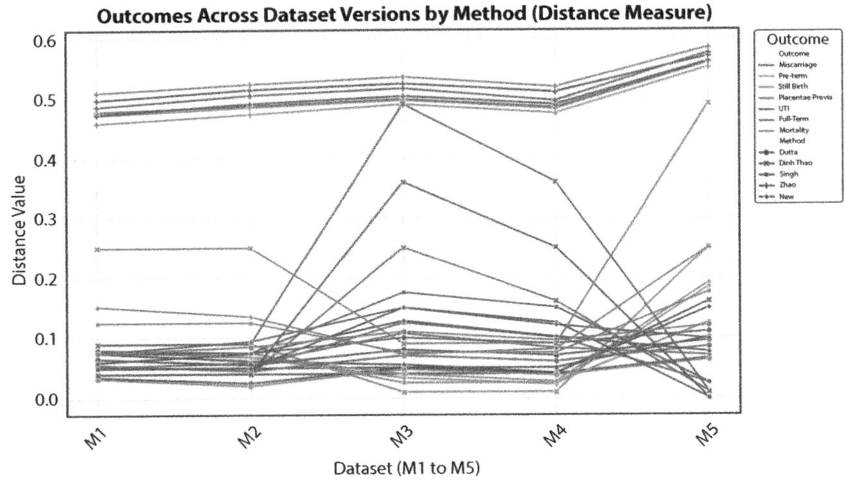

Figure 16.3 Line plot across the various picture fuzzy distance measures.

16.5 Conclusion

This study introduces a picture fuzzy distance measure highlighting a clear relationship between maternal risk factors and adverse pregnancy outcomes. The progressive increase in values from M1 to M5 emphasizes the necessity of early detection and proactive management of maternal complications to reduce the risk of severe outcomes like preterm birth, stillbirth, and mortality. Although lower-risk categories such as M1 and M2 show relatively stable outcomes, continuous monitoring remains essential to identify emerging issues. In contrast, patients classified under higher-risk groups, particularly M5, require urgent and concentrated medical attention due to significantly heightened risks, including Mortality. The data underscores the importance of personalized maternal care in improving maternal and neonatal health outcomes. Effective monitoring, early intervention, and targeted care for high-risk patients are crucial to minimizing complications. These findings are consistent with current clinical guidelines and highlight the ongoing need for research and innovation in maternal-fetal medicine to enhance risk stratification and intervention approaches. As demonstrated in this study, prioritizing at-risk patients through structured analysis can facilitate more precise and timely healthcare interventions, leading to better outcomes for mothers and their infants.

However, the results of this work focus the critical role of weighting in reducing distance measures across maternal conditions, thereby enhancing sensitivity refinement and prioritization of essential outcomes. This effect is particularly evident in conditions like preterm birth and miscarriage, where weighted distances consistently decrease. While physicians may already focus on these cases, this analysis, particularly for patients M1, M3, and M4, underscores their high correlation and susceptibility within the maternal dataset. These findings establish that weighting enables a more nuanced diversity of maternal outcomes, providing valuable discernments for medical and non-medical personnel in effectively managing risks in maternal healthcare. For future work, exploring more advanced picture fuzzy sets and complex models will be beneficial in further refining the analysis of maternal health risks and intervention strategies.

AI disclosure statement: The author confirms that no artificial intelligence (AI)-generated content or AI-assisted writing tools were used in the preparation of this chapter (including summaries and the abstract). All text, analysis, and conclusions are the result of the author's original work.

References

1. WHO, Maternal health, Accessed: Oct. 31, 2024. [Online]. Available: https://www.who.int/health-topics/maternal-health.
2. El-Makhzangy, I., Moeity, F., Anwer, M., Relationship Between Maternal Obesity And Increased Risk Of Preeclampsia. *Alexandria J. Med.*, 46, 2, 2010, doi: 10.4314/bafm.v46i2.61025.
3. Nwokoro, C.O., Inyang, U.G., Eyoh, I.J., Ejegwa, P.A., Intuitionistic Fuzzy Approach for Predicting Maternal Outcomes, in: *Fuzzy Optimization, Decision-making and Operations Research: Theory and Applications*, C. Jana, M. Pal, G. Muhiuddin, P. Liu (Eds.), pp. 399–421, Springer International Publishing, Cham, 2023, doi: 10.1007/978-3-031-35668-1_18.
4. Hackelöer, M., Schmidt, L., Verlohren, S., New advances in prediction and surveillance of preeclampsia: role of machine learning approaches and remote monitoring. *Arch. Gynecol. Obstet.*, 1–15, Dec. 2022, doi: 10.1007/s00404-022-06864-y.
5. Inyang, U.G., Eyoh, I.J., Nwokoro, C.O., Osang, F.B., Predictive Decision Support Analytic Model for Intelligent Obstetric Risks Management, in: *International Conference on Emerging Applications and Technologies for Industry 4.0 (EATI'2020)*, J.H. Abawajy, K.-K.R. Choo, H. Chiroma (Eds.), Lecture Notes in Networks and Systems, pp. 92–108, Springer International Publishing, Cham, 2021, doi: 10.1007/978-3-030-80216-5_8.
6. Bahado-Singh, R.O., Vishweswaraiah, S., Aydas, B., Radhakrishna, U., Placental DNA methylation changes and the early prediction of autism in

full-term newborns. *PLoS One*, 16, 7, e0253340, Jul. 2021, doi: 10.1371/journal.pone.0253340.

7. Nwokoro, C.O., Inyang, U.G., Eyoh, I.J., Umoh, U.A., Duke, O.A., Nwokoro, K.C., Opara, P.I., Obinachi, C., Kingsley, J.U., Enhancing Maternal Outcome Prediction Using Explainable Artificial Intelligence for Women of Childbearing Age. *Asian J. Sci. Appl. Technol.*, 12, 2, Dec. 2023, doi: 10.51983/ajsat-2023.12.2.4072.
8. WHO, Maternal mortality rates and statistics - UNICEF DATA, Accessed: Sep. 20, 2023. [Online]. Available: https://data.unicef.org/topic/maternal-health/maternal-mortality/.
9. UNICEF, Maternal and newborn health, UNICEF. Accessed: Oct. 31, 2024. [Online]. Available: https://www.unicef.org/health/maternal-and-newborn-health.
10. Zadeh, L.A., Fuzzy sets, in: *Fuzzy Sets, Fuzzy Logic, and Fuzzy Systems: Selected Papers by Lotfi A. Zadeh*, pp. 394–432, World Scientific Publishing Co., Singapore, 1996.
11. Atanassov, K., Intuitionistic fuzzy sets. *Fuzzy Sets Syst.*, 20, 1, 87–96, 1986.
12. Atanassov, K.T., Intuitionistic Fuzzy Sets, in: *Intuitionistic Fuzzy Sets: Theory and Applications*, K.T. Atanassov (Ed.), Studies in Fuzziness and Soft Computing, pp. 1–137, Physica-Verlag HD, Heidelberg, 1999, doi: 10.1007/978-3-7908-1870-3_1.
13. Garg, H., A new generalized improved score function of interval-valued intuitionistic fuzzy sets and applications in expert systems. *Appl. Soft Comput.*, 38, 988–999, Jan. 2016, doi: 10.1016/j.asoc.2015.10.040.
14. Garg, H. and Rani, D., Novel aggregation operators and ranking method for complex intuitionistic fuzzy sets and their applications to decision-making process. *Artif. Intell. Rev.*, 53, 5, 3595–3620, Jun. 2020, doi: 10.1007/s10462-019-09772-x.
15. Garg, H. and Kumar, K., Linguistic Interval-Valued Atanassov Intuitionistic Fuzzy Sets and Their Applications to Group Decision Making Problems. *IEEE Trans. Fuzzy Syst.*, 27, 12, 2302–2311, Dec. 2019, doi: 10.1109/TFUZZ.2019.2897961.
16. Garg, H. and Rani, D., Novel distance measures for intuitionistic fuzzy sets based on various triangle centers of isosceles triangular fuzzy numbers and their applications. *Expert Syst. Appl.*, 191, 116228, Apr. 2022, doi: 10.1016/j.eswa.2021.116228.
17. Rani, D. and Garg, H., Distance Measures between the Complex Intuitionistic Fuzzy Sets and their Applications to the Decision-Making Process. *Int. J. Uncertainty Quantif.*, 7, 5, 2017, doi: 10.1615/Int.J.UncertaintyQuantification.2017020356.
18. Ejegwa, P.A. and Onyeke, I.C., A Novel Intuitionistic Fuzzy Correlation Algorithm and Its Applications in Pattern Recognition and Student Admission Process. *Int. J. Fuzzy Syst. Appl. IJFSA*, 11, 1, 1–20, Jan. 2022, doi: 10.4018/IJFSA.285984.

19. Ejegwa, P.A. and Adamu, I.M., Distances between intuitionistic fuzzy sets of second type with application to diagnostic medicine. *Notes Intuitionistic Fuzzy Sets*, 25, 3, 53–70, Sep. 2019, doi: 10.7546/nifs.2019.25.3.53-70.
20. Ejegwa, P.A. and Onasanya, B.O., Improved intuitionistic fuzzy composite relation and its application to medical diagnostic process. *Notes Intuitionistic Fuzzy Sets*, 25, 1, 43–58, 2018, doi: 10.7546/nifs.2019.25.1.43-58.
21. Thao, N.X. and Smarandache, F., A new fuzzy entropy on Pythagorean fuzzy sets. *J. Intell. Fuzzy Syst.*, 37, 1, 1065–1074, Jan. 2019, doi: 10.3233/JIFS-182540.
22. Zhao, X., Wang, Y., Li, L., Developed dynamic PFSs for distance measures and parametric similarity measures to enhance multi-attribute decision-making. *Int. J. Comput. Intell. Syst.*, 8, 1, 32–45, 2015.
23. Duong, T.T.T. and Thao, N.X., A novel dissimilarity measure on picture fuzzy sets and its application in multi-criteria decision making. *Soft Comput.*, 25, 1, 15–25, Jan. 2021, doi: 10.1007/s00500-020-05405-6.
24. Van Dinh, P., Thao, T.P., Nguyen, Q.B., Distance and dissimilarity measures for PFSs to improve decision-making processes. *FAIR*, 10, 8, 104–109, 2017.
25. Dinh, N.V. and Thao, N.X., Some Measures of Picture Fuzzy Sets and Their Application. *J. Sci. Technol. Issue Inf. Commun. Technol.*, 3, 2, 35–40, 2017.
26. Dutta, P., Medical Diagnosis *via* Distance Measures on Picture Fuzzy Sets. *Adv. Model. Anal. A*, 54, 2, 657–672, 2017.
27. Pham, H.V., Thai, K.P., Nguyen, Q.H., Le, D.D., Le, T.T., Nguyen, T.X.D., Phan, T.T.K., Thao, N.X., Distance and entropy measures of picture fuzzy sets in decision support systems. *J. Intell. Fuzzy Syst.*, 44, 4, 6775–6791, Jan. 2023, doi: 10.3233/JIFS-221556.
28. Cuong, H.T., Ho, V.N., Nguyen, P.H., Picture Fuzzy Sets (PFSs), extending traditional fuzzy sets to handle uncertainty, indeterminacy, and neutrality. *J. Fuzzy Log. Syst.*, 12, 3, 112–124, 2013.
29. Riaz, M., Garg, H., Athar Farid, H.M., Chinram, R., Multi-Criteria Decision Making Based on Bipolar Picture Fuzzy Operators and New Distance Measures. *Comput. Model. Eng. Sci.*, 127, 2, 771–800, May 2021, doi: 10.32604/cmes.2021.014174.
30. Mahmood, T., Ali, Z., Aslam, M., Applications of complex picture fuzzy soft power aggregation operators in multi-attribute decision making. *Sci. Rep.*, 12, 1, Sep. 2022, doi: 10.1038/s41598-022-20239-y.
31. Cao, G., A novel similarity measure between picture fuzzy sets based on transformation techniques and its applications in mobile multimedia healthcare. *Multimedia Tools Appl.*, 83, 20, 58645–58688, Jun. 2024, doi: 10.1007/s11042-023-17723-6.
32. Khalil, A.M., Garg, H., Ma, S., Li, S.-G., Li, H., New operations on interval-valued picture fuzzy set, interval-valued picture fuzzy soft set and their applications. *IEEE Access*, 7, 51236–51253, 2021.

33. Zhu, S., Liu, Z., Ur Rahman, A., Novel Distance Measures of Picture Fuzzy Sets and Their Applications. *Arabian J. Sci. Eng.*, 49, 9, 12975–12988, Sep. 2024, doi: 10.1007/s13369-024-08925-7.
34. Devi, P., Kizielewicz, B., Guleria, A., Shekhovtsov, A., Gandotra, N., Saini, N., Sałabun, W., Dimensionality reduction technique under picture fuzzy environment and its application in decision making. *Int. J. Knowledge-Based Intell. Eng. Syst.*, 27, 1, 87–104, Jan. 2023, doi: 10.3233/KES-230031.
35. Wei, G., Some Similarity Measures for Picture Fuzzy Sets and their Applications. *Iran. J. Fuzzy Syst.*, 15, 1, 77–89, Mar. 2018, doi: 10.22111/ijfs.2018.3579.
36. Garg, H., Hussain, A., Ullah, K., Ashraf, A., Assessment of learning management systems based on Schweizer–Sklar picture fuzzy Maclaurin symmetric mean aggregation operators. *Comput. Appl. Math.*, 43, 7, 404, Sep. 2024, doi: 10.1007/s40314-024-02864-7.
37. Sirbiladze, G., Garg, H., Midodashvili, B., Parshutkin, I., Ghvaberidze, B., Decision-making framework with q-rung picture fuzzy linguistic information and its applications to logistics hubs during disaster response establishment. *Results Control Optim.*, 19, 100541, Jun. 2025, doi: 10.1016/j.rico.2025.100541.
38. Mohammed, S., Oleiwi, A.K., Asman, T., Saleh, H.M., Mahmood, A.M., Avci, I., A Survey of MCDM-Based Software Engineering Method. *Babylon. J. Math.*, 2024, 13–18, Feb. 2024, doi: 10.58496/BJM/2024/002.
39. Nwokoro, C.O. and Ejegwa, P.A., A Decade of Picture Fuzzy Sets in Multi-Criteria Decision-Making: A Comprehensive Review of Trends, Gaps, and Future Directions. *Knowl. Decis. Syst. Appl.*, 1, 145–164, May 2025, doi: 10.59543/kadsa.v1i.14051.
40. Ejegwa, P.A., Terna, A.M., Kausar, N., Nwokoro, C.O., Aydin, N., Yu, H., New Fermatean Fuzzy Distance Metric and Its Utilization in the Assessment of Security Crises using the MCDM Technique, Oct. 2024, doi: 10.3390/math12203214.
41. Peng, X. and Dai, J., Algorithm For Picture Fuzzy Multiple Attribute Decision-Making Based On New Distance Measure. *Int. J. Uncertainty Quantif.*, 7, 2, 2017, doi: 10.1615/Int.J.UncertaintyQuantification.2017020096.
42. Zhao, R., Luo, M., Li, S., A Dynamic Distance Measure of Picture Fuzzy Sets and Its Application. *Symmetry*, 13, 3, Mar. 2021, doi: 10.3390/sym13030436.
43. Son, L.H., Measuring analogousness in picture fuzzy sets: from picture distance measures to picture association measures. *Fuzzy Optim. Dec. Making*, 16, 3, 359–378, Sep. 2017, doi: 10.1007/s10700-016-9249-5.
44. Dutta, P., PFSs in medical diagnosis, particularly focusing on tropical diseases. *Expert Syst. Appl.*, 95, 102–118, 2018.
45. Sahu, R., Dash, S.R., Das, S., Career selection of students using hybridized distance measure based on picture fuzzy set and rough set theory. *Decis. Mak. Appl. Manag. Eng.*, 4, 1, Mar. 2021, doi: 10.31181/dmame2104104s.

46. Guleria, A. and Bajaj, R.K., A novel probabilistic distance measure for picture fuzzy sets with its application in classification problems. *Hacet. J. Math. Stat.*, 49, 6, Dec. 2020, doi: 10.15672/hujms.677920.
47. Khan, Z., Hussain, F., Rahim, T., Jan, R., Boulaaras, S., Distance measure and its application to decision making, medical diagnosis, and pattern recognition problems under complex picture fuzzy sets. *Eur. Phys. J. Plus*, 139, 3, 243, Mar. 2024, doi: 10.1140/epjp/s13360-024-04996-5.
48. Singh, S. and Ganie, A.H., Applications of picture fuzzy similarity measures in pattern recognition, clustering, and MADM. *Expert Syst. Appl.*, 168, 114264, Apr. 2021, doi: 10.1016/j.eswa.2020.114264.
49. Ganie, A.H. and Singh, S., A picture fuzzy similarity measure based on direct operations and novel multi-attribute decision-making method. *Neural Comput. Appl.*, 33, 15, 9199–9219, Aug. 2021, doi: 10.1007/s00521-020-05682-0.
50. Khan, M.J., Kumam, P., Deebani, W., Kumam, W., Shah, Z., Bi-parametric distance and similarity measures of picture fuzzy sets and their applications in medical diagnosis. *Egypt. Inform. J.*, 22, 2, 201–212, Jul. 2021, doi: 10.1016/j.eij.2020.08.002.
51. Jan, N., Mahmood, T., Zedam, L., Ali, Z., Multi-valued picture fuzzy soft sets and their applications in group decision-making problems. *Soft Comput.*, 24, 24, 18857–18879, Dec. 2020, doi: 10.1007/s00500-020-05116-y.
52. Kumar, S., Distance measures between picture fuzzy sets and its applications in medical diagnosis. *Advances in Engineering Science and Management,* 1, 13, 13–20, 2023.
53. Luo, M. and Zhang, Y., A new similarity measure between picture fuzzy sets and its application. *Eng. Appl. Artif. Intell.*, 96, 103956, Nov. 2020, doi: 10.1016/j.engappai.2020.103956.
54. Adak, A.K., Gunjan, M.K., Haghighi, A.M., Distance Measure of Picture Fuzzy Sets and its Application in Multi-Criteria Decision Making Problem.
55. Verma, R. and Rohtagi, B., Novel similarity measures between picture fuzzy sets and their applications to pattern recognition and medical diagnosis. *Granular Comput.*, 7, 4, 761–777, Oct. 2022, doi: 10.1007/s41066-021-00294-y.
56. Singh, P., Mishra, N.K., Kumar, M., Saxena, S., Singh, V., Risk analysis of flood disaster based on similarity measures in picture fuzzy environment. *Afr. Mat.*, 29, 1019–1038, 2018.
57. Dutta, P., Medical diagnosis based on distance measures between picture fuzzy sets. *Int. J. Fuzzy Syst.*, 7, 4, 15–36, 2018.
58. Saccone, G., Maruotti, G.M., Morlando, M., Visentin, S., De Angelis, C., Sarno, L., Cosmi, E., Torcia, F., Costanzi, F., Gragnano, E., Bartolini, G., La Verde, M., Borelli, F., Savoia, F., Schiattarella, A., De Franciscis, P., Locci, M., Guida, M., Randomized trial of screening for preterm birth in low-risk women—the preterm birth screening study. *Am. J. Obstet. Gynecol. MFM*, 6, 5, Supplement, 101267, May 2024, doi: 10.1016/j.ajogmf.2023.101267.

59. Doulaveris, G. and Berghella, V., Management of Preterm Labor, in: *Queenan's Management of High-Risk Pregnancy*, pp. 372–380, John Wiley & Sons, Ltd, UK, 2024, doi: 10.1002/9781119636540.ch42.
60. Mazza, G.R., Komatsu, E., Ponzio, M., Bai, C., Cortessis, V.K., Sasso, E.B., Progesterone therapy for prevention of recurrent spontaneous preterm birth in a minority patient population: a retrospective study. *BMC Pregnancy Childbirth*, 24, 1, 252, Apr. 2024, doi: 10.1186/s12884-024-06471-6.
61. Veenstra, J., Cohen, Z., Korteweg, F.J., van der Ham, D.P., Kuppens, S.M., Kroese, J.A., Hermsen, B.B., Kamphuis, M.M., Vanhommerig, J.W., van Pampus, M.G., Unplanned cesarean sections in advanced maternal age: A predictive model. *Acta Obstet. Gynecol. Scand.*, 103, 5, 927–937, 2024, doi: 10.1111/aogs.14765.
62. Yen, I.-W., *et al.*, Advanced maternal age-related clustering of metabolic abnormalities is associated with risks of adverse pregnancy outcomes. *J. Formos. Med. Assoc.*, 123, 3, 325–330, Mar. 2024, doi: 10.1016/j.jfma.2023.11.013.
63. Ahmad, M., Sechi, C., Vismara, L., Advanced Maternal Age: A Scoping Review about the Psychological Impact on Mothers, Infants, and Their Relationship. *Behav. Sci.*, 14, 3, Mar. 2024, doi: 10.3390/bs14030147.
64. Ou, M., Luo, L., Yang, Y., Yan, N., Yan, X., Zhong, X., Cheong, Y., Li, T., Ouyang, J., Wang, Q., Decrease in peripheral natural killer cell level during early pregnancy predicts live birth among women with unexplained recurrent pregnancy loss: a prospective cohort study. *Am. J. Obstet. Gynecol.*, 230, 6, 675.e1–675.e13, Jun. 2024, doi: 10.1016/j.ajog.2023.10.042.
65. Thompson, B.B., Holzer, P.H., Kliman, H.J., Placental Pathology Findings in Unexplained Pregnancy Losses. *Reprod. Sci.*, 31, 2, 488–504, Feb. 2024, doi: 10.1007/s43032-023-01344-3.
66. Chapuma, C., Mwaikambo, E.J.M., Broughton, E., Adeyemi, A.A., van der Heijden, A.M.M., van der Heijden, A.M.M., Van der Veer, C., Lissauer, D., The aetiology and antimicrobial resistance of bacterial maternal infections in Sub-Saharan Africa—a systematic review and meta-analysis. *BMC Infect. Dis.*, 24, 1, 978, Sep. 2024, doi: 10.1186/s12879-024-09855-3.
67. Pakdeesatitwara, N., Clark, I., Tamplin, J., A mixed-studies systematic review of self-administered music interventions (SAMIs) for psychological wellbeing in people with chronic health conditions: Meta-analysis and narrative summary. *Patient Educ. Couns.*, 118, 108006, Jan. 2024, doi: 10.1016/j.pec.2023.108006.
68. Allan, B., Amy J., G., Meredith J., A., A Review of Placental Abnormalities. *Top. Obstet. Gynecol.*, 44, 11, 1, Jul. 2024, doi: 10.1097/01.PGO.0001025336.48769.e0.
69. Sielhorst, J., Koether, K., Volkmann, N., Blanco, M., Vicioso, R., Baade, S., Kemper, N., de Mestre, A.M., Sieme, H., Occurrence of ultrasonographic assessed placental abnormalities, treatments, pregnancy outcome,

and subsequent fertility on a large warmblood stud farm: A retrospective field study. *J. Equine Vet. Sci.*, 137, 105076, Jun. 2024, doi: 10.1016/j.jevs.2024.105076.

70. Morales-Suárez-Varela, M., Peraita-Costa, I., Guerrero Cervera, B., Llopis-Morales, A., Botella Juan, L., Marcos Puig, B., Arterial hypertension and smoking in pregnant women in the Valencian Community: maternal and neonatal outcomes. *Med. Fam. Semergen*, 50, 4, 102171, May 2024, doi: 10.1016/j.semerg.2023.102171.
71. Kim, S., Exploring the Patterns of Substance Use Behaviors in a Nationally Representative Sample of Pregnant Women: a Latent Class Approach. *Int. J. Ment. Health Addict.*, 22, 1, 513–527, Feb. 2024, doi: 10.1007/s11469-022-00886-y.
72. Wimberly, C.E., Gulrajani, N.B., Russ, J.B., Landi, D., Wiemels, J.L., Towry, L., Wiencke, J.K., Walsh, K.M., Maternal Prenatal Use of Alcohol, Tobacco, and Illicit Drugs and Associations with Childhood Cancer Subtypes. *Cancer Epidemiol. Biomarkers Prev.*, 33, 3, 347–354, Mar. 2024, doi: 10.1158/1055-9965.EPI-23-1027.
73. Lim, C.W.C., Lustestica, I.E., Poon, W.B., Tan, W.C., Polyhydramnios associated with rare genetic syndromes: two case reports. *J. Med. Case Rep.*, 18, 1, 97, Feb. 2024, doi: 10.1186/s13256-024-04435-0.
74. Chen, X., Liang, Y., Zou, S., Liu, D., Qiu, C., Liu, Y., Wang, Y., Wang, C., Intrauterine inflammation exposure may increase the risk of late-onset sepsis in premature infants: a retrospective cohort study, Research Square, Oct. 18, 2024, doi: 10.21203/rs.3.rs-4967291/v1.
75. Tiruneh, G.T., Demissie, M., Worku, A., Berhane, Y., Community's experience and perceptions of maternal health services across the continuum of care in Ethiopia: A qualitative study. *PLoS One*, 16, 8, e0255404, Aug. 2021, doi: 10.1371/journal.pone.0255404.
76. Soobryan, N., Reddy, K., Ibrahim, U.H., Moodley, J., Kumar, A., Mackraj, I., Identification of gene signature markers in gestational hypertension and early-onset pre-eclampsia. *Placenta*, 145, 1–8, Jan. 2024, doi: 10.1016/j.placenta.2023.11.011.
77. Hu, H., Wang, L., Gao, J., Chen, Z., Chen, X., Tang, P., Zhong, Y., Risk factors of severe postpartum hemorrhage in pregnant women with placenta previa or low-lying placenta: a retrospective cohort study. *BMC Pregnancy Childbirth*, 24, 1, 674, Oct. 2024, doi: 10.1186/s12884-024-06876-3.
78. Christoffersen, M., Nielsen, S.B., Madvig, C.B., Agerholm, J.S., Potential risk factors for fetal loss due to umbilical cord torsion in the mare. *Theriogenology*, 214, 182–186, Jan. 2024, doi: 10.1016/j.theriogenology.2023.10.026.
79. Stephansson, O. and Sandström, A., Can short- and long-term maternal and infant risks linked to hypertension and diabetes during pregnancy be reduced by therapy? *J. Intern. Med.*, 296, 3, 216–233, 2024, doi: 10.1111/joim.13823.

80. Parker, J., Hofstee, P., Brennecke, S., Prevention of Pregnancy Complications Using a Multimodal Lifestyle, Screening, and Medical Model. *J. Clin. Med.*, 13, 15, Jan. 2024, doi: 10.3390/jcm13154344.
81. Root, A.L., Crossley, N.P., Heck, J.L., McCage, S., Proulx, J., Jones, E.J., Effects of Mindfulness-Based Interventions on Cardiometabolic-Related Adverse Pregnancy Outcomes: A Systematic Review. *J. Cardiovasc. Nurs.*, 39, 4, 335, Aug. 2024, doi: 10.1097/JCN.0000000000001054.
82. Patel, N., Mittal, N., Wilkinson, M.J., Taub, P.R., Unique features of dyslipidemia in women across a lifetime and a tailored approach to management. *Am. J. Prev. Cardiol.*, 18, 100666, Jun. 2024, doi: 10.1016/j.ajpc.2024.100666.
83. Lin, D., *et al.*, Risk factors for premature rupture of membranes in pregnant women: a systematic review and meta-analysis. *BMJ Open*, 14, 3, e077727, Mar. 2024, doi: 10.1136/bmjopen-2023-077727.
84. Walters, B., Midwinter, I., Chew-Graham, C.A., Smith, L.H., Pregnancy-Associated Cancer: A Systematic Review and Meta-Analysis. *Mayo Clin. Proc. Innov. Qual. Outcomes*, 8, 2, 188–199, Apr. 2024, doi: 10.1016/j.mayocpiqo.2024.02.002.
85. Brown, H.K. and Mitra, M., Perinatal health framework for people with intellectual disability. *Disabil. Health J.*, 17, 2, 101576, Apr. 2024, doi: 10.1016/j.dhjo.2023.101576.
86. Dadi, A.F., *et al.*, Association Between Preconception Maternal Mental Health-Related Hospitalisation (MHrH) and Outcomes During Pregnancy: A Population-Based Cohort Study in the Northern Territory, Australia. *Int. J. Ment. Health Addict.*, Apr. 2024, doi: 10.1007/s11469-024-01286-0.

17

Investigating the Digital Healthcare System Based on Knowledge-Based Systems

Sanjeev Kumar[1]*, Geeta Tiwari[2], Anil Kumar[3], Prateek Kumar Singhal[1] and Neeraj Tiwari[4]

[1]*Department of Electrical Engineering, Swami Keshvanand Institute of Technology, Management & Gramothan, Jaipur, Rajasthan, India*
[2]*Department of Computer Science and Engineering, Poornima College of Engineering, Jaipur, Rajasthan, India*
[3]*Department of Computer Science and Engineering, Manipal University Jaipur, Rajasthan, India*
[4]*Department of Computer Science and Engineering, School of Engineering and Technology, Jaipur National University, Jaipur, Rajasthan, India*

Abstract

Digital healthcare systems are innovative solutions for navigating the complex landscapes of modern healthcare, providing informed decision support and customized patient care. This chapter reviews knowledge-based systems (KBS) in relation to digital healthcare: KBS components, functions, and applications. It emphasizes the contribution of KBS in enhancing disease diagnosis, treatment planning, and prediction-related analytics, as well as assisting medical practitioners in clinical decision-making. It also discusses the enabling technologies like artificial intelligence (AI), natural language processing (NLP), and Internet of Medical Things (IoMT) of these systems that make them effective. It recognizes the challenges, including those around data privacy, ethical issues, and integration problems, but outlines innovative approaches and a path to the future to tackle these obstacles. Using real-world illustrations of Knowledge-Based Systems this chapter illustrates the ability of KBS to change the landscape of healthcare and build a digital healthcare ecosystem that is smarter and more resilient.

**Corresponding author*: sanjeev.85ee@gmail.com

Harish Garg (ed.) Decision Support Systems in Smart Computing: Embracing Uncertainty and Challenges, (531–550) © 2026 Scrivener Publishing LLC

Keywords: Knowledge-based systems, digital healthcare systems, clinical decision support, artificial intelligence in healthcare, predictive analytics in medicine, Internet of Medical Things

17.1 Introduction

Digital healthcare systems are rewriting the medical care paradigm by blending technology and information to provide solutions that are more educated and resource efficient. This evolution is driven by Knowledge-Based Systems (KBS) that serve as the brain behind clinical decision-making, treatment planning, and prediction analytics. Envision a hospital implementing AI and Natural Language Processing to listen and analyze the symptoms of a patient and provide accurate diagnoses — precious time and lives saved. This chapter will explore the components, functions and potential applications of KBS, as well as some drawbacks such as data privacy or integrated perspective challenges.

17.1.1 Overview of Digital Healthcare Systems

Digital systems that include sophisticated technologies such as NLP and KBS to support effective management of healthcare. These smart frameworks bring together data, expertise, and analytics that not only aid diagnosis, treatment planning, and patient management but in the long-term work towards improving and creating cost-effective healthcare solutions. AI-powered KBS have already come to help physicians make rare disease diagnoses through analyzing patient symptoms, data, and historical cases. KBS saves time and increases accuracy by recommending evidence-based treatments, which provide an effective solution, particularly for complex cases. The transformative potential of KBS is clear and it will lead to a smarter, more resilient approach to healthcare delivery despite various issues like data privacy and integration infrastructure.

17.1.2 Role of Knowledge-Based Systems in Modern Healthcare

By integrating Artificial Intelligence, Natural Language Processing, and the Internet of Medical Things, Knowledge-Based Systems are tackling unprecedented medical challenges to convert data into dire solutions. One example is IBM Watson Health, which assists oncologists in developing improved targeted cancer treatments. Already, KBS helps doctors to make better choices or make a good diagnosis of disease or provide more tailored care of each patient. Nevertheless, issues such as data privacy, ethical challenges, and system integration still exist. However, with KBS, we promise to provide healthcare solutions that are smarter, efficient, and tailored, leading the way to your future of health.

Knowledge-based systems in modern health care promote systematic knowledge development which enables effective accuracy of diagnosis and treatment decisions. Utilizing big data and machine learning powered by a knowledge capture, organization and application infrastructure to optimize decision-making and patient outcomes in a knowledge-intensive setting [18].

In the paper [13], authors introduce the health recommendations system (HRS) which permits patients to submit their query to the system at any point when they would like to couple with expert's knowledge and to inquest the remedy for the ailment. The authors describe big data, its use, and challenges of the big data knowledge system in health care and present a new framework utilizing big data and big data analytics [24].

17.1.3 Research Gaps and Merits of the Study

The digital healthcare ecosystem is changing fast, but there are still some critical gaps. Most of the systems that have been developed do not integrate knowledge-based tools and real-time clinical environments in a seamless manner. These systems have less flexibility to face uncertain or incomplete medical data. In addition, data privacy concerns, ethical constraints, and technical interoperability still stand in the way of their implementation at scale.

This study is intended to fill these gaps by conducting an in-depth analysis of KBS and its use in contemporary healthcare. This provides an in-depth evaluation on the role these technologies from artificial intelligence (AI) and natural language processing (NLP) to the Internet of Medical Things (IoMT) play in the delivery of decision support solutions and personalized care.

The major strengths of the work are its comprehensive perspective on digital health, practical focus on the real-world applications of KBS, and a recognition of the central challenges against which systems must be delivered. Finally, the chapter also describes the modern trends and provides realistic and constructive directions for future studies as well.

17.1.4 Major Contributions of the Study

1. Provides a comprehensive overview of Knowledge-Based Systems (KBS) in digital health, with a particular focus on their application in clinical decision making, diagnosis, and prediction.
2. Discussed the incorporation of modern technologies including AI, NLP, IoMT, and big data analytics with KBS for improving health care services and patient outcomes.
3. Highlights the most significant challenges related to data privacy, interoperability, and ethical considerations and offers recommendations to guide future system development.
4. Showcases real-world use-cases and worldwide examples to demonstrate the utility in practice and real-time transformative potential of KBS in healthcare services.

17.1.5 Objectives and Scope of the Chapter

The objective of this study is to provide an organized framework associated with KBS, investigate their architectural principles, discuss real-time applications, and outline both the opportunities and challenges posed by the use of artificial intelligence in the domain of intelligent healthcare systems.

NLP and KBS are major applications in healthcare; their roles in using EHR data for disease diagnosis, personalized care, predictive analytics, etc., are discussed in this chapter. Such as the implementation of Artificial Intelligence (AI), Natural Language Processing, and Internet of Medical Things technologies in KBS while creating awareness of data privacy and system integration challenges. IBM Watson Health is an example of KBS which supports clinicians with healthcare-specific recommendations for developing a precise treatment plan. In this chapter, vision of smarter, patient-centric digital healthcare ecosystem is presented that will close the gap between innovation and implementation.

17.2 Foundation of Knowledge-Based Systems

Knowledge-Based Systems form the core of Digital healthcare innovation. These systems are intelligent frameworks that mimic human expertise providing recommendations and answers to the complex challenges healthcare faces. KBS integrates a comprehensive library of knowledge, an inference engine for logical reasoning, and a user-friendly interface to improve decision-making. They take healthcare to the next level by leveraging AI, NLP, and IoMT to bring personalized outcomes across diagnostic, treatment planning, and patient care. The road ahead may not be smooth due to data privacy and integration challenges, however, KBSs have the potential to be extensively transformational and should be leveraged to create agile, intelligent, and efficient healthcare ecosystems that are essential for our future.

17.2.1 Definition and Characteristics of Knowledge-Based Systems

Knowledge-Based Systems are the workhorse behind intelligent decision-making in digital healthcare by following a systematic way to manage, process, and employ enormous quantities of medical knowledge in a format that is understandable to humans and machines alike. At their heart, KBS comprise a knowledge base—a store of domain-relevant information, an *inference engine* to apply logical reasoning to finding solutions to complex problems, and an intuitive user interface to connect the human and technological worlds.

These are the most important traits that KBS have, which make them far more transformative: they are adaptable, accurate, and scalable. They learn from fresh data, making them useful in ever-changing areas such as medicine, and they offer patient-specific predictions. They also scale seamlessly to interoperate with different healthcare applications. Additionally, they scale effortlessly to integrate with various healthcare applications.

Knowledge-based Systems are computer applications that use knowledge in the form of facts and rules to assist human decision-making. Features include processing large databases of diseases and symptoms, supporting clinical decisions, and improving the operational efficiency of healthcare without reducing the quality of service given to patients [8]. Predictions in healthcare predictive analytics may include patient readmission, early detection of diseases, and tailored methods of treatment. It uses data, modeling, and assessment methods to lower costs and increase the quality of care [23].

KBS lays a strong groundwork for more intelligent health-care systems, from facilitating individualized therapy to aiding clinicians in diagnostic decision-making. These systems transform how care is delivered by addressing the data overload and uncertainty challenges in the digital age to improve patient outcomes by utilizing AI, NLP, and IoMT.

17.2.2 Key Components of Knowledge-Based Systems

Knowledge-Based Systems are among the most important systems in digital healthcare, helping to make decisions and provide better patient care. There are three main components of KBS: the Knowledge Base, the Inference Engine, and the user interface.

Figure 17.1 illustrates the core components of knowledge-based systems which include knowledge acquisition, inference engine and the flow of information and interaction between the components necessary for automated reasoning and decision making.

Domain expertise is stored in a **knowledge base**. In health this can be medical guidelines, diagnostic criteria, case studies etc. It is the "brain" of the system, representing structured and deeply rich knowledge to be the basis for reasoning and decision-making.

Inference Engine – It is a problem-solving component. It processes the data contained in the Knowledge Base, uses logical rules to extract the data and make conclusions. For example, when diagnosing a disease, the engine compares patient symptoms to a repository of known medical facts and provides exact recommendations or predictions. By reducing not knowing this feature greatly improves clinical workflows.

Finally, the User Interface connects the technical system and the human user whether it is the doctor or nurse, or the patient themselves. An interface that has been thoughtfully designed will provide healthcare

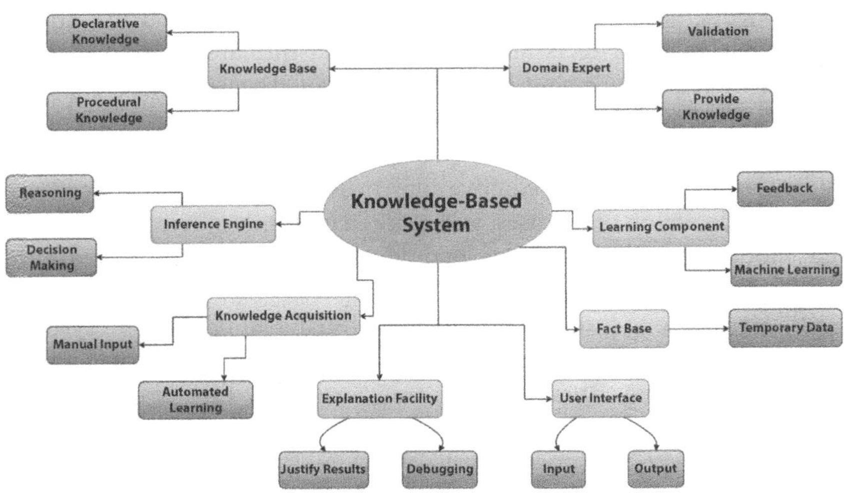

Figure 17.1 Architecture of a typical knowledge-based system.

professionals with the ability to easily access the software/app by either allowing them to input information themselves or receiving insights into the analysis that has been performed within the system.

All these elements become a seamless ecosystem that makes sense out of complexities in medical data and is paving the way for the future of efficient, tailored medicine delivery. Using a clever combination of the above, KBS changes the way healthcare is delivered, whilst overcoming issues such as scalability and usability.

17.2.3 Types of Knowledge-Based Systems in Healthcare

KBS is transforming the healthcare industry by providing tailored solutions to the most pressing problems of modern medicine. Divided into rule-based systems, expert systems, and hybrid systems, they represent best practices in clinical practice and research that fill knowledge gaps and provide guidance for clinicians when making decisions. With strategies such as rule-based systems which utilize if-then logic, expert systems that emulate the reasoning of medical professionals, and hybrid systems which combine these methods, all of this can be used to simulate predictions and provide personalized treatment recommendations. KBS is paving the way for a future of healthcare that is more efficient, accurate, and ultimately more patient-centered by streamlining processes and enhancing precision.

17.3 Applications of Knowledge-Based Systems in Digital Healthcare

Digital healthcare has been redefined by the adoption of Knowledge-based systems that use intelligent solutions to solve complex challenges. They are used in scope of everything from high accuracy in diagnosing diseases, prescription recommendations to tailor patient's care and anesthesia to predictive analytics. KBS provide healthcare professionals with powerful decision-making tools by utilizing AI, natural language processing, and IoMT. For example, they provide benefits to clinicians by aiding in real-time data capture and embedding evidence-based care management for quality patient care. While there are obstacles such as data privacy and system interoperability, KBS ushers in a smarter and adaptable healthcare system. Their goal, with innovation, is improved patient outcomes and a robust future for health care.

17.3.1 Disease Diagnosis and Treatment Recommendations

Knowledge-based systems offer increased patient care technology from the data, an essential step in the transformation of healthcare. Such systems leverage artificial intelligence, natural language processing, and the Internet of Medical Things to radically change how patients are diagnosed and treated. Able to assess patient symptoms almost instantly, compare the symptoms with millions of medical records, and provide the right set of diagnostic tests and treatment plans. KBS are proving to be quite promising in building a sustainable and efficacious digital healthcare ecosystem, tackling challenges like data privacy and ethical issues, improving clinical outcomes and trust in technology-induced healthcare.

17.3.2 Personalized Patient Care and Management in Digital Healthcare Systems

The growing demand for personalized patient care has encouraged healthcare professionals transiting to a knowledge-based system to assist them in providing patient care. Harnessing AI, machine learning, and predictive analytics, these systems can customize treatments for each patient according to their distinct needs, ensuring more targeted and efficacious outcomes. KBS contribute to more informed clinical decisions through integrating a wide array of medical data including patient history, laboratory and test results, and other personal and lifestyle factors to suggest individualized recommendations. This helps to improve the accuracy of diagnosing diseases and the effectiveness of treatment. Moreover, KBS are also extremely valuable in the context of chronic disease management, where they can provide continuous monitoring and prompt interventions to minimize hospital visits. Although there are hurdles in terms of data privacy and other challenges the future of personalized healthcare looks bright.

17.3.3 Decision Support for Medical Professionals

The use of AI and machine learning in healthcare is on the rise, as medical professionals are provided with greater decision-making power. KBS will transform clinical decision support by combining next-gen technologies like AI, NLP, and IoMT. Such systems can deliver accurate and timely suggestions related to disease diagnosis, treatment plan and patient care management. KBS aggregates' huge amount of medical data becomes the sources, and provides personalized insights, which can enhance healthcare and become decision-makers, and enhance outcomes. On the other hand, the future of KBS is bright, helping to create smarter, more efficient and person-centered care, even with challenges such as data privacy and ethical issues.

17.3.4 Predictive Analytics in Healthcare

An exciting change being added to the hospital setting is the use of predictive analytics utilizing Knowledge-Based Systems in healthcare. KBS offers real-time decision support when leveraging AI and IoMT, helping clinicians to make better diagnoses and treatment decisions. Through predictive analytics, historical patient information can be utilized to predict outcomes and last preventive measures, improving patient care and further increasing workflows. But there are still challenges such as data privacy, ethical and interoperability issues. However, these challenges are slowly starting to be surmounted due to technological breakthroughs such as AI-based models and the advent of natural language processing, and the future of predictive analytics in medicine looks bright.

This paper presents an application of predictive analytics in healthcare. The authors present machine learning approach to classify preeclampsia using three datasets. It employs various feature selection techniques and ensemble learning models, achieving high accuracy rates (over 95% AUC-ROC) in predictions, thus aiding timely clinical decisions in maternal health management [3].

Predictive analytics in healthcare refers to predicting the occurrence of diseases in the future, enabling early diagnosis and treatment. By leveraging historical data to identify patterns within the disease, it helps to mitigate risks and enhances outcomes by allowing informed and timely medical choices to be made [1]. Predictive analytics in healthcare aims at predicting when the disease will surface and provide early diagnosis and treatment. By unleashing the power of historical data to recognize patterns of disease, it helps reduce the risks and optimize outcomes at the patient level with timely and informed medical decisions [6].

17.4 Technologies Enabling Knowledge-Based Healthcare Systems

The health industry is changing rapidly with the supply of AI and ML applied sciences. Knowledge-Based Systems are changing the patient care

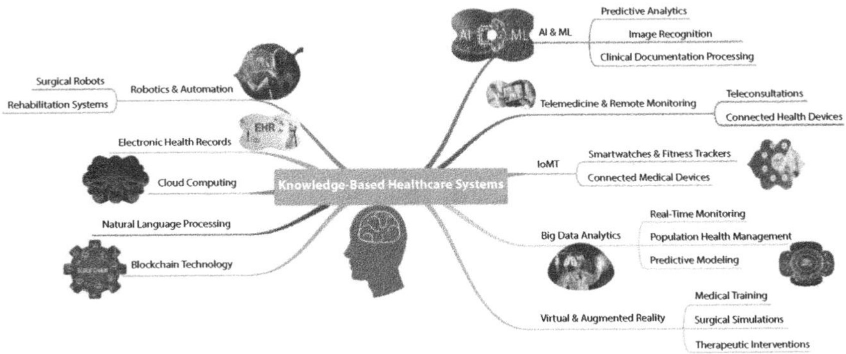

Figure 17.2 Technologies enabling knowledge-based healthcare systems.

by providing real-time insights and automating the diagnosis. The automated treatments and predicting the health outcomes by these systems make them more accurate and efficient. These systems are breaking free from traditional barriers as smart computing progresses, enhancing patient outcomes, and being introduced into the uncertainty of the real world to adapt with changing factors driven by new health care information.

Figure 17.2 illustrates the integration of various digital tools including EHRs, AI, IoMT, big data analytics and blockchain technology together these technologies improve clinical decision support, treatment, and generally efficacy of health care systems.

17.4.1 Artificial Intelligence and Machine Learning

Digital healthcare is being transformed by AI and Machine Learning through patient data processing and real-time insights. Especially in knowledge-based framework, these technologies can facilitate decision-making processes by recommending customized treatment plans, detecting pathogenic conditions at early stage, and optimizing functions of hospitals. Although issues such as data privacy or model interpretability stand as challenges that we need to address, the incorporation of AI and ML is essential for the progress of health care to provide more intelligent, adaptive solutions to emerge, enhancing care for patients while riding the wave of uncertainty that medical practice has always had to navigate.

In [15], author analyses machine learning's transformative applications across healthcare, finance, and IoT, highlighting challenges such as bias and data privacy. It emphasizes the importance of explainable AI to foster trust and ensure ethical practices in these sensitive domains.

Driven by data-oriented approaches, AI and ML are revitalizing healthcare by improving patient outcomes; developing patient-centered healthcare information systems; and enabling medical signal and image processing. The study highlights their paradigm-shifting potential, touches upon ethical considerations, and proposes avenues for future research [11]. Through machine learning, AI supports better patient well–being, drug building, and creates efficiencies in healthcare. Major applications are centered in medical image and smart devices, which are poised to not only reduce healthcare costs but also improve service delivery in the health systems [20]. Notably, a sub-branch of AI, Machine Learning, transforms various industries by demonstrating behaviors or patterns, assisted by statistical algorithms that analyze data using available data sets, and plays a huge role in areas like healthcare, with the various applications in electronic health records, medical imaging, and genomic data [21].

17.4.2 Natural Language Processing (NLP)

Machines analyzing and processing human language is where NLP is changing the landscape of healthcare systems. By transforming unstructured medical data into structured information, it helps cut through the noise and allows healthcare professionals to generate actionable insights. It helps in predicting outcomes, personalization and diagnosis of different diseases. It also enables voice-based virtual assistants and chatbots, which improve patient-provider communications. NLP as a field of study is the actual bridge between human language and machine language and as we see every single factor of decision-making, patient care, and health system needs to be dynamic and adaptive and above all it needs to be updated, therefore as NLP evolves it will surely contribute towards advancing the level of healthcare research.

In this article, the applications, advances and future directions of Natural Language Processing in health care are reviewed, emphasizing the potential for NLP to enhance patient care, clinical decision-making and operational efficiencies by providing data-driven insights and automation [19]. This paper investigates the current and future role of NLP in healthcare, analyzing the effects of NLP on clinical documentation, clinical decision support and patient-provider communication, as well as challenges pertaining to NLP in healthcare and possible solutions to achieve data-driven, personalized healthcare [25].

17.4.3 Big Data Analytics and Cloud Computing

In healthcare, big data analytics and cloud computing are imperative to help store, process and analyze huge amounts of medical data. They allow for early diagnosis and personalized treatment plans, which have served to enhance decision-making and the outcomes for patients. The complementary nature of Big Data and Cloud Computing allows healthcare professionals to collaborate reducing the ambiguity in diagnoses and treatment procedures. They hold the promise of enabling increasingly effective, systematized care as healthcare systems embrace these technologies.

The paper [5] reviews the current state of data-driven healthcare, highlighting its potential to improve patient outcomes through better data integration and analysis. However, it also addresses significant challenges, including data quality, privacy, and ethical concerns that must be navigated for successful implementation.

Karatas *et al.* [9] review the intersection of Industry 4.0, Big Data, and healthcare operations, highlighting applications in resource management and clinical processes, while addressing challenges and offering future perspectives on optimizing healthcare through advanced technologies and data utilization.

Big data analytics together with cloud computing improve the performance of the healthcare system through data-driven decision-making, predictive analytics, and data-sharing, leading to better patient outcomes, lower waiting time, and better system scalability [14]. The paper describes an architectural framework and methodology for big data analytics in healthcare, a.k.a. extract-answer-execute of very large data sets and increasingly hopeful territory for insight (at lower costs over time) into outcomes [10].

17.4.4 Internet of Medical Things (IoMT)

The medical devices now being better integrated into the cloud-based systems, the Internet of Medical Things is now allowing healthcare to monitor the health of patients in real-time. Such technology allows for the early identification of abnormalities and enables personalized care. IoMT offers an intelligent analysis layer, and when combined with Knowledge-Based Systems, it facilitates timely, well-informed decisions for clinicians. This would allow for the enhancement of the capabilities for prediction, enabling early identification of health threats. While focus is shifted from generic to personalized, efficient, and proactive healthcare, the role of IoMT and KBS will be crucial in overcoming challenges, including data overload, individual privacy, and weakening of security systems.

The Internet of Medical Things (IoMT) enhances healthcare through remote monitoring, intelligent systems, and real-time data collection. It leverages sensors, cloud computing, AI, and Blockchain, improving patient surveillance and monitoring, especially during public health crises like COVID-19 [22].

The proposed research implements a new based patient monitoring system based on IoT system, sensors that helps to monitor the vital signs of the patient (heartbeat data) and sends the data *via* a WSN to the cloud platform for all healthcare industry workers to use and process input of patient's data and control the output with the help of few experienced managers in the medical field [7]. This research paper proposes IoT-enabled healthcare system using wireless sensor networks for patient monitoring along with their processing and storage. It allows communication of critical health status conditions in real time, especially for the elderly, medical help can reach either without delay or particularly where there are no medical institutions [17].

17.5 Challenges in Implementing Knowledge-Based Digital Healthcare Systems

The incorporation of medical devices into health systems poses technical challenges that relate to data quality and interoperability. The integration of AI and machine learning models into existing infrastructure is fraught with technical challenges, and ethical issues, such as patient privacy, further complicate adoption. This can only be mitigated with more robust regulations, stricter data security measures, and constant upskilling of healthcare professionals.

17.5.1 Data Privacy and Security Concerns

The massive potential of knowledge-based technologies brings up the challenges of safeguarding sensitive medical information that health care systems collect and disseminate across various platforms, creating problems for data privacy and security. Such systems, usually deployed in the cloud, render them more susceptible to cyber-attacks, data breaches, and unauthorized access. These issues are why other positives strong encryption of data, securing data storage, making access controls tighter, etc.

Concerns regarding ethics and regulatory compliance, including Health Insurance Portability and Accountability Act (HIPAA), also play a vital role in establishing trust and facilitating efforts to enhance patient outcomes.

The paper [2] addresses cybersecurity threats in the Internet of Medical Things (IoMT) by proposing a secure framework that integrates blockchain technology and artificial intelligence. It emphasizes the importance of maintaining patient privacy through federated learning while collaboratively training models.

17.5.2 Handling Uncertainty and Incomplete Knowledge

The uncertainty and imperfect knowledge in human health create challenges for healthcare systems. KBS are built to solve these by evaluating vague or partial information and providing logical suggestions. Uncertain medical data is represented using fuzzy logic, probabilistic reasoning, and Bayesian networks. New data can be continuously learnt from and KBS is made progressively accurate over time. Digital healthcare systems are advancing and will continue to help clinical decision-making and individualized treatment delivery.

17.5.3 Integration with Existing Healthcare Infrastructure

Knowledge-based systems for patient care exist but have had specific challenges in incorporating KBS into healthcare systems. Integration is about being able to fit in with existing technology and workflows, but also about being strategic so that KBS can work with EHR, hospital management systems, and more clinical tools while minimizing disruption to existing work. One of the main challenges is the standardization of data since healthcare data can be present in different formats, therefore requiring standardized protocols such as HL7 or FHIR. KBS should be included in the education of healthcare professionals, ensuring that they work with KBS and trust its recommendations.

It notes that these include the unavailability of effective and transparent processes, lack of digitization, absence of relevant regulations, secure and safe data storage and use, lack of reliable systems, lack of change management and the importance of integrated health information and health systems. Such challenges inhibit the effective implementation of a knowledge-based digital healthcare solution [16]. This comprehensive review of the e-health implementation challenges outlines barriers to adoption and investment in the US, and initiatives to serve to overcome these, drawing on data from diverse sources as a basis to inform digital health practices globally [12].

17.5.4 Ethical and Legal Implications

KBS-supported healthcare systems pose considerable legal and ethical challenges. As these systems handle sensitive health information, ethical considerations such as the preservation of patient privacy and the security of these data are also a challenge. As you can imagine, consent is key to supplying your patients with information about how their data will be used. This leads to legal questions over accountability and transparency in decision-making. These systems are driven by AI and machine learning algorithms that make sure that treatment recommendations are fair. Therefore, addressing these concerns proactively, will ensure that the benefits of digital healthcare system materialize without compromising the ethical or legal aspects.

17.6 Case Studies and Real-World Applications

AI-driven systems are creating and facilitating real-world applications that broaden the reach of healthcare into the community. These systems are capable of revolutionizing early cancer detection, chronic disease management, and offering tailored insights. As these technologies mature, issues such as data privacy must be resolved, also indicating that the development of knowledge-based systems in health care needs to be extended.

17.6.1 Implementations of KBS in Healthcare

KBS in healthcare has proved to be transformational in a real-world context. IBM Watson Health combines AI with huge cancer medical databases for helping oncologists diagnose cancer and Zebra Medical Vision uses KBS-powered tools that can detect early signs of cancer, heart diseases and neurodegenerative diseases. Babylon Health uses KBS in their chronic disease management, offering virtual consultations that allow patients to get connected to monitor in real-time. The KBS analyze symptoms, suggest steps, and consistently improve both predictions and treatment recommendations from the endless stream of data from more patients. In short, these real-world applications show KBS and its augmented decision-making and diagnoses capabilities, and the result more intelligent tools to help patients and clinicians alike.

17.6.2 Learning from Global Deployments

Global deployments of Knowledge-Based Systems in healthcare demonstrate both potentials and pitfalls. The role of quality and integration of data and how Estonia delivered success through its eHealth are some of the key lessons. Nonetheless, hurdles such as privacy issues, data interoperability, and resistance to change linger. The other aspect is the local context adaptation, where all the systems might not fit into a different region due to varied socio-cultural-economic and healthcare infrastructure. Even with these challenges, KBS provides improved decision-making, individualized treatment, and better outcomes for patients.

17.7 Future Directions and Innovations

Knowledge-based systems are continuously bringing innovations to healthcare. KBS will provide timely and reliable diagnosis, treatment recommendations, and predictive analytics, as AI, big data and IoT advances. Wearable devices– this help in providing data for KBS that allows personalization and real-time solutions. Analyzing a huge amount of medical data, AI-driven platforms like IBM Watson Health help doctors in decision-making. KBS will improve patient management, lower costs, and address the unpredictability of clinical situations.

17.7.1 Advancements in AI-Driven Knowledge Systems

Using substantial volumes of medical data and cognitive computers, IBM has made steps toward reinventing health systems with AI knowledge systems that contribute to personalization of care and a higher precision diagnosis. Such systems can handle complicated patient data much more effectively than traditional systems, like Watson Health. Diagnosis letters with data-driven models like predictive analytics and diagnostic imaging are applied to medical records to suggest cancer treatment plans and customize treatment plans for patients. AI systems edit, continuously learn and improve from previous iterations which reduces errors, saves time, and leads to better patient outcomes, and will be a vital component of a fully digital healthcare system.

The digital healthcare revolution is increasingly integrating AI into healthcare information systems for decision-making. Despite advancements, gaps exist in standardized analysis and understanding AI's full impact. This study proposes a seven-category taxonomy for AI in healthcare decision-making, noting recent publications (2022-2024) and dominant use of Python and MATLAB [4].

17.7.2 Enhancing Interoperability and Scalability

IBM is using knowledge-based systems for enhanced interoperability and scalability in the healthcare domain. By allowing systems that employ machine learning and AI to interface between different healthcare platforms electronic health records, clinical decision supports (CDSS), medical devices, etc.), This seamless interoperability enables clinicians to remain connected to current data in customized spaces which enhances clinical decision-making and patient care. Equally, hospitals can introduce KBS applications (IBM Watson for Health) into use, and hemlock for health big data healthcare system development will be clawed and matured with wide use of KBS, which means there is still a long road for healthcare system development.

17.7.3 Potential for Improved Patient Outcomes

IBM Watson Health is a frontline player in digital healthcare using AI KBS for improving clinical decision support. These systems examine complicated medical data and suggest treatments tailored to a patient's particular health profile. With predictive analytics incorporated into KBS, potential health concerns can get forecast which can eventually lead to pre-emptive measures and a reduced requirement of emergency care. KBS makes the logical, progressive nature of KBS not only enhances the quality of care given to the patient but also arm the healthcare provider with evidence-based, timely information that aids in improved, better, prudent decision-making, enabling the patient to receive the utmost care for their well-being.

17.8 Conclusion

Knowledge-Based Systems (KBS) becomes the new normal in digital healthcare. They help clinicians make better decisions; use diagnose more accurately and prepare individually tailored treatment plans. The chapter explained the involvement of KBS in healthcare and the integration of KBS with technologies such as artificial intelligence (AI), natural language processing (NLP), and Internet of Medical Things (IoMT).

The study highlights that KBS could provide data-based insights that can greatly improve the quality of health services. They assist in the early diagnosis of diseases, minimize errors in diagnosis, and assist clinicians in real-time. AI has great promise for managing huge amounts of medical data and creating rapid, evidence-based recommendations, and the combination of AI and KBS is even more potent.

Even though KBS have many advantages, they still have several challenges. Such as data privacy issues, security issues, and absence of universal frameworks when it comes to integration of different systems. Also, in the case of providing healthcare, many healthcare providers face the problem of trusting the automated decisions if there is no rationale behind it. Moreover, there are not many quality examples of structured medical data available to train intelligent systems.

Future work should lean towards constructing hybrid KBS models, integrating rule-based reasoning capabilities into state-of-the-art deep learning models. Greater attention needs to be given to explainable AI in order to increase the trust and adoption of these systems by clinicians. The study also addresses the need for secure data-sharing protocols and enhanced interoperability with current healthcare systems. From this point, pilot implementations in real-world systems with broad variety of patterns of use can aid in validating these systems prior to their widespread adoption.

To conclude, KBS are not free from challenges but can lead us on the track to a smarter, responsive and patient-centered healthcare system.

AI disclosure statement: The author acknowledges the use of AI-based tools for minor language editing or grammatical correction. However, all intellectual contributions, analyses, and conclusions presented in this chapter are entirely the author's own.

References

1. Ahmad, A., Gupta, H., Singh, E.S., Predictive Analytics in Healthcare. *Int. J. Res. Appl. Sci. Eng. Technol.*, 12, V, 5624–5626, May 2024, https://doi.org/10.22214/ijraset.2024.62897.
2. Alsolai, H., Al-Wesabi, F.N., Al-Sharafi, A.M., Alshuhail, A., Darem, A.A., Alghamdi, B.M., Alallah, F.S., Alzahrani, A., A hybrid blockchain and AI-based approach for attack protection to secure internet of medical things networks. *Alexandria Eng. J.*, 128, 223–230, 2025, https://doi.org/10.1016/J.AEJ.2025.05.054.
3. Amin, P., Gulzar Ahmad, S., Khan, H.U., Munir, E.U., Ramzan, N., Predictive Analytics in Maternal Health: A Machine Learning Approach for Classification of Preeclampsia. *Int. J. Comput. Intell. Syst.*, 18, 1, 1–31, 2025, https://doi.org/10.1007/S44196-025-00825-4/FIGURES/20.

4. Amiri, Z., Taghavirashidizadeh, A., Khorrami, P., AI-Driven Decision-Making in Healthcare Information Systems: A Comprehensive Review. *J. Syst. Software*, 112470, 2025, https://doi.org/10.1016/J.JSS.2025.112470.
5. Amri, M.M. and Abed, S.A., The Data-Driven Future of Healthcare: A Review. *Mesopotamian J. Big Data*, 2023, 68–74, 2023, https://doi.org/10.58496/MJBD/2023/010.
6. Anand, G. and Vashisht, P., Predictive and Descriptive Analytics in Healthcare, in: *Data-Driven Analytics for Healthcare*, pp. 1–14, Apple Academic Press, New York, 2024, https://doi.org/10.1201/9781003558743-1.
7. Odirichukwu, J.C., Eze, E.O., Eze, V.C., Eze, E.I., Njoku, O.A., Chika-Ugada, P.K., Nwoke, J.C., Internet of Things (IoT) based patient information and heart beat monitoring system for health information system. *J. Firewall Software Networking*, 2, 1, 20–8, 2024.
8. Dubois, L. and Mack, P., Knowledge-based systems, in: *Artificial Intelligence in Process Fault Diagnosis: Methods for Plant Surveillance*, John Wiley & Sons, Ltd, New Jersey, pp. 300–342, 2024, https://doi.org/10.1002/9781119825920.CH10.
9. Karatas, M., Eriskin, L., Deveci, M., Pamucar, D., Garg, H., Big Data for Healthcare Industry 4.0: Applications, challenges and future perspectives. *Expert Syst. Appl.*, 200, 116912, 2022, https://doi.org/10.1016/J.ESWA.2022.116912.
10. Kushwaha, A. and Acharya, K., Big Data Analytics in Cloud Computing for Scientific Analytics. *Int. J. Res. Appl. Sci. Eng. Technol.*, 10, V, 1713–1717, 2022, https://doi.org/10.22214/ijraset.2022.42636.
11. Maithili, K., Ponmalar, A., Yamini, B., Karthikeyan, M., Anish, T.P., Maheswari, B., Siva Subramanian, R., Maithili, K., Ponmalar, A., Yamini, B., Karthikeyan, M., Anish, T.P., Maheswari, B., Siva Subramanian, R., Advances in AI and Machine Learning for Healthcare Informatics, Https://Services.Igi-Global.Com/Resolvedoi/Resolve.Aspx?Doi=10.4018/979-8-3693-3719-6.Ch001, 1–22, 1 C.E., https://doi.org/10.4018/979-8-3693-3719-6.CH001.
12. Mehta, A., Dias, L., da, S., Espinal, M., Jillellamudi, R., Mathew, R., Chauhan, A., Dhingra, K., Verma, S., E-Health Implementation Challenges: A Comprehensive Review of Digital Healthcare in the United States. *J. Knowl. Learn. Sci. Technol. ISSN 2959-6386 (Online)*, 3, 4, 233–246, 2024, https://doi.org/10.60087/JKLST.V2.N3.P233.
13. Mervin, R., Mavalaru, D., Thomas, T., Knowledge-Driven and Intelligent Computing in Healthcare, in: *Handbook of Intelligent Healthcare Analytics: Knowledge Engineering with Big Data Analytics*, pp. 167–188, John Wiley & Sons, Ltd, Beverly, MA, 2022, https://doi.org/10.1002/9781119792550.CH8.
14. Mishra, K., Jain, S.K., Varalakshmi, S., The Impact of Big Data Analytics and Cloud Computing on Healthcare System Performance. *2024 15th International Conference on Computing Communication and Networking Technologies, ICCCNT 2024*, 2024, https://doi.org/10.1109/ICCCNT61001.2024.10726051.

15. Mohammed, S.Y., The Transformative Applications of Machine Learning across Healthcare, Finance, IoT, and Emerging Domains: Challenges and Future Directions. *Babylon. J. Mach. Learn.*, 2024, 165–176, 2024, https://doi.org/10.58496/BJML/2024/017.
16. Mohanty, S.N., Singh, T., Goel, R., Baral, S.K., Challenges in Digital Health Care—A Hybrid-Decision Approach Understanding Key Challenges in India, in: *Lecture Notes in Electrical Engineering*, vol. 990 LNEE, pp. 91–101, Springer, Singapore, Singapore, 2023, https://doi.org/10.1007/978-981-19-9090-8_9.
17. Najim, A.H., Al-sharhanee, K.A.M., Al-Joboury, I.M., Kanellopoulos, D., Sharma, V.K., Hassan, M.Y., Issa, W., Abbas, F.H., Abbas, A.H., An IoT Healthcare System with Deep Learning Functionality for Patient Monitoring. *Int. J. Commun. Syst.*, 38, 4, e6020, 2025, https://doi.org/10.1002/DAC.6020.
18. Phan, A.C., Phan, T.C., Trieu, T.N., A Systematic Approach to Healthcare Knowledge Management Systems in the Era of Big Data and Artificial Intelligence. *Appl. Sci.*, 12, 9, 4455, 2022, https://doi.org/10.3390/APP12094455.
19. Rahim, F., Hameed, N.A., Salih, S.A., Jawad, A.M., Salman, H.M., Chornomordenko, D., Natural language processing for healthcare: Applications, progress, and future directions. *Edelweiss Appl. Sci. Technol.*, 8, 4, 2027–2041, 2024, https://doi.org/10.55214/25768484.V8I4.1579.
20. Ramyavarshini, P., Swetha, P.S., Malini, A., Shah, M.A., AI's implications in healthcare and medical systems, in: *Artificial Intelligence Technology in Healthcare: Security and Privacy Issues*, pp. 22–41, CRC Press, Boca Raton, 2024, https://doi.org/10.1201/9781003377818-2/AI-Implications-Healthcare-Medical-Systems-Ramyavarshini-Sai-Swetha-Malini-Mohd-Asif-Shah.
21. Shaik, F., Yelchuri, R., Dash, J.K., Fundamentals of Machine Learning in Healthcare, in: *Prediction in Medicine: The Impact of Machine Learning on Healthcare*, pp. 191–218, Bentham Science Publishers, 2024, https://doi.org/10.2174/9789815305128124010013.
22. Siddiq, A.I., A Comprehensive Review of the Internet of Medical Things in Healthcare. *Int. J. Electr. Electron. Eng. Telecommun.*, 13, 6, 415–426, 2024, https://doi.org/10.18178/IJEETC.13.6.415-426.
23. Srivastava, S.R. and Dubey, S., Knowledge-based systems in medical applications, in: *Computational Intelligence and Its Applications in Healthcare*, pp. 189–215, Academic Press,United Kingdom, 2020, https://doi.org/10.1016/B978-0-12-820604-1.00013-3.
24. Sujatha, P., Mahalakshmi, K., Sripriya, P., Big Data Knowledge System in Healthcare, in: *Handbook of Intelligent Healthcare Analytics: Knowledge Engineering with Big Data Analytics*, pp. 39–66, John Wiley & Sons, Ltd, USA, 2022, https://doi.org/10.1002/9781119792550.CH3.
25. Upadhyaya, N., Joshi, H., Agrawal, C., Upadhyaya, N., Joshi, H., Agrawal, C., Examining NLP for Smarter, Data-Driven Healthcare Solutions, Https://Services.Igi-Global.Com/Resolvedoi/Resolve.Aspx?Doi=10.4018/979-8-3693-8990-4.Ch017, 393–420, 1 C.E., https://doi.org/10.4018/979-8-3693-8990-4.CH017.

Part VI

EDUCATION AND PUBLIC SERVICES

18

DSS for Educational Resource Management Based on a Multicriteria Approach: A Case Study for Madagascar National Education

Rôlin Gabriel Rasoanaivo[1,2]* **and Pascale Zaraté**[1]

[1]*Faculté d'Informatique, Université Toulouse Capitole, Toulouse, France*
[2]*Ecole Normale Supérieure, Université de Toamasina, Toamasina, Madagascar*

Abstract

Focus: In this chapter, we present MADREN as a multi-criteria decision support system designed to rank the Regional Directorates of National Education (DREN) based on resource availability. It offers several options for evaluating these directorates: according to the school type and their location; taking into account all schools and locations. The multi-criteria decision-making methods Centroidous and Combined Compromise for Ideal Solution (CoCoFISo) were implemented to obtain the first DREN classification modality. To obtain a final ranking, the Minimum of Rank (MIRA) method has been added. MADREN has been tested for the case of Madagascar.

Finding: The application of the Centroidous method enabled the prioritization of these criteria according to the varying performance matrices, thereby demonstrating that the availability of materials emerged as the paramount criterion across all situations. Application of the CoCoFISo method gave different rankings of the regional directorate depending on school type and location. The aggregation of these disparate rankings through the MIRA method further allows proposing a global ranking.

Results: Following a thorough analysis of the results, it was noted that there is a discrepancy in resources across each directorate. This study is therefore vital for the Ministry of National Education in Madagascar, as the results produced by

**Corresponding author*: rolin-gabriel.rasoanaivo@ut-capitole.fr; rolin-gabriel.rasoanaivo@univ-toamasina.mg

Harish Garg (ed.) Decision Support Systems in Smart Computing: Embracing Uncertainty and Challenges, (553–606) © 2026 Scrivener Publishing LLC

MADREN will inform decision-makers. A key recommendation of this study is the reorganization of the distribution of resources among schools in each directorate to establish equity, thereby ensuring equal opportunities for students.

Keywords: Madagascar's National Education, multi-criteria decision support system, Centroidous, CoCoFISo, MIRA

18.1 Introduction

The evaluation of an institution is a social process aimed at establishing a picture of its value in comparison with other similar institutions, with a general standard or with defined or assigned objectives [1]. According to this definition, many educational institutions have been evaluated in the literature, but the used method varies according to the purpose of the evaluation.

Schools have been evaluated using a variety of mathematical and statistical methods, and we can mention a number of works on this subject. As part of the introduction of an academy dedicated to first-year students, a comparison of third-year student performance in Tennessee schools was carried out in relation to the previous situation [2]. Subsequently, an evaluation was made between the performance of these schools and that of traditional Tennessee high schools. To facilitate this analysis, a selection of three items was made, and the 2 x 2 Analysis of Variance (ANOVA) method was selected for data analysis. In the context of Quebec secondary schools, a subtractive method was used to evaluate the effects of student academic success [3]. The study encompassed a sample of 44,520 students, with the analysis incorporating nine distinct variables. The evaluation method entailed the examination of dependencies between variables, the examination of correlations, and regression analysis. A post-operational analysis of school infrastructure in the West Midlands, UK, was conducted to assess the effectiveness of a school building's services [4]. The research employed three methodological approaches: Cronbach's alpha, the one sample t-test, and the Kruskal-Wallis's test. In India, a geospatial study of roads was conducted in the Prayagraj district to support the government's efforts to enhance road infrastructure, with a focus on elementary schools [5]. A systematic approach was adopted, wherein a set of four criteria were meticulously considered, encompassing the home-school travel distance. The goal is to explore the use of Geographic Information Systems (GIS) in education. The study encompassed a total of 4,878 schools, thereby providing a comprehensive dataset for analysis.

The evaluation of educational establishments was also carried out using multi-criteria decision-making methods, some of which are described below. A research study was conducted to evaluate the performance of secondary schools in comparison to high schools for the case of Keles, located on the southern side of Mount Uludağ [6]. The objective of this study was to identify the most effective educational institution, considering both secondary and high schools, as well as those located in urban and rural settings. Five criteria were selected by applying the Preference Ranking Organization Method for Enrichment Evaluations (PROMETHEE) method. The evaluation and prioritization of schools in Tehran, Iran, was carried out with the objective of facilitating the selection of a suitable school for children by their parents [7]. The evaluation framework encompassed a total of ten criteria, subdivided into fifty-three sub-criteria. The evaluation was executed through the utilization of the Analytical Hierarchy Process (AHP) and Technique for Order Preference by Similarity to Ideal Solution (TOPSIS) methods. A comprehensive analysis of the academic performance of all high schools in Italy has been conducted [8]. The objective of this analysis was to establish a hierarchical ranking of schools based on their geographical location and the specific educational model to which they adhere. The evaluation process involved the consideration of three distinct criteria, with the PROMETHEE and "ÉLimination Et Choix Traduisant la RÉalité" (ELECTRE III) methods being implemented to analyze the data.

Guided by the pertinence of preceding studies, a decision was made to scrutinize the educational institutions situation in Madagascar, which, for the school year 2022-2023, includes 27,176 primary schools, 2,989 secondary schools and 583 high schools [9]. These institutions are dispersed throughout the 23 Regional Directorates of National Education (DREN), situated in all regions of Madagascar. Within a DREN, there are two distinct school locations: rural and urban. This is why we want to classify schools according to DREN, as the latter is responsible for implementing the policy of the Ministry of National Education in the region where it is located. Consequently, in the course of our data research, we identified criteria linked to the availability of human and material resources, as well as to student success in each type of school at each location. We therefore set ourselves the objective of evaluating the DRENs according to these criteria. As a result, we'll be able to offer a range of evaluation options for DRENs. Initially, it seemed necessary to evaluate DRENs according to school type and location. It would also be useful to know the evaluation of DREN by school type, combining the two locations. It would also be relevant to carry out an overall evaluation of DREN by including all schools while keeping each location distinct. Ultimately, this evaluation could be synthesized by considering all three schools (primary, secondary and high schools) and all locations (urban, rural, all areas) simultaneously.

After consulting the literature, we discovered that this DREN evaluation situation is part of a multi-criteria problem. "*Multi-criteria decision-making (MCDM) is one of the main decision-making problems which aims to determine the best alternative by considering more than one criterion in the selection process*" [10]. So, to remedy it, we would have to resort to multi-criteria approaches. The multi-criteria approach consists of two phases: the calculation of criteria weights and the evaluation of alternatives. Although a multitude of methods exist in the literature, we aim to implement the most recent multicriteria decision-making methods. We have identified a number of methods dating back to 2024 [11–18], including Centroidous method [19], which evaluates criteria weights, and CoCoFISo method [20], which examines alternatives. We are considering using CoCoFISo method to evaluate DRENs by school type and location because even though it is newly created, it has already been cited nineteen times in literature, and researchers have developed its extension in Fuzzy [21] and Grey [22]. However, to obtain an overall evaluation of DREN, we need to consider other method. Thus, we plan to aggregate the DREN ranks from our first analysis by applying the recent MIRA multi-criteria rank aggregation method [23].

Currently, systems implementing mathematical algorithms [24–26] have become popular for solving everyday problems. In order to streamline the acquisition of the evaluation, the algorithms of the selected methods and the evaluation process will be integrated into a decision support system called MADREN. This is a multi-criteria decision support system software; in that it integrates multi-criteria methods. Studies on multi-criteria decision support systems can be found in the literature, where multi-criteria methods are used in a variety of fields [27–31]. But, MADREN stands out for its specificity in relation to these systems mentioned in the literature. Initially, it uses multi-criteria decision-making methods (Centroidous and CoCoFISo) to rank DRENs according to school types in various locations. Then, a rank aggregation method (MIRA) was also implemented, across the various DREN rankings, to retrieve the latter and propose an overall DREN ranking. It can also be applied to various academic years.

To achieve this goal of evaluating DRENs, the remainder of this chapter will first present the research methodology describing the algorithms of the techniques we plan to apply. We then proceed to model the system and integrate the algorithms of these techniques into MADREN, where we outline the general scheme of MADREN. We then move on to the experimentation of MADREN, illustrating the study data and the evaluation results obtained, followed by an analysis. In the final section, we discuss the obtained results, concluding with our viewpoint on this study.

The main objective of this paper is to propose a Decision Support System for Decision makers at Ministry of National Education in Madagascar. This system is able to:

- Rank the Regional Directorate of the National Education at Madagascar considering the resources availability for primary, secondary and high schools;
- Apply a Multicriteria approach;
- Propose different ranks for each directorate: rural, urban and overall ranking linked to school's types;
- Use the MIRA methodology able to aggregate the different ranks of directorates to obtain a final rank.

18.2 Methodologies

In this study, we will implement three methods to achieve our goal. The initial two approaches are multi-criteria methods, which are utilized for decision support. The third approach is a rank aggregation technique derived from multi-criteria methods. The subsequent description of the algorithms for each method is given here.

18.2.1 Multi-Criteria Decision-Making Methods

In the application of multi-criteria methods, two phases are essential: the prioritization of criteria and the evaluation of alternatives. In this work, we opted for the Centroidous method for the first phase and the CoCoFISo method for the second. For each of these techniques, a performance matrix with n criteria and m alternatives is required, in accordance with Equation 18.1 below.

$$X = \begin{bmatrix} x_{11} & x_{12} & x_{13} \cdots & x_{1n} \\ x_{21} & x_{22} & x_{23} \cdots & x_{2n} \\ \cdot & \cdot & \cdot & \cdot \\ \cdot & \cdot & \cdot & \cdot \\ \cdot & \cdot & \cdot & \\ x_{m1} & x_{m2} & x_{m3} & x_{mn} \end{bmatrix} \tag{18.1}$$

Here's a step-by-step description of how these methods work.

18.2.1.1 Centroidous Method

Centroidous [19] is a technique for determining criteria weights without involving the decision-maker. It strives to determine the minimum distance between criteria values for all alternatives. The algorithm in question breaks down into five processes, which are detailed in Equations 18.2–18.6 below, m being the number of alternatives and n being the number of criteria.

- Performance matrix normalization

$$\widetilde{x_{ij}} = \frac{x_{ij}}{\sum_{i=1}^{m} x_{ij}} \tag{18.2}$$

- Centre of gravity

$$c_i = \frac{1}{n} \sum_{j=1}^{n} \widetilde{x_{ij}} \tag{18.3}$$

- Euclidean distance

$$d_j = \sqrt{\sum_{i=1}^{m} (\widetilde{x_{ij}} - c_i)^2} \tag{18.4}$$

- Euclidean distance normalization

$$\widetilde{d_j} = \frac{j^{\min(d_j)}}{d_j} \tag{18.5}$$

- Criteria weight

$$w_j = \frac{\widetilde{d_j}}{\sum_{j=1}^{n} \widetilde{d_j}} \tag{18.6}$$

18.2.1.2 CoCoFISo Method

CoCoFISo [20] is a recently developed method for evaluating alternatives, which requires the presence of weights corresponding to the criteria. It is designed to find an ideal solution by optimizing the algorithm of the combined compromise solution method, which seeks a balance between the weighted sum and the weighted product. Its algorithm relies on processes to determine the ranking of alternatives according to Equations 18.7–18.13 below.

- Performance matrix normalization

$$r_{ij} = \frac{x_{ij}}{\sqrt{\sum_{i=1}^{m}(x_{ij})^2}} \tag{18.7}$$

- comparability sequence weighting

$$S_i = \sum_{j=1}^{n}(w_j r_{ij}) \tag{18.8}$$

$$P_i = \sum_{j=1}^{n}(r_{ij})^{w_j} \tag{18.9}$$

- Deduction of aggregation strategies from comparability sequences

$$k_{ia} = \frac{P_i + S_i}{\sum_{i=1}^{m}(P_i + S_i)} \tag{18.10}$$

$$k_{ib} = \left(\frac{S_i + P_i}{1 + \frac{S_i}{1+S_i} + \frac{P_i}{1+P_i}} \right) \tag{18.11}$$

$$k_{ic} = \frac{\lambda(S_i) + (1-\lambda)(P_i)}{(\lambda \max_i S_i + (1-\lambda)\max_i P_i)}; 0 \le \lambda \le 1 \tag{18.12}$$

$$k_i = (k_{ia}k_{ib}k_{ic})^{\frac{1}{3}} + \frac{1}{3}(k_{ia} + k_{ib} + k_{ic}) \tag{18.13}$$

In this way, the rank of the alternatives will be deduced from the *Ki* value whose maximum value has the highest rank.

18.2.2 Rank Aggregation Methods: MIRA

MIRA [23] is a rank aggregation technique derived from multicriteria methods for decision support. Initially, it can be used to synthesize the different rankings obtained by various multicriteria methods for a specific use case. Furthermore, in the context of group decision-making using a multi-criteria approach, the involvement of various decision-makers will lead to varied evaluations of alternatives, but also, in this context, with regard to the existence of different ranking variants of alternatives derived from a multi-criteria method. In general, this process involves two phases, suggesting a correlation test of the ranks obtained *via* multi-criteria methods before and after the implementation of MIRA presented in the Equations 18.14–18.16 below.

- Kendall's correlation coefficient test

$$r_k = \frac{2(N_c - N_d)}{N_a(N_a - 1)} \tag{18.14}$$

Where:
N_c: number of concordant pair
N_d: number of discordant pair
N_a: number of alternatives

- Creation of the rank matrix

$$R = \begin{bmatrix} r_{11} & r_{12} & r_{13} & \cdots & r_{1n} \\ r_{21} & r_{22} & r_{23} & \cdots & r_{2n} \\ \cdot & \cdot & \cdot & & \cdot \\ \cdot & \cdot & \cdot & & \cdot \\ \cdot & \cdot & \cdot & & \cdot \\ r_{n1} & r_{n2} & r_{n3} & \cdots & r_{nn} \end{bmatrix} \tag{18.15}$$

- Rank sum

$$M_i^+ = \sum_{j=1}^{n} r_{ij} \tag{18.16}$$

Consequently, a decrease in the value of *Mi* corresponds to an improvement in the ranking of the alternative.

18.3 MADREN: From Modeling to Implementation

MADREN is a special system designed to evaluate the regional directorates of national education (DREN). This system offers various options for evaluating the DRENs.

Initially, the evaluation of DRENs will be based more on the availability of resources within primary schools, secondary schools or high schools, depending on their location, whether rural, urban or a combination of the two. For instance, the ranking of DRENs can be observed in its entirety or exclusively for the urban or rural area, depending on the availability of resources at secondary schools. The same applies to primary schools and high schools. This initial assessment is proposed by the Centroidous method, which determines the weight of the criteria and CoCoFISo method ranks the DRENs according to the establishment selected and the location chosen by the user.

Secondly, MADREN proposes a general ranking of the DRENs based on the distinction between urban, rural, or a combination of the two. This general ranking is captivating because it synthesizes the various DREN rankings obtained according to school type to generate a new ranking, thereby considering the availability of resources in all primary schools, secondary schools, and high schools. However, the decision of whether to consult the overall ranking for the rural area, the urban area, or a general ranking that takes both areas into account is left to the user. The MIRA method will be applied to combine the different rankings and obtain an overall ranking.

Figures 18.1 and 18.2 demonstrate the structure of the relational database. Figure 18.1 shows the class diagram, which defines the six distinct classes and their interrelationships. Figure 18.2 shows the physical data model, which lists the nine tables to be managed in the database.

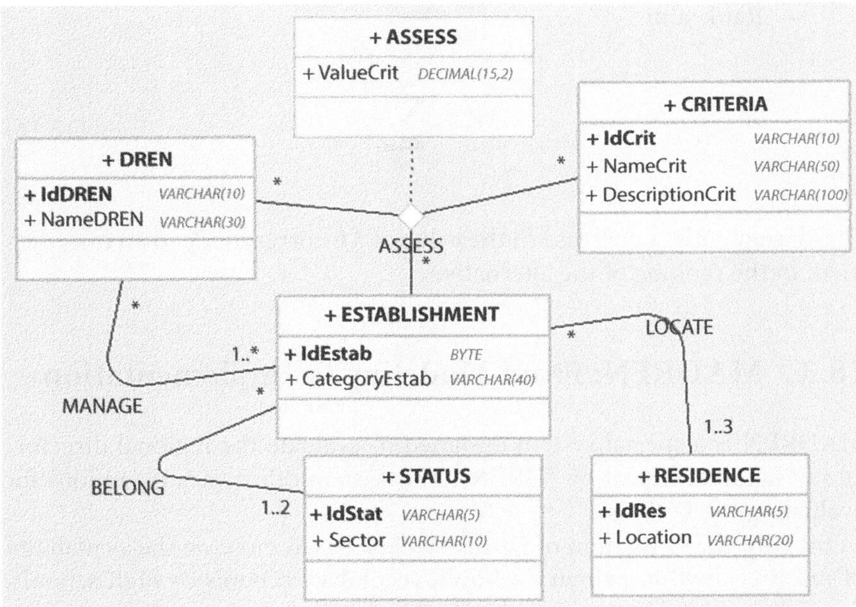

Figure 18.1 MADREN class diagram.

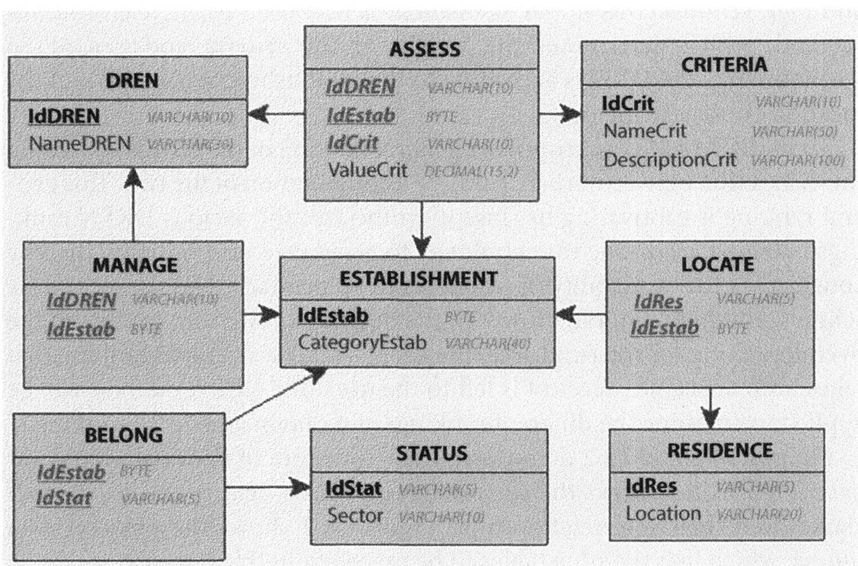

Figure 18.2 MADREN logical data model.

Interaction with the system is initiated through the utilization of MADREN's main menu, as depicted in Figure 18.3. The user is initially prompted to enter data by pressing each button in a specific sequence. The sequence begins with accessing the basic data input, followed by the DREN evaluation. The data input components include DREN, Establishment, Residence, Status, and Criteria. The **DREN** is to register the various regional directorates of national education to be evaluated. The **Establishment** is required to record the three categories of schools, including primary school, secondary school, and high school. The **Residence** is to indicate location (rural, urban, and all). The **Status** is to identify whether schools are public or private, and the **Criteria** is to list the various criteria applied. Subsequent to the collection of the aforementioned information, it is now necessary to enter the value of the criteria according to establishment type and location by selecting the **DREN evaluation** button (Figure 18.3). In this case, a new window will appear on the screen, as shown in Figure 18.4. This functionality will empower users to select the establishment and location, facilitating the entry of information into the performance matrix.

As illustrated in Figure 18.4, the presentation of the results is preceded by a preparatory phase. The initial tab displays the results according to

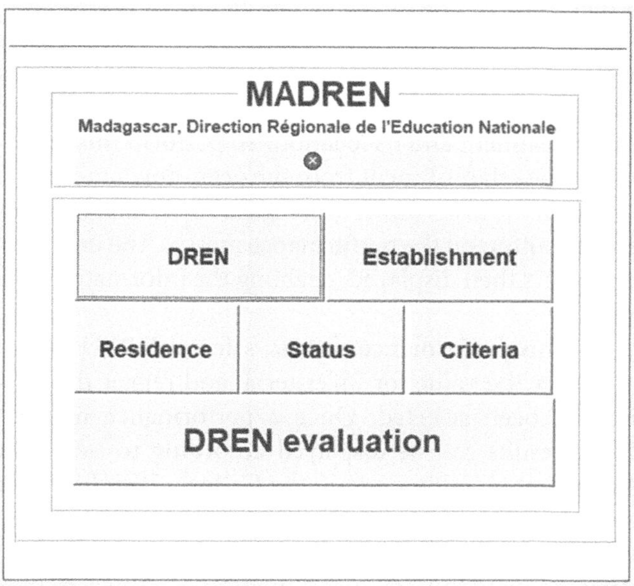

Figure 18.3 MADREN's main menu.

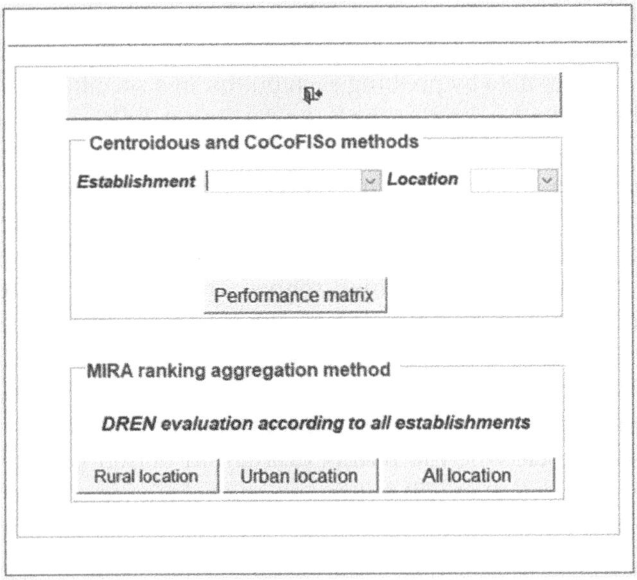

Figure 18.4 Preparing to view results.

the type of establishment and location, employing the Centroidous and CoCoFISo methods. The subsequent tab facilitates access to the overall evaluation using the MIRA method according to location. However, this process necessitates the completion of the performance matrix prior to the entry of data. The performance matrix data will be entered according to the type of establishment and its location. To perform this action, the user must first select the establishment from the drop-down menu and the relevant location from the drop-down list (Figure 18.4). Subsequently, the user should press the button on the performance matrix. The interface shown in Figure 18.5 below is then displayed, enabling the information in the matrix to be added.

To complete this performance matrix, select a DREN from the drop-down menu, enter the value for its criteria, and repeat this process until all DRENs have been selected. Once a performance matrix has been completed, the results can be displayed according to establishment and location. As illustrated in Figure 18.5, the **Criteria Weight** button demonstrates the weights of the criteria calculated through the centroid method. Furthermore, the **DREN's Ranking** button enables direct access to DREN assessment according to the CoCoFISo method. However, in the event that all performance matrices for the various establishments and locations are complete, the user can return to Figure 18.4 and access the second tab.

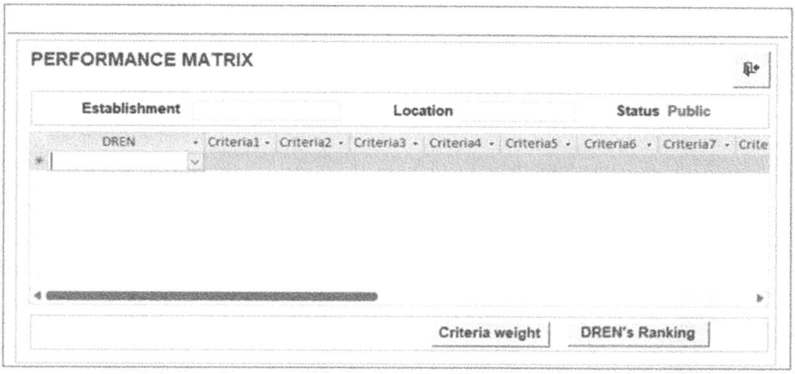

Figure 18.5 Empty performance matrix (add data).

There, they will find the overall ranking of DRENs by location using the MIRA rank aggregation method.

Given that MADREN offers two types of evaluation for regional education departments. Figures 18.6 and 18.7 present the activity diagrams that

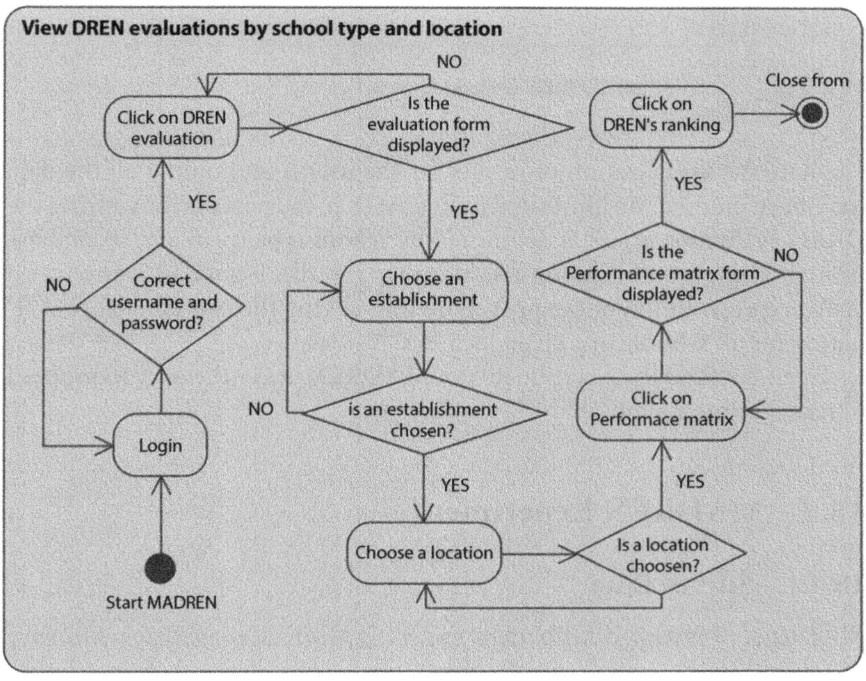

Figure 18.6 Visualization of DREN evaluation by CoCoFISo method.

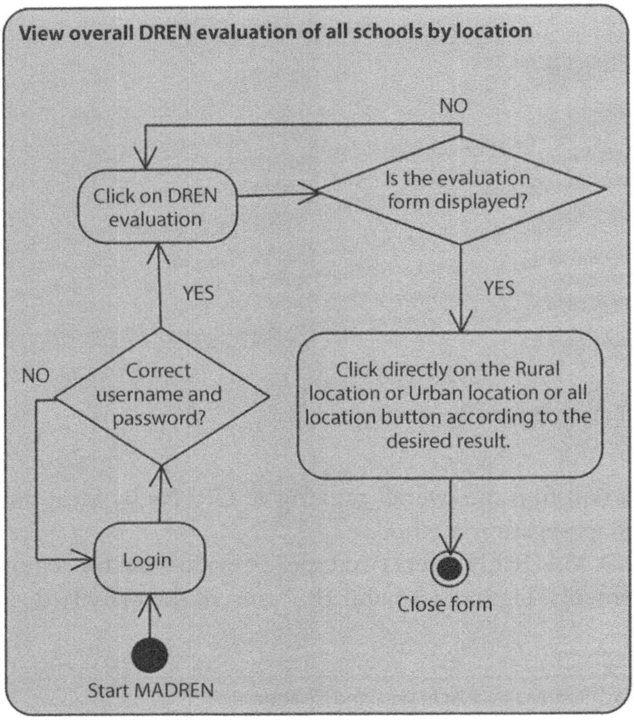

Figure 18.7 Visualization of DREN evaluation by MIRA method.

facilitate the visualization of results for the user if and only if all the data have been entered. As illustrated in Figure 18.6, the process for viewing the DREN evaluation result is delineated by school type (primary, secondary, or high school) and location (rural, urban, or all). Figure 18.7 provides a visual representation of the procedure for viewing the overall DREN evaluation for all schools in a given location.

To understand the functionality of MADREN, it is necessary to proceed to its experimental phase.

18.4 MADREN Experiment

18.4.1 Survey Data

MADREN was tested with data collected from Madagascar's Ministry of Education. Following our investigations, we located a document published annually on the Ministry's website, entitled "Annuaire statistique".

This document compiles statistics on various schools under the supervision of the regional directorates of national education in Madagascar. We therefore selected the most recent version of the document, which covers the 2022-2023 school year. Consequently, there are twenty-three DRENs to be examined, each located in a specific region of Madagascar and bearing the name of that region. Table 18.1 below provides a list of these DRENs, which have been integrated into MADREN in alphabetical order.

To assess the 23 DRENs, nine criteria were identified and organized into three categories: availability of human resources, availability of material resources, and exam success. The factors affecting the availability of human resources include the number of students enrolled for an academic year (STUD), the number of non-teaching administrative staff (STAFF), and the rate of teachers paid by the national budget (TEACH). The elements that make up the availability of material resources include the number of blackboards (BOARD), the number of classrooms (CLASS), the number of schools in operation (SCHO), the number of seats available on desks (SEAT), as well as all the textbooks in various subjects supplied by the state (MANU). The third criterion is predicated on the results achieved

Table 18.1 Twenty-three DREN of Madagascar.

ID	Name	ID	Name
01DREN	Alaotra Mangoro	13DREN	Diana
02DREN	Amoron'i Mania	14DREN	Fitovinany
03DREN	Analamanga	15DREN	Haute Matsiatra
04DREN	Analanjirofo	16DREN	Ihorombe
05DREN	Androy	17DREN	Itasy
06DREN	Anosy	18DREN	Melaky
07DREN	Atsimo Andrefana	19DREN	Menabe
08DREN	Atsimo Atsinanana	20DREN	Sava
09DREN	Atsinanana	21DREN	Sofia
10DREN	Betsiboka	22DREN	Vakinakaratra
11DREN	Boeny	23DREN	Vatovavy
12DREN	Bongolava		

on end-of-school-year exams, with the overall success rate of students in higher grades being a contributing factor (SUC). Table 18.2 shows the nine criteria added to MADREN.

The criteria are based on the raw data in the documents, but there are also those that have been processed. The subsequent discourse herein delineates the data processing process for two of the aforementioned criteria.

The first one is the student success rate (SUC). Instead, the document shows the number of students who repeat a year (STU REP). To calculate the student success rate (SUC), we first subtracted the number of repeaters (STU REP) from the total number of students enrolled (STUD) to obtain the number of students admitted. We then determine the percentage of students admitted in relation to the total number of students enrolled. This operation is summarized by the following formula.

$$SUC = \frac{STUD - STU\ REP}{STUD} \times 100$$

The data concerning the percentage of teachers paid by the state budget (TEACH) has also been processed. Initially, the document mentions five categories of teachers: civil servants (CISE), state-paid contract teachers

Table 18.2 Nine DREN evaluation criteria.

ID	Criteria	Description
BOARD	Blackboard	Whole number of blackboards
CLASS	Classroom	Total number of classrooms
MANU	Manuals	Total number of manuals for all subjects combined by the State
SCHO	School	Total number of schools according to establishment
SEAT	Seating	Number of seats available according to bench table
STAFF	Staff	Number of administration staff
STUD	Student	Number of all students registered for a school year
SUC	Success	Student success rate in promotion exams
TEACH	Teacher	Percentage of teachers paid by the state budget

(COTE), those financed by the parents' association (FRAM), those who do not receive funding from the parents' association (NOTFRAM), and another unspecified type (OTHER). These teachers were first classified into two categories. The first category includes civil servant and contract teachers paid by the state. The second includes the other three types of teachers. Subsequently, we determined the ratio of teachers in the first category by the second to ascertain the TEACH ratio according to the formula below.

$$TEACH = \frac{CISE + COTE}{FRAM + NOTFRAM + OTHER} \times 100$$

Consequently, for each DREN and criterion, information is available in three variants depending on school location: urban, rural, and a combination of the two. The data for each school is presented below, according to these three locations which will be the performance matrix. Initially, Figures 18.8 to 18.10 below show the availability of resource according to the location of public primary school by DREN. To begin with, Figure 18.8 below sets out the DREN performance matrix according to resources for public elementary school in rural areas.

Establishment Primary school **Location** Rural **Status** Public

DREN	Student	Succes	Class	Seat	Board	School	Teacher	Staff	Manuals
ALAOTRA MANGORO	165 172	73,91%	4 538	132 587	5 954	1 195	36,46%	108	524 679
AMORON'I MANIA	126 172	70,28%	3 742	96 289	4 093	943	37,29%	34	332 324
ANALAMANGA	187 021	78,73%	5 924	167 387	7 226	1 542	55,40%	355	560 979
ANALANJIROFO	170 231	72,13%	5 319	135 499	6 471	1 374	35,09%	45	557 453
ANDROY	252 128	76,38%	2 661	51 213	3 517	1 428	33,50%	63	205 238
ANOSY	143 054	77,86%	1 497	42 928	1 887	774	29,44%	86	145 806
ATSIMO ANDREFANA	299 366	85,90%	3 810	66 265	5 191	1 805	25,80%	326	283 962
ATSIMO ATSINANANA	251 967	70,55%	4 053	103 790	5 126	1 437	30,21%	48	339 151
ATSINANANA	230 868	65,52%	5 769	153 145	7 550	1 706	37,72%	68	540 594
BETSIBOKA	58 278	74,88%	1 169	28 205	1 322	478	42,81%	22	104 763
BOENY	92 750	73,87%	1 715	42 864	1 888	682	56,98%	75	178 230
BONGOLAVA	78 585	75,61%	1 994	47 449	2 160	636	28,71%	32	171 754
DIANA	94 543	76,60%	2 134	62 581	2 786	799	48,46%	43	163 999
FITOVINANY	166 484	73,89%	3 280	81 016	3 875	994	26,34%	56	240 839
HAUTE MATSIATRA	178 452	69,57%	4 601	111 966	4 954	1 088	40,95%	122	469 598
IHOROMBE	58 837	70,00%	1 270	23 387	1 613	654	55,13%	16	120 407
ITASY	87 230	74,66%	2 417	63 977	2 730	613	43,49%	49	251 592
MELAKY	52 858	75,18%	738	14 409	934	418	51,87%	30	63 972
MENABE	86 162	78,23%	1 250	25 874	1 491	553	47,16%	91	118 906
SAVA	189 243	71,69%	4 563	141 214	5 672	1 358	39,87%	65	404 023
SOFIA	284 268	74,02%	7 372	189 297	8 504	2 453	26,84%	103	636 367
VAKINAKARATRA	221 132	77,72%	5 449	165 444	6 198	1 316	50,67%	98	664 641
VATOVAVY	197 851	66,16%	3 304	94 907	4 533	1 437	28,89%	43	287 775

Figure 18.8 Performance matrix: rural public primary school.

The initial performance matrix delineates the DREN's stance on the accessibility of resources within public elementary schools situated in rural zones. It is evident that resources are distributed heterogeneously across different DREN. To provide a comprehensive overview of the situation of public primary schools, we have summarized the minimum, maximum, and average values for each DREN in the Table 18.3 presentation below. For instance, on average, 39.52% of teachers in all DREN receive compensation from the state budget. The Atsimo Andrefana DREN exhibits the lowest proportion of teachers compensated by the state, at 25.80%, while the Boeny DREN demonstrates the highest, at 56.98%.

To continue, Figure 18.9 below illustrates the DREN performance matrix according to resources for public primary school in urban areas.

This second matrix presents information on public elementary school in urban areas. As in the previous matrix, the values of the criteria vary considerably from DREN to DREN. In terms of administrative staff, the Bongolava DREN has just 9 employees, unlike the 269 in the Analamanga DREN, which is the largest. These public elementary schools located in rural areas have an average of 69 administrative staff spread across all DREN. Table 18.4 below summarizes the minimum, maximum, and average values of the DREN evaluation criteria.

Let's move on to the performance matrix, which summarizes the availability of resources to elementary school, regardless of location.

We have now reached the third matrix, which presents an overall panorama of public elementary school, taking into account all aspects of the two locations. This is a summary table of the availability of resources within public elementary school, organized by DREN. As a result, there are 445 elementary school in operation in the Melaky DREN, compared with 2,527 in the Sofia DREN. This figure highlights the inequality of resources between the different DRENs. On average, we recorded 1,182 elementary

Table 18.3 Variation in values for public primary school in rural areas.

Variation	Stud	Suc	Class	Seat	Board	Scho	Teach	Staff	Manu
Min	52 858	65,52%	738	14 409	934	418	25,80%	16	63 972
Max	299 366	85,90%	7 372	189 297	8 504	2 453	56,98%	355	664 641
Average	159 681	74,06%	3 416	88 769	4 160	1 117	39,52%	86	320 307

Establishment Primary school **Location** Urban **Status** Public

DREN	Student	Succes	Class	Seat	Board	School	Teacher	Staff	Manuals
ALAOTRA MANGORO	17 571	76,07%	371	11 874	427	80	64,10%	83	71 525
AMORON'I MANIA	15 814	70,44%	428	12 873	511	98	52,53%	37	40 838
ANALAMANGA	55 829	78,22%	993	40 580	1 196	175	66,09%	269	159 983
ANALANJIROFO	20 151	75,19%	469	14 183	578	87	72,68%	72	64 434
ANDROY	20 590	74,37%	159	5 659	217	58	55,26%	32	24 139
ANOSY	20 476	78,57%	247	9 869	313	49	46,14%	47	28 983
ATSIMO ANDREFANA	35 457	85,35%	425	12 624	651	117	32,49%	175	57 738
ATSIMO ATSINANANA	11 922	69,27%	199	6 236	212	24	49,83%	32	18 632
ATSINANANA	26 880	74,52%	465	15 418	593	77	64,45%	135	67 260
BETSIBOKA	6 680	76,50%	109	4 450	130	32	75,36%	16	11 312
BOENY	25 510	79,76%	429	15 395	454	76	65,35%	88	51 285
BONGOLAVA	3 925	70,75%	58	2 825	66	10	58,67%	9	8 347
DIANA	27 511	77,77%	540	18 695	670	95	74,91%	81	47 514
FITOVINANY	17 469	68,61%	284	9 091	374	64	32,49%	40	33 076
HAUTE MATSIATRA	22 671	75,50%	395	14 940	436	61	66,67%	93	65 410
IHOROMBE	4 817	69,07%	68	2 674	80	12	71,43%	14	10 712
ITASY	14 050	74,89%	308	9 086	353	61	56,65%	19	41 041
MELAKY	6 111	71,82%	77	2 365	81	27	93,75%	13	11 956
MENABE	13 436	75,83%	203	6 444	208	52	69,52%	58	28 776
SAVA	20 050	75,51%	339	13 297	345	49	73,22%	47	48 133
SOFIA	19 585	76,16%	425	11 197	454	74	59,45%	105	42 844
VAKINAKARATRA	21 740	76,17%	434	16 428	511	72	77,65%	90	73 473
VATOVAVY	7 907	70,22%	151	4 615	190	43	63,55%	29	16 072

Figure 18.9 Performance matrix: urban public primary school.

Table 18.4 Variation in values for public primary school in urban areas.

Variation	Stud	Suc	Class	Seat	Board	Scho	Teach	Staff	Manu
Min	3 925	68,61%	58	2 365	66	10	32,49%	9	8 347
Max	55 829	85,35%	993	40 580	1 196	175	93,75%	269	159 983
Average	18 963	74,81%	329	11 340	393	65	62,71%	69	44 499

school across all DRENs. Table 18.5 below summarizes the minimum, maximum, and average values for the DREN evaluation criteria.

Now that we've looked at the situation in public elementary school, let's move on to secondary schools. Figures 18.11 and 18.13 present data on the availability of data from institutions of public secondary schools in both rural and urban areas for each DREN. Let's start with Figure 18.11, which shows the situation of secondary schools in rural areas.

This figure shows the first college matrix and compiles the state of play in the rural zone as observed by the DREN. In the course of our analysis,

Establishment	Primary school	Location	All	Status	Public

DREN	Student	Succes	Class	Seat	Board	School	Teacher	Staff	Manuals
ALAOTRA MANGORO	182 743	74,12%	4 909	144 461	6 381	1 275	38,69%	191	596 204
AMORON'I MANIA	141 986	70,30%	4 170	109 162	4 604	1 041	39,13%	71	373 162
ANALAMANGA	242 850	78,62%	6 917	207 967	8 422	1 717	57,24%	624	720 962
ANALANJIROFO	190 382	72,45%	5 788	149 682	7 049	1 461	38,59%	117	621 887
ANDROY	272 718	76,22%	2 820	56 872	3 734	1 486	35,14%	95	229 377
ANOSY	163 530	77,95%	1 744	52 797	2 200	823	32,33%	133	174 789
ATSIMO ANDREFANA	334 823	85,84%	4 235	78 889	5 842	1 922	26,51%	501	341 700
ATSIMO ATSINANANA	263 889	70,49%	4 252	110 026	5 338	1 461	31,18%	80	357 783
ATSINANANA	257 748	66,46%	6 234	168 563	8 143	1 783	40,54%	203	607 854
BETSIBOKA	64 958	75,05%	1 278	32 655	1 452	510	45,56%	38	116 075
BOENY	118 260	75,14%	2 144	58 259	2 342	758	58,58%	163	229 515
BONGOLAVA	82 510	75,38%	2 052	50 274	2 226	646	29,64%	41	180 101
DIANA	122 054	76,86%	2 674	81 276	3 456	894	53,91%	124	211 513
FITOVINANY	183 953	73,39%	3 564	90 107	4 249	1 058	26,92%	96	273 915
HAUTE MATSIATRA	201 123	70,24%	4 996	126 906	5 390	1 149	43,25%	215	535 008
IHOROMBE	63 654	69,92%	1 338	26 061	1 693	666	56,17%	30	131 119
ITASY	101 280	74,69%	2 725	73 063	3 083	674	45,11%	68	292 633
MELAKY	58 969	74,83%	815	16 774	1 015	445	56,33%	43	75 928
MENABE	99 598	77,91%	1 453	32 318	1 699	605	50,24%	149	147 682
SAVA	209 293	72,05%	4 902	154 511	6 017	1 407	42,75%	112	452 156
SOFIA	303 853	74,15%	7 797	200 494	8 958	2 527	28,52%	208	679 211
VAKINAKARATRA	242 872	77,58%	5 883	181 872	6 709	1 388	53,03%	188	738 114
VATOVAVY	205 758	66,32%	3 455	99 522	4 723	1 480	30,32%	72	303 847

Figure 18.10 Performance matrix: all public primary school.

Table 18.5 Variation in values for public primary school in all areas.

Variation	Stud	Suc	Class	Seat	Board	Scho	Teach	Staff	Manu
Min	58 969	66,32%	815	16 774	1 015	445	26,51%	30	75 928
Max	334 823	85,84%	7 797	207 967	8 958	2 527	58,58%	624	738 114
Average	178 644	74,17%	3 745	100 109	4 553	1 182	41,72%	155	364 806

we noticed that the Melaky DREN has a minimal number of classrooms, 69, compared to the Analamanga DREN, which has 1,685. In terms of the number of students enrolled, a classroom in the Melaky DREN for secondary schools can host 53 students, while the Analamanga DREN can host 42. Of all the DRENs, Melaky has the highest number of students in a classroom for secondary schools in rural location. To give an overview of the situation, the Table 18.6 below shows the minimum, maximum, and average values for the DREN evaluation criteria.

Establishment Secondary school **Location** Rural **Status** Public

DREN	Student	Succes	Class	Seat	Board	School	Teacher	Staff	Manuals
ALAOTRA MANGORO	38 916	88,55%	967	36 115	1 077	183	57,26%	210	71 481
AMORON'I MANIA	24 904	86,67%	809	22 454	814	155	55,52%	102	39 782
ANALAMANGA	70 408	87,78%	1 685	64 638	1 895	237	71,10%	778	131 083
ANALANJIROFO	35 349	88,08%	968	34 880	1 124	166	46,74%	166	57 504
ANDROY	18 420	84,31%	266	6 676	300	85	22,09%	120	8 742
ANOSY	14 235	86,91%	234	9 113	276	68	33,47%	81	12 334
ATSIMO ANDREFANA	31 529	87,44%	456	13 588	524	112	33,00%	235	32 101
ATSIMO ATSINANANA	31 593	80,89%	626	19 866	792	158	40,05%	130	24 938
ATSINANANA	27 068	84,18%	668	24 249	770	136	56,49%	155	33 170
BETSIBOKA	7 972	88,23%	173	6 530	206	43	60,46%	46	5 449
BOENY	11 144	90,66%	217	8 877	237	43	67,91%	87	15 896
BONGOLAVA	12 436	94,32%	375	10 544	386	75	54,19%	30	12 437
DIANA	15 822	90,59%	365	13 346	386	87	58,79%	29	11 502
FITOVINANY	18 462	87,86%	486	14 970	494	108	36,99%	146	19 116
HAUTE MATSIATRA	39 412	85,39%	1 056	29 194	1 046	183	51,84%	201	58 279
IHOROMBE	4 582	82,89%	112	3 674	125	25	77,78%	36	5 828
ITASY	18 482	89,81%	492	15 799	516	86	62,74%	71	23 184
MELAKY	3 690	89,21%	69	2 667	77	17	63,16%	28	4 024
MENABE	8 391	90,73%	163	5 313	184	40	47,24%	98	8 714
SAVA	32 994	88,97%	716	28 854	817	136	63,00%	109	29 153
SOFIA	50 300	91,27%	1 220	42 363	1 291	299	39,32%	209	54 312
VAKINAKARATRA	42 973	92,43%	1 021	37 711	1 130	180	66,04%	188	64 053
VATOVAVY	19 373	82,17%	402	14 361	526	126	47,75%	98	17 907

Figure 18.11 Performance matrix: rural public secondary school.

Table 18.6 Variation in values for public secondary school in rural areas.

Variation	Stud	Suc	Class	Seat	Board	Scho	Teach	Taff	Manu
Min	3 690	80,89%	69	2 667	77	17	22,09%	28	4 024
Max	70 408	94,32%	1 685	64 638	1 895	299	77,78%	778	131 083
Average	25 150	87,80%	589	20 251	652	119	52,74%	146	32 217

The next situation of secondary schools is focusing on the current state within urban location presented by the Figure 18.12 below.

This matrix illustrates the distribution of resources in the urban area by DREN, thus representing the situation of the secondary schools. With regard to seating arrangements, the Analamanga DREN demonstrates a notable lead with 21,134 seats, in comparison to the 550 available in the Ihorombe DREN. It is important to note that the availability of seating is contingent on the number of students enrolled, which differs significantly between the two DRENs (26,576 and 2,081, respectively). However, with

Establishment Secondary school **Location** Urban **Status** Public

DREN	Student	Succes	Class	Seat	Board	School	Teacher	Staff	Manuals
ALAOTRA MANGORO	8 961	87,78%	159	6 167	166	15	83,19%	105	21 512
AMORON'I MANIA	4 939	88,28%	130	4 383	142	15	83,22%	66	19 006
ANALAMANGA	26 576	86,01%	459	21 134	470	33	80,85%	472	73 924
ANALANJIROFO	11 229	82,64%	228	9 986	250	18	76,73%	80	16 443
ANDROY	3 868	91,08%	44	1 890	49	4	66,39%	31	4 385
ANOSY	5 241	86,64%	72	5 619	81	7	49,45%	70	5 458
ATSIMO ANDREFANA	9 610	88,89%	106	5 861	106	15	56,11%	117	16 349
ATSIMO ATSINANANA	3 759	86,88%	62	3 130	48	6	85,09%	51	8 594
ATSINANANA	16 302	84,59%	225	11 304	246	17	85,57%	175	25 363
BETSIBOKA	2 201	85,78%	41	1 758	72	3	92,00%	22	3 038
BOENY	10 671	83,65%	150	6 179	147	12	81,34%	149	37 716
BONGOLAVA	2 814	94,14%	35	1 795	35	2	72,97%	12	9 441
DIANA	11 630	87,85%	234	9 320	204	21	77,80%	87	25 207
FITOVINANY	3 080	88,08%	76	2 244	79	9	61,93%	51	35 432
HAUTE MATSIATRA	8 882	82,73%	175	8 117	151	11	93,33%	110	29 922
IHOROMBE	2 081	77,27%	19	550	25	1	70,37%	5	3 873
ITASY	4 997	90,15%	106	4 249	109	11	74,78%	65	14 219
MELAKY	2 005	87,73%	39	1 314	38	3	89,86%	20	5 232
MENABE	3 882	88,61%	73	3 290	93	6	64,25%	74	8 176
SAVA	12 278	86,14%	140	8 612	111	8	84,04%	62	9 832
SOFIA	11 977	83,89%	181	9 281	183	12	84,99%	164	18 254
VAKINAKARATRA	10 523	87,70%	197	9 559	225	10	90,66%	114	25 041
VATOVAVY	2 898	89,34%	32	1 702	37	2	78,13%	28	2 699

Figure 18.12 Performance matrix: urban public secondary school.

respect to functional colleges in urban locations, the Ihorombe DREN is notable for its singularity, while the Analamanga DREN stands out with its 33 secondary schools. Table 18.7 below recaps the minimum, maximum, and average values for the DREN evaluation criteria.

Let's move on the performance matrix in Figure 18.13 below who reviews the overall availability of resources to secondary schools.

The third matrix offers a synopsis of the preceding two cases pertaining to the colleges. It ensures the availability of resources in both locations. The Melaky DREN has 115 blackboards, which is the minimum compared to the 2,365 blackboards in the Analamanga DREN, which is the maximum quantity. The classrooms in the two DRENs are 108 and 2,144, respectively.

Table 18.7 Variation in values for public secondary school in urban areas.

Variation	Stud	Suc	Class	Seat	Board	Scho	Teach	Staff	Manu
Min	2 005	77,27%	19	550	25	1	49,45%	5	2 699
Max	26 576	94,14%	459	21 134	470	33	93,33%	472	73 924
Average	7 844	86,78%	130	5 976	133	10	77,52%	93	18 222

Establishment	Secondary school	Location	All	Status	Public

DREN	Student	Succes	Class	Seat	Board	School	Teacher	Staff	Manuals
ALAOTRA MANGORO	47 877	88,41%	1 126	42 282	1 243	198	61,32%	315	92 993
AMORON'I MANIA	29 843	86,94%	939	26 837	956	170	60,09%	168	58 788
ANALAMANGA	96 984	87,29%	2 144	85 772	2 365	270	73,21%	1 250	205 007
ANALANJIROFO	46 578	86,77%	1 196	44 866	1 374	184	53,78%	246	73 947
ANDROY	22 288	85,49%	310	8 566	349	89	26,74%	151	13 127
ANOSY	19 476	86,84%	306	14 732	357	75	36,86%	151	17 792
ATSIMO ANDREFANA	41 139	87,78%	562	19 449	630	127	38,53%	352	48 450
ATSIMO ATSINANANA	35 352	81,52%	688	22 996	840	164	44,20%	181	33 532
ATSINANANA	43 370	84,34%	893	35 553	1 016	153	66,65%	330	58 533
BETSIBOKA	10 173	87,70%	214	8 288	278	46	65,52%	68	8 487
BOENY	21 815	87,23%	367	15 056	384	55	73,30%	236	53 612
BONGOLAVA	15 250	94,29%	410	12 339	421	77	56,13%	42	21 878
DIANA	27 452	89,43%	599	22 666	590	108	65,64%	116	36 709
FITOVINANY	21 542	87,89%	562	17 214	573	117	40,14%	197	54 548
HAUTE MATSIATRA	48 294	84,90%	1 231	37 311	1 197	194	57,98%	311	88 201
IHOROMBE	6 663	81,13%	131	4 224	150	26	76,51%	41	9 701
ITASY	23 479	89,88%	598	20 048	625	97	65,04%	136	37 403
MELAKY	5 695	88,69%	108	3 981	115	20	70,83%	48	9 256
MENABE	12 273	90,06%	236	8 603	277	46	51,45%	172	16 890
SAVA	45 272	88,20%	856	37 466	928	144	67,14%	171	38 985
SOFIA	62 277	89,85%	1 401	51 644	1 474	311	45,69%	373	72 566
VAKINAKARATRA	53 496	91,50%	1 218	47 270	1 355	190	70,06%	302	89 094
VATOVAVY	22 271	83,10%	434	16 063	563	128	50,47%	126	20 606

Figure 18.13 Performance matrix: all public secondary school.

However, observations indicate that the number of blackboards in the Diana and Haute Matsiatra DRENs is 590 and 1,197, respectively, while the number of classrooms is 599 and 1,231. This discrepancy could potentially indicate a shortage of blackboards in the colleges within these two DRENs. Within Diana DREN, this discrepancy can be attributed to the number of blackboards falling short of the number of classrooms in the urban area (204<234). Conversely, in the Haute Matsiatra DREN, a similar trend is evident in both zones (rural: 151<175; urban: 1,046<1,056). Table 18.8 below recaps the minimum, maximum, and average values for all locations of the DREN evaluation criteria according to the secondary schools.

Table 18.8 Variation in values for public secondary school in all areas.

Variation	Stud	Suc	Class	Seat	Board	Scho	Teach	Staff	Manu
Min	5 695	81,13%	108	3 981	115	20	26,74%	41	8 487
Max	96 984	94,29%	2 144	85 772	2 365	311	76,51%	1 250	205 007
Average	32 994	87,36%	719	26 227	785	130	57,27%	238	50 439

We have already presented the performance matrices for primary and secondary schools, so what remains is to present those for high schools. The data presented in Figures 18.14 and 18.16 below illustrate the availability of resources according to the location of the public high schools collected by DREN.

This is the first Performance Matrix developed to assess the availability of resources in rural high schools, grouped by DREN. The number of students enrolled exhibits variation across the DRENs, ranging from 1,008 in the Melaky DREN to 25,265 in the Analamanga DREN. The average number of students enrolled in rural high schools within the DRENs is 6,090. When the average number of textbooks supplied by the State to high schools is considered, which is 6,097, it is evident that this figure exceeds the number of students. However, the allocation of these textbooks among the high schools within each DREN does not align proportionally with the number of students enrolled. A total of eight out of twenty-three DRENs received more textbooks than the number of students. A notable exception is the Vakinakaratra DREN, which has 10,226 students and 16,169 textbooks, indicating a supply that exceeds its student population. Conversely, in the remaining fifteen DRENs, the number of textbooks is found to be inadequate in comparison to the number of students enrolled. For instance,

Establishment High school **Location** Rural **Status** Public

DREN	Student	Succes	Class	Seat	Board	School	Teacher	Staff	Manuals
ALAOTRA MANGORO	9 266	92,32%	168	7 946	188	27	64,51%	87	12 861
AMORON'I MANIA	5 622	93,77%	147	5 431	164	24	76,62%	66	5 748
ANALAMANGA	25 262	90,65%	572	27 448	621	77	81,93%	438	33 745
ANALANJIROFO	7 397	93,17%	128	6 913	156	20	70,93%	54	5 208
ANDROY	3 399	83,85%	32	1 552	40	11	56,06%	26	2 213
ANOSY	3 561	90,12%	66	2 711	66	16	53,93%	31	3 798
ATSIMO ANDREFANA	8 027	87,13%	114	5 075	125	28	58,20%	84	3 073
ATSIMO ATSINANANA	5 120	87,36%	86	5 199	105	21	66,37%	40	2 903
ATSINANANA	5 095	93,44%	95	5 110	110	15	73,86%	71	7 063
BETSIBOKA	1 555	93,18%	34	1 512	40	11	53,47%	16	714
BOENY	3 189	91,97%	69	2 903	73	9	74,38%	40	5 029
BONGOLAVA	3 861	91,27%	91	3 725	108	13	68,68%	26	3 427
DIANA	2 754	93,46%	61	2 070	73	11	65,85%	11	1 415
FITOVINANY	4 654	88,40%	78	3 762	79	14	60,99%	33	3 312
HAUTE MATSIATRA	13 423	86,15%	274	11 477	308	50	75,44%	110	12 948
IHOROMBE	1 266	90,05%	23	1 034	24	5	85,71%	13	1 121
ITASY	3 986	89,89%	89	3 489	105	19	71,43%	29	4 052
MELAKY	1 008	94,05%	11	686	16	3	80,00%	12	537
MENABE	1 974	88,80%	33	1 652	39	7	52,94%	29	2 389
SAVA	5 677	95,54%	82	4 945	100	15	57,59%	15	3 333
SOFIA	9 928	91,07%	191	8 355	186	39	52,81%	70	8 352
VAKINAKARATRA	10 226	90,94%	200	9 811	234	34	69,96%	81	16 169
VATOVAVY	3 818	80,23%	71	3 230	79	16	74,40%	49	831

Figure 18.14 Performance matrix: rural public high school.

Table 18.9 Variation in values for public high school in rural areas.

Variation	Stud	Suc	Class	Seat	Board	Scho	Teach	Staff	Manu
Min	1 008	80,23%	11	686	16	3	52,81%	11	537
Max	25 262	95,54%	572	27 448	621	77	85,71%	438	33 745
Average	6 090	90,30%	118	5 480	132	21	67,22%	62	6 097

the Vatovavy DREN, with 3,818 students, received 831 textbooks, which falls short of the required number. Table 18.9 above recaps the minimum, maximum, and average values for rural location of the DREN evaluation criteria according to the high schools.

Let's move on to the availability of resources at high schools in the urban location, shown in Figure 18.15 below.

As illustrated in Figure 18.15, the second variant of the performance matrix demonstrates the availability of resources in rural high schools. The number of functional high schools is limited compared to what was previously observed in rural areas, ranging from 1 (in Ihorombe DREN) to 11 (in Analamanga DREN), with a total average of 4 high schools. With regard to the composition of the teacher, most of them are paid from the

Establishment High school **Location** Urban **Status** Public

DREN	Student	Succes	Class	Seat	Board	School	Teacher	Staff	Manuals
ALAOTRA MANGORO	5 341	93,02%	90	3 474	92	4	86,30%	70	14 162
AMORON'I MANIA	3 141	90,04%	73	3 419	84	4	89,31%	40	9 689
ANALAMANGA	16 565	89,77%	326	17 639	346	11	84,68%	305	54 669
ANALANJIROFO	5 981	91,47%	93	5 224	95	5	85,89%	61	8 131
ANDROY	2 142	93,46%	38	1 561	34	3	75,00%	24	1 609
ANOSY	2 913	90,32%	51	1 898	43	3	77,98%	45	4 276
ATSIMO ANDREFANA	6 063	93,25%	84	5 576	90	7	64,08%	139	7 310
ATSIMO ATSINANANA	1 936	87,55%	32	923	32	2	88,31%	24	1 972
ATSINANANA	5 994	92,18%	103	5 544	112	4	81,45%	102	24 039
BETSIBOKA	1 309	84,95%	20	987	20	2	76,60%	14	490
BOENY	3 850	90,83%	84	4 069	89	6	78,02%	59	7 972
BONGOLAVA	1 340	87,99%	27	1 192	27	1	86,89%	13	2 484
DIANA	9 375	92,73%	137	7 507	135	8	85,16%	78	9 289
FITOVINANY	2 680	81,08%	60	3 428	60	4	82,95%	41	5 600
HAUTE MATSIATRA	5 408	91,55%	105	5 305	132	6	92,50%	85	11 125
IHOROMBE	1 207	79,70%	15	880	15	1	91,67%	7	1 280
ITASY	3 564	90,15%	60	2 926	66	4	87,15%	45	7 314
MELAKY	834	95,32%	14	758	18	2	82,05%	10	3 391
MENABE	2 292	84,55%	40	2 000	42	4	88,66%	36	1 314
SAVA	9 667	92,86%	115	7 850	110	4	75,11%	47	4 870
SOFIA	8 327	90,36%	140	7 549	138	7	80,28%	105	11 892
VAKINAKARATRA	5 577	89,30%	83	4 260	87	4	92,92%	66	10 155
VATOVAVY	2 475	93,17%	27	1 230	27	2	87,14%	21	268

Figure 18.15 Performance matrix: urban public high school.

state budget. The percentage of which varies from one DREN to another, ranging from 64.08% (Atsimo Andrefana DREN) to 92.92% (Vakinakaratra DREN). Table 18.10 below recaps the minimum, maximum, and average values for the DREN evaluation criteria.

To conclude with the performance matrices, Figure 18.16 shows the overall situation of the high schools.

This matrix provides a summary of the general availability of resources in the high schools according to the two sites. The administrative staff has indicated a discrepancy in the provision of resources across the DRENs, with a minimum of 20 in Ihorombe DREN compared with a maximum of 743 in Analamanga DREN. Furthermore, the ratio of students to

Table 18.10 Variation in values for public high school in urban areas.

Variation	Stud	Suc	Class	Seat	Board	Scho	Teach	Staff	Manu
Min	834	79,70%	14	758	15	1	64,08%	7	268
Max	16 565	95,32%	326	17 639	346	11	92,92%	305	54 669
Average	4 695	89,81%	79	4 139	82	4	83,48%	62	8 839

Establishment High school **Location** All **Status** Public

DREN	Student	Succes	Class	Seat	Board	School	Teacher	Staff	Manuals
ALAOTRA MANGORO	14 607	92,57%	258	11 420	280	31	71,66%	157	27 023
AMORON'I MANIA	8 763	92,43%	220	8 850	248	28	80,54%	106	15 437
ANALAMANGA	41 827	90,30%	898	45 087	967	88	82,86%	743	88 414
ANALANJIROFO	13 378	92,41%	221	12 137	251	25	77,74%	115	13 339
ANDROY	5 541	87,57%	70	3 113	74	14	61,98%	50	3 822
ANOSY	6 474	90,21%	117	4 609	109	19	63,07%	76	8 074
ATSIMO ANDREFANA	14 090	89,77%	198	10 651	215	35	60,88%	223	10 383
ATSIMO ATSINANANA	7 056	87,41%	118	6 122	137	23	72,00%	64	4 875
ATSINANANA	11 089	92,76%	198	10 654	222	19	77,74%	173	31 102
BETSIBOKA	2 864	89,42%	54	2 499	60	13	60,81%	30	1 204
BOENY	7 039	91,35%	153	6 972	162	15	76,32%	99	13 001
BONGOLAVA	5 201	90,42%	118	4 917	135	14	73,25%	39	5 911
DIANA	12 129	92,89%	198	9 577	208	19	78,84%	89	10 704
FITOVINANY	7 334	85,72%	138	7 190	139	18	69,03%	74	8 912
HAUTE MATSIATRA	18 831	87,70%	379	16 782	440	56	79,65%	195	24 073
IHOROMBE	2 473	85,00%	38	1 914	39	6	88,14%	20	2 401
ITASY	7 550	90,01%	149	6 415	171	23	77,96%	74	11 366
MELAKY	1 842	94,63%	25	1 444	34	5	81,08%	22	3 928
MENABE	4 266	86,52%	73	3 652	81	11	68,98%	65	3 703
SAVA	15 344	93,85%	197	12 795	210	19	65,77%	62	8 203
SOFIA	18 255	90,74%	331	15 904	324	46	63,87%	175	20 244
VAKINAKARATRA	15 803	90,36%	283	14 071	321	38	76,97%	147	26 324
VATOVAVY	6 293	85,32%	98	4 460	106	18	77,62%	70	1 099

Figure 18.16 Performance matrix: all public high school.

Table 18.11 Variation in values for public high school in all areas.

Variation	Stud	Suc	Class	Seat	Board	Scho	Teach	Staff	Manu
Min	1 842	85,00%	25	1 444	34	5	60,81%	20	1 099
Max	41 827	94,63%	898	45 087	967	88	88,14%	743	88 414
Average	10 785	89,97%	197	9 619	214	25	73,34%	125	14 937

administrative personnel was determined, exhibiting a range from 63 in DREN Atsimo Andrefana to 136 in Diana DREN. The mean ratio across all DRENs is 86. This ratio serves as a metric for the number of students cared for by a single administrative staff member. Table 18.11 above recaps the minimum, maximum, and average values for rural location of the DREN evaluation criteria according to the high schools.

A total of nine performance matrices are available, with three matrices allocated for each category of school, depending on location. We can now proceed to visualize the results.

18.4.2 Results and Analysis

The result is divided into two variants. The initial evaluation of the DRENs is based on the nine performance matrices. These results will be organized by school type and location, according to the Centroidous and CoCoFISo methods. The second result builds on the first. The aim is to consolidate the different rankings by using the additive MIRA method to summarize the evaluation of DRENs according to their location. These results are provided in the following section.

18.4.2.1 DREN Evaluation Results by School Type and Location

The initial phase in the implementation of multi-criteria methods in MADREN involves the determination of the importance of the criteria through the utilization of the Centroidous method. To this end, the nine performance matrices will be considered. This approach will yield the weights of the criteria according to each matrix. The subsequent step involves the utilization of the Centroidous method to ascertain the relative importance of the criteria. This is achieved by examining the nine performance matrices, thereby deriving the weights of the criteria according to each matrix. The subsequent Table 18.12 presents the weights of the

Table 18.12 Weight of criteria by school type and location.

Establishment	Location	Class	Board	School	Seat	Manuals	Student	Teacher	Staff	Success
Primary school	Rural	0,16	0,16	0,16	0,11	0,11	0,13	0,06	0,04	0,08
	Urban	0,17	0,17	0,13	0,10	0,09	0,17	0,04	0,06	0,05
	All	0,14	0,19	0,14	0,12	0,12	0,12	0,06	0,04	0,07
Secondary school	Rural	0,15	0,19	0,10	0,15	0,07	0,19	0,05	0,05	0,05
	Urban	0,17	0,17	0,14	0,14	0,08	0,14	0,06	0,07	0,06
	All	0,14	0,19	0,10	0,14	0,08	0,19	0,05	0,05	0,05
High school	Rural	0,16	0,16	0,16	0,13	0,06	0,21	0,04	0,05	0,04
	Urban	0,18	0,18	0,12	0,14	0,05	0,14	0,05	0,09	0,05
	All	0,19	0,19	0,12	0,12	0,05	0,19	0,04	0,06	0,04

criteria obtained according to school type and location, in accordance with the performance matrices.

The evaluation of the DREN will be influenced by the importance attached to these criteria. It was observed that Centroidous demonstrated the capacity to categorize the criteria according to each school's location and its corresponding category. Weights were calculated according to the specificity of this method. It was noticed that for each category of school and location, some criteria were more important than others. In some cases, the weight value of a specific criterion varies between schools and across locations, though these variations are not significant. However, Table 18.13 presents a synthesis of the average weights of the criteria for all school types and locations combined.

This average weighting facilitated the determination of the general classification of the nine DREN evaluation criteria. It was observed that the initial five criteria exhibited significant average weights, ranging from 0.13 to 0.16, while the final four demonstrated low weights, ranging from 0.05 to 0.08. Of the five criteria deemed important, four belong to the group relating to the availability of material resources and one to the group relating to the availability of human resources. This observation underscores the significance accorded to material resource availability in the context of the study, as determined by Centroidous method.

In order to verify this hypothesis, the weights assigned to the criteria evaluated by Centroidous according to the material and human resource availability groups for each school category and location were aggregated. The accompanying illustration demonstrates that the group pertaining to the availability of material resources exhibits a fluctuation in weights ranging from 0.65 to 0.71, while that relating to the availability of human resources varies from 0.22 to 0.30. Figure 18.17 below shows the variation in weights between these resources.

Now that the criteria weights are available, we can move on to the results of the first DREN evaluation.

Given our access to the weights of the criteria, we are able to conduct the assessment of the DRENs using the CoCoFISo method. To facilitate comprehension of the results, the ranking derived from the performance

Table 18.13 Average weights of the criteria.

Board	**Class**	**Student**	**School**	**Seat**	**Manuals**	**Staff**	**Teacher**	**Success**
0,18	0,16	0,16	0,13	0,13	0,08	0,06	0,05	0,05

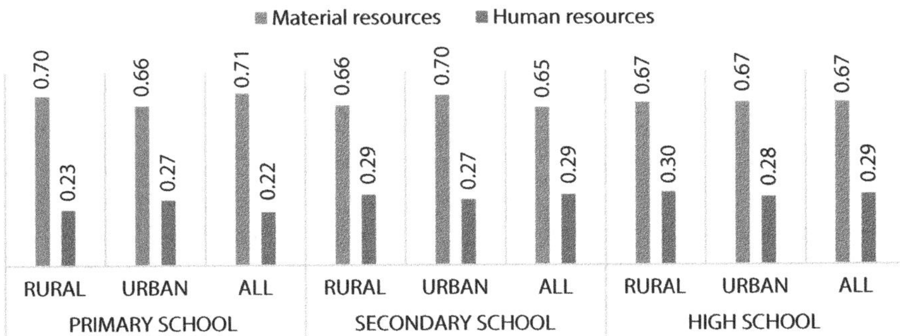

Figure 18.17 Comparison of availability weights for material and human resources.

matrices according to school type and location has been extracted from the MADREN system. The ensuing Table 18.14 offers a synopsis of the CoCoFISo evaluation of the DRENs.

The various rankings obtained using the CoCoFISo method are based on each performance matrix and the weights of the criteria, according to each type of school and its location. It is important to note that rankings vary significantly between different types of schools and across various locations. To comprehend this variation, an examination of the circumstances by school type is necessary.

First, an analysis of the primary school result is in order. A comprehensive evaluation of the all locations reveals that Analamanga DREN and Sofia DREN are the leading contenders. The Atsinanana, Vakinakaratra, Analanjirofo, and Alaotra Mangoro DRENs follow in third and sixth place, respectively. The Atsimo Andrefana and Sava DRENs are positioned in seventh place. The Haute Matsiatra DREN ranks ninth, and the Atsimo Atsinanana DREN is in tenth place. So, the two DRENs Vatovavy and Amoron'i Mania were also ranked eleventh. From the thirteenth to the twenty-third rank, there are successively the DRENs Fitovinany, Androy, Diana, Itasy, Boeny, Anosy, Bongolava, Menabe, Ihorombe, Betsiboka, and Melaky. The simultaneous evaluation of the DRENs across the all location provides insight into the availability of DREN resources. It is noteworthy that the weight accorded to the group of criteria pertaining to the availability of material resources (0,71) is more substantial than that allocated to the other groups of criteria. This observation has a pronounced effect on the final ranking of the DRENs, with those possessing substantial material resources attaining a distinct advantage. This is why the Analamanga and Sofia DRENs are the best DRENs for elementary school in all location, as they have greater material resources at their disposal than the other

Table 18.14 CoCoFISo ranking of DREN by school type and location.

DREN	Primary school			Secondary school			High school		
	Rural	Urban	All	Rural	Urban	All	Rural	Urban	All
SOFIA	1	9	1	2	5	2	4	2	3
ANALAMANGA	2	1	1	1	1	1	1	1	1
ATSINANANA	3	4	3	9	2	7	9	4	8
VAKINAKARATRA	3	5	4	3	5	3	3	9	4
ALAOTRA MANGORO	5	9	6	4	9	4	5	9	5
ANALANJIROFO	5	6	5	6	4	6	6	8	6
ATSIMO ANDREFANA	7	2	7	11	10	10	8	6	6
SAVA	7	12	7	7	10	8	12	6	10
HAUTE MATSIATRA	9	8	9	4	7	4	2	4	2
ATSIMO ATSINANANA	10	18	10	10	17	10	10	18	15
VATOVAVY	11	19	11	12	22	15	15	23	18
AMORON'I MANIA	12	11	11	8	12	9	6	12	9
FITOVINANY	12	13	13	13	14	14	14	14	14
ANDROY	14	17	14	17	18	19	19	17	19
DIANA	15	2	15	15	3	12	18	3	10
ITASY	15	15	16	13	13	13	11	13	12
ANOSY	17	14	18	18	14	17	15	15	16
BOENY	17	7	17	19	7	16	17	11	13
BONGOLAVA	19	23	19	16	21	18	12	19	17
MENABE	20	16	20	20	16	20	20	16	19
IHOROMBE	21	22	21	22	23	22	22	22	22
BETSIBOKA	22	20	22	21	19	21	21	20	21
MELAKY	23	21	23	23	20	23	23	21	23

DRENs. This situation can be verified by analyzing the performance matrix (Figure 18.10). Not only did we observe this situation at primary school, but we also obtained results concerning the distribution of these overall resources between all locations. This leads us to highlight the variation in results between rural and urban areas. This variation in DREN rankings, according to the availability of resources in the primary school located in each location, is shown in Figure 18.18 below.

This illustration has enabled us to observe that some DRENs are ideally positioned in rural location, but less favorably positioned in urban location, and vice versa. But there are also DRENs with the same rank in both locations. A categorization of DRENs can be derived from the aforementioned situation. The initial group categorizes DRENs as being well-placed in rural location but poorly situated in urban location. These are referred to as ***rural-oriented DREN***. The second group encompasses DRENs that demonstrate proficiency in urban location but exhibit deficiencies in rural settings. These are referred to as ***urban-oriented DREN***. Finally, DRENs that demonstrate equivalent performance in both rural and urban contexts are designated as ***balanced DREN***. Table 18.15 lists the DRENs in each category for elementary school.

As we have already presented and analyzed the results of the DREN evaluation for elementary school, let's continue with that for secondary schools.

A comparison of the DREN rankings in Table 18.14 for secondary schools and those for elementary schools reveals that, in all locations, the

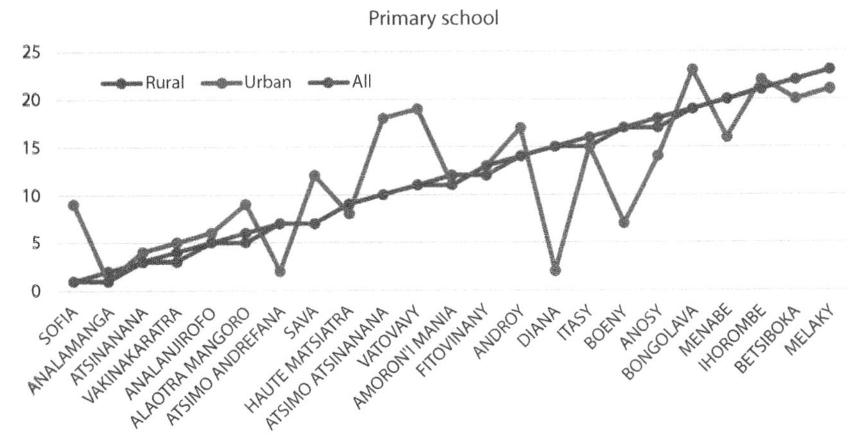

Figure 18.18 Variation in elementary school of DREN rankings by location.

Table 18.15 Categorization of DREN by elementary school resources.

Category	DREN
Rural oriented	Sofia, Atsinanana, Vakinakaratra, Alaotra Mangoro, Analanjirofo, Sava, Atsimo Atsinanana, Vatovavy, Fitovinany, Androy, Bongolava, Ihorombe.
Urban oriented	Analamanga, Atsimo Andrefana, Haute Matsiatra, Amoron'i Mania, Diana, Anosy, Boeny, Menabe, Betsiboka, Melaky.
Balanced	Itasy

DREN rankings exhibit significant variation. CoCoFISo had placed the Analamanga DREN as the best following its availability of resources for the case of secondary schools. The Sofia and Vakinakaratra DRENs followed, with the former ranking second and the latter third. The Alaotra Mangoro and Haute Matsiatra DRENs were positioned in a tie for fourth place. The Analanjirofo, Atsinanana, Sava, and Amoron'i Mania DRENs followed, with the latter three ranking sixth through ninth, respectively. Conversely, the Atsimo Andrefana and Atsimo Atsinanana DRENs occupied the tenth position. The DRENs Diana, Itasy, Fitovinany, Vatovavy, Boeny, Anosy, Bongolava, Androy, Menabe, Betsiboka, Ihorombe, and Melaky are positioned from twelfth to twenty-third place, respectively. The strategic placement of these DRENs by CoCoFISo method has been determined by their respective availability of material and human resources. However, an analysis of the DRENs' rankings in their respective rural and urban locations reveals a general variation in their performance as shown in the Figure 18.19 below.

This variation leads us to classify the DRENs into three categories. In this context of secondary schools, we observe the presence of DREN who ranked so highly in rural location compared to urban of which there are twelve. These DREN belong to the ***rural-oriented*** group. The second group consists of DRENs, which demonstrate higher efficacy in urban areas but lower efficacy in rural areas. These are the ***urban-oriented*** DRENs, of which there are nine in the case of secondary schools. The third category comprises DRENs that demonstrate consistent rankings in both rural and urban contexts. These ***balanced*** DRENs, of which there are two. Table 18.16 provides a comprehensive categorization of DRENs based on their performance in urban and rural contexts.

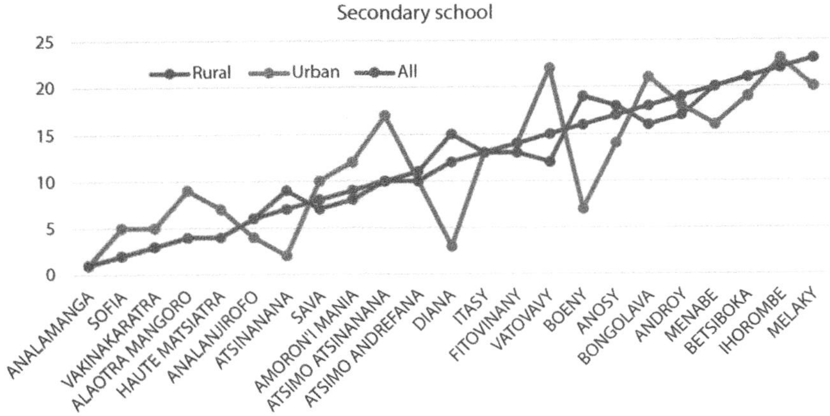

Figure 18.19 Variation in secondary school of DREN rankings by location.

Table 18.16 Categorization of DREN by secondary school resources.

Category	DREN
Rural oriented	Sofia, Vakinakaratra, Alaotra Mangoro, Sava, Haute Matsiatra, Atsimo Atsinanana Vatovavy, Amoron'i Mania, Fitovinany, Androy, Bongolava, Ihorombe.
Urban oriented	Atsinanana, Analanjirofo, Atsimo Andrefana, Diana, Anosy, Boeny, Menabe, Betsiboka, Melaky.
Balanced	Analamanga, Itasy.

In the context of high schools, CoCoFISo had prioritized the Analamanga DREN. The subsequent DRENs, in descending order, are the Haute Matsiatra, Sofia, Vakinakaratra, and Alaotra Mangoro DRENs. Conversely, DREN Atsimo Andrefana and Analanjirofo occupied the sixth position. The eighth and ninth positions were occupied by DREN Atsinanana and Amoron'i Mania, respectively. The tenth position is shared by the Sava and Diana DRENs. From twelfth to eighteenth place, we have DREN Itasy, Boeny, Atsimo Atsinanana, Anosy, Bongolava, and Vatovavy, respectively. Equally, the Androy and Menabe DRENs attained the nineteenth position concurrently. Finally, the Betsiboka, Ihorombe, and Melaky DRENs secured the twenty-first to twenty-third positions. It is imperative to note that this ranking is contingent upon the availability of resources at high schools. However, as in the case of elementary school and secondary school, we noted the difference in ranking of the same DREN from

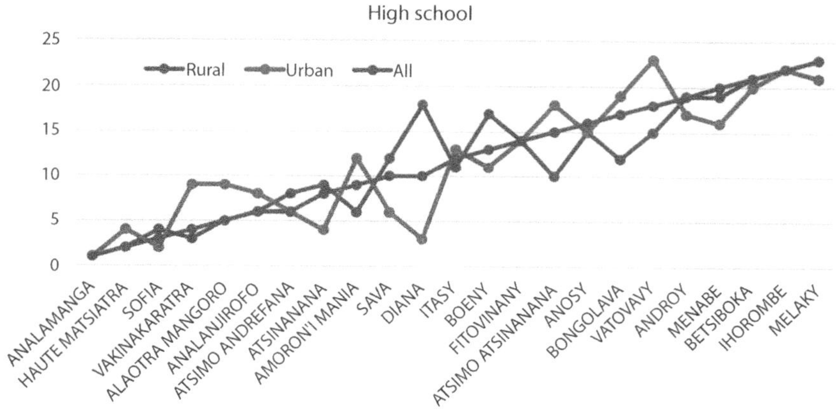

Figure 18.20 Variation in high school of DREN rankings by location.

one location to another, based on the availability of resources at the high schools. Figure 18.20 above illustrates this variation in DREN rankings for rural and urban locations, compared to both together.

The variation in DREN rankings by location allows us to group these DRENs into three categories based on the resources available to the high schools. The initial category comprises eight DRENs with a rural orientation. The second group includes thirteen DRENs in urban-oriented. On the other hand, two DRENs had stable ranks and belonged to the third group. The group membership of each DREN is delineated in the Table 18.17 presentation that follows.

The ranking of DRENs by school type and location was presented using the Centroidous method, which calculated the weight of the criteria an CoCoFISo method evaluated the DRENs. It was observed that the rankings

Table 18.17 Categorization of DREN by high school resources.

Category	DREN
Rural oriented	Vakinakaratra, Alaotra Mangoro, Analanjirofo, Haute Matsiatra, Atsimo Atsinanana Vatovavy, Itasy, Bongolava.
Urban oriented	Sofia, Sava Atsinanana, Atsimo Andrefana, Diana, Anosy, Boeny, Menabe, Betsiboka, Melaky, Amoron'i Mania, Fitovinany, Androy.
Balanced	Analamanga, Ihorombe.

exhibited variability among different schools and locations. Subsequent to this, we will proceed to the second DREN evaluation modality, which employs the MIRA method.

18.4.2.2 DREN Rank Aggregating by MIRA Method

The aim of this second type of result is to summarize the different DREN rankings derived from the CoCoFISo method in order to obtain an overall evaluation of the DRENs, taking into account all three categories of schools. The MIRA additive algorithm will be utilized, as it has been integrated into the MADREN system. The resultant summary is to be presented in three distinct versions: one for rural location, another for urban location, and finally a version combining these two types of locations, but without distinguishing between all types of schools. Let's present these three results in turn.

It is imperative to note that the implementation of the MIRA method necessitates the existence of a rank matrix. The rank matrix employed in this study is derived from Table 18.14, which encompasses all the ranks of elementary schools (PS), secondary schools (SS), and high schools (HS) by location. The subsequent Table 18.18 and Table 18.19 present the ranks matrix from rural and urban location respectively.

Prior to the implementation of the MIRA method, it is recommended to conduct a correlation coefficient test on the rank matrices. This is to ascertain whether the ranks derived from the CoCoFISo method will align in a consistent direction. The outcomes of this test for the case of Kendall's tau are presented in Table 18.20 for the rural rank matrix and in Table 18.21 for the urban rank matrix.

The Kendall rank correlation coefficients obtained exhibited positive rates. In the context of schools located in rural areas, the rates ranged from 0.70 to 0.84, while for those in urban areas, they ranged from 0.73 to 0.84. This finding suggests that school rankings in both contexts are highly correlated and exhibit a similar trend. Notwithstanding, the MIRA method remains applicable.

The comprehensive evaluation of DREN in rural location, encompassing all schools, is presented in Figure 18.21. Additionally, Figure 18.22 presents the comprehensive evaluation of DREN in urban settings, encompassing all schools within this context.

Table 18.18 Rural rank matrix.

DREN	PS	SS	HS
SOFIA	1	2	4
ANALAMANGA	2	1	1
ATSINANANA	3	9	9
VAKINAKARATRA	3	3	3
ALAOTRA MANGORO	5	4	5
ANALANJIROFO	5	6	6
ATSIMO ANDREFANA	7	11	8
SAVA	7	7	12
HAUTE MATSIATRA	9	4	2
ATSIMO ATSINANANA	10	10	10
VATOVAVY	11	12	15
AMORON'I MANIA	12	8	6
FITOVINANY	12	13	14
ANDROY	14	17	19
DIANA	15	15	18
ITASY	15	13	11
ANOSY	17	18	15
BOENY	17	19	17
BONGOLAVA	19	16	12
MENABE	20	20	20
IHOROMBE	21	22	22
BETSIBOKA	22	21	21
MELAKY	23	23	23

Table 18.19 Urban rank matrix.

DREN	PS	SS	HS
ANALAMANGA	1	1	1
ATSIMO ANDREFANA	2	10	6
DIANA	2	3	3
ATSINANANA	4	2	4
VAKINAKARATRA	5	5	9
ANALANJIROFO	6	4	8
BOENY	7	7	11
HAUTE MATSIATRA	8	7	4
SOFIA	9	5	2
ALAOTRA MANGORO	9	9	9
AMORON'I MANIA	11	12	12
SAVA	12	10	6
FITOVINANY	13	14	14
ANOSY	14	14	15
ITASY	15	13	13
MENABE	16	16	16
ANDROY	17	18	17
ATSIMO ATSINANANA	18	17	18
VATOVAVY	19	22	23
BETSIBOKA	20	19	20
MELAKY	21	20	21
IHOROMBE	22	23	22
BONGOLAVA	23	21	19

Table 18.20 Rural Kendall rank correlation.

Rural		Kendall's tau
PS	SS	0,83
PS	HS	0,70
SS	HS	0,84

Table 18.21 Urban Kendall rank correlation.

Urban		Kendall's tau
PS	SS	0,84
PS	HS	0,77
SS	HS	0,84

DREN's ranking

MIRA rank aggregation

Rural location for all establishments

DREN	Rank sum	Rank
ANALAMANGA	4	1
SOFIA	7	2
VAKINAKARATRA	9	3
ALAOTRA MANGORO	14	4
HAUTE MATSIATRA	15	5
ANALANJIROFO	17	6
ATSINANANA	21	7
AMORON'I MANIA	26	8
ATSIMO ANDREFANA	26	8
SAVA	26	8
ATSIMO ATSINANANA	30	11
VATOVAVY	38	12
ITASY	39	13
FITOVINANY	39	13
BONGOLAVA	47	15
DIANA	48	16
ANDROY	50	17
ANOSY	50	17
BOENY	53	19
MENABE	60	20
BETSIBOKA	64	21
IHOROMBE	65	22
MELAKY	69	23

Figure 18.21 Overall assessment of DREN in rural.

DREN's ranking
MIRA rank aggregation

Urban location for all establishments

DREN	Rank sum	Rank
ANALAMANGA	3	1
DIANA	8	2
ATSINANANA	10	3
SOFIA	16	4
ANALANJIROFO	18	5
ATSIMO ANDREFANA	18	5
HAUTE MATSIATRA	19	7
VAKINAKARATRA	19	7
BOENY	25	9
ALAOTRA MANGORO	27	10
SAVA	28	11
AMORON'I MANIA	35	12
ITASY	41	13
FITOVINANY	41	13
ANOSY	43	15
MENABE	48	16
ANDROY	52	17
ATSIMO ATSINANANA	53	18
BETSIBOKA	59	19
MELAKY	62	20
BONGOLAVA	63	21
VATOVAVY	64	22
IHOROMBE	67	23

Figure 18.22 Overall assessment of DREN in urban.

In order to verify the aggregation of the ranks obtained from the MIRA method, it is recommended to carry out a correlation test of the ranks with those obtained in the rank matrix. Accordingly, Kendall's rank correlation coefficient was calculated and presented in Table 18.22 for rural location and Table 18.23 for urban location, respectively.

Table 18.22 Rural Kendall's rank correlation of MIRA.

Rural		Kendall's tau
MIRA+	PS	0,85
	SS	0,96
	HS	0,86

Table 18.23 Rural Kendall's rank correlation of MIRA.

Urban		Kendall's tau
MIRA +	PS	0,88
	SS	0,93
	HS	0,89

The aggregation of ranks obtained using the MIRA method is confirmed in both locations, as evidenced by the proximity of these rates to 1.

The DREN aggregated ranks by MIRA method illustrate the availability of resources in primary, secondary, and high schools, collectively, according to their geographical location. In all rural areas, the top seven DRENs are Analamanga, Sofia, Vakinakaratra, Alaotra Mangoro, Haute Matsiatra, Analanjirofo, and Atsinanana. Conversely, the Amoron'i Mania, Atsimo Andrefana, and Sava DRENs are positioned in eighth place. In contrast, DRENs with limited resources are at the bottom of the scale, with Menabe, Betsiboka, Ihorombe, and Melaky ranking twentieth to twenty-third in this rural environment assessment. In all urban areas, the top four DRENs are Analamanga, Diana, Sofia, and Atsinanana. DRENs in a similar position are Analanjirofo and Atsimo Andrefana, ranked fifth, while Haute Matsiatra and Vakinakaratra are seventh. However, Melaky, Bongolava, Vatovavy, and Ihorombe are the last four urban DRENs, ranking twentieth to twenty-third respectively.

The ensuing findings are of particular interest, as they offer a comprehensive overview of the DRENs by taking a holistic approach to the three schools. The evaluation has been presented by location in order to understand the strengths and weaknesses of the DRENs based on the availability of resources in each location.

The subsequent analysis will focus on the culmination of this evaluation, which is the establishment of the comprehensive ranking of the DRENs, concurrently integrating the resources of primary, secondary, and high schools in all locations. The ensuing discussion will focus on the corresponding rank matrix, as depicted in Table 18.24 below (extract from Table 18.14).

Table 18.24 Rural and urban rank matrix.

DREN	Rural			Urban		
	PS	SS	HS	PS	SS	HS
ALAOTRA MANGORO	5	4	5	9	9	9
AMORON'I MANIA	12	8	6	11	12	12
ANALAMANGA	2	1	1	1	1	1
ANALANJIROFO	5	6	6	6	4	8
ANDROY	14	17	19	17	18	17
ANOSY	17	18	15	14	14	15
ATSIMO ANDREFANA	7	11	8	2	10	6
ATSIMO ATSINANANA	10	10	10	18	17	18
ATSINANANA	3	9	9	4	2	4
BETSIBOKA	22	21	21	20	19	20
BOENY	17	19	17	7	7	11
BONGOLAVA	19	16	12	23	21	19
DIANA	15	15	18	2	3	3
FITOVINANY	12	13	14	13	14	14
HAUTE MATSIATRA	9	4	2	8	7	4
IHOROMBE	21	22	22	22	23	22
ITASY	15	13	11	15	13	13
MELAKY	23	23	23	21	20	21
MENABE	20	20	20	16	16	16
SAVA	7	7	12	12	10	6
SOFIA	1	2	4	9	5	2
VAKINAKARATRA	3	3	3	5	5	9
VATOVAVY	11	12	15	19	22	23

Table 18.25 Rural and urban Kendall rank correlation.

School and location		Kendall's tau
PS RUR	SS RUR	0,83
PS RUR	HS RUR	0,70
PS RUR	PS URB	0,53
PS RUR	SS URB	0,57
PS RUR	HS URB	0,55
PS URB	SS URB	0,84
PS URB	HS URB	0,77
SS RUR	HS RUR	0,84
SS RUR	PS URB	0,47
SS RUR	SS URB	0,54
SS RUR	HS URB	0,54
SS URB	HS URB	0,84
HS RUR	PS URB	0,49
HS RUR	SS URB	0,52
HS RUR	HS URB	0,53

Given our intention to employ the MIRA rank aggregation approach, an initial step was taken to ascertain the Kendall rank correlation coefficients for the designated ranking matrix. Consequently, Table 18.25 presents these coefficients as a function of each school's ranking in all localities.

We have observed that these rates are all positive, ranging from 0.47 to 0.85. In this way, we are able to apply the MIRA technique to arrive at the final evaluation of these DRENs. As a result, the MADREN system produced this assessment, which is illustrated in Figure 18.23 below.

To confirm this final MIRA ranking of the DRENs, we checked the Kendall rank correlation coefficient of the latter against the rank matrix just used to obtain it. Table 18.26 below shows the results of these correlation coefficients.

Given the positivity of these coefficients and their substantial values, the final DREN rankings determined by the MIRA method are substantiated. These rankings illustrate the accessibility of resources following DREN across all schools and locations. Consequently, across all the resources examined in this study, the Analamanga DREN stands out as the best in Madagascar. The DRENs of Sofia, Vakinakaratra, Atsinanana, Haute Matsiatra, Analanjirofo, Alaotra Mangoro, Atsimo Andrefana, Sava, and Diana are then ranked from second to tenth. Conversely, the DRENs of Menabe, Bongolava, Betsiboka, Melaky, and Ihorombe are positioned at the lower end of the spectrum, occupying the nineteenth to twenty-third

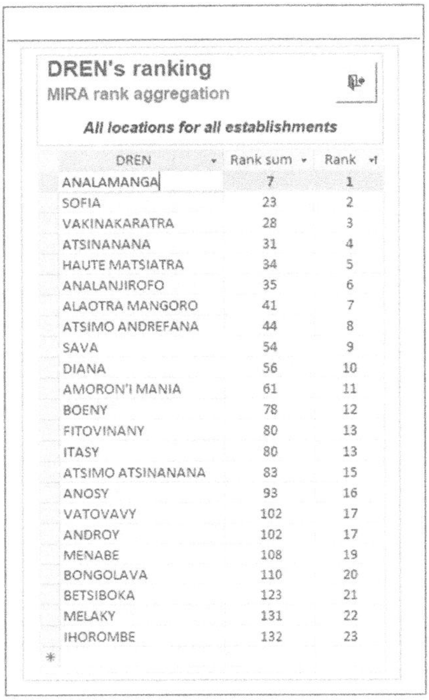

DREN's ranking

MIRA rank aggregation

All locations for all establishments

DREN	Rank sum	Rank
ANALAMANGA	7	1
SOFIA	23	2
VAKINAKARATRA	28	3
ATSINANANA	31	4
HAUTE MATSIATRA	34	5
ANALANJIROFO	35	6
ALAOTRA MANGORO	41	7
ATSIMO ANDREFANA	44	8
SAVA	54	9
DIANA	56	10
AMORON'I MANIA	61	11
BOENY	78	12
FITOVINANY	80	13
ITASY	80	13
ATSIMO ATSINANANA	83	15
ANOSY	93	16
VATOVAVY	102	17
ANDROY	102	17
MENABE	108	19
BONGOLAVA	110	20
BETSIBOKA	123	21
MELAKY	131	22
IHOROMBE	132	23

Figure 18.23 DREN final ranking by MIRA.

Table 18.26 Kendall rank correlation coefficient of the MIRA+ method.

Rural and urban		Kendall's tau
MIRA+	PS RUR	0,77
	SS RUR	0,75
	HS RUR	0,71
	PS URB	0,72
	SS URB	0,79
	HS URB	0,78

positions, respectively, in this comprehensive evaluation of Madagascar's DRENs.

However, it is imperative to comprehend the orientation of the DRENs in relation to the resources at their disposal. This variability arises from the manner in which the Ministry of National Education and the Malagasy State allocate resources, which exhibits variation among DRENs and across different geographical locations. The Figure 18.24 below shows the variation in DREN rankings for all schools by location.

Subsequent to a thorough examination of the outcomes of rank aggregation employing the MIRA method, it is feasible to categorize the DRENs into three discrete groups. The first group, comprising 39% of the total, is focused on rural areas. The second group, with 48% of the total, is focused on urban areas. The third group, with 13% of the total, has balanced resources. The following illustration provides an overview of this DREN trend. The Table 18.27 below summarizes the final categorization of these DRENs according to the result obtained by the MIRA.

This orientation of the DREN could serve as a potential tool to help the manager make decisions concerning resource allocation within the Ministry in charge of National Education. We now turn to the discussion and conclusion of this study.

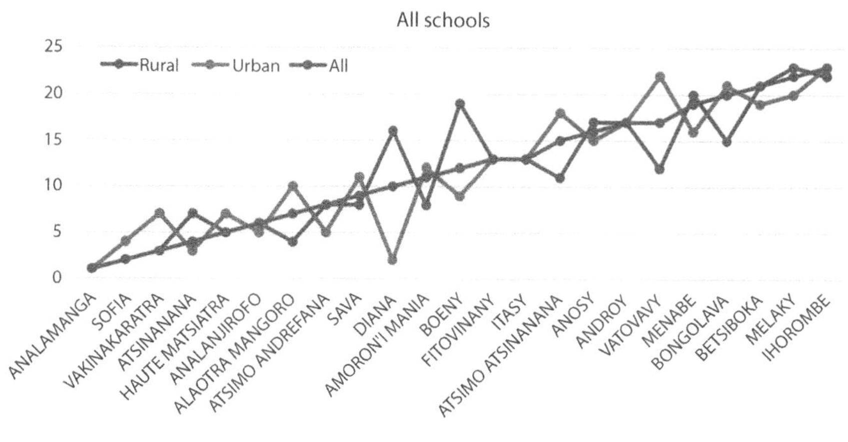

Figure 18.24 Variation in DREN according to rank aggregated by MIRA.

Table 18.27 Categorization of DREN by all schools' resources in all locations.

Category	DREN
Rural oriented	Sofia, Vakinakaratra, Alaotra Mangoro, Amoron'i Mania, Sava, Atsimo Atsinanana, Vatovavy, Bongolava, Ihorombe.
Urban oriented	Haute Matsiatra, Analanjirofo, Atsinanana, Atsimo Andrefana, Itasy, Diana, Anosy, Boeny, Menabe, Betsiboka, Melaky.
Balanced	Analamanga, Fitovinany, Androy.

18.5 Discussion and Conclusion

18.5.1 Discussion

Giving to the result of the CoCoFISo method, the evaluation of DRENs in terms of resources in primary schools revealed that their rankings vary from rural to urban contexts. However, it was observed that the rank of DRENs in both location is contingent on their position in the rural location. In essence, for the case of primary schools, the rank of a DREN in rural areas is indicative of its performance in these settings in general, and vice versa. A case in point is Atsinanana DREN, which ranked third in rural areas, fourth in urban areas, and maintained its third position overall for both environments. A parallel example is Diana DREN, which ranked fifteenth in rural areas, second in urban areas, and maintained its fifteenth position overall for both locations.

The same context applies to the evaluation of DRENs for colleges, whose rankings vary according to location. Furthermore, the position of DREN in different localities is strongly influenced by its rural ranking. For instance, Atsinanana DREN is ranked ninth in the rural sector, second in the urban sector, and seventh overall across both environments. Conversely, Diana DREN occupies the fifteenth position in the rural sector, the third position in the urban sector, and the twelfth position overall across both types of localities.

A comparison of DREN evaluations between the two previous establishments reveals no significant disparities when considering high schools. However, there is a fluctuation in DREN positions depending on location. Consequently, DRENs' assessments of resource availability in high schools are influenced by their rural location. For instance, Atsinanana DREN occupies the ninth position in rural areas, the fourth position in urban areas, and the eighth position in both environments. Equally, Diana DREN rankings are eighteenth in a rural context, third in an urban context, and tenth overall for both locations.

These variations in rankings have led us to propose three distinct categories for grouping DRENs. DRENs with high rural rankings but low urban rankings are referred to as rural-oriented DRENs. The second category groups those with high urban rankings but low rural rankings, referred to as urban-oriented DRENs. The third group identifies DRENs that have similar rankings in both locations, known as balanced DRENs. Consequently, twelve out of twenty-three DREN maintain constant orientations in primary, secondary and high schools. For instance, DREN Vakinakaratra and DREN Alaotra Mangoro are rural-oriented, while Atsimo Andrefana DREN and Diana DREN are urban-oriented. The remaining eleven DRENs fall into diverse orientations, categorized by school type. For instance, Atsinanana DREN adopts a rural orientation for primary schools, but an urban orientation for secondary and high schools. Itasy DREN exhibits a rural orientation in primary schools, belongs to the balanced group in secondary schools, and changes to the urban orientation in high schools.

To summarize these rankings, the MIRA method was employed to combine these positions. The objective of this approach was to ascertain the comprehensive DREN ranking, encompassing all educational institutions. The application of the MIRA method yielded three conclusions regarding the overall assessment of DREN in rural, urban, and combined locations. For all these options, Analamanga DREN is identified as the leading institution. In the rural context, DRENs Sofia and Vakinakaratra ranked second and third, respectively, while in the urban setting, DRENs Diana and Atsinanana ranked second and third, respectively. In deduction, the final ranking, which combined the three schools and two locations, showed that the Sofia, Vakinakaratra, Atsinanana, and Haute Matsiatra DRENs occupied second to fifth place, respectively. This comprehensive evaluation underscores the persistent dominance of the top three DRENs in rural areas, as evidenced by their consistent leadership in the final ranking across all schools and locations. We also set out the final orientations of the DRENs, whether rural, urban, or balanced.

Why is it relevant to understand DREN rankings by school type and location, as well as overall DREN rankings taking all schools and locations into consideration?

This research will provide a relevant indication of the availability of resources in schools under the responsibility of Madagascar's Ministry of National Education. For instance, it has demonstrated that the group of criteria related to the availability of material resources has a more significant weight. This finding suggests that DRENs with greater material resources may have a competitive advantage over those with fewer resources. Consequently, this study underscores the disparity in resource allocation among schools under the purview of DRENs. The assessment of the resource availability situation within a DREN can be made on the basis of its final ranking versus its rankings by school type and location. To illustrate this point, consider the example of DREN Atsinanana shows by Figure 18.25 below.

Consequently, by knowing the specific assessment situation of each DREN, the Malagasy State, through the Ministry in charge of National Education, will be able to increase the availability of resources within a given DREN. Let's consider again the case of Atsinanana DREN illustrated in Figure 18.25 below. Given that this DREN ranks 4th in its final ranking among all schools and locations, an additional allocation of resources could propel it to the level of the best DREN (DREN Analamanga). On the basis of this overall ranking, taking all schools together, we note that Atsinanana DREN stands out for its excellent performance at primary level (3rd), but is less well placed at secondary (7th) and high school level (8th). So, where exactly should we be boosting resources, at secondary and high schools? If we now look at locations, we see that Atsinanana DREN ranks 3rd among all schools in urban areas, but 7th in rural areas. It's obvious, then, that the increase in resources will have to be achieved in the rural context. This circumstance is defensible, because we note that in rural areas, as far as secondary and high schools are concerned, the Atsinanana

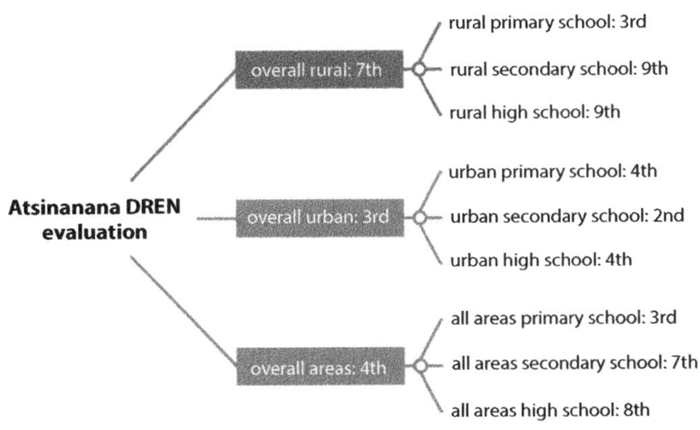

Figure 18.25 Assessment of Atsinanana DREN.

DREN ranks 9th. So, when the State chooses to provide more resources to the Atsinanana DREN for middle and high schools in rural areas, the situation will improve.

By evaluating each DREN in this manner, this study will serve as a decision-making instrument in the context of resource allocation among DRENs.

18.5.2 Conclusion

This study underscores the significance of a multi-criteria decision support system in addressing a prevalent challenge encountered by managerial personnel. The objective of this research is to furnish decision support for the allocation of resources to primary schools, secondary schools, and high schools under the authority of the Regional Directorate of National Education in Madagascar. To this end, the latter were evaluated based on nine criteria focusing on the availability of human and material resources. To comprehensively address these criteria, we have developed a multi-criteria decision support system called MADREN. The system under consideration offers two options for evaluating DRENs. The first approach is contingent upon the school type and its geographical location, while the second is an overall evaluation of the DRENs. MADREN, in its capacity as a multi-criteria decision support system, employs multi-criteria methods. Initially, the Centroidous method is used to determine the importance of criteria, while the CoCoFISo method is implemented to rank the DRENs by school type and location. These approaches are dedicated to the initial evaluation of DRENs. Subsequently, the MIRA method compiles the various ranks of each school category according to location to establish an overall evaluation of the DRENs. This comprehensive approach is instrumental in deriving the final DREN rankings.

The findings suggest that the MADREN experiment has been successful. The Centroidous method was employed to calculate the weights of the criteria according to the nine distinct performance matrices associated with the three school categories and the three location options. Consequently, the set of criteria pertaining to the availability of material resources possessed a weight that exceeded twice that of the group of criteria concerning the availability of human resources in all versions of the matrices. Accordingly, the CoCoFISo method assigned DRENs giving to the order of priority of the criteria and the availability of resources at the DRENs, considering both the type of school and its location. The MIRA method then aggregated the various DREN rankings resulting from the CoCoFISo method.

The experiment focused on the Malagasy context in public primary, secondary and high schools for the 2022-2023 school year. The findings indicated MADREN's capacity to tackle the issue of DREN evaluation. For future research, it would be worthwhile to consider the situation of private schools for comparison with that of the public sector. Additionally, the integration of artificial intelligence algorithms into MADREN could facilitate the prediction of resource allocation to each DREN, with the aim of aligning the best DREN's situation.

Highlights

- Centroidous, CoCoFISo, and MIRA methods have made it possible to assess the situation of public schools in Madagascar;
- MADREN software, which implements these hybrid methods, facilitates the evaluation of the Regional Directorates of National Education based on the availability of resources;
- Initially, different regional directorate ranks were obtained by school type (primary, secondary and high schools) and location (urban, rural, all);
- Overall ranking of regional directorate was obtained by aggregating the different rankings;
- To help the Ministry of National Education allocate resources fairly among schools, the use of MADREN is recommended.

AI disclosure statement: The author confirms that no artificial intelligence (AI)-generated content or AI-assisted writing tools were used in the preparation of this chapter (including summaries and the abstract). All text, analysis, and conclusions are the result of the author's original work.

References

1. Perrenoud, P., L'évaluation des établissements scolaires, un nouvel avatar de l'illusion scientiste?, 1994. Retrieved March 17, 2025, from https://www.unige.ch/fapse/SSE/teachers/perrenoud/php_main/php_1994/1994_16.html.
2. Thornton, K., A Quantitative Study Comparing Traditional High Schools and High Schools Implementing Freshman Academies in the State of Tennessee, Electronic Theses and Dissertations, 2009, Retrieved from https://dc.etsu.edu/etd/1838.

3. Guay, R. and Riopel, M., L'évaluation des établissements scolaires – le cas du collégial. *Rev. Des. Sci. Éduc.*, *47*, 1, 165–200, 2021, https://doi.org/10.7202/1081476ar.
4. Ahmed, H., Edwards, D.J., Lai, J.H.K., Roberts, C., Debrah, C., Owusu-Manu, D.-G., Thwala, W.D., Post Occupancy Evaluation of School Refurbishment Projects: Multiple Case Study in the UK. *Buildings*, *11*, 4, 169, 2021, https://doi.org/10.3390/buildings11040169.
5. Meena, D.K., Tripathi, R., Agrawal, S., An evaluation of primary schools and its accessibility using GIS techniques: a case study of Prayagraj district, India. *GeoJournal*, *88*, 2, 1921–1951, 2023, https://doi.org/10.1007/s10708-022-10715-3.
6. Murat, S., Kazan, H., Coskun, S.S., An Application for Measuring Performance Quality of Schools by Using the PROMETHEE Multi-Criteria Decision-Making Method. *Procedia Social Behav. Sci.*, *195*, 729–738, 2015, https://doi.org/10.1016/j.sbspro.2015.06.344.
7. Li, P., Edalatpanah, S.A., Sorourkhah, A., Yaman, S., Kausar, N., An Integrated Fuzzy Structured Methodology for Performance Evaluation of High Schools in a Group Decision-Making Problem. *Systems*, *11*, 3, 159, 2023, https://doi.org/10.3390/systems11030159.
8. Mancini, P. and Marcarelli, G., A multi-criteria approach for ranking Italian high schools. *Qual. Quant.*, *57*, 6, 5533–5549, 2023, https://doi.org/10.1007/s11135-023-01621-y.
9. MEN, M., Annuaire statistique national 2022-2023, 2023. Retrieved November 11, 2024, from https://www.instat.mg/p/men-annuaire-statistique-de-leducation-2022-2023.
10. Taherdoost, H. and Madanchian, M., Multi-Criteria Decision Making (MCDM) Methods and Concepts. *Encyclopedia*, *3*, 1, 77–87, 2023, https://doi.org/10.3390/encyclopedia3010006.
11. Kizielewicz, B., Shekhovtsov, A., Więckowski, J., Wątróbski, J., Sałabun, W., The Compromise-COMET Method for Identifying an Adaptive Multi-Criteria Decision Model. *IEEE Access*, *12*, 157083–157106, 2024, https://doi.org/10.1109/ACCESS.2024.3485798.
12. Mendoza Luis Fernando, M., Perez Escobedo, J.L., Azzaro-Pantel, C., Pibouleau, L., Domenech, S., Aguilar-Lasserre, A., Selecting the best portfolio alternative from a hybrid multiobjective GA-MCDM approach for New Product Development in the pharmaceutical industry, in: *2011 IEEE Symposium on Computational Intelligence in Multicriteria Decision-Making (MDCM)*, pp. 159–166, 2011, https://doi.org/10.1109/SMDCM.2011.5949271.
13. Puška, A., Štilić, A., Pamučar, D., Božanić, D., Nedeljković, M., Introducing a Novel multi-criteria Ranking of Alternatives with Weights of Criterion (RAWEC) model. *MethodsX*, *12*, 102628, 2024, https://doi.org/10.1016/j.mex.2024.102628.

14. Sepehri, M., Linh, N.T.T., Pouya, H.N., Bahramloo, R., Sadeghian, J., Ghermezcheshme, B., Thanh, P.N., Developing a new multi-criteria decision-making for flood prioritization of sub-watersheds using concept of D numbers. *Acta Geophys.*, *72*, 3, 2027–2039, 2024, https://doi.org/10.1007/s11600-023-01119-z.
15. Keskes, M.A., Zouari, A., Houssin, R., Dhouib, D., Renaud, J., A new multi-criteria, multi-phase, and multi-decision makers' approach to the agricultural sustainability problem. *Environ. Syst. Dec.*, *44*, 2, 433–455, 2024, https://doi.org/10.1007/s10669-023-09946-7.
16. Kamari, M.S.M., Rodzi, Z.M., Kamis, N.H., Pythagorean Neutrosophic Method Based on the Removal Effects of Criteria (PNMEREC): An Innovative Approach for Establishing Objective Weights in Multi-Criteria Decision-Making Challenges. *Malays. J. Fundam. Appl. Sci.*, *21*, 1, 1678–1696, 2025, https://doi.org/10.11113/mjfas.v21n1.3600.
17. Kumari, A. and Acherjee, B., A novel hybrid multi-criteria decision methodology for assessing tool materials in friction stir welding process. *Int. J. Interact. Des. Manuf. (IJIDeM)*, *18*, 7, 4963–4986, 2024, https://doi.org/10.1007/s12008-024-01783-5.
18. Tian, H., Zhang, S., Garg, H., Liu, X., An extended SECA-GDM method considering flexible linguistic scale optimization and its application in occupational health and safety risk assessment. *Alexandria Eng. J.*, *88*, 317–330, 2024, https://doi.org/10.1016/j.aej.2024.01.026.
19. Vinogradova-Zinkevič, I., Centroidous Method for Determining Objective Weights. *Mathematics*, *12*, 14, 2269, 2024, https://doi.org/10.3390/math12142269.
20. Rasoanaivo, R.G., Yazdani, M., Zaraté, P., Fateh, A., Combined compromise for ideal solution (CoCoFISo): A multi-criteria decision-making based on the CoCoSo method algorithm. *Expert Syst. Appl.*, 124079, 2024, https://doi.org/10.1016/j.eswa.2024.124079.
21. Chang, H., Decision Algorithm for Digital Media and Intangible-Heritage Digitalization Using Picture Fuzzy Combined Compromise for Ideal Solution in Uncertain Environments. *Symmetry*, *17*, 3, 443, 2025, https://doi.org/10.3390/sym17030443.
22. Sen, H. and Toksoy, M.S., Green Supplier Selection with CoCoFISo-G. *Eurasia Proc. Sci. Technol. Eng. Math.*, *32*, 257–265, 2024, https://doi.org/10.55549/epstem.1598450.
23. Rasoanaivo, R.G. and Zaraté, P., A rank aggregating method based on several multi-criteria methodologies "minimum of ranks": a case study for student's room allocation. *Int. J. Decis. Support Syst.*, *5*, 1, 75–101, 2024, https://doi.org/10.1504/IJDSS.2024.137246.
24. Li, Y., Pérez, I.J., Cabrerizo, F.J., Garg, H., Morente-Molinera, J.A., A belief rule-based classification system using fuzzy unordered rule induction algorithm. *Inf. Sci.*, *667*, C, 2024, https://doi.org/10.1016/j.ins.2024.120462.

25. Sirbiladze, G., Garg, H., Khutsishvili, I., Midodashvili, B., Gugunava, O., Associated Probabilities' Aggregations in Fuzzy Collaborative Filtering Recommender System Prediction. *Int. J. Fuzzy Syst.*, *27*, 1, 204–236, 2025, https://doi.org/10.1007/s40815-024-01772-6.
26. Rasoanaivo, R.G. and Zaraté, P., SAGeLogE: A Decision Support System for Students' Accommodation Management. *J. Comput. Commun.*, *12*, 3, 107–145, 2024, https://doi.org/10.4236/jcc.2024.123008.
27. Alam Bhuiyan, M.M. and Hammad, A., A Hybrid Multi-Criteria Decision Support System for Selecting the Most Sustainable Structural Material for a Multistory Building Construction. *Sustainability*, *15*, 4, 3128, 2023, https://doi.org/10.3390/su15043128.
28. Huang, H. and Burgherr, P., MCDA Calculator: A Streamlined Decision Support System for Multi-criteria Decision Analysis, in: *Decision Support Systems XIV. Human-Centric Group Decision, Negotiation and Decision Support Systems for Societal Transitions*, S.P. Duarte, A. Lobo, B. Delibašić, D. Kamissoko (Eds.), pp. 31–45, Springer Nature Switzerland, Cham, 2024, https://doi.org/10.1007/978-3-031-59376-5_3.
29. Naik, M.G., Kishore, R., Dehmourdi, S.A.M., Modeling A Multi-Criteria Decision Support System for Prequalification Assessment of Construction Contractors Using CRITIC and EDAS Models. *Oper. Res. Eng. Sci. Theory Appl.*, *4*, 2, 79–101, 2021, https://doi.org/10.31181/oresta20402079n.
30. Paradowski, B., Shekhovtsov, A., Bączkiewicz, A., Kizielewicz, B., Sałabun, W., Similarity Analysis of Methods for Objective Determination of Weights in Multi-Criteria Decision Support Systems. *Symmetry*, *13*, 10, 1874, 2021, https://doi.org/10.3390/sym13101874.
31. Rasoanaivo, R.G. and Tata, J.A., A New Technique of Ranking Madagascar's Universities Using CoCoFISo Method in a Multi-Criteria Decision Support System: MadUrank. *Int. J. Sci. Res. Comput. Sci. Eng.*, *12*, 4, 18–31, 2024.

Part VII

ADVANCED FUZZY AND SOFT COMPUTING TECHNIQUES

19

Interval Valued Fermatean Fuzzy Emergency Decision-Making Method with Weighted Distance-Based Approximation and Similarity Measures

Murat Kirişci

Istanbul University-Cerrahpaşa, Cerrahpaşa, Medicine Faculty, Istanbul, Türkiye

Abstract

When making decisions to protect people's lives, simple but robust solutions with a high degree of certainty are sought. Unfortunately, there is no simple technical decision-making method for selecting protective actions. Simple rules do not work in all conditions or even for a wide set of conditions. A checklist approach is practical but probably will not make the best decision. This study presents a decision support mechanism to help select the best shelter construction project based on criteria obtained from the official shelter guide and the necessity of using shelters in emergencies. The selection is made by considering the five basic criteria in the Civil Defense Guidelines and optimizing the construction of the projects by the standards. Ensuring an acceptable shelter meets the safety standards required to prevent disasters and their consequences is important. Valued by intervals, an efficient and adaptable method of capturing indeterminacy is using the interval form of a Fermatean fuzzy set, represented by membership and non-membership. In order to handle specific comparative problems,. this study has used chiefly a novel score function for an interval-valued Fermatean fuzzy number. Then, a novel distance metric has been proposed for interval-valued Fermatean fuzzy sets with several parameters. The objective weights were determined using an entropy metric based on an interval-valued Fermatean fuzzy set. Next, the algorithm for weighted distance-based approximation was applied. The foundation of the weighted distance-based approximation technique is that the best option could be near the negative-ideal solution (AIP-worst plan) and far from the positive-ideal

Email: mkirisci@hotmail.com; murat.kirisci@iuc.edu.tr

Harish Garg (ed.) Decision Support Systems in Smart Computing: Embracing Uncertainty and Challenges, (609–636) © 2026 Scrivener Publishing LLC

solution (PIS-best plan). The characteristics of the developed entropy, distance, and similarity metrics have also been examined. We introduce two interval-valued Fermatean fuzzy decision-making techniques based on multiparametric similarity measure and weighted distance-based approximation. Since the establishment and improvement of urban emergency shelter systems have become indispensable in the new era to guarantee the safety and development of cities, the results obtained with the proposed methods facilitate the selection of the most appropriate shelter project according to the regulation criteria. Considering the situations that necessitate staying in the shelter, the selected project should be designed to protect human life and provide a comfortable life for a while. In the decision-making problem, the projects were evaluated using the criteria, and the projects that could protect healthy, sound, solid, and hygienic conditions were selected.

***Keywords*:** Entropy, interval-valued Fermatean fuzzy set, weighted distance-based approximation, similarity measures

19.1 Introduction

Making significant judgments under time constraints, uncertainty, and urgency—often with insufficient information—is known as emergency decision-making, or EDM. This DM type is essential when quick action is needed to stop harm, lower risks, or deal with unforeseen circumstances. In EDM, decisions must be made quickly and frequently in seconds or minutes. Information could be unclear, lacking, or changing quickly. Decisions might have significant repercussions, like preventing harm, saving lives, or safeguarding property. Decision-makers frequently work under extreme pressure, which affects their ability to think clearly. Teams or cooperation between several organizations, including first responders, governmental organizations, or healthcare practitioners, are frequently involved in EDs.

EDM manages mass reactions to artificial or natural disasters, including industrial accidents, storms, earthquakes, and terrorist attacks. Decisions can affect entire nations, regions, or villages during a disaster. The government, non-governmental organizations, and the corporate sector must collaborate. Rapid situational change necessitates constant evaluation and flexibility.

In classical decision theory, a decision can be defined as a set of decision alternatives, states of nature, and a utility function that assigns each pair of decisions, specifies a result, and ranks the results according to necessity. The DM process, on the other hand, proceeds based on subjective values when there is no precise numerical information. When deciding certainty, the decision maker knows which situation he expects and selects the highest utility decision alternative from the given valid state space. When deciding on risk, the decision maker does not know which situation will occur; he only knows the probability function of the situation. Therefore, this time, the DM becomes more difficult. In certain real-world DM situations, professionals can find it difficult to precisely communicate their thoughts with a certain number due to a lack of knowledge. However, they might be represented by an interval number in unit interval.

An expansion of Fermatean fuzzy sets (FFS) is the concept of IVFFSs. Interval-valued Fermatean fuzzy sets (IVFFS) [15] reflect the degree of hesitation of fuzzy information more logically than FFSs since they define $\mathscr{M}$ and cubic $\mathscr{N}$ using interval-valued data. In contrast, IVFFSs are an extension of IVIFSs and IVPFSs. To have a larger space than IVIFSs and IVPFSs, IVFFSs must have a sum of cubic $\mathscr{M}$ and cubic $\mathscr{N}$ that does not exceed one. Because of the loosened restriction, IVFFSs are more suited to managing more complicated uncertainty than IVIFSs and IVPFSs. As a result, IVFFNs are better at characterizing the nuanced level of uncertainty that decision-makers experience while weighing options and aiding in minimizing information loss.

DM is the process of choosing from multiple options. In other words, DM is the art of making choices. The DM process is a process that aims to solve problems or issues. DM is a process that evaluates the past and makes decisions for the future. Multi-criteria decision-making (MCDM) is the process of assigning values to alternatives by evaluating many criteria together. MCDM represents both an approach and encompasses techniques or methods designed to help people facing problems characterized by multiple, unequal, and conflicting criteria make choices consistent with their value judgments. There is just one goal that the MCDM technique can achieve. The objective is to find the most advantageous and economical solution to the choice dilemma. There are different MCDM studies. For example, the study in [32] reviews the advantages and disadvantages of different DM techniques, specifically in software engineering. David and Alamoodi [5] have presented a bibliometric analysis of research conducted over the last five years concerning MCDM and its application in the energy sector.

The Weighted Distance Based Approximation (WDBA) technique is an important method. This technique takes into account the distance between points. It also helps make more precise and meaningful estimates by assigning weights to different data points. Data science has evolved as a disruptive field, allowing firms to gain important insights from massive amounts of data. However, data scientists encounter two significant challenges in pursuing meaningful information: noise and outliers. Noise refers to random changes or inaccuracies in data, whereas outliers are data points that differ significantly from the mean. To solve these problems, weighting is required, which can reduce the impact of such data and provide more robust results for the model. This is a strong feature of WDBA. WDBA provides more effective learning by better reflecting the structure of the local data. Weight functions can be changed depending on the structure of the data and the problem. This allows the method to be easily adapted to different application areas. In some cases, distances can become meaningless in high-dimensional data, meaning that even minor differences can lead to large distances. WDBA is a suitable method to alleviate this problem. From these explanations, it is understood that WDBA enables obtaining more reliable results by increasing the accuracy and robustness of distance-based models.

Fallout shelters are structures designed to protect people against events such as nuclear explosions, nuclear facility accidents, or the spread of radioactive material. They are constructed based on certain engineering principles. The primary purposes of radioactive fallout shelters are to protect against radiation, to prevent the entry of nuclear fallout particles, and to ensure the long-term survival of people inside. Fallout shelters should be secure structures with thick walls, air filters, water, and food storage. It is recommended that underground construction be done for the best protection, and air tightness is significant. Such a shelter can significantly increase the chance of survival in a nuclear threat. The construction of radioactive fallout shelters is subject to MCDM because it depends on various criteria.

19.1.1 Research Motivation

A. IVFFSs provide greater accuracy and flexibility when managing ambiguous and uncertain data. IVFFSs are crucial in DM scenarios, data processing, and modeling. IVFFSs offer a strong and adaptable instrument for simulating ambiguity and uncertainty, which makes them useful in domains where conventional FSs or other extensions might not be sufficient.

B. To qualify as an MCDM problem, an EDM method selection problem must meet several requirements and alternatives. However, experts who evaluate these problems can only evaluate the qualitative norms linguistically. While MCDM techniques transform these valuations into a numerical structure, fuzzy type logic may handle the ambiguity in linguistic formations.

C. WDBA, defined by Rao and Singh [36], measures the distance between alternatives' best or ideal value and the non-optimal point or worst value. Lastly, an appropriateness index is used to rank the options. The option with the greatest appropriateness index value is ordered last, followed by the lowest value.

D. To calculate the measures such as entropy, distance, and similarity, of two IVFFSs, a unique approach for creating distance and similarity measures that rely on three elements has been described. The different criteria's effect on the options' ranking is also displayed.

19.1.2 Objective of Study

It is essential to build a safe and effective shelter to protect people, their lives, and vital living and non-living values from the impacts of nuclear and conventional weapons, chemical and biological warfare agents, and natural disasters. For this, the choice of method is important, and it is desired that this method is the best. Military officials, engineers, security experts, and public health professionals must choose the most appropriate shelter project to address shelter construction adequately. This procedure can be framed as an MCDM problem, requiring the evaluation of numerous tangible and intangible criteria for shelter-building alternatives and selecting the best technique. The conclusions drawn from implementing these findings can help decision-makers create strategic plan to put workable ideas into practice and encourage the choice of the best shelter-building method. The main objectives can be expressed as follows:

- Determine which criteria should be used to choose shelter-building projects in the nuclear security system.
- To ascertain how significant the weights assigned to the established evaluation criteria are.
- Introducing a new weight counting method to avoid the influence of the objective and subjective aspects.
- To decide which project is most suited for creating a shelter.
- To demonstrate the consistency of the results and compare the suggested strategy with other well-known MCDM techniques.

19.1.3 Originality and Gaps

Because they can occur at any time and output in or potentially output in environmental damage, economic and social harm, or property or human casualties. Public health problems, natural disasters, social security, and accidents are all seen as emergencies since they necessitate the preparation and application of an emergency plan. In addition to causing significant losses of life or property, emergencies can also result in serious environmental harm, societal panic, and even secondary disasters, making it challenging to achieve sustainable development goals. Nuclear shelters are the safest places to be protected from a possible nuclear attack or accident. These shelters protect from radioactive fallout and explosion effects. The materials used during the construction of nuclear shelters are of great importance in terms of the durability and reliability of the shelters. Radioactive material exposure can have major negative effects on one's health. Radioactive shelters provide the best protection against such dangers. These shelters are constructed using materials resistant to exceptionally high radioactive levels. Radioactive fallout shelters are specially designed to minimize leaks and radiation.

This study presents new fuzzy MCDM methods for assessing emergency fallout shelter construction. This approach incorporates the similarity measure and weighted fallout distance-based approximation methods specified by IVFFS. An emergency fallout shelter-build problem can be categorized as an MCDM problem since it has multiple criteria and choices. However, experts evaluating these problems can only evaluate the qualitative criteria linguistically.

In order to prioritize emergency fallout shelter-builds, model the corresponding uncertainty, and maximize their benefits, this work utilizes MCDM methods according to IVFFSs. The listing and assessment of shelter projects to be constructed in order to guard against the negative impacts of radioactive fallout is one pressing topic that the suggested technique tackles.

Research Gap:

- (i) Define weighted distance-based approximation based on IVFFS.
- (ii) Define new weighted distance and similarity measures using IVFFS and examine their properties.
- (iii) To provide new WDBA and MCDM algorithms with similarity measures.

(vi) To determine the effectiveness of projects related to shelters to be built to protect from radioactive fallout according to the determined criteria.
(v) Selecting the best and most effective emergency fallout shelter construction projects using IVFFS.
(vi) The consistency of the results is shown by comparing them with other well-known MCDM techniques.

19.1.4 Contribution

According to the work's methodological section, a system based on IVFFSs has been created to rank the potential for building a shelter for radioactive fallout. A radioactive fallout shelter-build assessment has looked at an MCDM issue. Furthermore, comparison analyses are conducted to confirm the accuracy of the recommended decisions and procedures. The application section clearly shows how much attention is paid to this construction work by listing the successes of the fallout shelter construction projects in solving the problems that endanger human health and safety. However, potential issues may arise.

The main contributions:

1. In order to mitigate the impact of subjective and objective criteria, a novel weight-determining paradigm is put forth.
2. A novel WDBA and information measure (distance, entropy, similarity measures) for IVFFSs is initiated.
3. New algorithms are proposed.
4. With the application example, the applicability, robustness, and precision of MCDM algorithms are obtained.
5. Comparison demonstrates the consistency of the suggested technique.

19.2 Literature

After Zadeh's pioneering work [48], Atanassov [3] added IFS, and Yager [47] developed PFS. IFSs and PFSs exist in the literature. Ejegwa *et al.* [6] identified the disadvantages of FF-type correlation coefficients (CC) in the literature and obtained a novel FFCC method using Spearman's CC method. Garg *et al.* [9] presented a DM environment to work cognitive wireless communication, the model utilized to combine cognitive radio technology with wireless communication systems using the idea of circular-complex-IFSs. In [10], the complex IF-Hamacher Choquet integral average and geometric operators are given by addressing the theory of complex IFSs. A novel distance measure for IFS according to the difference between the cross-evaluation factors' min and max, the $\mathscr{M}$ and $\mathscr{N}$, has been proposed in [11]. The paper of Garg *et al.* [12] has included some developed Dombi operational laws according to circular developed PFSs. The notion of Fibonacci statistical convergence on an IF-normed space has been defined in [16]. Kirisci [17] presented methods with respect to the IF-parametrized SSs and Riesz mean methods. Riaz *et al.* have introduced a new method for changing selection in the healthcare industry's supply chain by presenting a topological evaluation of data in the domain of a circular IFS [38].

Senapati and Yager [43] defined FFS and studied its basic properties. In a short time, FFS began to be used in a vast area: The problem of the best valve for drip irrigation systems with the CoCoSo method using the 2-tuple linguistic FF-weighted averaging operator has been solved [2]. Using an MCDM process, a novel FF-distance measure is introduced to assess insecurity in Nigeria's North-Central Region [7]. Farid *et al.* [8] examined the topological properties of FFSs and improved the FF-CODAS approach. A concept of FFS in a multiset framework is developed to take care of complex DM involving repeated criteria, and the fundamentals of the multiset framework are discussed illustratively [50]. An innovative group DM method characterized by Fermatean fuzzy information has been developed recently, including new similarity and distance measures and aggregation operators [13]. Rong *et al.* [39] proposed an IVFF-FMEA model for risk prioritization by combining the IVFF-Hamy mean operator, IVFF-LOPCOW model, and IVFF-ARAS method, and improved new aggregation operators based on Aczel-Alsina norms [39]. Tan *et al.* [46] created an integrated MCGDM risk investment evaluation framework by combining prospect theory with the MABAC approach in an FF scenario. A novel CCs and weighted CCs have been proposed to appraise the relationship between two FFSs [18]. Four kinds of CCs are given for Fermatean hesitant FSs and IVF hesitant FSs by developing the least common multiple expansion techniques to figure out the problem of different cardinalities of Fermatean hesitant FSs and IVF hesitant FSs [19]. Kiri¸sci [20] proposed a new method to build other similarity measures between FFSs according to cosine similarity and Euclidean distance measures, considering that the cosine measure does not satisfy the axiom of a similarity measure. In [22], the definition of the FF-soft entropy has been presented. In order to help decision-makers handle the physical design and attack risks of autonomous vehicles, evaluate their uncertainty, and control cyber hazards, Kirisci [23] has suggested a new integrated IVFF-based MCDM strategy that combines the AHP, TOPSIS, and MABAC methodologies. The FF-ELECTRE I method for MCGDM has been given by Kirisci *et al.* [24]. A new DM approach is proposed using the cumulative prospect theory and TODIM method based on FFSs with entropy for applying breast cancer risk assessment [27]. In [25], an IVFF-linguistic kernel principal component analysis model is proposed. An integrated MCDM method with of IVFF-based DEMATEL, AHP, and TOPSIS methods is proposed to identify, categorize, and rate multiple risks associated with decentralized finance, and the IVFF-ARAS method is used for performance evaluation and validation [28]. Several new distance metrics for complex FFSs and their weighted counterparts based on the Hausdorff, Hellinger, Euclidean, and Hamming distances have been introduced by Liu *et al.* [29]. Luqman *et al.*'s research [30] aimed to create a new method for multi-objective optimization in the context of hesitant FFSs and a new distance measure. After combining the Hausdorff metric and the Hamming distance, they also developed a framework to measure the difference between hesitation Fermatean fuzziness. In [31], a new FF-Archimedean copula-based Maclaurin symmetric mean operator and similarity measures and an extended COPRAS were utilized for renewable energy source selection. Riaz *et al.* [37] developed an FF-prioritized weighted average and geometric operator. Then, they proposed a new and revolutionary convolutional neural network (CNN) with robust graphics processing units (GPUs) that provides realistic, low-cost, energy-efficient solutions according to real-time camera occupancy detection and recognition techniques across different sensor types. FF-Dombi Generalized Maclaurin Symmetric Mean operators for MCGDM problems have been investigated by Saha *et al.* [40]. Seikh and Mandal [41] have developed IVFF-Dombi weighted averaging (geometric) operators and have presented an integrated DM methodology, which includes PROMETHEE II and SWARA. In [42], a novel MAGDM method integrating SWARA and ARAS based on FSSs has been proposed to determine the most promising renewable energy sources. A novel model for GDM techniques in which experts' preferences can be stated as incomplete FF preference relations has been offered by Simsek and Kirisci [44]. By combining interval-valued sets with fuzzy, IF, and PFS, IVFSs, IFVFSs [4], and IVPFSs [49] were defined, and these new sets played an essential role in solving DM problems. With similar thinking, Jeevaraj defined IVFFS by combining interval-valued sets with FFS [15].

In the study of Peng and Garg [33], a new score function is given for IV-fuzzy soft sets, distance, entropy, and similarity measures are introduced, and algorithms according to WDBA, CODAS, and similarity measures are offered. A mine EDM problem is studied as an application example of these algorithms. Peng and Li [34] gave algorithms for EDM based on multi-parameter similarity measures and WDBA using IVPFS. A mine EDM problem later demonstrates the algorithms' validity by examining the impact of various parameters on the ranking. Hao *et al.* [45] developed the IF-Bayesian network method and combined it with prospect theory to create a new algorithm.

WDBA is a method used in various computational and mathematical applications, particularly in optimization, machine learning, and numerical analysis. It involves approximating a function, value, or solution by considering weighted distances between known data points or reference points. Unlike standard distance-based methods, this method assigns weights to different points, emphasizing some over others based on importance, relevance, or reliability. The method provides flexibility by allowing emphasis on specific data points. Improves approximation accuracy in non-uniform datasets. Can handle uncertainty by adjusting weights dynamically.

19.3 Preliminaries

Definition 3.1. *[43] For ζ_C, $\eta_C \in [0, 1]$ and $0 \le \zeta_C^3 + \eta_C^3 \le 1$, the set $C = \{(a, \zeta_C(a), \eta_C(a)) : a \in \mathscr{E}\}$ is said to be FFS, where $\mathscr{E}$ is an initial set.*

$\theta_C = (1 - \zeta_C^3 + \eta_C^3)^{1/3}$ demonstrate the degree of hesitation.

Definition 3.2. *[15] Consider CIS$[0, 1]$, whisch is the set of all closed subintervals of unit interval. Then, $C = \{(a, \zeta_C(a), \eta_C(a)) : a \in \mathscr{E}\}$ is called IVFFS, where $\zeta_C(a), \eta_C(a) \in \mathscr{I}[0,1]$ with $0 < \sup_a(\zeta_C(a))^3 + \sup_a(\eta_C(a))^3 \le 1$.*

IVFFS can also be illustrated as follows.

$$C = \{(a, [\zeta_{C_L}(a), \zeta_{C_U}(a)], [\eta_{C_L}(a), \eta_{C_U}(a)]) : a \in \mathscr{E}\}.$$

Here, $0 \le (\zeta_{C_U}(a))^3 + (\eta_{C_U}(a))^3 \le 1$ and $\theta_C = [\theta_{C_L}, \theta_{C_U}] = [(1 - \zeta_{C_L}^3 + \eta_{C_L}^3)^{1/3}, (1 - \zeta_{C_U}^3 + \eta_{C_U}^3)^{1/3}]$.

Definition 3.3. *[15] For IVFFSs $C = ([\zeta_{C_L}(a), \zeta_{C_U}(a)], [\eta_{C_L}(a), \eta_{C_U}(a)])$,*

$$C_1 = ([\zeta_{C_{1L}}(a), \zeta_{C_{1U}}(a)], [\eta_{C_{1L}}(a), \eta_{C_{1U}}(a)],$$
$$C_2 = ([\zeta_{C_{2L}}(a), \zeta_{C_{2U}}(a)], [\eta_{C_{2L}}(a), \eta_{C_{2U}}(a)],$$

- $C_1 \cup C_2 = ([\max(\zeta_{C_{1L}}, \zeta_{C_{2L}}), \max(\zeta_{C_{1U}}, \zeta_{C_{2U}})], [\min(\eta_{C_{1L}}, \eta_{C_{2L}}), \min(\eta_{C_{1U}}, \eta_{C_{2U}})])$
- $C_1 \cap C_2 = ([\min(\zeta_{C_{1L}}, \zeta_{C_{2L}}), \min(\zeta_{C_{1U}}, \zeta_{C_{2U}})], [\max(\eta_{C_{1L}}, \eta_{C_{2L}}), \max(\eta_{C_{1U}}, \eta_{C_{2U}})])$
- $C^c = ([\eta_{C_L}, \eta_{C_U}], [\zeta_{C_L}, \zeta_{C_U}])$
- $C_1 \oplus C_2 = \left(\left[\sqrt[3]{(\zeta_{C_{1L}}(a))^3 + (\zeta_{C_{2L}}(a))^3 - (\zeta_{C_{1L}}(a))^3 \cdot (\zeta_{C_{2L}}(a))^3}, \sqrt[3]{(\zeta_{C_{1U}}(a))^3 + (\zeta_{C_{2U}}(a))^3 - (\zeta_{C_{1U}}(a))^3 \cdot (\zeta_{C_{2U}}(a))^3}\right], [\eta_{C_{1L}}\eta_{C_{2L}}, \eta_{C1U}\eta_{C_{2U}}]\right)$
- $C_1 \otimes C_2 = \left([\zeta_{C_{1L}}\zeta_{C_{2L}}, \zeta_{C_{1U}}\zeta_{C_{2U}}], \left[\sqrt[3]{(\eta_{C_{1L}}(a))^3 + (\eta_{C_{2L}}(a))^3 - (\eta_{C_{1L}}(a))^3 \cdot (\eta_{C_{2L}}(a))^3}, \sqrt[3]{(\eta_{C_{1U}}(a))^3 + (\eta_{C_{2U}}(a))^3 - (\eta_{C_{1U}}(a))^3 \cdot (\eta_{C_{2U}}(a))^3}\right]\right)$
- $\lambda C = \left(\left[\sqrt[3]{1-(1-\zeta_{C_L}^3)^\lambda}, \sqrt[3]{1-(1-\zeta_{C_U}^3)^\lambda}\right], [\eta_{C_L}^\lambda, \eta_{C_U}^\lambda]\right)$
- $C^\lambda = \left([\zeta_{C_L}^\lambda, \zeta_{C_U}^\lambda], \left[\sqrt[3]{1-(1-\eta_{C_L}^3)^\lambda}, \sqrt[3]{1-(1-\eta_{C_U}^3)^\lambda}\right]\right)$

For $C = ([\zeta_{C_L}(a), \zeta_{C_U}(a)], [\eta_{C_L}(a), \eta_{C_U}(a)]$, the score, accuracy and normalized score functions [35] are:

$$\begin{aligned}
P(C) &= \frac{1}{2}([\zeta_{C_L}(a)^3 + \zeta_{C_U}(a)^3] - [\eta_{C_L}(a)^3 + \eta_{C_U}(a)^3]), \\
D(C) &= \frac{1}{2}([\zeta_{C_L}(a)^3 + \zeta_{C_U}(a)^3] + [\eta_{C_L}(a)^3 + \eta_{C_U}(a)^3]), \\
\bar{P}(C) &= \frac{1}{2}(P(C)+1).
\end{aligned}$$

The equation

$$IVFFWG(C_1, C_2, \cdots, C_n) = \left(\left[\prod_{i=1}^{n}(\zeta_{C_{iL}})^{w_i}, \prod_{i=1}^{n}(\zeta_{C_{iU}})^{w_i}\right], \left[\sqrt[3]{\left(1-\prod_{i=1}^{n}\left(1-\eta_{C_{iL}}^3\right)^{w_i}\right)}, \sqrt[3]{\left(1-\prod_{i=1}^{n}\left(1-\eta_{C_{iU}}^3\right)^{w_i}\right)}\right]\right). \tag{19.1}$$

is called IVFF-weighted geometric operator, where w_k is a influence weight.

Definition 3.4. *[26] For* $C=([\zeta_{C_L}(a),\zeta_{C_U}(a)],[\eta_{C_L}(a),\eta_{C_U}(a)])$, *the new score function is defined as*

$$P(C) = \frac{\zeta_{C_L}^3+\zeta_{C_U}^3-\eta_{C_L}^3-\eta_{C_U}^3}{2}+\frac{\zeta_{C_L}^3-\zeta_{C_L}^3\eta_{C_U}^3-\zeta_{C_L}^3}{2(\zeta_{C_L}^3-\eta_{C_U}^3\eta_{C_L}^3-\eta_{C_L}^6+1)}. \tag{19.2}$$

Theorem 3.5. *[26] For two IVFFSs* $C=([\zeta_{C_L}(a),\zeta_{C_U}(a)],[\eta_{C_L}(a),\eta_{C_U}(a)])$ *and* $D=([\zeta_{D_L}(a),\zeta_{D_U}(a)],[\eta_{D_L}(a),\eta_{D_U}(a)])$, *if* $D \le C$, *then* $P(D) \le P(C)$.

Corollary 3.6. *[26] For* $C=([\zeta_{C_L}(a),\zeta_{C_U}(a)],[\eta_{C_L}(a),\eta_{C_U}(a)])$,

1. $-1 \le P(C) \le 1$.
2. If $\zeta_{C_L}=\zeta_{C_U}=X$ *and* $\eta_{C_L}=\eta_{C_U}=\sqrt[3]{1-X^3}$, *then* P(C) = $2X^3 - 1$.
3. *If* $C = [(1, 1), (0, 0)]$, *then* $P(C) = 1$ *and If* $C = [(0, 0), (1, 1)]$, *then* $P(C) = -1$

The normalized score function can be given as

$$\bar{P}(F) = \frac{1}{2}(P(F)+1).$$

Definition 3.7. *[21] For two IVFFSs C and D, the entropy for IVFFSs is defined as* $E: IVFFS(\mathscr{E}) \to [0,1]$. *The entropy function holds the following conditions:*

A real-valued function $E: IVFFS(\mathscr{E}) \to [0,1]$ *is called an entropy for IVFFSs with the following properties:*

E1. $E(C) \in [0, 1]$,
E2. The entropy of C is equal to 0 iff C is a crisp set,
E3. The entropy of C is equal to 1 iff $(\zeta_{Ci}^-)(a_i)=(\eta_{Ci}^-)(a_i)$, $(\zeta_{Ci}^+)(a_i)=(\eta_{Ci}^+)(a_i)$,
E4. $E(C) = E(C^c)$,
E5. $E(C) \le E(D) \Leftrightarrow$

- *If* $(\zeta_{Ci}^-)(a_i)\le(\eta_{Ci}^-)(a_i)$, $(\zeta_{Ci}^+)(a_i)\le(\eta_{Ci}^+)(a_i)$, *then* $C \subseteq D$,
- *If* $(\zeta_{Ci}^-)(a_i)\ge(\eta_{Ci}^-)(a_i)$, $(\zeta_{Ci}^+)(a_i)\ge(\eta_{Ci}^+)(a_i)$, *then* $C \supseteq D$.

Theorem 3.8. *[21] The equation*

$$E_t(C) = 1 - \sqrt[t]{\frac{1}{2n}\sum_{i=1}^{n}\left(\left|((\zeta_{Ci}^{-})(a_i))^3 - ((\eta_{Ci}^{-})(a_i))^3\right|^t + \left|((\zeta_{Ci}^{+})(a_i))^3 - ((\eta_{Ci}^{+})(a_i))^3\right|^t\right)}, \tag{19.3}$$

is called the entropy measure, where t is parameter-varying.

19.3.1 Similarity Measures

Definition 3.9. *For the two IVFFSs C and D, the equation*

$$\mathrm{D_{EW}}(\mathrm{C,D}) = \left(\frac{1}{2^{p+1} n u_y^p}\sum_{i=1}^{n}\omega_i\left(\left|(uy-1)[(\zeta_C^{-})(a_i)^3 + (\zeta_C^{+})(a_i)^3 - (\zeta_D^{-})(a_i)^3\right.\right.\right.$$

$$\left. - (\zeta_D^{+})(a_i)^3] - [(\eta_C^{-})(a_i)^3 + (\eta_C^{+})(a_i)^3 - (\eta_D^{-})(a_i)^3 - (\eta_D^{+})(a_i)^3]\right|^p$$

$$+ \left|(u_y - y)[(\zeta_C^{-})(a_i)^3 + (\zeta_C^{-})(a_i)^3 - (\zeta_D^{-})(a_i)^3 - (\zeta_D^{-})(a_i)^3]\right.$$

$$\left.\left.\left. - [(\eta_C^{-})(a_i)^3 + (\eta_C^{-})(a_i)^3 - (\eta_D^{-})(a_i)^3 - (\eta_D^{-})(a_i)^3]\right|^p\right)\right)^{1/p}$$

is said to be the weighted distance measure(WDM).

($p = L_p norm$; k=slope; u_y= the level of uncertainty according to y; $y \geq 0$; $u_y \geq y + 1$).

Theorem 3.10. *For two IVFFSs C and D, D_{EW} (C, D) is the WDM between C and D.*

Proof. It will be shown that the distance measure properties are provided.

(i.) For $0 \leq \zeta_C^{-}(a_i), \zeta_D^{-}(a_i), \zeta_C^{+}(a_i), \zeta_D^{+}(a_i), \eta_C^{-}(a_i), \eta_D^{+}(a_i), \eta_D^{-}(a_i), \eta_D^{+}(a_i) \leq 1$, then $1 - u_y \leq (u_y - 1)[(\zeta_C^{-}(a_i))^3 - (\zeta_D^{-})(a_i)^3] \leq u_y - 1$ and $-1 \leq (\eta_C^{-}(a_i))^3 - (\eta_C^{-}(a_i))^3 \leq 1$. Therefore,

$$-u_y \leq (u_y - 1)[(\zeta_C^-(a_i))^3 - (\zeta_D^-(a_i))^3 - (\eta_C^-(a_i))^3 - (\eta_D^-(a_i))^3] \leq u_y,$$
$$-u_y \leq (u_y - 1)[(\zeta_C^+(a_i))^3 - (\zeta_D^+(a_i))^3 - (\eta_C^+(a_i))^3 - (\eta_D^+(a_i))^3] \leq u_y,$$
$$-u_y \leq (u_y - y)[(\eta_C^-(a_i))^3 - (\eta_D^-(a_i))^3 - y[(\zeta_C^-(a_i))^3 - (\zeta_D^-(a_i))^3] \leq u_y,$$
$$-u_y \leq (u_y - y)[(\eta_C^+(a_i))^3 - (\eta_D^+(a_i))^3 - y[(\zeta_C^+(a_i))^3 - (\zeta_D^+(a_i))^3] \leq u_y.$$

Hence, the inequalities are hold:

$$-2u_y \leq (u_y - 1)[(\zeta_C^-(a_i))^3 - (\zeta_C^+(a_i))^3 - (\zeta_D^-(a_i))^3 - (\zeta_D^+(a_i))^3]$$
$$-[(\eta_C^-(a_i))^3 + (\eta_C^+(a_i))^3 - (\eta_D^-(a_i))^3 - (\eta_D^+(a_i))^3] \leq 2u_y,$$
$$-2u_y \leq (u_y - y)[(\eta_C^-(a_i))^3 - (\eta_C^+(a_i))^3 - (\eta_D^-(a_i))^3 - (\eta_D^+(a_i))^3]$$
$$-y.[(\zeta_C^-(a_i))^3 + (\zeta_C^+(a_i))^3 - (\zeta_D^-(a_i))^3 - (\zeta_D^+(a_i))^3] \leq 2u_y.$$

It means that

$$0 \leq |(u_y - 1)[(\zeta_C^-(a_i))^3 - (\zeta_C^+(a_i))^3 - (\zeta_D^-(a_i))^3 - (\zeta_D^+(a_i))^3]$$
$$-[(\eta_C^-(a_i))^3 + (\eta_C^+(a_i))^3 - (\eta_D^-(a_i))^3 - (\eta_D^+(a_i))^3]|^p \leq (2u_y)^p,$$
$$0 \leq |(u_y - y)[(\eta_C^-(a_i))^3 - (\eta_C^+(a_i))^3 - (\eta_D^-(a_i))^3 - (\eta_D^+(a_i))^3]$$
$$-y.[(\zeta_C^-(a_i))^3 + (\zeta_C^+(a_i))^3 - (\zeta_D^-(a_i))^3 - (\zeta_D^+(a_i))^3]|^p \leq (2u_y)^p.$$

Therefore, we can find $0 \leq D_{EW}(C, D) \leq 1$.

It can be easily shown that conditions $D_{EW}(C, D) = D_{EW}(D, C)$, $D_{EW}(C, D) = 0 \Leftrightarrow C = D$, and $D_{EW}(C, C^c) = 1 \Leftrightarrow C$ is a crisp set are met.

(v.) Consider $C \subseteq D \subseteq F$. Thus,

$$\zeta_C^-(a_i) \leq \zeta_D^-(a_i) \leq \zeta_F^-(a_i), \quad \zeta_C^+(a_i) \leq \zeta_D^+(a_i) \leq \zeta_F^+(a_i),$$
$$\eta_C^-(a_i) \geq \eta_D^-(a_i) \geq \eta_F^-(a_i), \quad \eta_C^+(a_i) \geq \eta_D^+(a_i) \geq \eta_F^+(a_i),$$

and from here,

$$
\begin{aligned}
&(u_y-1)[(\zeta_C^-(a_i))^3+(\zeta_C^+(a_i))^3-((\eta_C^-(a_i))^3+(\eta_C^+(a_i))^3)]\\
&\geq (u_y-1)[(\zeta_D^-(a_i))^3+(\zeta_D^+(a_i))^3-((\eta_D^-(a_i))^3+(\eta_D^+(a_i))^3)]\\
&\geq (u_y-1)[(\zeta_C^-(a_i))^3+(\zeta_C^+(a_i))^3-((\eta_C^-(a_i))^3+(\eta_C^+(a_i))^3)],\\
&(u_y-y)[(\zeta_F^-(a_i))^3+(\zeta_F^+(a_i))^3-y.((\eta_F^-(a_i))^3+(\eta_F^+(a_i))^3)]\\
&\leq (u_y-y)[(\zeta_D^-(a_i))^3+(\zeta_D^+(a_i))^3-((\eta_D^-(a_i))^3+(\eta_D^+(a_i))^3)]\\
&\leq (u_y-1)[(\zeta_C^-(a_i))^3+(\zeta_C^+(a_i))^3-((\eta_C^-(a_i))^3+(\eta_C^+(a_i))^3)].
\end{aligned}
$$

Consequently,

$$
\begin{aligned}
&|(u_y-1))[(\zeta_C^-(a_i))^3+(\zeta_C^+(a_i))^3-((\zeta_D^-(a_i))^3-(\zeta_D^+(a_i))^3-((\eta_C^-(a_i))^3\\
&\qquad+(\eta_D^+(a_i))^3-(\eta_D^-(a_i))^3-(\eta_D^+(a_i))^3)|\\
&\leq |(u_y-1))[(\zeta_C^-(a_i))^3+(\zeta_C^+(a_i))^3-((\zeta_F^-(a_i))^3-(\zeta_F^+(a_i))^3)-((\eta_C^-(a_i))^3\\
&\qquad+(\eta_C^+(a_i))^3-(\eta_F^-(a_i))^3-(\eta_F^+(a_i))^3)|,\\
&|(u_y-y))[(\zeta_C^-(a_i))^3+(\zeta_C^+(a_i))^3-((\zeta_D^-(a_i))^3-(\zeta_D^+(a_i))^3)-y.((\eta_C^-(a_i))^3\\
&\qquad+(\eta_C^+(a_i))^3-(\eta_D^-(a_i))^3-(\eta_D^+(a_i))^3)|\\
&\leq |(u_y-y))[(\zeta_C^-(c_i))^3+(\zeta_C^+(c_i))^3-((\zeta_F^-(a_i))^3-(\zeta_F^+(a_i))^3)-y.((\eta_C^-(a_i))^3\\
&\qquad+(\eta_C^+(a_i))^3-(\eta_F^-(a_i))^3-(\eta_F^+(a_i))^3)|.
\end{aligned}
$$

Hence, $D_{EW}(C, D) \leq D_{EW}(C, F)$. Further, $D_{EW}(D, F) \leq D_{EW}(C, F)$.

Definition 3.11. *For two IVFFSs C and D, the equation $S_{EW}(C, D) = 1 - D_{EW}(C, D)$ is called the similarity measure between C and D.*

19.4 Proposed Methodology

The DM problem is a well-known decision analysis technique used to handle ambiguous and fuzzy information related to human beings. Fuzziness is involved in every field of life, such as social decision-making, artificial intelligence, computational problems, and many other complicated real-life applications. Using different decision algorithms, we can evaluate suitable optimal options by considering prominent characteristics or attribute information. Sometimes, existing decision algorithms cannot handle incomplete and redundant human details. To serve such situations, the proposed DM algorithm:

STAGE A. Problem Design:
Let A_i, K_j, w_j ($w_j \in [0, 1]$) ($i = 1, 2, \cdots, m$; $j = 1, 2, \cdots, n$) be the set of alternatives, criteria and weighted vector, respectively. Suppose that the assessment of the A_i w. r. t. K_j is indicated by IVFF-matrix $R = (r_{ij})_{m\times n} = ([\zeta_{C_{ijL}}, \zeta_{C_{ijU}}], [\eta_{C_{ijL}}, \eta_{C_{ijU}}])$.

STAGE B. The process for figuring out the combined weights:
Step 1: Using the entropy method to identify the objective weights: From Theorem 3.8, IVFF entropy E_j of jth criteria is computed as:

$$E_j = 1 - \sqrt[p]{\frac{1}{2n}\sum_{i=1}^{n}\left(\left|((\zeta_{ijL})(a_i))^3 - ((\eta_{ijL}^{-})(a_i))^3\right|^p + \left|((\zeta_{ijU}^{+})(a_i))^3 - ((\eta_{ijU}^{+})(a_i))^3\right|^p\right)}. \tag{19.4}$$

The equation

$$\omega_j = \frac{1 - E_j}{n - \sum_{j)1}^{n} E_j}. \tag{19.5}$$

calculates the weight ω_j of the jth parameter.
Step 2: The linear weighted comprehensive technique is utilized to identify the combined weights.

Think of $\varpi = \{\varpi_1, \varpi_2, \cdots, \varpi_n\}$ $(\varpi_j \in [0,1], \sum_{j=1}^{n} \varpi_j = 1)$ as the subjective weight that the experts themselves provided. Equation 19.5 is utilized to identify the objective weight's vector. Therefore, the equation

$$\varpi_j = \frac{w_j * \omega_j}{\sum_{j=1}^{n}(w_j * \omega_j)}, \tag{19.6}$$

calculates the vector of the combined weight, where $(\varpi_j \in [0,1], \sum_{j=1}^{n} \varpi_j = 1)$.

STAGE C. IVFF-WDBA Method:
Using the IVFF information, the distance between the minimum value of points and the maximum value of points will be determined. Thus, alternatives will be ranked using the suitability index.

Step 3: A new matrix is obtained ($\hat{P} = (\hat{p}_{ij})_{m\times n}$) by normalizing a matrix containing benefit and cost criteria with the following equation:

$$\hat{p}_{ij} = \begin{cases} ([\zeta_{F_L}, \zeta_{F_U}],[\eta_{F_L}(k), \eta_{F_U}]), & \textit{for benefit criterion,} \\ ([\eta_{F_L}, \eta_{F_U}],[\zeta_{F_L}(k), \zeta_{F_U}]), & \textit{for non-benefit criterion.} \end{cases} \tag{19.7}$$

Step 4: The equation

$$\hat{t}_{ij} = \frac{\zeta_{ijL}^3 + \zeta_{ijU}^3 - \eta_{ijL}^3 - \eta_{ijU}^3}{2} + \frac{\zeta_{ijL}^3 - \zeta_{ijL}^3 \eta_{ijU}^3 - \zeta_{ijL}^6}{2(\zeta_{ijL}^3 - \eta_{ijU}^3 \eta_{ijL}^3 - \eta_{ijL}^6 + 1)}$$

computes the score function $\hat{t}_{ij}$ of $\hat{p}_{ij}$.
Step 5: The standardized matrix, an average value matrix, and a standard deviation matrix have been given as

$$\widehat{SM}_{ij} = \frac{\hat{t}_{ij} - \overline{AV}_j}{\widehat{SD}_j},$$

$$\widehat{AV}_j = \frac{1}{m}\sum_{i=1}^{m} \hat{t}_{ij},$$

$$\widehat{SD}_j = \sqrt{\frac{1}{m}\sum_{i=1}^{m} (\hat{t}_{ij} - \overline{AV}_j)^2}$$

respectively.
Step 6: Using the normalized matrix, the PIS and AIP are

$$PIS = \left\{\max_i\{\widehat{SM}_{i1}\}, \max_i \widehat{SM}_{i2}, \cdots, \max_i\{\widehat{SM}_{in}\}\right\}$$

$$AIP = \left\{\min_i\{\widehat{SM}_{i1}\}, \min_i \widehat{SM}_{i2}, \cdots, \min_i\{\widehat{SM}_{in}\}\right\}.$$

Step 7: Compute the WED as

$$\widehat{W}_i^{PIS} = \sqrt{\sum_{j=1}^{n} \omega_j \left(\widehat{SM}_{ij} - PIS\right)^2}$$

$$\widehat{W}_i^{AIP} = \sqrt{\sum_{j=1}^{n} \omega_j \left(\widehat{SM}_{ij} - AIP\right)^2}.$$

Step 8: The equation

$$\widehat{SI}_i = \frac{\widehat{W}_i^{AIP}}{\widehat{W}_i^{PIS} + \widehat{W}_i^{AIP}}.$$

computes the suitability index $(\widehat{SI})$.

A suitable alternative is closer to the ideal alternative if its $\widehat{SI}$ is bigger. The best option is the one with the greatest value of $\widehat{SI}$ for alternatives. The greater the $\widehat{SI}$, the bigger the ordering is substituted.

Stage D. IVFF-Similarity Measure:

The new similarity measure among IVFFSs is used for decision-making.

Step 9: Steps 3-5 in Stage C are taken similarly.

Step 10: Calculate the similarity measure as

$$S_{EW}(C_i, C*) = 1 - \sqrt[p]{\begin{array}{l} \frac{1}{2^p +^1 u_y^p} \sum_{i=1}^{n} \omega_i \left(\left|(u_y - 1)[(\zeta_C^-)(a_i)^3 + ((\zeta_C^+)(a_i)^3 - 2) - [(\eta_C^-)(a_i)^3 + (\eta_C^+)(a_i)^3\right|^p \right. \\ \left. + \left|(u_y - y)[(\eta_C^-)(a_i)^3 + (\eta_C^+)(a_i)^3 - y.[(\zeta_C^-)(a_i)^3 + ((\eta_C^-)(a_i)^3 - 2\right|^p \right) \end{array}}$$

where $C*$ is the ideal alternative as the IVFFN $a_j* = ([1, 1], [0, 0])$ for $\forall j$.

Step 11: Rank the alternatives.

19.5 Scenario-Based Application

In parallel with technological developments, the power and capabilities of weapons and weapon systems have also increased today. As a natural result, concepts such as front and border have entirely disappeared, and the entire country and civilians have entered the attack area. In addition to the precautions to be taken by the Armed Forces against these great dangers and other measures, importance should also be given to the construction of shelters. Otherwise, it is natural that there will be much loss of life and property. However, the following three important principles must be considered before constructing shelters to obtain the expected benefit from shelters: 1. The shelter's location must be well determined. 2. The people who will benefit from the shelter must be planned. 3. The shelter to be built must be usable for other purposes.

Shelters are places of protection constructed to shield the living and non-living values essential to human survival and the nation's military power from the effects of biological, chemical, and nuclear weapons, as well as traditional and contemporary weapons. The purpose of shelter construction is to minimize loss of life and property, to provide deterrence by giving the image of preparedness, and to create mass protection opportunities at low cost.

During a war, emergency shelters are being considered to be built in the event of a nuclear attack on important cities of the country. Shelters to guard against the consequences of nuclear weapons' radioactive fallout have been specified. These features are determined as [1]:

C_1: Size - In fallout shelters, at least 1 square meter of space is allocated per person. The interior height cannot be less than 2 meters 40 centimeters.
C_2: Wall Thickness - The wall thickness of fallout shelters shall be at least 60 cm of concrete, 75 cm of brick or stone, or 90 cm of compressed soil or other equivalent material.
C_3: Entrance - The shelter's entrance shall have an iron door and at least one right-angle return.
C_4: Ventilation - Regardless of the type of shelter, both mechanical and natural ventilation shall be sufficient, natural ventilation shall be provided with vents and mechanical ventilation shall be provided with an air conditioner. A filter system shall be used to prevent radioactive fallout and chemical gases from entering the ventilation.

C_5: Hygienic Measures - If possible, toilets shall be connected to the sewer system, and toilet-type toilets shall be used. Food waste shall be collected in closed containers in nylon bags.

Five different projects (P_i, $i = 1, 2, 3, 4, 5$) have been proposed to construct shelters. The decision-making team consists of five experts: U_1: economic experts, U_2: construction experts, U_3: military experts, U_4: public health experts, and U_5: safety experts. The domain expert gives a set of previous weights as $w = (w_1, \cdots, w_5) = (0.13, 0.28, 0.24, 0.12, 0.23)$.

The assessment of fallout shelter plans from the domain expert's survey and the construction of an IVFF matrix are shown in Table 19.1.

Calculations according to combine weight determination and the steps of IVFF-WDBA are as follows:

Entropy values are $E_j = (0.178, 0.118, 0.129, 0.083, 0.109)$ and from here the weights are $\omega_j = (0.188, 0.201, 0.199, 0.209, 0.203)$. Therefore, combined weights are found as $\varpi_j = (0.122, 0.281, 0.239, 0.125, 0.233)$.

Table 19.1 IVFF matrix.

	C1	C2	C3	C4	C5
P1	[(0.42, 0.66), (0.50, 0.74)]	[(0.70, 0.28), (0.80, 0.33)]	[(0.85, 0.35), (0.92, 0.18)]	[(0.36, 0.72), (0.39, 0.77)]	[(0.33, 0.68), (0.44, 0.78)]
P2	[(0.49, 0.70), (0.43, 0.68)]	[(0.34, 0.85), (0.29, 0.73)]	[(0.68, 0.40), (0.56, 0.39)]	[(0.32, 0.66), (0.96, 0.10)]	[(0.40, 0.72), (0.42, 0.61)]
P3	[(0.67, 0.51), (0.57, 0.44)]	[(0.74, 0.35), (0.61, 0.45)]	[(0.85, 0.27), (0.80, 0.32)]	[(0.91, 0.13), (0.86, 0.10)]	[(0.80, 0.35), (0.75, 0.28)]
P4	[(0.53, 0.55), (0.63, 0.60)]	[(0.32, 0.75), (0.38, 0.80)]	[(0.72, 0.37), (0.75, 0.39)]	[(0.92, 0.23), (0.91, 0.13)]	[(0.41, 0.70), (0.75, 0.19)]
P5	[(0.29, 0.77), (0.34, 0.74)]	[(0.37, 0.69), (0.44, 0.72)]	[(0.54, 0.51), (0.58, 0.48)]	[(0.43, 0.65), (0.58, 0.69)]	[(0.78, 0.26), (0.82, 0.27)]

Every parameter is a benefit parameter. Consequently, normalizing the matrix is not necessary. Score function values as

$$t_{ij} = \begin{bmatrix} -0.065 & 0.064 & 0.155 & -0.0296 & 0.0251 \\ 0.009 & 0.131 & 0.142 & -0.0487 & -0.0252 \\ 0.0526 & 0.149 & 0.126 & 0.062 & 0.045 \\ -0.0366 & -0.22 & 0.128 & 0.088 & -0.0606 \\ -0.096 & 0.09 & 0.146 & 0.027 & 0.064 \end{bmatrix}$$

According to the average and standard deviation values, the standardized matrix is obtained as follows:

$$\widehat{SM}_{ij} = \begin{bmatrix} -0.4186 & 0.5375 & 1.101 & -0.0517 & -0.82 \\ 0.157 & 0.653 & 0.787 & -1.95 & 0.35 \\ 1.418 & 0.236 & -1.22 & -1.036 & 0.6 \\ -16.45 & -22.813 & 14.087 & 22.753 & 2.42 \\ 0.33 & -0.762 & 0.76 & -1.53 & 1.17 \end{bmatrix}$$

for $\overline{AV}_1 = -0.0326, \overline{AV}_2 = 0.0428, \overline{AV}_3 = 0.1394, \overline{AV}_4 = 0.01974,\ \overline{AV}_5 = 0.01$ and $\widehat{SD}_1 = 0.0774, \widehat{SD}_2 = 0.135, \widehat{SD}_3 = 0.011, \widehat{SD}_4 = 0.003, \widehat{SD}_5 = 0.0462$.

According to the *PIS* and *AIP* values, weighted Euclidean distances are computed. Then, $\widehat{SI}$ values are obtained as $\widehat{SI}_j = (1.223, 0.935, 0.844, 0.5, 0.7)$. If the alternatives are ranked according to $\widehat{SI}$, then, $P_1 > P_2 > P_3 > P_5 > P_4$. That is, it is seen that the most suitable shelter plan to be constructed to protect from the radioactive fallout effects of nuclear weapons is P_1. When the same calculations are made according to IVFF-Similarity measures, it is seen that the ranking and the result do not change.

19.6 Discussion

19.6.1 Comparative Analysis

The continuum of selecting and evaluating alternatives from a big or small pool based on relevant criteria is known as MCDM. As part of MCDM, numerous options are assessed based on several criteria. DMs can find the best and most desired solution for these problems using MCDM approaches. As a result, researchers have proposed many MCDM solutions. In this part, two MCDM techniques were tested in the context of FFS. Comparing the recommended and accepted practices has confirmed their validity and correctness.

A comparative analysis with IF-Bayesian Network(IFBN) and Prospect Theory [14], IVPFS-WDBA and multiparametric Similarity measure [34], and IV-fuzzy soft settings, the suggested method's robustness will be confirmed using WDBA, CODAS, and similarity measurements [33].

- An IFBN was established in [14] to determine the practical attribute weights in an uncertain environment. Subsequently, a dynamic DM approach incorporating prospect theory has been refined to address risk DM issues.
- In [34], two IVPF DM methods according to multiparametric similarity measures and WDBA are presented.
- In [33], three algorithmic steps to unravel IV-fuzzy soft DM problems, WDBA, CODAS, and similarity measures, have been proposed.

The identical decision matrices and sub-criteria weights were used in the computations of the comparative approaches. The results in Table 19.2 are the outcome of the comparisons. The differences between the compared methodologies are shown in Table 19.2. Shelters and projects to be built to protect against the effects of radioactive fallout from nuclear weapons were evaluated with the selected methods for comparison according to the criteria. In all applicable methodologies, the first alternative was obtained as P_1. With a few minor adjustments, the results of the "IF-Bayesian Network(IFBN) and Prospect Theory," "IVPFS-WDBA and multiparametric Similarity measure," and "IV fuzzy soft sets WDBA, CODAS, and similarity measures" approaches are comparable to those of this study. Therefore, the proposed method's applicability, robustness, and sensitivity are revealed. Since the suggested methods analyze criteria and alternatives using IVFFSs rather than traditional techniques, they aid in addressing MCDM issues more sensibly and practically.

Different MCDM techniques may produce different results depending on the situation. Since different approaches have varied methodological impacts and aims, it makes perfect sense to have a variety of findings (Table 19.2). According to the data, there have also been some slight changes, which makes sense given the unique characteristics of every DM process.

Table 19.2 Ranking comparison.

IF-Bayesian Network and Prospect Theory [14]	$P_1 > P_3 > P_2 > P_5 > P_4$
IV fuzzy soft sets WDBA and CODAS [33]	$P_1 > P_2 > P_3 > P_5 > P_4$
IVPFS-WDBA and multiparametric Similarity measure [34]	$P_1 > P_2 > P_5 > P_3 > P_4$

FFS's several membership tiers and organizational structure enable it to generate precise and adaptable outcomes. Consequently, the analysis validates the precision of the outcomes of the suggested approach.

19.6.2 Advantages of the Method

The results of the accessible methodologies and the offered approach are comparable according to the existing analysis and comparison results. The primary superiority of the presented method on readily available DM solutions is that it addresses data uncertainty by including additional information and considering factors like $\mathscr{M}$ and $\mathscr{N}$ of criteria. The item's information might be examined more precisely and impartially. It is also helpful for handling imprecise and erroneous data in the DM process. The expected information loss subsequently takes place since the reasoning for giving one parameter a score value has no bearing on the other values.

Conversely, there is no discernible loss of information with our suggested method. By determining the degree of similarity and differentiation among data, the intended methodology avoids making ill-informed decisions, which gives it an advantage over existing methodologies. The DM process can be aided by combining unclear and inaccurate information.

19.6.3 Limitations

This study still raises several issues. First, risk and uncertainty are not the same thing. This study primarily concerns the consequences of risk selection rather than promoting ambiguity. Risk aversion is an important type of uncertainty aversion because it may be difficult to forecast if shelters will be constructed to guard against the effects of radioactive fallout from nuclear weapons. A more comprehensive evaluation is necessary to identify possible issues with shelters designed for radioactive fallout. Consequently, it could not recognize the benefit and loss domains linked to shelters. Future research should concentrate on combining general risk choice criteria with particular shelter risk indicators.

In the WDBA method, choosing optimal weights can be complex and problem-dependent. Computationally expensive for large datasets if not optimized properly. Sensitive to outliers if not regularized. While similarity measures are powerful tools in data science, machine learning, and information retrieval, they also come with limitations and challenges. Some measures (e.g., Euclidean distance) are heavily influenced by differences in scale. In high-dimensional spaces, distances become less meaningful as most points are equidistant. Outliers can distort similarity measures, especially with Euclidean and Manhattan distances. Pairwise similarity computation in large datasets is slow. Despite the benefits of the proposed IVFF-type method, its implementation in specific DM scenarios is constrained by its incapacity to assess the different choices thoroughly. It is easier to create IVFFSs when more criteria and options are available.

19.7 Conclusion

Different kinds of emergencies have begun to happen more regularly in recent decades. Their complexity and effect have grown dramatically, posing significant obstacles to establishing sustainable economies, societies, and environments. Making emergency decisions is essential to managing crises and accomplishing sustainable development objectives. EDM is essential for countries or communities to increase the legitimacy and effectiveness of emergency response, which can significantly lower economic loss, casualties, and environmental harm. When evaluating emergency decisions, serious inaccuracy, fuzziness, and ambiguity are the main issues. Civil defense guidelines generally recommend survival based on isolation in a shelter for at least two weeks. During this period, the shelter should have an environment where basic needs such as uncontaminated water, food, temperature regulation and ventilation systems, and medical supplies can be kept. Shelters become important during the war, as well as global terrorist attacks, industrial accidents, and environmental hazards. In all these cases, it is essential to evaluate projects for a shelter to be built and to choose the optimal project by considering the appropriate precautions and procedures to be taken according to specific risks. This paper establishes a novel DM approach for crises and addresses the challenge of choosing projects for radioactive fallout shelters. The IVFF-WDBA and IVFF-similarity measurement techniques were developed as a result. In WDBA, weighted distances between known data points or reference points approximate a function, value, or solution. Similarity measures are mathematical functions that quantify how alike two objects, data points, or sets are. IVFF-similarity measure computes the information measure of two IVFFSs.

As expressed in this study, designing shelters that are idealized for protection is a complex process that requires comprehensive planning, attention to detail, and a reasonable budget. Because a poorly designed shelter can turn into a deadly structure instead of protecting life. The projects envisaged for this study have been evaluated according to the criteria in the guidelines for the ideal shelter construction, and the most suitable project has been selected.

Their validity and effectiveness were assessed by comparing the suggested methods with previous studies. The comparison analysis shows that the proposed approaches are more competitive and robust in managing uncertainty in DM circumstances than other MCDM tactics.

Future research can apply the methodology described in this study to other areas of uncertainty. Furthermore, this approach can be investigated using techniques like Chouqet integral and TOPSIS.

AI disclosure statement: The author confirms that no artificial intelligence (AI)-generated content or AI-assisted writing tools were used in the preparation of this chapter (including summaries and the abstract). All text, analysis, and conclusions are the result of the author's original work.

References

1. Republic of Türkiye, Ministry of Interior, Disaster and Emergency Management Presidency, Shelters (Turkish), https://www.afad.gov.tr/afadem/siginaklar (Access: March 10, 2025).
2. Akram, M. and Niaz, Z., 2-Tuple linguistic Fermatean fuzzy decision-making method based on COCOSO with CRITIC for drip irrigation system analysis. *J. Comput. Cogn. Eng.*, 3, 186–202, 2024.
3. Atanassov, K., Intuitionistic fuzzy sets. *Fuzzy Sets Syst.*, 20, 87–96, 1986.
4. Atanassov, K. and Gargov, G., Interval valued intuitionistic fuzzy sets. *Fuzzy Sets Syst.*, 31, 343–349, 1989.
5. David, D. and Alamoodi, A., A bibliometric analysis of research on multiple criteria decision making with emphasis on Energy Sector between (2019-2023). *Appl. Data Sci. Anal.*, 143–149, 2023.
6. Ejegwa, P.A., Kausar, N., Aydin, N., Feng, Y., Olanrewaju, O.A., A new Fermatean fuzzy Spearman-like correlation coefficient and its application in evaluating insecurity problem via multi-criteria decision-making approach. *Heliyon*, 10, 22, 2024.

7. Ejegwa, P.A., Anum, M.T., Kausar, N., Nwokoro, C.O., Aydin, N., Yu, H., New Fermatean fuzzy distance metric and its utilization in the assessment of security crises using the MCDM technique. *Mathematics*, 12, 3214, 2024.
8. Farid, H.M.A., Bouye, M., Riaz, M., Jamil, N., Fermatean Fuzzy CODAS Approach with Topology and Its Application to Sustainable Supplier Selection. *Symmetry*, 15, 1–26, 2023.
9. Garg, H., Ali, Z., Emam, W., A decision-making algorithm with circular complex intuitionistic fuzzy information and their application in cognitive wireless communications. *Alexandria Eng. J.*, 115, 501–519, 2025.
10. Garg, H., Ayaz, K., Emam, W., Multi attribute decision-making algorithms using Hamacher Choquet-integral operators with complex intuitionistic fuzzy information. *AIMS Math.*, 9, 35860–35884, 2024.
11. Garg, H., Dutta, D., Dutta, P., Gohain, B., An extended group decision-making algorithm with intuitionistic fuzzy set information distance measures and their applications. *Comput. Ind. Eng.*, 197, 110537, 2024.
12. Garg, H., Waqas, M., Ali, Z., Emam, W., EDAS method for circular pythagorean fuzzy with improved Dombi power aggregation operators and their application in policy analysis and decision support systems. *Alexandria Eng. J.*, 106, 172–193, 2024.
13. Garg, H., Khan, F.M., Ahmed, W., Fermatean Fuzzy Similarity Measures-Based Group Decision-Making Algorithm and Its Application to Dengue Disease. *Iran. J. Sci. Technol. Trans. Electr. Eng.*, 48, 2, 687–703, 2024.
14. Hao, Z., Xu, Z., Zhao, H., Fujita, H., A Dynamic Weight Determination Approach Based on the Intuitionistic Fuzzy Bayesian Network and Its Application to Emergency Decision Making. *IEEE Trans. Fuzzy Syst.*, 26, 4, 1893–1907, 2018.
15. Jeevaraj, S., Ordering of interval-valued Fermatean fuzzy sets and their applications. *Expert Syst. Appl.*, 185, 115613, 2021.
16. Kirişci, M., Fibonacci statistical convergence on intuitionistic fuzzy normed spaces. *J. Intell. Fuzzy Syst.*, 4, 1–14, 2019.
17. Kirişci, M., Comparison of the medical decision-making with Intuitionistic fuzzy parameterized fuzzy soft set and Riesz Summability. *New Math. Nat. Comput.*, 15, 351–359, 2019.
18. Kirişci, M., Correlation Coefficients of Fermatean Fuzzy Sets with Their Application. *J. Math. Sci. Model.*, 5, 2, 16–23, 2022.
19. Kirişci, M., Data analysis for panoramic X-ray selection: Fermatean fuzzy type correlation coefficients approach. *Eng. Appl. Artif. Intell.*, 126, 106824, 2023.
20. Kirişci, M., New cosine similarity and distance measures for Fermatean fuzzy sets and TOPSIS approach. *Knowl. Inf. Syst.*, 65, 855–868, 2023.
21. Kirişci, M., Medical Waste Management Based on an Interval-Valued Fermatean Fuzzy Decision-Making Method. *J. Math. Sci. Model.*, 7, 128–145, 2024.

22. Kirişci, M., Measures of Distance and Entropy Based on the Fermatean Fuzzy-Type Soft Sets Approach. *Univ. J. Math. Appl.*, 7, 12–29, 2024.
23. Kirişci, M., Interval-valued Fermatean fuzzy based risk assessment for self-driving vehicles. *Appl. Soft Comput.*, 152, 111265, 2024.
24. Kirişci, M., Demir, I., Simsek, N., Fermatean fuzzy ELECTRE multi-criteria group decision-making and most suitable biomedical material selection. *Artif. Intell. Med.*, 127, 102278, 2022.
25. Kirişci, M. and Simsek, N., A novel kernel principal component analysis with application disaster preparedness of hospital: interval-valued Fermatean fuzzy set approach. *J. Supercomput.*, 79, 19848–19878, 2023.
26. Kirisci, M., Kuzu, S., Kablan, A., Ongel, V., The New Integrated Interval-Valued Fermatean Fuzzy Decision-Making Approach with the Implementation of Green Supply Chain Management. *Axioms*, 14, 3, 187, 2025.
27. Kirişci, M., Risk Assessment for Breast Cancer with Integrated Group Decision-Making Method. *Fundam. Contempl. Math. Sci.*, 6, 1, 1–18, 2025.
28. Kirişci, M., An integrated decision-making process for risk analysis of decentralized finance. *Neural Comput. Appl.*, 37, 6021–6051, 2025.
29. Liu, Z., Zhu, A., Senapati, T., Deveci, M., Pamucar, D., Yager, R.R., New distance measures of complex Fermatean fuzzy sets with applications in decision making and clustering problems. *Inf. Sci.*, 686, 121310, 2025.
30. Luqman, A., Siddique, S., Shahzadi, G., Akram, M., Multi-criteria group decision making through full multiplicative form under hesitant Fermatean fuzzy environment. *Granular Comput.*, 9, 51, 2024.
31. Mishra, A.R., Rani, P., Saha, A., Senapati, T., Hezam, I.M., Yager, R.R., Fermatean fuzzy copula aggregation operators and similarity measures-based complex proportional assessment approach for renewable energy source selection. *Complex Intell. Syst.*, 8, 5223–5248, 2022.
32. Mohammed, S.Y., Oleiwi, A.K., kh.Asman, T., Saleh, H.M., Mahmood, A.M., Avci, I., A Survey of MCDM-Based Software Engineering Method. *Babylonian J. Math.*, 13–18, 2023.
33. Peng, X.D. and Garg, H., Algorithms for interval-valued fuzzy soft sets in emergency decision making based on WDBA and CODAS with new information measure. *Comput. Ind. Eng.*, 119, 439–452, 2018.
34. Peng, X. and Li, W., Algorithms for Interval-Valued Pythagorean Fuzzy Sets in Emergency Decision Making Based on Multiparametric Similarity Measures and WDBA. *IEEE Access*, 7, 7419–7441, 2019.
35. Rani, P. and Mishra, A.R., Interval-valued fermatean fuzzy sets with multi-criteria weighted aggregated sum product assessment-based decision analysis framework. *Neural Comput. Appl.*, 34, 8051–8067, 2022.
36. Rao, R.V. and Singh, D., Weighted Euclidean distance based approach as a multiple attribute decision making method for plant or facility layout design selection. *Int. J. Ind. Eng. Comput.*, 3, 365–382, 2012.

37. Riaz, M., Farid, H.M.A., Shakeel, H.M., Arif, D., Cost effective indoor HVAC energy efficiency monitoring based on intelligent decision support system under fermatean fuzzy framework. *Sci. Iran.*, 30, 2143–2161, 2023.
38. Riaz, M., Qamar, F., Tariq, S., Alsager, K., AI-Driven LOPCOW-AROMAN Framework and Topological Data Analysis Using Circular Intuitionistic Fuzzy Information: Healthcare Supply Chain Innovation. *Mathematics*, 12, 3593, 2024.
39. Rong, Y., Yu, L., Liu, Y., Simic, V., Garg, H., The FMEA model based on LOPCOW-ARAS methods with interval-valued Fermatean fuzzy information for risk assessment of R&D projects in industrial robot offline programming systems. *Comput. Appl. Math.*, 43, 1, 25, 2024.
40. Saha, A., Dabic-Miletic, S., Senapati, T., Simic, V., Pamucar, D., Ala, A., Arya, L., Fermatean fuzzy Dombi generalized Maclaurin symmetric mean operators for prioritizing bulk material handling technologies. *Cognit. Comput.*, 16, 3096–3121, 2025.
41. Seikh, M.R. and Mandal, U., Interval-valued Fermatean fuzzy Dombi aggregation operators and SWARA based PROMETHEE II method to bio-medical waste management. *Expert Syst. Appl.*, 226, 120082, 2023.
42. Seikh, M.R. and Chatterjee, P., Determination of best renewable energy sources in India using SWARA-ARAS in confidence level based interval-valued Fermatean fuzzy environment. *Appl. Soft Comput.*, 155, 111495, 2024.
43. Senapati, T. and Yager, R.R., Fermatean fuzzy sets. *J. Ambient Intell. Hum. Comput.*, 11, 663–674, 2020.
44. Simsek, N. and Kirişci, M., Incomplete Fermatean Fuzzy Preference Relations and Group Decision Making. *Topol. Algebra Appl.*, 11, 20220125, 2023.
45. Su, W., Chen, L., Gao, X., Emergency Decision Making: A Literature Review and Future Directions. *Sustainability*, 14, 10925, 2022.
46. Tan, J., Liu, Y., Senapati, T., Garg, H., Rong, Y., An extended MABAC method based on prospect theory with unknown weight information under Fermatean fuzzy environment for risk investment assessment in B&R. *J. Ambient Intell. Humaniz. Comput.*, 14, 13067–13096, 2023.
47. Yager, R.R., Pythagorean fuzzy subsets. *Proc. Joint IFSA World Congress and NAFIPS Annual Meeting*, 2013.
48. Zadeh, L.A., Fuzzy sets. *Inf. Comput.*, 8, 338–353, 1965.
49. Zhang, X.L., A novel approach based on similarity measure for Pythagorean fuzzy multiple criteria group decision making. *Int. J. Intell. Syst.*, 31, 593–611, 2016.
50. Zuakwagh, D., Ejegwa, P.A., Akwu, A.D., Fermatean fuzzy sets in multiset framework with application in diagnostic process based on composite relations, in: *Strategic Fuzzy Extensions and Decision-Making Techniques*, pp. 195–210, CRC Press, 2024.

20

An Innovative MADM Framework Utilizing Some Dombi Shapley Choquet Integral Operators with Picture Fuzzy Information

Pankaj Kakati

Department of Mathematics, Jagannath Barooah University, Jorhat, Assam, India

Abstract

The picture fuzzy set extends boundaries of intuitionistic fuzzy sets (IFS) by proficiently capturing intricate states of acceptance, rejection, and neutrality within information. Further, Dombi operations, well-known for their unmatched flexibility, surpass the limitations of traditional Algebraic and Einstein operations, courtesy of a versatile general parameter. In this study, the fusion of Dombi operations with the generalized Shapley Choquet integral gives rise to novel operators like the Picture Fuzzy Dombi Generalized Shapley Choquet Integral (PFDGSCI) and the Picture Fuzzy Dombi Generalized Shapley Geometric Choquet Integral (PFDGSGCI). Then, these proposed operators are studied to uncover their special properties. Utilizing these new operators fosters a novel approach for multiattribute decision making (MADM) that involves interrelated and intricate attributes. To portray the approach's effectiveness, a detailed quantitative demonstration is presented, emphasizing its applicability. This study aims to widen the range of decision-making approaches, contributing to the refinement and progress within this field.

Keywords: Picture fuzzy set, Dombi operations, generalized Shapley function, Choquet integral, MADM

Email: pankaj07kakati@gmail.com

Harish Garg (ed.) Decision Support Systems in Smart Computing: Embracing Uncertainty and Challenges, (637–664) © 2026 Scrivener Publishing LLC

20.1 Background Study

In practical decision-making scenarios, the available information is usually portrayed by uncertainty and ambiguity. Zadeh's formulation of the fuzzy set (FS) [1] addresses the representation of imprecise information by attributing a membership grade varying between 0 and 1, which reflects the extent of agreement. Nonetheless, conventional fuzzy sets [1] fails to effectively represent instances of non-acceptance or rejection. In response, Atanassov introduced intuitionistic fuzzy sets (IFSs) [2, 3], incorporating nonmembership degrees alongside membership degrees for each element. The IFS [2, 3] quantifies the level of disagreement or rejection in decision-making contexts. Notably, while IFS has wide applications in decision-making problems [4–9], it remains insufficient in capturing decision-maker preferences beyond mere membership and non-membership degrees. Let us consider the scenario of an election where voters can choose to vote for, against, abstain, or refuse to vote for a candidate. IFS falls short in expressing instances like abstention or refusal to vote. Addressing this limitation, Cuong introduced picture fuzzy sets (PFSs) [10, 11] as a significant advancement in the domain of computational intelligence systems [12]. PFSs are identified by three membership grades, namely the positive membership, neutral membership, and non-membership. Subsequently, decision-making models under the PFS framework [10, 11] have emerged. Various researchers have expanded this field significantly. Singh proposed a correlation coefficient for PFSs [13], while Thong introduced the clustering analysis approach under PFSs [14]. Son formulated a similarity measure for PFSs [14], and utilized it in clustering investigation [15]. Wang *et al.* [16] developed some new picture fuzzy similarity measures grounded in fuzzy strict negations and proposed a multi-attributive border approximation area comparison (MABAC) model built on the prospect theory. Jin *et al.* [17] presented an advanced score function to overcome the limitations of the existing picture fuzzy distance measures (PFDMs) and picture fuzzy similarity measures (PFSMs). Further, developed a MCDM approach by integrating the newly developed PFDM and VIKOR method and applied it to medical diagnosis problems. Ma *et al.* [18] extended the power Bonferroni mean (PBM) operator by incorporating Aczel-Alsina operational laws with picture fuzzy sets, proposed several Aczel-Alsina power Bonferroni mean operators and developed a MADM approach. Moreover, Wang *et al.* [19] developed a hybrid fuzzy decision-making method under the picture fuzzy set. It was particularly utilized in energy performance contracting projects. Garg [20] introduced picture fuzzy weighted averaging operators. Additionally, Wang *et al.* [21] offered picture fuzzy geometric aggregation operators for solving MADM problems. Later, developed a MADM method [22] using the Muirhead mean within PFSs. Khan *et al.* [23] introduced picture fuzzy Einstein weighted aggregation operators along with a MADM method. Tian *et al.* [24] introduced the weighted picture fuzzy power Choquet ordered geometric (WPFPCOG) operator and its power Shapley Choquet ordered geometric variant (WPFPSCOG), establishing a decision-making approach utilizing these operators. Wei [25] introduced picture fuzzy Hamacher and Dombi aggregation operators, and further introduced operations expressing priority variation employing Dombi triangular-norms [26]. Seikh *et al.* [27] proposed several intuitionistic fuzzy Dombi weighted average operators and applied them to MADM problems. Liu *et al.* [28] defined several Dombi Bonferroni means for multiattribute group decision-making within IFSs. Additionally, Chen & Ye [29] developed a decision-making framework employing Dombi AOs under single-valued neutrosophic environment. Mohanasundari & Mohana [30] introduced Dombi weighted AOs within quadri-partitioned single-valued neutrosophic sets. He [31] offered a methodology for Typhoon disaster estimation using Dombi hesitant fuzzy AOs. Shi & Ye [32] expanded Dombi operations to neutrosophic cubic sets, introducing the neutrosophic cubic Dombi weighted arithmetic average (NCDWAA) and the neutrosophic cubic Dombi weighted geometric average (NCDWGA) operators. Akram *et al.* [33] proposed some new Dombi weighted aggregation operators within Pythagorean fuzzy sets. Jana *et al.* [34] developed picture fuzzy Dombi weighted operators for tackling MADM problems.

Real-life decision-making often involves attribute correlations. Fuzzy measure [35, 36] based Choquet integral [35] is suitable for depicting attribute interactions. Beliakov and Divakov [38] studied the marginal representation of fuzzy measures, building them from experimental data *via* optimization. They further introduced k-interactivity, reducing constraints and complexity in each constraint [39, 40]. Tan & Chen [51] introduced the intuitionistic fuzzy Choquet integral (IFCI). Wei [52] progressed the IFCI by proposing the interval-valued intuitionistic fuzzy Choquet integral (IIFCI). Lucca *et al.* [41–44] extended Choquet Copula-based aggregation operators, providing broader applications. Dimuro *et al.* [45] introduced the $C_F 1\ F2$ -integral based on pseudo pre-aggregation pairs (F_1, F_2). Bustince *et al.* [46] generalized the Choquet integral, replacing argument differences with a dissimilarity function. Wieczynski *et al.* [47] applied CT-integrals for MCDM with heterogeneous information, extending the Group Modular Choquet Random TOPSIS (GMC-RTOPSIS) method. Additionally, Dimuro [48] provided a state-of-the-art overview of Choquet integrals generalizations in MCDM problems.

During collective decision-making with the Choquet integral, the significance of the ordering of element often gets overlooked. Moreover, defining fuzzy measures over the power set poses challenges in obtaining measures for subsets within a large criteria set. To address these issues, the Shapley function [50] has been introduced as an alternative to solving fuzzy measures. Shapley function-based Choquet integral operators offer advantages over their fuzzy measure-based counterparts:

- *Computational Complexity:* Effectiveness of Choquet integral operators are based on fuzzy measures or Shapley functions in depicting attribute interactions in decision-making. Higher computational complexity in the fuzzy measure-based Choquet integral in contrast to the Shapley function-based operators.
- *Evaluation of Attributes in MADM Problems:* Practical decision-making scenarios often involve numerous attributes, leading to exponential computational complexity in MADM problems. To obtain the overall evaluation of MADM scenarios with n attributes using the fuzzy measure-based Choquet integral, it is necessary to calculate $2^n - 1$ components of fuzzy measures. Hence, computational complexity increases exponentially for large number of attributes. Shapley function-based Choquet integrals exhibit superior efficiency in handling this complexity compared to their fuzzy measure-based counterparts.
- *Representation of Attribute Importance:* Fuzzy measure-based Choquet integral operators tend to overlook the comprehensive importance of attributes, while Shapley function-based counterparts consistently reflect the global significance of attributes within real-life MADM problems.
- *Practical Applications:* Shapley function-based Choquet integrals find effective applications across various domains such as Big Data analytics [58], Pattern recognition [59, 60], and Medical diagnosis [61–63]. Their particular suitability lies in scenarios with extensive datasets, making them invaluable tools.

For an extensive investigation into the Shapley function and aggregation operators rooted in it, consider the works as cited in the literature [53–57]. Based on this review, the primary motivations driving this current investigation can be encapsulated as follows:

1. Picture fuzzy sets [10, 11], an enhanced version of the FSs [1] and IFSs [2, 3], offer an effective way to articulate uncertainty and imprecision within practical decision-making scenarios.
2. Several existing MADM methods [20, 23] fail to account for attribute interactions, a common aspect in real-life problems, demonstrated by the Picture fuzzy set (PFS) models.
3. While the fuzzy measure-based Choquet integrals [35] consider only adjacent attribute interactions, Shapley function-based Choquet integrals [50], estimate overall correlations among random attributes. Moreover, the computational complexity in solving MADM problems with extensive attribute sets can be reduced using the Shapley function, overcoming the intricacies of the fuzzy measure approach.
4. The Dombi operations [26, 34] on PFSs ensure better adaptability compared to than Algebraic and Einstein operations, due to the incorporation of a general variable.

Hence, driven by the aforementioned considerations, merging the Shapley Choquet integral and the Dombi operations within PFSs results in the introduction of Picture fuzzy Dombi generalized Shapley Choquet integral (PFDGSCI) and Picture fuzzy Dombi generalized Shapley geometric Choquet integral (PFDGSGCI). The absence of prior studies on Dombi operations-based Choquet integral operators within the picture fuzzy context underscores the significance of this study, specifically in addressing attribute interactions within practical MADM contexts.

Upcoming sections of this chapter are outlined as: Section 20.2 offers an overview of fundamental concepts. Section 20.3 introduces the PFDGSCI and PFDGSGCI, discussing their respective special unique characteristics. Section 20.4 presents a MADM procedure centered around these operators. Section 20.5 illustrates the applicability of this approach through a numerical example, including a comparative assessment with several existing approaches. Finally, Section 20.6 encapsulates the key concluding remarks.

20.2 Essential Concepts

This section establishes the groundwork for the progression of this study, based on concepts extracted from related literature [10, 11, 35, 36, 50].

Definition 2.1. [10, 11] A picture fuzzy set (PFS) on V is defined as

$$P = \{\langle y, \xi_p(y), \eta_p(y), \zeta_p(y)\rangle \mid y \in V\},$$

where $\xi_p(y)$, $\eta_p(y)$, $\zeta_p(y) \in [0, 1]$, accordingly, depict degrees of positive, neutral, and negative memberships such that $0 \in \xi_p(y) + \eta_p(y) + \zeta_p(y) \in 1$ for each $y \in V$. Further, the refusal degree is defined as $\pi_p(y) = 1 - \xi_p(y) - \eta_p(y) - \zeta_p(y)$ for all $y \in V$. The triplet $P = \langle \xi_p, \eta_p, \zeta_p \rangle$ is referred to as a picture fuzzy number (PFN).

Definition 2.2. [64] Assume $\beta = \langle \xi_\beta, \eta_\beta, \zeta_\beta \rangle$ as a PFN, then the Score $S(\beta)$ and Accuracy $H(\beta)$ functions are presented as follows:

$S(\beta) = \xi_\beta - \zeta_\beta,\ S(\beta) \in [-1, 1]$

$H(\beta) = \xi_\beta + \eta_\beta + \zeta_\beta,\ H(\beta) \in [0, 1]$

Definition 2.3. [64] Suppose $\alpha = \langle \xi_\alpha, \eta_\alpha, \zeta_\alpha \rangle$ and $\beta = \langle \xi_\beta, \eta_\beta, \zeta_\beta \rangle$ represent two PFNs. The following rules hold:

(S.1) if $S(\alpha) < S(\beta)$, then $\alpha \prec \beta$

(S.2) if $S(\alpha) = S(\beta)$, then,

(T.1) if $H(\alpha) < H(\beta)$, then $\alpha \prec \beta$

(T.2) if $H(\alpha) = H(\beta)$, then $\alpha = \beta$.

Definition 2.4. [36] Consider a fuzzy measure on a fixed domain V as a mapping $\tau : 2^v \to [0, 1]$, which fulfills the conditions outlined below:

(i) $\tau(\varnothing) = 0,\ \tau(V) = 1$

(ii) if $B_1 \subseteq B_2 \subseteq V$, then $\tau(B_1) \leqslant \tau(B_2)$.

In order to simplify the perplexity of solving fuzzy measures, Sugeno [36] introduced a particular type of fuzzy measure known as the λ-fuzzy measure.

Definition 2.5. [36] Consider a λ-fuzzy measure on a fixed domain $\boldsymbol{V}$ as a mapping $\tau_\lambda : 2^v \to [0, 1]$, which fulfills the conditions outlined below:

(i) $\tau_\lambda(\emptyset) = 0,\ \tau_\lambda(\boldsymbol{V}) = 1$

(ii) if $B_1 \subseteq B_2 \subseteq \boldsymbol{V}$, then $\tau_\lambda(B_1) \leqslant \tau_\lambda(B_2)$

(iii) $\tau_\lambda(B_1 \cup B_2) = \tau_\lambda(B_1) + \tau_\lambda(B_2)$
$+\lambda\tau_\lambda(B_1)\tau_\lambda(B_2),\ \lambda \in (-1, +\infty),$
$\forall\, B_1, B_2 \in 2^V$, and $B_1 \cap B_2 = \emptyset$.

In particular, when $\lambda = 0$, the λ-fuzzy measure simplifies to the standard additive measure:

$$\tau_\lambda(B_1 \cup B_2) = \tau_\lambda(B_1) + \tau_\lambda(B_2),$$
$$\forall B_1, B_2 \subseteq \boldsymbol{V}, \text{and } B_1 \cap B_2 = \emptyset.$$

When all components of $\boldsymbol{V}$ non-interacting, it follows that $\tau_\lambda(B) = \sum_{s \in B} \tau_\lambda(\{s\})$

Further, $\forall$ B $\subseteq$ $\boldsymbol{V}$, Sugeno [36] presented the following:

$$\tau_\lambda(B) = \begin{cases} \frac{1}{\lambda}\left(\prod_{s \in B}[1 + \lambda\tau_\lambda(\{s\})] - 1\right), & \text{if } \lambda \neq 0 \\ \sum_{s \in B} \tau_\lambda(\{s\}), & \text{if } \lambda = 0 \end{cases} \tag{20.1}$$

Given that $\tau_\lambda(\boldsymbol{V}) = 1$, λ is uniquely derived by resolving the expression below.

$$\lambda + 1 = \prod_{s \in V}(1 + \lambda\tau_\lambda(\{s\})) \tag{20.2}$$

Definition 2.6. [37] Assume g as a positive real-valued function on $V = \{v_1, v_2, \ldots, v_p\}$, and let τ be the fuzzy measure on V. The Choquet integral of g using fuzzy measure τ, is defined as:

$$\mathcal{CH}_\tau(\mathfrak{g}) = \sum_{s=1}^{p} \mathfrak{g}(V_{(i)})(\tau(B_{(s)}) - \tau(B_{(s-1)})),$$

here $(\cdot)$ specifies a permutation on $\boldsymbol{V}$ ensuring that $\mathfrak{g}(v_{(1)}) \geqslant \mathfrak{g}(v_{(2)}) \geqslant \cdots \geqslant \mathfrak{g}(v_{(p)})$ with $B_{(s)} = \{v_{(1)}, v_{(2)}, \ldots, v_{(s)}\}$ for $s \geqslant 1$ and $B_{(0)} = \emptyset$.

Shapley [49] and Marichal [50] presented the idea of the generalized Shapley index, which evaluates the collective effect of each group of alternatives instead of evaluating individual alternative. The generalized Shapley index [49, 50] is furnished as,

$$\varphi_{B_1}(\tau, V) = \sum_{B_2 \subset \mathcal{V} \setminus B_1} \frac{(|V| - |B_1| - |B_2|)!\,|B_2|!}{(|V| - |B_1| + 1)!}(\tau(B_1 \cup B_2) - \tau(B_2)) \tag{20.3}$$

here τ is a fuzzy measure on $\boldsymbol{V}$. $|\boldsymbol{V}|$, $|B_1|$ and $|B_2|$ denote the sizes of alternative's groups B_1, B_2 and $\boldsymbol{V}$, accordingly.

Dombi [26] introduced the Dombi t-norm and t-conorm.

Definition 2.7. [26] Suppose $\gamma > 0$ be a real number and $v_1, v_2 \in [0, 1]$, the Dombi t-norm and t-conorm are characterized as

$$T_\gamma(v_1, v_2) = \frac{1}{1+\left(\left(\frac{1-v_1}{v_1}\right)^\gamma + \left(\frac{1-v_2}{v_2}\right)^\gamma\right)^{\frac{1}{\gamma}}} \tag{20.4}$$

$$T_\gamma^*(v_1, v_2) = 1 - \frac{1}{1+\left(\left(\frac{v_1}{1-v_1}\right)^\gamma + \left(\frac{v_2}{1-v_2}\right)^\gamma\right)^{\frac{1}{\gamma}}} \tag{20.5}$$

Definition 2.8. [34] Consider $\alpha = \langle \xi_\alpha, \eta_\alpha, \zeta_\alpha \rangle$ and $\beta = \langle \xi_\beta, \eta_\beta, \zeta_\beta \rangle$ as two PFNs, and $k, \gamma > 0$, then

(i) $$\alpha \oplus_D \beta = \left\langle 1 - \frac{1}{1+\left(\left(\frac{\xi_\alpha}{1-\xi_\alpha}\right)^\gamma + \left(\frac{\xi_\beta}{1-\xi_\beta}\right)^\gamma\right)^{1/\gamma}}, \frac{1}{1+\left(\left(\frac{1-\eta_\alpha}{\eta_\alpha}\right)^\gamma + \left(\frac{1-\eta_\beta}{\eta_\beta}\right)^\gamma\right)^{1/\gamma}}, \frac{1}{1+\left(\left(\frac{1-\zeta_\alpha}{\zeta_\alpha}\right)^\gamma + \left(\frac{1-\zeta_\beta}{\zeta_\beta}\right)^\gamma\right)^{1/\gamma}} \right\rangle$$

(ii) $$\alpha \otimes_D \beta = \left\langle \frac{1}{1+\left(\left(\frac{1-\xi_\alpha}{\xi_\alpha}\right)^\gamma + \left(\frac{1-\xi_\beta}{\xi_\beta}\right)^\gamma\right)^{1/\gamma}}, 1 - \frac{1}{1+\left(\left(\frac{\eta_\alpha}{1-\eta_\alpha}\right)^\gamma + \left(\frac{\eta_\beta}{1-\eta_\beta}\right)^\gamma\right)^{1/\gamma}}, 1 - \frac{1}{1+\left(\left(\frac{\zeta_\alpha}{1-\zeta_\alpha}\right)^\gamma + \left(\frac{\zeta_\beta}{1-\zeta_\beta}\right)^\gamma\right)^{1/\gamma}} \right\rangle$$

(iii) $$k\alpha = \left\langle 1 - \frac{1}{1+\left(k\left(\frac{\xi_\alpha}{1-\xi_\alpha}\right)^\gamma\right)^{1/\gamma}}, \frac{1}{1+\left(k\left(\frac{1-\eta_\alpha}{\eta_\alpha}\right)^\gamma\right)^{1/\gamma}}, \frac{1}{1+\left(k\left(\frac{1-\zeta_\alpha}{\zeta_\alpha}\right)^\gamma\right)^{1/\gamma}} \right\rangle$$

(iv) $$\alpha^k = \left\langle \frac{1}{1+\left(k\left(\frac{1-\xi_\alpha}{\xi_\alpha}\right)^\gamma\right)^{1/\gamma}}, 1 - \frac{1}{1+\left(k\left(\frac{\eta_\alpha}{1-\eta_\alpha}\right)^\gamma\right)^{1/\gamma}}, 1 - \frac{1}{1+\left(k\left(\frac{\zeta_\alpha}{1-\zeta_\alpha}\right)^\gamma\right)^{1/\gamma}} \right\rangle$$

20.3 The Innovative PFDGSCI and PFDGSGCI

Here, we introduce several picture fuzzy Dombi generalized Shapley Choquet integral operators, namely PFDGSCI and PFDGSGCI, then explore certain desired properties

Definition 3.1. Let $\beta_t = \{\langle \xi_{\beta_t}, \eta_{\beta_t}, \zeta_{\beta_t} \rangle \mid 1 \leqslant t \leqslant q\}$ be a collection of PFNs on V and τ be a fuzzy measure on V, then the picture fuzzy Dombi generalized Shapley Choquet integral (PFDGSCI) operator is expressed as

$$\text{PFDGSCI}(\beta_1,\beta_2,\ldots,\beta_q)=\bigoplus_{t=1}^{q}{}_{D}(\varphi_{B_{(t)}}(\tau,V)-\varphi_{B_{(t-1)}}(\tau,V))\beta_{(t)}, \tag{20.6}$$

where $(\cdot)$ denotes a permutation of $\{\beta_1, \beta_2, \ldots, \beta_q\}$, so that $\beta_{(1)} \geqslant \beta_{(2)} \geqslant \cdots \geqslant \beta_{(q)}$, and $B_{(t)} = \{\beta_{(1)}, \beta_{(2)}, \ldots, \beta_{(t)}\}$, $B_{(0)} = \emptyset$. Also, here $\bigoplus_D$ represents the Dombi sum of PFNs.

Theorem 3.1. Suppose $\beta_t = \{\langle \xi_{\beta_t}, \eta_{\beta_t}, \zeta_{\beta_t} \rangle \mid t = 1, 2, \ldots, q\}$ as an accumulation of PFNs on V *and* τ *be a fuzzy measure on* V, *then the* PFDGSCI *is described as:*

$$\begin{aligned}
&\text{PFDGSCI}(\beta_1,\beta_2,\ldots,\beta_q)\\
&=\left\langle 1-\frac{1}{1+\left(\sum_{t=1}^{q}(\varphi_{B_{(t)}}(\tau,v)-\varphi_{B_{(t-1)}}(\tau,v))\left(\frac{\xi_{\beta_{(t)}}}{1-\xi_{\beta_{(t)}}}\right)^{\gamma}\right)^{\frac{1}{\gamma}}},\right.\\
&\frac{1}{1+\left(\sum_{t=1}^{q}(\varphi_{B_{(t)}}(\tau,v)-\varphi_{B_{(t-1)}}(\tau,v))\left(\frac{1-\eta_{\beta_{(t)}}}{\eta_{\beta_{(t)}}}\right)^{\gamma}\right)^{\frac{1}{\gamma}}},\\
&\left.\frac{1}{1+\left(\sum_{t=1}^{q}(\varphi_{B_{(t)}}(\tau,v)-\varphi_{B_{(t-1)}}(\tau,v))-\left(\frac{1-\zeta_{\beta_{(t)}}}{\zeta_{\beta_{(t)}}}\right)^{\gamma}\right)^{\frac{1}{\gamma}}}\right\rangle
\end{aligned} \tag{20.7}$$

Definition 3.2. Suppose $\beta_t = \{\langle \xi_{\beta_t}, \eta_{\beta_t}, \zeta_{\beta_t} \rangle \mid t = 1, 2, \ldots, q\}$ as an accumulation of PFNs on V and τ be a fuzzy measure on V, then the picture fuzzy Dombi generalized Shapley geometric Choquet integral (PFDGSGCI) operator is viewed as

$$\text{PFDGSGCI}(\beta_1,\beta_2,\ldots,\beta_q)=\bigotimes_{t=1}^{q}{}_{D}\,\beta_{(t)}^{\left(\varphi_{B_{(t)}}(\tau,v)-\varphi_{B_{(t-1)}}(\tau,v)\right)}, \tag{20.8}$$

where $(\cdot)$ denotes a permutation of $\{\beta_1, \beta_2, \ldots, \beta_q\}$, so that $\beta_{(1)} \geqslant \beta_{(2)} \geqslant \cdots \geqslant \beta_{(q)}$, and $B_{(t)} = \{\beta_{(1)}, \beta_{(2)}, \ldots, \beta_{(t)}\}$, $B_{(0)} = \emptyset$. Also, here $\bigotimes_D$ expresses the Dombi product of PFNs.

Theorem 3.2. *Suppose* $\beta_t = \{\langle \xi_{\beta_t}, \eta_{\beta_t}, \zeta_{\beta_t} \rangle \mid 1 \leqslant t \leqslant q\}$ *as an accumulation of PFNs on* $\boldsymbol{V}$ *and* τ *be a fuzzy measure on* $\boldsymbol{V}$*, then the* PFDGSGCI *can be represented as*

$$
\begin{aligned}
&\text{PFDGSGCI}(\beta_1, \beta_2, \ldots, \beta_q) \\
&= \left\langle \frac{1}{1+\left(\sum_{t=1}^{q}\left(\varphi_{B_{(t)}}(\tau,\nu)-\varphi_{B_{(t-1)}}(\tau,\nu)\right)\left(\frac{1-\xi_{\beta_{(t)}}}{\xi_{\beta_{(t)}}}\right)^{\gamma}\right)^{\frac{1}{\gamma}}}, \right. \\
&1-\frac{1}{1+\left(\sum_{t=1}^{q}\left(\varphi_{B_{(t)}}(\tau,\nu)-\varphi_{B_{(t-1)}}(\tau,\nu)\right)\left(\frac{\eta_{\beta_{(t)}}}{1-\eta_{\beta_{(t)}}}\right)^{\gamma}\right)^{\frac{1}{\gamma}}}, \\
&1-\frac{1}{1+\left(\sum_{t=1}^{q}\left(\varphi_{B_{(t)}}(\tau,\nu)-\varphi_{B_{(t-1)}}(\tau,\nu)\right)\left(\frac{\zeta_{\beta_{(t)}}}{1-\zeta_{\beta_{(t)}}}\right)^{\gamma}\right)^{\frac{1}{\gamma}}}
\end{aligned}
\tag{20.9}
$$

The PFDGSCI and PFDGSGCI exhibit several particular instances, which are such as:

Corollary 3.1. *If for each set of attribute* $\varphi_{B_{(t)}}(\tau, \mathbf{V}) = \tau(B_{(t)})\ (1 \leqslant t \leqslant q)$*, the* PFDGSCI, *and* PFDGSGCI *operators respectively, reduce to the picture fuzzy Dombi Choquet integral* (PFDCI), *and the picture fuzzy Dombi geometric Choquet integral* (PFDGCI) *and are given as follows:*

$$
\begin{aligned}
\text{PFDCI}(\beta_1, \beta_2, \ldots, \beta_q) = &\left\langle 1-\frac{1}{1+\left(\sum_{t=1}^{q}\left(\tau(B_{(t)})-\tau(B_{(t-1)})\right)\left(\frac{\xi_{\beta_{(t)}}}{1-\xi_{\beta_{(t)}}}\right)^{\gamma}\right)^{\frac{1}{\gamma}}}, \right. \\
&\frac{1}{1+\left(\sum_{t=1}^{q}\left(\tau(B_{(t)})-\tau(B_{(t-1)})\right)\left(\frac{1-\eta_{\beta_{(t)}}}{\eta_{\beta_{(t)}}}\right)^{\gamma}\right)^{\frac{1}{\gamma}}}, \\
&\left. \frac{1}{1+\left(\sum_{t=1}^{q}\left(\tau(B_{(t)})-\tau(B_{(t-1)})\right)\left(\frac{1-\zeta_{\beta_{(t)}}}{\zeta_{\beta_{(t)}}}\right)^{\gamma}\right)^{\frac{1}{\gamma}}} \right\rangle
\end{aligned}
\tag{20.10}
$$

$$\mathrm{PFDGCI}(\beta_1,\beta_2,\ldots,\beta_q)=\left\langle \frac{1}{1+\left(\sum_{t=1}^{q}\left(\rho(B_{(t)})-\tau(B_{(t-1)})\right)\left(\frac{1-\xi_{\beta(t)}}{\xi_{\beta(t)}}\right)^{\gamma}\right)^{\frac{1}{\gamma}}},\right.$$
$$1-\frac{1}{1+\left(\sum_{t=1}^{q}(\tau(B_{(t)})-\tau(B_{(t-1)}))\left(\frac{\eta_{\beta(t)}}{1-\eta_{\beta(t)}}\right)^{\gamma}\right)^{\frac{1}{\gamma}}},$$
$$\left. 1-\frac{1}{1+\left(\sum_{t=1}^{q}\left(\tau(B_{(t)})-\tau(B_{(t-1)})\right)\left(\frac{\zeta_{\beta(t)}}{1-\zeta_{\beta(t)}}\right)^{\gamma}\right)^{\frac{1}{\gamma}}}\right\rangle \tag{20.11}$$

Corollary 3.2. *If the attributes are non-interacted, then* $\tau(\{v_t\})=\sum_{t=1}^{|B|}w_t,\forall v_t\in B\subseteq \mathbf{V}$, *where* $w_t=\varphi_{B_{(t)}}(\tau,\mathbf{V})-\varphi_{B_{(t-1)}}(\tau,\mathbf{V})$ *and* $\sum_{t=1}^{q}w_t=1$. *In this case, the* PFDGSCI *simplifies to the picture fuzzy Dombi ordered weighted average* (PFDOWA) [34].

$$\mathrm{PFDOWA}(\beta_1,\beta_2,\ldots,\beta_q)=\left\langle 1-\frac{1}{1+\left(\sum_{t=1}^{q}w_t\left(\frac{\xi_{\beta_{(t)}}}{1-\xi_{\beta_{(t)}}}\right)^{\gamma}\right)^{\frac{1}{\gamma}}},\right.$$
$$\left.\frac{1}{1+\left(\sum_{t=1}^{q}w_t\left(\frac{1-\eta_{\beta_{(t)}}}{\eta_{\beta_{(t)}}}\right)^{\gamma}\right)^{\frac{1}{\gamma}}},\frac{1}{1+\left(\sum_{t=1}^{q}w_t\left(\frac{1-\zeta_{\beta_{(t)}}}{\zeta_{\beta_{(t)}}}\right)^{\gamma}\right)^{\frac{1}{\gamma}}}\right\rangle \tag{20.12}$$

Corollary 3.3. *If the attributes are non-interacted, then* $\tau(\{v_t\})=\sum_{t=1}^{|B|}w_t\forall v_t\in B\subseteq \mathbf{V}$, *where* $w_t=\varphi_{B_{(t)}}(\tau,\mathbf{V})-\varphi_{B_{(t-1)}}(\tau,\mathbf{V})$ *and* $\sum_{t=1}^{q}w_t=1$. *In this case, the* PFDGSGCI *simplifies to the picture fuzzy Dombi ordered weighted geometric* (PFDOWG) [34].

$$\text{PFDOWG}(\beta_1,\beta_2,\ldots,\beta_q)=\left\langle \frac{1}{1+\left(\sum_{t=1}^{q} w_t\left(\frac{1-\xi_{\beta_{(t)}}}{\xi_{\beta_{(t)}}}\right)^{\gamma}\right)^{\frac{1}{\gamma}}}, 1-\frac{1}{1+\left(\sum_{t=1}^{q} w_t\left(\frac{\eta_{\beta_{(t)}}}{1-\eta_{\beta_{(t)}}}\right)^{\gamma}\right)^{\frac{1}{\gamma}}}, 1-\frac{1}{1+\left(\sum_{t=1}^{q} w_s\left(\frac{\zeta_{\beta_{(t)}}}{1-\zeta_{\beta_{(t)}}}\right)^{\gamma}\right)^{\frac{1}{\gamma}}} \right\rangle \tag{20.13}$$

Remark 1. From Corollary 3.1, it is clear that the PFDGSCI, and PFDGSGCI can be reduced to several novel Dombi Choquet integral such as the PFDCI and PFDGCI operators.

Remark 2. Corollaries 3.2 and 3.3, show that the PFDGSCI, and PFDGSGCI operators are extensions of some existing Dombi weighted aggregation operators such as the PFDOWA [34], and PFDOWG [34].

20.3.1 Properties of PFDGSCI and PFDGSGCI

Theorem 3.3 (Idempotency). *Let* $\beta_t = \{\langle \xi_{\beta_t}, \eta_{\beta_t}, \zeta_{\beta_t}\rangle \mid 1 \leqslant t \leqslant q\}$ *be an accumulation of* PFNs *on* V. *If* $\beta_t = \beta \ \forall\ t(1 \leqslant t \leqslant q)$, *then*

$$\text{PFDGSCI}(\beta_1, \beta_2, \ldots, \beta_q) = \beta$$
$$\text{PFDGSGCI}(\beta_1, \beta_2, \ldots, \beta_q) = \beta$$

Theorem 3.4 (Commutativity). *Let* $\beta_t = \{\langle \xi_{\beta_t}, \eta_{\beta_t}, \zeta_{\beta_t}\rangle \mid 1 \leqslant t \leqslant q\}$ *be an accumulation of* PFNs *on* V, *and* $\beta'_t = \{\langle \xi_{\beta'_t}, \eta_{\beta'_t}, \zeta_{\beta'_t}\rangle \mid 1 \leqslant t \leqslant q\}$ *be a reordering of* β_t. *Then*

$$\text{PFDGSCI}(\beta_1, \beta_2, \ldots, \beta_q) = \text{PFDGSCI}(\beta'_1, \beta'_2, \ldots, \beta'_q)$$
$$\text{PFDGSGCI}(\beta_1, \beta_2, \ldots, \beta_q) = \text{PFDGSGCI}(\beta'_1, \beta'_2, \ldots, \beta'_q)$$

Theorem 3.5 (Comonotonicity). *If* $\alpha_t = \langle \xi_{\alpha_t}, \eta_{\alpha_t}, \zeta_{\alpha_t}\rangle$, $\beta_t = \langle \xi_{\beta_t}, \eta_{\beta_t}, \zeta_{\beta_t}\rangle$ $(1 \leqslant t \leqslant)$ *be two accumulations of* PFNs *on* V, *such that* $\xi_{\alpha(t)} \leqslant \xi_{\beta(t)}, \eta_{\alpha(t)} \geqslant \eta_{\beta(t)}$, *and* $\zeta_{\alpha(t)} \geqslant \zeta_{\beta(t)}$ *for all s, then*

$$\text{PFDGSCI}(\alpha_1, \alpha_2, \ldots, \alpha_q) \preccurlyeq \text{PFDGSCI}(\beta_1, \beta_2, \ldots, \beta_q)$$
$$\text{PFDGSGCI}(\alpha_1, \alpha_2, \ldots, \alpha_q) \preccurlyeq \text{PFDGSGCI}(\beta_1, \beta_2, \ldots, \beta_q)$$

here, $(\cdot)$ *indicates a reordering on* V.

Theorem 3.6 (Boundedness). *Let* $\beta_t = \{\langle \xi_{\beta_t}, \eta_{\beta_t}, \zeta_{\beta_t} \rangle \mid 1 \leqslant t \leqslant q\}$ *be an accumulation of* PFNs *on* V. *Then,*

$$\beta^- \preccurlyeq \text{PFDGSCI}(\beta_1, \beta_2, \ldots, \beta_q) \preccurlyeq \beta^+$$
$$\beta^- \preccurlyeq \text{PFDGSGCI}(\beta_1, \beta_2, \ldots, \beta_q) \preccurlyeq \beta^+$$

where,

$$\beta^- = \langle \min(\xi_{\beta_t}), \max(\eta_{\beta_t}), \max(\zeta_{\beta_s}) \rangle$$
$$\beta^+ = \langle \max(\xi_{\beta_t}), \min(\eta_{\beta_t}), \min(\zeta_{\beta_t}) \rangle$$

20.4 A Novel MADM Approach Based on PFDGSCI and PFDGSGCI

A novel MADM approach utilizing PFDGSCI and PFDGSGCI operators is presented here. Facilitate the characterization of alternative assessment data by employing PFNs. Consider $B = \{B_1, B_2, \ldots, B_p\}$ as an accumulation of alternatives and $\mathfrak{C} = \{\mathfrak{C}_1, \mathfrak{C}_2, \ldots, \mathfrak{C}_q\}$ a group of attributes. Suppose that the assessment data of B_s's $(s = 1, 2, \ldots, p)$ based upon each attribute $\mathfrak{C}_t \in \mathfrak{C}$ $(1 \leqslant t \leqslant q)$ is portrayed *via* PFNs.

The proposed MADM framework comprises of the subsequent stages.

Step 1. Express the evaluation data of B_s's $(s = 1, 2, \ldots, p)$ related to $\mathfrak{C}_t$ $(1 \leqslant t \leqslant q)$ into the picture fuzzy decision matrix $\mathfrak{D} = [\beta_{st}]_{p\times q}$, where each β_{st} is a PFN, and is given by $\beta_{st} = \langle \xi_{\beta_{st}}, \eta_{\beta_{st}}, \zeta_{\beta_{st}} \rangle, (s = 1, 2, \ldots, p; t = 1, 2, \ldots, q)$. The terms $\xi_{\beta_{st}}, \eta_{\beta_{st}}$, and $\zeta_{\beta_{st}}$ respectively, represent the degrees of positive, neutral, and negative memberships such that $\xi_{\beta_{st}}, \eta_{\beta_{st}}, \zeta_{\beta_{st}} \subset [0, 1]$ with $0 \leqslant \xi_{\beta_{st}} + \eta_{\beta_{st}} + \zeta_{\beta_{st}} \leqslant 1$.

Step 2. Compute fuzzy measures τ for every arrangement by applying Equations (20.1) and (20.2), and generalized Shapley indices φ_S (τ, N) through Equation (20.3).

Step 3. Employ score and accuracy functions [64] to re-arrange the β_{st}'s for each $1 \leqslant s \leqslant p$ so as $\beta_{s(1)} \succ \beta s(2) \succ \cdots \succ \beta s(q)$.

Step 4. Utilize the PFDGSCI (or PFDGSGCI) operator expressed in Equation (20.7) (or Equation (20.8)), to aggregate the re-ordered partial evaluation $\beta_{s(t)}$ $(1 \leqslant s \leqslant p; 1 \leqslant t \leqslant q)$ for obtaining the overall evaluation values β_s $(1 \leqslant s \leqslant p)$ corresponding to each alternative B_s $(1 \leqslant s \leqslant p)$.

Step 5. Evaluate the score $S(\beta_s)$ and accuracy $H(\beta_s)$ of the overall evaluation values β_s $(1 \leqslant s \leqslant p)$ to assess the alternative B_s $(1 \leqslant s \leqslant p)$ and specify the most favorable choice.

Step 6. Finalization.

A flowchart of the proposed MADM is shown in Figure 20.1 as follows:

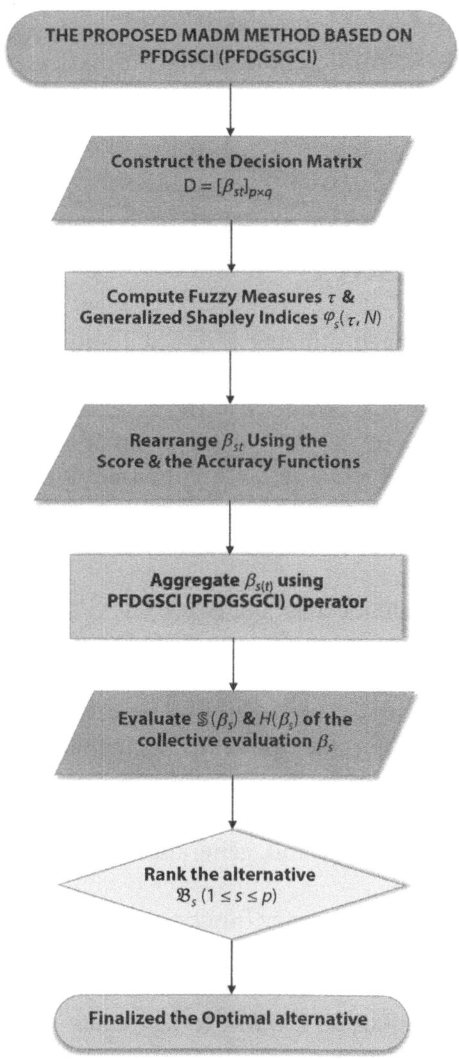

Figure 20.1 Flowchart of the proposed MADM approach.

20.5 Detailed Depiction

Suppose a construction firm assessing potential production partners to establish a global partnership. The firm needs to identify the most viable option from four different alternatives B_s $(1 \leqslant s \leqslant 4)$, determined by the attributes outlined as: (i) $\mathfrak{C}_1$: Manufacturing capabilities, (ii) $\mathfrak{C}_2$: Quality control, (iii) $\mathfrak{C}_3$: Time management, (iv) $\mathfrak{C}_4$: Potential market.

Stage 1. The alternatives B_s $(1 \leqslant s \leqslant 4)$ relative to the attributes $\mathfrak{C}_t$ $(1 \leqslant t \leqslant 4)$ are expressed by the picture fuzzy decision matrix $\mathfrak{D} = [\beta_{st}]_{4\times 4}$, as described in Table 20.1.

Stage 2. Identify the fuzzy measure τ such that for individual attribute C_t $(1 \leqslant t \leqslant 4)$, the value $\tau(\{C_t\})$ represents the importance of C_t $(1 \leqslant t \leqslant 4)$. Assuming experts' opinion, suppose the fuzzy measures of the attributes be constructed as: $\tau(\emptyset) = 0$, $\tau(\{C_1\}) = 0.23$, $\tau(\{C_2\}) = 0.17$, $\tau(\{C_3\}) = 0.22$ and $\tau(\{C_4\}) = 0.25$. By employing Equation (20.2), the value of λ is obtained as $\lambda = 0.43$.

Table 20.1 The picture fuzzy decision matrix $\mathfrak{D}$.

	$\mathfrak{C}_1$	$\mathfrak{C}_2$	$\mathfrak{C}_3$	$\mathfrak{C}_4$
B_1	⟨0.52, 0.32, 0.08⟩	⟨0.56, 0.34, 0.06⟩	⟨0.68, 0.17, 0.07⟩	⟨0.74, 0.13, 0.05⟩
B_2	⟨0.76, 0.18, 0.06⟩	⟨0.14, 0.65, 0.08⟩	⟨0.62, 0.07, 0.23⟩	⟨0.72, 0.06, 0.09⟩
B_3	⟨0.56, 0.32, 0.05⟩	⟨0.07, 0.76, 0.08⟩	⟨0.71, 0.13, 0.04⟩	⟨0.08, 0.67, 0.16⟩
B_4	⟨0.09, 0.78, 0.04⟩	⟨0.67, 0.22, 0.03⟩	⟨0.06, 0.69, 0.07⟩	⟨0.55, 0.26, 0.06⟩

Again using Equation (20.1), we have

$$\tau(\{\mathfrak{C}_1,\mathfrak{C}_2\}) = 0.42,\ \tau(\{\mathfrak{C}_1,\mathfrak{C}_3\}) = 0.47,$$
$$\tau(\{\mathfrak{C}_1,\mathfrak{C}_4\}) = 0.50,\ \tau(\{\mathfrak{C}_2,\mathfrak{C}_3\}) = 0.41,$$
$$\tau(\{\mathfrak{C}_2,\mathfrak{C}_4\}) = 0.44,\ \tau(\{\mathfrak{C}_3,\mathfrak{C}_4\}) = 0.49,$$
$$\tau(\{\mathfrak{C}_1,\mathfrak{C}_2,\mathfrak{C}_3\}) = 0.68,\ \tau(\{\mathfrak{C}_1,\mathfrak{C}_2,\mathfrak{C}_4\}) = 0.71,$$
$$\tau(\{\mathfrak{C}_1,\mathfrak{C}_3,\mathfrak{C}_4\}) = 0.77,\ \tau(\{\mathfrak{C}_2,\mathfrak{C}_3,\mathfrak{C}_4\}) = 0.70,$$
$$\tau(\{\mathfrak{C}_1,\mathfrak{C}_2,\mathfrak{C}_3,\mathfrak{C}_4\}) = 1.$$

Again, by applying Equation (20.3), generalized Shapley indices [50] for all coalitions are obtained as:

$$\varphi_{\varnothing}(\tau,\nu) = 0,\qquad \varphi_{\mathfrak{C}_1}(\tau,\nu) = 0.26,$$
$$\varphi_{\mathfrak{C}_2}(\tau,\nu) = 0.22,\qquad \varphi_{\mathfrak{C}_3}(\tau,\nu) = 0.25,$$
$$\varphi_{\mathfrak{C}_4}(\tau,\nu) = 0.27,\qquad \varphi_{\{\mathfrak{C}_1,\mathfrak{C}_2\}}(\tau,\nu) = 0.50,$$
$$\varphi_{\{\mathfrak{C}_1,\mathfrak{C}_3\}}(\tau,\nu) = 0.54,\qquad \varphi_{\{\mathfrak{C}_1,\mathfrak{C}_4\}}(\tau,\nu) = 0.56,$$
$$\varphi_{\{\mathfrak{C}_2,\mathfrak{C}_3\}}(\tau,\nu) = 0.46,\qquad \varphi_{\{\mathfrak{C}_2,\mathfrak{C}_4\}}(\tau,\nu) = 0.48,$$
$$\varphi_{\{\mathfrak{C}_3,\mathfrak{C}_4\}}(\tau,\nu) = 0.52,\qquad \varphi_{\{\mathfrak{C}_1,\mathfrak{C}_2,\mathfrak{C}_3\}}(\tau,\nu) = 0.75,$$
$$\varphi_{\{\mathfrak{C}_1,\mathfrak{C}_2,\mathfrak{C}_4\}}(\tau,\nu) = 0.77,\qquad \varphi_{\{\mathfrak{C}_1,\mathfrak{C}_3,\mathfrak{C}_4\}}(\tau,\nu) = 0.78,$$
$$\varphi_{\{\mathfrak{C}_2,\mathfrak{C}_3,\mathfrak{C}_4\}}(\tau,\nu) = 0.73,\qquad \varphi_{\{\mathfrak{C}_1,\mathfrak{C}_2,\mathfrak{C}_3,\mathfrak{C}_4\}}(\tau,\nu) = 1.$$

Stage 3. Applying Definition 2.2, the score values of the evaluation values β_{st} $(1 \leqslant t \leqslant 4)$ of each alternative B_s $(1 \leqslant s \leqslant 4)$ are organized in descending order. The score values β_{1t} $(1 \leqslant t \leqslant 4)$ relative to the alternative B_1 are computed as $\mathbb{S}(\beta_{11}) = 0.70$, $\mathbb{S}(\beta_{12}) = 0.72$, $\mathbb{S}(\beta_{13}) = 0.81$, $\mathbb{S}(\beta_{14}) = 0.85$. Since $\mathbb{S}(\beta_{14}) > \mathbb{S}(\beta_{13}) > \mathbb{S}(\beta_{12}) > \mathbb{S}(\beta_{11})$, hence, by Definition 2.2, β_{st} $(1 \leqslant s \leqslant 4)$ relative to the alternative B_1 is re-ordered as $\beta_{14} \succ \beta_{13} \succ \beta_{12} \succ \beta_{11}$. The fuzzy measures $\tau(\mathcal{G})\ \forall\ \mathcal{G} \subseteq V$ of each attribute $\mathfrak{C}_t$ $(1 \leqslant s \leqslant 4)$ relative to the alternative B_1 are computed as:

$$\left.\begin{aligned}
\tau(\mathcal{G}_{1(1)}) &= \rho(\mathfrak{C}_4) = 0.25,\\
\tau(\mathcal{G}_{1(2)}) &= \rho(\mathfrak{C}_4,\mathfrak{C}_3) = 0.49,\\
\tau(\mathcal{G}_{1(3)}) &= \rho(\mathfrak{C}_4,\mathfrak{C}_3,\mathfrak{C}_2) = 0.70,\\
\tau(\mathcal{G}_{1(4)}) &= \rho(\mathfrak{C}_4,\mathfrak{C}_3,\mathfrak{C}_2,\mathfrak{C}_1) = 1.
\end{aligned}\right\} \tag{20.14}$$

Moreover, the generalized Shapley indices [50] relative to the alternative B_1 are given by :

$$\varphi_{\mathcal{G}_{1(1)}}(\tau,\mathbf{V}) = \varphi_{\mathfrak{C}_4}(\tau,\mathbf{V}) = 0.27,$$
$$\varphi_{\mathcal{G}_{1(2)}}(\tau,\mathbf{V}) = \varphi_{\{\mathfrak{C}_4,\mathfrak{C}_3\}}(\tau,\mathbf{V}) = 0.52,$$
$$\varphi_{\mathcal{G}_{1(3)}}(\tau,\mathbf{V}) = \varphi_{\{\mathfrak{C}_4,\mathfrak{C}_3,\mathfrak{C}_1\}}(\tau,\mathbf{V}) = 0.78,$$
$$\varphi_{\mathcal{G}_{1(4)}}(\tau,\mathbf{V}) = \varphi_{\{\mathfrak{C}_4,\mathfrak{C}_3,\mathfrak{C}_1,\mathfrak{C}_2\}}(\tau,\mathbf{V}) = 1.$$

In a similar manner, the reshuffling of the partial evaluations β_{st} (s = 2, 3, 4; $1 \leqslant t \leqslant 4$) and the generalized Shapley indices associated with the alternatives B_s (s = 2, 3, 4) are indicated in Table 20.2.

Stage 4. Utilizing the PFDGSCI operator with $\gamma = 1$ the overall evaluations β_s ($1 \leqslant s \leqslant 4$) relative to each alternative B_s ($1 \leqslant s \leqslant 4$) are computed as:

$$\beta_1 = \langle 0.6514, 0.2000, 0.0623 \rangle,$$
$$\beta_2 = \langle 0.6655, 0.1007, 0.0879 \rangle,$$
$$\beta_3 = \langle 0.5046, 0.2875, 0.0616 \rangle,$$
$$\beta_4 = \langle 0.4468, 0.3697, 0.0450 \rangle.$$

Table 20.2 Reordering of the partial evaluations β_{st}.

Choices	Reshuffling of the partial evaluations	Generalized Shapley indices
B_2	$\beta_{21} \succ \beta_{24} \succ \beta_{23} \succ \beta_{22}$	$\varphi_{\mathcal{G}_{2(1)}}(\tau,V) = \varphi_{\mathfrak{C}_1}(\tau,V) = 0.26$, $\varphi_{\mathcal{G}_{2(2)}}(\tau,V) = \varphi_{\{\mathfrak{C}_1,\mathfrak{C}_4\}}(\tau,V) = 0.56$, $\varphi_{\mathcal{G}_{2(3)}}(\tau,V) = \varphi_{\{\mathfrak{C}_1,\mathfrak{C}_4,\mathfrak{C}_3\}}(\tau,V) = 0.78$, $\varphi_{\mathcal{G}_{2(4)}}(\tau,V) = \varphi_{\{\mathfrak{C}_1,\mathfrak{C}_4,\mathfrak{C}_3,\mathfrak{C}_2\}}(\tau,V) = 1$
B_3	$\beta_{33} \succ \beta_{31} \succ \beta_{32} \succ \beta_{34}$	$\varphi_{\mathcal{G}_{3(1)}}(\tau,V) = \varphi_{\mathfrak{C}_3}(\tau,V) = 0.25$, $\varphi_{\mathcal{G}_{3(2)}}(\tau,V) = \varphi_{\{\mathfrak{C}_3,\mathfrak{C}_1\}}(\tau,V) = 0.54$, $\varphi_{\mathcal{G}_{3(3)}}(\tau,V) = \varphi_{\{\mathfrak{C}_3,\mathfrak{C}_1,\mathfrak{C}_2\}}(\tau,V) = 0.75$, $\varphi_{\mathcal{G}_{3(4)}}(\tau,V) = \varphi_{\{\mathfrak{C}_3,\mathfrak{C}_1,\mathfrak{C}_2,\mathfrak{C}_4\}}(\tau,V) = 1$
B_4	$\beta_{42} \succ \beta_{44} \succ \beta_{41} \succ \beta_{43}$	$\varphi_{\mathcal{G}_{4(1)}}(\tau,V) = \varphi_{\mathfrak{C}_2}(\tau,V) = 0.22$, $\varphi_{\mathcal{G}_{4(2)}}(\tau,V) = \varphi_{\{\mathfrak{C}_2,\mathfrak{C}_4\}}(\tau,V) = 0.48$, $\varphi_{\mathcal{G}_{4(3)}}(\tau,V) = \varphi_{\{\mathfrak{C}_2,C_4,\mathfrak{C}_1\}}(\tau,V) = 0.77$, $\varphi_{\mathcal{G}_{2(4)}}(\tau,V) = \varphi_{\{\mathfrak{C}_2,\mathfrak{C}_4,\mathfrak{C}_1,\mathfrak{C}_3\}}(\tau,V) = 1$

Stage 5. The score values $\mathbb{S}(\beta_s)$ $(1 \leqslant s \leqslant 4)$ of the overall evaluations β_s $(1 \leqslant s \leqslant 4)$ relative to each alternative B_s $(1 \leqslant s \leqslant 4)$ are computed as: $\mathbb{S}(\beta_1) = 0.7964$, $\mathbb{S}(\beta_2) = 0.8256$, $\mathbb{S}(\beta_3) = 0.7185$, $\mathbb{S}(\beta_4) = 0.6774$. Since $\mathbb{S}(\beta_2) > \mathbb{S}(\beta_1) > \mathbb{S}(\beta_3) > \mathbb{S}(\beta_4)$, therefore the order of preference of the alternatives is $B_2 \succ B_1 \succ B_3 \succ B_4$. Hence the alternative B_2 emerges the ultimate option.

20.5.1 A Comparative Analysis

A comparative analysis of the proposed MADM method with several existing methods [20, 21, 34] is provided here. Suppose that weight vector associated with the attributes be $w = (0.3, 0.2, 0.1, 0.4)^T$ and Dombi parameter $\gamma = 1$. The outcomes of relative analysis are derived by employing the existing methods [20, 21, 34] to the example in Section 20.5, and shown in Table 20.3.

The comparative analysis provides the following key observations based on Table 20.3 and Figure 20.2.

- The alternative B_2 appears as the optimal choice across all methods.
- The proposed MADM method based on PFDGSCI and PFDGSGCI is more suitable for handling interdependent attributes and effectively reflects global importance of attributes on the alternatives. Therefore, it is more applicable to practical life problems.
- From Table 20.3 and Figure 20.2, it's evident that the proposed method utilizing PFDGSCI shows significantly higher ranking values compared to the existing methods [20, 21, 34].
- Similar to PFDGSCI, the optimal outcome obtained by using PFDGSGCI is also B_2, thereby maintaining the consistency in the ranking order, although the corresponding ranking values are comparatively lower.
- The alternative with lowest ranking according to Garg [20] and Jana *et al.* [34] is B_3, whereas Wang *et al.* [21] and the proposed methods identifies B_4 as the last alternative. This indicates minor difference between B_3 and B_4, due to the influence of attribute weights and variation of the Dombi parameter.

Table 20.3 A relative analysis of different MADM methods.

Method	Operators	Score	Ordering
Garg [20]	PFWA [20]	$\mathbb{S}(\beta_1) = 0.4671, \mathbb{S}(\beta_2) = 0.5591, \mathbb{S}(\beta_3) = 0.4104, \mathbb{S}(\beta_4) = 0.4113.$	$B_2 \succ B_1 \succ B_4 \succ B_3$
Wang *et al.* [21]	PFWG [21]	$\mathbb{S}(\beta_1) = 0.4593, \mathbb{S}(\beta_2) = 0.5683, \mathbb{S}(\beta_3) = 0.4302, \mathbb{S}(\beta_4) = 0.4109.$	$B_2 \succ B_1 \succ B_3 \succ B_4$
Jana *et al.* [34]	PFDWA [34]	$\mathbb{S}(\beta_1) = 0.5071, \mathbb{S}(\beta_2) = 0.5865, \mathbb{S}(\beta_3) = 0.4770, \mathbb{S}(\beta_4) = 0.4876.$	$B_2 \succ B_1 \succ B_4 \succ B_3$
Proposed method	PFDGSCI	$\mathbb{S}(\beta_1) = 0.7964, \mathbb{S}(\beta_2) = 0.8256, \mathbb{S}(\beta_3) = 0.7185, \mathbb{S}(\beta_4) = 0.6774.$	$B_2 \succ B_1 \succ B_3 \succ B_4$
Proposed method	PFDGSGCI	$\mathbb{S}(\beta_1) = 0.4565, \mathbb{S}(\beta_2) = 0.5428, \mathbb{S}(\beta_3) = 0.3771, \mathbb{S}(\beta_4) = 0.2591.$	$B_2 \succ B_1 \succ B_3 \succ B_4$

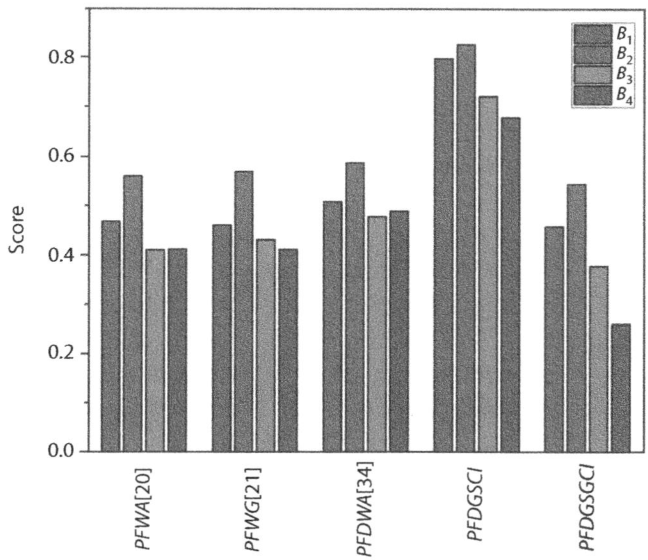

Figure 20.2 Comparative analysis of alternative rankings based on various methods.

Thus the comparative analysis demonstrate that despite differences in the frameworks of all the existing methods [20, 21, 34] and the proposed MADM method, all the methods offer the same optimal outcome B_2. This ensures the applicability of the proposed method. Further, the proposed operators PFDGSCI and PFDGSGCI are more cognizant of the interdependencies between the attributes. Hence, it is considered more competent than the existing methods [20, 21, 34] in situations where such interactions can't be ignored.

20.5.2 Advantages of the Proposed Study

The proposed study offers several key advantages which can be summarized as follows:

- The proposed operators PFDGSCI and PFDGSGCI based on the Shapley function reduces the computational complexity of solving fuzzy measures, hence more effective even for MADM problems with large data set.
- The Shapley function is a useful tool for reflecting the global importance of individual attributes, whereas the fuzzy measure reflect only the local importance of the attributes during the collective decision-making process. Hence, the proposed method based on PFDGSCI and PFDGSGCI appears to be more effective than the contemporary methods.
- The proposed MADM method is grounded in the picture fuzzy sets (PFSs) Environment, which allows for a more appropriate representation of the ambiguity, hesitancy, and imprecision compared to other fuzzy set extensions.
- The proposed operators PFDGSCI and PFDGSGCI are built on Dombi operations. Further, Dombi *t*-norms are more flexible than the Algebraic and the Einstein *t*-norms due to the presence of an additional parameter, consequently, the overall result obtained by the using PFDGSCI and PFDGSGCI are more robust and accurate.
- Due to less computational complexity the proposed method based on PFDGSCI and PFDGSGCI are more effective to tackle Big Data than some contemporary methods.

20.6 Conclusions

In this study, two innovative operators are introduced, namely the Picture Fuzzy Dombi Generalized Shapley Choquet Integral (PFDGSCI) and the Picture Fuzzy Dombi Generalized Shapley Geometric Choquet Integral (PFDGSGCI), which combine Dombi operations with the generalized Shapley Choquet integral. These operators, designed to handle intricate states of acceptance, rejection, and neutrality within information, extend the capabilities of intuitionistic fuzzy sets (IFS). Moreover, the study investigates various special cases and features of PFDGSCI and PFDGSGCI, emphasizing their application within the MADM framework, where attributes interact within the Picture fuzzy environment. The proposed MADM method is demonstrated through a detailed numerical example, showcasing its effectiveness and applicability. The versatility of these operators suggests potential applications beyond decision-making, extending to areas such as optimization, pattern recognition, neural networks, and image processing.

The major contributions of this study can be summarized as:

- Introduction of two novel operators, Picture Fuzzy Dombi Generalized Shapley Choquet Integral (PFDGSCI) and the Picture Fuzzy Dombi Generalized Shapley Geometric Choquet Integral (PFDGS-GCI) by combining the Dombi operational rules with Shapley Choquet integral.
- Properties and special cases of PFDGSCI and PFDGSGCI are studied.
- A new approach for MADM utilizing these proposed operators is designed.
- The proposed MADM approach is demonstrated with a numerical example.
- Some key advantages of the proposed operators are discussed.

Despite these contributions, this study has certain limitations:

- The final result obtained by using the proposed operators PFDGSCI and PFDGSGCI may be influenced by Dombi operations, due to their dependency on parameter variations and may require intelligent expert assessment.

- Although, the proposed operators PFDGSCI and PFDGSGCI are suitable for solving MADM problems with large dataset due to less computational complexity of the Shapley function compared to fuzzy measures, complexity may still arise while solving decision-making problems involving extremely large datasets.
- The present MADM algorithm is formulated to tackle individual decision-making scenarios. However, the present study hasn't been extended to support group decision-making problems. Upgrading the present MADM algorithm to accommodate group decision-making scenarios could be considered as a future research direction.

Further, the present study can contribute towards the following research directions:

- The present study can enhance the data-driven techniques such as machine learning, deep learning, big data analytics, etc. by appropriately tuning the Dombi parameter values.
- The proposed MADM approach can enhance Shapley-based estimation techniques to reduce computational complexity and processing time of large datasets.
- The proposed approached can be extended to support group decision-making scenarios, such as supplier selection, medical equipment procurement, construction project assessment, waste management, water resource establishment.
- The proposed approach can be applied to study various advanced areas, such as big data analytics, medical diagnosis, pattern recognition, image processing.

Acknowledgments

The author acknowledges the anonymous referees for their insightful comments and suggestions in refining this chapter.

AI disclosure statement: The author confirms that no artificial intelligence (AI)-generated content or AI-assisted writing tools were used in the preparation of this chapter (including summaries and the abstract). All text, analysis, and conclusions are the result of the author's original work.

References

1. Lotfi, A.Z., Fuzzy sets. *Inf. Control*, 8, 3, 338–353, 1965.
2. Atanassov, K.T., Intuitionistic fuzzy sets. *Fuzzy Sets Syst.*, 20, 1, 87–96, 1986.
3. Atanassov, K.T., More on intuitionistic fuzzy sets. *Fuzzy Sets Syst.*, 33, 1, 37–45, 1989.
4. Li, D.F., Multiattribute decision making models and methods using intuitionistic fuzzy sets. *J. Comput. Syst. Sci.*, 70, 1, 73–85, 2005.
5. Xu, Z.S., Models for multiple attribute decision making with intuitionistic fuzzy information. *Int. J. Uncertainty Fuzziness Knowledge Based Syst.*, 15, 3, 285–297, 2007.
6. Li, D.F., Extension of the LINMAP for multiattribute decision making under Atanassov's intuitionistic fuzzy environment. *Fuzzy Optim. Dec. Making*, 7, 1, 17–34, 2008.
7. Liu, H.W. and Wang, G.J., Multi-criteria decision-making methods based on intuitionistic fuzzy sets. *Eur. J. Oper. Res.*, 179, 1, 220–233, 2007.
8. Liu, P. and Zhang, X., Approach to multi-attributes decision making with intuitionistic linguistic information based on dempster-shafer evidence theory. *IEEE Access*, 6, 1, 52969–52981, 2018.
9. Szmidt, E. and Kacprzyk, J., Using intuitionistic fuzzy sets in group decision making. *Control Cybern.*, 31, 1055–1057, 2002.
10. Cuong, B.C., Picture fuzzy sets-first results. part 1, seminar neuro-fuzzy systems with applications. Tech. rep., Institute of Mathematics, Hanoi, 2013.
11. Cuong, B.C., Picture fuzzy sets-first results. part 2, seminar neuro-fuzzy systems with applications. Tech. rep., Institute of Mathematics, Hanoi, 2013.
12. Siddique, N. and Adeli, H., *Computational intelligence: synergies of fuzzy logic, neural networks and evolutionary computing*, John Wiley & Sons, Chichester, West Sussex, UK, 2013.
13. Singh, P., Correlation coefficients for picture fuzzy sets. *J. Intell. Fuzzy Syst.*, 28, 2, 591–604, 2015.
14. Thong, P.H., A novel automatic picture fuzzy clustering method based on particle swarm optimization and picture composite cardinality. *Knowledge-Based Syst.*, 109, 48–60, 2016.
15. Son, L.H., Measuring analogousness in picture fuzzy sets: from picture distance measures to picture association measures. *Fuzzy Optim. Dec. Making*, 16, 359–378, 2017.
16. Wang, T., Wu, X., Garg, H., Liu, Q., Chen, G., A prospect theory-based MABAC algorithm with novel similarity measures and interactional operations for picture fuzzy sets and its applications. *Eng. Appl. Artif. Intell.*, 126, 106787, 2023.
17. Jin, J., Garg, H., You, T., Generalized picture fuzzy distance and similarity measures on the complete lattice and their applications. *Expert Syst. Appl.*, 220, 119710, 2023.

18. Ma, L., Jabeen, K., Karamti, W., Ullah, K., Khan, Q., Garg, H., Yin, S., Aczel-Alsina power bonferroni aggregation operators for picture fuzzy information and decision analysis. *Complex Intell. Syst.*, 10, 3, 3329–3352, 2024.
19. Wang, L., Peng, J.J., Wang, J.Q., A multi-criteria decision-making framework for risk ranking of energy performance contracting project under picture fuzzy environment. *J. Cleaner Prod.*, 191, 105–118, 2018.
20. Garg, H., Some picture fuzzy aggregation operators and their applications to multicriteria decision-making. *Arabian J. Sci. Eng.*, 42, 12, 5275–5290, 2017.
21. Wang, C., Zhou, X., Tu, H., Tao, S., Some geometric aggregation operators based on picture fuzzy sets and their application in multiple attribute decision making. *Ital. J. Pure Appl. Math.*, 37, 477–492, 2017.
22. Wang, R., Wang, J., Gao, H., Wei, G., Methods for MADM with picture fuzzy muirhead mean operators and their application for evaluating the financial investment risk. *Symmetry*, 11, 1, 6, 2019.
23. Khan, S., Abdullah, S., Ashraf, S., Picture fuzzy aggregation information based on Einstein operations and their application in decision making. *Math. Sci.*, 13, 3, 213–229, 2019.
24. Tian, C., Peng, J.J., Zhang, S., Zhang, W.Y., Wang, J.Q., Weighted picture fuzzy aggregation operators and their applications to multi-criteria decision-making problems. *Comput. Ind. Eng.*, 137, 106037, 2019.
25. Wei, G., Picture fuzzy Hamacher aggregation operators and their application to multiple attribute decision making. *Fundam. Inform.*, 157, 3, 271–320, 2018.
26. Dombi, J., A general class of fuzzy operators, the DeMorgan class of fuzzy operators and fuzziness measures induced by fuzzy operators. *Fuzzy Sets Syst.*, 8, 2, 149–163, 1982.
27. Seikh, M.R. and Mandal, U., Intuitionistic fuzzy Dombi aggregation operators and their appli- cation to multiple attribute decision-making. *Granular Comput.*, 1–16, 2019.
28. Liu, P., Liu, J., Chen, S.M., Some intuitionistic fuzzy Dombi Bonferroni mean operators and their application to multi-attribute group decision making. *J. Oper. Res. Soc.*, 1–26, 2017.
29. Chen, J. and Ye, J., Some single-valued neutrosophic Dombi weighted aggregation operators for multiple attribute decision-making. *Symmetry*, 9, 6, 82, 2017.
30. Mohanasundari, M. and Mohana, K., Quadripartitioned Single valued Neutrosophic Dombi Weighted Aggregation Operators for Multiple Attribute Decision Making. *Neutrosophic Sets Syst.*, 32, 1, 9, 2020.
31. He, X., Typhoon disaster assessment based on Dombi hesitant fuzzy information aggregation operators. *Nat. Hazard.*, 90, 3, 1153–1175, 2018.
32. Shi, L. and Ye, J., Dombi aggregation operators of neutrosophic cubic sets for multiple attribute decision-making. *Algorithms*, 11, 3, 29, 2018.

33. Akram, M., Dudek, W.A., Dar, J.M., Pythagorean Dombi fuzzy aggregation operators with application in multicriteria decision-making. *Int. J. Intell. Syst.*, 34, 11, 3000–3019, 2019.
34. Jana, C., Senapati, T., Pal, M., Yager, R.R., Picture fuzzy Dombi aggregation operators: Application to MADM process. *Appl. Soft Comput.*, 74, 99–109, 2019.
35. Choquet, G., Theory of capacities. *Ann. Inst. Fourier*, 5, 131–295, 1954.
36. Sugeno, M., Theory of fuzzy integrals and its applications, Doctorial Thesis, Tokyo Institute of technology, 1974.
37. Murofushi, T. and Sugeno, M., An interpretation of fuzzy measures and the Choquet integral as an integral with respect to a fuzzy measure. *Fuzzy Sets Syst.*, 29, 2, 201–227, 1989.
38. Beliakov, G. and Divakov, D., On representation of fuzzy measures for learning Choquet and Sugeno integrals. *Knowledge-Based Syst.*, 189, 105134, 2020.
39. Beliakov, G. and Wu, J.Z., Learning fuzzy measures from data: simplifications and optimisation strategies. *Inf. Sci.*, 494, 100–113, 2019.
40. Beliakov, G. and Wu, J.Z., Learning k-maxitive fuzzy measures from data by mixed integer programming. *Fuzzy Sets Syst.*, 412, 41–52, 2021.
41. Lucca, G., Dimuro, G.P., Fernández, J., Bustince, H., Bedregal, B., Sanz, J.A., Improving the Performance of Fuzzy Rule-Based Classification Systems Based on a Nonaveraging Generalization of CC-Integrals Named C_F1 *F*2-Integrals. *IEEE Trans. Fuzzy Syst.*, 27, 1, 124–134, 2018.
42. Lucca, G., Sanz, J.A., Dimuro, G.P., Bedregal, B., Mesiar, R., Kolesárová, A., Bustince, S.H., Pre-aggregation functions: construction and an application. *IEEE Trans. Fuzzy Syst.*, 24, 2, 260, 2016.
43. Lucca, G., Sanz, J.A., Dimuro, G.P., Bedregal, B., Bustince, H., A proposal for tuning the β α parameter in $C_\beta C$ C α C-integrals for application in fuzzy rule-based classification systems. *Nat. Comput.*, 19, 3, 533–546, 2020.
44. Lucca, G., Sanz, J.A., Dimuro, G.P., Bedregal, B., Asiain, M.J., Elkano, M., Bustince, H., CC-integrals: Choquet-like copula-based aggregation functions and its application in fuzzy rule-based classification systems. *Knowledge-Based Syst.*, 119, 32–43, 2017.
45. Dimuro, G.P., Lucca, G., Bedregal, B., Mesiar, R., Sanz, J.A., Lin, C.T., Bustince, H., Generalized CF1F2-integrals: from Choquet-like aggregation to ordered directionally monotone func- tions. *Fuzzy Sets Syst.*, 378, 44–67, 2020.
46. Bustince, H., Mesiar, R., Fernández, J., Galar, M., Paternain, D., Altalhi, A., Takác ˇ, Z., d-choquet integrals: Choquet integrals based on dissimilarities. *Fuzzy Sets Syst.*, 414, 1–27, 2021.
47. Wieczynski, J.C., Dimuro, G.P., Borges, E.N., Santos, H.S., Lucca, G., Lourenzutti, R., Bustince, H., Generalizing the GMC-RTOPSIS Method using CT-integral Pre-aggregation Functions, in: *2020 IEEE International Conference on Fuzzy Systems*, 2020, July, IEEE, pp. 1–8.

48. Dimuro, G.P., Fernández, J., Bedregal, B., Mesiar, R., Sanz, J.A., Lucca, G., Bustince, H., The state-of-art of the generalizations of the Choquet integral: from aggregation and pre-aggregation to ordered directionally monotone functions. *Inf. Fusion*, 57, 27–43, 2020.
49. Shapley, L.S., A Value for n-Person Games, in: *W: Contributions to the Theory of Games*, vol. 2, 28, pp. 307–317, Princeton University Press, NJ, USA, 1953.
50. Marichal, J.L., The influence of variables on pseudo-Boolean functions with applications to game theory and multicriteria decision making. *Discrete Appl. Math.*, 107, 1-3, 139–164, 2000.
51. Tan, C. and Chen, X., Intuitionistic fuzzy Choquet integral operator for multi-criteria decision making. *Expert Syst. Appl.*, 37, 1, 149–157, 2010.
52. Wei, G., Interval-valued intuitionistic fuzzy choquet integral operator. *J. Inf. Comput. Sci.*, 5, 6, 2545–2551, 2008.
53. Grabisch, M., Alternative representations of discrete fuzzy measures for decision making. *Int. J. Uncertainty Fuzziness Knowledge Based Syst.*, 5, 5, 587–607, 1997.
54. Meng, F., Zhang, Q., Cheng, H., Approaches to multiple-criteria group decision making based on interval-valued intuitionistic fuzzy Choquet integral with respect to the generalized λ-Shapley index. *Knowledge-Based Syst.*, 37, 237–249, 2013.
55. Meng, F., Chen, X., Zhang, Q., Generalized Hesitant Fuzzy Generalized Shapley-Choquet Integral Operators and Their Application in Decision Making. *Int. J. Fuzzy Syst.*, 16, 3, 2014.
56. Wei, G. and Zhang, N., A multiple criteria hesitant fuzzy decision making with Shapley value- based VIKOR method. *J. Intell. Fuzzy Syst.*, 26, 2, 1065–1075, 2014.
57. Kakati, P. and Borkotokey, S., Generalized interval-valued intuitionistic fuzzy Hamacher generalized Shapley Choquet integral operators for multicriteria decision making. *Iran. J. Fuzzy Syst.*, 17, 1, 121–139, 2020.
58. Yakubu, H. and Kwong, C.K., Using Online Big Data for Determining the Importance of Product Attributes, in: *2020 IEEE International Conference on Industrial Engineering and Engineering Management*, IEEE, pp. 691–695, 2020.
59. Grabisch, M., A new algorithm for identifying fuzzy measures and its application to pattern recognition, in: *Proceedings of 1995 IEEE International Conference on Fuzzy Systems*, vol. 1, IEEE, pp. 145–150, 1995.
60. Santosh, K.C. and Wendling, L., Pattern recognition based on hierarchical description of deci- sion rules using choquet integral, in: *International Conference on Recent Trends in Image Processing and Pattern Recognition*, Springer, pp. 146–158, 2016.
61. Ameur, S.T.B., Cloppet, F., Dorra, S., Wendling, L., Choquet Integral based feature selection for early breast cancer diagnosis from MRIs, in: *ICPRAM*, pp. 351–358, 2016.

62. Trabelsi Ben Ameur, S., Sellami, D., Wendling, L., Cloppet, F., Breast Cancer Diagnosis System Based on Semantic Analysis and Choquet Integral Feature Selection for High Risk Subjects. *Big Data Cognit. Comput.*, 3, 3, 41, 2019.
63. Anzilli, L. and Giove, S., Multi-criteria and medical diagnosis for application to health insurance systems: a general approach through non-additive measures. *Dec. Econ. Finance*, 43, 2, 559–582, 2020.
64. Chen, S.M. and Tan, J.M., Handling multicriteria fuzzy decision-making problems based on vague set theory. *Fuzzy Sets Syst.*, 67, 2, 163–172, 1994.

21

Fuzzy Approach to Replacement Problems Using Pentagonal Fuzzy Numbers

Krishnaveni G., Sudha G., Melita Vinoliah E. and Balaganesan M.*

Department of Mathematics, College of Engineering and Technology, SRM Institute of Science and Technology, Kattankulathur, Chengalpattu, Tamil Nadu, India

Abstract

In real-world scenarios, uncertainties are pervasive, and the fuzzy set theory provides a powerful mathematical framework to handle imprecise and uncertain information. One area where this is particularly useful is in replacement decisions, where various parameters such as capital cost, maintenance cost, the estimated value of an asset and interest rates are uncertain. This paper focuses on analyzing and solving replacement problems using fuzzy set techniques, particularly with pentagonal fuzzy numbers, to model the uncertainty associated with these parameters. Pentagonal fuzzy numbers provide a more general and versatile framework compared to traditional triangular or trapezoidal fuzzy numbers. This study explores the application of pentagonal fuzzy numbers in solving fuzzy replacement problems, aiming to improve decision accuracy and offer practical solutions to real-world replacement scenarios, such as machinery replacement in industries, system upgrades. This method offers a simple and easy-to-apply approach for solving practical fuzzy replacement problems and it effectively addresses uncertainties or imprecision in decision-making processes. A practical numerical example is presented to highlight the ease and efficiency of the proposed approach, showcasing its straightforward application in real-world situations to achieve optimal decision-making outcomes.

***Keywords*:** Pentagonal fuzzy number (PFN), pentagonal fuzzy replacement model, core and spread of PFN, operations on PFN, ranking of PFN

**Corresponding author*: balaganm@srmist.edu.in

Harish Garg (ed.) Decision Support Systems in Smart Computing: Embracing Uncertainty and Challenges, (665–684) © 2026 Scrivener Publishing LLC

21.1 Introduction

In today's rapidly changing and constantly advancing world, the replacement of machinery and facilities has become a persistent and complex challenge, driven by rapid technological advancements and globalization. This issue is a common concern for business owners, as maintaining operational efficiency is critical to staying competitive. Maintenance, a planned and systematic process, ensures that equipment, systems, or facilities function as intended, preventing unexpected downtime and service disruptions. To achieve consistent performance, safety, and reliability, regular maintenance activities are essential to keep systems and facilities in optimal working condition. While maintenance increases operational costs, it also enhances production efficiency and profitability by preserving and improving the performance of machinery and facilities, ultimately contributing to higher revenues.

For businesses to remain competitive, it is crucial to evaluate whether to continue maintaining existing equipment or replace it entirely. This choice is influenced by factors including maintenance expenses, resale value, initial investment, and interest rates.

The concept of equipment replacement in industries was first introduced [1], utilizing the principles of renewal theory. Over time, numerous researchers have explored replacement models within a classical framework. However, it was recognized that real-world replacement models often involve imprecise or ill-defined costs, leading to the incorporation of fuzzy environments—demonstrated through applications like street-lighting problems [2]. Further advancements employed the fuzzy hierarchy process (HP) to tackle replacement problems, highlighting the effectiveness of fuzzy methods in handling uncertainty and imprecision in decision-making [3].

Traditionally, equipment replacement decisions have been approached in a deterministic and precise manner. However, in real-world applications, uncertainty and vagueness are inherent in factors such as cost, time, and other variables due to various unpredictable reasons. Consequently, it is more practical to consider a range of acceptable values rather than relying on exact figures when determining the optimal time to replace equipment. To address such scenarios, the concept of fuzzy set theory was introduced [4], providing a robust framework for handling imprecision and uncertainty. This approach has become a valuable tool for decision-making in complex and ambiguous situations.

The economic lifespan of equipment has been evaluated using ranking methods that convert FRM into classical models [5, 6], with comprehensive overviews provided in these approaches. Ranking principles have been successfully applied to solve fuzzy fractional programming problems [7], while trapezoidal fuzzy numbers (TFNs) have been transformed into crisp values to address fuzzy multi-objective programming problems [8]. The economic life of equipment has been examined considering both changing and constant monetary values [9–11], with extensions made to an intuitionistic fuzzy framework. Recent research has advanced the field of fuzzy replacement models, offering valuable insights into practical applications for optimizing equipment replacement decisions [12]. This work focuses on maintaining operational continuity while addressing challenges, though shortages are not explicitly considered. A flexible random sampling methodology was introduced that accommodates both with-replacement and without-replacement selection strategies [13]. Replacement concepts have been analyzed using membership and non-membership grades for both group and individual cases [14, 15]. Maintenance optimization under uncertainty has been formulated as a Markov Decision Process [16], solved through a modified Reinforcement Learning approach capable of handling infinite horizons for stochastic and deterministic scheduling. Optimal preventive replacement strategies for single-unit systems subject to external shocks and stochastic degradation were investigated [17]. Additionally, the present worth factor was incorporated into replacement models [18]. For military applications, a fuzzy Multi-Criteria Decision-Making (MCDM) model was developed specifically for dump truck selection, emphasizing critical factors including construction specifications, purchase costs, and maintenance expenses [19].

21.1.1 Research Gaps in Fuzzy Replacement Models

Despite significant advancements in fuzzy replacement models, several critical research gaps remain unaddressed in current literature. The triangular or trapezoidal fuzzy numbers used in most existing models are imprecise enough to not convey the complex, multi modal uncertainty present in real-world replacement decisions. During optimization, many existing methods lose essential uncertainty information by turning fuzzy models into crisp forms, which degrades the quality of the solutions. Pure fuzzy form methods that preserve uncertainty representation during the whole decision-making process without defuzzification have also not been thoroughly investigated. Furthermore, even though environmental factors are becoming more and more important in sustainable industrial operations, the majority of replacement models do not sufficiently take them into account. Finally, more reliable techniques that can handle several unknown aspects at once, such as costs, interest rates, and depreciation rates, with higher precision and usefulness are still desperately needed. The aforementioned deficiencies highlight the necessity of more sophisticated fuzzy methods for equipment replacement modeling.

21.1.2 Motivation and Novelties of the Study

Failure to properly implement machinery replacement strategies can lead to severe environmental consequences, such as air and water pollution. Outdated or poorly maintained equipment often operates inefficiently, consuming more energy and emitting higher levels of harmful pollutants into the atmosphere. Additionally, aging machinery may leak hazardous chemicals or waste into water sources, contaminating ecosystems and posing risks to human health. By neglecting timely replacement and maintenance, industries not only compromise operational efficiency but also contribute to environmental degradation. Adopting sustainable replacement practices is essential to minimize pollution, conserve resources, and promote a cleaner, healthier environment.

In environments characterized by uncertainty, fuzzy set theory serves as a powerful tool for addressing decision-making challenges and applications across various engineering fields. The primary goal of this research paper is to solve the fuzzy replacement problem by leveraging pentagonal fuzzy numbers. This is achieved through the following steps:

1. Representing input parameters using pentagonal fuzzy numbers.
2. Creating arithmetic operations for pentagonal fuzzy numbers using core and spread principles, encompassing addition, subtraction, scalar multiplication, and the product of two PFNs.
3. Identifying a strategy to ensure optimality is the most challenging step in transforming a fuzzy replacement model into a precise version. It is essential to verify the accuracy of the solution, as the crisp model derived from the fuzzy model may not fully address the original problem. The crisp model often

fails to effectively capture the inherent uncertainty and complexity of the fuzzy optimization model. For this purpose, the numerical example provided in this study is solved entirely in its fuzzy form, avoiding conversion to a crisp model, which guarantees a more precise and realistic solution.

This chapter is organized as follows. Section 21.2 introduces the fundamental concepts of PFN, their ranking and arithmetic operations. Section 21.3 describes the proposed algorithm and flow chart for the presented model. Section 21.4 demonstrates the replacement model using a real-life example. Lastly, Section 21.5 summarizes the key findings and conclusions of the research.

21.2 Operational Framework and Techniques

Definition 2.1 [20]: A fuzzy number $\tilde{p}$ represents a convex and normalized fuzzy set on the real line R, characterized by a membership function and it is piecewise continuous in segments and it is denoted by $\tilde{p} = (p_1, p_2, p_3, p_4, p_5)$, where $p_1 \le p_2 \le p_3 \le p_4 \le p_5$ are real numbers is given by

$$\mu_{\tilde{p}}(x) = \begin{cases} m\dfrac{x-p_1}{p_2-p_1} & \text{if} \quad p_1 \le x \le p_2 \\ 1-(1-m)\dfrac{x-p_2}{p_3-p_1} & \text{if} \quad p_2 \le x \le p_3 \\ 1 & \text{if} \quad x = p_3 \\ 1-(1-m)\dfrac{p_4-x}{p_4-p_3} & \text{if} \quad p_3 \le x \le p_4 \\ m\dfrac{p_5-x}{p_5-p_4} & \text{if} \quad p_4 \le x \le p_5 \\ 0 & \text{otherwise} \end{cases}$$

And its visual representation is shown in the following figure (Figure 21.1):

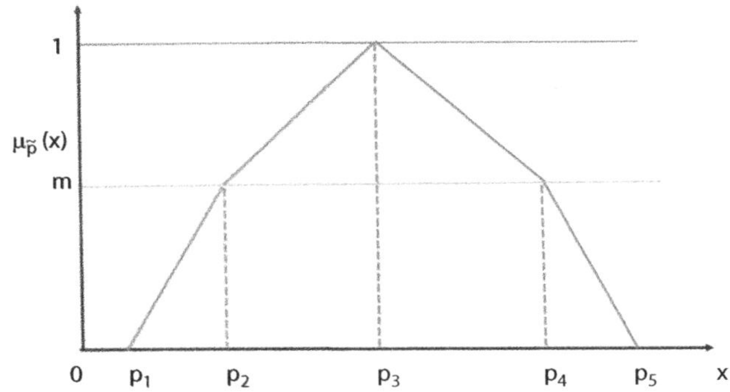

Figure 21.1 Pentagonal fuzzy number $\tilde{p} = (p_1, p_2, p_3, p_4, p_5)$.

21.2.1 Pentagonal Fuzzy Number and Its Alternate Representation

A fuzzy number can be expressed using its core (c), left spread (u), and right spread (v). For a triangular fuzzy number, the core represents a single point, while for a trapezoidal case it is represented as an interval.

This study presents the pentagonal fuzzy number in the structure of $\tilde{p} = (c, u_1, u_2, v_1, v_2)$ as given in the following figure (Figure 21.2):

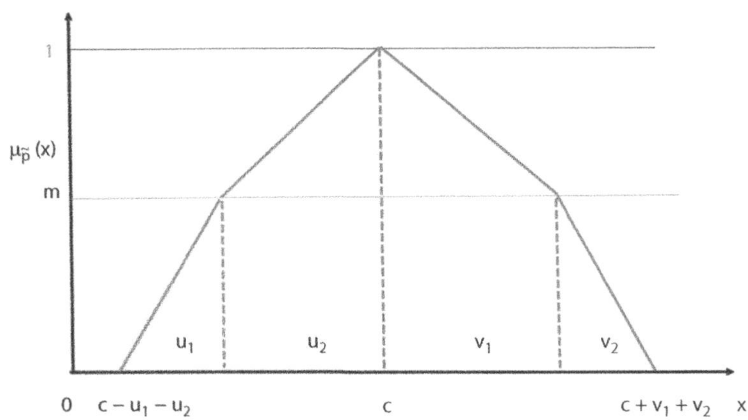

Figure 21.2 Alternative representation of the PFN.

Here, c represents the centroid point, u_1 denotes the distance of the left spread from c to $(c-u_1)$ and u_2 signifies the distance of the left spread from $(c-u_1)$ to $(c-u_1-u_2)$.

Furthermore, v_1 signifies the distance of the right spread from c to $c+v_1$ and v_2 gives the right spread from $(c+v_1)$ to $(c+v_1+v_2)$.

21.2.2 Arithmetic Operations of PFNs

Based on [21], we define the arithmetic operations between $\tilde{p}=(c_1,x_1,x_2,y_1,y_2)$ and $\tilde{q}=(c_2,j_1,j_2,k_1,k_2)$, which are given by:

Addition:

$$\begin{aligned}\tilde{p}+\tilde{q}&=(c_1,x_1,x_2,y_1,y_2)+(c_2,j_1,j_2,k_1,k_2)\\&=\{(c_1+c_2,),\max(x_1,j_1),\max(x_2,j_2),\max(y_1,k_1),\max(y_2,k_1)\}\end{aligned}$$

Subtraction:

$$\begin{aligned}\tilde{p}-\tilde{q}&=(c_1,x_1,x_2,y_1,y_2)-(c_2,j_1,j_2,k_1,k_2)\\&=\{(c_1-c_2,),\min(x_1,j_1),\min(x_2,j_2),\min(y_1,k_1),\min(y_2,k_1)\}\end{aligned}$$

Multiplication:

$$\begin{aligned}\tilde{p}\times\tilde{q}&=(c_1,x_1,x_2,y_1,y_2)\times(c_2,j_1,j_2,k_1,k_2)\\&=\{(c_1\times c_2,),\max(x_1,j_1),\max(x_2,j_2),\max(y_1,k_1),\max(y_2,k_1)\}\end{aligned}$$

Division:

$$\begin{aligned}\tilde{p}\div\tilde{q}&=(c_1,x_1,x_2,y_1,y_2)\div(c_2,j_1,j_2,k_1,k_2)\\&=\{(c_1\div c_2,),\min(x_1,j_1),\min(x_2,j_2),\min(y_1,k_1),\min(y_2,k_1)\}\end{aligned}$$

Here both spreads are following the lattice rule.

21.2.3 Ranking of PFN

In scenarios involving uncertain or imprecise data, the ability to rank fuzzy numbers plays a crucial role in processes of decision-making. Determining the order of fuzzy numbers is necessary to identify the highest and lowest values to make decisions. Numerous studies [22–24] have introduced different approaches to rank fuzzy numbers effectively. This paper employs an enhanced ranking function that utilizes graded mean values to facilitate the comparison of fuzzy numbers.

$$R(\tilde{p}) = \frac{V + 4c - U}{4}$$

Here $U = u_1 + u_2$ and $(V = v_1 + v_2)$.

The comparison of two pentagonal fuzzy numbers $\tilde{p} = (c_1, u_1, u_2, v_1, v_2)$ and $\tilde{q} = (c_2, u_1', u_2', v_1', v_2')$ is

$$\begin{aligned}
&(i) \quad \tilde{p} \succeq \tilde{q} \;\; if \;\; R(\tilde{p}) \geq R(\tilde{p}) \\
&(ii) \quad \tilde{p} \preceq \tilde{q} \;\; if \;\; R(\tilde{p}) \leq R(\tilde{p}) \\
&(iii) \quad \tilde{p} \approx \tilde{q} \;\; if \;\; R(\tilde{p}) = R(\tilde{p})
\end{aligned}$$

21.3 Replacement Model with Pentagonal Fuzzy Numbers

Theorem 3.1: Optimum Replacement Policy [25]

1. Replacement is not needed if the pentagonal fuzzy maintenance cost for the upcoming period is less than the pentagonal fuzzy average total cost of the prior period.
2. If the pentagonal fuzzy maintenance cost for the next period exceeds the pentagonal fuzzy average total cost (PFAC) of the previous period, the old equipment should be replaced with new equipment.

Proof:

Let $\widetilde{PC}$, $\widetilde{PS_n}$ and $\widetilde{PR_n}$ be pentagonal fuzzy capital cost (PFC), pentagonal fuzzy scrap value (PFS) and pentagonal fuzzy running cost (PFR) respectively. In this context, n is a discrete variable, and the value of money changes as time progresses.

The present worth of all discounted costs at the end of every n years is

$$\widetilde{PP}_n = \left(\widetilde{PC} + \widetilde{PR}_1\right)\left[1 + \widetilde{Pv}^n + \widetilde{Pv}^{2n} + \cdots\right] + \widetilde{PR}_2\tilde{v}\left[1 + \widetilde{Pv}^n + \widetilde{Pv}^{2n} + \cdots\right]$$

$$+ \cdots + \widetilde{PR}_n\widetilde{Pv}^{n-1}\left[1 + \widetilde{Pv}^n + \widetilde{Pv}^{2n} + \cdots\right]$$

$$= \left(\widetilde{PC} + \widetilde{PR}_1 + \widetilde{PR}_2\widetilde{Pv} + \cdots + \widetilde{PR}_n\widetilde{Pv}^{n-1}\right)\left[1 + \widetilde{Pv}^n + \widetilde{Pv}^{2n} + \cdots\right]$$

$$= \left(\widetilde{PC} + \widetilde{PR}_1 + \widetilde{PR}_2\tilde{v} + \cdots + \widetilde{PR}_n\widetilde{Pv}^{n-1}\right)\left[\frac{1}{1 - \widetilde{Pv}^n}\right]$$

$$= \frac{\widetilde{PF}_n}{1 - \widetilde{Pv}^n}$$

Here $\widetilde{PF}_n = \begin{cases} \widetilde{PC} + \sum \widetilde{PR}_n\widetilde{Pv}^{n-1}, \textit{ if the is no solvage value} \\ \widetilde{PC} - \widetilde{PS}_n\widetilde{Pv}^n + \sum \widetilde{PR}_n\widetilde{Pv}^{n-1}, \textit{ if the is solvage value} \end{cases}$

Similarly $\widetilde{PP}_{n+1} = \dfrac{\widetilde{PF}_{n+1}}{1 - \widetilde{Pv}^{n+1}}$

$\widetilde{PP}_n$ is minimum if $\widetilde{PP}_{n+1} - \widetilde{PP}_n > 0 > \widetilde{PP}_n - \widetilde{PP}_{n-1}$

That is if, $\dfrac{\widetilde{PF}_{n+1}}{1 - \widetilde{Pv}^{n+1}} - \dfrac{\widetilde{PF}_n}{1 - \widetilde{Pv}^n} > 0 > \dfrac{\widetilde{PF}_n}{1 - \widetilde{Pv}^n} - \dfrac{\widetilde{PF}_{n-1}}{1 - \widetilde{Pv}^{n-1}}$

Now $\dfrac{\widetilde{PF}_{n+1}}{1 - \widetilde{Pv}^{n+1}} - \dfrac{\widetilde{PF}_n}{1 - \widetilde{Pv}^n} = \dfrac{(1 - \widetilde{Pv}^n)\widetilde{PF}_{n+1} - (1 - \widetilde{Pv}^{n+1})\widetilde{PF}_n}{(1 - \widetilde{Pv}^{n+1})(1 - \widetilde{Pv}^n)}$

$$= \frac{\widetilde{PF}_{n+1} - \widetilde{PF}_n + \widetilde{PF}_n\widetilde{Pv}^{n+1} - \widetilde{PF}_{n+1}\widetilde{Pv}^n}{(1 - \widetilde{Pv}^{n+1})(1 - \widetilde{Pv}^n)}$$

But $\widetilde{PF}_{n+1} = \widetilde{PF}_n + \widetilde{PR}_{n+1}\widetilde{Pv}^n$

$$= \frac{\widetilde{PR}_{n+1}\widetilde{Pv}^n + \widetilde{PF}_n\widetilde{Pv}^{n+1} - \widetilde{Pv}[\widetilde{PF}_n + \widetilde{PR}_{n+1}\widetilde{Pv}^n]}{(1 - \widetilde{Pv}^{n+1})(1 - \widetilde{Pv}^n)}$$

$$= \frac{\widetilde{PR}_{n+1}\widetilde{Pv}^n[1 - \widetilde{Pv}^n] + \widetilde{PF}_n\widetilde{Pv}^n[\widetilde{Pv} - 1]}{(1 - \widetilde{Pv}^{n+1})(1 - \widetilde{Pv}^n)}$$

$$= \frac{\widetilde{Pv}^n[1 - \widetilde{Pv}][\widetilde{PR}_{n+1}\left(\dfrac{1 - \widetilde{Pv}^n}{1 - \widetilde{Pv}}\right) - \widetilde{PF}_n]}{(1 - \widetilde{Pv}^{n+1})(1 - \widetilde{Pv}^n)}$$

That is, $\widetilde{PP}_n$ is minimum if

$$\frac{\widetilde{Pv}^n[1-\widetilde{Pv}][\widetilde{PR}_{n+1}\left(\frac{1-\widetilde{Pv}^n}{1-\widetilde{Pv}}\right)-\widetilde{PF}_n]}{(1-\widetilde{Pv}^{n+1})(1-\widetilde{Pv}^n)}>0>\frac{\widetilde{Pv}^{n-1}[1-\tilde{v}][\widetilde{PR}_n\left(\frac{1-\widetilde{Pv}^{n-1}}{1-\widetilde{Pv}}\right)-\widetilde{PF}_{n-1}]}{(1-\widetilde{Pv}^n)(1-\widetilde{Pv}^{n-1})}$$

$$\frac{\widetilde{Pv}^n[\widetilde{PR}_{n+1}\left(\frac{1-\widetilde{Pv}^n}{1-\widetilde{Pv}}\right)-\widetilde{PF}_n]}{(1-\widetilde{Pv}^{n+1})}>0>\frac{\widetilde{Pv}^{n-1}[\widetilde{PR}_n\left(\frac{1-\widetilde{Pv}^{n-1}}{1-\widetilde{Pv}}\right)-\widetilde{PF}_{n-1}]}{(1-\widetilde{Pv}^{n-1})}$$

$$\frac{\widetilde{Pv}\left[\widetilde{PR}_{n+1}\left(\frac{1-\widetilde{Pv}^n}{1-\widetilde{Pv}}\right)-\widetilde{PF}_n\right]}{(1-\widetilde{Pv}^{n+1})}>0>\frac{\left[\widetilde{PR}_n\left(\frac{1-\widetilde{Pv}^{n-1}}{1-\widetilde{Pv}}\right)-\widetilde{PF}_{n-1}\right]}{(1-\widetilde{Pv}^{n-1})}$$

$$\widetilde{PR}_{n+1}\left(\frac{1-\widetilde{Pv}^n}{1-\widetilde{Pv}}\right)-\widetilde{PF}_n>0>\widetilde{PR}_n\left(\frac{1-\widetilde{Pv}^{n-1}}{1-\widetilde{Pv}}\right)-\widetilde{PF}_n+\widetilde{PR}_n\,\widetilde{Pv}^{n-1}$$

$$\widetilde{PR}_{n+1}\left(\frac{1-\widetilde{Pv}^n}{1-\widetilde{Pv}}\right)>\widetilde{PF}_n>\widetilde{PR}_n\left[\left(\frac{1-\widetilde{Pv}^{n-1}}{1-\widetilde{Pv}}\right)+\widetilde{Pv}^{n-1}\right]$$

$$\widetilde{PR}_{n+1}>\widetilde{PF}_n\left(\frac{1-\widetilde{Pv}}{1-\widetilde{Pv}^n}\right)>\widetilde{PR}_n$$

$$\widetilde{PR}_{n+1}>\frac{\widetilde{PF}_n}{1+\widetilde{Pv}^1+\widetilde{Pv}^2+\cdots+\widetilde{Pv}^{n-1}}>\widetilde{PR}_n$$

$$\widetilde{PR}_{n+1} > \frac{\widetilde{PF}_n}{\sum_{r=0}^{n-1} \widetilde{Pv}^r} > \widetilde{PR}_n$$

Here $\frac{\widetilde{PF}_n}{\sum_{r=0}^{n-1} \tilde{v}^r}$ is the pentagonal fuzzy weighted average cost $(\widetilde{PW})$ of previous n years with weights $0, 1, \widetilde{Pv}, \widetilde{Pv}^2, \ldots, \widetilde{Pv}^{n-1}$ respectively.

Which leads the proof of the theorem. That is

$$\widetilde{PR}_n < \widetilde{PW}_n < \widetilde{PR}_{n+1}$$

21.3.1 Procedure to Find the Pentagonal Fuzzy Equipment Replacement Time

To identify the best time for replacement, follow this strategy.

Step 1. By Using c, U and V, reformulate the given PFNs into the structure of $\tilde{p} = (c_1, u_1, u_2, v_1, v_2)$
Step 2. Calculate the total accumulated pentagonal maintenance cost $\sum \widetilde{PR}_n$ for n = 1,2,3, …
Step 3. Using interest rate, find pentagonal present worth factor (PPWF), $\widetilde{Pv}^n$, $\widetilde{Pv}^{n-1}$ and accumulated value $\sum \widetilde{Pv}^{n-1}$.
Step 4. By using steps 2 and 3, determine $\sum \widetilde{PR}_n \widetilde{Pv}^{n-1}$.
Step 5. Evaluate $\widetilde{PC} - \widetilde{PS}_n \widetilde{Pv}^n + \sum \widetilde{PR}_n \widetilde{Pv}^{n-1}$, by using PFC and step 4.
Step 6. Divide step 5 value by $\sum \widetilde{Pv}^{n-1}$ to find the PFAC, $\widetilde{PW}(n)$
Step 7. Utilize the proposed graded mean methodology to calculate the precise value of PFAC.
Step 8. The optimal replacement time for the equipment is determined by applying Theorem 3.1.

21.3.2 Process Flow for Determining Pentagonal Fuzzy Equipment Replacement Timing

The structure of the proposed approach is illustrated in Figure 21.3.

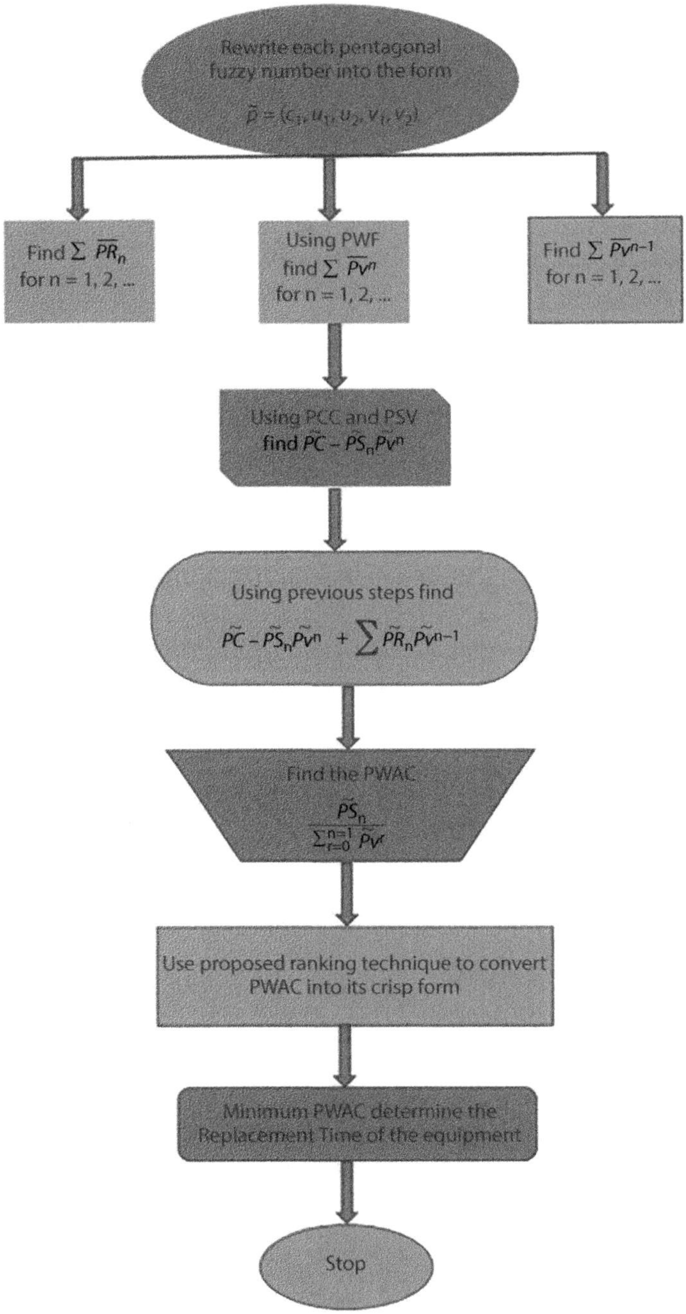

Figure 21.3 Diagram outlining the process for determining PFRT.

21.4 Numerical Simulation

A real-world numerical example is referenced from. The PFR and PFS of a machine together with its PFC (5950, 6050, 6100, 6150, 6200) are detailed below (Table 21.1). Consider the fuzzy interest rate as (0.08, 0.09, 0.10, 0.12, 0.14) annually, reflecting market variations. Calculate the optimal time to replace the machine.

Table 21.1 Pentagonal fuzzy maintenance outlays and salvage valuation.

Year(n)	Running cost (PRC) (In tens)	Salvage value (PSV) (In tens)
1	(90, 95, 100, 105, 110)	(240, 260, 320, 390, 400)
2	(120, 125, 130, 135, 140)	(134, 142, 165, 190, 200)
3	(160, 169, 171, 178, 185)	(70, 78, 100, 114, 120)
4	(210, 224, 235, 249, 260)	(52, 54, 56, 58, 60)
5	(280, 294, 299, 320, 340)	(42, 44, 46, 48, 50)
6	(370, 390, 420, 444, 460)	(32, 34, 36, 38, 40)
7	(470, 498, 500, 520, 550)	(32, 34, 36, 38, 40)

Due to market volatility, the uncertain interest rate is projected to be (0.08, 0.09, 0.10, 0.12, 0.14) per year.

Therefore, $\tilde{v} = (1+\tilde{r})^{-1} = (0.91, 0.01, 0.01, 0.02, 0.02)$.

The table (Table 21.2) yields the alternative representation of PFR, PFS and PFPWF.

Table 21.2 Alternative form of PFR, PFS, and PFPWF.

Year(n)	$\widetilde{PR}_n$	$\widetilde{PS}_n$	$\widetilde{Pv}^n$
1	(100, 5, 5, 5, 5)	(320, 60, 20, 70, 10)	(0.91, 0.01, 0.01, 0.02, 0.02)
2	(130, 5, 5, 5, 5)	(165, 23, 8, 25, 10)	(0.83, 0.01, 0.01, 0.02, 0.02)
3	(171, 2, 1, 7, 7)	(100, 22, 8, 14, 6)	(0.75, 0.01, 0.01, 0.02, 0.02)
4	(235, 11, 14, 14, 11)	(56, 2, 2, 2, 2)	(0.69, 0.01, 0.01, 0.02, 0.02)
5	(299, 5, 14, 21, 20)	(46, 2, 2, 2, 2)	(0.62, 0.01, 0.01, 0.02, 0.02)
6	(420, 30, 20, 24, 16)	(36, 2, 2, 2, 2)	(0.57, 0.01, 0.01, 0.02, 0.02)
7	(500, 2, 28, 20, 30)	(36, 2, 2, 2, 2)	(0.52, 0.01, 0.01, 0.02, 0.02)

Table 21.3 Table to assess the optimal schedule for replacement strategies.

Year (n)	$\widetilde{PR_n}$	$\widetilde{PS_n}$	$\widetilde{Pv}^{n-1}$	$\sum \widetilde{PR_n}\,\widetilde{Pv}^{n-1}$	$\widetilde{PS_n}\,\widetilde{Pv}^{n}$	$\sum \widetilde{Pv}^{n-1}$	$\widetilde{PW(n)}$	$R[\widetilde{PW(n)}]$
1	(100, 5, 5, 5, 5)	(320, 60, 20, 70, 10)	(1, 0.01, 0.01, 0.02, 0.02)	(100, 5, 5, 5, 5)	(291.2, 60, 20, 70, 1)	(1, 0.01, 0.01, 0.02, 0.02)	(418.8, 0.01, 0.01, 0.02, 0.02)	418.805
2	(130, 5, 5, 5, 5)	(165, 23, 8, 25, 10)	(0.91, 0.01, 0.01, 0.02, 0.02)	(218.3, 5, 5, 5, 5)	(136.95, 23, 8, 25, 10)	(1.91, 0.01, 0.01, 0.02, 0.02)	(361.9633, 0.01, 0.01, 0.02, 0.02)	361.9683
3	(171, 2, 1, 7, 7)	(100, 22, 8, 14, 6)	(0.83, 0.01, 0.01, 0.02, 0.02)	(360.23, 5, 5, 7, 7)	(75, 22, 8, 14, 6)	(2.74, 0.01, 0.01, 0.02, 0.02)	(326.7263, 0.01, 0.01, 0.02, 0.02)	326.7313
4	(235, 11, 14, 14, 11)	(56, 2, 2, 2, 2)	(0.75, 0.01, 0.01, 0.02, 0.02)	(536.48, 11, 14, 14, 11)	(38.64, 2, 2, 2, 2)	(3.49, 0.01, 0.01, 0.02, 0.02)	(317.4327, 0.01, 0.01, 0.02, 0.02)	317.4377
5	(299, 5, 14, 21, 20)	(46, 2, 2, 2, 2)	(0.69, 0.01, 0.01, 0.02, 0.02)	(742.79, 11, 14, 21, 20)	(28.52, 2, 2, 2, 2)	(4.18, 0.01, 0.01, 0.02, 0.02)	(316.811, 0.01, 0.01, 0.02, 0.02)	316.816
6	(420, 30, 20, 24, 16)	(36, 2, 2, 2, 2)	(0.62, 0.01, 0.01, 0.02, 0.02)	(1003.19, 30, 20, 24, 20)	(20.52, 2, 2, 2, 2)	(4.8, 0.01, 0.01, 0.02, 0.02)	(331.8063, 0.01, 0.01, 0.02, 0.02)	331.8113
7	(500, 2, 28, 20, 30)	(36, 2, 2, 2, 2)	(0.57, 0.01, 0.01, 0.02, 0.02)	(1288.19, 30, 28, 24, 30)	(18.72, 2, 2, 2, 2)	(5.37, 0.01, 0.01, 0.02, 0.02)	(349.9944, 0.01, 0.01, 0.02, 0.02)	349.9994

From the Table (21.3), The minimum pentagonal weighted average cost in parametric form is (316.811, 0.01, 0.01, 0.02, 0.02). The replacement period of the equipment should be at the end of the 5th year.

21.4.1 Results and Discussion

Without altering the uncertain conditions, the suggested algorithm concludes that the loader's replacement is optimal after the fifth year. Therefore, the fifth year minimum PWAC is Rs. (316.811, 0.01, 0.01, 0.02, 0.02), that is (3167.91, 3168.01, 3168.11, 3168.31, 3168.51). Figure 21.4, which is more vagueness reduced than the PWAC (3064.86, 3151.07, 3197.80, 3266.70, 3327.92) obtained in [26].

Compared to more straightforward fuzzy models like triangular or trapezoidal fuzzy numbers, Pentagonal Fuzzy Numbers (PFNs) offer a more sophisticated framework for capturing and managing uncertainty. This is achieved by utilizing their five-point membership representation (b_1, b_2, b_3, b_4, b_5) to provide greater precision and adaptability. More accurate modeling of asymmetric, skewed, and multimodal uncertainties is made possible by this increased precision. In complex decision-making, risk analysis, and optimization tasks where intermediate conditions between extremes are essential, PFNs provide enhanced flexibility and are particularly well-suited for capturing linguistic variables that span a wide range (such as "very very low" to "very very high"). They work especially well at simulating real-world events with non-linear behaviors or irregular distributions; economic patterns, sensor readings, and human judgments are a

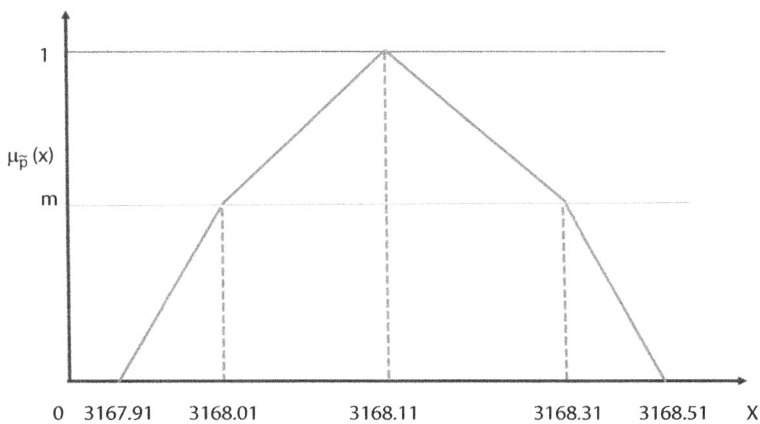

Figure 21.4 Graphical representation of the proposed result.

few examples. Because of these features, PFNs are very useful in domains where datasets frequently show multiple peaks or varying degrees of certainty, such as time-series prediction, financial analysis, and reliability research. Additionally, PFNs are completely compatible with both traditional fuzzy arithmetic (such as addition, subtraction, multiplication, and division) and well-known defuzzification methods like the centroid and weighted average methods, guaranteeing straightforward interpretability and ease of integration in real-world applications.

Through a variety of unique approaches, Pentagonal Fuzzy Numbers (PFNs) offer effective techniques for handling uncertainties in the real world. By defining membership functions which are frequently determined by expert insights, statistical studies, or clustering techniques data fuzzification converts exact numerical data into PFNs. For instance, historical data can be mapped into a pentagonal format for supply chain demand forecasting, where b_1 represents the lowest recorded demand, b_2 the lower quartile, b_3 the median, b_4 the higher quartile, and b_5 the maximum demand. By using weighted average approaches to reach collective judgments, PFNs also make it easier to synthesize the viewpoints of different experts, which is very helpful in risk assessment. In computational analysis, PFNs improve fuzzy neural networks by allowing them to process ambiguous or uncertain inputs using PFN-based activation mechanisms, and they enrich fuzzy regression by adding pentagonal fuzzy coefficients. PFNs offer a more thorough and adaptable framework for multi-criteria analysis when making decisions in the face of uncertainty. This enables decision-makers to distinguish between closely related risk categories, such as "low risk" (0.2, 0.3, 0.4, 0.7, 0.8) and "high risk" (0.5, 0.7, 0.8, 0.9, 1.0), supporting more precise and sophisticated decisions in complex situations.

While Pentagonal Fuzzy Numbers (PFNs) are more complex than triangular/trapezoidal ones, modern tools (MATLAB, Python libraries) streamline their implementation. Our arithmetic operations extend beyond pentagonal to hexagonal, octagonal and other polygonal systems, maintaining simplicity while reducing computational complexity.

21.4.2 Comparative Analysis

The proposed mathematical operations, algorithmic process, and framework achieve a 95% confidence level in clarifying uncertainties compared to the results reported in [26]. The comparative analysis of two diagrammatic representation is given detailed in the following figure (Figure 21.5).

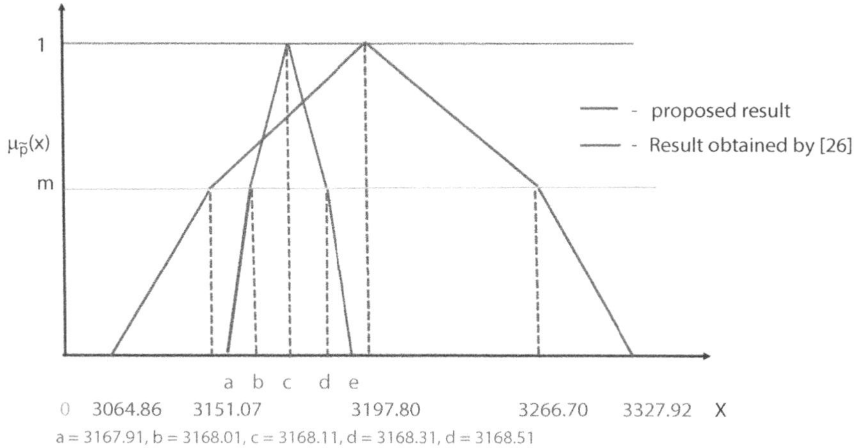

Figure 21.5 Comparative analysis.

21.5 Conclusion

Owing to the existence of unpredictable elements, uncertainty significantly influences replacement decisions encountered in practical situations. This study presents a numerical illustration that integrates fuzziness into replacement analysis while maintaining its imprecise form, providing a simple and effective method to evaluate equipment robustness and longevity and it is easy to conclude that the ambiguity in the solution derived from our proposed method is significantly reduced compared to the approach referenced in [26]. Although many researchers have tackled replacement issues using fuzzy approaches, their findings often converged to definitive values. In this work, a mathematical framework is established to demonstrate that the proposed method retains the ambiguous characteristics of the results without compromising their uncertain quality. Future research could extend this approach to hexagonal and octagonal fuzzy replacement models, assuming a monetary value that remains both fixed and adaptable over time and this approach ensures consistency while accommodating fluctuations.

AI disclosure statement: The author confirms that no artificial intelligence (AI)-generated content or AI-assisted writing tools were used in the preparation of this chapter (including summaries and the abstract). All text, analysis, and conclusions are the result of the author's original work.

References

1. Lotka, A.J., A contribution to the theory of self-renewing aggregates with special reference to industrial replacement. *Ann. Math. Stat.*, 10, 1–25, 1939, http://dml.mathdoc.fr/item/1177732243/.
2. Kai-Yuan, C. and Chuan-Yuan, W., Street-lighting lamps replacement. A fuzzy viewpoint. *Fuzzy Sets Syst.*, 37, 2, 161–172, 1990, https://doi.org/10.1016/0165-0114(90)90039-9.
3. Tolga, E., Demircan, M.L., Kahraman, C., Operating system selection using fuzzy replacement analysis and analytic hierarchy process. *Int. J. Prod. Econ.*, 97, 1, 89–117, 2005, DOI:10.1016/j.ijpe.2004.07.001.
4. Zadeh, L.A., Fuzzy sets. *Inf. Control*, 8, 338–353, 1965, https://doi.org/10.1016/S0019-9958(65)90241-X.
5. Biswas, P. and Pramanik, S., Application of fuzzy ranking method to determine the replacement time for fuzzy replacement problem. *Int. J. Comput. Appl.*, 25, 11, 41–47, 2011, DOI:10.5120/3154-4359.
6. El-Kholy, A.M. and Abdelalim, A.M., A comparative study for fuzzy ranking methods in determining economic life of equipment. *Int. J. Constr. Eng. Manag.*, 5, 2, 42–54, 2016, DOI:10.5923/j.ijcem.20160502.02.
7. Mitlif, R.J., An efficient algorithm for fuzzy linear fractional programming problems *via* ranking function. *Baghdad Sci. J.*, 19, 1, 0071, 2022, DOI: https://doi.org/10.21123/bsj.2022.19.1.0071.
8. Mitlif, R.J. and Hussein, I.H., Ranking function to solve a fuzzy multiple objective function. *Baghdad Sci. J.*, 18, 1, 144–148, 2021, DOI:https://doi.org/10.21123/bsj.2021.18.1.0144.
9. Balaganesan, M. and Ganesan, K., Fuzzy approach to determine optimum Economic life of equipment with change in money value. *Adv. Intell. Syst. Comput.*, 1040, 647–655, 2020, DOI:10.1007/978-981-15-1451-7_66.
10. Balaganesan, M. and Ganesan, K., An approach to solve replacement problems under intuitionistic fuzzy nature. *J. Phys. Conf. Ser.*, 1000, 1, 012018, 2018, DOI:10.1088/1742-6596/1000/1/012018.
11. Balaganesan, M., Melita Vinoliah, E., Krishnaveni, G., A New Replacement Model under Trapezoidal Fuzzy Number Environment. *Baghdad Sci. J.*, 21, 11, 3520–7, 2024.
12. Anees Fathima, M., Nandakumar, C.D., Srinivasan, S., Fuzzy numerous productive model with limited amount of replacement excluding shortages. *Telematique*, 21, 1, 7839–7845, 2022, https://www.provinciajournal.com/index.php/telematique/article/view/1343.
13. Kesemen, O., Tiryaki, B.K., Tezel, O., Ozkul, E., Naz, E., Random sampling with fuzzy replacement. *Expert Syst. Appl.*, 185, 115602, 2021, https://doi.org/10.1016/j.eswa.2021.115602.
14. Singh, R.P. and Tiwari, C.M., Individual and group replacement policy under intuitionistic fuzzy environment. *Telematique*, 21, 1, 2703–2718, 2022, https://www.provinciajournal.com/index.php/telematique/article/view/341.

15. Singh, R.P. and Tiwari, C.M., A study on intuitionistic fuzzy replacement model. *Telematique*, 21, 1, 2687–2702, 2022.
16. Hu, J., Wang, Y., Pang, Y., Liu, Y., Optimal maintenance scheduling under uncertainties using linear programming-enhanced reinforcement learning. *Eng. Appl. Artif. Intell.*, 109, 104655, 2022, https://doi.org/10.1016/j.engappai.2021.104655.
17. Dong, W., Liu, S., Cao, Y., Javed, S.A., Scheduling optimal replacement policies for a stochastically deteriorating system subject to two types of shocks. *ISA Trans.*, 112, 292–301, 2021, https://doi.org/10.1016/j.isatra.2020.12.017.
18. Biswas, P. and Pramanik, S., Fuzzy approach to replacement problem with value of money changes with time. *Int. J. Comput. Appl.*, 30, 10, 28–33, 2011, DOI:10.5120/3676-5151.
19. Tesic, D., Bozanic, D., Puska, A., Milic, A., Marinkovic, D., Development of the MCDM Fuzzy Lmaw-Grey Marcos Model for Selection of a Dump Truck. *Rep. Mech. Eng.*, 4, 1, 1–17, 2023.
20. Arulselvam, B., Merceline Anita, A., Bharathi, T., Mike Dison, E., New Operations for Linear Pentagonal Fuzzy Numbers. *J. Propul. Tech.*, 45, 2, 4159–4170, 2024, https://doi.org/10.52783/tjjpt.v45.i02.6601.
21. Ma, M., Friedman, M., Kandel, A., A new fuzzy arithmetic. *Fuzzy Sets Syst.*, 108, 1, 83–90, 1999, DOI:10.1016/S0165-0114(97)00310-2.
22. Abbasbandy, S. and Hajjari, T., A new approach for ranking of trapezoidal fuzzy numbers. *Comput. Math. Appl.*, 57, 413–419, 2009, DOI: 10.1016/j.camwa.2008.10.090.
23. Deshmukh, A., Fuzzy Transportation Problem by Using Triangular Fuzzy Numbers with Ranking Using Area of Trapezium, Rectangle and Centroid at Different Level Of α-Cut. *TURCOMAT*, 12, 12, 3941–3951, 2021.
24. Chakraborty, Mondal, S.P., Alam, S., Ahmadian, A., Senu, N., De, D., Salahshour, S., The pentagonal fuzzy number: its different representations, properties, ranking, defuzzification and application in game problems. *Symmetry*, 11, 2, 1–29, 2019, DOI: 10.3390/sym11020248.
25. Swarup, K., Gupta, P.K., Mohan, M., *Operations research*, 13th edition, Chand and company LTD, New Delhi, 2007.
26. Ikram, S.N. and Rajkumar, A., Replacement Model Analysed by Using Pentagonal Fuzzy number. *IJPAM*, 119, 9, 107–112, 2018.

Index

Printed and bound by CPI Group (UK) Ltd, Croydon, CR0 4YY
29/09/2026
14971772-0005